Simulation

with

Visual SLAM

and

AweSim

Simulation with
Visual SLAM and AweSim

A. Alan B. Pritsker
Pritsker Corporation and Purdue University

Jean J. O'Reilly
Pritsker Corporation

David K. LaVal
Pritsker Corporation

John Wiley & Sons
New York • Chichester • Brisbane

Systems Publishing Corporation
West Lafayette, Indiana

Distributed by:

John Wiley & Sons, Inc., New York

and

Systems Publishing Corporation
P.O. Box 2161
West Lafayette, Indiana 47906

Library of Congress Cataloging in Publication Data Available Upon Request

Printed in the United States of America
10 9 8 7 6 5 4 3 2 1

To Anne, many thanks for many happy years
Alan

To Michael, husband and best friend
Jean

To Nora, wife, friend and colleague
for her support, advice and love
David

Preface

This textbook presents a process for problem resolution, policy crafting and decision making based on the use of modeling and simulation. Detailed descriptions of the methods by which Visual SLAM® and AweSim® support this process are presented throughout the book.

The text introduces general information on the use of simulation in industry and government. Information is presented on modeling perspectives (Chapter 2), modeling and simulation process (Chapter 3) and applications of simulation (Chapter 15). Chapter 16 describes standard statistical distributions and random sampling procedures. Chapter 17 presents general statistical methods for estimating performance from simulation outputs. Specific uses of statistical techniques are included throughout the many examples in the text.

Chapters 4 through 13 provide a detailed description of Visual SLAM. The organizational structure provided by Visual SLAM for building models is explained, illustrated and applied. Input procedures and output reports are described in the 26 examples, 27 illustrations and hundreds of explanations of Visual SLAM components. Problem-solving support for simulation using databases, interactive processing and graphics capabilities is detailed in Chapter 14 where the capabilities of AweSim are presented. Exercises are given at the end of each chapter which require the application of the material presented.

Visual SLAM is an advanced simulation language for building models of systems and for automatically simulating the models to produce performance measures. Visual SLAM supports the three world views of network, discrete event and continuous modeling. By combining these world views, Visual SLAM is a Simulation Language for Alternative Modeling. Visual SLAM also includes a hierarchical network view that includes object-oriented subnetworks. This hierarchical network capability is a major technical advance in network simulation. The interfaces between the alternative modeling approaches are explicitly defined to allow new conceptual views of systems to be explored. User inserts and event routines can be developed in either the Visual Basic or C languages.

To support the entire problem resolution process AweSim provides a database, project maintainer, interactive execution environment (IEE), standard textual and graphical reports and concurrent and postprocess animation facilities. AweSim has links to other application programs for documentation, communication, statistical

---

® Visual SLAM and AweSim are registered trademarks of Pritsker Corporation.

analysis, board room presentation preparation and report writing. Furthermore, the AweSim environment provides for file management, model component management, model reuse and updating, database management of simulation outputs and, in general, problem-solving support.

The GERT/GASP/SLAM family of products has been well received and has contributed to the tremendous increase in the use of modeling and simulation throughout the world. A key ingredient of their success is the development, maintenance and support provided by Pritsker Corporation which will continue for the Visual SLAM and AweSim products. Upward compatibility has been maintained so that models developed with SLAMSYSTEM can be translated for use with Visual SLAM.

There are many ways to use this textbook for teaching simulation from a modeling perspective. Chapters 1 through 8 and 14-16 provide for a one-quarter course on network modeling and simulation analysis. When using AweSim, there is complete documentation of the Visual SLAM language online. This facilitates building models, translating them for processing and obtaining simulation outputs. AweSim's database facilitates the statistical analysis of simulation outputs as it maintains the individual simulated observations. AweSim provides the tools necessary to learn simulation modeling and its use in the problem-solving process.

For a semester course, Chapters 9 and 10 can be added to present the flavor of discrete event and continuous modeling using networks as a foundation. Chapters 11 and 12 provide for detailed modeling of systems using discrete event and continuous world views with all three world views combined in the models presented in Chapter 13.

Chapters 9 and 11 deal with user inserts and discrete events which may be coded in either Visual Basic or C. For student convenience, Chapters 9 and 11 are provided in two flavors: Visual Basic or C with the letters VB or C appended to the chapter numbers. In Chapters 10, 12, 13 and 14 where models contain user-written code, both Visual Basic and C versions of the code are provided where appropriate. For these chapters, the figures which contain code have the letters VB or C appended to the figure number. This textbook on simulation modeling with Visual SLAM and AweSim is the first to present three different modeling world views with user extensions being able to be written in Visual Basic or C. When using the C version of Visual SLAM, the data structures important to modeling and simulation can be explored and developed. With the Visual Basic version, an object-oriented view of simulation modeling can be presented.

From a teaching perspective, Visual SLAM and AweSim represent a significant advance. The programs are completely extensible and are easy to use for those familiar with Windows-based products. The open-ended nature of Visual SLAM and AweSim will allow you to pursue many topics associated with modeling and simulation based on your expertise. This includes the introduction to queueing and inventory theory as well as scheduling and optimization algorithmic evaluation and development.

Simulation languages are developed in an evolutionary manner. For Visual SLAM and AweSim, this has occurred over a thirty year period starting with the developments of GASP for discrete event and continuous modeling and Q-GERT for network modeling. For those interested in the development and evolution of these languages, the book *Papers • Experiences • Perspectives* is recommended. The design, development, documentation and testing of Visual SLAM and AweSim was a team effort and, in addition to the authors, the team included Bill Lilegdon, Janet Reust, Cathy Stein and Brad Resner. The authors thank Bill, Janet Cathy and Brad for their efforts.

We would like to thank Jim Wilson for his continuous support and significant contributions to Chapter 17; Bill Lilegdon for the Excel macros to provide the statistical outputs directly from the AweSim database; Michael Schmeiser, Janet Reust and Dave Martin for their support in the develoment of the ULAMjr example; UNOS for granting us permission to use material on organ transplantation; Lt. Col. Steven Parker for providing a preliminary version of the retirement evaluation model; and David Vaughan and Dave Withers of Lexis-Nexis for their suggestions and review regarding the development of visual subnetworks.

This book directly uses material contained in the books and papers by Thomas Schriber, George S. Fishman and Bruce Schmeiser. We thank these friends for granting us permission to use this material. Our thanks and appreciation go to Miriam Walters and Donna Kuipers for their efforts in the typing and preparation of numerous copies of the manuscript and to Anne Pritsker for reviewing and editing the manuscript.

A Solutions Manual for the exercises at the end of each chapter is available from Systems Publishing Corporation, P.O. Box 2161, West Lafayette, IN 47906. We wish you success in mastering the modeling concepts and simulation pro-cedures described in this book. When you do, you will have a modeling frame-work and a simulation tool to solve meaningful problems.

A. Alan B. Pritsker
Jean J. O'Reilly
David K. Laval

West Lafayette, Indiana
January 1997

Table of Contents

Examples

Illustrations

Simulation

with

Visual SLAM

and

AweSim

CHAPTER 1

Introduction to Modeling
and Simulation

1.1 PROBLEM SOLVING

The problems facing industry, commerce, government and society in general continue to grow in size and complexity. The need for procedures and techniques for resolving such problems is apparent. This book advocates the use of modeling and, in particular, simulation modeling for the resolution of problems. Simulation models can be employed at five levels:

- As explanatory devices to define a system or problem;
- As analysis vehicles to determine critical elements, components and issues;
- As design assessors to synthesize and evaluate proposed solutions;
- As predictors to forecast and aid in planning future developments;
- As part of a system to provide on-line monitoring, status projections and decision support.

1

In order to resolve a problem using simulation models, it is necessary to understand and to define the problem within the context of the system within which the problem exists (4). In our judgment, models should be developed to resolve specific problems. The form of the model, although dependent on the problem solver's background, requires an organized structure for investigating system changes. A simulation language provides such a vehicle. It also translates a model description into a form acceptable by a computing system. The computer is used to exercise the model to provide outputs that can be analyzed in order that changes to achieve problem resolution can be made.

The goal of this book is to provide useful information for problem solving. The book is both an introduction to simulation methodology and an introduction to the visual simulation language for alternative modeling, Visual SLAM. Visual SLAM supports the modeling of systems from diverse points of view and thus the book contains information on different methods of structuring models of systems (7).

AweSIM is a simulation problem-solving environment for Visual SLAM. Among other capabilities, AweSIM provides extensive input, output and integration capabilities to facilitate the use of Visual SLAM by engineers, managers and researchers. Since many of today's problems are statistical in nature, the input and output capabilities require a background in probability and statistics. Thus, chapters of this book are devoted to presenting probabilistic and statistical concepts related to problem solving using simulation models.

In this chapter, we present general discussions and definitions of simulation-related topics including data acquisition for model building.

1.2   SYSTEMS

A system is a collection of items from a circumscribed sector of reality that is the object of study or interest. Therefore, a system is a relative thing. In one situation, a particular collection of objects may be only a small part of a larger system—a subsystem; in another situation that same collection of objects may be the primary focus of interest and would be considered as the system. The scope of every system, and of every model of a system, is determined solely by its reason for being identified and isolated. The scope of every simulation model is determined by the particular problems the model is designed to solve (8).

To consider the scope of a system, one must contemplate its boundaries and contents. The boundary of a system may be physical; however, it is better to think of a boundary in terms of cause and effect. Given a tentative system definition, some external factors may affect the system. If they completely govern its behavior, there is no merit in experimenting with the defined system, that is, the system definition is insufficient. If they partially influence the system, there are several possibilities:

The system definition may be enlarged to include them.
They may be ignored.
They may be treated as inputs to the system.

If treated as inputs, it is assumed that the factors are functionally specified by prescribed values, tables or equations. For example, when defining the model of a company's manufacturing system, if the sales of the company's product are considered as inputs to the manufacturing system, the model does not contain a cause and effect relation between meeting due dates and sales; it only includes a statistical description of historical or predicted sales, which is used as an input. In such a model of the manufacturing system, the sales organization is outside the boundaries of the "defined" system. In systems terminology, objects that are outside the boundaries of the system, but can influence it, constitute the environment of the system, Thus, systems are collections of mutually interacting objects that are affected by outside forces. Figure 1-1 shows such a system.

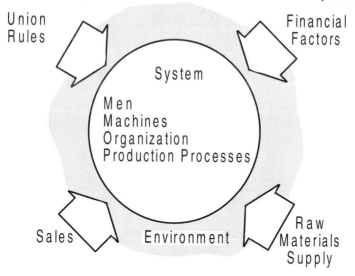

Figure 1-1 Manufacturing system model showing external influences.

1.3   MODELS

Models are *descriptions* of systems. In the physical sciences, models are usually developed based on theoretical laws and principles. The models may be scaled physical objects (iconic models), mathematical equations and relations (abstract models), or graphical representations (visual models). The usefulness of models has been demonstrated in describing, designing and analyzing systems. Many students are educated in their discipline by learning how to build and use models. Model building is a complex process and in most fields is an art. The modeling of a system is made easier if: 1) physical laws are available that pertain to the system; 2) a pictorial or graphical representation can be made of the system; and 3) the variability of system inputs, elements and outputs is manageable.

The modeling of complex, large-scale systems is often more difficult than the modeling of physical systems for the following reasons: 1) few fundamental laws are available; 2) many procedural elements are involved which are difficult to describe and represent; 3) policy inputs are required which are hard to quantify; 4) random components are significant elements; and 5) human decision making is an integral part of such systems. Through the use of a simulation approach, we will illustrate methods for alleviating these difficulties.

1.4   MODEL BUILDING

Since a model is a description of a system, it is also an abstraction of a system. To develop an abstraction, a model builder must decide on the elements of the system to include in the model. To make such decisions, a purpose for model building should be established. Reference to this purpose should be made when deciding if an element of a system is significant and, hence, should be modeled. The success of a modeler depends on how well he or she can define significant elements and the relationships between elements.   Principles for simulation modeling (7) and maxims for performing simulation modeling (6) to enhance the probability of success have been developed.

A pictorial view of our model building approach is shown in Figure 1-2. The definition of a system's objects and their function is subjective. It depends on the individual who is defining the system. Because of this, the first step of our approach is the development of a purpose for modeling that is based on a stated problem or project goal. Based on this purpose, the boundaries of the system and a level of modeling detail are established. This abstraction results in a model that smooths out many of the ill-defined edges of the actual system. We also include in the model the desired performance measures and design alternatives to be evaluated. These can be considered as part of the model or as inputs to the model. Assessments of design alternatives in terms of the specified performance measures are considered as model outputs. Typically, the assessment process requires redefinitions and redesigns. In fact, the entire model building approach is performed iteratively. When recommendations can be made based on the assessment of alternatives, an implementation phase is initiated. Implementation should be carried out in a well-defined environment with an explicit set of recommendations. Major decisions should have been made before implementation is attempted.

Simulation models are ideally suited for carrying out the problem-solving approach illustrated in Figure 1-2. Simulation provides the flexibility to build either aggregate or detailed models. It also supports the concepts of iterative model building by allowing models to be embellished through simple and direct additions. These aspects of simulation models are described in Chapter 2.

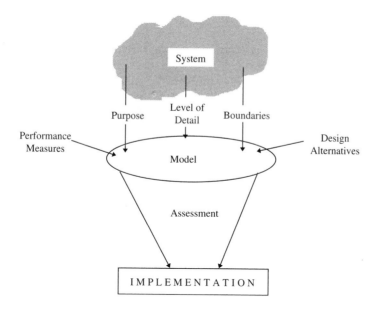

Figure 1-2 A model building approach for problem solving.

1.5   DEFINITION OF SIMULATION

In its broadest sense, computer simulation is the process of designing a mathematical-logical model of a real system and experimenting with this model on a computer (9). Thus simulation encompasses a model building process as well as the design and implementation of an appropriate experiment involving that model. These experiments, or simulations, permit inferences to be drawn about systems:

- Without building them, if they are only proposed systems.
- Without disturbing them, if they are operation systems that are costly or unsafe to experiment with;
- Without destroying them, if the object of an experiment is to determine their limits of stress.

In this way, simulation models can be used for design, procedural analysis and performance assessment.

Simulation modeling assumes that we can describe a system in terms acceptable to a computing system. In this regard, a key concept is that of a *system state description*. If a system can be characterized by a set of variables, with each combination of variable values representing a unique state or condition of the system, then manipulation of the variable values simulates movement of the system from state to state. A simulation experiment involves observing the dynamic behavior of a model by moving from state to state in accordance with well-defined operating rules designed into the model.

Changes in the state of a system can occur continuously over time or at discrete instants in time. The discrete instants can be established deterministically or stochastically depending on the nature of model inputs. Although the procedures for describing the dynamic behavior of discrete and continuous change models differ, the basic concept of simulating a system by portraying the changes in the state of the system over time remains the same. In the next section, we will illustrate the type of dynamic behavior obtained from a simulation experiment with a discrete change model.

1.6   SIMULATION OF A BANK TELLER

As an example of the concept of simulation, we examine the processing of customers by a teller at a bank. Customers arrive to the bank, wait for service by the teller if the teller is busy, are served, and then depart the system. Customers arriving to the system when the teller is busy wait in a single queue in front of the teller. For simplicity, we assume that the time of arrival of a customer and the service time by the teller for each customer are known. These values are given in Table 1-1. Our objective is to manually simulate the above system to determine the percent of time the teller is idle and the average time a customer spends at the bank.

Table 1-1 Customer arrival and service times.

Customer Number	Time of Arrival (Minutes)	Service Time (Minutes)
1	3.2	3.8
2	10.9	3.5
3	13.2	4.2
4	14.8	3.1
5	17l7	2.4
6	19.8	4.3
7	21.5	2.7
8	26.3	2.1
9	32.1	2.5
10	36.6	3.4

Since a simulation is the dynamic portrayal of the changes in the state of a system over time, the states of the system must be defined. For this example, they can be defined by the status of the teller (busy or idle) and by the number of customers at the bank. The state of the system is changed by: 1) a customer arriving to the bank; and 2) the completion of service by the teller and subsequent departure of the customer. To illustrate a simulation, we will determine the state of the system over time by processing the events corresponding to the arrival and departure of customers in a time-ordered sequence.

The manual simulation of this example corresponding to the values in Table 1-1 is summarized in Table 1-2 by customer number. It is assumed that initially there are no customers in the system, the teller is idle, and the first customer is to arrive at time 3.2.

In Table 1-2, columns (1) and (2) are taken from Table 1-1. The start of service time given in column (3) depends on whether the preceding customer has departed the bank. It is taken as the larger value of the arrival time of the customer and the departure time of the preceding customer. Column (4), the departure time, is the sum of the column (3) value and the service time for the customer given in Table 1-1. Values for time in queue and time in bank for each customer are computed as shown in Table 1-2. Average values per customer for these variables are 2.61 minutes and 5.81 minutes respectively.

Table 1-2 presents a good summary of information concerning the customer but does not provide information about the teller and the queue size for the teller. To portray such information, it is convenient to examine the events associated with the situation.

Table 1-2 Manual simulation of bank teller.

Customer Number (1)	Arrival Time (2)	Service Time (3)	Start Departure Time (4)	Time in Queue (5)=(3)-(2)	Time in Bank (6)=(4)-(2)
1	3.2	3.2	7.0	0.0	3.8
2	10.9	10.9	14.4	0.0	3.5
3	13.2	14.4	18.6	1.2	5.4
4	14.8	18.6	21.7	3.8	6.9
5	17.7	21.7	24.1	4.0	6.4
6	19.8	24.1	28.4	4.3	8.6
7	21.5	28.4	31.1	6.9	9.6
8	26.3	31.1	33.2	4.8	6.9
9	32.1	33.2	35.7	1.1	3.6
10	36.6	36.6	40.0	0.0	3.4

The logic associated with processing the arrival and departure events depends on the state of the system at the time of the event. In the case of the arrival event, the disposition of the arriving customer is based on the status of the teller. If the teller is idle, the status of the teller is changed to busy and the departure event is scheduled for the customer by adding his service time to the current time. However, if the teller is busy at the time of an arrival, the customer cannot begin service at the current time and, therefore, he enters the queue (the queue length is increased by 1). For the departure event, the logic associated with processing the event is based on queue length. If a customer is waiting in the (?) queue, the teller status remains busy, the queue length is reduced by 2, and the departure event for the first waiting customer is scheduled. However, if the queue is empty, the status of the teller is set to idle.

An event-oriented description of the bank teller status and the number of customers at the bank is given in Table 1-3 where the events are listed in chronological order. A graphic portrayal of the status variables over time is shown in Figure 1-3. These results indicate that the average number of customers at the bank in the first 40 minutes is 1.4525 and that the teller is idle 20 percent of the time.

In order to place the arrival and the departure events in their proper chronological order, it is necessary to maintain a record or calendar of future events to be processed. This is done by maintaining the times of the next arrival event and next departure event. The next event to be processed is then selected by comparing these event times. For situations with many events, an ordered list of events would be maintained which is referred to as an event file or event calendar.

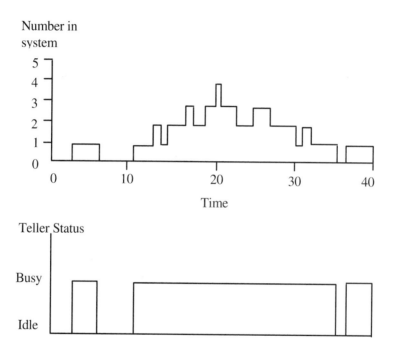

Figure 1-3 Graphic portrayal of bank teller simulation.

There are several important concepts illustrated by this example. We observe that at any instant in simulated time, the model is in a particular state. As events occur, the state of the model may change as prescribed by the logical-mathematical relationships associated with the events. Thus, the events define the dynamic structure of the model. Given the starting state, the logic for processing each event, and a method for specifying sample values, our problem is largely one of bookkeeping. An essential element in our bookkeeping scheme is an event calendar which provides a mechanism for recording and sequencing future events. Another point to observe is that we can view the state changes from two perspectives: the process that the customer encounters as he seeks service (the customer's view); or the events that cause the state of the teller to change (the teller's or bank's view). These so-called world views are described in detail in Chapter 3.

Table 1-3 Event-oriented description of bank teller simulation.

Event Time	Customer Number	Event Type	Number in Queue	Number in Bank	Teller Status	Teller Idle Time
0.0	–	Start	0	0	Idle	–
3.2	1	Arrival	0	1	Busy	3.2
7.0	1	Departure	0	0	Idle	
10.9	2	Arrival	0	1	Busy	3.9
13.2	3	Arrival	1	2	Busy	
14.4	2	Departure	0	1	Busy	
14.8	4	Arrival	1	2	Busy	
17.7	5	Arrival	2	3	Busy	
18.6	3	Departure	1	2	Busy	
19.8	6	Arrival	2	3	Busy	
21.5	7	Arrival	4	5	Busy	
24.1	5	Departure	1	2	Busy	
26.3	8	Arrival	2	3	Busy	
28.4	6	Departure	1	2	Busy	
31.1	7	Departure	0	1	Busy	
32.1	9	Arrival	1	2	Busy	
33.2	8	Departure	0	1	Busy	
35.7	9	Departure	0	0	Idle	
36.6	10	Arrival	0	1	Busy	0.9

1.7   DATA COLLECTION AND ANALYSIS

As seen in the bank teller illustration of Section 1.6, an essential function in simulation modeling is the collection and analysis of data. This function is required both in defining inputs for the model and in obtaining performance measures from experimentation with the model. In this section, we will review some of the important statistical concepts applicable to data collection and analysis.

1.7.1 Data Acquisition

Data acquisition is the process of obtaining data on a phenomenon of interest. There are a variety of methods by which the data can be acquired. In some cases, the data are available in existing documents, and the problem is that of locating and accessing the data. In other cases, data acquisition may involve the use of questionnaires, field surveys and physical experimentation.

In aggregate models such as those of urban or economic systems, the required data can frequently be obtained from existing documentation. Common sources of data for these models include census reports, the Statistical Abstract of the United States, United Nations publications, and other publications of governmental and international organizations. Sometimes such data are available on CD-ROM or computer disks.

In models of business systems, a valuable source of data is the accounting and engineering records of the company. These records are sometimes sufficient to form the basis for estimating product demand, production cost, and other relevant data. Normally, however, they only represent a starting point. Questionnaires and field surveys are also potential methods for obtaining data for industrial models. With the advent of on-line collection systems, data acquisition is a semi-continuous process and makes data readily available in databases or as computer records. Manufacturing, communications, transportation and medical-related fields led in the introduction of such data acquisition capabilities.

Physical experimentation is commonly the most expensive and time consuming method for obtaining data. This process includes measurement, recording and editing of the data. Considerable care must be taken in planning the experiment to assure that the experimental conditions are representative and that the data are recorded correctly. For a discussion of experimental design considerations in data collection, the reader is referred to the text by Bartee (2).

In some cases, there may be no existing data and the available budget or nature of the system may preclude experimentation. An example of such a case would be the use of simulation modeling to compare several proposed assembly line layouts. A possible approach to data acquisition in such cases is the use of synthetic or predetermined data (1). In this method, estimates of activity durations are synthesized by using tables of standard data. Thus, this method permits activity times to be estimated before the process is actually in operation. Another method is to use data obtained from similar or analogous activities.

1.7.2 Descriptive Statistics

In both collecting data for defining inputs to the model and collecting data on system performance from the model, we encounter the problem of how to convert the raw data to a usable form. Hence, we are interested in treatments designed to summarize or describe important features of a set of data. These treatments summarize the data with a loss of individual measurements contained within the data.

Grouping Data. One method for transforming data into a more manageable form is to group the data into classes or cells. The data is then summarized by tabulating the number of data points which fall within each class. This kind of table is called a frequency distribution table and normally gives a good overall picture of the data. An example of a frequency distribution table for data collected on customer waiting times is depicted below.

Waiting time (Seconds)	Number of Customers
$0 \rightarrow 20$	21
$20 \rightarrow 40$	35
$40 \rightarrow 60$	42
$60 \rightarrow 80$	35
$80 \rightarrow 100$	19
$100 \rightarrow 120$	10
> 120	10

The numbers in the right-hand column denote the number of customers falling into each class and are called the class frequencies. The numbers in the left-hand column define the range of values in each class and are referred to as the class limits. The difference between the upper class limit and lower class limit in each case is called the class width. Classes with an unbounded upper or lower class limit are referred to as open. If a class has bounded limits, it is denoted as closed. Frequently the first and/or last class in a frequency distribution will be open.

There are several variations of the class frequency tables which are useful for displaying grouped data. One variation is the cumulative frequency which is obtained by successively adding the frequencies in the frequency table. The cumulative frequency table for the customer waiting time data is depicted below.

Waiting time Less Than	Cumulative Number of Customers
$0 \rightarrow 20$	21
$20 \rightarrow 40$	35
$40 \rightarrow 60$	42
$60 \rightarrow 80$	35
$80 \rightarrow 100$	19
$100 \rightarrow 120$	10
> 120	10

The values in the right-hand column represent the cumulative or total number of customers whose waiting time was less than the upper class limit specified in the left-hand column. Another variation is obtained by converting the class frequency table (or cumulative table) into a corresponding frequency distribution by dividing each class frequency (cumulative frequency) by the total number of data points. Frequency distributions are particularly useful when comparing two or more distributions.

The frequency and cumulative distribution are sometimes presented graphically in order to enhance the interpretability of the data. The most common among graphical presentations is the histogram which displays the class frequencies as rectangles whose heights are proportional to the class frequency. Figure 1-4 depicts a histogram for the customer waiting time data.

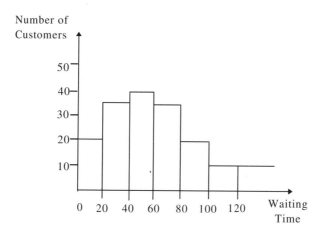

Figure 1-4 Histogram for customer waiting time data.

The primary consideration in the construction of frequency distributions is the specification of the number of classes and the upper and lower class limits for each class. These choices depend upon the nature and ultimate use of the data; however, the following guidelines are offered.

1. Whenever possible, the class widths should be of equal length. Exceptions to this are the first and last classes which are frequently open.

2. Class intervals should not overlap and all data points should fall within a class. In other words, each data point should be assignable to one and only one class.

3. Normally at least five but no more than twenty classes are used.

Parameter Estimation. If a set of data points consists of all possible observations of a random variable, we refer to it as a population; if it contains only part of these observations, we refer to it as a sample. Another method for summarizing a set of data is to view the data as a *sample* which is then used to estimate the parameters of the parent or underlying population. The population parameters of most frequent interest are the mean which provides a measure of centrality, and the variance which provides a measure of dispersion.

To illustrate, consider again the data on customer waiting times. This data can be viewed as a sample from the population which consists of all possible customer waiting times. We can use this sample data to estimate the mean customer waiting time and the variance of the customer waiting time for the population of all possible customers.

Different symbols are used to distinguish between population parameters and estimates of these parameters based upon a sample. The greek letters μ and σ^2 are often used to denote the population mean and variance, respectively. The corresponding estimates of these parameters based upon the sample record x_1, $x_2,\ldots,x_I$ are the average, denoted as $\overline{X}_I$ and the variance estimate, denoted as s_x^2. In order to further distinguish between descriptions of populations and descriptions of samples, the first are referred to as parameters and the second are referred to as statistics.

Before proceeding with this discussion of descriptive statistics, a clarifying point regarding the notation used to describe random samples and experimental values of a random variable or stochastic sequence is necessary. Before an experimental value is observed, it is a random variable denoted by X_I. After a value is observed it is denoted by x_i. By the sample mean, $\overline{X}_I$, we refer to a random variable that is the sum of I random samples before they are observed divided by I. The average, $\overline{X}_I$, however, is the sum of I observed values x_i divided by I. In an analogous fashion, s_x^2 is the random variable describing an estimate of the sample variance before experimental values are observed and s_x^2 is the estimate of the variance of observed values.

In constructing estimates of the population parameters from sample data, there are two distinct cases to consider. In the first case, we consider a sample record where we are concerned only with the value of each observation and not with the times at which the observations were recorded. The data on customer waiting times is an example of such a record. Statistics derived from a time-independent sample record are referred to as statistics based upon observations.

The second case is for variables which have values defined over time. For example, the number of busy tellers in a bank is a random variable that has a value which is defined over time. In this case, we require knowledge of both the values assumed by the random variable and the time periods for which each value persisted. Statistics derived from time-dependent records are referred to as *statistics on time-persistent variables*.

The formulas for calculating $\overline{X}_i$ and s_x^2 for statistics based upon observations and statistics on time-persistent variables are summarized in Table 1-4. For the time-persistent case the sample mean is designated by $\overline{X}_T$ where T is the total time interval observed. Sometimes the formulas for s_x^2 are given in a slightly different form; however the form shown is the most convenient for computational purposes. Note that for statistics based upon observations, the $\sum_{i=1}^{I} x_i$, the $\sum_{i=1}^{I} x_i^2$ and the number of samples I, are sufficient to compute both $\overline{x}_I$ and s_x^2. Similarly, for statistics on time-persistent variables $\int_0^T x\,dt$, $\int_0^T x^2\,dt$, and T are required.

Another statistic which is commonly employed in summarizing a set of data is the coefficient of variation $s_x / \overline{x}_I$. The coefficient of variation expresses the sample standard deviation relative to the sample mean. The use of the coefficient of variation is advantageous when comparing the variation between two or more sets of data.

Distribution Estimation. A related but more difficult problem is the use of the sample record to identify the distribution of the population. This problem frequently arises in modeling because of the need to characterize random elements of a system by particular distributions. Although an understanding of the properties of the theoretical distributions described in Chapter 16 will aid the modeler in hypothesizing an appropriate distribution, it is frequently desired to test the hypothesis by applying one or more goodness-of-fit tests to the sample record. The chi-square and Kolmogorov-Smirnov are probably the best known tests, and descriptions and examples of these can be found in most statistics and simulation textbooks (3,5). A discussion of identifying a distribution function that fits a sample record and for fitting a nonstandard distribution function to data is given in Chapter 16.

Table 1-4 Formulas for calculating the average and variance of a sample record.

Statistic	Formula	
	Statistics based upon Observations	Statistics for Time Persistent Variables
Sample Mean	$\overline{x}_I = \dfrac{\sum\limits_{i=1}^{I} x_i}{I}$	$\overline{x}_T = \dfrac{\int\limits_{0}^{T} x(t)\,dt}{T}$
Sample Variance	$s_X^2 = \dfrac{\sum\limits_{i=1}^{I} x_i^2 - I\overline{x}_I^2}{I-1}$	$s_X^2 = \dfrac{\int\limits_{0}^{T} x^2(t)\,dt}{T} - \overline{x}_T^2$

1.8   CHAPTER SUMMARY

Simulation is a technique that has been employed extensively to solve problems. Simulation models are abstractions of systems. They should be built quickly, explained to all project personnel, and changed when necessary. The implementation of recommendations to improve system performance is an integral part of the simulation methodology.

1.9   EXERCISES

1-1. Define the elements shown in Figure 1-2 for a specific problem related to your organization. Include proposed design alternatives, assessment procedures, and one possible implementation outcome. Repeat this exercise from your supervisor's (instructor's) perspective.

1-2. Build a diagram similar to Figure 1-1 for the University System. Build an explanatory model of the University System from a student's point of view.

1-3. How does a simulation language support modeling?

1-4. In the simulation of the bank teller, hypothesize a relation between the average time in the bank per customer and average number of customers in the bank. Determine if your hypothesis holds for average time in queue and average number in queue.

1-5. Discuss how a simulation language impacts on model building.

1-6. Describe the operation of a machine tool.

1-7. Describe the events associated with maintaining accounting records.

1-8. Discuss the types of data that are needed to build a structural model of a system. Discuss the type of data that is needed to estimate parameters of a model. Give examples of structural data and detailed data.

1.10   REFERENCES

1. Barnes, R. M., *Motion and Time Study: Design and Measurement of Work*, Sixth Edition, John Wiley, 1968.

2. Bartee, E. M., *Engineering Experimental Design Fundamentals*, Prentice-Hall, 1968.

3. Bratley, P., B. L. Fox, and L. E. Schrage, *A Guide to Simulation*, Second Edition, Springer-Verlag, 1987.

4. Emshoff, J. R. and R. L. Sisson, *Design and Use of Computer Simulation Models*, Macmillan, 1970.

5. Law, A. M. and W. D. Kelton, *Simulation Modeling and Analysis*, Second Edition, McGraw-Hill, 1991.

6. Musselman, K. J., "Guidelines for Success" in *Handbook of Simulation*, J.Banks, Ed., John Wiley, 1997.

7. Pritsker, A. A. B., "Modeling for Simulation Analysis," in *Handbook of Industrial Engineering*, Second Edition, G. Salvendy, Ed., John Wiley, 1992, pp. 2533-2547.

8. Pritsker, A. A. B. , *Papers • Experiences • Perspectives*, Wadsworth/ Duxbury Publishers, 1990.

9. Pritsker, A. A. B., "Compilation of Definitions of Simulation," *Simulation*, Vol. 33, 1979, pp. 61-63.

CHAPTER 2

Simulation Modeling Perspectives

2.1 INTRODUCTION

In developing a simulation model, an analyst needs to select a conceptual framework for describing the system to be modeled. The framework or perspective contains a "world view" within which the system functional relationships are perceived and described. If the modeler is employing a simulation language, the world view will normally be implicit within the language. However, if the modeler elects to employ a general purpose language such as FORTRAN, C or C++, the perspective for organizing the system description is the responsibility of the modeler. In either case, the world view employed by the modeler provides a conceptual mechanism for articulating the system description. In this chapter, we summarize the alternative world views for simulation modeling and introduce the unified modeling framework of Visual SLAM.

2.2   MODELING WORLD VIEWS

Models of systems can be classified as either discrete change or continuous change. Note that these terms describe the model and not the real system. In fact, it may be possible to model the same system with either a discrete change (hereafter referred to simply as discrete) or a continuous change (continuous) model. In most simulations, time is the major independent variable. Other variables included in the simulation are functions of time and are the dependent variables. The adjectives discrete and continuous when modifying simulation refer to the behavior of the dependent variables.

Discrete simulation occurs when the dependent variables change discretely at specified points in simulated time referred to as event times. The time variable may be either continuous or discrete in such a model, depending on whether the discrete changes in the dependent variable can occur at any point in time or only at specified points.

The bank teller problem discussed in Chapter 1 is an example of a discrete simulation. The dependent variables in that example were the teller status and the number of waiting customers. The event times corresponded to the times at which customers arrived to the system and departed from the system following completion of service by the teller. In general, the values of the dependent variables for discrete models do not change between event times. An example response for a dependent variable in a discrete simulation is shown in Figure 2-1.

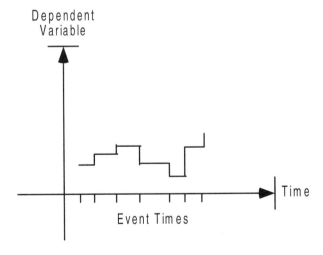

Figure 2-1 Response measurement from a discrete event simulator.

In *continuous simulation* the dependent variables of the model may change continuously over simulated time. A continuous model may be either continuous or discrete in time, depending on whether the values of the dependent variables are available at any point in simulated time or only at specified points in simulated time. Examples of response measurements for continuous simulations are shown in Figure 2-2 and Figure 2-3.

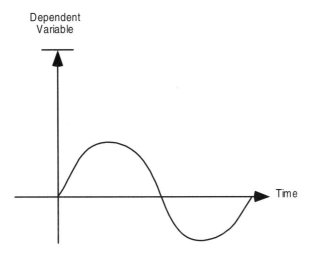

Figure 2-2 Response measurement from a continuous simulator.

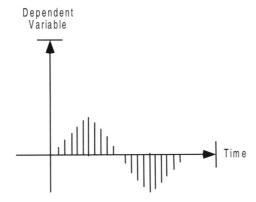

Figure 2-3 Response measurement from a continuous simulator using discrete time steps.

The modeling of the concentration of a reactant in a chemical process or the position and velocity of a spacecraft are illustrations of situations where a continuous representation is appropriate. However, in some cases, it is also useful to model a discrete system with a continuous representation by considering the entities in the system in the aggregate rather than as individual entities. For example, we would probably prefer to model the population of a particular species in a lake using a continuous representation, even though in reality the population changes discretely.

In combined simulation the dependent variables of a model may change discretely, continuously, or continuously with discrete jumps superimposed. The time variable may be continuous or discrete. The most important aspect of combined simulation arises from the interaction between discretely and continuously changing variables. For example, when the concentration level of a reactant in a chemical process reaches a prescribed level, the process may be shut down. A combined simulation language must contain provisions for detecting the occurrence of such conditions and for modeling their consequences. An example of a response from a combined simulation model is shown in Figure 2-4.

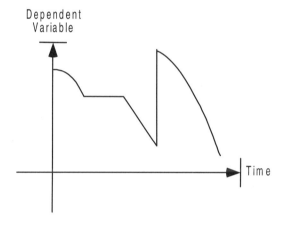

Figure 2-4 Response measurement from a combined simulator.

2.3   DISCRETE SIMULATION MODELING

The objects within the boundaries of a discrete system, such as people, equipment, orders, and raw materials are called entities. There are many types of entities and each has various characteristics or attributes. Although they engage in different types of activities, entities may have a common attribute requiring that they be grouped together. Groupings of entities are called files. Inserting an entity into a file implies that it has some relation with other entities in the file.

The aim of a discrete simulation model is to reproduce the activities that the entities engage in and thereby learn something about the behavior and performance potential of the system. This is done by defining the states of the system and constructing activities that move it from state to state. The state of a system is defined in terms of the alphanumeric values assigned to the attributes of the entities. A system is said to be in a particular state when all of its entities are in states consonant with the range of attribute values that define that state. Thus, simulation is the dynamic portrayal of the states of a system over time.

In discrete simulation, the state of the system can change only at event times. Since the state of the system remains constant between event times a complete dynamic portrayal of the state of the system can be obtained by advancing simulated time from one event to the next. This timing mechanism is referred to as the next event approach and is used in most discrete simulation languages.

A discrete simulation model can be formulated by: 1) defining the changes in state that occur at each event time; 2) describing the activities in which the entities in the system engage; or 3) describing the process through which the entities in the system flow. The relationship between the concept of an *event*, an *activity*, and a *process* is depicted in Figure 2-5. An event takes place at an isolated point in time at which decisions are made to start or end activities. A process is a time-ordered sequence of events and may encompass several activities. These concepts lead naturally to three alternative world views for discrete simulation modeling. These world views are commonly referred to as the event, activity scanning, and process interaction orientations, and are described in the following sections. A manufacturing simulation language, FACTOR/AIM, built on the process interaction perspective shown in Figure 2-5, has been developed (5,9).

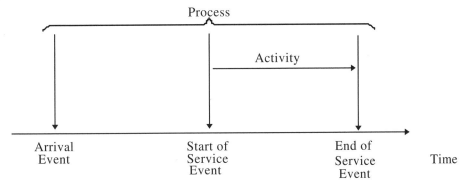

Figure 2-5 Relationship of events, activities and processes.

3 WORLD VIEWS FOR DISCRETE MODELING.

 • EVENT

 • ACTIVITY SCANNING

 • PROCESS INTERACTION.

2.3.1 Event Orientation

· SCHEDULED EVENTS.

In the event-oriented world view, a system is modeled by defining the changes that occur at event times. The task of the modeler is to determine the events that can change the state of the system and then to develop the logic associated with each event type. A simulation of the system is produced by executing the logic associated with each event in a time-ordered sequence(1).

To illustrate the event orientation, consider again the bank teller problem discussed in Chapter 1. Customers arrive to the system, possibly wait, undergo service by the teller, and then exit the system. The state of the system is defined by the status of the teller and the number of waiting customers. The state of the system remains constant except when a customer arrives to the system or departs from it. Therefore, the event model for this system consists of describing what happens at a customer arrival time and at an end-of-service time. Since a change in the state of the system can occur only at these event times, the customer arrival and end-of-service events can be used to completely describe the dynamic structure of the system. At the event time, the simulation clock stands still and only status changes are made. However, future events can be placed on the event calendar which represents times in the future at which status changes may take place.

Consider first the logic associated with the customer arrival event. The first action taken is to schedule the next arrival. This is done to provide a sequence of arrivals. Hence, once the first arrival is scheduled, a continuing stream of arrivals will occur. The disposition of the current customer arrival depends upon the state of the system at the customer arrival time. If the teller is busy, the arriving customer must wait, and therefore the state of the system is changed by increasing the number of waiting customers by one. Otherwise, the arriving customer can be placed immediately into service. In this case, the state of the system is changed by setting the status of the teller to busy. In addition, the end-of-service event for the customer must be scheduled to occur at the current simulated time plus the time it takes the teller to serve the customer.

Next, consider the logic associated with processing the end-of-service event. In this event, both the disposition of the customer and the teller must be specified. We assume the customer departs the bank after being served. For the teller who is completing service on the current customer, we first test to see if additional customers are waiting for service by the teller. If customers are waiting, we reduce the number waiting by 1 and schedule the end-of-service event for the first waiting customer. Otherwise, we set the teller to idle status.

To create a simulation of the bank teller problem using the event orientation, we would maintain a calendar of events and cause their execution at the proper points in simulated time. The event calendar would initially contain an event notice corresponding to the first arrival event. As the simulation proceeds, additional arrival events and end-of-service events would be scheduled onto the calendar as prescribed by the logic associated with the events. Each event would be executed in a time-ordered sequence, with simulated time being advanced from one event to the next. The event orientation of simulation represents a large decomposition of the modeling effort. To obtain the dynamic behavior of a model, the status variable need only be examined at event times. The specification of a limited number of events reduces the modeling effort by allowing the same logic to be used at the event occurrences.

If the modeler employs a general purpose language to code a discrete event model, then a considerable amount of programming effort will be directed at developing the event calendar and a timing mechanism for processing the events in their proper chronological order. Since this function is common to all discrete event models, simulation languages like Visual SLAM provide special features for event scheduling, as well as other functions which are commonly encountered in discrete event models.

2.3.2 Activity Scanning Orientation

In the activity scanning orientation, the modeler describes the activities in which the entities in the system engage and prescribes the conditions which cause an activity to start or end. The events which start or end the activity are not scheduled by the modeler, but are initiated from the conditions specified for the activity. As simulated time is advanced, the conditions for either starting or ending an activity are scanned. If the prescribed conditions are satisfied, then the appropriate action for the activity is taken. To insure that each activity is accounted for, it is necessary to scan the entire set of activities at each time advance.

For certain types of problems, the activity scanning approach can provide a concise modeling framework. This approach is particularly well suited for situations where an activity duration is indefinite and is determined by the state of the system satisfying a prescribed condition. However, because of the need to scan each activity at each time advance, the approach is relatively inefficient when compared to the discrete event orientation. As a result, the activity scanning orientation has not been widely adopted as a modeling framework for discrete simulations. However, a number of languages employ specific features which are based on the concept of activity scanning. Visual SLAM includes two methods for incorporating activities whose start and end times are based on system status. These are described in Chapters 4 and 9.

2.3.3 Process Interaction Orientation

'SEQUENCE OF EVENTS IN PRESCRIBED PATTERN.

Many simulation models include sequences of elements which occur in defined patterns, for example, a queue where entities wait for processing by a server. The logic associated with such a sequence of events can be generalized and defined by a single statement. A simulation language can then translate such statements into the appropriate sequence of events. A process oriented language employs such statements to model the flow of entities through a system (3). These statements define a sequence of events which are automatically executed by the simulation language as the entities move through the process. Pritsker has developed the concepts for network simulation languages (8) that capture the process interaction world view. For example, the following network describes the process interactions for the bank teller problem.

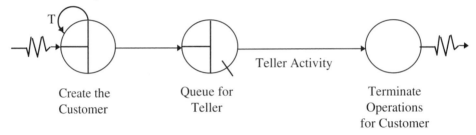

| Create the Customer | Queue for Teller | Terminate Operations for Customer |

The first node creates the arrivals of customers to the system with a time between arrivals of T time units. T could be specified to be a constant or to be a sampled value. The QUEUE FOR TELLER NODE specifies that the entity is to wait until the teller is idle. The TELLER ACTIVITY models the elapsed time during which the customer is served by the teller. Following completion of service, the customer is terminated from the system. The teller is then available to process any waiting entities at the QUEUE FOR TELLER NODE.

From the above example we see that the process interaction orientation provides a description of the flow of the entities through a process. Its simplicity is derived from the fact that the event logic associated with the statements is contained within the symbols of the simulation language. However, since we are normally restricted to a set of standardized symbols provided by the simulation language, our modeling flexibility is not as great as with the event orientation.

2.4   CONTINUOUS SIMULATION MODELING

In a continuous simulation model, the state of the system is represented by dependent variables which change continuously over time. To distinguish continuous change variables from discrete change variables, the former are referred to as state variables. A continuous simulation model is constructed by defining equations for a set of state variables whose dynamic behavior simulates the real system. Models of continuous systems are frequently written in terms of the derivatives of the state variables. The reason for this is that it is often easier to construct a relationship for the rate of change of the state variable than to devise a relationship for the state variable directly. Equations of this form involving derivatives of the state variables are referred to as differential equations. For example, our modeling effort might produce the following differential equation for the state variable, s, over time, t, together with an initial condition at time 0.

$$\frac{ds(t)}{dt} = s^2(t) + t^2$$
$$s(0) = k$$

The first equation specifies the rate of change of s as a function of s and t and the second equation specifies the initial condition for the state variable. The simulation analyst's objective is to determine the response of the state variable over simulated time.

In some cases, it is possible to determine an analytical expression for the state variable, s, given an equation for ds/dt. However, in many cases of practical importance, an analytical solution for s will not be known. As a result we must obtain the response, s, by integrating ds/dt over time using an equation of the following type:

$$s(t_2) = s(t_1) + \int_{t_1}^{t_2} \left(\frac{ds}{dt}\right) dt$$

In Visual SLAM this integration is performed using numerical integration methods which divide the independent variable (normally time) into small slices referred to as steps. The values for the state variables requiring integration are obtained by employing an approximation to the derivative of the state variable over time.

The accuracy of these methods depends upon the order of the approximation method and the size of the step, with greater accuracy resulting from higher-order approximations and smaller step sizes. Since higher-order approximations and smaller step sizes result in more computations, a trade-off exists between accuracy of state variable calculations and computer run time. A description of numerical integration algorithms can be found in introductory texts for numerical analysis (2,10). The numerical integration scheme employed by Visual SLAM for simulating continuous models involving differential equations is described in Chapter 12.

Sometimes a continuous system is modeled using difference equations. In these models, the time axis is decomposed into time periods of length Δt. The dynamics of the state variables are described by specifying an equation which calculates the value of the state variable at period $k + 1$ from the value of the state variable at period k. For example, the following difference equation could be employed to describe the dynamics of the state variable S:

$$S_{k+1} = S_k + r*\Delta t$$

When using difference equations, the continuous simulation model reflects the change in S during Δt by the product of a rate r and Δt and adds it to S_k to project the value of the state variable at period k+1, that is, S_{k+1}. A combination of differential and difference equations can be included in the same model. Also, sets of differential-difference equations can be a part of a simulation model.

2.5 COMBINED DISCRETE-CONTINUOUS MODELS

In combined discrete-continuous models, the dependent variables may change both discretely and continuously. The world view of a combined model specifies that the system can be described in terms of entities, their associated attributes, and state variables. The behavior of the system model is simulated by computing the values of the state variables at small time steps and by computing the values of attributes of entities at event times.

There are three fundamental interactions which can occur between discretely and continuously changing variables. First, a discrete change in value may be made to a continuous variable. Examples of this type of interaction are: 1) the completion of a new power station which instantaneously increases the total energy available within a system; and 2) the chemical spraying of a lake which instantaneously decreases the population of a particular species in the lake. Second, an event involving a continuous state variable achieving a threshold value may cause an event to occur or to be scheduled. As examples consider: 1) a chemical process that is completed when a prescribed concentration level is obtained and the process is shut down for cleaning and maintenance activities; and 2) the shutdown of a refinery when the level of crude oil available for input is below a prescribed value. Third, the functional description of continuous variables may be changed at discrete time instants. Examples of this are: 1) the discharge of a pollutant into an ecosystem that immediately alters the growth relationships governing species populations; and 2) the completion of a docking operation of a space vehicle which requires the use of new equations for simulating the space vehicle's motion.

The interaction between the continuous and discrete change state variables in a combined discrete-continuous change system necessitates a broader interpretation of an event than is normally used in discrete change languages. For combined simulation models, Pritsker (7) defined an event as follows:

> An event occurs at any point in time beyond which the status of
> the system cannot be projected with certainty.

Note that this definition allows the system status to change continuously without an event occurring, as long as the change has been prescribed in a well-defined manner.

There are two types of events that can occur in combined simulations. *Time-events* are those events which are scheduled to occur at specified points in time. They are commonly thought of in terms of discrete simulation models. In contrast, *state-events* are not scheduled, but occur when the system reaches a particular state. For example, as illustrated in Figure 2-6, a state-event could be specified to occur whenever state variable SS(1) crosses state variable SS(2) in the positive direction. Note that the idea of a state-event is similar to the concept of activity scanning in that the event is not scheduled but is initiated by the state of the system. The possible occurrence of a state-event must be tested at each time advance in the simulation.

These constructs were first implemented in GASP IV (4,7). This language provided a formalized world view which combined the discrete event orientation for modeling discrete systems with the state variable equation orientation for continuous system modeling. The analysis of systems using combined simulation models continues to be a fertile area for research, development and application (6,11,12,13).

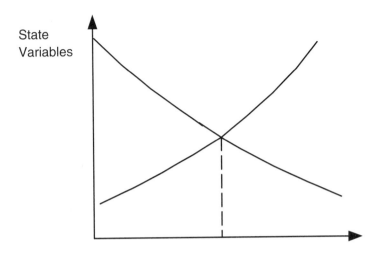

State
Variables

Figure 2-6 Example of a state-event occurrence.

2.6 Visual SLAM: A UNIFIED MODELING FRAMEWORK

In the preceding sections, we described several alternate world views for simulation modeling. Each of these views presumes a framework within which the system is described. The diversity of world views has persisted because each has certain advantages and disadvantages. For example, the process orientation provides a concise and easy to learn modeling framework, but may lack flexibility. On the other hand, the event orientation is normally more difficult to learn but, once mastered, provides a highly flexible modeling framework.

In Visual SLAM, the alternate modeling world views are combined to provide a unified modeling framework. A discrete change system can be modeled within an event orientation, a process orientation, or *both*. Continuous change systems can be modeled using either differential or difference equations. Combined discrete-continuous change systems can be modeled by combining the event and/or the process orientation with the continuous orientation. In addition, Visual SLAM incorporates a number of features which correspond to the activity scanning orientation.

The process orientation of Visual SLAM employs a network structure as illustrated in Section 2.3.3 which consists of specialized symbols called nodes and *branches*. These symbols model elements in a process such as queues, servers and decision points. The modeling task consists of combining these symbols into a network model which pictorially represents the system of interest. In short, a network is a pictorial representation of a process. The entities in the system (such as people and items) flow through the network model.

In the event orientation of Visual SLAM, the modeler defines the events and the potential changes to the system when an event occurs. The mathematical-logical relationships prescribing the changes associated with each event type are coded by the modeler as Visual Basic or C procedures. A set of standard subprograms is provided by Visual SLAM for use by the modeler to perform common discrete event functions such as event scheduling, file manipulations, statistics collection, and random sample generation. The executive control program of Visual SLAM controls the simulation by advancing time and initiating calls to the appropriate event subroutines at the proper points in simulated time. Hence, the modeler is completely relieved of the task of sequencing events to occur chronologically.

A continuous model is coded in Visual SLAM by specifying the differential or difference equations which describe the dynamic behavior of the state variables. These equations are coded by the modeler in Visual SLAM by employing a set of special Visual SLAM defined storage arrays. The value of Ith state variable is maintained as variable $SS(I)$ and the derivative of the Ith state variable, when required, is maintained as the variable $DD(I)$. The immediate past values for state variable I and its derivative are maintained as $SSL(I)$ and $DDL(I)$, respectively. When differential equations are included in the continuous model, they are automatically integrated by Visual SLAM to calculate the values of the state variables within an accuracy prescribed by the modeler.

An important aspect of Visual SLAM is that alternate world views can be combined within the same simulation model. There are six specific interactions which can take place between the network, discrete event, and continuous world views of Visual SLAM:

1. Entities in the network model can initiate the occurrence of discrete events.
2. Events can alter the flow of entities in the network model.
3. Entities in the network model can cause instantaneous changes to values of the state variables.
4. State variables reaching prescribed threshold values can initiate entities in the network model.
5. Events can cause instantaneous changes of the values of state variables.
6. State variables reaching prescribed threshold values can initiate events.

2.7 CHAPTER SUMMARY

In this chapter, we described the alternate world views of simulation modeling and introduced the unified modeling framework of Visual SLAM. In Chapters 5 through 14 we describe the network, event, continuous, and combined modeling features of Visual SLAM. As the reader masters each of these orientations within the unified framework of Visual SLAM, the need for a simulation language with the alternative modeling concepts and relationships discussed in this chapter should become clear.

2.8 EXERCISES

2-1 Consider the operation of a physician's office. Specify the boundaries of the system, and describe its operation in terms of entities, attributes, relationships, and activities.

2-2 Give an example of a situation in which the end of an activity cannot be scheduled in advance but must be based on the status of the system.

2-3 A paint shop employs six workers who prepare jobs to be spray painted. The preparation time is lengthy compared to the spraying operation and, hence, only two spraying machines are available. After a worker completes the preparation of a job, he proceeds to a spraying machine where he waits if necessary for a free spraying machine. Jobs to be prepared and painted are always available to the workmen. Describe this system using the event orientation and the process orientation.

2-4. Describe a residential heating and cooling system in terms of state variables, time-events and state-events.

2-5. Model an elevator system to ascertain energy usage. The elevator services five floors. Assume the arrival of passengers at each floor is a random variable and that the probability associated with the passenger's floor to floor transition are known. Note that energy use is a function of the dynamic characteristic of the elevator's motion.

2-6. Write a simulation model of a single-server queueing system using general purpose programming language such as FORTRAN, Visual Basic or C. Assume that the time between customer arrivals is exponentially distributed with mean of 5 time units and the service time is uniformly distributed between 2 and 6 time units. Estimate the average queue length, server utilization, and time-in-system based on 1000 customers.

   Embellishment: Change the model to include two parallel servers and a finite queue capacity of 10 customers.

2.9   REFERENCES

1. Banks, J., J. S. Carson, II, and B. L. Nelson, *Discrete-Event System Simulation*, Prentice Hall, Second Edition, 1996.

2. Carnahan, B., H. A. Luther, and J. O. Wilkes, *Applied Numerical Methods*, John Wiley, 1969.

3. Franta, W. R., *The Process View of Simulation*, North Holland, 1977.

4. Hurst, N. R., "GASP IV: A Combined Continuous/Discrete FORTRAN Based Simulation Language," Unpublished Ph.D. Thesis, Purdue University, 1973.

5. Lilegdon, W. R., D. L. Martin and A. A. B. Pritsker, FACTOR/AIM: A Manufacturing Simulation System, *Simulation*, Vol. 62, June 1994, pp. 367-372.

6. Morito, S., K. Nakano and R. Aizawa, *Intoduction to Simulation Using SLAM II* (in Japanese), Koza Keikaku Engineering, Tokyo, Japan, 1993.

7. Pritsker, A. A. B., *The GASP IV Simulation Language*, John Wiley, 1974.

8. Pritsker, A. A. B., *Modeling and Analysis Using Q-GERT Networks*, Halsted Press and Pritsker & Associates, Inc., Second Edition, 1979.

9. Pritsker, A. A. B., *Introduction to Simulation and SLAM II*, Fourth Edition, Systems Publishing Corporation and John Wiley, 1995.

10. Shampine, L. F. and R. C. Allen, Jr., *Numerical Computing: An Introduction*, W. B. Saunders, 1973.

11. Sigal, C. E. and A. A. B. Pritsker, "SMOOTH: A Combined Continuous-Discrete Network Simulation Language," *Simulation*, Vol. 21, 1974, pp. 65-73.

12. Washam, W., "GASPPI: GASP IV With Process Interaction Capabilities," Unpublished M.S. Thesis, Purdue University, 1976.

13. Wortman, D. B., S. D. Duket et al, Simulation Using SAINT: A User-Oriented *Instruction Manual, AMRL-TR-77-61, Aerospace Medical Research Laboratory*, Wright-Patterson AFB, Ohio, 1978.

CHAPTER 3

Modeling and Simulation Process

3.1   INTRODUCTION

The modeling and simulation process focuses on formulating and solving a problem. The modeling process is iterative because the act of modeling reveals important information piecemeal. This information supports actions that make the model and its output measures more relevant and accurate. The modeling process continues until additional detail or information is no longer necessary for problem resolution. During this iterative process, relationships between the system under study and the model are continually defined and redefined. The resulting correspondence between the model and the system establishes a tool that has value and relevance to the participating problem solvers.

Figure 3-1 presents the suggested steps in performing a project in which modeling and simulation are used (7,13). The six steps in the process are: 1) formulate problem, 2) specify model, 3) build model, 4) simulate model, 5) use model, and 6) support decision making. The iterative nature of the process is indicated by the feedback branches in Figure 3-1. Within step 3, build model, the substeps of develop simulation model, collect data, and define experimental controls are performed concurrently. These substeps are dependent on the information generated by each other. This is also the case for the run model, verify model, and validate model substeps which are a part of step 4, simulate model. Each of the six steps in the modeling and simulation process are described in this chapter.

3.2   FORMULATE PROBLEM

The first step in the problem solving process is to formulate the problem by understanding the problem context, identifying project goals, specifying system performance measures, setting specific modeling objectives, and defining the system to be modeled. These functions serve to guide and bound a project.

A project typically starts with a broad problem statement such as planned production quantities are not being met by the factory. Faced with this situation, basic questions should be asked to understand the problem context:

1. What operations and functions produce the systems output?
2. What procedural elements exist in the systems operation?
3. What interactions occur between functional units of the system?
4. What information is available to characterize the operations, functions, and procedures of the system?

The answers to these questions help to formulate a problem statement and to determine if modeling is an appropriate and efficient way to solve the problem. Modeling may not be appropriate because of data unavailability or because the resources required are more costly than the potential savings from solving the problem.

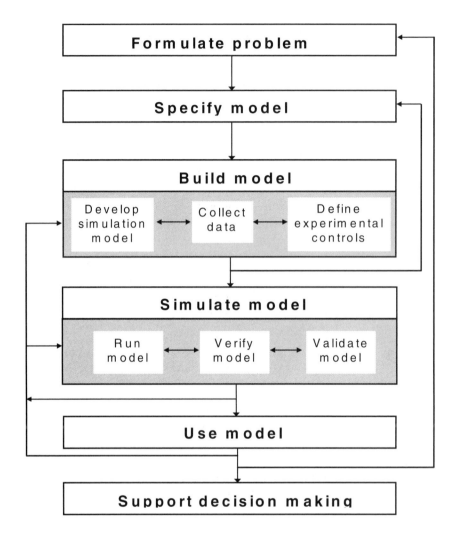

Figure 3-1 Modeling and simulation process.

Measures of system performance are typically profits or costs which are a function of operational measures such as utilization, throughput, inventory levels, and quality. Project goals specify what is to be achieved in terms of these performance measures of the system. An example of a project goal is to lower in-process inventory in a factory without decreasing production rates.

Modeling objectives are statements of desired results in terms of performance measures. For example, if a goal is to cut operating costs through a reduction in inventory costs then an objective may be to introduce a control system to decrease inventory levels below 500 units without changing plant capacity. Objectives should be stated in such a way that an action can be taken or a decision can be made if the objective is met.

Once objectives are established, the system to be modeled can be defined. System boundaries and components (subsystems) should be determined based on the performance measures to be estimated. For example, if the throughput of an inspection station is to be estimated, then the inspection station must be included in the model. If the utilization of inspectors is a performance measure, then the inspectors and the inspection station must be represented.

After defining the project goal, critical performance measures, modeling objectives, and the system to be modeled, the use of a model should again be re-examined. In defining the problem, an obvious solution may become evident or the system definition may be too imprecise to warrant a modeling effort.

Problem formulation is extremely important and often is not given sufficient attention. When this step is performed correctly, modeling and analysis efforts are better focused. This leads to effective problem solving and large returns from the investment made in the project. Good problem formulation helps to avoid projects where the wrong problem is solved or where a model is developed when it is not needed.

3.3 SPECIFY MODEL

There is an art to conceptualizing a model. The modeler must understand the structure and operating rules of the system and be able to extract the essence of the system without including unnecessary detail. Good models tend to be easily understood, yet have sufficient detail to reflect realistically the important characteristics of the system. The crucial questions in model specification focus on what simplifying assumptions are reasonable to make, what components should be included in the model, and what interactions occur among the components. The amount of detail included in the model should be based on the modeling objectives established. Only those components that could cause significant differences in decision making need be considered.

Close interaction among project personnel is required when formulating a problem and specifying a model. This interaction causes inaccuracies to be discovered quickly and corrected efficiently. Most important is that interactions induce confidence between the modeler and the decision maker which helps to achieve the positive interactions necessary to obtain a successful implementation of results.

The second step, specify model, identifies the data requirements for the model. By conceptualizing the model in terms of the structural elements of the system and product flows through the system, a good understanding of the detailed data requirements can be projected. It establishes the schedules, algorithms, and controls required for the model. These decision components are typically the most difficult aspect of a modeling effort.

Models analyzed by simulation are easily changed, which facilitates making iterations between the problem formulation and the model specification steps. This is not the case for other model analysis techniques. Examples of the types of changes that can be made in simulation models which encourage flexibility in model specification are:

1. Setting arrival patterns and activity times to be constant, to be samples from a theoretical distribution, or to use a history of values.

2. Setting due dates based on historical records, finite capacity planning procedures, or sales information.

3. Setting decision variables based on a heuristic procedure or calling a decision-making subprogram that uses an optimization technique.

4. Including fixed rules or expert-system setting rules directly in the model.

3.3.1   Model Specification Illustration

In a recent study of a flexible manufacturing system (FMS), a detailed model specification was prepared (2). The project goal was to determine if the FMS could achieve the designed throughput rate. The modeling objectives were to estimate the utilization of work centers, carrousels, material handling equipment, and tools sets, and to provide a tool for analyzing alternative designs and graphically animating the operation of the FMS.

A conceptual model of the flow of parts through the FMS system is shown in Figure 3-2. For each component of the production process depicted in Figure 3-2, a specification was written from which a model could be developed. In addition, the flow of orders was described. The specification provided basic characteristics, assumptions, operation sequences, resource contention issues, and input data requirements for each component in the production process. To illustrate, the model specifications are given for the flow of orders in Figure 3-3 and the review station in Figure 3-4.

3.4   BUILD MODEL

The build model step consists of three substeps: develop simulation model, collect data, and define experimental controls. In the first substep, the simulation model is developed which contains the structural and procedural elements that represent a system. Experimental controls describe the procedures for performing a simulation and analysis of the model. The term scenario is used to refer to a particular combination of a simulation model, data, and experimental controls.

3.4.1 Develop Simulation Model

One secret to being a good modeler is the ability to remodel. Model building should be interactive and graphical because a model is not only defined and developed but is continually refined, updated, modified, and extended. An up-to-date model provides the basis for future models. The following five model building themes support this approach and should be used where feasible:

1.   Develop generalized input schemes.
2.   Divide the model into relatively small logical elements.
3.   Differentiate between physical movement and information flow in the model.
4.   Develop and maintain clear documentation directly in the model.
5.   Leave hooks in the model to insert extensions or more detail.

Throughout this book, Visual SLAM network models are used to illustrate these model building procedures.

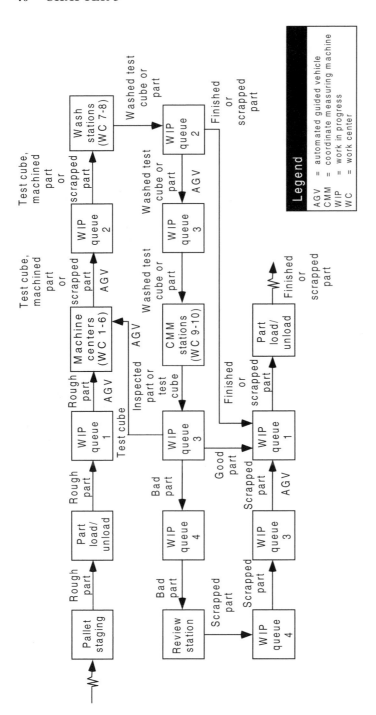

Figure 3-2 Flow of parts through a proposed flexible manufacturing system. Source (2).

FMS Model Specification: Order Processing

Basic characteristics

- There are 57 different part types.
- Each part type requires 1, 2, or 3 passes through the FMS.
- Parts are fixtured, machined, washed, and possible inspected and reviewed.
- Part-operations are processed individually.
- Parts with multiple machining operations leave the FMS between operations.

Assumptions

- A scheduler module generates an order arrival sequence for the FMS based on current machining center backlogs, up/down states, and toolkit states.
- The sequence generated by the scheduler is an input to the simulation model.
- The scheduler is invoked at simulation start up time and also whenever required.
- The objectives of the scheduler are to: balance the load across the machining centers, be on time with respect to order due dates, limit toolkit changes at the machining centers, limit fixture changes on pallets, and limit resource contention blockages.
- The first parts on the schedule determine the toolkits initially installed at the machines.
- Parts are diverted from a down machining center toward one that is functional.
- Scrapped parts are monitored so that the scheduler can adjust the production schedule accordingly.

Operation Sequences   Figure 3-2 presents the flow of parts through the system.

Resource contention issues   None

Model inputs

- For each order
  - Part identifications
  - Scheduled start date
  - Scheduled due date
- For each part of the order
  - Part identification
  - Operation identification
  - Time to load part into fixture
  - Identification of the required toolkit
  - Time to perform the machining operation
  - Time to wash the part
  - Inspection requirement
  - Time to inspect the part
  - Probability of failing inspection
- Time to review a part
- Time to unload part from fixture

Figure 3-3 Model specification for FMS order processing. Source (2).

FMS Model Specification: Review Station

Basic characteristics

- There is 1 review station.
- Parts are reviewed at the review station to determine why they failed inspection.
- After review, parts exit the system through WIP queue 1 carrousel.

Assumptions

- The review station has a capacity of 1 part.
- The review station is blocked until the reviewed part is removed from the input/output shuttle and loaded onto the carrousel.
- A shuttle can have preventative maintenance and failures.

Operation Sequences

- Load bad part onto review station.
- Free input/output shuttle of review station.
- Review part.
- Wait for/seize space in work-in-process queue of carrousel.
- Wait for/seize input/output shuttle of review station.
- Remove reviewed part from review station and place on shuttle.
- Wait for/seize control of carrousel.
- Free review station.
- Rotate shuttle 180 degrees.

Contention issues

- At input/output shuttle entities have the following priorities:

Priority	Contending system entity
1	Scrapped parts at the review station.
2	Bad parts in WIP queue 4 carrousel.

Model inputs

- Time to transfer a part from the shuttle to the review station.
- Time to review a part for each part-operation combination.
- Probability that a part passes the review for each part-operation combination.
- Time to transfer a part from the review station to the shuttle.

Figure 3-4 Model specification for review station. Source (2)

In developing a Visual SLAM network model, entities are defined that move through the network. An entity represents an object, part, person, or message. It can be thought of as an information packet with a set of attributes as shown in Figure 3-5 where the value of attribute 1 is 22, attribute 2 is 1 and so on. As an entity moves through a network model, its information content is changed. Some changes only modify the characteristics of the entity while other changes identify a new type of entity. For example, a raw material entity, after a processing step, is converted to an unfinished part entity; a demand entity is transformed into a sale entity; a sick patient entity is transformed into a hospitalized patient entity; and an information record entity is converted to a patient entity. Entities are created, cloned, and terminated. These changes to entities are reflected in changes made to the attributes of the entity.

As an entity moves through a network model, decisions are made at nodes to hold it at the node, to start an activity that explicitly models a delay in its movement through the network, to route it or its clone to specific nodes, to collect information based on its reaching a node, to allocate resources to it, or to determine if it should be combined with other entities. The nodes and activities defined to perform these operations on entities constitute the network modeling language. The symbols and syntax associated with the network language are the inputs to a simulation processor that is used to simulate the network model. The network portion of the Visual SLAM language is presented in Chapters 4, 5, 6 and 7. User-written procedures for augmenting the decision logic within a Visual SLAM network are presented in Chapters 9 and 10. AweSim is a software system which includes Visual SLAM and supports the modeling and simulation process described in this chapter. AweSim provides a means for producing a documentation trail regarding model development, analysis, and use (6).

Attribute Type	Attribute number			
	4	3	2	1
Real	100.	17.	1.	22.
Integer			−3	6
String			Red	

Figure 3-5. An entity with attribute values.

3.4.2   Collect Data

The types of data which need to be collected to support the modeling and simulation process include data describing the system, data measuring the actual performance of the system, and data describing the alternatives to be evaluated. Data which describes the system is concerned with the system structure, the individual components of the system, component interactions, and system operations. The possible states of the system are established from this information.

As discussed in Chapter 1, data collection may involve performing detailed time studies, getting information from equipment manufacturers, talking to system operators or accessing databases of data collection systems. Actual system performance histories are collected whenever possible to help validate model outputs. Data describing proposed solutions are used to modify the basic model for each alternative to be evaluated. Each alternative is typically evaluated individually but performance data across alternatives are displayed together. The model specifications presented in Figures 3-3 and 3-4 provide a good list of the type of data needed for simulating the flow of parts in a manufacturing system.

3.4.3   Define Experimental Controls

A simulation run is an experiment which calculates and records model status from an initial state to a final state. In a network model, model status is reflected by the number of entities in the network and their location on activities and at nodes. For example, an entity on a machining activity indicates that the machine's status is busy performing an operation. The number of entities waiting at a node preceding this same activity provides the status of the number of jobs waiting for processing by the machine. Other indicators of model status are the number of resource units allocated to entities, the number of entities that have completed an activity or reached a node, and observations made on model variables and attributes of entities during the course of the run.

One of the key advantages of simulation is that model status changes are clearly identified with and related to system status changes. Evaluations made for model variables may be directly translated into evaluations for system variables. Statistical techniques used to analyze system variables can be applied directly to model variables.

In defining experimental controls, the following type of information is specified:

1. Project title and modeler identification

2   Beginning and ending times, number of runs, and control information

3. Report types and frequency desired

4. Status variables on which performance is desired and the form in which outputs are to be presented, such as plots, tables, histograms, charts and spreadsheets

5. Initial values for status variables and initial location of entities in the model

6. Statistical estimation procedures including warm-up time periods, variance estimation procedures, confidence and tolerance interval calculation methods, and variance reduction techniques

7. Files, spreadsheets and databases where input data exists and output values are to be stored

3.4.4   Build Model Interactions

Figure 3-1 shows that the three substeps of develop simulation model, collect data, and define experimental controls are performed concurrently. Several examples are given to illustrate how these substeps are interdependent.

After a first-cut model is developed, it may be necessary to include weekend operations into the model. This modeling decision may require that the data collected on jobs be divided into those that can be performed on the weekend and those that must be performed during the weekday. The inclusion of weekend activity may also require that experimental controls be established to collect statistics to estimate utilization by weekday and by weekend. In collecting data on operators, it may be uncovered that different skill levels are used on weekends, and the time to perform a job must be based on the skill level of the personnel available. This could entail including different resource types in the model and different job processing times which are dependent on resource type. It might further require additional statistics collection to ascertain the number of jobs completed by resource type and by day of the week. As can be seen, the three substeps of the build model step have a high degree of interdependence.

After completing the build model step, it is typically necessary to update the model specification. Although not always done, maintaining an up-to-date model specification makes reuse of the model possible and future extensions probable. In addition to updating the model specification, there are projects on which the model is not completely specified initially. For example, a weekly review of job priorities may have been omitted from the original specification. If this is the case, then it is necessary to establish how priorities are assigned to jobs and how jobs are to be reordered If a planning system is used for establishing job priorities through due dates, then it is necessary to specify what aspects of the planning system need to be included in the model. In some projects, it is determined that the level of detail of the model need not be as extensive as specified. In such an instance, it is necessary to question why the specification included the items now being considered for deletion. If deletion is confirmed, then the specification should be shortened.

3.5   SIMULATE MODEL

The simulate model step requires that the build model step be completed at least once. The experimental controls establish an initial state of the model. A network simulation advances time in accordance with the movement of entities through the nodes and activities of the model. This is the run model substep. Before the model can be used to support decision making, it must be shown to run in accordance with model specifications. This is accomplished as a verification substep, which consists of determining that the simulation model behaves as intended. A validation substep seeks to establish that the simulation model is a reasonable representation of the system. These substeps are performed concurrently and usually require a return to earlier steps in the modeling and simulation process as described in Section 3.5.4.

3.5.1 Run Model

The running of a Visual SLAM model is facilitated by embedding Visual SLAM in a simulation support system that is programmed for specific computer platforms. AweSim provides procedures for simulating Visual SLAM models on personal computers. The input of Visual SLAM models is handled through graphical and forms input. The linking of Visual SLAM networks with user inserts is performed automatically. The storage of models for reuse as the basis of new models is provided. The capabilities for watching entity movement on a step-by-step basis or over an interval of time are available. Animations of model status changes on system diagrams can be presented to support model understanding. Outputs can be presented during a run or stored for display following a completed run. AweSim supports the steps of a modeling and simulation project and simplifies the process of using the computer as a simulation vehicle. These capabilities are described in detail in Chapter 14.

3.5.2 Verify Model

Verification is the process of determining that a simulation run is executing as intended, that is, according to specifications as described in Section 3.3 (1,8). One method of verification is to check that each model element is described correctly and that modeling elements are interfaced as specified. Model verification can be a manual process of reviewing data inputs and outputs and insuring that no significant discrepancies exist between expected and observed model performance. AweSim contains the Interactive Execution Environment which allows modelers to watch the running of a model as each status change occurs or at defined breakpoints established by the user. At these breakpoints, the modeler can incrementally execute the simulation, examining the changes of the state of the model caused by simulation events.

The Interactive Execution Environment is also used to follow the logical flow described in the model. The modeler can simulate to a decision point, save the system status, and execute the simulation further from that breakpoint. The modeler can then examine the model's response to alternate inputs by restoring the simulation to the previously saved state, changing the appropriate inputs, and then restarting the simulation from the breakpoint. In this way, the verification process is supported by allowing the user to make runs interactively and to access model status variables during an interactive session. A description of the Interactive Execution Environment is presented in Chapters 8 and 14.

3.5.3 Validate Model

Validation is the process of determining that the simulation model is a useful or reasonable representation of the system (3, 4, 9, 10) Typically, validation is made with respect to requirements established during the formulate problem step described in Section 3.1. Validation is usually performed in levels involving an examination of data inputs, model elements, subsystems, and interface points. Validation of simulation models is a significantly easier task than validating other types of models because there is a correspondence between model elements and system components. Testing for reasonableness involves a comparison of a model's organization with the system's structure as well as comparing the number of times elements in the model are exercised with data describing the number of times tasks in the system are performed.

Specific validation procedures evaluate reasonableness using all constant or expected values or assessing the sensitivity of outputs to parametric variation of data inputs. In making validation studies, the comparison yardstick should encompass both past system outputs and experiential knowledge of system behavior. A point to remember is that past system outputs are but one sample record of what could have happened.

For models of existing systems, validation is typically done in two ways. First, the structure and operation of the system is compared to the structure and operation of the model. Individual components as well as component interfaces are examined. Second, the values of the critical performance measures of the entire system and any identifiable subsystems are compared to the outputs of the entire model and the parts of the model representing the subsystems. If discrepancies exist, then the performance measure values for the system may have been incorrectly determined, or the data describing the system may contain errors. Both types of data should be checked before rebuilding the model.

For models of new system designs, the validation process is more difficult because model outputs cannot be compared to measures of actual system performance. The first means of validating a new system design is to compare the structure and expected operation of the system design to the structure and operation of the model. Each individual component and the interface between components are examined. The second means of validating new designs is to review model outputs for reasonableness considering the performance of similar existing systems. Individuals familiar with the system play a valuable role in validating a model. To support them, it is important to develop reports, traces, and graphical outputs that are expressed in the context of their system.

3.5.4   Simulate Model Interactions

The dependent nature of the run, verify, and validate model substeps is intuitive. To verify that the model is operating as intended, it is necessary to run the model. The same is true for the validation substep. In verification, preliminary runs of the model are made with all randomness removed. Counts are made on the number of times an event occurs and on the number of entities that are processed through various portions of the model. These counts are checked against the number expected as calculated from the model specification. Runs of the model are then made with randomness included and counts are compared to expected values. Verification also involves making parameter changes and ascertaining if performance measures change in an expected manner. For example, as arrival rates increase, utilizations of resources are expected to increase. The validation substep typically questions the occurrence of events and combinations of events in the simulation run. For example, why did a robot resource fail twice in the first 100 hours of the run? Validation is facilitated by watching animations of the model and comparing them to the operation of the real system. If system data is available , then it can be input into the animation system and the animation of the model can be compared to the animation of the system data. In the course of validating a model, verification questions arise concerning whether the model is operating in accordance with system operating rules.

Feedback from the simulate model step to the build model step is common. During verification, if an incorrect processing of jobs is uncovered, a new job processing algorithm may be required for the model. During validation, a shortfall in throughput for a given set of conditions may be observed. After establishing that the model was incorrectly developed, the model is rebuilt to eliminate the shortfall in throughput. A direct feedback from the simulate model step to the specify model step is not shown in Figure 3-1. Typically, a return from the simulate model step is made to the build model step from which a return to the specify model step can be made.

3.6 USE MODEL

The use of the model involves the making of runs and the interpretation and presentation of the outputs. When simulation results are used to draw inferences or to test hypotheses, statistical methods should be employed. Planning for the use of the model entails strategic and tactical considerations (5, 11, 12).

A simulation model does not require a method for determining an optimal solution. Rather, the model specifies a means to obtain experimental data from which an alternative can be selected. For example, to determine the number of machines needed at a particular station to achieve a production rate of 150 parts per day, runs are made with 4 machines, then 5 machines, then 6 machines until the desired production rate is achieved. The key point here is that the simulation model does not determine the number of machines needed, it only evaluates the performance of systems with specified machine level alternatives. Augmenting the simulation model with algorithms to specify the next alternative is a common practice.

In addition to evaluating alternatives, the procedure to be followed when evaluating alternatives is also defined. The order in which alternatives are evaluated is important, especially if the results of one evaluation are used to specify the next alternative. For example, if a bottleneck at a station is alleviated by adding additional equipment, another station may then become the bottleneck. Runs are then made to alleviate this second bottleneck. If additional alternatives arise, their impact on the entire analysis is considered. When using the model, the specification of the type and form of outputs is extremely important. When possible, model outputs should relate directly to system outputs. A listing of the types of outputs from Visual SLAM models is presented in Chapter 8.

3.6.1   Use Model Interactions

After the use model step is completed, there is a potential return to the simulate model step, build model step, or formulate problem step. After using the model and analyzing outputs, a better setting of a resource level may be discovered. This parameter change is easily made at the simulate model step where the model is rerun under the new resource level. In another situation, the outputs from the model may indicate that the scheduling system is not as robust as necessary. In this case, a return to the build model step is made where a new scheduling system is developed. It may be necessary to first determine if the model can accommodate a new scheduling procedure. If it cannot, then a return to the specify model step is made where the scheduling procedure must be specified before the model is embellished to contain it.

In some cases, after examining outputs from the model, it is determined that the scope of the problem is broader than anticipated and that the modeling objectives need revision. This should lead to a return to the formulate problem step. Examples of a broader type of scope are the need to purchase a new material handling system to alleviate a bottleneck or the incorporation of a production control system to provide for the efficient release of orders to the shop floor. When a return is made to the formulate problem step, the decision maker should be brought back into the process to provide information regarding the feasibility and desirability of any proposed change in scope or objectives. In many instances, the knowledge that a bottleneck will exist or a production control system is necessary provides sufficient information to take an action to meet the modeling objectives or the project goal.

3.7   SUPPORT DECISION MAKING

The final step in the modeling and simulation process is to support decision making. No simulation project should be considered complete until its results are used in the decision-making process. A key activity in having results used is the presentation and documentation of the model and its outputs. Remember that the model supports communication in many forms. Documentation is required to support the presentation of results and their use. The success of the decision-support step is largely dependent upon the degree to which the modeler has successfully performed the other steps. Decision support is not an end-of-project activity. If the problem formulation and underlying assumptions are not effectively communicated early in the project, then it is more difficult to have recommendations implemented, regardless of the elegance and validity of the simulation model. On the other hand, if the model builder and model user have worked closely together throughout the project and both understand the model, its outputs and its uses, then it is likely that the results of the project will be implemented with vigor.

3.8   SUMMARY

Simulation is a technique that has been employed extensively to solve problems. Simulation models are abstractions of systems . They should be built efficiently, explained to all project personnel, and changed when necessary. The steps outlined in this chapter are rarely performed in a structured sequence beginning with problem formulation and ending with decision making and implementation. A project may involve false starts, erroneous assumptions, reformulation of the modeling objectives, and repeated redesign of the model. If properly performed, however, this iterative process yields new knowledge of the system and management policy. It promotes communication and leads to alternative designs for equipment and operations. It is the essence of the modeling and simulation process and results in properly assessed alternatives and improved systems.

3.9   EXERCISES

3-1. Discuss the types of data that are needed to build a structural model of a system. Discuss the types of data that are needed to estimate parameters of a model. Give examples of structural data and detailed data.

3-2. Discuss the different uses of statistics in each of the steps of the modeling and simulation process.

3-3. Models are used as explanatory vehicles, design accessors, and as a basis for control mechanisms. Give a definition of each model use and prepare an illustration to demonstrate each type of use.

3-4. Build an explanatory model of the university system from the point of view of an undergraduate student. Describe the activities that are required in each of the steps of the modeling and simulation process that estimates the utilization of the scarcest resource in your definition of the university system.

3-5. Develop the steps involved in applying a modeling and optimization process. Compare the steps to the process described in this chapter.

3-6. Compare the procedures used in problem formulation between seeking an optimal solution and using a satisficing approach (Section 1.7) to alternative selection. In a dynamic analysis, how is optimal defined?

3-7. A model of a system can be viewed as data describing the system. Develop a database schema that can be used to store models.

3-8. For each step in the modeling and simulation process described in this chapter, make a list of decisions that are required to accomplish each step. Describe the types of information necessary to make the decisions that you have listed.

3-9. Specify methods for obtaining time estimates for each data input specified in the order processing illustration given in Figure 3-3.

3.10 REFERENCES

1. Balci, O., "Validation, Verification and Testing Techniques Throughout the Life Cycle of a Simulation Study," *Annals of Operations Research*, Vol. 53, 1994, pp. 121-174.

2. Gaskins, R. J. and J. P. Whitford, "Simulation Model Specification for a Flexible Manufacturing System for an Aerospace Company," Pritsker & Associates, West Lafayette, IN, 1988.

3. Gass, S. I., "Decision-aiding Models: Validation, Assessment, and Related Issues for Policy Analysis," *Operations Research*, Vol. 31, 1983, pp. 601-631.

4. Kleijnen, J. P. C., "Theory and Methodology of Simulation Models," *European Journal of Operational Research,* Vol. 82, 1995, pp. 145-162.

5. Law, A. M., and W. D. Kelton, *Simulation Modeling and Analysis*, Second Edition, McGraw-Hill, New York, 1982.

6. O'Reilly, J. J., *AweSim Quick Reference Manual*, Pritsker Corporation, West Lafayette, IN, 1996.

7. Pritsker, A. A. B., C. E. Sigal and J. Hammesfahr, *SLAM II Network Models for Decision Support*, The Scientific Press, 1994.

8. Sargent, R. G., "An Expository on Verification and Validation of Simulation Models," *Proceedings, Winter Simulation Conference*, 1994.

9. Schlesinger, S., and others, "Terminology for Model Credibility," *Simulation*, Vol. 32, No. 3, 1979, pp. 103-104.

10. Van Horn, R. L., "Validation of Simulation Results," *Management Science*, Vol. 17, 1971, pp. 247-258.

11. Welch, P. D., "The Statistical Analysis of Simulation Results," *Computer Performance Modeling Handbook*, S. S. Lavenberg, ed., Academic Press, Palisades, NY, 1983.

12. Wilson, J. R., "Statistical Aspects of Simulation," *Proceedings, IFORS*, 1984, pp. 825-841.

13. Withers, B.D., A.A.B. Pritsker and D.H. Withers, "A Structured Definition of the Modeling Process," *Proceedings, Winter Simulation Conference*, 1993, pp. 1109-1117.

Basic Network Modeling

4.1   INTRODUCTION

In Chapter 3, we introduced Visual SLAM as a simulation language which allows the modeler to select the "world view" that is most applicable to the system under study. As such, the Visual SLAM user can employ any combination of the following perspectives when modeling a system: process, event, continuous and activity scanning. This chapter begins the description of the process orientation or network modeling procedures available in Visual SLAM. The task of the analyst is to use network concepts to formulate a model which reflects the important characteristics of the system. In approaching network modeling using Visual SLAM, the analyst confronts two related problems: 1) deciding what detail to include in the model and 2) deciding how to represent that detail with the Visual SLAM network framework.

In modeling and simulation, the level of detail to include in a model is relative to the purpose of the model. By knowing the purpose of the model, the relative worth of including specific details can be assessed. Only those elements that could cause significant differences in decision making resulting from the outputs from simulation need be considered. In addition, for larger models it is often advantageous to decompose the models into stages of development. The decomposition could consist of initially developing an aggregate model which crudely approximates the system under study, and then improving the model through embellishments in subsequent stages, or it could consist of segmenting the total system into subsystems each of which are modeled separately and then combined. In any case, the prerequisite step in developing a network model of a system is to construct a problem statement which defines the purpose so that the specific detail level to be included in the model can be decided.

Once the problem statement is complete, the system can be represented as entities which flow through a network of nodes and activities. The first step in this modeling process is to define the elements which are to be represented as entities. Recall that an entity is any object, person, unit of information, or combination thereof which defines or can alter the state of the system. Therefore the entities to be modeled can be identified by defining the variables that represent the system state and determining the changes in state that can occur. For example, in a radio inspection problem, the status of the system could be represented by the number of busy inspectors and the number of radios waiting for inspection. Status changes are due entirely to the movement of a radio through the system; therefore, the entity to be modeled is the radio. For more complicated problems, the entities may be more abstract and there may be more than one entity type within the simulation.

The next and most challenging step in developing a network model is the synthesis of a network of nodes and activities which represents the process through which the entities flow. Although the synthesis can be done using either the graphic or statement form of the network elements, the initial development most often takes place using the graphic symbols. The advantage of using the graphic symbols is that they provide a logical and visual medium for both conceptualization and communication. The graphic symbols of Visual SLAM play a role for the simulation analyst similar to that of the free body diagram for mechanical engineers or the circuit diagram for electrical engineers. Once the graphic model is complete, the transcribing of the graphic model into a statement representation is automatic as AweSim provides for statement generation (2).

As an introduction to Visual SLAM network modeling let us consider a simple queueing system in which items arrive, wait, are processed by a single server, and then depart the system. Such a sequence of events, activities, and decisions is referred to as a *process*. *Entities* flow through a process. Thus, items are considered as entities. An entity can be assigned *attribute* values that enable a modeler to distinguish between individual entities of the same type or between entities of different types. For example, the time an entity enters the system could be an attribute of the entity. Such attributes are attached to the entity as it flows through the network. The resources of the system could be servers, tools, or the like for which entities compete while flowing through the system. A resource is busy when processing an entity, otherwise it is idle.

Visual SLAM provides a framework for modeling the flow of entities through processes. The framework is a network structure consisting of specialized nodes and branches that are used to model resources, queues for resources, activities, and entity flow decisions. In short, a Visual SLAM network model is a representation of a process and the flow of entities through the process.

4.2   A VISUAL SLAM NETWORK OF A SINGLE SERVER QUEUEING SYSTEM

To illustrate the basic network concepts and symbols of Visual SLAM, we will construct a model of an inspection process in the manufacturing of transistor radios. In this system, manufactured radios are delivered to an inspector at a central inspection area. The inspector examines each radio. After this inspection, the radio leaves the inspection area. Although we could model the entire manufacturing process, we are only interested in the operations associated with the inspection of radios. Therefore, we concern ourselves with the following three aspects of the system

1. The arrival of radios to the inspection area;

2. The buildup of radios awaiting inspection; and

3. The activity of inspecting radios by a single inspector.

This is a single resource queueing system, and is similar to the bank teller system described in previous chapters. The radios are the system's entities. The inspector is the resource and will be modeled as a *server*. The *service activity* is the actual inspection, and the buildup of the radios awaiting service is the queue. A pictorial diagram of this inspection system is shown below.

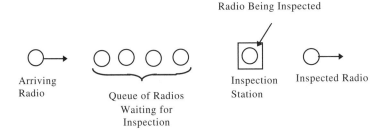

Radio Being Inspected

Arriving
Radio

Queue of Radios
Waiting for
Inspection

Inspection
Station

Inspected Radio

4.2.1   Modeling Queues and Servers

Let us now build a network for this one server system. The passage of time is represented by a *branch*. Branches are the graphical representation of activities. Clearly, the service operation (the inspection of the radios) is an activity and, hence, is modeled by a branch. If the service activity is ongoing, that is, the server (the inspector) is busy, arriving entities (radios) must wait. Waiting occurs at a QUEUE node. Thus, a one-server, single-queue operation is depicted in Visual SLAM by a QUEUE node and a branch as follows:

QUEUE Node

In our example, radios wait for service at the queue. When the inspector is free, he removes a radio from the queue and performs the service activity. The procedure for specifying the time to perform the service operation will be discussed later. A wide variety of service time distributions are available for use in Visual SLAM.

Since there may be many queues and service activities in a network, each can be identified numerically. Entities waiting at queues are maintained in files, and a file number, IFL, is associated with a queue. Service activities are assigned a value to indicate the number, N, of parallel servers described by the branch, that is, the number of possible concurrent processings of entities. Activities can also be given an activity number, A, for identification and statistics collection purposes. The notation shown on the following page is the procedure for labeling these elements of the network.

The file number is put on the right-hand side of the node. The procedure for ranking entities in the file is specified separately by a PRIORITY statement and is not shown on the graphic model. Also specified for a QUEUE node are the initial number of entities at the QUEUE node, IQ, and the capacity of the queue, QC. This latter quantity is the largest number of entities that can wait for service at the QUEUE node. Arriving entities to a full queue will either balk or be blocked. A QUEUE node has a "hash" mark in the lower right-hand corner to make the symbol resemble the letter Q. For the service activity, the number of parallel servers is put in a circle below the branch, and the activity number is put in a square below the branch.

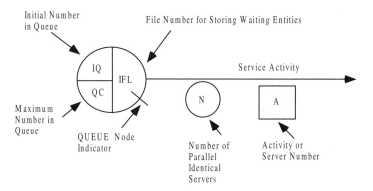

4.2.2   Modeling the Arrival of Entities

Turning our attention to the entities (the individual radios), we must model the arrival of radios to the system. In Visual SLAM, entities are inserted into a network by CREATE nodes. The symbol for the CREATE node is shown below.

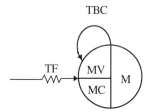

where
   TF is the time at which the first entity is to be created and sent into the network;
   TBC is the time between creations of entities;
   MV is the variable in which the creation or mark time is to be maintained;
   MC is the maximum number of entities that can be created at this node; and
   M is the maximum number of branches along which a created entity can be routed from this node (referred to as the M-number or "max take" value).

There are several important features to note about the CREATE node. At a prescribed time, TF, a first entity will be created. If desired, the time at which an entity is created can be saved in the variable MA of the entity. This time is usually referred to as the "mark" time. The created entity will be routed over the branches emanating from the node in accordance with the M-number. If M is equal to one and there are two branches emanating from the node, the entity will only be routed over one of the two branches. Procedures for selecting which branch over which to route the entity will be described later. If all branches are to be taken, M need not be specified.

The second entity created at the node will occur at time TF + TBC where TBC is the time between creation of entities. For the radio example, TBC is the time between the arrivals of radios which can be a constant, a Visual SLAM variable, or a random variable. This is described in the section on specifying attribute or duration assignments. The variable MC prescribes a maximum number of entities that can be created at the node. If no limit is specified, entities will continue to be created until the end of the simulation run.

4.2.3   Modeling Departures of Entities

We have now modeled the arrival pattern of entities and the waiting and service operations. All that remains is the modeling of the departure process for the entity. For our simple system, we will let the entities leave the system following the completion of service. The modeling of the departure of an entity is accomplished by a TERMINATE node as shown below.

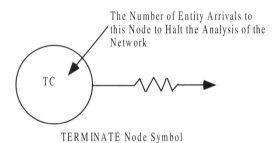

The Number of Entity Arrivals to this Node to Halt the Analysis of the Network

TC

TERMINATE Node Symbol

A squiggly line is used on the output side of a node to indicate that entities are to be terminated or destroyed at the node. TERMINATE nodes are one way to specify the stopping procedure to be used when analyzing a Visual SLAM network. Each simulation of a network is referred to as a run. The TERMINATE node can be used to specify that TC entity arrivals at the TERMINATE node are required to complete one run. As we shall see, the stopping condition can also be based on a time period. For example, a run could be made for 1000 hours of operation.

4.2.4 Combining Modeling Concepts

We are now ready to combine the arrival, service, and departure operations to obtain a complete network model of the one server, single queue process. This Visual SLAM model is shown below with data values prescribed for the variables associated with the network symbols. This network depicts the flow of an entity and all the potential processing steps associated with the entity. The first entity arrives at the CREATE node at time 7. The next entity is scheduled to arrive 10 time units later which would be at time 17. The first entity is routed to the service activity by the branch to the QUEUE node. The branch represents the activity of traveling to the server and is prescribed to be 3 time units in duration. When the entity arrives at the QUEUE node, it will immediately be serviced if server 3 is idle. If this occurs. the entity flows from the QUEUE node to the TERMINATE node in 9 time units. During this time, server 3 is busy.

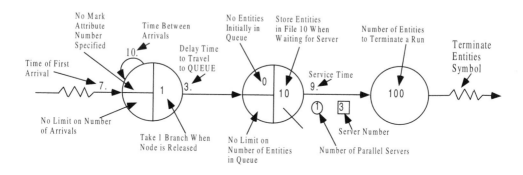

Other entities will also follow the pattern described above. However, if server 3 is busy when an entity arrives at the QUEUE node, the entity is placed in file 10 which models the queue of entities waiting for server 3. When an entity joins a queue, a rule is used that specifies the order in which the entities are ranked in the queue. (The ranking rule for the queue is characteristic of the file and is not specified on the graphical model.) If no ranking rule is specified, a first-in, first-out (FIFO) procedure is used, that is, entities are taken from the queue in the order in which they arrived to the queue. After entities are served by server 3, they reach the TERMINATE node where the entity is removed from the system since its routing through the process is completed.

4.3   VISUAL SLAM NETWORK MODELING

A Visual SLAM network model consists of a set of interconnected symbols that depict the operation of the system under study. The symbols can be converted into a form for input to a program that analyzes the model using simulation techniques. The input corresponding to a graphic Visual SLAM model is in the form of statements. To provide an illustration of a statement model, the network model presented previously is given in statement form below. A semicolon is used to indicate the end of the data on a particular record. Comments can be given following a semicolon. The sequence of statements must correspond to the process an entity encounters as it flows through the network.

```
CREATE,10.,7.,,,1;        TIME BETWEEN ARRIVALS = 10
ACTIVITY,,3.;             TIME TO REACH QUEUE NODE IS 3
QUEUE,10,;                USE FILE 10 FOR QUEUE
ACTIVITY,3,9.,,,1;        SERVICE TIME = 9
TERMINATE,100;            RUN MODEL FOR 100 ENTITIES
```

This illustration is only to indicate the similarity of the graphic model and the statement model. AweSim provides the capability to build Visual SLAM networks graphically at a terminal. AweSim then converts the graphic network to the input required for the Visual SLAM processor, that is, the list of statements. The modeler is not required to prepare the statements as it is only necessary to fill in dialog boxes. The statements are used as a means to list the model in a textual form for presentation and review. Later in this section, a description of the basic Visual SLAM symbols, statements and AweSim definitions are presented.

As previously seen, a network consists of an interrelated set of nodes and branches. The nodes and branches can be considered as elements that are combined and integrated into a system description. The task of the modeler is to integrate the elements into a network model for the system of interest.

Before presenting the basic Visual SLAM symbols and statements, several comments on general sequencing and entity flow are in order. The flow of entities normally follows the directed branches indicated on the network. Node labels are used to identify non-standard flows of entities. In statements, node labels are used as statement labels in a fashion similar to statement labels in a C program. Node labels can be appended to any node. On the graphic model, they are placed below the node symbol. On the statement, they precede the node name and are followed by a colon (:).

As described previously, branches are used to depict activities. In some situations, it is desired to have entities flow from one node to another node with no intervening activity. Such transfers are depicted on the network by branches with no specifications or by broken (nonsolid) lines, and are referred to as connectors. No statements are required in the statement model to describe connectors.

4.3.1   Routing Entities from Nodes (Branching)

Entities are routed along the branches emanating from nodes. The maximum number of branches, M, that can be selected is specified on the right-hand side of the node through the value assigned to M. The default value for M is ∞. When M equals 1, at most one branch will be taken. If probabilities are assigned to the branches emanating from a node that has M = 1, then the node is said to have *probabilistic branching*. If no conditions or probabilities are prescribed for the branches, and M equals the number of branches emanating from the node then *deterministic branching* is specified. Deterministic branching causes an entity to be cloned and routed over every branch emanating from the node.

The branching concept prescribed by the value of M is quite general. It allows the routing of entities over a subset of branches for which conditions are prescribed. For example, if M is equal to 2 and there are five branches emanating from the node, then the entity would be routed over the first two branches for which the condition is met.

An even more complex situation involves a combination of probabilistic and conditional branching. Letting p_i be the probability of routing an entity over branch i and letting c_j be the condition for routing over branch j, consider the following situation:

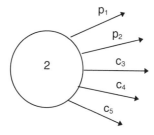

The node type shown above is the GOON node. Every entity that arrives to a GOON node causes it to be "released." The 2 inside the node specifies the M-value previously mentioned. The statement syntax for the GOON node is

GOON,M;

For this example, M is equal to 2 which signifies that at most two of the five Branches are to be taken. Assuming the branches are evaluated in the order 1, 2, 3, 4, and 5, a random selection between branches 1 and 2 will be made ($p_1 + p_2$ must equal 1) and then branch 3 will be taken if condition 3 (c_3) is satisfied. If not, c_4 is tested and then c_5. If c_3 is satisfied, the other branches would not be taken even though c_4 or c_5 were satisfied. In the statement model, when branches (activities) emanate from a node, a statement describing each activity is placed immediately after the statement describing the node. The order of the activity statements defines the order in which the conditions are evaluated. Additional information on the GOON node will be presented in Section 4.11.

4.3.2   Visual SLAM Variables, Function and Random Variables

Table 4-1 presents Visual SLAM variables and their definitions. The vectors ATRIB, LTRIB and STRIB define the attributes of an entity as it flows through the network. Each entity has its own attribute vector which is attached to the entity as it moves through nodes and across branches. Reference is sometimes made to the current entity which is the entity that has just been created or has completed an activity and is arriving to a node in the network. The variable II is an integer variable that is frequently used as an index for other Visual SLAM variables, for example, ATRIB[II]. The variables XX[I], LL[I], and SZ[I] are variables that maintain a value until reset by the user within the model.

ARRAY[I,J] provides a means for storing tables of values in a row and column format. An ARRAY statement is provided for initializing the ARRAY table. The variables DD[I] and SS[I] have special definitions which are used to model continuous status variables. Specifically, DD[I] is defined as the first derivative of SS(I) when differential equations are used to model system status.

The current simulation time is represented by the variable TNOW. TNOW is maintained automatically in Visual SLAM and is advanced in accordance with the time at which variables in the model may change value. TNOW is used to communicate to the modeler the current simulation clock time.

Table 4-1 Visual SLAM variables.

Variable Name	Definition
ATRIB[I]	Real Attribute I of a current entity
LTRIB[I]	Integer Attribute I of a current entity
STRIB[I]	String Attribute I of a current entity
ETYPE	Integer attribute to give current entity a type number
ENUM	Read-only unique integer identifier of current entity
ERETURN	Value stored with current entity at last return from a subnetwork
II	An integer global variable; II is frequently used as an index
XX[I]	Real system or global vector
LL[I]	Integer system or global vector
SZ[I]	String system or global vector
ARRAY[I,J]	System or global array
SS[I]	State variable I
DD[I]	Derivative of SS[I]
TNOW	Current time

Table 4-2 presents the Visual SLAM network functions and random variables which are used to model the logical and stochastic aspects of a system.

Function GGTBLN(IRX, IRY, XVALUE) is a Visual SLAM table lookup function that can be used directly on a network to retrieve a value corresponding to XVALUE. The first two arguments of function GGTBLN provide row numbers of ARRAY which contain values of a dependent variable Y corresponding to values of an independent variable X. If IRY=5 and IRX=3 then the value of Y stored in ARRAY(5,K) corresponds to the value of X stored in ARRAY(3,K). XVALUE is the X value for which a corresponding Y value is desired. As an example, consider the following table:

K	ARRAY (3, K)	ARRAY (5, K)
1	100	10
2	200	20
3	400	10
4	1000	0

The specification GGTBLN(3,5,400) assigns a value of 10 to the network location in which GGTBLN is invoked. Linear interpolation is used for intermediate values so that a value of 5 is obtained when GGTBLN(3, 5, 700) is specified. Values outside of the range of the independent variable are assigned the end values for the dependent variable. For example, an XVALUE less than 100 results in an assignment of 10 and an XVALUE greater than 1000 results in an assignment of 0.

Table 4-2 Visual SLAM network functions.

Function	Definition
ASSERT(VAL,LOW,HIGH)	Function to range check a value and make sure it is between two numbers. The return value is VAL. An error is generated if VAL is out of range.
GETEXCEL(SHEET,IROW,ICOL)	Get data from an EXCEL spreadsheet SHEET from row IROW, column ICOL.
GGTBLN(IRX,IRY,XVALUE)	Table lookup from row IRY of global array by interpolating XVALUE between independent variable values in row IRX.
NNACT(I)	Number of active entities in activity I at current time
NNCNT(I)	The number of entities that have completed activity I
NNGAT(I)	Status of gate I at current time. (1: open, 0: closed)
NNRSC(I)	Current number of units of resource type I available
NRUSE(I)	Current number of units of resource type I in use
NNGRP(I)	Current number of units of group type I available
NGUSE(I)	Current number of units of group type I in use
NNQ(I)	Number of entities in file I at current time
PROB(P)	Only legal in condition field of ACTIVITY. Returns TRUE if a random number between 0.0 and 1.0 is less than P. P must be between 0.0 and 1.0
USERF(N)	A value obtained from the user-written function USERF with user function number N
DRAND(IS)	A pseudo-random number obtained from random number stream IS.
EXPON(XMN,IS)	A sample from an exponential distribution with mean XMN using random number stream IS.
UNFRM(ULO,UHI,IS)	A sample from a uniform distribution in the interval ULO to UHI using random number stream IS.
WEIBL(ALPHA,BETA,IS)	A sample from a Weibull distribution with scale parameter ALPHA and shape parameter BETA using random number stream IS.
TRIAG(XLO,XMODE,XHI,IS)	A sample from a triangular distribution in the interval XLO to XHI with mode XMODE using random number stream IS.
RNORM(XMN,STD,IS)	A sample from a normal distribution with mean XMN and standard deviation STD using random number stream IS.
RLOGN(XMN,STD,IS)	A sample from a lognormal distribution with mean XMN and standard deviation STD using random number stream IS.
ERLNG(EMN,XK,IS)	A sample from a Erlang distribution which is the sum of XK exponential samples each with mean EMN using random number stream IS.
GAMA(BETA,ALPHA,IS)	A sample from a gamma distribution with parameters BETA and ALPHA using random number stream IS.
BETA(THETA,PHI,IS)	A sample from a beta distribution with parameters THETA and PHI using random number stream IS.
NPSSN(XMN,IS)	A sample from a Poisson distribution with mean XMN using random number stream IS.
DPROBN(IRCUM,IRVAL,IS)	A sample from a probability mass function where the cumulative probabilities are in row IRCUM of ARRAY and the corresponding sample values are in row IRVAL of ARRAY using random number stream IS.

NNACT, NNCNT, NNGAT, NNQ, NNRSC, NRUSE, NNGRP and NGUSE are Visual SLAM status variables that are updated automatically by Visual SLAM as the number of entities and the status of the entities in activities, gates, resources, groups and files changes over time. For example, NNQ(3) describes the number of entities in file 3 at the current time, TNOW. If the user wants to model a decision which is dependent on the number of entities in file 3, NNQ(3) would be used as part of the logical expression representing the decision.

The function USERF(N) is a function that can be inserted throughout a network model to include user-written Visual Basic or C code into the model. The argument N is a code that differentiates the various invocations of function USERF by the modeler. Function USERF can be used as part of an expression on a Visual SLAM network in any location where an expression is permitted to use a Visual SLAM variable. This allows extensive modeling flexibility using Visual SLAM networks.

The remainder of the entries in Table 4-2 represent functions from which samples can be obtained in accordance with a specified distribution function. The equations for the distribution functions associated with the random sampling functions presented in Table 4-2 are included in Chapter 16. The arguments for the random sampling routines relate to the parameters of the distribution functions associated with the random variables. A description of the random variables and the functional form of the distribution functions describing the random variables is given in Chapter 16.

Visual SLAM provides the function DPROBN(IC,IV,IS) to obtain a sample from a probability mass function. The cumulative probabilities associated with the probability mass function are stored in row IC of the global variable ARRAY and the corresponding sample values are stored in row IV of ARRAY. IS is a random number stream. The use of function DPROBN is similar to the use of the table lookup function GGTBLN with a random number being used as the independent value for which a random sample is to be obtained. Additional functions for obtaining statistical values are described in Chapter 11, Table 11-2.

4.3.3   EQUIVALENCE Statement for Visual SLAM Variables

Visual SLAM provides an EQUIVALENCE statement so that textual names can be used for the Visual SLAM variables on a network model. The format for the EQUIVALENCE statement is

EQUIVALENCE{{Visual SLAM variable,name},repeats};

The equivalence between a name for a Visual SLAM variable in network and statement models provides for increased readability for the non-Visual SLAM user. For the experienced Visual SLAM user, knowledge of the type of variable that is being used in a model provides additional information regarding the structure of the model. The degree to which textual names are included in models should be dependent upon the model, the modeler, and the use to which the model is to be made. In this book, the use of the EQUIVALENCE statement will be kept to a minimum so that the basic understanding of the use of entities, attributes, global variables and the random sampling functions can be seen directly.

The EQUIVALENCE statement:

EQUIVALENCE{ATRIB[1],PROC_TIME};

specifies that the name PROC_TIME may be used in place of ATRIB[1]. In the network model, statistics can be collected on PROC_TIME by the following statement:

COLCT,,PROC_TIME;

This statement causes PROC_TIME to be collected for each arriving entity, that is, ATRIB[1] of the arriving entity is collected.

Below an EQUIVALENCE statement is used to indicate that INVENTORY can be used in place of the global variable XX[1] and REORDER_PT for XX[2].

EQUIVALENCE{{XX[I],INVENTORY},
            {XX[2],REORDER_PT},
            {UNFRM(4,6),REVIEW_TIME}}:

In addition, the name REVIEW TIME may be used in place of the random sampling function UNFRM(4,6). To illustrate the use of these equivalences, the statement

ACTIVITY,,REVIEW_TIME,INVENTORY<=REORDER_PT;

specifies an activity whose duration is REVIEW_TIME, that is, a sample from a uniform distribution between 4 and 6, and whose condition for performing the activity is that the INVENTORY is less than or equal to the REORDER_PT.

4.3.4   ARRAY Statement

The ARRAY statement is used to INITIALIZE a row of the Visual SLAM global table, ARRAY. The number of elements in a row of ARRAY can vary and, hence, the table is referred to as a ragged table. The format for the ARRAY statement is

ARRAY,IROW,NELEMENTS,{initial value, repeats};

where IROW is an integer constant defining the row for which initial values are being provided; NELEMENTS is the number of elements in this row; and initial values are constants to be inserted in the order of the columns for the row. For example, the statement

ARRAY,2,4,{5,4,2,7.3};

defines ARRAY[2,1] to be 5; ARRAY[2,2] to be 4; ARRAY[2,3] to be 2; and ARRAY[2,4] to be 7.3.

Elements of ARRAY may be referenced on a Visual SLAM network where a Visual SLAM variable is allowed. ARRAY subscripts may be constants or variables. For example, if an entity has ATRIB[1] defined as a job type, ATRIB[2] as its next job step, and ATRIB[3] as the machine number for the next job step and the table ARRAY is organized such that machine numbers are the values included in the table with each row defined by a job type and each column by a job step, then

ATRIB[3] = ARRAY[ATRIB[1],ATRIB[2]]

assigns a machine number to attribute 3 based on an entity's job type and current job step value.

ARRAY can be used in conjunction with the EQUIVALENCE statement to make a model more readable. Continuing with the above example, we will equivalence JOBTYPE to ATRIB[1], JOBSTEP to ATRIB[2] and MACHINE to ATRIB[3]. These equivalences are shown on the following EQUIVALENCE statement.

EQUIVALENCE {ATRIB[1],JOBTYPE},
            {ATRIB[2],JOBSTEP},
            {ATRIB[3],MACHINE};

With these equivalences made, the above replacement statement becomes

MACHINE = ARRAY[JOBTYPE,JOBSTEP]

ARRAY elements are accessible from user-written C code as well as from network statements. The functions GETARY, PUTARY, and SETARY are used to: get values of an element of ARRAY; put or insert a new value into an element of ARRAY; and set a complete row of ARRAY. These functions are described in detail in Chapter 9.

4.4   INTRODUCTION TO BASIC NETWORK ELEMENTS

There are seven basic network elements in Visual SLAM. These network elements are: CREATE node, QUEUE node, TERMINATE node, ASSIGN node, ACTIVITY branches, GOON node and COLCT node. With these basic network elements, many diverse network models can be built.

The CREATE node is a method for creating entities for arrival or insertion into the network. The QUEUE node is used to model the complex decision processes involved when an entity arrives to a service operation where the disposition of the entity is dependent upon the status of the server and the number entities already waiting for the server in a queue. The TERMINATE node is used to delete entities from the network. The ASSIGN node is used to assign new or updated values to Visual SLAM variables. When an entity arrives to an ASSIGN node, the assignments specified at the ASSIGN node are made. ACTIVITY branches represent explicit time delays for entities traversing the network. Service activities are used to represent machines, operators. and the like which can process a limited number of entities concurrently. Preceding a service activity, a buffer or waiting area must be prescribed which is accomplished through the use of a QUEUE node. Activities which model explicit delays but do not have a limit on the number of concurrent entities are referred to as regular activities. GOON nodes are used to separate activities and can model branching logic to route entities following the completion of an activity. Statistical information on entities and Visual SLAM variables is obtained through the use of the COLCT node. Each of these basic network elements will now be described in detail.

4.5   CREATE NODE

The CREATE node generates entities and routes them into the system over activities that emanate from the CREATE node. A time for the first entity to be created by the CREATE node is specified by the value of TF. The time between creations of entities after the first is specified by the variable TBC. TBC can be specified as a constant or an expression. Entities will continue to be created until a limit is reached. This limit is specified as MC, the maximum number of creations allowed at the node. When MC entities have been input to the system, the CREATE node stops creating entities.

The time at which the entity is created can be assigned to a variable, MV. This time is referred to as the *mark time* of the entity and it is stored in the given variable. The symbol, statement and AweSim dialog box for the CREATE node are shown below.

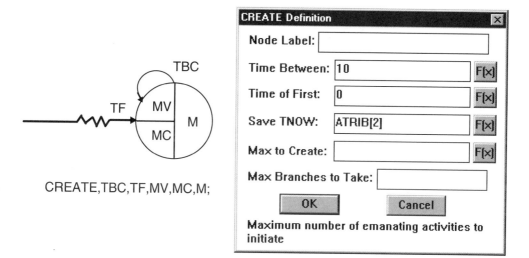

CREATE,TBC,TF,MV,MC,M;

The dialog box is presented when a CREATE node is added to a network diagram in AweSim. The node description is completed by filling in the entry boxes or by selecting a function or variable name using the F(x) pushbutton.

The following are examples of the CREATE node.

1. Create entities starting at time zero and every 10 time units thereafter. Put the mark time into attribute 2 of the entity. Take all branches emanating from the CREATE node.

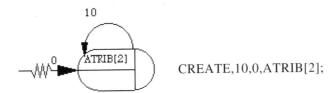 CREATE,10,0,ATRIB[2];

The default values taken are: MC = ∞ and M = ∞.

2. Create fifty entities starting at time 100.0. The time between creations should be 30. Take at most 2 branches emanating from the node.

 CREATE,30,100,,50,2 ;

The default value for MV is not to mark the entities created.

3. Create 1 entity at time 75 and take all branches emanating from the node.

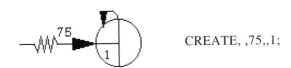 CREATE, ,75,,1;

The default values are: no marking; TBC = ∞; and M = ∞.

4. Create entities that model a Poisson arrival process, that is, an exponential time between arrivals, with a mean time of 10.

 CREATE,EXPON(10);

The default values are taken for all parameters except the time between creations.

5. Create entities based on user written function 1.

USERF(1)

CREATE,USERF(1);

Function USERF(I) would need to be written to return USERF as the TBC value to be employed. USERF(I) with argument 1 would be called at time 0 since TF by default is 0 and then at times specified by the values given to USERF. In writing Function USERF(I), all C or Visual Basic statement types are available. For example, an external file could be read to obtain arrival times from historical records.

4.6   QUEUE NODE

A QUEUE node is a location in the network where entities wait for service. When an entity arrives at a QUEUE node, its disposition depends on the status of the server that follows the QUEUE node. If the server is idle, the entity passes through the QUEUE node and goes immediately into the service activity. If no server is available, the entity waits at the QUEUE node until a server can process it. When a server does become available, the entity will automatically be taken out of the queue and service will be initiated. Visual SLAM assumes that no delay is involved from the time a server becomes available and the time service is started on an entity that was waiting in the QUEUE node.

When an entity waits at a QUEUE node, it is stored in a file which maintains the entity's attributes and the relative position of the entity with respect to other entities waiting at the same QUEUE node. The order in which the entities wait in the QUEUE is specified outside the network on a PRIORITY statement which defines the ranking rule for the file associated with the QUEUE. Files can be ranked on: first-in, first-out (FIFO); last-in, first-out (LIFO); low-value first based on an expression (LVF(expr)); and high-value first based on an expression (HVF(expr)). FIFO is the default priority for files.

Entities can initially reside at queues, as the initial number of entities at a QUEUE node, IQ, is part of the description of the QUEUE node. These entities all start with attribute values equal to zero. When IQ>0, all service activities emanating from the QUEUE node are assumed to be busy initially working on entities with all attribute values equal to zero. QUEUE nodes can have a capacity which limits the number of entities that can reside at the queue at a given time. The basic symbol, statement and AweSim dialog box for the QUEUE node are shown below.

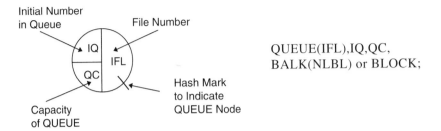

QUEUE(IFL),IQ,QC,
BALK(NLBL) or BLOCK;

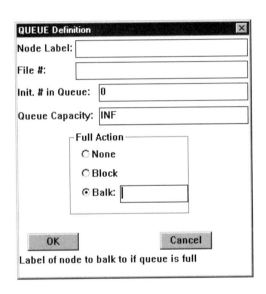

When an entity arrives at a QUEUE node which is at its capacity, its disposition must be determined. This decision is based on a specification at the QUEUE node as to whether the entity should balk or be blocked. In the case of balking, the entity can be routed to another node of the network. This node is specified by providing the label of the node. If no balking node label is specified, the entity is deleted from the system. The symbol for balking is shown below where balking can occur from one QUEUE node to another QUEUE node labeled QUE2. There is no restriction on the type of node to which entities can balk.

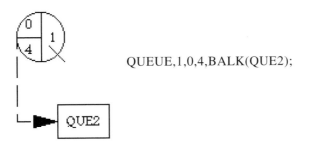

QUEUE,1,0,4,BALK(QUE2);

When an entity is blocked by a QUEUE node, it waits until a free space is available in the queue. The activity which just served the entity that is blocked is also considered as blocked. A blocked entity will join the queue when a space is available. At that time, the blocked activity becomes free to process other entities waiting for it. *Queue nodes may only block service activities.* No time delay is associated with these deblocking operations. The symbol and statement for blocking at a QUEUE node are shown below.

QUEUE,3,2,10,BLOCK;

The file number for the QUEUE node can be specified as a range of values, using the ASSERT function. This specification for the file number, IFL, has the syntax ASSERT(VAR,LOW,HIGH). LOW through HIGH are the allowable file numbers specified by VAR. As an example, consider the following

QUEUE,ASSERT(LTRIB[2],3,5),0;

where LTRIB[2] defines the file number which can be 3, 4 or 5.

When more than one service activity follows a queue and the service activities are not identical, a selection of the server to process an entity must be made. This selection is not made at the QUEUE node but at a SELECT node that is associated with the QUEUE node. The label of the SELECT node associated with a QUEUE node is entered on the QUEUE statement. When an entity arrives at a QUEUE node, its associated SELECT node is interrogated. When a SELECT node finds a free server, the entity arriving at the QUEUE node is transferred to the SELECT node and is immediately put into service. Direct transfers of this type are shown in Visual SLAM through the use of dashed lines called connectors. An illustration of a QUEUE node-SELECT node combination is shown below.

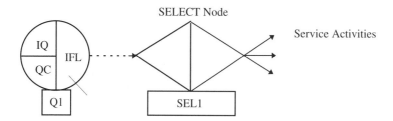

Multiple SELECT nodes may be associated with a QUEUE node. When this occurs, the order in which the SELECT nodes are listed on the QUEUE statement specifies the order in which SELECT nodes are interrogated to find an available server. Multiple servers and a selection rule would be given for each SELECT node. Additional information on SELECT nodes is given in Chapter 6. The following are examples of QUEUE nodes:

1. Cause arriving entities to wait in file 7 if the number of waiting entities is less than 6 and the following server is busy.

       QUEUE,7,,6;

    The default values are: IQ = 0 implying no initial entities are at the QUEUE node; no balking node is specified, implying that entities arriving to the queue when it is full are lost to the system; no SELECT nodes are specified, implying a single type of service activity is represented by the branch that follows the QUEUE node.

2. Cause arriving entities to be blocked if two entities are waiting in the QUEUE node called QUE1. Entities at QUE1 wait in file 3. Two servers can process entities arriving to the QUE1. Initially there is one entity waiting at QUE 1.

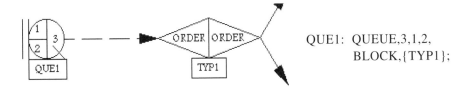

QUE1: QUEUE,3,1,2,
        BLOCK,{TYP1};

In this example, the branch incident to QUE1 represents a service activity that will be blocked if it finishes processing an entity when two entities are already waiting at QUE1 (in file 3). The service activities that process entities waiting in QUE1 are represented by the branches following SELECT node TYP1.

4.7   TERMINATE NODE

The TERMINATE node is used to destroy or delete entities from the network. It can be used to specify the number of entities to be processed on a simulation run. This number of entities is referred to as the termination count or TC value. When multiple TERMINATE nodes are employed, the first termination count reached ends the simulation run. If a TERMINATE node does not have a termination count, the entity is destroyed and no further action is taken. The symbol, statement and AweSim dialog box for the TERMINATE node are shown below.

TERMINATE,TC;

TERMINATE Definition	✕
Node Label:	
Term. Count:	INF

OK   Cancel

Label of this node. Used for branching and reports

As an example, consider the ending of a simulation run after 25 entities arrive to node DONE. This would be modeled as shown below.

DONE: TERMINATE,25;

4.8   ASSIGN NODE

The ASSIGN node is used to prescribe values to the attributes of an entity passing through the ASSIGN node or to prescribe values to system variables that pertain to the network in general. The ASSIGN node can also change values pertaining to discrete and continuous models that can be a part of Visual SLAM. The variables to which assignments can be made are those given in Table 4-1 with the exception of TNOW and ENUM. In addition, a special assignment can be made to the variable STOPA to cause the completion of an activity. This feature is described further in Section 4.9.1.

A value assigned to a variable can be used as an activity duration, as a routing condition, and in program inserts. In combined simulations, assignments can be used to change the values of variables that are part of the discrete or continuous model. This latter concept will be described in more detail in later chapters.

The values assigned to variables at an ASSIGN node can take on a wide variety of forms. The value can be a constant, one of the variables described above, a network status variable, the current time, a sample from a probability distribution or a value set in a user-written function (a program insert). Table 4-2 presented the names of the variables and functions that can be used to obtain values for inclusion in the calculations within the ASSIGN node. The symbol, statement and AweSim dialog box for the ASSIGN node are shown below.

ASSIGN,{{VAR,VALUE},Repeats},M;

Basically each line in the ASSIGN node can be considered as a C replacement statement with a left-hand side variable being restricted to those presented in Table 4-1 with the exception that assignments to the clock time TNOW and entity number ENUM are not allowed. The right-hand side expression can involve operations using the constants and variables defined in Tables 4-1 and 4-2. In evaluating the right-hand side expression, multiplication and division are evaluated first, then addition and subtraction. The expression is evaluated from left to right. Note that ASSIGN, XX[3]= 5./ 10.*2.; sets XX[3] to 1.0.

The parameters used in the probability functions are those described in the equations presented in Section 4.3.2. Each parameter for a distribution can be specified as a constant or an expression. In network assignments, the stream number, IS, can be omitted and a default stream number is used. The default stream number is 9 for random variables and 10 for probabilistic branching. An example of the ASSIGN node is shown below.

In this example, the value of attribute 2 of the entity passing through the node is changed to 7.0. The value of attribute 3 is replaced by its current value divided by XX[2]. The third assignment specifies that XX[1] be given a value that is a sample from a normal distribution whose mean is 4 and whose standard deviation is 2. The value of M is set to 1 to indicate that the entity is to be routed through only one branch. Since the statement is long, it is divided and placed on separate lines as long as a comma ends the preceding line (the details associated with statement continuation and input procedures are described in Chapter 8).

As another example of the flexibility of the ASSIGN node, consider the setting of XX[l] equal to a sample from an exponential distribution whose mean is taken as ATRIB[1] using stream 2. This is accomplished with the following statement:

ASSIGN,{XX[1],EXPON(ATRIB[1],2)};

The variables to which attributes are assigned can be used for many purposes. The primary uses involve the routing of entities and the duration of activities based on assigned values. Specific examples of the use of assignments will be deferred until these concepts are presented.

In summary, an attribute of the entity passing through the ASSIGN node is changed if any of the assignments involve the variables ATRIB[I], LTRIB[I], STRIB[I] or ETYPE on the left-hand side of the replacement statement. Global system variables are not associated with entities but are changed by the passage of an entity through an ASSIGN node. A global variable retains its value until another entity passes an ASSIGN node at which the global variable is recomputed. Following the assignments, the entity arriving to the ASSIGN node is routed in accordance with the M-number prescribed for the node.

4.9   ACTIVITIES

Branches are used to model activities. Only at branches are explicit time delays prescribed for entities flowing through the network. Activities emanating from QUEUE or SELECT nodes are referred to as service activities. Service activities restrict the number of concurrent entities flowing through them to be equal to the number of servers represented by the activity. Activities represented by branches emanating from other node types have no restriction on the number of entities that can simultaneously flow through them. The duration of an activity is the time delay that an entity encounters as it flows through the branch representing the activity.

Each branch has a start node and an end node. When an entity is to be routed from the start node, the branch may be selected as one through which the entity should be routed. The selection can be probabilistic in which case a probability is part of the activity description. The selection can be conditional in which case a condition is specified as part of the activity description. Service activities cannot have prescribed conditions, as their availability is limited and they must be allocated when free. If no probability or condition is specified (a common situation), the activity will be selected unless the M-number associated with its start node has been satisfied.

Activities can be given activity numbers. If the number I is prescribed for an activity then statistics are maintained and reported on the number of entities that are currently being processed through the activity, NNACT(I), and the number of entities that have completed the activity, NNCNT(I). A range of numbers can be prescribed for the activity number, for example, ASSERT(LTRIB[2],3,5) specifies that the activity number is taken from integer attribute 2 of the entity traversing the activity. The activity number can be 3, 4, or 5.

For service activities, the number of parallel identical servers represented by the activity needs to be specified if different from one. (For non-service activities, the number of parallel processes is assumed as infinite.) For service activities, Visual SLAM automatically provides utilization statistics.

The symbol, statement, and AweSim dialog box for a branch representing an activity is shown below.

DUR,PROB OR COND

ACTIVITY,A,DUR,PROB OR COND,NLBL,N,ID;

ACTIVITY Definition

Activity #:

Duration: F(x)

Condition: F(x)

End Node Label: F(x)

# of Servers:

Identifier:

OK   Cancel

Activity number for statistics collection

where

N is the number of parallel identical servers if the activity represents servers;

A is an activity number (an integer or a range of integers);

DUR is the duration specified for the activity;

PROB is a probability specification for selecting the activity;

COND is a condition for selecting the activity if the activity is a non-server;

NLBL is the end node label and is only required if the end node is not the next node listed; and

ID is an activity identification that provides a label for activity statistics.

4.9.1   Activity Durations

Activity durations (DUR) can be specified by any expression containing the variables described in Tables 4-1 and 4-2. Thus, a duration can be assigned a value in the same way as an attribute or system variable is assigned a value. For example, a duration can be taken as the value of attribute 3 by specifying DUR to be ATRIB[3] or as a sample from an exponential distribution whose mean is ATRIB[3], that is, EXPON(ATRIB[3]). If a sample from a probability distribution is negative, and the sample is used for an activity duration, Visual SLAM assumes a zero value for the activity's duration.

The duration can be made to depend on the release time of a node of the network by specifying that the activity continue until the next release of the node. This is accomplished using the REL(NLBL) specification. When the duration is specified in this manner, the activity will continue in operation, holding the entity being processed until the next release of the node with the label NLBL. The REL specification corresponds to an activity scanning orientation as described in Chapter 3. By release of a node is meant the act of an entity arriving at the node and the attempt to route it from the node. In Chapter 6, the ACCUMULATE node is described where entities arrive but may not release (pass through) the node

The duration can also be made to depend on an assignment made at an ASSIGN node. This is accomplished using the STOPA(NTC) specification where NTC is an integer code to distinguish entities in such activities. The value of NTC can be specified as any integer expression and will be truncated to the nearest integer. The duration of an activity specified by STOPA will continue in operation holding the entity being processed until an assignment is made in which STOPA is set equal to NTC. Thus, STOPA is similar to a wait until specification. For example, the activity statement

ACT,,STOPA(1);

will cause each entity to wait in the activity until STOPA is set to 1 at an ASSIGN node. Every entity in this activity or other STOPA specified activities with an NTC value of 1 will be allowed to proceed when the assignment is made. By specifying the NTC code as an attribute of an entity or as a random variable, a modeler can assign different entity codes to entities within the same activity or for different activities. One use of the STOPA specification is as a switch for entity types. If the attribute ETYPE has been defined, then

ACT,,STOPA(ETYPE);

will require an assignment of STOPA=1 to release type 1 entities from the activity, an assignment of STOPA=2 to release type 2 entities, and so on. In Chapter 9, additional information on the use of STOPA is given.

4.9.2   Probability Specification for Branches

A probability is specified for a branch as an argument to the PROB function. The argument is any expression which yields a value between 0.0 and 1.0. The sum of the probabilities of those branches with probabilities emanating from the same node need not be one. Probabilities may be assigned to branches emanating from QUEUE nodes. In this case, the activities emanating from the QUEUE node are assumed to be the same server(s) and the probabilities can be used to obtain different duration specifications or different routings for entities processed by the same server(s).

Examples of probability specifications are: PROB(0.7), PROB(1-XX[3]) and PROB (NNQ(2)/100).

4.9.3   Condition Specification for Branches

A condition specification is only allowed for regular activities. Service activities must be initiated if an entity is waiting. Conditions are prescribed in the form:

VALUE operator VALUE

VALUE can be any expression, a Visual SLAM variable, or a Visual SLAM random variable (see Tables 4-1 and 4-2). OPERATOR is one of the standard C relational codes defined below.

Relational Code	Definition
<	Less than
<=	Less than or equal to
==	Equal to
!=	Not equal to
>	Greater than
>=	Greater than or equal to

Examples of condition codes are:

Condition			Take branch if
TNOW	>=	100.0	Current time greater than or equal to 100.
ATRIB[1]	<	DRAND(2)	Attribute 1 of the current entity is less than a random number obtained from stream 2.
NNQ(7)	==	10	The number of entities in file 7 is equal to 10.

The union and intersection of two or more conditions can be prescribed for an activity using && and ‖ specifications. Thus, a possible conditional expression for a branch could be

TNOW>=100&&ATRIB[2]<5.0

which specifies TNOW to be greater than 100 and ATRIB[2] less than 5.0. An example of the use of the union of two conditions is the following which specifies that the activity is to be taken if NNQ(7) equals 10 or II is not equal to 4.

NNQ(7)==10‖II !=4

If more than two conditions are combined using the && and ‖ specifications then the conditions are tested sequentually from left to right. Complicated logic may be expressed using parentheses.

4.10   ILLUSTRATIONS

In this section, we present illustrations that combine the node and activity concepts into networks. Both network and statement models are presented.

4.10.1   Illustration 4-1. Two Parallel Servers

Consider a situation involving the processing of customers at a bank with two tellers and a single waiting line. A network that models this situation is shown below.

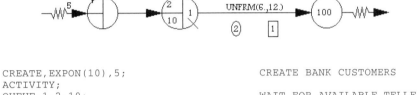

```
CREATE,EXPON(10),5;                  CREATE BANK CUSTOMERS
ACTIVITY;
QUEUE,1,2,10;                        WAIT FOR AVAILABLE TELLER
ACTIVITY,1,UNFRM(6.,12.),,,2;        TWO TELLERS IN PARALLEL
TERM,100;                            END SIMULATION WHEN 100
;                                    CUSTOMERS HAVE BEEN SERVED
```

In this example, two parallel servers (tellers) are associated with activity 1. The service time of each server is uniformly distributed between 6 and 12 time units. Entities (customers) that arrive at the QUEUE node when both servers are busy wait in file 1. Initially, there are two entities in the queue which causes both servers to be busy. Thus, there are four in the system initially; two in service and two waiting at the QUEUE node. A capacity of ten entities has been assigned to the queue. Since no BLOCK or BALK specification is made, customers arriving when the bank is full will be terminated upon arrival. A warning message is provided for this event.

The TERMINATE node indicates that the model is to be analyzed until 100 entities have completed processing. The time between arrivals is prescribed at the CREATE node as samples from an exponential distribution with a mean of 10. The first entity is scheduled to arrive at time 5.

4.10.2   Illustration 4-2. Two Types of Entities

Consider a situation involving two types of jobs that require processing by the same server. The job types are assumed to form a single queue before the server. The network and statement model of this situation is shown below.

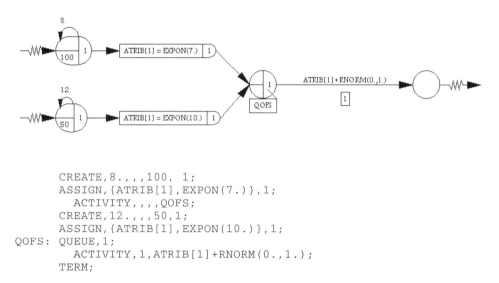

```
        CREATE,8.,,,,100, 1;
        ASSIGN,{ATRIB[1],EXPON(7.)},1;
          ACTIVITY,,,,QOFS;
        CREATE,12.,,,,50,1;
        ASSIGN,{ATRIB[1],EXPON(10.)},1;
QOFS:   QUEUE,1;
          ACTIVITY,1,ATRIB[1]+RNORM(0.,1.);
        TERM;
```

In this model, one type of entity is scheduled to arrive every 8 time units and only 100 of them are to be created. These entities have a service time estimated to be a sample from an exponential distribution with a mean time of 7. This service time is assigned to attribute 1 at an ASSIGN node. For the other type of entity the time between arrivals is 12 time units and 50 of these entities are to be created. The estimated service time for each of these entities is exponentially distributed with a mean time of 10. Both types of entities are routed to a QUEUE node whose label is QOFS. Entities at QOFS wait in file 1 and are ranked on small values of attribute one. This priority specification is made through a PRIORITY statement that will be described in Section 4.13. The server is modeled as activity 1 where the service time is specified as attribute 1 plus a sample from a normal distribution. Thus, the actual processing time is equal to the estimated processing time plus an error term that is assumed to be normally distributed. This model might be used to represent a job shop in which jobs are performed in the order of the smallest estimated service time.

Many default values were assumed in the above statement model. Both entity types have their first arrival at time zero and neither are marked. The default value for the initial number in the QUEUE node is zero and the capacity of the QUEUE node is assumed to be infinite. No specification for the termination count is made at the TERMINATE node and, hence, the run is completed when all entities created have passed through the system, which in this case is 150. (Note: this termination condition cannot be determined absolutely from the model description, as a completion time for the network could have been prescribed. The procedure for specifying a completion time is discussed in Section 4.13.)

To illustrate the use of the EQUIVALENCE statement to make the model more readable, the statement model is redone below.

```
EQUIVALENCE,{{ESERVET,ATRIB[1]},
             {NOISE,RNORM(0.,1.)}};
NETWORK;
;
;CREATE AND ASSIGN ESTIMATES OF PROCESSING TIME
;
     CREATE,8.,,100,1;
     ASSIGN,{ESERVET,EXPON(7.)},1;
        ACTIVITY,,,,QOFS;
     CREATE,12.,50,1;
     ASSIGN,{ESERVET,EXPON(10.)},1;
QOFS:  QUEUE,1;
;
; ACTIVITY TIME IS ESTIMATE + ERROR IN ESTIMATE
;
        ACTIVITY,1,ESERVT+NOISE;
     TERM;
```

The estimated service time is defined as ESERVET and equivalenced to ATRIB[l]. The error of the estimate of the service time is defined as NOISE and equivalenced to RNORM(0.0,1.0). As can be seen, the use of the EQUIVALENCE statement improves the readability of a Visual SLAM statement model.

4.10.3   Illustration 4-3. Blocking and Balking from QUEUE Nodes

Consider a company with a maintenance shop that involves two operations in series. When maintenance is required on a machine and four machines are waiting for operation 1, the maintenance operations are subcontracted to an external vendor. This situation is modeled below.

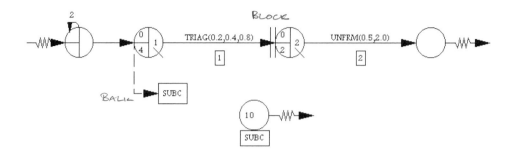

```
CREATE,2;
;
;BALK FROM QUEUE OF FIRST OPERATION IF 4 ITEMS ARE WAITING
;
   QUEUE,1,0,4,BALK(SUBC);
      ACT,1,TRIAG(0.2,0.4,0.8);
;
; SERVICE ACTIVITY 1 IS BLOCKED IF SECOND QUEUE HAS
; 2 ITEMS WAITING
;
   QUEUE,2,0,2,BLOCK;
     ACT,2,UNFRM(0.5,2.0);
   TERM;
;
; TERMINATE THE SIMULATION IF 10 ITEMS SUBCONTRACTED
;
SUBC: TERM,10;
```

In this model, entities are created every two time units and routed directly to a QUEUE node that has a capacity of four. At this node, entities are stored in file 1 and, if an entity arrives when there are four other entities in file 1, it balks to the TERMINATE node SUBC. When ten entities balk to node SUBC, the run is to be ended. The service time for activity 1 is triangularly distributed with a mode of 0.4 and minimum and maximum values of 0.2 and 0.8, respectively. When service activity 1 is completed, entities are routed directly to a second QUEUE node. File 2 is used to store waiting entities for server 2. If two entities are already waiting for server 2, the entity is blocked and service activity 1 must hold the blocked entity. No further service activities can be started for server 1 even though entities are waiting in file 1. When the number of entities in file 2 decreases below 2, the blocked entity is routed to file 2 and another service activity for server 1 can be started. The processing time for server 2 is uniformly distributed between 0.5 and 1. The example to be presented in Section 4.14 is similar to this illustration and provides the inputs to and outputs from the Visual SLAM processor.

4.10.4   Illustration 4-4. Conditional and Probabilistic Branching

Consider a situation involving an inspector and an adjustor. Presume that seventy percent of the items inspected are routed directly to packing and thirty percent of the items require adjustment. Following adjustment, the items are returned for reinspection. We will let the inspection time be a function of the number of items waiting for inspection (NNQ(1)) and the number waiting for adjustment (NNQ(2)). The model corresponding to this description is shown below.

```
CREATE,10.,,,,1;
;
;ASSIGN INSPECTION TIME BASED ON THE NUMBER AWAITING INSPECTION
;
        ACTIVITY,,0,NNQ(1)<=5;
        ACTIVITY,,0,NNQ(1)<9&&NNQ(2)<=2,"NORM";
        ACTIVITY,,,,"SECS";
ABNM: ASSIGN,{{ATRIB[1],6}},1;
        ACTIVITY,,,,"QUE1";
NORM: ASSIGN,{{ATRIB[1],8}},1;
        ACTIVITY,,,,"QUE1";
;
; INSPECTION PROCESSING
;
QUE1: QUEUE,1;
        ACTIVITY,1,ATRIB[1],PROB(0.3);
        ACTIVITY,1,ATRIB[1],PROB(0.7),"PACK";
;
; ADJUSTMENT PROCESSING
;
QUE2: QUEUE,2;
        ACTIVITY,2,EXPON(10.),,"QUE1";
PACK: TERMINATE,300;
SECS: TERMINATE,20;
```

In this model, conditional branching is specified from the CREATE node where the M-number is one, that is, a maximum of one of the three branches emanating from the CREATE node is to be taken. The entity is routed to node ABNM, if the number of entities in file 1 is less than or equal to 5. At ASSIGN node ABNM, ATRIB[1] is set equal to 6 time units. ATRIB[1] will be used in this illustration to represent the processing time for an entity. The branch from the CREATE node to the ASSIGN node NORM is taken if the number of entities in file 1 is less than 9 and the number of entities in file 2 is less than or equal to 2. When this occurs, a processing time of 8 time units is stored in ATRIB[1] at the ASSIGN node NORM.

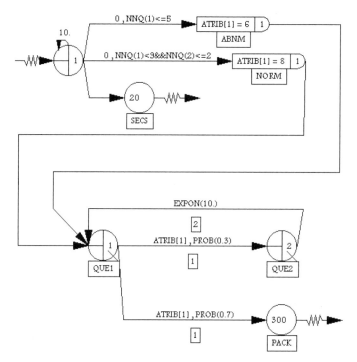

No condition is specified on the branch from the CREATE node to the TERM node SECS. Since the conditions are evaluated in the order prescribed by the statement model, this branch will only be taken if the preceding two branches are not taken. This branch represents a non-processing of an entity through the server process. If 20 such occurrences materialize, the run is to be completed.

QUE1 is the QUEUE node for server 1. With probability 0.3, the entity is routed to QUE2. With probability 0.7, it is routed to the TERM node PACK. Both of these activities represent service activity 1. The service time is set equal to ATRIB[1] previously defined at the ASSIGN nodes. AT QUE2, the entity goes through a second service activity whose service time is exponentially distributed with a mean time of 10. Entities are then routed back to QUE1 for additional processing by server 1. At TERMINATE node PACK, a requirement of 300 entity arrivals is indicated in order to complete one run of the network. Thus, a run can be terminated by an entity arrival to either node PACK or node SECS.

4.10.5   Illustration 4-5. Service Time Dependent on Node Release

Consider an assembly line that is paced so that units can only be completed at the end of ten-minute intervals. This model depicts two identical servers with a single queue and is similar to the model presented in Illustration 4-1. However, for this model the service time duration is specified as the next release time of CREATE node TlMR. CREATE node TIMR is released for the first time at time 10 and every 10 time units thereafter. This specifies that the duration for service activity 1 will end at a multiple of 10. If service activity 1 starts at time 13 then the end time will be 20. Thus, the service duration will be 7.

If an entity is put into service at time 49, it will complete service at time 50 and its duration will be 1. Other aspects of this illustration were described previously. The model for this situation is given below.

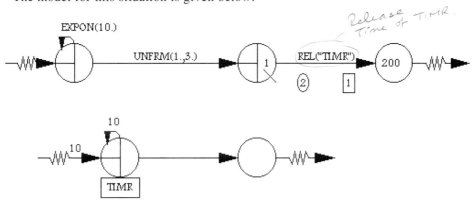

```
; SUBNETWORK FOR ARRIVAL AND PROCESSING OF PARTS
;
      CREATE,EXPON(10.);
         ACTIVITY,,UNFRM(1.,3.);
      QUEUE,1;
; PROCESSING TIME BASED ON RELEASE OF PACING TIMER
         ACTIVITY,1,REL("TIMR"),,,2;
      TERMINATE,200;
;
; SUBNETWORK FOR PACING SERVER IN ACTIVITY 1
;
TIMR: CREATE,10,10;
         ACTIVITY;
       TERMINATE;
```

4.11   GOON NODE

The GOON node is included as a continue type or go-on node. The symbol, and statement and dialog box for the GOON node are shown below.

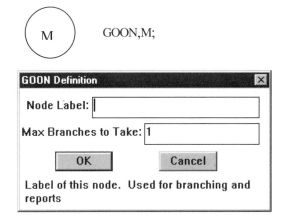

The GOON node is used in the modeling of sequential activities since two consecutive activity statements are used to model parallel activities. This should be clear from the following two network segments.

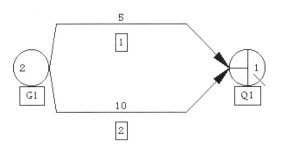

```
;MODEL OF TWO ACTIVITIES IN PARALLEL
  G1: GOON,2;
        ACT,1,5;
        ACT,2,10;
  Q1: QUEUE,1;
```

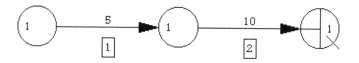

```
MODEL OF TWO ACTIVITIES IN SERIES
     GOON,1;
        ACT,1,5;
     GOON,1;
        ACT,2,10;
     QUEUE,1;
```

Note that for each entity arriving to GOON node Gl, two entities are routed to QUEUE node Q1. The attributes of the two entities are the same as the attributes of the entity arriving to node Gl except that a new ENUM is given to the cloned entity that is routed over activity 2. For the model of two activities in series, each arriving entity is routed over activity l first, then activity 2.

4.11.1   Illustration 4-6. Attribute Specified File and Service Activity Numbers

In this illustration, the use of an attribute to specify a file number and a service activity number will be demonstrated. The situation to be modeled consists of entities that arrive to a system every five time units. Each arriving entity is to be processed sequentially by servers 1, 2, and 3. Entities waiting for server I are stored in file I with I equal to 1, 2, or 3. This situation will be modeled by a single QUEUE node-service activity combination where the file number and service activity number are specified by the value of (LTRlB[1]). The value of LTRIB[1] is set initially to 1 and then indexed each time a service is performed on the entity. When the value of LTRIB[1]==3, the entity is routed to a TERM node because processing on the entity is completed. The service time for each server is assumed to be exponentially distributed with a different mean service time given by XX[II], II= 1,2,3. It will be assumed that these values of XX are set through initial conditions or in a disjoint network not shown in this illustration. The network model and statements are shown below.

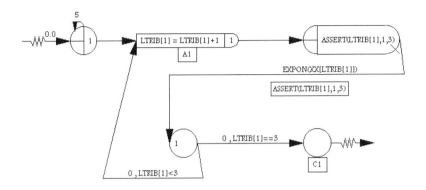

```
    CREATE,5,0.0,,,1;
;
; LTRIB[1] = Next server station, XX[station] = Mean service time
;
A1: ASSIGN,{{LTRIB[1],LTRIB[1]+1}},1;
;
; Set file number = Server station number
;
    QUEUE,ASSERT(LTRIB[1],1,3);
        ACTIVITY,ASSERT(LTRIB[1],1,3),EXPON(XX[LTRIB[1]]);
    GOON,1;
        ACTIVITY,,0,LTRIB[1]==3;
        ACTIVITY,,0,LTRIB[1]<3,"A1";
C1: TERMINATE;
```

Basically the above model consists of a single queue-service activity combination with the use of an ASSIGN node and conditional branching to allow for different definitions of the file and server numbers. For this illustration, it may be just as easy to model the situation with three queue-server combinations in series. However, for a larger number of serial operations, the above procedure for indirectly specifying the file number and server number can condense the size of a network significantly. Although this illustration has entities flowing through servers in a prescribed order, it is easy to modify the network so that the value of LTRIB[1] is changed in accordance with a routing structure defined for each entity type, that is, an attribute could be used to define an entity type and then, based on the entity type, different server numbers can be prescribed for LTRIB[1].

4.12 COLCT NODE

Statistics can be collected on any expression at a COLCT node. Expressions commonly used include:

1. Time-of-first arrival (FIRSTARRIVE). Only one value is recorded during each run.

2. Time-of-all arrivals (TNOW). Every time an entity arrives to the node, its arrival time is added to all previous arrival times. At the end of a run, an average time of arrival is computed.

3. Time between arrivals (TNOW-LASTARRIVE). The time of first arrival is used as a reference point. On subsequent arrivals, the time between arrivals is collected as an observation of the statistic of interest.

4. Internal statistics (TNOW-ATRIB(I)). This statistic relates to the arrival time of an entity minus an attribute value of the entity. The attribute value would have been set earlier as a mark time at a CREATE node or by assignment at an ASSIGN node.

5. Visual SLAM expression. The value of a Visual SLAM expression is recorded as an observation every time an entity arrives to the node. Note that USERF(I) may be part of a Visual SLAM expression.

For any observed expression, estimates for the mean and standard deviation of the variable are obtained. In addition, a histogram of the values that are collected at a COLCT node can be obtained. This is accomplished by specifying on input the number of cells, NCEL; the upper limit of the first cell, HLOW; and a cell width, HWID, for the histogram.

The number of cells specified, NCEL, is the number of interior cells, each of which will have a width of HWID. Two additional cells will be added that contain the interval (- ∞,HLOW} and (HLOW + NCEL*HWID, ∞). The cells are closed at the high value. Thus, if HLOW=0, the value 0 will be included in the first cell. For the specification: NCEL = 5; HLOW = 0; and HWID = 10, the number of times the expression on which statistics are being maintained is in the following intervals would be presented as part of the standard Visual SLAM summary report:

(-∞,0], (0,10], (10,20], (20,30], (30,40], (40,50], and (50, ∞).

If the number of cells is not specified, no histogram will be prepared. A string identifier, enclosed in quotes, can be associated with a COLCT node. This identifier, denoted ID, will be printed on the Visual SLAM summary report to identify the output associated with the COLCT node. In order to identify values stored by a particular COLCT node in user written subprograms, an integer expression, COLCT #, can also be defined. The symbol, statement and dialog box for the COLCT node are:

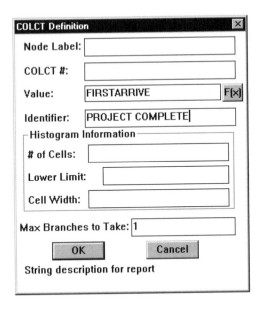

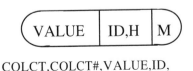

COLCT,COLCT#,VALUE,ID,
NCEL,HLOW,HWID,M;

Since histograms are not always requested, a single field identified as "H" is used on the symbol where it is implied that H represents NCEL/HLOW/HWID. Examples of the COLCT node are given below.

1. Collect statistics on the completion time of a project with no histogram required.

   COLCT,,FIRSTARRIVE,
                         "PROJECT COMPLETE",,,,1;

2. Collect statistics on the time in the system of an entity whose time of entering the system is maintained in ATRIB[3]. No histogram is requested for this COLCT node and the entity is to be routed over one branch. The COLCT node should be identified as the seventh collect variable.

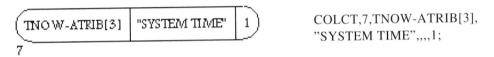   COLCT,7,TNOW-ATRIB[3],
                         "SYSTEM TIME",,,,1;

7

3. Collect statistics on the value of global variable, XX[2], every time an entity passes through the COLCT node. Identify the statistical output with the identifier SAFETY STOCK. Prepare a histogram consisting of 20 cells for which the first cell interval is $(-\infty, 10]$ and the width of the next 20 cells is 5. Set the maximum number of branches to be taken to 2.

COLCT,,XX[2],"SAFETYSTOCK",20,10,5,2;

← HISTOGRAM SPECIFICATION.

In this illustration, XX[2] can be considered as an inventory level and the entity arriving to the COLCT node represents a replenishment of the units in inventory.

4. Collect time in system statistics on 10 entity types. The entity types are numbered 1 through 10 and are stored in attribute ETYPE. The entity time of arrival is stored in ATRIB[0]. The identifier for the Visual SLAM summary report for each collection should be "TIS-TYPE #"

ETYPE

COLCT,ETYPE,TNOW-ATRIB[0],
    STRCAT("TIS-TYPE ",ITOA (ETYPE)),,,,1;

In this illustration, the COLCT# is specified as an attribute, ETYPE, and the identifier is an expression involving a string concatenation of the string "TIS-TYPE " and the entity type number which is changed from an integer to an alphanumeric by the function ITOA. On the summary report, the 10 entity types are printed out individually. In this way, Visual SLAM avoids the branching and 10 COLCT node specifications that would be required to obtain statistics on 10 entity types. The intrinsic functions available for constructing expressions are given in Table 4-3.

Table 4-3   Visual SLAM intrinsic functions

Function	Definition
ABS(RVAL)	Absolute value of RVAL
ACOS(RVAL)	Arc cosine of value
ASIN(RVAL)	Arc sine of value
ATAN(RVAL)	Arc tangent of value
ATAN2(A,B)	Arc tangent of (A/B)
ATOI(SZVAL)	Converts string into integer value
ATOF(SZVAL)	Converts string into double value
CEIL(RVAL)	Returns double equal to smallest integer >= RVAL
CHAR(IVAL)	Converts an integer into the ASCII character
COS(RADIAN)	Cosine of angle
COSH(RADIAN)	Hyperbolic cosine of angle
DBLE(IVAL)	Convert integer value into double
DIM(RV1,RV2)	Returns the positive difference between RV1 and RV2
DPROD(RV1,RV2)	Double-precision product
EXP(RVAL)	Returns e raised to the power RVAL
FLOOR(RVAL)	Returns double equal to largest integer <= RVAL
FMOD(RV1,RV2)	Returns remainder of RV1 / RV2
FTOA(RVAL)	Converts double into string
IILEN(SZVAL)	Returns the length of string SZVAL not counting any trailing whitespace
INDEX(SZ1,SZ2)	Finds the offset of string SZ2 within SZ1
INT(RVAL)	Truncate RVAL and return integer
ITOA(IVAL)	Converts integer into string
LDEXP(RVAL,IEXP)	Calculates the value RVAL * 2 raised to the IEXP power
LEN(SZVAL)	returns the length of the character string SZVAL
LLE(SZ1,SZ2)	Returns TRUE if string SZ1 <= string SZ2
LGE(SZ1,SZ2)	turns TRUE if string SZ1 >= string SZ2
LGT(SZ1,SZ2)	Returns TRUE if string SZ1 > string SZ2
LLT(SZ1,SZ2)	Returns TRUE if string SZ1 < string SZ2
LOG(RVAL)	Natural logarithm of value
LOG10(RVAL)	Common logarithm of value
MAX(VAL1,VAL2)	Returns maximum of VAL1 and VAL2
MIN(VAL1,VAL2)	Returns minimum of VAL1 and VAL2
MOD(IVAL,IBASE)	Returns remainder of IVAL / IBASE
NINT(RVAL)	Round RVAL to nearest integer
POW(RV1,RV2)	Calculates RV1 raised to the power of RV2
SIGN(RV1,RV2)	if RV2 < 0.0 returns -abs(RV1) else abs(RV1)
SIN(RADIAN)	Sine of angle
SINH(RADIAN)	Hyperbolic sine of angle
SQRT(RVAL)	Square root of value
STRCAT(SZ1,SZ2)	Returns string SZ2 concatenated onto SZ1
TAN(RADIAN)	Tangent of angle
TANH(RADIAN)	Hyperbolic tangent of angle

4.13   INTRODUCTION TO EXAMPLES AND CONTROL STATEMENTS

Throughout this book, a standard format is employed in the presentation of examples. First, the problem statement is presented which describes the system to be modeled including the objective of the analysis. A Concepts Illustrated section is then given which describes the major concepts which the example is intended to illustrate. The Visual SLAM Model is then presented. Lastly, a Summary of Results is presented including a reproduction of the Visual SLAM Summary Report where appropriate.

The final step in developing a network simulation is to combine the network description statements with the necessary control statements. Control statements provide information about the simulation experiment to be performed. At a minimum, the control statements GENERAL, LIMITS, and FINISH must be included. Other control statements such as PRIORITY, MONTR and INITIALIZE are included as required to specify the operation of the simulation runs. The TIMST statement is used to collect statistics on time-persistent variables and the ENTRY statement causes entities to be inserted into files.

In this section, the format of these control statements will be presented in abbreviated form. In Chapter 8, a complete discussion of the general format conventions for network and control statements is given along with a complete description of each field on a control statement. The abbreviated form for the GENERAL or GEN statement is shown below.

GEN,NAME,PROJECT,DATE,NNRNS;

The fields on the GEN statement are for the name of the modeler, the project title and the date of the run. The value specified for NNRNS is the number of runs to be made.

The format of the LIMITS or LIM statement is shown below:

LIM,MXX,MLL,MSZ,MATRIB,MLTRIB,MSTRIB,MNTRY;

This defines the maximum index for global variables (XX,LL or SZ), attributes (ATRIB,LTRIB or STRIB) and the largest number of concurrent entities expected in the model.

The abbreviated form of the NETWORK statement consist of a single field as shown below:

NETWORK;

and specifies that a network description follows.

The format for the INTLC statement is

INTLC,{{VAR = value}, repeats};

INTLC is used to assign initial values to Visual SLAM variables.

The abbreviated format for the INITIALIZE or INIT statement is shown below

INIT,TTBEG,TTFIN,JJCLR;

where TTBEG is the beginning time for the simulation, TTFIN is the desired ending time for the simulation, and JJCLR is used to specify if statistics are to be maintained separately for each run.

The abbreviated format for the TIMST statement is:

TIMST,STAT#,EXPR,"ID";

where EXPR is a Visual SLAM expression whose value persists for a time duration, for example, XX[l]. ID is an alphanumeric identifier printed in the Visual SLAM Summary Report to identify the summary statistics calculated for VAR. STAT# is the statistics index number, which may be defaulted.

The format for the ENTRY statement is shown below.

ENTRY,IFILE,NLBL,{attribute values};

The ENTRY statement is used to place initial entities into files or schedule entity arrivals to nodes. An ENTRY statement is specified by entering the file number, IFILE, or a node label, NLBL, followed by the attributes of the entry enclosed in braces.

The format of the PRIORITY statement is shown below:

PRIORITY,{{IFILE,ranking},repeats};

where IFILE is the file for which the ranking priority is being specified, and ranking is the priority specification. The options for the ranking are: FIFO, first-in, first-out; LIFO, last-in, first-out; HVF(expr), entities with a higher value of the expression are given priority, that is, a high-value-first priority; and LVF(expr) entities with a lower value of the expression are given priority, that is, a low-value-first priority.

The format for the MONTR statement is shown below:

MONTR,option,TFRST,TSEC,{expressions};

For the present, only the TRACE and CLEAR options are considered. TRACE specifies that a list of events is to be printed starting at the time TFRST and ending at time TSEC. Expressions is a list of Visual SLAM expressions whose value is to be displayed at each event time. The CLEAR option causes statistics to be discarded at time TFRST. CLEAR is used to eliminate statistics collected during a transient period.

The FIN statement consists of a single field as shown below

FIN;

and denotes the end of all Visual SLAM input statements. The SIMULATE or SIM statement consists of a single field as shown below

SIM;

and denotes the end of the Visual SLAM input statements for one run. A SIM statement is not required for a run if a FIN statement is the last statement.

4.14   EXAMPLE 4-1. WORK STATIONS IN SERIES

The maintenance facility of a large manufacturer performs two operations. These operations must be performed in series; operation 2 always follows operation 1. The units that are maintained are bulky, and space is available for only eight units including the units being worked on. A proposed design leaves space for two units between the work stations, and space for four units before work station 1. The proposed design is illustrated in Figure 4-1. Current company policy is to subcontract the maintenance of a unit if it cannot gain access to the in-house facility (1).

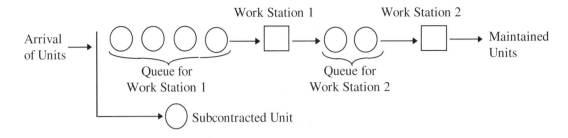

Figure 4-1 Schematic diagram of work stations in series.

Historical data indicates that the time interval between requests for maintenance is exponentially distributed with a mean of 0.4 time units. Service times are also exponentially distributed with the first station requiring on the average 0.25 time units and the second station, 0.5 time units. Units are transported automatically from work station 1 to work station 2 in a negligible amount of time. If the queue of work station 2 is full, that is, if there are two units waiting for work station 2, the first station is blocked and a unit cannot leave the station. A blocked work station cannot serve other units.

To evaluate the proposed design, statistics on the following variables are to be obtained over a period of 300 time units:

1. work station utilization;
2. time to process a unit through the two work stations;
3. time between the subcontracting of units;
4. number of units waiting for each work station; and
5. fraction of time that work station I is blocked.

Concepts Illustrated. This example will illustrate the general Visual SLAM network modeling procedure which consists of identifying the entities to be modeled; and constructing a graphical model of the entity flow process through the system. Specific network modeling concepts illustrated by this example include the creation of entities by a CREATE node, the modeling of a service system with a QUEUE node and ACTIVITY, balking and blocking at QUEUE nodes and statistics collection at a COLCT node.

Visual SLAM Model. The maintenance facility described in this example is representative of a large class of queueing-type systems in which units can be represented by entities that flow through the work stations. In this example, the entity flow process can be conveniently modeled by representing the storage area preceding each work station by a QUEUE node. The QUEUE node for work station

2 is prescribed to have a blocking capability to stop the processing of units by work station 1 when work station 1 has completed processing a unit and the queue before work station 2 is at its capacity. Each work station is represented by a service ACTIVITY with one server associated with each work station.

The Visual SLAM graphical model for this system is depicted in Figure 4-2.

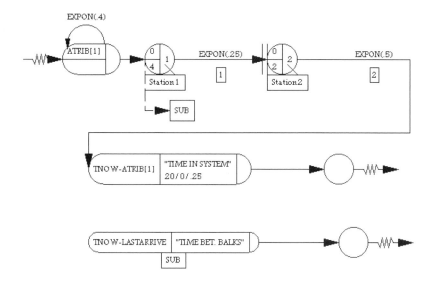

Figure 4-2 Visual SLAM network model of maintenance facility.

Entities representing the units are created at the CREATE node with the time between entities specified to be exponentially distributed with mean of 0.4 time units. Each entity's ATRIB[1] is marked with its time of creation at the CREATE node. Marking is specified to permit interval statistics to be collected on the time in the system for each entity. The entity is sent to the first QUEUE node which is used to represent the waiting area for work station 1. The parameters for this QUEUE node specify that the queue is initially empty, has a capacity of four and that entities waiting in the queue are placed in file 1. The subcontracting for the maintenance of units is modeled by the balking option for this QUEUE node. Entities which arrive to the system when the queue is full are denied access to the queue and are routed to the COLCT node labeled SUB. The COLCT node collects values on the time between entity arrivals which corresponds to the time between the subcontracting of units. The first work station is represented by activity 1 emanating from the QUEUE node with the service time specified as exponentially distributed with a mean of 0.25 time units.

Following completion of service at work station 1, the entity attempts to enter the second QUEUE node which is used to model the storage area for work station 2. The parameters for this node specify that the QUEUE node is initially empty, has a capacity of two and that entities waiting in the queue are placed in file 2. In addition, the blocking option is specified as indicated by the parallel lines preceding the QUEUE node. Thus, if an entity completes service activity 1 when there are two entities waiting in file 2, work station 1 will be blocked from further processing until work station 2 completes service on an entity. Work station 2 is represented by activity 2 and has a service time specified as exponentially distributed with mean of 0.5 time units.

Following completion of service by work station 2, the entity proceeds to a COLCT node where statistics are collected on the interval of time between the time recorded in ATRIB[1] of the entity and the current simulated time. Since the entity was marked at the CREATE node, ATRIB[1] is the time of arrival of the entity to the system. Thus, the interval of time represents the total processing time of the entity in the system. Following the COLCT node, the entity is terminated.

Once the graphical representation of the system is completed, AweSim translates the graphical representation of the system into the equivalent Visual SLAM statement representation according to the format specifications described in Chapter 8. The statement representation for this example is shown in Figure 4-3. Note that the sequence numbers along the left side of the figure are included to simplify statement referencing and are not part of the input data. Note also that the comments appearing on the right of the statement listing occur after the line terminator character (the semicolon) and are ignored by the Visual SLAM processor. Not shown on the network model are the activity identifiers which appear as labels on the summary report.

```
1    GEN, "PRITSKER", "SERIAL WORK STATIONS", 1/1/96, 1;
2    LIMITS,,,,1;
3    NETWORK;
4         CREATE, EXPON(.4), , ATRIB[1];       CREATE ARRIVALS
5    Station1: QUEUE, 1, 0, 4, BALK(SUB);           STN1 QUEUE
6         ACT, 1, EXPON(.25),,,,"STATION1 SVC TIME";
7    Station2:  QUEUE, 2, 0, 2, BLOCK;                STN2 QUEUE
8         ACT, 2, EXPON(.50),,,,"STATION2 SVC TIME";
9         COLCT,,TNOW-ATRIB[1],"TIME IN SYSTEM",10,0,.25;
10        TERM;
11   SUB:  COLCT, , TNOW-LASTARRIVE, "TIME BET. BALKS";
12        TERM;
13        END;
14   INIT, 0, 300;
15   FIN;
```

Figure 4-3 Input statements for maintenance facility model.

The first statement in the simulation program listing has the code GEN in field 1 and is used to provide general project information including the simulation author's name, project title, date, and number of simulation runs. This statement is followed by the LIMITS statement which specifies that the maximum index for ATRIB is 1. This is followed by the NETWORK statement which specifies that the simulation includes a network model with the network statement representation beginning with the next statement.

The network statement representation of the system parallels closely the graphical network representation of the system. The CREATE statement (line 4) specifies that entities are marked in ATRIB[1]. The time between entity arrivals is specified to be exponentially distributed with a mean of 0.4 time units. Since the time of first creation is not specified, a zero value is used. Also, there is no limit to the number of entities generated at this node. Each entity proceeds to Station1, the QUEUE statement (line 5). The parameters for the QUEUE statement specify that entities residing in the queue waiting for service are stored in file 1, initially there are no entities in the queue, the queue has a capacity of four and entities arriving to the queue when the queue is at capacity balk to the node labeled SUB. The ACT statement (line 6) following the QUEUE statement is a service activity representing work station 1 with a service time exponentially distributed with a mean of 0.25 time units.

Following completion of service at work station 1, the entities continue to Station2, the second QUEUE node (line 7). The parameters for this QUEUE statement specify that entities waiting in the queue for service are stored in file 2, the queue is initially empty, has a capacity of two and incoming entities (and service activities) are blocked when the queue is at capacity. The ACT statement (line 8) following the QUEUE statement is a service activity representing work station 2 with a service time that is exponentially distributed with a mean of 0.5 time units.

Following completion of service at work station 2, the entities arrive at the COLCT node (line 9) which collects interval statistics using the mark time in ATRIB[1] as a reference time, with the output statistics labeled TIME IN SYSTEM. A histogram is requested with 10 cells, with the upper limit of the first cell set equal to 0, and with a cell width equal to 0.5 units. Entities are then terminated as specified by the TERM statement (line 10).

The subcontracting of units which cannot gain access to the in-house facility is modeled by the balking of entities from the QUEUE statement (line 5) to the COLCT node labeled SUB (line 11). The options listed for the COLCT statement specify that statistics are to be collected on the time betweem entity arrivals to SUB, and that the output statistics are to be labeled TIME BET. BALKS. No histogram is requested. The entities representing the subcontracted units are then destroyed by the TERM statement (line 12). The END statement (line 13) denotes an end to the network description portion of the simulation program.

The simulation is initialized by the INIT statement (line 14) which sets the beginning time of the simulation (TTBEG) to 0 and the ending time of the simulation (TTFIN) to 300 time units. The FIN statement (line 15) denotes an end to all Visual SLAM simulation input.

Summary of Results. The results for the simulation are summarized by the Visual SLAM summary report depicted in Figure 4-4. The first category of statistics is for variables based upon observations. For this example, these statistics were collected by the network model at the COLCT nodes and include the interval statistics for TIME IN SYSTEM and the between statistics for TIME BET. BALKS. During the 300 simulated time units, there were a total of 586 units processed by the in house facility. The average time in the system for these units was 2.761 time units with a standard deviation of 1.278 time units and times ranged from 0.100 to 7.191 time units. The distribution for time in the system is depicted by the histogram generated by AweSim and included as Figure 4-5. There was a total of 179 observations of time between balks and, therefore, there were 180 units that were subcontracted. Recall that the time of first release of the COLCT node is not included as a value for between statistics because it may not be a representative value. It is only used to establish the reference value for LASTARRIVE.

The second category of statistics for this example is the file statistics. The statistics for file 1 and file 2 correspond to the units waiting for service at work stations 1 and 2, respectively. Thus, the average number of units waiting at work station 1 was 2.043 units, with a standard deviation of 1.515 units, a maximum of 4 units waited, and at the end of the simulation there were no units in the queue.

The last category of statistics for this example is statistics on service activities. The first row of service activity statistics corresponds to the server at work station 1 who was busy 47.0 percent of the time and blocked 40.4 percent of the time. Since the capacity of the server is one, the values 2.205 and 4.478 refer to the maximum length of the server idle period and busy period, respectively.

A number of additional statistics not provided by the Visual SLAM Summary Report can be obtained by straightforward analysis using the statistics provided. For example, an estimate of the average time that units spent waiting for service (2.011) can be obtained by subtracting the sum of the mean service times (0.75) from the average time in the system (2.761). The fraction of time idle (.126) for the server at work station 1 can be determined by simply subtracting the sum of the average utilization (.470) and average blockage (.404) from 1.

The main conclusion from the simulation results is that work station 2 does not have the capacity to satisfy the anticipated work load on the facility. The service time for work station 2 must be decreased if less subcontracting of units is desired.

```
            ** AweSim SUMMARY REPORT **

  Simulation Project : SERIAL WORK STATIONS
  Modeler : PRITSKER
  Date : 1/1/1996
  Scenario : EX41

  Run number 1 of 1
  Current simulation time    : 300.000000
  Statistics cleared at time : 0.000000


         ** OBSERVED STATISTICS REPORT for scenario EX41 **

  Label            Mean      Standard    Number of     Min.       Max.
                   Value     Deviation   Observations  Value      Value

  TIME IN SYSTEM   2.761     1.278          586        0.100      7.191
  TIME BET. BALKS  1.545     3.291          179        0.013      27.567


          ** FILE STATISTICS REPORT for scenario EX41 **

  File    Label or    Average  Standard   Max.    Current  Average
  Number  Input Loc.  Length   Deviation  Length  Length   Wait Time

  1 QUEUE    STATION   2.043    1.515        4       0      1.039
  2 QUEUE    STATION   1.556    0.727        2       2      0.792
  0 Event Calendar     3.413    0.512        4       4      0.455


         ** SERVICE ACTIVITY STATISTICS REPORT for scenario EX41 **

  Activity  Label or        Server    Entity   Average      Standard
  Number    Input Location  Capacity  Count    Utilization  Deviation

  1 STATION1 SVC TIM          1        589      0.470        0.499
  2 STATION2 SVC TIM          1        586      0.942        0.234

  Activity  Current      Average   Maximum    Maximum
  Number    Utilization  Blockage  Idle Time  Busy Time
                                   or Servers or Servers

     1          1        0.404     2.205      4.478
     2          1        0.000     2.580      69.433
```

Figure 4-4 Visual SLAM summary report for serial work station model.

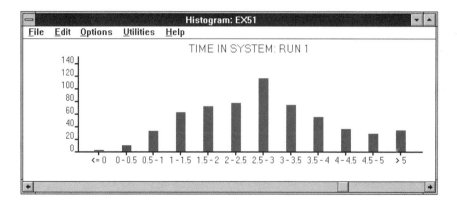

Figure 4-5 AweSim histogram for time in system, serial work station model.

4.15   EXAMPLE 4-2. INSPECTION AND ADJUSTMENT STATIONS ON A PRODUCTION LINE

The problem statement for this example is taken from Schriber (3) who presents a GPSS model of the problem. A Q-GERT model of this example is presented by Pritsker (1). Assembled television sets move through a series of testing stations in the final stage of their production. At the last of these stations, the vertical control setting on the TV sets is tested. If the setting is found to be functioning improperly, the offending set is routed to an adjustment station where the setting is adjusted. After adjustment, the television set is sent back to the last inspection station where the setting is again inspected. Television sets passing the final inspection phase, whether for the first time or after one or more routings through the adjustment station, are routed to a packing area.

The situation described is pictured in Figure 4-6 where "circles" represent television sets. "Open circles" are sets waiting for final inspection whereas "circled x's" are sets whose vertical control settings are improper. These sets are either being serviced at the adjustment station or waiting for service there.

The time between arrivals of television sets to the final inspection station is uniformly distributed between 3.5 and 7.5 minutes. Two inspectors work side-by-side at the final inspection station. The time required to inspect a set is uniformly distributed between 6 and 12 minutes. On the average, 85 percent of the sets pass inspection and continue on to the packing department. The other 15 percent are routed to the adjustment station which is manned by a single worker. Adjustment of the vertical control setting requires between 20 and 40 minutes, uniformly distributed.

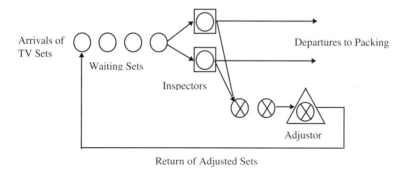

Return of Adjusted Sets

Figure 4-6 Schematic diagram of inspection and adjustment stations.

The inspection station and adjustor are to be simulated for 480 minutes to estimate the time to process television sets through this final production stage and to determine the utilization of the inspectors and the adjustor.

Concepts Illustrated. This example illustrates the uses of a service activity to model parallel identical servers. In addition, this example illustrates the use of regular activities for probabilistic branching. The procedure for obtaining a Visual SLAM trace through the use of a MONTR statement is illustrated.

Visual SLAM Model. The entities to be modeled in this system are the television sets. The television sets arrive and are routed to the inspection station. The two inspectors at the inspection station are represented as servers. If both inspectors are busy, a queue of television sets forms. This process can be conveniently modeled in Visual SLAM with a QUEUE node that precedes a service activity that represents two servers. Following the service activity representing the inspectors, 85 percent of the entities are accepted and depart to packing. The remaining 15 percent of the televisions do not pass inspection and are routed to the adjustor. If the adjustor is busy, a queue would form of televisions waiting for the adjustor. The adjustment process can be modeled as a QUEUE node followed by a service activity with a capacity of one. Following the adjustment operation, the entity is routed back to the queue of the inspectors.

The above describes the complete processing and routing of television sets through the inspection and adjustment stations. The Visual SLAM graphical model can be built directly from this discussion and is shown in Figure 4-7. Entities representing the television sets are created by the CREATE node with the time between entities uniformly distributed between 3.5 and 7.5 time units. The entity's arrival time is recorded as attribute 1. Each entity proceeds to the QUEUE node labeled INSP, and will proceed directly into service if an inspector represented by the emanating service activity is free. Recall that the 2 in the circle under the service ACTIVITY denotes two parallel identical servers. The service time for each server is specified as uniformly distributed between 6 and 12. Entities which arrive to the QUEUE node when both servers are busy wait in the QUEUE node which prescribes that they be stored in file 1.

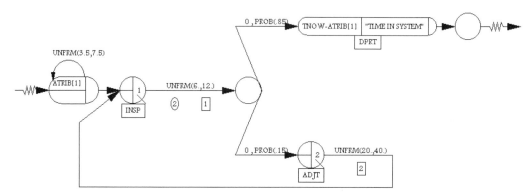

Figure 4-7 Visual SLAM network of TV inspection and adjustment stations.

Following inspection, the entities arrive at a GOON node where they are probabilistically routed since the M-number of the GOON node is 1 and probabilities are associated with the two activities emanating from the GOON node. One activity leads to the COLCT node labeled DPRT representing departure to the packing area. The other activity leads to the QUEUE node labeled ADJT representing the waiting line for the adjustment operation. Entities in the QUEUE node ADJT wait for the adjustor in file 2. The adjustment operation is represented by the emanating service activity whose duration is uniformly distributed between 20 and 40 time units. Following adjustment, television entities are routed back to the QUEUE node INSP. Entities which are routed to the COLCT node DPRT have interval statistics collected based on the time of creation which was stored in ATRIB[1] at the CREATE node. This interval of time corresponds to the total time that the television set spends in the inspection and adjustment process. The entities are then terminated.

The Visual SLAM statement listing follows directly from the network model and is shown in Figure 4-8. In the network statements, entities representing televisions are created by the CREATE statement (line 1) with a time between creations that is uniformly distributed in the range (3.5, 7.5) time units. The arrival time is marked as attribute 1 at the CREATE node. The entity is routed to the QUEUE node INSP where they wait in file 1 for a free server. The two parallel inspectors are represented by an ACTIVITY statement (line 4). The 2 indicates two parallel identical servers and the duration for each is specified as uniformly distributed between 6 and 12. Entities completing inspection arrive at the GOON statement (line 5) which has two emanating activities. The first activity (line 6) has a default duration of zero. and is taken with a probability of 0.85 and routes the entity to the statement labeled DPRT. The second activity (line 7) has a default duration of zero, and is taken with a probability of 0.15 and routes the entity to the statement labeled ADJT. Entities which arrive to this QUEUE node wait in file 2 for the adjustor. The adjustor is represented by the emanating service activity (line 12) which has a duration uniformly distributed from 20 to 40 and routes entities to the statement labeled INSP. Entities which arrive to the DPRT statement (line 8) have interval statistics collected from the mark time recorded in ATRIB[1], and the statistics are labeled TIME IN SYSTEM. The entities then continue to the TERM statement (line 10) where they are destroyed.

```
Network statements:
  1 CREATE,UNFRM(3.5,7.5),,ATRIB[1];
  2   ACTIVITY;
  3 INSP: QUEUE,1;
  4   ACT,1,UNFRM(6.,12.),,,2,"INSPECTION";
  5 GOON;
  6   ACTIVITY,,0,PROB(.85);
  7   ACTIVITY,,0,PROB(.15),"ADJT";
  8 DPRT: COLCT,,TNOW-ATRIB[1],"TIME IN SYSTEM";
  9   ACTIVITY;
 10 TERM;
 11 ADJT: QUEUE,2;
 12   ACTIVITY,2,UNFRM(20.,40.),,"INSP",,"ADJUSTMENT";
Control statements:
  1 GEN,"PRITSKER","TV INSP. AND ADJUST.",1/1/1995,1;
  2 LIMITS,-1,-1,-1,1,-1,-1;
  3 NETWORK;
  4 INIT,0,480;
  5 ;
  6 ;    WRITE A TEXT TRACE FROM TIME 0 TO TIME 60,
  7 ;    PRINT THE VALUE OF ATRIB(1), NNQ(1), AND NNQ(2)
  8 MONTR,TRACE,0,60,{ ATRIB[1], NNQ(1), NNQ(2) };
  9 FIN;
```

Figure 4-8 Statement model for television set inpsection and adjustment stations.

In the control statements, the LIMITS statement specifies that the highest index for ATRIB[1] is 1. The highest index for other variables is shown as -1 because a 0 would indicate that the highest index is zero. The MONTR definition (line 8) initiates the tracing of events at time 0, stops the tracing of events at time 60, and specifies that the value of ATRIB[1] be printed along with the number in the inspector's queue, NNQ(1) and the number in the adjustor's queue, NNQ(2). The trace output is shown in Figure 4-9. Each trace event consists of 2 or more lines. The first gives the time of the event, the node type, the line in the network model for the node type, the event type and the entity number. The second line provides the values of the variables requested. Procedures are available within AweSim to stylize the trace outputs. Trace lines are then printed to provide information on any activities that are released.

Summary of Results. The results for this simulation are summarized in the Visual SLAM Summary Report shown in Figure 4-10. The first category of statistics for this example, is statistics for variables based on observations. It consists of the interval statistics on the TIME IN SYSTEM collected by the COLCT statement (line 8). During the 480 minutes of simulated operation, a total of 84 television sets completed processing with the sets spending an average of 26.63 minutes in the system. However, there was a high variability in times in the system between television sets as reflected by the minimum and maximum times and the high standard deviation. This is to be expected since a fraction of the television sets have much larger times in the system due to their being adjusted. Also, 480 time units is insufficient to reach steady-state values. The second category of statistics for this example is the file statistics. The results show that there was an average of .851 television sets waiting for inspection in file 1 and 1.465 television sets waiting for adjustment in file 2. Again, the high standard deviations relative to the average indicate a high degree of variation in queue length over time.

The final category of statistics is the service activity statistics. In this example, there are two service activities corresponding to the inspectors and adjustors, respectively. The first service activity represents the inspectors and they had an average utilization of 1.906. Note that since this activity has a capacity of 2, the maximum idle and busy values refer to the number of servers. The output indicates that both servers were idle at one point during the simulation and that both servers were busy at one point during the simulation. The second service activity represents the adjustor who had an average utilization of 0.871. The longest period of time for which the adjustor was idle was 48.365 minutes and the longest period of time for which the adjustor was busy was 245.403 minutes.

The summary report also indicates that one television is waiting for adjustment and that both inspectors and the adjustor are busy at the end of the simulation run. Adding these four television sets to the 84 that were completely processed indicates that 88 television sets were created. This is comparable to the 480/5.5 or approximately 87 arrivals expected.

```
0.000000 CREATE     (NEX42.net:1) Arrival of entity 10.000000  0  0
                    release ACTIVITY (NEX42.net:2) dur. 0.000000
0.000000 QUEUE      INSP(NEX42.net:3) Arrival of entity 1
        0.000000  0  0
0.000000 QUEUE      INSP(NEX42.net:3)
                    release ACTIVITY #1(NEX42.net:4) dur. 11.602716
0.000000  0  0
4.710670 CREATE     (NEX42.net:1) Arrival of entity 2
        4.710670  0  0
                    release ACTIVITY (NEX42.net:2) dur. 0.000000
4.710670 QUEUE      INSP(NEX42.net:3) Arrival of entity 2
        4.710670  0  0
4.710670 QUEUE      INSP(NEX42.net:3)
                    release ACTIVITY #1(NEX42.net:4) dur. 8.825559
        4.710670  0  0
8.773881 CREATE     (NEX42.net:1) Arrival of entity 3
        8.773881  0  0
                    release ACTIVITY (NEX42.net:2) dur. 0.000000
8.773881 QUEUE      INSP(NEX42.net:3) Arrival of entity 3
        8.773881  0  0
11.602716 QUEUE      INSP(NEX42.net:3)
                    release ACTIVITY #1(NEX42.net:4) dur. 8.210622
        8.773881  0  0
11.602716 GOON       (NEX42.net:5) Arrival of entity 1
        0.000000  0  0
                    release ACTIVITY (NEX42.net:6) dur. 0.000000
                    ACTIVITY (NEX42.net:7) not released
11.602716 COLCT      DPRT(NEX42.net:8) Arrival of entity 1
        0.000000  0  0
                    release ACTIVITY (NEX42.net:9) dur. 0.000000
11.602716 TERMINATE  (NEX42.net:10) Arrival of entity 1
        0.000000  0  0
13.536229 GOON       (NEX42.net:5) Arrival of entity 2
        4.710670  0  0
                    ACTIVITY (NEX42.net:6) not released
                    release ACTIVITY (NEX42.net:7) dur. 0.000000
13.536229 QUEUE      ADJT(NEX42.net:11) Arrival of entity 2
        4.710670  0  0
13.536229 QUEUE      ADJT(NEX42.net:11)
                    release ACTIVITY #2(NEX42.net:12) dur. 26.394796
        4.710670  0  0
15.716344 CREATE     (NEX42.net:1) Arrival of entity 4
        15.716344  0  0
                    release ACTIVITY (NEX42.net:2) dur. 0.000000
15.716344 QUEUE      INSP(NEX42.net:3) Arrival of entity 4
        15.716344  0  0
15.716344 QUEUE      INSP(NEX42.net:3)
                    release ACTIVITY #1(NEX42.net:4) dur. 7.201519
        15.716344  0  0
```

Figure 4-9 Trace report for television set inspection and adjustment stations.

The information on the Visual SLAM Summary Report can be used to assess system performance relative to questions such as: Are the queue storage areas large enough? Is the allocation of manpower between the inspection station and adjustor station proper? Is the time to process a television too long? In general, "what if" type questions are readily addressed using Visual SLAM.

```
** AweSim SUMMARY REPORT **

   Simulation Project : TV INSP. AND ADJUST.
   Modeler : PRITSKER
   Date : 1/1/1995
   Scenario : EX42

   Run number 1 of 1
   Current simulation time    : 480.000000
   Statistics cleared at time : 0.000000


              ** OBSERVED STATISTICS REPORT for scenario EX42 **

Label              Mean      Standard   Number of      Minimum     Maximum
                   Value     Deviation  Observations   Value       Value

TIME IN SYSTEM   26.632     35.910         84          6.381       162.182

              ** FILE STATISTICS REPORT for scenario EX42 **

File    Label or   Average   Standard   Max.      Current   Average
Number  Input Loc. Length    Deviation  Length    Length    Wait Time

1 QUEUE INSP        0.851     0.776        3         0        4.047
2 QUEUE ADJT        1.465     1.195        4         1       46.882
0 Event Calendar    4.902     0.491        6         5       10.793


              ** SERVICE ACTIVITY STATISTICS REPORT for scenario EX42 **

Activity   Label or    Server     Entity   Average      Standard
Number     Input Loc.  Capacity   Count    Utilization  Deviation

   1       INSPECTION     2         99      1.906        0.292
   2       ADJUSTMENT     1         13      0.871        0.335

Activity   Current      Average    Maximum       Maximum
Number     Utilization  Blockage   Idle Time     Busy Time
                                   or Servers    or Servers

   1          2         0.000       2.000         2.000
   2          1         0.000      48.365       245.403
```

Figure 4-10 Summary report for TV inspection and adjustment stations.

4.16   EXAMPLE 4-3. QUARRY OPERATIONS

In this example, the operations of a quarry are modeled. In the quarry, trucks deliver ore from three shovels to a crusher. A truck always returns to its assigned shovel after dumping a load at the crusher. There are two different truck sizes in use, twenty-ton and fifty-ton. The size of the truck affects its loading time at the shovel, travel time to the crusher, dumping time at the crusher and return trip time from the crusher back to the appropriate shovel. For the twenty-ton trucks, these loading, travel, dumping and return trip times are: exponentially distributed with a mean 5; a constant 2.5; exponentially distributed with mean 2; and a constant 1.5. The corresponding times for the fifty-ton trucks are: exponentially distributed with mean 10; a constant 3; exponentially distributed with mean 4; and a constant 2. To each shovel is assigned two twenty-ton trucks and one fifty-ton truck. The shovel queues are all ranked on a first-in, first-out basis. The crusher queue is ranked on truck size, largest trucks first. A schematic diagram of the quarry operations is shown in Figure 4-11. It is desired to analyze this system over 480 time units to determine the utilization and queue lengths associated with the shovels and crusher (1).

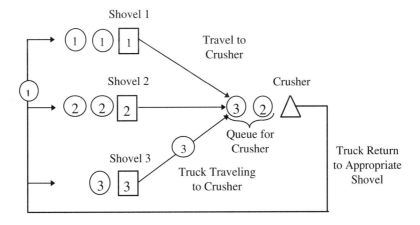

Figure 4-11 Quarry operations schematic diagram.

Concepts Illustrated. In the previous examples, entities have been entered into the network by the CREATE node. In this example, we illustrate an alternate approach of directly inserting entities into the network using the ENTRY statement. The use of an attribute of an entity to define a file number of a QUEUE node and to specify a service activity number is demonstrated. Additional concepts illustrated by this example include the specification of activity durations as a function of the attributes of the entities, the ranking of entities at a QUEUE node based upon an attribute value and EQUIVALENCE statements for relating textual names to Visual SLAM variables.

Visual SLAM Model. The network modeling of the quarry operations involves the routing of two distinct entity types representing the twenty-ton and fifty-ton trucks. Each entity is assigned five attribute values consisting of: 1) truck tonnage (either 20 or 50); 2) shovel number to which the truck is assigned; 3) mean shovel loading duration; 4) mean crusher dumping duration; and 5) return trip time. The Visual SLAM network model for processing the entities through the quarry operations is depicted in Figure 4-12. Note that entities are neither created or terminated within the graphical model. Therefore, to initiate the simulation, we must insert six entities representing the twenty-ton trucks and three entities representing the fifty-ton trucks directly into the network. These entities will continue to cycle through the network until the simulation is terminated. However, before discussing the procedure for inserting the truck entities into the network, we will complete our description of the network model.

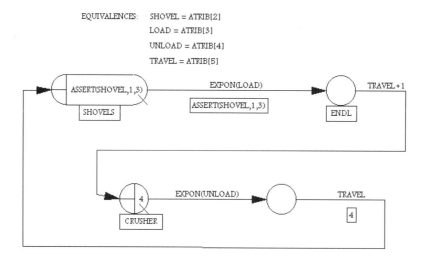

Figure 4-12 Network representation of quarry operations.

We begin our description at the far left at QUEUE node SHOVELS. Entities arriving to the node SHOVELS represent trucks completing their return trip from the crusher. SHOVEL is an attribute of the truck entity and contains the shovel number to which the truck is assigned. Each shovel queue is represented by the QUEUE node SHOVELS with the loading operation represented by an emanating ACTIVITY. Through the use of the attribute SHOVEL, the queue file numbers and service activity numbers for all three shovels can be represented in a single QUEUE-ACTIVITY combination. The duration of the service ACTIVITY is specified to be exponentially distributed with a mean given by the attribute LOAD. LOAD is equal to 5 or 10 depending upon whether the entity represents a twenty or fifty-ton truck. Therefore the duration of the ACTIVITY is dependent upon the type of entity being processed. After completing the loading operation, the entity then undertakes the ACTIVITY with duration TRAVEL+ 1 representing the loaded travel time. The entity continues to QUEUE node CRUSHER representing the queue of trucks waiting to dump ore at the crusher. Entities in the QUEUE node are waiting for the CRUSHER in file 4 which is ranked on high values of attribute 1 (HVF(ATRIB[1])). Since the first attribute denotes truck tonnage, priority is given to the fifty-ton trucks. The dumping operation is represented by the service ACTIVITY emanating from the QUEUE node CRUSHER and is exponentially distributed with a mean given by the UNLOAD attribute of a truck entity. Following completion of the dumping operation, the entity arrives to the GOON node and then continues through the emanating ACTIVITY representing the return trip. This ACTIVITY has a duration given by TRAVEL, an activity index of 4 and routes the entity back to QUEUE node SHOVELS.

The statement model for this example is shown in Figure 4-13. The PRIORITY statement (line 3) specifies that file 4 corresponding to the crusher queue is ranked on HVF(ATRIB[1]). The network model consists of statements 9 - 21 and follows the network description given above.

The initial insertion of truck entities into the network is accomplished by the ENTRY statements (line 25-33). Recall that each ENTRY statement places an entity into the file specified with attribute values as listed. For example, the first three ENTRY statement places three entities into file 1 with attribute values of (20,1,5,2,1.5), (20,1,5,2,1.5), and (50,1,10,4,2). These entities correspond to two twenty-ton trucks and one fifty-ton truck. Since file 1 is a queue for one of the shovels, the filing of an entity into file 1 is processed as an arrival to node SHOVELS. Likewise, entities filed in file 2 and file 3 are processed as arrivals to node SHOVELS. Therefore the ENTRY statements place two twenty-ton and one fifty-ton truck in each shovel queue even though a single QUEUE node is used to model all three shovel queues.

```
 1 GEN, "PRITSKER", "QUARRY OPERATIONS", 1/1/1996, 1;
 2 LIMITS,,,,5;
 3 PRIORITY,{4,HVF(ATRIB[1])};
 4 EQUIVALENCE, { { SHOVEL, ATRIB[2] },
 5                 {   LOAD, ATRIB[3] },
 6                 { UNLOAD, ATRIB[4] },
 7                 { TRAVEL, ATRIB[5] } };
 8 NETWORK;
 9 ;
10 ;ATRIB(1)=TONNAGE,ATRIB(2)=SVL NO.,ATRIB(3)=SVL TIME
11 ;ATRIB(4)=CRSR TIME,ATRIB(5)=RETURN TRIP TIME
12 ;
13 SHOVELS: QUEUE, ASSERT(SHOVEL,1,3);
14       ACT, ASSERT(SHOVEL,1,3), EXPON(LOAD),,,,"LOAD SHOVEL";
15 ENDL: GOON;
16       ACT, , TRAVEL+1;
17 CRSR: QUEUE, 4;
18       ACT,5, EXPON(UNLOAD),,,,"UNLOAD SHOVEL";
19       GOON;
20       ACT, 4, TRAVEL, ,"SHOVELS", , "TRUCK RETURN";
21       END;
22 INIT, 0, 480;
23 ;
24 ;     PLACE TWO 20 TON AND ONE 50 TON TRUCK IN EACH SHOVEL QUEUE
25 ENTRY,1,SHOVELS,0,20,1,5,2,1.5};
26 ENTRY,1,SHOVELS,0,20,1,5,2,1.5};
27 ENTRY,1,SHOVELS,0,50,1,10,4,2};
28 ENTRY,2,SHOVELS,0,20,2,5,2,1.5};
29 ENTRY,2,SHOVELS,0,20,2,5,2,1.5};
30 ENTRY,2,SHOVELS,0,50,2,10,4,2};
31 ENTRY,3,SHOVELS,0,20,3,5,2,1.5};
32 ENTRY,3,SHOVELS,0,20,3,5,2,1.5};
33 ENTRY,3,SHOVELS,0,50,3,10,4,2};
34 FIN;
```

Figure 4-13 Statement model of quarry operations.

Summary of Results. The results for this example are summarized by the Visual SLAM Summary Report shown in Figure 4-14. Note that in addition to statistics on queue lengths and server utilizations, statistics are also provided on each numbered ACTIVITY. Activity 4 represents the return trip from the crusher to the shovels. The results show that 152 trucks completed the return trip during the 480 time units of simulation, and that there was an average of 0.541 trucks in transit between the crusher and the shovels. The maximum number of trucks on the return road at any one time was five.

```
** AweSim SUMMARY REPORT **

   Simulation Project : QUARRY OPERATIONS
   Modeler : PRITSKER
   Date : 1/1/1996
   Scenario : EX43

   Run number 1 of 1
   Current simulation time    : 480.000000
   Statistics cleared at time :   0.000000
```

** FILE STATISTICS REPORT for scenario EX43 **

File Number	Label or Input Loc.	Average Length	Standard Deviation	Maximum Length	Current Length	Average Wait Time
1 QUEUE	SHOVELS	0.516	0.757	2	1	4.502
2 QUEUE	SHOVELS	0.556	0.773	2	2	4.945
3 QUEUE	SHOVELS	0.507	0.746	2	1	4.682
4 QUEUE	CRUSHER	3.046	2.250	8	0	9.495
0 Event	Calendar	5.374	1.370	10	6	4.037

** ACTIVITY STATISTICS REPORT for scenario EX43 **

Activity Number	Label or Input Loc.	Average Util.	Standard Deviation	Entity Count	Maximum Util.	Current Util.
4	TRUCK RETURN	0.541	0.743	152	5	1

** SERVICE ACTIVITY STATISTICS REPORT for scenario EX43 **

Activity Number	Label or Input Loc.	Server Capacity	Entity Count	Average Util.	Standard Deviation	Current Util.
1 LOAD	SHOVEL	1	53	0.707	0.455	1
2 LOAD	SHOVEL	1	51	0.642	0.479	1
3 LOAD	SHOVEL	1	50	0.707	0.455	1
5 UNLOAD	SHOVEL	1	153	0.911	0.284	1

Activity Number	Average Blockage	Maximum Idle Time or Servers	Maximum Busy Time or Servers
1	0.000	20.808	62.683
2	0.000	18.433	47.819
3	0.000	18.586	57.893
5	0.000	5.271	84.135

Figure 4-14 Visual SLAM Summary Report for quarry operations example.

4.17   SUMMARY OF SYMBOLS AND STATEMENTS

Table 4-4 presents the basic symbols and statements of Visual SLAM network modeling. The basic node types are: CREATE, QUEUE, TERMINATE, ASSIGN, GOON and COLCT. There is only one activity symbol and it is used to represent both service and non-service activities. An explicit delay in the processing of an entity can only be modeled by using an activity. The capability to model and analyze systems with 7 graphical elements demonstrates the power and flexibility of the Visual SLAM network approach. The default values associated with Visual SLAM network statements are presented in Chapter 8, Table 8-1. A complete description of each network element is provided in the *Visual SLAM Quick Reference Manual* (2).

Table 4-4 Basic symbols and statements for Visual SLAM networks.

Name	Symbol	Statement
ACTIVITY	DUR,PROB or COND (N) [A]	ACTIVITY, A,DUR, PROB or COND, NLBL, N, ID;
ASSIGN	VAR=Value M	ASSIGN,{{VAR=Value}, repeats}, M;
CREATE	TBC TF MV / MC M	CREATE, TBC, TF, MV, MC, M;
COLCT	VALUE | ID, H | M	COLCT, N,VALUE,NCEL, HLOW, HWID, M;
GOON	(M)	GOON, M;

Table 4-4 Basic symbols and statements for Visual SLAM networks (continued).

Name	Symbol	Statement
QUEUE		QUEUE, IFL, IQ, QC, BLOCK or BALK(NLBL), {SLBLs, repeats},
TERMINATE		TERMINATE, TC;
Special Symbols		
BLOCK		BLOCK
BALK		BALK (NLBL)
Node label	NLBL	NLBL

4.18   EXERCISES

4-1.   Develop a Visual SLAM portion of a network in which the time to traverse an activity is normally distributed with a mean of 10, a standard deviation of 2, a minimum value of 7 and a maximum value of 15. State your assumptions regarding the type of truncation used.

4-2.   Perform a manual simulation of the following network for 28 time units by preparing tables similar to those given in Tables 1-2 and 1-3. (Note: Since entities are initially in the QUEUE nodes, the servers are busy and all entities initially in the system have an ATRIB[1] value equal to zero.) Compute the utilization of each server, the fraction of time server 1 is blocked, the average number in each queue and the average time spent in the system by an entity.

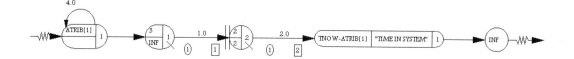

4-3.   Develop a Visual SLAM network model for the following situation. State any assumptions necessary to model the situation in network form. A machine shop contains two drills, one straightener and a finishing area. Drilling time is normally distributed with a mean of 10 minutes and a standard deviation of one minute. For those parts that need to be straightened, it takes 15 time units on the average and this time is exponentially distributed. To perform the finishing operations on a part takes five minutes and only one part can be finished at a time.

The machine shop processes two types of parts. Type 1 parts arrive every 30 minutes and it takes two minutes for the arriving part to be routed to the drill area. Type 1 parts require the drilling operation, straightening and finishing. Type 2 parts arrive every 20 minutes and require only drilling and finishing. The time to route a Type 2 part from its arrival to the drilling area is 10 minutes. Assume no time delays between drilling, straightening and finishing operations. Assume operators are always available if a machine is available. The network is to be used to obtain information on throughput of parts through the machine shop and utilization of the drills, straightener and finishing area. Throughput by each part type is also desired. A histogram of the time for each part type to be processed through the machine area is to be obtained. The initial condition of the machine shop is that it is empty.

Embellishments:

a)   Estimate the expected time in the system for each part type under the assumption that there are 20 drills, 10 straighteners and 15 finishing operators. Estimate the variance of the time in the system for each part type.

b)   "Guess" at the expected time in system for each part type in the original model.

c)   Revise your network model to include a probability that finishing operations have to be repeated 10% of the time. How would this change your expected time operations estimates given in your answer to Embellishment(b)?

d)   If a part type 1 has been routed through finishing twice but still needs to be refinished, it must be restraightened. Include this in your model. Estimate the fraction of parts that will need to be restraightened.

4-4.   Build the following Visual SLAM network. Set up the input data to make 10 independent replications with each run processing the 500 entities completely through the network.

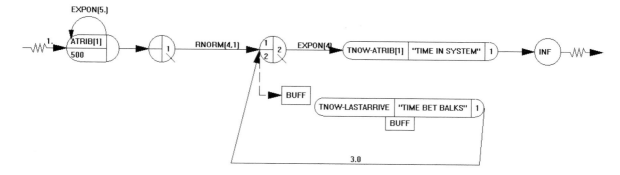

4-5.   Redo the input data for Exercise 4-4 to stop each simulation run at time 2500 or following the processing of 500 entities, whichever occurs first. Clear the statistical arrays at time 200 on each run using the MONTR statement.

4-6.   Given the following input statements, draw the equivalent Visual SLAM network and describe the system.

```
GEN,EXERCISE 4-6,INVERT,6/1/1996,2;
LIMITS,,,,,2;
PRIORITY,1,LVF(2)
NETWORK;
        CREATE,EXPON(4.0),, ATRIB[1];
        ASSIGN,{ATRIB[2],1.0};
        ACT,,,,WAIT;
        CREATE,EXPON(2.0),, ATRIB[1];
        ASSIGN,{ATRIB[2],2.0};
WAIT:   QUEUE,1;
        ACT,,EXPON(1.0);
        COLCT,TNOW-ATRIB[1],"TIME IN SYSTEM":
        TERM;
        ENDNETWORK;
INIT,0,1000;
FIN;
```

4-7.   For the maintenance facility situation involving work stations in series, Example 4-1, analyze the results and redistribute the six storage spaces to work station 1 and work station 2. Test your alternative design using Visual SLAM . If you were to begin a research and development program for improving the production line, on what quantity would you place your initial efforts?

4.8.   For the maintenance facility situation, Example 4-1, the output from the simulation indicates that the time in workstation 1 is subsumed by the time in workstation 2. Under this assumption, the situation could be modeled as a single workstation with the service time being that of work station 2 which has a queue with a capacity of 7 units. Perform a Visual SLAM simulation of this situation and compare the results with the original model.

Embellishment: Perform a mathematical analysis of the single queue, single server system described in this exercise and compare the values obtained with the simulation results.

4.9.　Modify the Visual SLAM model of the inspection and adjustment stations, Example 4-2, to accommodate the following changes:

    a)　an arrival of television sets to the inspection station involves two television sets to be inspected;

    b)　the adjustor routes 40% of the adjusted sets directly to packing and 60% back to the inspectors;

    c)　add a step to the inspection process which decreases the probability of sending a set to an adjustor to 0.10; the added step takes 5 minutes.

Redraw the network to indicate these changes. For one of the above situations, run the model and analyze the results.

4.10.　A new design has been proposed for the television inspection and adjustment situation presented in Example 4-2 so that television sets requiring a third adjustment are sent to a rebuild operation. The rebuild operation is not modeled. For this proposal develop the network. Assume the adjustor spends more time on a television set the second time it is adjusted. (Increase both limits on the uniform distribution by 2). Because of this added time, the probability of requiring a third adjustment is reduced to 0.10.

4.11.　For a one server, single queue situation, develop the Visual SLAM network model when the service time is sample from the probability mass function as shown below.

Probability	Service Time (min.)
.2	4
.3	6
.1	7
.4	10

The interarrival times are exponentially distributed with a mean of 7.75 minutes.

4.19　REFERENCES

1.　Pritsker, A. A. B., *Modeling and Analysis Using Q-GERT Networks*, Second Edition, Halsted Press and Pritsker & Associates, Inc. 1979.

2.　Pritsker Corporation, *Visual SLAM Quick Reference Manual*, 1996.

3.　Schriber, T., *Simulation Using GPSS*, John Wiley, 1974.

CHAPTER 5

Resources and Gates

5.1   INTRODUCTION

In a network model, an entity is advanced in accordance with the duration of activities. The flow of an entity is regulated by the status of servers. When a service activity is encountered, the entity waits in a queue for the server to become idle. Servers are a particular type of resource that remain stationary, that is, a service activity is only associated with the entity while the entity is flowing through the branch that represents the service activity. Situations arise where an entity requires a resource for a set of activities. Visual SLAM provides the capability to model this situation through the definition of resource types. For each resource type, the number of units available to be allocated to entities is defined. We refer to the total number of resource units available as the capacity of the resource.

An entity that requires a resource, multiple resources, or a resource that is in a group of resources waits at an AWAIT node. When an entity arrives to an AWAIT node, it proceeds through it to the activity emanating from the node if sufficient units of the resource are available. Otherwise, its flow is halted. A file is associated with the AWAIT node to maintain entities waiting for resources. An entity is removed from the file associated with the AWAIT node when units of the resource required by the entity can be assigned to it. Regular activities follow an AWAIT node since resources are allocated to the entity for all their activities until they are released for reallocation at a FREE node.

To allow an entity to acquire a resource currently allocated to an entity that has a lower priority, a PREEMPT node is employed. If a resource cannot be preempted, then the entity waits in a file prescribed at the PREEMPT node in a fashion similar to that for the AWAIT node.

Resources are allocated to entities waiting in AWAIT and PREEMPT nodes in a prescribed order. This order is established through the use of a RESOURCE block. Also defined at the RESOURCE block is the initial capacity of the resource type.

When an entity no longer requires the use of a resource, it is routed to a FREE node where a specified number of units of the resource are freed (made available for reallocation). The PREEMPT and AWAIT nodes associated with the resource type are then interrogated to determine if the freed units can be allocated to waiting entities.

The capacity of a resource type can be changed by routing an entity through an ALTER node. ALTER nodes are used to increase or decrease the level of resource availability and can be used to model resource level changes due to machine maintenance, employee breaks and daily shifts.

In Visual SLAM, a vehicle for accomplishing the stopping and starting of entity flow is a GATE. Entities can be routed to AWAIT nodes which require that a specified GATE be open before the entity can proceed through the AWAIT node. If the GATE associated with the AWAIT node is closed, the entity waits in a file until the GATE is opened. A GATE is opened when an entity flows through an OPEN node. It can be closed by an entity passing through a CLOSE node. The files in which entities may be waiting for a GATE to be opened are defined at a GATE block. When a gate is opened, all entities waiting at AWAIT nodes for the gate are permitted to pass through the AWAIT node and are routed to the branches emanating from the AWAIT node. For example, a gate can be used to stop the flow of passenger entities in a bus system until a bus entity arrives to an OPEN node. When the passenger entities are loaded on the bus, the bus entity is routed through a CLOSE node to restrict the flow of passenger entities onto the bus.

In this chapter, RESOURCES and GATES are described. The modeling of systems using nodes associated with these concepts is presented. Basically, the flow of entities is controlled through the requirements of an entity for units of a resource or for an open gate. The standard branching process for entities presented in Chapter 4 is not changed. Hence, no new ACTIVITY capabilities are required. In fact, only regular activities are needed when modeling systems with RESOURCES and GATES.

5.2 RESOURCE BLOCK

The RESOURCE block is used to identify: the resource name or label, RLBL; the initial resource capacity, that is, the number of resource units available, CAP; and the order in which files associated with AWAIT and PREEMPT nodes are to be polled to allocate freed units of the resource to entities. The word "block" is employed instead of "node" because the RESOURCE block has no inputs or outputs as entities do not flow through it. Basically, the RESOURCE block is a definitional vehicle to specify a resource label (RLBL), the available number of units for the resource type, and an allocation procedure for entities waiting for units of the resource. On the network diagram, blocks can be placed together to form a legend. Visual SLAM assigns numeric codes to each resource name. The resource defined by the first resource block in the NETWORK statements is given a code of 1, the second a code of 2, and so on. The user may specify the resource number, RNUM, directly.

The RESOURCE, generically referred to as RES, is used in AWAIT, PREEMPT, FREE and ALTER nodes to identify the resource type associated with the nodes. The label RLBL can be any string of characters beginning with an alphanumeric and excluding the special characters [, / ( ) + −* ';]. The numeric code can also be used to reference a RESOURCE at AWAIT, PREEMPT, FREE and ALTER nodes. In addition, a variable can carry the numeric code to define the RESOURCE to be acted upon. The initial resource capacity, CAP, is the number of units of the resource that can be allocated at the beginning of a run. During a run, the level of resource capacity can be increased or decreased by entities passing through ALTER nodes. The number of units of a particular resource in use is the number assigned to entities at AWAIT and PREEMPT nodes that have not been released at FREE nodes. The Visual SLAM variable NRUSE(RES) maintains the value of the number of units of resource RES in use. NNRSC(RES) is the value of the number of units of RES currently available. Statistics are automatically collected on resource utilization and availability and are printed as part of the Visual SLAM summary report.

At the RESOURCE block, file numbers are listed in the order in which the PREEMPT and AWAIT nodes for this resource type are to be polled. The RESOURCE block symbol, statement and AweSim dialog box are shown below.

| RNUM | RLBL | CAP | | IFL | repeats |

RESOURCE,RNUM,RLBL,CAP,{IFL,repeats};

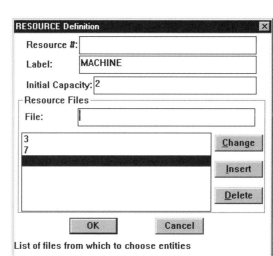

As an example of a RESOURCE block statement, consider a resource with the label MACHINE which has a capacity of 2 and for which it is desired that files 3 and then 7 be polled for entities waiting for a MACHINE. The resource block statement would be written as

RESOURCE,,MACHINE,2,{3,7};

If this were the first resource block in the list of statements, MACHINE would be identified by Visual SLAM as resource number 1. For example, the number of units of MACHINE in use could be accessed on a Visual SLAM network by NRUSE(MACHINE) or NRUSE(1).

If it is desired to specify explicitly that MACHINE be resource 1, then the resource block statement definition would be as shown below:

RESOURCE,1,MACHINE,2,{3 ,7};

If a specified numeric value is not assigned to a resource then it is assigned a number sequentially in accordance with either the order in which the RESOURCE statements appear in the statement model or the next number if the last specified resource was assigned a number.

5.3   AWAIT NODE

AWAIT nodes are used to store entities waiting for UR units of resource RES or waiting for gate GATE to open. When an entity arrives to an AWAIT node and the units of resource required are available or the GATE is opened, the entity passes directly through the node and is routed according to the M-number prescribed for the node. If the entity has to wait at the node, it is placed in file IFL in accordance with the priority assigned to that file. Regular activities emanate from the AWAIT node. The symbolism, statement and AweSim dialog box for the AWAIT node are shown below.

```
AWAIT,IFL,{{RESORGATE,UR},repeats},
RULE,QC,BLOCK or BALK(NLBL),M;
```

Normally, RESORGATE is specified by a resource label, by a gate label, or by a group (See Section 5.7). The file number, IFL, queue capacity, QC, and blocking and balking specifications are identical to those used for QUEUE nodes. IFL can be specified as a variable, such as ASSERT(ATRIB[I],J,K), where I is the attribute number and J through K are the allowable file numbers specified by ATRIB[I]. With respect to the file number, AWAIT nodes differ from QUEUE nodes in that the same file number can be associated with more than one AWAIT node. This allows entities requiring the same resource to wait in one file at different AWAIT nodes. The resource, RES, and number of units, UR, can be integers or variable expressions. In the latter case, the expression yields the resource code or number of units required.

Multiple resources can be required at an AWAIT node, and the "How to Allocate" rule specifies how to select from the list of resources. The default rule is ALL, meaning that an entity must wait until all listed resources are available, and this would apply if only one resource is listed. If the rule is ONE, the first resource in the list which is available will be allocated. In this case, the entry box beside the rule is used to specify a variable (typically an attribute) which will save the number of the resource actually allocated so that it may be used later to specify the resource to release. The third RULE option, ALLOC, would invoke a user-written resource allocation rule. If the rule is ALLOC, no specific resources need to be listed at the AWAIT node. The user-written allocation rule is discussed in Chapter 9.

Consider an entity that arrives to the following AWAIT node.

AWAIT,1,{BOOKS,2},,,,1;

The entity that arrives requires two units of the resource BOOKS. If two units of the resource BOOKS are available at the time of arrival of the entity, the two books are allocated to the entity and the entity branches from the AWAIT node in accordance with the M number which is 1. If two books are not available, the entity waits in file 1. No limit is prescribed for the number of entities that can wait in file 1.

The following AWAIT node is the same as the one above except that the number of books required by an arriving entity is prescribed by the value of ATRIB[4].

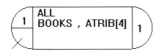

AWAIT,1,{BOOKS,ATRIB[4]},,,,1;

Thus, each entity may require a different number of books before being processed. The resource BOOKS will only be allocated to the first entity in file 1 when BOOKS are available. Thus, if an entity requires 3 BOOKS and it has a higher priority than an entity that requires 1 BOOKS, then the entity that requires 1 BOOKS would wait even though one of the BOOKS was available to be allocated.

The AWAIT node below illustrates that the resource can be specified by an attribute of the arriving entity and that a capacity can be set on the number of entities waiting at an AWAIT node. Specifically, an arriving entity requests one unit of the resource defined by the value of LTRIB[3]. If the entity has to wait, it waits in file 2. If there are 4 entities waiting in file 2, then the newly arriving entity will balk to the node labeled QUE2.

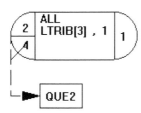

AWAIT,2,{LTRIB[3],1},,4,BALK(QUE2),1;

As an example of the ONE allocation rule, consider the following AWAIT node.

AWAIT,3,{{LOADER1,1}, {LOADER2,1}},
    ONE(LTRIB[2]),,,1;

In this situation, either LOADER1 or LOADER2 may be assigned, with the preferred resource being LOADER1 (the first resource listed). The number of the resource actually allocated would be stored in LTRIB[2] of the seizing entity.

In the following node, the file in which an entity waits is described by a range of values given by integer attribute 2 of the arriving entity. Each arriving entity requests 1 unit of the resource TELEX and the RESOURCE block for TELEX indicates a capacity of 3 with the priority for allocations given to entities waiting in file 4 first, then in file 5 followed by those in file 3. In this

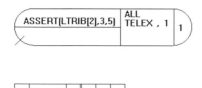

AWAIT,ASSERT(LTRIB[2],3,5),{TELEX,1},,,,1;

situation, an entity that is waiting at this AWAIT node is placed in file 3, 4, or 5 depending on its integer attribute 2 value. The priority of entities in files 3, 4, and 5 is specified on PRIORITY statements. When 1 unit of TELEX is made available, it will be allocated to the first entity waiting in file 4. If no entities are waiting in file 4, then entities waiting in file 5 will be considered. Similarly, those entities in file 3 will have to wait until all entities in files 4 and 5 are allocated units. A complete description of the allocation and reallocation of resources is given in Chapter 9.

5.4   FREE NODE

FREE nodes are used to release units of a resource type when an entity arrives to the node. Every entity arriving to a FREE node releases UF units of resource type RES where UF and RES are specified values for the FREE node. UF can be a constant or a Visual SLAM variable. The freed units are then allocated to entities waiting in PREEMPT and AWAIT nodes in the order prescribed by the RESOURCE block. Multiple resources may be freed at a single FREE node. The entity arriving to the FREE node is then routed in accordance with the M-number associated with the FREE node. The symbol, statement and AweSim dialog box for the FREE node are shown below.

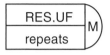

FREE{{RES,UF},repeats},M;

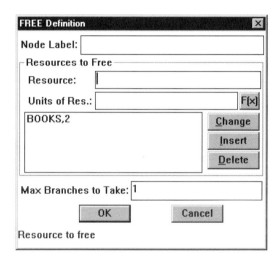

The resource RES can be a resource label or a resource number specified as an expression. If RES is not specified, all resource units that have been allocated to the entity are freed.

Consider an entity that arrives to the following FREE node.

At this FREE node, two BOOKS are made available for reallocation when an entity arrives. The reallocation is made to entities in accordance with the list of file numbers in the RESOURCE block specification. The file numbers are polled in order and, if entities are waiting, the entities are allocated the BOOKS and they are placed in the appropriate activity following the AWAIT node. The entity arriving to the FREE node is routed from the FREE node. The routing for this entity is done before the completion of an activity for any entity that has been reallocated the BOOKS resources.

FREE,{BOOKS,2},1;

BOOKS , ATRIB[4]   1

FREE,{BOOKS,ATRIB[4]},1;

The FREE node to the right frees one unit of the resources defined by the third and fourth integer attributes of an arriving entity.

The FREE node to the left causes ATRIB[4] number of BOOKS to be available for reallocation where ATRIB[4] is the value of the fourth attribute of the entity arriving to the FREE node.

LTRIB[3] , 1
LTRIB[4] , 1   1

FREE,{{LTRIB[3],1},{LTRIB[4],1}},1;

The reallocation of resource units is a complex process as there may be entities waiting in different files which require the resource, entities in the same file requiring different units of the resource, or entities in different files requiring different units of the resource. The following describes the procedures used within Visual SLAM for reallocating resources that are made available. First, the freed resources are added to the current number of idle resources of the same type. Resources may be idle and entities waiting if an insufficient number of units of the resource are not available. For example, an entity may require 2 units and only 1 is available. A polling of the files associated with the resource type is then initiated. The files are checked in the order listed on the RESOURCE block. For each file, the first entity in the file is polled to determine if sufficient resources are available to satisfy the needs of the entity ranked first. If sufficient resources are not available, the polling continues to the next file. A search for entities in the file is not made as it is assumed that the entity that is ranked first takes precedence over other entities in the file. If resources are sufficient to satisfy the first entity's requirement, that entity is removed from the file and scheduled from the AWAIT node associated with the file. The resources available are then decreased by the amount allocated. The next entity in the file is then polled to see if its resource requirements can be satisfied. The above process continues until either insufficient units of the resource are available to reallocate to entities that are ranked first in each file or there are no further entities waiting in any of the files for the resource type that was freed.

When multiple resources are freed at a FREE node, the reallocation is done in the following steps:

1.   All resources are freed;

2.   The next listed resource at the FREE node is considered for reallocation at the files listed in its resource block. If the AWAIT node associated with the file requires other resources, they will also be allocated including any resources that were freed in Step 1 above.

3. The list of resources at the FREE node to be reallocated is updated in accordance with the allocations made in Step 2. If all resources have been considered, the procedure is completed. If resources have not been considered, a return is made to Step 2.

Example 5-4 on port operations illustrates the reallocation of multiple resources from a FREE node.

5.5 ILLUSTRATIONS OF THE USE OF RESOURCES

5.5.1 Illustration 5-1. Resource Usage for Sequential Operations

Consider the situation in which a radio inspector performs an inspection operation and, if the radio requires adjustment, the inspector also performs that operation. Assume that fifteen percent of the radios manufactured require adjustment. In this situation, the inspector can be thought of as a resource that is allocated or assigned to the processing (inspection and adjustment) of the radio. Thus the inspector is not always available to perform another inspection because he may be required to perform the adjustment operation. The modeling of this situation is shown below in both a network and statement form.

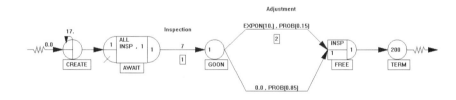

```
            RESOURCE,1,INSP,1,{1};
CREATE:     CREATE,17.,0.0;
            ACTIVITY;
AWAIT:      AWAIT,1,{{INSP,1}};                Wait for inspector
            ACTIVITY,1,7;                      Inspection activity
GOON:       GOON,1;
            ACTIVITY,2,EXPON(10.),PROB(0.15);  Adjustment time
            ACTIVITY,,0.0,PROB(0.85);          No adjustment
FREE:       FREE,{{INSP,1}};                   Free inspector
            ACTIVITY;
TERM:       TERMINATE,200;
            END;
```

In this model, the RESOURCE block indicates that the resource INSP has an initial capacity of one and that it is allocated at an AWAIT node where file 1 is used to maintain waiting entities. After an entity is created, it is routed to the AWAIT node and, if the inspector resource is available, it is processed through ACTIVITY 1. At the GOON node, it is routed either through the adjustment activity (ACTIVITY 2) with probability 0.15 or to an activity that requires zero time with probability 0.85. In either case, the entity flows through the FREE node to make the inspector available to process the next radio waiting in file 1. After freeing the inspector, the radio entity that was inspected and possibly adjusted is terminated at the TERM node. When 200 radios depart the network, one run is completed.

5.5.2   Illustration 5-2. Single Resource Processing Different Entity Types

Consider the situation in which a professor (PROF) meets with students. Forty percent of the students are classified as type A or B while 60 percent are classified as type C or F. The PROF serves the students on a first-come, first-serve basis but would like to determine the amount of time she spends counseling the two types of students and the amount of time per visit that each type of student spends waiting or being advised. She would also like to have aggregate statistics on her time spent with students and the time required to counsel a student for each type. The network and statement models for this situation are shown in Figure 5-1 and Figure 5-2.

At the CREATE node, the interarrival time between students is exponentially distributed with a mean of 60. One of the two branches is selected from the CREATE node with 40 percent going to the AWAIT node AWAB and 60 percent going to the AWAIT node AWCF. Both AWAIT nodes reference file 1 so that all students are waiting in file 1 for one unit of the PROF. The RESOURCE block specifies a capacity of 1 for PROF with entities waiting for PROF in file 1. The time to process an A-B type is normally distributed with a mean of 10 and a standard deviation of 10. This is identified as activity 1 on the network. Since negative times are truncated to 0, a fraction of the A-B types will require very little or 0 time (approximately 16 percent). Following servicing, the PROF is available to serve another student if one is waiting. The A-B type who has been counseled is routed to a COLCT node where statistics on the student's time in the system are collected. The entity is then routed to node COMBS where statistics on all students are collected.

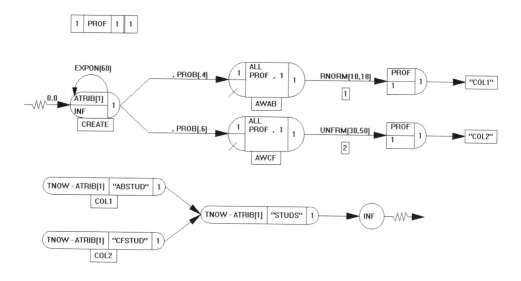

Figure 5-1 Network model of student processing.

A C-F type is routed to AWAIT node AWCF where one unit of the PROF is requested. If the PROF is not available, the student waits in file 1. When the PROF is allocated to the C-F student, the entity is routed over activity 2 which has a counseling time that is uniformly distributed between 30 and 50. Following counseling, one unit of the PROF is freed and statistics are collected on C-F types individually and collectively with the A-B types at node COMBS. Statistics on the PROF's time spent with A-B types are recorded automatically since it is the time that activity 1 is in use. Statistics on the time the PROF spends with C-F types are recorded from the data maintained by Visual SLAM for activity 2. Resource statistics for PROF will provide information on her total utilization. The number of students waiting and the average waiting time for students will be an output from statistics for file 1. This illustration demonstrates how two classes of entities can be served by a single resource and how statistics by entity class can be obtained. By using the same file number with two AWAIT nodes, a single priority can be applied to a class of entities that require a particular resource for processing.

```
RESOURCE,1,PROF,1,{1};
;
CREATE:  CREATE,EXPON(60),0.0,ATRIB[1],,1;    Create students wanting help
         ACTIVITY,,0,PROB(.4);                 40% are A to B students
         ACTIVITY,,0,PROB(.6),"AWCF";          60% are C to F students
;
; A to B Student Processing
;
AWAB:    AWAIT,1,{{PROF,1}};
         ACTIVITY,1,RNORM(10,10);
         FREE,{{PROF,1}};
         ACTIVITY;
COL1:    COLCT,,TNOW-ATRIB[1],"ABSTUD";
         ACTIVITY;
;
; Collect statistics on all students
;
COMBS:   COLCT,,TNOW-ATRIB[1],"STUDS";
         ACTIVITY;
         TERMINATE;
;
; C to F Student Processing
;
AWCF: AWAIT,1,{{PROF,1}};
         ACTIVITY,2,UNFRM(30,50);
         FREE,{{PROF,1}};
         ACTIVITY;
COL2:    COLCT,,TNOW-ATRIB[1],"CFSTUD";
         ACTIVITY,,,,"COMBS";
       END;
```

Figure 5-2 Statement model of student processing.

5.5.3   Illustration 5-3. A Flexible Machining System

A flexible manufacturing system (FMS) which performs machining operations on castings was described in Section 4.4. In this illustration, a portion of that system will be modeled which consists of 10 horizontal milling machines which can perform any of three operations. It is desired to evaluate a design in which five of the milling machines are dedicated to performing operation 10, one of the machines is dedicated to perform operation 20, and two of the machines are dedicated to perform operation 30. Two of the 10 milling machines are classified as flexible and the tooling necessary for these machines to perform any of the three operations is made available.

The arrival of castings is scheduled to occur every 22 minutes and the processing times to perform operations 10, 20 and 30 are 120, 40 and 56 minutes respectively. When a casting arrives, it is placed in a queue for one of the four categories of mills described above. Once placed in a queue for a dedicated mill it will not be processed by the flexible mill even if the flexible mill is idle. The network and statement models for this situation are presented in Figure 5-3 and Figure 5-4.

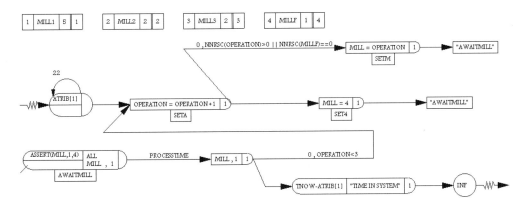

Figure 5-3 Network model of a flexible machining system.

At the CREATE node, castings are inserted into the network every 22 time units and real attribute 1 is established as the arrival time. At node SETA, the first integer attribute of the arriving casting is set with LTRIB[1] defined as the operation number. On the resource statements, the mills dedicated to operation 10 are defined as resource 1, those dedicated to operation 20 as resource 2, those dedicated to operation 30 as resource 3, and the flexible mills are identified as resource 4.

The activities emanating from node SETA determine if a casting should be routed to a dedicated machine or to a flexible mill. It is assumed that a dedicated machine will be used if one is available or if no flexible mill is available. An activity with this condition is shown on the network leading to the ASSIGN node SETM. The availability of a resource is obtained through the Visual SLAM network variable NNRSC so the joint condition described above is

$$\text{NNRSC(OPERATION)>0||NNRSC(MILLF)==0}$$

that is, the activity condition either represents that the mill for the current operation is available or that the flexible mill, MILLF, is not available. In either case, the casting is assigned by setting MILL = OPERATION where MILL is equivalenced to LTRIB[2]. MILL is used later as a file number and resource number.

```
GEN,"PRITSKER","FMS",2/8/1995;
LIMITS,,,,1,2;
ARRAY,1,3,{120,40,56};
EQUIVALENCE,{{OPERATION,LTRIB[1]},{MILL,LTRIB[2]},
            {PROCESSTIME,ARRAY[1,OPERATION]}};
INITIALIZE,0,2400;
NETWORK;
;
;   Define 10 mills as 4 resource types
;
RESOURCE,1,MILL1,5,{1};
RESOURCE,2,MILL2,1,{2};
RESOURCE,3,MILL3,2,{3};
RESOURCE,4,MILLF,2,{4};
;
CREATE,22,,ATRIB[1];
;
;   Increment operation number and branch to
;   dedicated mill if available, flexible ill otherwise
;
SETA:   ASSIGN,{{OPERATION,OPERATION+1}},1;
        ACTIVITY,,,NNRSC(OPERATION)>0||NNRSC(MILLF)==0;
        ACTIVITY,,,,"SET4";
SETM:   ASSIGN,{{MILL,OPERATION}};

;
;   Process at the mill
;
AWAITMILL:  AWAIT,ASSERT(MILL,1,4),{{MILL,1}};
            ACTIVITY,,PROCESSTIME;
            FREE,{{MILL,1}},1;
;
; Check for another operation
;
        ACTIVITY,,0,OPERATION<3,"SETA";
        ACTIVITY;
        COLCT,,TNOW-ATRIB[1],"TIME IN SYSTEM";
        TERMINATE;
SET4:   ASSIGN,{{MILL,4}};
        ACTIVITY,,,,"AWAITMILL";
        END;
FIN;
```

Figure 5-4 Statement model of a flexible machining system.

If the above condition is not satisfied, then a dedicated machine for OPERATION is not available and a flexible mill is available. In this case, MILL is set to 4 to indicate that the flexible mill is to perform the operation. At AWAIT node AWAITMILL, the casting entity awaits for one unit of the mill as defined by MILL. The casting entity waits in file 1, 2, 3 or 4. When the appropriate mill is freed, the casting entity proceeds through the activity whose duration is specified by PROCESSTIME which is equivalenced to ARRAY(1,OPERATION). An ARRAY statement sets the processing times to 120, 40 and 56.

Following processing by the mill, the mill is freed at a FREE node and the casting entity is routed back to node SETA if an additional operation is to be performed, that is, OPERATION is less than 3. Otherwise, the casting entity has completed all three operations and is routed to a COLCT node where the time the casting was in the FMS system is recorded.

This illustration demonstrates how a complex situation can be reduced in scope in order to get a fast working model of the situation. The scope has been reduced by eliminating portions of the total system such as raw material, lathes, inspection station, and load and unload areas. In addition, the scope of the modeling effort was reduced by making assumptions concerning the routing of castings, that is, the assignment of a casting to a mill made at the time the casting was available to be processed.

5.6   ALTER NODE

The ALTER node is used to change the capacity of resource type RES by CC units. CC can be a constant or an expression. If CC is positive, the number of available units is increased. If CC is negative, the capacity is decreased. The symbol, statement and AweSim dialog box for the ALTER node are shown below.

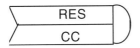   ALTER,RES,CC,M;

ALTER Definition	✕
Node Label:	
Resource:	
Capacity Change:	F(x)
Max Branches to Take:	1

OK   Cancel

Label of this node. Used for branching and reports

When the ALTER node is used to decrease availability (CC is negative), the change is invoked only if a sufficient number of units of the resource are not in use. If this is not the case, the capacity is reduced to the current number in use. Further reductions then occur when resources are freed at FREE nodes. In no case will the capacity of a resource be reduced below zero. Any additional reductions requested when the capacity has been reduced to zero are ignored.

RES can be specified in alphanumeric form by a resource label RLBL previously defined in a resource block. RES can also be specified as an expression which defines a resource code to be altered. For example, when an entity arrives to the node

ALTER,MACHINE,-1;

the capacity of the resource MACHINE is decreased by one unit. If a machine is currently not in use, this change occurs immediately; otherwise the change is made as soon as a MACHINE is freed.

As another example, the node and statement

ALTER,LTRIB[2],LTRIB[3];

causes a change in the capacity of the resource corresponding to the value which is carried in LTRIB[2] of an arriving entity. The change in capacity is carried in LTRIB[3] of the arriving entity.

An ALTER node differs from a PREEMPT node in the following respects:

1. An entity arriving to an ALTER node requests a change in the capacity of the resource. The arriving entity is always routed from the ALTER node. An entity that arrives to a PREEMPT node either causes a preemption immediately, in which case the arriving entity is routed from the PREEMPT node, or the entity is queued in the file associated with the PREEMPT node.
2. An entity that arrives to an ALTER node causes the number of available units of the resource, NNRSC, to be decreased by the requested capacity change. Thus, NNRSC can have a negative value which indicates that all units are in use and there are requests to decrease the capacity of the resource.
3. It is not necessary to specify a disposition for the entity which has a resource at an ALTER node since altering a resource's capacity does not stop the processing of any entity. At a PREEMPT node, this is not the case and a send node must be specified.

5.7   EXAMPLE 5-1. INVENTORY SYSTEM WITH LOST SALES AND BACKORDERS

A large discount house is planning to install a system to control the inventory of a particular radio (1,2). The time between demands for a radio is exponentially distributed with a mean time of 0.2 weeks. In the case where customers demand the radio when it is not in stock, 80 percent will go to another nearby discount house to find it, thereby representing lost sales, while the other 20 percent will backorder the radio and wait for the next shipment arrival. The store employs a periodic review-reorder point inventory system where the inventory status is reviewed every four weeks to decide if an order should be placed. The company policy is to order up to the stock control level of 72 radios whenever the inventory position, consisting of the radios in stock plus the radios on order minus the radios on backorder, is found to be less than or equal to the reorder point of 18 radios. The procurement lead time (the time from the placement of an order to its receipt) is constant and requires three weeks.

The objective of this example is to simulate the inventory system for a period of six years (312 weeks) to obtain statistics on the following quantities:

1. number of radios in stock;
2. inventory position;
3. safety stock (radios in stock at order receipt times); and
4. time between lost sales.

The initial conditions for the simulation are an inventory position of 72 and no initial backorders. In order to reduce the bias in the statistics due to the initial starting conditions, all the statistics are to be cleared at the end of the first year of the six year simulation period.

Concepts Illustrated. This example illustrates the use of: a RESOURCE block for modeling an inventory level; an AWAIT node for holding backorders; a FREE node for satisfying backorders; the logical operator for specifying the condition for selecting an activity; the CLEAR option on the MONTR statement for clearing statistics; and the TIMST statement for obtaining time-persistent statistics.

Visual SLAM Model. The inventory system for this example can be thought of in terms of two separate processes. The first process is the customer arrival process and consists of arriving customers demanding radios. If no radio is available, the customer either backorders a radio or balks to a nearby competitor. The second process is the inventory review through which radios are replenished. This process consists of a review, every four weeks, of the inventory position. If the inventory position is less than or equal to the reorder point, an order is placed. The size of the order is equal to the stock control level minus the inventory position, thus increasing the inventory position to the stock control level. Receipt of the order occurs three weeks later. The radios received are first used to satisfy backorders. Any remaining radios are used to increase the number of radios on-hand.

The two processes described above are modeled in Visual SLAM as shown in Figure 5-5 by representing the radios on-hand as a resource named RADIO whose capacity is 72 units. The buying and backordering of radios in the customer arrival process can be modeled as entities representing customers arriving to an AWAIT node. Likewise, the replenishment of radios in the inventory review process can be modeled as an entity representing a radio shipment arriving to an ALTER node. Thus, the resource RADIO is depleted in the customer arrival process by entities representing customers and replenished in the inventory review process by entities representing radio shipments.

The Visual SLAM statement model for this example is presented in Figure 5-6. The model employs three XX variables equivalenced to INV_POS, REORDER_PT, and SCL. The INTLC statement (line 8) assigns initial values to these variables of 72, 18, and 72, respectively. The TIMST statement (line 9) causes time-averaged statistics to be collected on the inventory position and the results to be printed using the label INV. POSITION. The RESOURCE block (line 11) is used to define the radios on-hand resource and sets the initial level (availability) to 72. It identifies file 1 as the location of customers awaiting radios. The average number of radios on-hand is equal to the average availability of this resource.

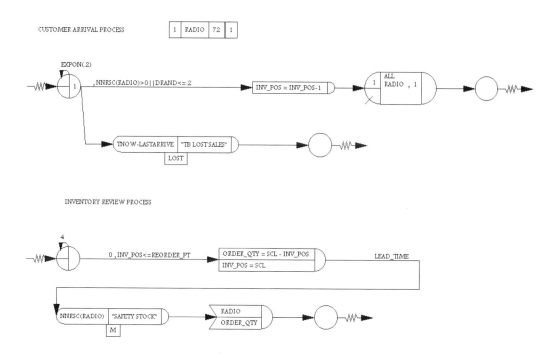

Figure 5-5 Network model for inventory example.

```
1 GEN, "PRITSKER", "INVENTORY PROBLEM", 1/1/96, 1, Y, N;
2 LIMITS,, 3,,,1;
3 EQUIVALENCE, { { INV_POS, XX[1] },
4                { REORDER_PT, XX[2] },
5                { SCL, XX[3] },
6                { ORDER_QTY, ATRIB[1] },
7                { LEAD_TIME, 3 } };
8 INTLC, { { INV_POS, 72 }, { REORDER_PT, 18 }, { SCL, 72 } };
9 TIMST, 1, INV_POS, "INV. POSITION";
10 NETWORK;
11    RESOURCE,1, "RADIO", 72, { 1 };
12 ;
13 ;      CUSTOMER ARRIVAL PROCESS
14 ;      -----------------------
15 ;
16    CREATE, EXPON(.2), , , , 1;           CREATE ARRIVALS
17    ACT,,,NNRSC(RADIO)>0||DRAND<=.2;      RADIO AVAIL OR P<=.2
18    ACT, , , ,"LOST";                     ELSE BRANCH TO LOST SALE
19    ASSIGN, {INV_POS, INV_POS-1};         DECREMENT INVENTORY POSITION
20    AWAIT,1, { RADIO,1};                   SEIZE A RADIO
21    TERM;                                 LEAVE THE SYSTEM
22 LOST: COLCT,,TNOW-LASTARRIVE,"TB LOST SALES";COLLECT STATSON LOST SALES
23       TERM;                                        LEAVE THE SYSTEM
24
25 ;      INVENTORY REVIEW PROCESS
26 ;      -----------------------
27 ;
28    CREATE, 4;                            CREATE A REVIEW ENTITY
29    ACT, , 0, INV_POS<=REORDER_PT;    IF POSITION BELOW REORDER PT
30    ASSIGN, { { ORDER_QTY, SCL - INV_POS },
31            { INV_POS, SCL } };      ORDER UP TO STOCK CTRL LVL
32    ACT, , LEAD_TIME;                     DELAY RECEIPT BY LEAD TIME
33    COLCT, , NNRSC(RADIO),"SAFETY STOCK"; COLLECT STATS, SAFETY STOCK
34    ALTER, RADIO, ORDER_QTY;          INCREMENT RADIOS ON HAND
35    TERM;                                 END REVIEW
36 END;
37 INIT, 0, 312;
38 MONTR, CLEAR, 52;
39 FIN;
```

Figure 5-6 Statement model of inventory example.

The customer arrival process is modeled by statements 16 through 23. Entities representing customers are generated by the CREATE node with an interarrival time that is exponentially distributed with mean of 0.2 weeks. A maximum of 1 emanating activity is taken at each release of the CREATE statement. The first emanating ACTIVITY (line 17) is taken by entities that represent the non-balking customers; that is, the customers who purchase an available radio or the 20 percent of the customers who backorder a radio when no radio is available. The duration of this ACTIVITY is zero and it is taken conditionally if the current number of available units of RADIO is greater than zero or if the random number DRAND is less than or equal to 0.2. The non-balking customers arrive at the ASSIGN node (line 19) where the inventory position is decremented by 1. The entities then continue to the AWAIT node where they either immediately seize (buy) or wait for one unit of RADIO. Each entity exiting the AWAIT node is destroyed at the TERM statement (line 21) corresponding to the departure of the customer from the system.

The second ACTIVITY (line 18) following the CREATE node has a duration of zero, is selected unconditionally, and ends at the COLCT node (line 22) labeled LOST. Since the CREATE node specifies that at most one emanating ACTIVITY is to be taken at each release, the second ACTIVITY will be taken if and only if the first ACTIVITY is not taken. The entities undertaking this ACTIVITY represent balking customers and are therefore lost sales. These entities are routed by the ACTIVITY to the COLCT node where statistics are collected on the time between lost sales. Each entity is then destroyed at the TERM node.

The inventory review process is modeled by statements 28 through 35. The CREATE node (line 28) creates an entity representing a review every four weeks. The emanating ACTIVITY is taken if the inventory position is less than or equal to the reorder point; otherwise no activity is selected and the review entity is destroyed. At the ASSIGN node (line 29), the first attribute of the entity, the ORDER QTY, is set equal to the stock control level minus the inventory position and then the inventory position is reset to the stock control level. The exiting entry represents a radio shipment with the number of radios in the shipment specified by the ORDER_QTY (ATRIB[1]). The entity next takes the ACTIVITY representing the shipment delay time or lead time. LEAD_TIME is equivalenced to 3 in an EQUIVALENCE statement. At the completion of the ACTIVITY, the entity arrives at the COLCT node (line 33) where statistics are collected on the number of available units of resource RADIO. This value corresponds to the inventory on hand level at the order receipt time. This quantity is referred to as the safety stock. The entity next moves to the ALTER node (line 34) where the number of units of resource RADIO added to the system is the ORDER_QTY. These radios are then available to the entities representing non-balking customers in the arrival segment of the model. The TERM statement (line 35) then destroys the entity.

The clearing of statistics in order to reduce any bias due to the starting conditions is accomplished by the MONTR statement (line 38) with the CLEAR option. This statement causes all statistical arrays including the file statistics to be cleared at time 52. Therefore, the statistical results for the simulation are based upon values recorded during the last 260 weeks of simulated operation.

This example is easily modified to change the characteristics of the inventory policy and the ordering assumptions. The ease of changing the model, and hence, the simulation analysis, supports the assertion that the original problem formulation for simulation analysis need not be a time consuming process.

Summary of Results. The Visual SLAM Summary Report for this example is given in Figure 5-7. The report provides statistics on time between lost sales, safety stock, and inventory position which were requested by the user. Automatically obtained are file 1 statistics corresponding to backordered radios and resource statistics corresponding to the average resource utilization or the average number of radios seized. The average number of radios on-hand is the average availability of the RADIO resource and is 28.64. The current utilization of the RADIO resource, 1478, provides a count of the number of radios sold. The values from the summary report can be used to compute the average profit for the inventory decision policy employed in the model. An investigation of different parameter settings for this policy can be made by changing the input values of the reorder point, the stock control level, and the time between reviews.

```
          ** AweSim SUMMARY REPORT **
   Simulation Project : INVENTORY PROBLEM
   Modeler : PRITSKER
   Date : 1/1/1996
   Scenario : EX51
   Run number 1 of 1
   Current simulation time    : 312.000000
   Statistics cleared at time : 52.000000
          ** OBSERVED STATISTICS REPORT for scenario EX51 **
```

Label	Mean Value	Standard Deviation	Number of Observations	Minimum Value	Maximum Value
TB LOST SALES	2.069	6.112	134	0.002	49.203
SAFETY STOCK	0.300	0.923	20	0.000	4.000

```
       ** TIME-PERSISTENT STATISTICS REPORT for scenario EX51 **
```

Label	Mean Value	Standard Deviation	Minimum Value	Maximum Value	Time Interval	Current Value
INV. POSITION	43.011	19.265	-3.000	72.000	260.000	42.000

```
          ** FILE STATISTICS REPORT for scenario EX51 **
```

File Number	Label or Input Loc.	Average Length	Standard Deviation	Maximum Length	Current Length	Average Wait Time
1	RES. RADIO	0.101	0.528	5	0	0.022
0	Event Calendar	3.231	0.421	8	3	0.567

```
          ** RESOURCE STATISTICS REPORT for scenario EX51 **
```

Resource Number	Resource Label	Average Util.	Standard Deviation	Current Util.	Maximum Util.	Current Capacity
1	RADIO	848.226	354.040	1478	1478	1520

Resource Number	Average Available	Current Available	Minimum Available	Maximum Available
1	28.643	42	0	75

Figure 5-7   Visual SLAM summary report for inventory example.

5.8   GROUP BLOCK

The GROUP block provides a method of grouping resources such that any member of the group can be used to provide service for an entity. The selection of which resource of the GROUP to allocate to an entity is made at an AWAIT node. The selection process is specified at the GROUP block. The concept of a selection process is similar to the server selection concept that was described in the previous section for the SELECT node. At the GROUP block, a list of resource numbers, GRNUM, is specified which may be allocated to entities arriving to or waiting at AWAIT and PREEMPT nodes. Only one resource of the GROUP may be allocated at a time. The GROUP label, GRLBL, is the name used at the AWAIT or PREEMPT node where a resource name is normally used. The file number of the AWAIT or PREEMPT node must still appear in the list of files for each individual resource that is a member of the resource group. The resource selection rule determines the order in which the resources are considered for allocation to an incoming entity. The resource selection rule, GRSELRULE can be one of the following: ORDER, CYCLIC, LBUSY, SBUSY, LIDLE, SIDLE, RANDOM or NRS (expr) with ORDER being the default rule. The definition of these rules is given in Table 5-1. When a resource of a group becomes free, it is allocated in accordance with its ordered list of files specified on its RESOURCE block.

Table 5-1 Definition of rules.

Code	Definition
ORDER	Select from free resources in a preferred order.
CYCLIC	Select resources in a cyclic manner. That is, select the next free resource starting with the last resource selected.
LBUSY	Select the resource that has the largest amount of usage (busy time) to date.
SBUSY	Select the resource which has the smallest amount of usage (busy time) to date.
LIDLE	Select the resource which has been idle for the longest period of time.
SIDLE	Select the resource which has been idle for the shortest period of time.
RANDOM	Select randomly from free resources according to preassigned probabilities.
NRS(expr)	User written routine to select a resource. The value of expr is passed as an integer code to routine NRS along with the await node.

The symbol, statement and AweSim dialog box for the GROUP block are presented below.

| GRNUM | GRLBL | {RESNUM, ...} | GRSELRULE |

GROUP, GRNUM, GRLBL, {RESNUM, ...}, GRSELRULE;

To allocate a resource of a group, the GRLBL for the group is used as the resource label at an AWAIT node. A selection among groups can be made by listing multiple GRLBLs at the AWAIT node. In addition, resource labels can be included in the list of GRLBLs. This concept is illustrated in Example 5-2.

The concept of a resource group requires that a FREE node be able to free resources that have been allocated to an arriving entity. A FREE node in which no resource is specified frees all resources that are currently allocated to the arriving entity. For a FREE node which has a list of resources specified, only the resources listed are freed when the FREE node is released. If a GROUP label is specified, then all resources belonging to the GROUP that have been allocated to the entity are freed.

5.9   EXAMPLE 5-2. ANALYSIS OF AGENTS AT AN AIRPORT COUNTER

At an airport counter, there are two lines for passengers waiting to check in or to purchase tickets. One of the two lines is for first class passengers and passengers who receive priority treatment due to the number of miles they fly with the airline. The second line is for coach passengers. The airline maintains 6 agents to process passengers during a peak period. Two agents process priority passengers but will serve coach passengers if no priority passengers are waiting. Two of the agents select their passengers from either of the two lines with a preference for passengers waiting in the priority line if both dedicated agents are busy. If no one is waiting in the priority line, then these agents select the next passenger waiting from the coach line. The last 2 agents are dedicated to coach passengers. If more than 1 of the coach agents are idle, the agents have an informal rule that the agent that has been idle the longest serves the next incoming passenger. Passengers in the priority line are served by the closest available agent that serves priority passengers.

Priority passengers arrive during the peak period according to an exponential distribution with a mean time between arrivals of 5 minutes. Coach passengers also arrive with an exponential distribution but with a mean time between arrivals of 2 minutes. For priority passengers, the service time is uniformly distributed between 2 and 20 minutes as they require different types of service. Coach passengers have a processing time that is triangularly distributed with a modal value of 6 minutes, a low value of 3 minutes and a high value of 12 minutes. It is desired to estimate the amount of time each type of passenger waits in the system and to assess the utilization of the 6 agents, both individually and as part of the first class and coach groups. A schematic of the system is shown in Figure 5-8.

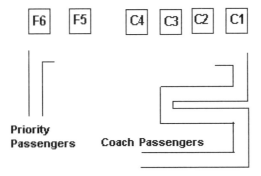

Figure 5-8 Schematic diagram of airport counter.

Concepts Illustrated. This example demonstrates the use of resource groups for processing different types of entities. A resource group is formed in order to collect statistics on a set of resources. The multiple run capability of Visual SLAM is demonstrated and a multiple-run summary report is presented. MONTR statements are used to clear statistics after an initial period of each run.

Visual SLAM Model. The Visual SLAM network model consists of two disjoint network segments involving the arrival of passengers, the waiting for an agent, the processing by the agent, the freeing of the agent and the collection of time-in-the-system statistics. These functions are modeled by a CREATE node, AWAIT node, ACTIVITY, a FREE node, a COLCT node and a TERM node. The network model is shown in Figure 5-9. In the network, resources are placed into groups. GROUP 1 is named ALLAGNTS and consists of 6 agents who have RESOURCE names F6, F5, C4, C3, C2, and C1 with corresponding resource numbers. Resources F6 and F5 are agents dedicated to serve priority passengers. Agent F6 has the line of priority passengers directly in front of her with Agent F5 being to her left. The coach agents, Resources C4, C3, C2, and C1 are to the left of Agent F5 and Resources group ALLAGNTS is used in this example to collect statistics on all 6 agents as a group. Resource GROUP 2, COACHAGNTS, consists of resources C1, C2, C3, and C4. The coach line is in front of Agent C1 and Agents C2, C3, and C4 are to the right of Agent C1. The agent that has been idle the longest processes a newly arriving coach passenger and this is indicated on the GROUP block by the code LIDLE. GROUP 3 consists of resources F6 and F5 and is identified as First Class Agents, FCAGNTS. The GROUP FCAGNTS is used to obtain statistical information of the combined use of F5 and F6.

In Figure 5-9, the label of the AWAIT node in each network segment indicates whether the segment is for priority passengers or coach passengers. The arrival time is assigned at the CREATE nodes and placed in ATRIB[0] for each arriving passenger entity. The entity is then routed to an AWAIT node where it waits, if necessary, in File 1 for priority service or File 2 for coach service. For priority service, a selection is made of one of the resources in GROUP ALLAGNTS. The coach passenger entities wait in File 2 for one of the resources in GROUP COACHAGNTS. The agent or resource number allocated to a passenger is stored in LTRIB[0] as indicated at the AWAIT nodes. Activities 1 and 2 model the agent processing time. For priority passengers the processing time is uniformly distributed between 2 and 20. For coach passengers the processing time is triangularly distributed with parameters 3, 6 and 12 indicating the distributions of the low, modal and high values. After being processed, the passenger entity arrives at a FREE node where the resource allocated at the AWAIT node is freed. Next, the time in the system, TNOW-ATRIB[0], is collected at COLCT nodes which are numbered as 1 and 2. The entities are then terminated as they have received service from an agent.

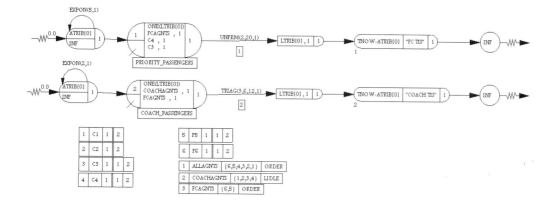

Figure 5-9 Network Model for Airport Agent Model, Example 5-2.

The statement model for the network is shown in Figure 5-10. The control statements indicate that the model is to be run from time 0 to time 300 and that statistics are to be cleared at time 60. Thus, statistics are cleared after 60 minutes and are collected over a 240 minute period on each run. Clearing is necessary as the system is starting in an empty and idle state and the analysis is for a 240 minute peak period. In 60 minutes, there will be 12 priority arrivals and 20 coach arrivals. Ten runs of the network are to be made and it is necessary to clear statistics for each run. Statistics over multiple runs are obtained and are available from the Multiple Run Summary Report. In AweSim, this report is obtained by selecting Reports and Outputs on the Executive Window. A selection is then made of the type of report desired from the resulting list. (See Chapter 14.)

Summary of Results. The SLAM II Multiple Run Summary Report for this example is given in Figure 5-11. The values shown in the summary report are for 10 runs. The time for first class and priority passengers to be processed by an agent is on the average 13.183 minutes over the 10 runs. The smallest average observed in one of the runs was 10.461 minutes, and the largest was 15.966 minutes. The standard deviation is computed about the average value for the 10 runs and represents the amount of variation in the 10 observations. The standard error is computed as the standard deviation divided by the square root of the number of runs which is 0.530 minutes. The standard error is used to compute confidence intervals relative to the average value as a sample from the distribution of average values. A confidence interval specifies an interval about the average which has a specified probability of containing the theoretical mean. (See Section 17.7.1).

```
; Control Statements

    GEN,"PRITSKER","AIRPORT",8-24-96,10,YES,YES,2;
    LIMITS,,,,1,1,,100;
    MONTR,CLEAR,60;
    INITIALIZE,0.0,300,YES;
    REPORT,80,YES,YES,LAST,{{ ,3}};
    NET;
    SIMULATE;
    MONTR,CLEAR,60;
    SIMULATE;
    MONTR,CLEAR,60;
    SIMULATE;
    MONTR,CLEAR,60;
    SIMULATE;
    MONTR,CLEAR,60;
    SIMULATE;
    MONTR,CLEAR,60;
    SIMULATE;
    MONTR,CLEAR,60;
    SIMULATE;
    MONTR,CLEAR,60;
    SIMULATE;
    MONTR,CLEAR,60;
    SIMULATE;
    MONTR,CLEAR,60;
    SIMULATE;
    MONTR,CLEAR,60;
    SIMULATE;
    MONTR,CLEAR,60;
    FIN;

; Network Statements

    RESOURCE,1,C1,1,{2};
    RESOURCE,2,C2,1,{2};
    RESOURCE,3,C3,1,{1, 2};
    RESOURCE,4,C4,1,{1, 2};
    RESOURCE,5,F5,1,{1, 2};
    RESOURCE,6,F6,1,{1,2};
    GROUP,1,ALLAGNTS,{6,5,4,3,2,1},ORDER;
    GROUP,2,COACHAGNTS,{1,2,3,4},LIDLE;
    GROUP,3,FCAGNTS,{6,5},ORDER;
    CREATE,EXPON(5,1),0.0,ATRIB[0],INF,1;
          ACTIVITY;
    PRIORITY_PASSENGERS: AWAIT,1,{{FCAGNTS,1},{C4,1},{C3,1}},
                         ONE(LTRIB[0]), ,NONE,1;
          ACTIVITY,1,UNFRM(2,20,1), , , ,"FCLASS";
    FREE,{{LTRIB[0],1}},1;
          ACTIVITY;
    COLCT,1,TNOW-ATRIB[0],"FC TIS", , , ,1;
          ACTIVITY;
    TERMINATE,INF;
    CREATE,EXPON(2,1),0.0,ATRIB[0],INF,1;
          ACTIVITY;
    COACH_PASSENGERS: AWAIT,2,{{COACHAGNTS,1},{FCAGNTS,1}},
                      ONE(LTRIB[0]), ,NONE,1;
          ACTIVITY,2,TRIAG(3,6,12,1), , , ,"COACH";
    FREE,{{LTRIB[0],1}},1;
          ACTIVITY;
    COLCT,2,TNOW-ATRIB[0],"COACH TIS", , , ,1;
          ACTIVITY;
    TERMINATE,INF;
    END;
```

Figure 5-10 Statement model for airport agent model, Example 5-2.

The 95% confidence interval for the mean time in the system for high priority passengers based on the 10 observations is 13.183 ± 1.83*0.530 = (12.213, 14,153). Since the number of observations is relatively small, the critical value used is based on the t-distribution. Specifically, the confidence interval (12.213, 14,153) specifies that only one out of twenty confidence intervals calculated in the manner described would not contain the mean time in the system.

The time in the system for a coach passenger is on the average 19.928 minutes. The coefficient of variation of this statistic is the standard deviation divided by the average value which yields a coefficient of variation of 0.619. This is approximately sixty percent of the value of the coefficient of variation for the exponential distribution which is considered to have a high degree of variability. Since the mean service time for a coach passenger is 7 minutes, the average waiting time of a coach passenger is approximately 13 minutes.

In the file statistics, it is seen that high priority passengers have an extremely small line with the average number of passengers waiting being 0.5. The average waiting time for a high priority passenger is 2.292 minutes. For coach passengers the average length is 7.128 with an average waiting time of 12.626 minutes. Note that the Multiple Run Summary Report does not show the largest size of the waiting line. This would be obtained from individual run summary reports or from a histogram of the maximum length on each run. These values are stored in the AweSim database and procedures for displaying them are described in Chapter 14.

The activity statistics show that an average of 2.239 and 3.336 passengers are being served concurrently. Thus, 5.575 passengers are being served concurrently on the average. This value is also seen as the average utilization of GROUP ALLAGNTS which is 5.575. The individual agent breakdown is given under resource statistics and it is seen that the coach agents C1, C2, C3 and C4 are busy over 92% of the time, Agent F6 is busy .933% of the time, and Agent F5 is busy .917% of the time. Agent F5 has a lower utilization because Agent F6 is selected first, when available, by high priority passengers.

Statistics relative to groups indicate that 5.575 out of the 6 agents are busy on the average. On at least one of the 10 runs, the average utilization was 6.0 indicating that all agents were busy during the peak traffic period. The average utilization of coach agents was 3.724 out of 4. The GROUP FCAGENTS has an average utilization of 1.851 agents out of 2. Based on these output statistics, alternative scenarios for the use of the 6 agents are easily identified. For example, one scenario to evaluate is to dedicate agent C3 to coach passengers: another scenario would be to increase the number of agents to 7, but to make the number of agents flexible based on the length of the priority and coach queues.

```
              ** AweSim! MULTIPLE RUN SUMMARY REPORT **

     Simulation Project : AIRPORT
     Modeler : PRITSKER
     Date : 8-24-96
     Scenario: AIRPORT
     Number of runs 10

              ** OBSERVED STATISTICS for scenario AIRPORT **
```

Label	Mean Value	Standard Deviation	Standard Error	Minimum Avg. Value	Maximum Value Avg.
FC TIS	13.183	1.675	0.530	10.461	15.966
COACH TIS	19.928	12.345	3.904	7.818	41.062

```
              ** FILE STATISTICS for scenario AIRPORT **
```

File Number	Label or Input Loc.	Average Length	Standard Deviation	Standard Error	Maximum Avg. Length	Average Wait Time
1 RES.	C3	0.506	0.247	0.078	0.835	2.292
2 RES.	C1	7.128	6.428	2.033	18.083	12.626

```
              ** ACTIVITY STATISTICS for scenario AIRPORT **
```

Activity Number	Label or Input Loc.	Average Util.	Standard Deviation	Standard Error	Maximum Avg. Util.	Minimum Avg. Util.
1	FCLASS	2.239	0.406	0.129	2.876	1.409
2	COACH	3.336	0.245	0.078	3.700	2.822

```
              ** RESOURCE STATISTICS for scenario AIRPORT **
```

Resource Number	Resource Label	Average Util.	Standard Deviation	Standard Error	Average Available	Maximum Average Util.
1	C1	0.924	0.076	0.024	0.076	1.000
2	C2	0.924	0.081	0.026	0.076	1.000
3	C3	0.930	0.069	0.022	0.070	1.000
4	C4	0.947	0.057	0.018	0.053	1.000
5	F5	0.917	0.099	0.031	0.083	1.000
6	F6	0.933	0.080	0.025	0.067	1.000

Resource Number	Minimum Average Utilization	Maximum Average Available	Minimum Average Available
1	0.769	0.231	0.000
2	0.750	0.250	0.000
3	0.809	0.191	0.000
4	0.816	0.184	0.000
5	0.700	0.300	0.000
6	0.759	0.241	0.000

```
              ** GROUP STATISTICS for scenario AIRPORT **
```

Group Number	Group Label	Average Util.	Standard Deviation	Standard Error	Average Available	Maximum Average Util.
1	ALLAGNTS	5.575	0.452	0.143	0.425	6.000
2	COACHAGNTS	3.724	0.279	0.088	0.276	4.000
3	FCAGNTS	1.851	0.178	0.056	0.149	2.000

Group Number	Minimum Average Utilization	Maximum Average Available	Minimum Average Available
1	4.603	1.397	0.000
2	3.144	0.856	0.000
3	1.459	0.541	0.000

Figure 5-11 Multiple-run summary for airport agent model.

5.10 PREEMPT NODE

The PREEMPT node is a special type of AWAIT node in which an entity can preempt one unit of a resource that has been allocated to some other entity. If the entity using the resource came from an AWAIT node, preemption will always be attempted. The preemption will also be attempted if the priority assigned to the PREEMPT node is greater than the priority of the PREEMPT node from which the entity currently using the resource type came. The symbolism, statement and AweSim dialog box for the PREEMPT node are shown below.

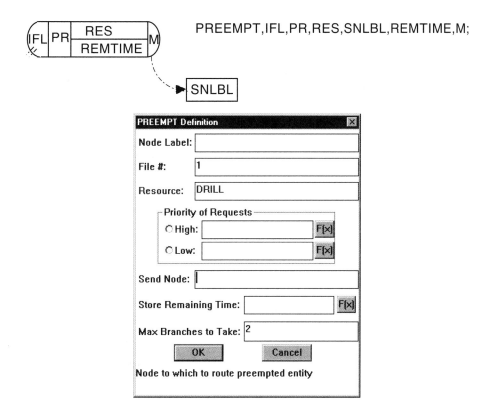

PREEMPT,IFL,PR,RES,SNLBL,REMTIME,M;

The definitions of IFL and RES for the PREEMPT node are identical to the specifications for these variables at the AWAIT node and identify the file number and the resource requested at the PREEMPT node. The priority, PR, is specified as LOW(K) or HIGH(K) where K is an expression. The incoming entity will attempt to preempt another entity if the expression gives it a higher priority. A preemption attempt is not satisfied if the resource is currently in use by an entity that: 1) is being processed in a service activity; 2) is in a file; or 3) is performing an activity with an indefinite duration (REL or STOPA). Entities that do not cause a preemption to occur wait for the resource in file IFL.

An entity that is preempted is routed to a node as specified by the send node label SNLBL. The time remaining to process the entity when it is preempted is stored in the variable REMTIME. If no send node label is specified then the preempted entity is routed to the AWAIT or PREEMPT node at which it was allocated the resource. At that node, it is established as the first entity waiting for the resource. When the resource is reassigned to the preempted entity, its remaining processing time will be used.

As described above, some restrictions are associated with the PREEMPT node. First, if a resource capacity is greater than 1 and all units are busy, only the last unit seized can be preempted. Second, an entity holding a resource that currently is in a QUEUE or AWAIT node will not be preempted. Also, if the entity is in a service activity or an activity of indefinite duration, it will not be preempted.

PREEMPT nodes only apply to resources as the concept of preempting a GATE is not meaningful. The PREEMPT node

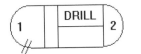   PREEMPT,1,DRILL,,,2;

specifies that when an entity arrives to it, the DRILL should be preempted. No ranking is given so the default ranking for preemptions, FIFO, is used. Thus, if an entity had already preempted the DRILL, the current entity would wait in file 1 until the DRILL becomes available. Default values are also used for the send node label, SNLBL, and the variable for storing the remaining activity time. In this situation, when the preemption occurs, the entity that is preempted will be held out of the network, and Visual SLAM will automatically maintain the remaining processing time for the activity from which it was preempted. The entity that was preempted will start its reprocessing from the activity from which it was preempted. The M-number of 2 specifies that the preemption entity will, after preemption occurs, take at most two branches from the PREEMPT node.

The following PREEMPT node provides values for the SNLBL and REMTIME fields.

   PREEMPT,1,,DRILL,AWT2,ATRIB[3];

This situation is similar to the one presented above except that the preempted entity will go to a node whose label is AWT2 and the remaining processing time will be stored in ATRIB[3].

To illustrate a ranking for preemptions, consider the following PREEMPT node.

PREEMPT,1,LOW(ATRIB[2]),DRILL,,,2;

In this case, if the entity that arrived to the PREEMPT node has a smaller value of ATRIB[2] than an entity that previously preempted the DRILL, then the new arriving entity will preempt the previous preemptor. Since the entity that is preempted was itself a preempt entity, it will return to the PREEMPT node from which it preempted the DRILL.

The following PREEMPT node shows that the specification of the resource to be preempted can be an expression.

PREEMPT,1,LTRIB[4],,,2;

In this case, the resource to be preempted is defined by LTRIB[4] of the arriving entity to the PREEMPT node. This capability allows the same PREEMPT node to be used for different machine failures by assigning a numeric resource code to LTRIB[4] and routing all such entities to the PREEMPT node.

5.11 ILLUSTRATION 5-4. MACHINE BREAKDOWNS

Consider the situation in which packages are to be processed through a scale. The scale encounters failures which stop the processing of packages until the scale is repaired. In this situation, the scale is modeled as a resource and the packages as entities that require one unit of the resource. An entity representing scale status is modeled in a disjoint network. It is delayed by the time to failure, after which the scale status entity arrives to a PREEMPT node. The PREEMPT node stops the weighing of a package by the scale. The package is routed to node HAND where manual weighing is done. The time to weigh by manual methods is twice the remaining process time. The network and statement models for this illustration are as follows:

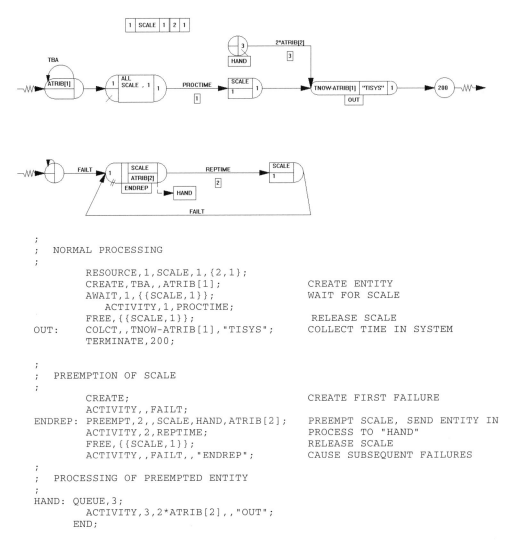

```
;
;   NORMAL PROCESSING
;
        RESOURCE,1,SCALE,1,{2,1};
        CREATE,TBA,,ATRIB[1];                   CREATE ENTITY
        AWAIT,1,{{SCALE,1}};                     WAIT FOR SCALE
            ACTIVITY,1,PROCTIME;
        FREE,{{SCALE,1}};                        RELEASE SCALE
OUT:    COLCT,,TNOW-ATRIB[1],"TISYS";            COLLECT TIME IN SYSTEM
        TERMINATE,200;


;
;   PREEMPTION OF SCALE
;
        CREATE;                                  CREATE FIRST FAILURE
        ACTIVITY,,FAILT;
ENDREP: PREEMPT,2,,SCALE,HAND,ATRIB[2];          PREEMPT SCALE, SEND ENTITY IN
        ACTIVITY,2,REPTIME;                      PROCESS TO "HAND"
        FREE,{{SCALE,1}};                        RELEASE SCALE
        ACTIVITY,,FAILT,,"ENDREP";               CAUSE SUBSEQUENT FAILURES
;
;   PROCESSING OF PREEMPTED ENTITY
;
HAND: QUEUE,3;
        ACTIVITY,3,2*ATRIB[2],,"OUT";
        END;
```

A repair time for the scale is scheduled from the PREEMPT node. Following the repair time, the scale is freed and a waiting package, if there is one, can be processed. The next failure of the scale is scheduled by routing the status-of-scale entity back through an activity representing the failure time.

5.12   EXAMPLE 5-3. A MACHINE TOOL WITH BREAKDOWNS

A schematic diagram of job processing and machine breakdown for a machine tool is given in Figure 5-12. Jobs arrive to a machine tool on the average of one per hour. The distribution of these interarrival times is exponential. During normal operation, the jobs are processed on a first-in, first-out basis. The time to process a job in hours is normally distributed with a mean of 0.5 and a standard deviation of 0.1. In addition to the processing time, there is a set-up time that is uniformly distributed between 0.2 and 0.5 of an hour. Jobs that have been processed by the machine tool are routed to a different section of the shop and are considered to have left the machine tool area (3).

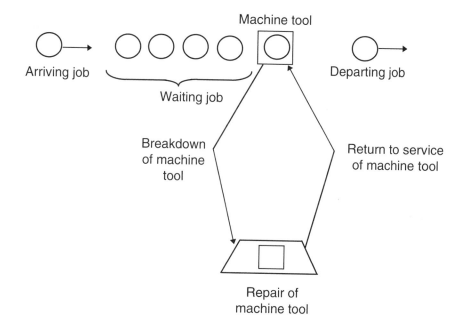

Figure 5-12   Schematic diagram of a machine tool that has breakdowns.

The machine tool experiences breakdowns during which time it can no longer process jobs. The time between breakdowns is normally distributed with a mean of 20 hours and a standard deviation of 2 hours. When a breakdown occurs, the job being processed is removed from the machine tool and is placed at the head of the queue of jobs waiting to be processed. Jobs preempted restart from the point at which they were interrupted.

When the machine tool breaks down, a repair process is initiated which is accomplished in three phases. Each phase is exponentially distributed with a mean of 3/4 of an hour. Since the repair time is the sum of independent and identically distributed exponential random variables, the repair time is Erlang distributed. The machine tool is to be analyzed for 500 hours to obtain information on the utilization of the machine tool and the time required to process a job. Statistics are to be collected for five simulation runs.

Concepts Illustrated. This example illustrates the concept of preemption of a resource through the use of a PREEMPT node.

Visual SLAM Model. The machine tool can be considered as a single server. Service involves two operations: job setup and job processing. Since two operations are involved, a resource will be used to model the machine tool. Entities representing jobs will arrive and await the availability of the machine tool if necessary. The jobs will be set up and processed when the machine tool is available and, following processing, will depart the system.

The breakdown of the machine tool will be modeled using a breakdown entity which preempts the machine tool and holds it while a repair operation is performed. The breakdown entity is processed through a disjoint network.

The Visual SLAM network model of the machine tool processing with breakdowns is shown in Figure 5-13. The corresponding statement model is given in Figure 5-14. Consider first the flow of job entities through the first network segment. Jobs are created at the CREATE node with an exponential time between arrivals having a mean of one hour. The job entities are routed to the AWAIT node. If a TOOL is available they proceed to activity 1. If a TOOL is not available, they wait in file 1. Activity 1 represents the setup time and is uniformly distributed between 0.2 and 0.5 hours. Following setup, the job entity proceeds to activity 2 which represents the machine tool processing operation which is normally distributed with a mean of 0.5 and a standard deviation of 0.1 hours.

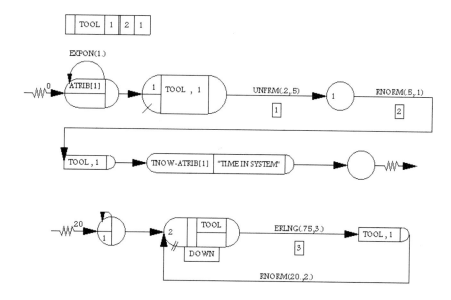

Figure 5-13 Visual SLAM network model of a machine tool with breakdowns.

```
GEN, "PRITSKER", "MACHINE BREAKDOWN", 1/1/96,5;
LIMITS,,,, 1;
NETWORK;
    RESOURCE, , "TOOL", 1, { 2, 1 };
    CREATE, EXPON(1.), 0, ATRIB[1];          CREATE ARRIVALS
    AWAIT, 1, { TOOL, 1 };                    AWAIT THE TOOL
      ACT, 1, UNFRM(.2,.5);                   SET UP
    GOON, 1;
      ACT, 2, RNORM(.5,.1);                   PROCESSING
    FREE, { TOOL, 1 };                        FREE THE TOOL
    COLCT,,TNOW-ATRIB[1],"TIME IN SYSTEM";    COLLECT STATISTICS
    TERM;
;
    CREATE, , 20, , 1;                        CREATE FIRST BREAKDOWN
DOWN: PREEMPT, 2, , TOOL;                      PREEMPT THE TOOL
      ACT, 3, ERLNG(.75,3.);                  DOWN TIME
    FREE, { TOOL, 1 };                        FREE THE TOOL
      ACT, , RNORM(20.,2.), ,"DOWN";          TIME BETWEEN FAILURES
    END;
 INITIALIZE,0,500;
 FIN;
```

Figure 5-14 Visual SLAM statement model of a machine tool with breakdowns.

Following processing, the machine tool is made available by having the job entity pass through a FREE node. The machine tool resource would then be used to process another job if one was waiting in file 1. The job entity proceeds to the COLCT node where time-in-system statistics are computed for the job entity. The job entity is then terminated.

The second network segment illustrates the processing of breakdown entities. The first breakdown is generated at time 20 hours. The CREATE note indicates that only one machine breakdown entity is to be generated. This machine breakdown entity will be recycled in the network segment as machine breakdown times are conditioned upon the time that the machine tool completes repair. Following the creation of the machine breakdown entity it is routed to a PREEMPT node where the resource TOOL is captured. If TOOL was processing a job entity, the entity is interrupted. We will discuss what happens to the interrupted job following the description of this network segment. The machine breakdown entity is then processed by activity 3 which represents the repair time which is Erlang distributed as prescribed. Following repair, the machine tool resource is made available by routing the entity through a FREE node. The next machine breakdown is then scheduled by routing the entity back to the PREEMPT node DOWN through an activity that represents the time between breakdowns which is normally distributed with a mean of 20 and a standard deviation of 2 hours.

Consider now the disposition of the job entity that was preempted. At the PREEMPT node the remaining processing time attribute and the SEND node label were defaulted. The default values for these quantities are to route the entity back to the AWAIT node where it captured the resource, and to save the remaining processing time. In this case, the job that was preempted is replaced in file 1 since that is the file number associated with the AWAIT node where the job entity captured the resource TOOL. The job entity is made the first entity in file 1. When the resource TOOL is made available, following the completion of the repair activity (activity 3), the job entity that was preempted will be removed from file 1 and will be placed in the activity from which it was preempted. The time to perform the activity will be the remaining service time for the activity. In this case, the job entity can be preempted from either activity 1 or activity 2 and hence, following repair, it will be reinserted in either activity 1 or activity 2, with the time to perform the activity as the processing time remaining when the job was interrupted.

The control statements shown in Figure 5-14 indicate that five runs are to be made with each run lasting for 500 hours.

Summary of Results. A summary of the output reports from Visual SLAM is shown in Table 5-2. The results show a high variability in the average time in the system for jobs. This can be attributed to the high variability in both the interarrival times and the service times. A different job arrival sequence was used on each run so that an entirely different 500 hour simulation was performed on each run. The variability of the service times is due to service being the sum of the setup time and the processing time and then sometimes including a machine tool repair time. In 500 hours, 22 machine tool breakdowns are expected. that is, (500-20)/(2.25 + 20).

Table 5-2 Summary of 5 runs for machine breakdown example.

Run Number	Average Time in System	Average Number of Jobs Waiting	Tool Status Percentages		
			In-Use	Idle	In-Repair
1	12.06	12.80	90	1	9
2	7.46	6.69	86	4	10
3	6.39	5.53	86	4	10
4	5.33	4.24	82	7	11
5	9.48	9.58	82	7	11

When a breakdown occurs, all jobs in the system are delayed by the repair time. Based on the results, a large buffer area for holding jobs waiting for processing will be required. Furthermore, if tight due dates are set on jobs, many jobs will be late. Methods should be investigated for better scheduling of job arrivals and for reducing the number of breakdowns.

5.13 EXAMPLE 5-4. PORT OPERATIONS

This problem statement is taken from Schriber (3). A port in Africa is used to load tankers with crude oil for overwater shipment. The port has facilities for loading as many as three tankers simultaneously. The tankers, which arrive at the port every 11± 7 hours, are of three different types. The relative frequency of the various types, and their loading time requirements, are as follows:

Type	*Relative Frequency*	*Loading Time, Hours*
1	.25	18±2
2	.55	24±3
3	.20	36±4

"There is one tug at the port. Tankers of all types require the services of this tug to move into a berth, and later to move out of a berth. When the tug is available, any berthing or deberthing activity takes about one hour. Top priority is given to the berthing activity.

"A shipper is considering bidding on a contract to transport oil from the port to the United Kingdom. He has determined that 5 tankers of a particular type would have to be committed to this task to meet contract specifications. These tankers would require 21±3 hours to load oil at the port. After loading and deberthing, they would travel to the United Kingdom, offload the oil, and return to the port for reloading. Their round-trip travel time, including offloading, is estimated to be 240±24 hours.

"A complicating factor is that the port experiences storms. The time between the onset of storms is exponentially distributed with a mean of 48 hours and a storm lasts 4±2 hours. No tug can start an operation until a storm is over.

"Before the port authorities can commit themselves to accommodating the proposed 5 tankers, the effect of the additional port traffic on the in-port residence time of the current port users must be determined. It is desired to simulate the operation of the port for a one-year period (8640 hours) under the proposed new commitment to measure in-port residence time of the proposed additional tankers, as well as the three types of tankers which already use the port." All durations given as ranges are uniformly distributed.

Concepts Illustrated. This example illustrates the use of the AWAIT and FREE nodes to model constrained resources. The ALTER node is used to reduce and increase the capacity of a resource during the simulation. An expression is used to define the number of a COLCT node and its identifier, ID.

Visual SLAM Model. In this example, entities representing tankers flow through a network model of the port facilities. The port facilities are constrained by the three berths and one tug. In the previous examples, resources have been modeled as service activities. However, in this example, the tug is required for both the berthing and the deberthing operation and its availability can be altered by storms. In addition, a tanker requires both a berth and a tug before berthing can be undertaken. Therefore, a network model of the port operations can most easily be constructed by using explicit resources to model both the tug and the berths.

The network model for this example is presented in Figure 5-15 and the statement listing is given in Figure 5-16. The explanation of the model will be given in terms of the statement model. The first statement in the network section is the RESOURCE block (line 4) which defines the resource BERTH. The resource BERTH is assigned a capacity of 3 and entities waiting for a BERTH reside in file 1. The resource TUG is defined in statement 5 and has a capacity of one. Entities waiting for the TUG reside in either file 2 or file 1. Recall that the priority for allocating free resources to waiting entities is determined by the order in which these files are listed in the RESOURCE block. Therefore entities waiting in file 2 for a TUG have priority over entities waiting in file 1 for both a berth and a TUG.

The statement model for this example can be divided into three major segments. The first segment represents the arrival process for the system and consists of statements 9 through 23. The second segment models the port operations and consists of statements 27 through 38. The last segment models the storm process and includes statements 42 through 47.

The arrival process for this problem is composed of two classes of arrivals. The first arrival class represents the existing tanker traffic consisting of tanker types 1, 2 and 3. These entities are generated by the CREATE node (line 9) and are routed probabilistically by the three emanating ACTIVITY's to either ARV1, ARV2, or ARV3 ASSIGN nodes. At these ASSIGN nodes, ATRIB[1] is set equal to the appropriate loading time and attribute ETYPE is set equal to the appropriate tanker type. Following any of these ASSIGN nodes, the entity is routed to the ASSIGN node labeled PORT.

The second arrival class involves inserting five entities representing the proposed type 4 tankers into the network. The entities are created by the CREATE node (line 20) which generates an entity every 48 time units, with the first entity at time 0, and a maximum of five entities created. At an ASSIGN node (line 22) labeled ARV4, ATRIB[1] is set equal to the loading time and ETYPE is set equal to the tanker type. The entities then continue to the PORT ASSIGN node (line 27).

The second major segment in the model represents the port operations and begins with the ASSIGN statement labeled PORT. Entities arriving to this statement represent tankers arriving to the port. The PORT ASSIGN node records the time of arrival to the port as ATRIB[2] of the entity. The entity then proceeds to the AWAIT node (line 28) where it waits for a BERTH and a TUG in file 1. Thus, entities which arrive to the AWAIT node when either a BERTH or a TUG is not available reside in file 1. When a BERTH and a TUG are available, the entity moves across an ACTIVITY (line 29) which represents the berthing operation that has a duration of one hour. Following berthing, the entity arrives at a FREE node (line 30) which frees one unit of the resource TUG.

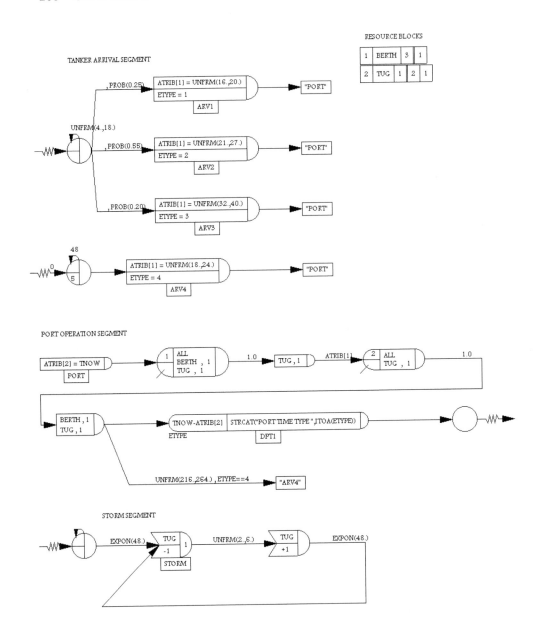

Figure 5-15   Visual SLAM network model of port operations.

```
 1 GEN,"PRITSKER","AFRICA PORT",1/1/1996,1;
 2 LIMITS,-1,-1,-1,3,-1,-1;
 3 NETWORK;
 4    RESOURCE,1,BERTH,3,{1};
 5    RESOURCE,2,TUG,1,{2,1};
 6 ;
 7 ; TANKER ARRIVAL SEGMENT
 8 ;
 9    CREATE,UNFRM(4.,18.);
10        ACTIVITY,,,PROB(0.25);
11        ACTIVITY,,,PROB(0.55),"ARV2";
12        ACTIVITY,,,PROB(0.20),"ARV3";
13  ARV1: ASSIGN,{{ATRIB[1],UNFRM(16.,20.)},{ETYPE,1}};
15        ACT,,,,"PORT";
16  ARV2: ASSIGN,{{ATRIB[1],UNFRM(21.,27.)},{ETYPE,2}};
17        ACT,,,,"PORT";
18  ARV3: ASSIGN,{{ATRIB[1],UNFRM(32.,40.)},{ETYPE,3}};
19        ACT,,,,"PORT";
20    CREATE,48,0,,5;
21        ACTIVITY,,,,"ARV4";
22  ARV4: ASSIGN,{{ATRIB[1],UNFRM(18.,24.)},{ETYPE,4}};
23        ACTIVITY,,,,"PORT";
24 ;
25 ; PORT OPERATION SEGMENT
26 ;
27  PORT: ASSIGN,{{ATRIB[2],TNOW}};
28   AWAIT,1,{{BERTH,1},{TUG,1}},ALL,,NONE;
29        ACTIVITY,,1.0,,,,"TRAVEL TO BERTH";
30   FREE,{ { TUG, 1 } };
31        ACTIVITY,,ATRIB[1];
32   AWAIT,2,{{TUG,1}},ALL,,NONE;
33        ACTIVITY,,1.0;
34   FREE,{{BERTH,1},{TUG,1}};
35        ACTIVITY,,,,"DPT1";
36        ACTIVITY,,UNFRM(216.,264.),ETYPE==4,"ARV4";
37   DPT1: COLCT,ETYPE,TNOW-ATRIB[2],
                   STRCAT("PORT TIME TYPE ",ITOA(ETYPE));
38 TERM;
39 ;
40 ; STORM SEGMENT
41 ;
42    CREATE;
43        ACT,,EXPON(48.);
44   STORM: ALTER,TUG,-1,1;
45        ACT,,UNFRM(2.,6.),,,,"DURATION OF STORM";
46    ALTER,TUG,+1;
47        ACTIVITY,,EXPON(48.),,"STORM",,"SCHEDULE THE NEXT STORM";
48    END;
49 INIT,0,8640;
50 FIN;
```

Figure 5-16   Statement model for port operations example.

Since file 2 is listed before file 1 in the RESOURCE block for the TUG, the TUG will be allocated to the deberthing first. The ACTIVITY (line 31) which follows represents the tanker loading activity that has a duration of ATRIB[1]. Recall that the appropriate loading time for the tanker entity was previously assigned to ATRIB[1] in the arrival segment of the model. Following the loading operation, a tanker requires a tug before the deberthing operation can begin. The next AWAIT node (line 32) models this requirement by causing the entity to wait in file 2 for a TUG. The ACTIVITY (line 33) with a duration of one hour represents the deberthing operation. When a TUG is finished deberthing, the BERTH and the TUG (line 34) are freed. When multiple resources are freed at a FREE node, all resources are first made available, and then they are allocated in accordance with the order in which the resources are listed at the FREE node. In this case, one unit of berth and one unit of tug are made available. Since the berth is listed first, file 1 is polled to determine if a tanker is waiting to be berthed. If there is, then the the berth and a tug are allocated to the berthing operation. If there is not a tanker to be berthed then the berth is made idle and the allocation of the tug is made in accordance with the files listed in the tug resource block. If it is desired to use the tug for a deberthing operation first, then the tug should be listed first at the FREE node that involves the two resources.

Statements 35 through 37 represent the tanker departure process from the port. After freeing the TUG, all tanker entities are routed (line 35) to COLCT node DPT1. Tanker type 4 is also routed across an activity (line 36) which models the round trip travel time to the United Kingdom and back for tankers of type 4, that is, routes the entity back to the ARV4 ASSIGN node. Therefore the five type 4 tankers continue to cycle through the model until the simulation is terminated after 8640 hours of operations.

The entities routed to COLCT node DPTI (line 37) record the time in port for all 4 tanker types. This is accomplished by using the attribute ETYPE of the entity to define the COLCT node number and using the string concatenation operator, STRCAT, to provide the COLCT node identifier, ID, as "PORT TIME TYPE" with ETYPE using the integer to alphanumeric function ITOA. The use of expressions for node parameters can condense network modeling. The storm segment of the model starts with the creation of a storm entity at a CREATE node (line 42). The first storm is delayed by an exponentially distributed time with a mean of 48 by an ACTIVITY (line 45). At the node with label STORM (line 44), the TUG resource is requested to be altered by -1 units. This decrease in capacity will occur immediately if the tug is not in use or at the end of the tug's current operation. Thus, the tug does not abandon a tanker in stormy waters. The storm duration is uniformly distributed between 2 and 6. This ACTIVITY starts immediately and does not depend on the status of the resource TUG. At the end of the storm, the TUG resource capacity is increased by 1 at an ALTER node (line 46). The next storm is then scheduled by an ACTIVITY (line 47) and the storm entity is routed back to node STORM. This completes the description of the model.

Summary of Results. The Visual SLAM Summary Report for this example is shown in Figure 5-17. The first category of statistics is for variables based on observations and consists of the in-port times collected on each tanker type at the COLCT node DPTI. This is followed by the file statistics for files 1 and 2 which correspond to tankers awaiting a berth and a tug for berthing, and loaded tankers awaiting a tug for deberthing, respectively. The last category of statistics for this example is the resource statistics. The results show on the average of 2.849 of the 3 BERTH's were utilized and that the TUG was busy 21.5 percent of the time.

```
              ** AweSim SUMMARY REPORT **
    Simulation Project : AFRICA PORT
      Modeler : PRITSKER
      Date : 1/1/1996
      Scenario : EX54

      Run number 1 of 1
      Current simulation time    : 8640.000000
      Statistics cleared at time : 0.000000

          ** OBSERVED STATISTICS REPORT for scenario EX54 **

      Label              Mean     Standard   Number of     Minimum    Maximum
                         Value    Deviation  Observations  Value      Value

    PORT TIME TYPE 1  35.080    14.243        183         18.183     77.327
    PORT TIME TYPE 2  39.621    12.935        449         23.077     85.188
    PORT TIME TYPE 3  51.681    12.967        141         34.147     93.075
    PORT TIME TYPE 4  36.868    13.451        156         20.176     75.678

          ** FILE STATISTICS REPORT for scenario EX54 **

    File    Label or       Average  Standard  Maximum  Current   Average
    Number  Input Location Length   Deviation Length   Length    Wait Time

      1    RES. BERTH      1.464    1.530        7         0       13.602
      2    RES. TUG        0.036    0.199        2         0        0.334
      0    Event Calendar 10.114    0.728       11         9       21.646

          ** RESOURCE STATISTICS REPORT for scenario EX54 **

    Resource   Resource     Average    Standard    Current    Maximum
    Number     Label        Util.      Deviation   Util.      Util.

      1       BERTH         2.849      0.405          1          3
      2       TUG           0.215      0.411          0          1

    Resource   Current    Average    Current    Minimum    Maximum
    Number     Capacity   Available  Available  Available  Available

      1         3         0.151         2          0          3
      2         1         0.713         1         -1          1
```

Figure 5-17 Visual SLAM summary report for port operations model.

The outputs indicate a high utilization of berths and the potential for a large queue of tankers waiting for berths. At one time during the year as many as nine tankers were waiting for a berth. Based on this information, port management should not accept the proposed five new tankers unless an additional berth is constructed or loading times are reduced. The model should be rerun to ascertain the effects of such changes.

5.14   GATE BLOCK

A GATE block is used to define the GATE named GLBL, the initial status of the GATE, and the file numbers associated with entities waiting for a gate to be opened at AWAIT nodes. The naming convention for gates is the same as for resources. Also, the default numeric codes for GATES are made in accordance with the GATE block's location in the network input statements. The GATE on the first GATE statement is given a numeric code of 1, the second is given a code of 2, and so on. GATE blocks are not connected to other nodes and are used only to provide the above definitional information. The symbol, statement and AweSim dialog box for the GATE block are shown below:

| NUM | GLBL | OPEN or CLOSE | IFL1 | : : : |

GATE,NUM,GLBL,OPEN or
CLOSE,{IFL,repeats};

GATE Definition

Gate #:

Label:

┌─ Initial Status ─
  ⦿ Open   ○ Closed

┌─ Gate Files ─
Files:

Change

Insert

Delete

OK   Cancel

Gate number. Used to access gate

5.15   OPEN NODE

An OPEN node is used to open a GATE with name GLBL or a GATE code specified by an expression. Each entity arriving to an OPEN node causes GATE to be opened. When this occurs, all entities waiting for GATE are removed from the files associated with the AWAIT nodes for GATE and are routed in accordance with the M-number of the AWAIT node. The entity that caused GATE

to be opened is then routed from the OPEN node. The symbol, statement and AweSim dialog box for the OPEN node are shown below.

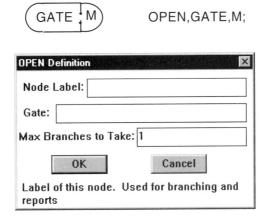

$$\text{GATE}\ \vdots\ \text{M} \qquad \text{OPEN,GATE,M;}$$

5.16   CLOSE NODE

A CLOSE node is used to close a GATE with name GLBL or a GATE code specified by an expression. An entity arriving to a CLOSE node causes the GATE referenced to be closed. Any entity arriving to an AWAIT node after the GATE is closed will wait for it to be opened. The entity that caused the GATE to be closed at the CLOSE node is routed in accordance with the M-number associated with the CLOSE node. The symbol, statement and AweSim dialog box for the CLOSE node are shown below.

$$\text{GATE}\ \vdots\ \text{M} \qquad \text{CLOSE,GATE,M;}$$

CLOSE Definition   [X]

Node Label: [   ]

Gate: [   ]

Max Branches to Take: [1   ]

[OK   ]   [Cancel]

Label of this node. Used for branching and
reports

5.17   ILLUSTRATION 5-5.   GATES TO MODEL SHIFTS

Consider the situation in which packages arrive to a post office over a 24-hour period; however, they are only weighed, stamped, and loaded into trucks during the day shift. This can be modeled by having the packages, as represented by entities, created and then routed to an AWAIT node that is associated with a gate called DSFT. In a disjoint network, an entity is created that closes the gate after eight hours and then opens it sixteen hours later. The network and statement models for this illustration are shown below. The model involving the processing of the packages through the operations on the day shift has not been detailed.

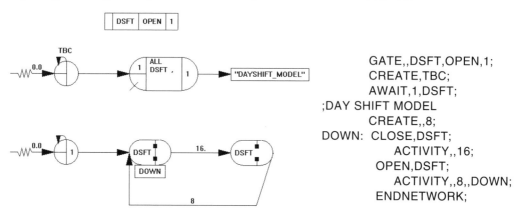

```
GATE,,DSFT,OPEN,1;
CREATE,TBC;
AWAIT,1,DSFT;
;DAY SHIFT MODEL
CREATE,,8;
DOWN:  CLOSE,DSFT;
       ACTIVITY,,16;
       OPEN,DSFT;
       ACTIVITY,,8,,DOWN;
ENDNETWORK;
```

5.18   EXAMPLE 5-5.   SINGLE-LANE TRAFFIC ANALYSIS

The system to be modeled in this example consists of the traffic flow from two directions along a two-lane road, one lane of which has been closed for 500 meters for repairs (1). Traffic lights have been placed at each end of the closed lane to control the flow of traffic through the repair section. The lights allow traffic to flow for a specified time interval from only one direction. This arrangement is depicted in Figure 5-18. When a light turns green, the waiting cars start and pass the light every two seconds. If a car arrives at a green light when there are no waiting cars, the car passes through the light without delay. The car arrival pattern is exponentially distributed, with an average of 12 seconds between cars from direction 1 and 9 seconds between cars from direction 2. A light cycle consists of green in direction 1, both red, green in direction 2, both red, and then the cycle is repeated. Both lights remain red for 55 seconds to allow the cars in transit to leave the repair section before traffic from the other direction can be initiated.

The objective is to simulate the above system to determine values for the green time for direction 1 and the green time for direction 2 which yield a low average waiting time for all cars.

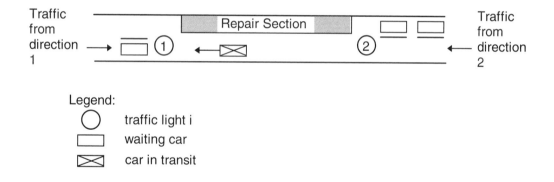

Figure 5-18   Schematic diagram of traffic lights.

Concepts Illustrated. This example illustrates the use of the OPEN and CLOSE nodes in conjunction with a gate to control entity flow through a system. Multiple simulation runs are made and activity durations are specified as XX[.] values to facilitate the changing of durations between runs.

Visual SLAM Model. There are three separate processes in this system consisting of: traffic flow from direction 1; traffic flow from direction 2; and information flow representing the traffic light cycle. Each of these processes is modeled by the movement of an entity through a subnetwork. We will model the traffic lights by the gates LIGHT1 and LIGHT2 where an open gate represents a green light and a closed gate represents a red light. To insure that only one car passes through the light at a time, a resource with a capacity of one is employed in conjunction with each gate. These resources are named START1 and START2 corresponding to LIGHT1 and LIGHT2 and represent the starting location before each light. The starting location is seized by each car entity before passing through the light and then freed immediately after it passes the light. In this way only one car can pass through the starting location at a time.

The network model for this example is depicted in Figure 5-15. Since the decision logic for the traffic flow from both directions is the same, a single network will be used to model both traffic flows with attributes employed to specify the resources and gates required. We will use ATRIB[2] to maintain the resource number and file number associated with the first location before each light. If ATRIB[2] equals 1, the car entity requires the resource START1. If ATRIB[2] equals 2 then resource START2 is required. The numeric values for the resources are defined by the order in which they are specified in the resource block or resource statement. A similar procedure is used for gates, and the GATE LIGHT1 has a numeric code of 1 and the GATE LIGHT2 has a numeric code of 2. Thus we can use ATRIB[2] to indicate the numeric value associated with entities flowing in a particular direction, that is, ATRIB[2]=I where I is the direction of traffic flow and the entities require RESOURCE I and GATE I.

Entities representing cars are created at two CREATE nodes, one for each direction. The time between car arrivals is exponentially distributed, and for direction 1 has a mean of 9 seconds and for direction 2 has a mean of 12 seconds. Following the creation of the entities, ATRIB[2] is set to 1 for direction 1 and set to 2 for direction 2. Entities that wait for a light change will be put in file 3 or 4 and we use ATRIB[3] to indicate these numbers. Thus, entities are assigned an ATRIB[3] value of 3 for direction 1 and 4 for direction 2. Entities from both directions are then routed to the AWAIT node with label QUE where they wait for the START resource as defined by ATRIB[2]. Once an entity is allocated the starting location, it proceeds to the next AWAIT node where it waits for the gate defined by ATRIB[2], that is, either LIGHT1 or LIGHT2. If the appropriate light is closed, the entities will wait in file 3 or file 4 in accordance with the value given by ATRIB[3]. Note that VISUAL SLAM uses the internal information presented in the GATE block which specifies that entities should wait in file 3 if gate number 1 is requested and should wait in file 4 if gate number 2 is requested.

A COLCT node is used to record values of the waiting time of the car at the light and the entity is then routed through one of the two emanating ACTIVITY's since an M-number of 1 is specified. A car that stopped has an arrival time different from the current time, TNOW. The condition specified on the first activity is for those cars that stopped and causes a two second delay for the car to pass the light. Since the M-value of the COLCT node is 1, the second ACTIVITY is taken if and only if the first is not taken. This ACTIVITY models the passage of moving cars that do not incur a delay. The resource defined by ATRIB[2] is then freed and the entity is terminated.

The traffic light segment of the model controls the changes in the traffic lights and consists of a series of OPEN and CLOSE nodes separated by ACTIVITY's. In this segment of the model, gates are referred to by the labels given them in the GATE blocks. A single entity is entered into the subnetwork by a CREATE node. It is delayed 55 seconds (both lights are red) before opening GATE LIGHT1. The information entity is then delayed by XX[1] seconds before closing GATE LIGHT1. Next, it is delayed by 55 seconds, opens LIGHT2, is delayed XX[2] seconds, closes LIGHT2, and then loops back after a delay of 55 seconds. By specifying the green time for LIGHT1 and LIGHT2 as XX[1] and XX[2] respectively, we can experiment with different values by prescribing new values for XX[1] and XX[2] in INTLC statements.

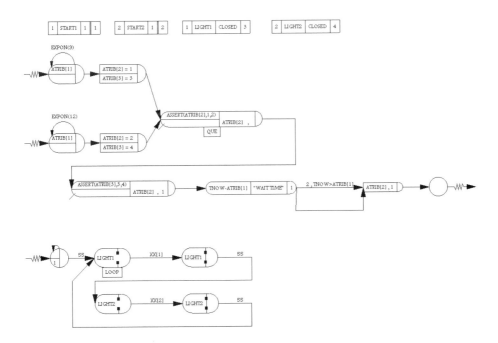

Figure 5-19 Visual SLAM network model of a traffic light situation.

The Visual SLAM statement model for this example is given in Figure 5-20 and follows directly from the network model. As specified on the input, three separate runs were made with the following values for XX[1] and XX[2].

Run Number	XX(1)	XX(2)
1	60	45
2	80	60
3	40	30

```
 1 GEN, "PRITSKER", "TRAFFIC LIGHTS", 1/1/96, 3;
 2 LIMITS,500,,, 3;
 3 INTLC, { { XX[1], 60 }, { XX[2], 45 } };
 4 NETWORK;
 5     RESOURCE, ,START1, , { 1 };   DEFINE STARTING PLACES
 6     RESOURCE, ,START2, , { 2 };
 7     GATE, , LIGHT1, CLOSE,  3  ; DEFINE TRAFFIC LIGHTS
 8     GATE, , LIGHT2, CLOSE,  4  ;
 9 ;TRAFFIC LANES
10 ;-----------------------
11     CREATE, EXPON(9);              CREATE ARRIVALS, DIRECTION 1
12     ASSIGN,{{ATRIB[1],TNOW},
13        { ATRIB[2],1},{ATRIB[3],3 }}; REQUIRES START1, LIGHT1
14      ACT, , , ,"QUE";
15     CREATE, EXPON(12);              CREATE ARRIVALS, DIRECTION 2
16     ASSIGN, {{ATRIB[1],TNOW},
17        {ATRIB[2],2},{ATRIB[3],4}}; REQUIRES START2, LIGHT2
18 QUE: AWAIT,ASSERT(ATRIB[2]),1,2;AWAIT STARTING PLACE
19     AWAIT,ASSERT(ATRIB[3],3,4),{ATRIB[2]}; AWAIT GREEN LIGHT
20     COLCT,,TNOW-ATRIB[1],"WAIT TIME",,,,1;
21      ACT, , 2, TNOW>ATRIB[1];        CAR BEGAN STOPPED
22      ACT;                            CAR BEGAN MOVING
23     FREE, { ATRIB[2] };             FREE THE STARTING PLACE
24     TERM;
25 ;TRAFFIC LIGHTS
26 ;--------------
27     CREATE, , , , 1;
28      ACT, , 55;                     BOTH LIGHTS RED
29 LOOP: OPEN, LIGHT1;                  LIGHT1 TURNS GREEN
30      ACT, , XX[1];                  GREEN TIME 1
31     CLOSE, LIGHT1;                   LIGHT1 TURNS RED
32      ACT, , 55;                     BOTH LIGHTS RED
33     OPEN, LIGHT2;                    LIGHT2 TURNS GREEN
3       ACT, , XX[2];                  GREEN TIME 2
35     CLOSE, LIGHT2;                   LIGHT 2 TURNS RED
36      ACT, , 55, ,"LOOP";            BEGIN NEW CYCLE
37     END;
38 INIT, 0, 3600;
39 SIMULATE;
40 INTLC, {{XX[1],80},{XX[2],60}};
41 SIMULATE;
42 INTLC,{{XX[1],60},{XX[2],45}};
43 FIN;
```

Figure 5-20 Visual SLAM statement model of traffic light situation.

Summary of Results. The results of primary interest for this problem are the average waiting times for cars in direction 1 and direction 2. The results for the three runs are summarized in the following table. Note that the statistics include the cars that waited for zero time units.

Run Number	Green Times		Average Waiting Time	
	Direction 1	Direction 2	Direction 1	Direction 2
1	60	45	62.35	74.92
2	80	60	66.06	75.79
3	40	30	185.43	185.30

These results indicate that the best combination of green times was obtained from run 1 and suggest that additional simulations should be performed with green times in the range of 60 seconds for direction 1 and 45 seconds for direction 2. After further exploration, we should check the statistical stability of the results by making several runs (replications) with different random number seed values for the values of XX[1] and XX[2] that resulted in the smallest average waiting times.

5.19 CHAPTER SUMMARY

The symbols and statements associated with resources and gates are summarized in Table 5-3. Four node types are used for modeling with resources and three node types are associated with gates. Resources and gates greatly increase the modeling flexibility available with Visual SLAM as shown by the illustrations and three examples presented in this chapter.

5.20 EXERCISES

5-1. Entities are generated at a node whose label is START. The first entity is to be generated at time 5. Thereafter the time between entity arrivals is exponentially distributed with a mean of 2 time units. An unlimited number of entities can be generated at node START. Entities are routed to QUEUE node Q1 if gate G1 is open. The time to reach node Q1 is equal to the capacity of the queue which is 5 minus the current number of entities in Q1. Entities that balk from Q1 leave the

Table 5-3 Symbols and statements for resources and gates

Name	Symbol	Statement
ALTER	RES / CC / M	ALTER,RES,CC,M;
AWAIT	IFL / QC / RULE RESORGATE,UR repeats / M	AWAIT,IFL, {{RESORGATE,UR},repeats}, RULE,QC, FULLCOND,M;
CLOSE	GATE M	CLOSE,GATE,M;
FREE	RES,UF / repeats / M	FREE{{RES,UF},repeats},M;
GATE	NUM GLBL OPEN or CLOSE IFL1,...	GATE,GLBL,OPEN or CLOSE,{IFL,repeats};
GROUP	GRNUM GRLBL {RNUM, repeats} GRSELRULE	GROUP,GRLBL,{RNUM,repeats} GRSELRULE;
OPEN	GATE M	OPEN,GATE,M;
PREEMPT	IFL PR RES REMTIME M → SNLBL	PREEMPT,IFL,PR,RES, SNLBL,REMTIME,M;
RESOURCE	RNUM RLBL CAP IFL1, repeats	RESOURCE,RNUM, RLBL,CAP,{IFL,repeats};

system. Initially, there are no entities at Q1 and file 1 is used to store entities waiting at Q1. Two servers process entities waiting at Q1. Processing time of these servers is normally distributed with a mean of 3 and a standard deviation of 1. After service, an entity leaves the system. If an entity's time in the system is greater than 10, gate G1 is closed. Gate G1 is open when an entity spends less than 2 time units in the system or when an arrival finds no one waiting at queue node Q1. It is desired to collect the time between departures for all entities that have arrived to the system. Draw the Visual SLAM network of the processing of entities as described above.

5-2. A barber has categorized his customers according to the type of haircut desired. He has determined that the time for a regular haircut is uniformly distributed between 15 and 20 minutes whereas the time for customers who desire a stylilzed haircut is exponentially distributed with a mean of 20 minutes. The barber has determined that 60 percent of his customers request a hair styling. Assuming that the time between customer arrivals is triangularly distributed with a mode of 20, a minimum of 15 and a maximum of 40, draw a SLAM II network to represent this situation. Include in the network the collection of statistics on the time spent in the system by each type of customer and by both types of customers collectively.

5-3. Modify the inventory model presented in Example 5-1 to include a variable representing stock-on-hand. Determine whether it is still necessary to use resources to model the inventory situation.

5-4. A certain machine repair shop consists of a work station where incoming units are repaired and an inspection station where the repaired units are either released from the shop or recycled. The work station has three parallel servers. and the inspection station has one inspector. Units entering this system have interarrival times which are exponentially distributed with a mean of 10.25 time units. The repair time for a unit is Erlang distributed with mean 22 and variance 242. The "shortest processing time" priority dispatching rule is used at the work station: the unit with the smallest repair time is served first. Repaired units queue up for inspection on a FIFO basis. The inspection of a unit requires 6 time units; the unit is then rejected with a probability p^n, where $p=.15$ and $n=$the number of times the unit has already been repaired. Rejected units queue up at the work station to be repaired again. The initial conditions are: two servers are busy with service completions scheduled for times 1.0 and 1.5, respectively; the first new arrival will occur at time 0; and the inspector is idle.

Simulate the operation of this shop for 2000 time units to obtain

estimates of the following quantities: server utilization; mean, standard deviation, and histogram of total waiting time for each repaired unit; mean, standard deviation, and histogram of total time spent in the system by each unit; average number of units in the system; and mean, standard deviation, and histogram of number of repair cycles required of a unit before it leaves the shop.

Embellishments:

(a) Modify the priority dispatching rule used at the work station so that recycled items are processed ahead of new arrivals. Among recycled units, priority is based on time spent in the system.

(b) Let the repair time be uniformly distributed in the range 0-48.

(c) Modify the original problem so that all units arriving before time 2000 are processed, and statistics concerning these items are included in the overall statistics for the simulation.

(d) Evaluate the effect of a lognormally distributed inspection time with mean 6 and standard deviation 1.5.

5-5.   Perform an analysis of the situation presented in Illustration 5-3 to determine the number of dedicated mills required to produce 173 castings in 80 hours.

5-6.   For the flexible milling system described in Illustration 5-3, assume that the use of a flexible mill to perform an operation increases the operation time by 10 percent. Illustrate the modeling changes required to model this situation.

Embellishment: Instead of an increase in processing time when an operation is performed by a flexible mill, add a setup time to the processing time for a flexible mill if the operation number performed by the flexible mill changes. The setup time for changing a flexible mill from operation 10 to 20 is five minutes, from 20 to 30 is eight minutes, from 10 to 30 is seven minutes, from 20 to 10 is ten minutes, from 30 to 10 is eight minutes, and from 30 to 20 is six minutes. Make the modeling changes required to include this setup time for the flexible mills.

5-7.   Cargo arrives at an air terminal in unit loads at the rate of two unit loads per minute. At the freight terminal there is no fixed schedule, and planes take off as soon as they can be loaded to capacity. Two types of planes are available for transporting cargo. There are three planes with a capacity of 80 unit loads and two planes with a capacity of 140 unit loads. The round trip time for any plane is normally distributed with a mean of 3 hours, a standard deviation of 1 hour, and minimum and maximum times of 2 and 4 hours, respectively. The loading policy of the terminal manager is to employ smaller planes whenever possible. Only when 140 unit loads are available will a plane of type 2 be employed. Develop a Visual SLAM network to model this system to estimate the number of unit loads waiting and the utilization of the two types of planes over a 100 hour period. Assume at first that the loading time of planes is negligible. Embellish the model to include a one minute per unit loading time.

5-8.   Change the model presented in Example 5-3 so that the utilization of the machine tool does not include the repair time of the machine tool.

5-9.   A machine tool processes two different types of parts. The time between arrivals of Type 1 parts is triangularly distributed with a mode of 30 minutes, a minimum of 20 minutes, and a maximum of 50 minutes. The interarrival time of Type 2 parts is a sample from a triangular distribution with a mode of 50 minutes, a minimum of 35 minutes, and a maximum of 60 minutes. Processing time for Type 1 parts is exponentially distributed with a mean of 20 minutes. For Type 2 parts, processing time is a sample from a uniform distribution with a minimum of 15 minutes and a maximum of 20 minutes. Processing time includes an inspection of the completed part. Fifteen percent of the parts fail inspection and return to the end of the queue of parts awaiting processing. Assume that parts which fail inspection have a rework time equal to 90% of the previous processing time. Develop a Visual SLAM network to collect statistics on the time spent in the system by a part and the utilization of the machines. Simulate this system for 2400 minutes.

Embellishments:
(a) Include a downtime of one-half hour after 4 simulated hours, recurring every 8 hours. This allows for preventive maintenance. Assume that preventive maintenance is performed after the completion of the current job and that the machine is always placed back into service at the end of the scheduled maintenance period.
(b) Any part which fails inspection more than once is scrapped. Collect statistics on the time between scraps. Run this model and identify the effect on throughput and in-process inventory.

5.21 REFERENCES

1. Pritsker, A. A. B., *Introduction to Simulation and SLAM II*, Fourth Edition, Systems Publishing Corporation and John Wiley, 1995.

2. Pritsker A. A. B., C. E. Sigal, R. D. J. Hammesfahr, *SLAM II Network Models for Decision Support*, boyd & fraser publishing company, 1994.

3. Schriber, T., *Simulation Using GPSS*, John Wiley, 1974.

CHAPTER 6

Logic and Decision Nodes

6.1 INTRODUCTION

Many systems involve logical operations and complex rules for deciding among sets of alternatives. As examples of the type of logic and decision processes that need to be modeled, consider the following rules and situations:

- Wait until three people arrive before sending a bus to the airport.
- Do not start a military engagement until confirming intelligence signals from two different sources are received.
- A pallet requires 24 cartons to be loaded before it is to be moved.
- Route a job to the shortest queue.
- Select Professor A's course unless there are over 80 students in it, in which case select Professor B's course.

- Assign a patient an examining room only after the patient's insurance has been verified and the patient's records have been received.
- Start an assembly operation after receiving at least one nut, one bolt and one washer.
- Select the next job to be done from different types of jobs based on the longest waiting time of the first job of each type.
- Start the car after the doors are closed, seat buckles are fastened and the key is inserted.

As can be seen from the above list, the modeling of diverse systems involves extensive logic and procedural specifications. Visual SLAM provides the capability to model such situations through the use of logic and decision nodes.

There are five nodes in Visual SLAM which perform logic and decision operations. The ACCUMULATE node is used to accumulate a specified number of entities. The BATCH node generalizes the concept of the ACCUMULATE node and allows the identity of each entity put into a batch to be maintained. The UNBATCH node causes individual entities of a batch to be rerouted into the network. The MATCH node is used to identify entities that have a common characteristic and to cause entities to wait until a prescribed set of entities with the common characteristic have reached the MATCH node. The SELECT node is used for routing purposes. It provides rules for selecting a QUEUE node from a set of parallel QUEUE nodes. It also provides decision logic to select an entity from a set of parallel QUEUE nodes when a server becomes available. A third use of the SELECT node is to select a service activity from among a set of available service activities when an entity arrives to a QUEUE node. One of the queue selection rules for the SELECT node is ASSEMBLY which requires an entity in each QUEUE node.

The logic and decision nodes described in this chapter perform operations on an entity or a set of entities. This differs from the branching logic on an activity which is applied to a single entity to determine its route through a network.

6.2   ACCUMULATE NODE

The ACCUMULATE node or ACCUM node accumulates entities until a prescribed number is reached. When the number is achieved, the node is released. The release of an ACCUMULATE node causes branching from the node to be initiated. At the ACCUMULATE node, a release specification is required. This specification involves the number of incoming entities needed to release the node for the first time (FR), the number required for subsequent releases (SR), and a rule for deciding which entity's attributes to save when more than one incoming entity is required to release the node (SAVE). The possible rule specifications are:

Save the attributes of the first entity arriving to the node (FIRST);

Save the attributes of the entity that causes the release of the node (LAST);

Save the attributes of the incoming entity for which an expression is highest (HIGH(expr));

Save the attributes of the incoming entity for which an expression is lowest (LOW(expr));

Create a new entity whose attributes are equal to the sum of the attributes of all incoming entities (SUM);

Create a new entity whose attributes are equal to the product of the attributes of all incoming entities (MULT).

The symbol, statement and AweSim dialog box for the ACCUMULATE node are:

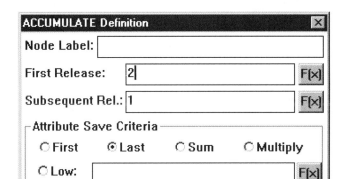

As an example of the release mechanism specification, consider that two in-coming entities are required to release the node for the first time and only one incoming entity is required to release the node on subsequent times. On the first release, it is desired to save the attributes of the second arriving entity. The ACCUMULATE node for this example is:

$$\text{ACC,2,1,LAST;}$$

where the default value of M = infinity is used. If the SAVE criterion was specified as SUM, then the sum of the real and integer attributes of the first two entities arriving would be maintained as the attributes of the entity routed from the node. In this case, the string attributes of the first arriving entity would be saved. By using this criterion and by specifying zero attribute values for selected attributes for each entity, a mixture of attribute values can be obtained.

The ACCUMULATE node is used extensively in project planning networks   (1, 3, 5, 6) where multiple activities must be completed prior to the start of additional activities. The SAVE criterion can be used to maintain information about entities that cause the ACCUMULATE node to be released.

FR and SR may also be specified by an expression evaluated for the first arriving entity following a release of the accumulate node. For example,

ACCUM,2,ATRIB[1],SUM, 1;

specifies that 2 entities cause the first release and that subsequent releases require ATRIB[1] entity arrivals where ATRIB[1] of the first of these arrivals provides the SR value. The default for the SAVE criterion is LAST.

6.3   EXAMPLE 6-1. ANALYSIS OF A PERT-TYPE NETWORK

PERT is a technique for evaluating and reviewing a project consisting of interdependent activities (4). A number of books have been written that describe PERT modeling and analysis procedures (1, 3, 6). A PERT network is a graphical illustration of the relations between the activities of a program. A PERT network model of a repair and retrofit project (5) is shown in Figure 6-1 and activity descriptions are given in Table 6-1. All activity times will be assumed to be triangularly distributed. For ease of description, activities have been aggregated. The activities relate to power units, instrumentation, and a new assembly and involve standard types of operations.

In the following description of the project, activity numbers are given in parentheses. At the beginning of the project, three parallel activities can be performed that involve: the disassembly of power units and instrumentation (1); the installation of a new assembly (2); and the preparation for a retrofit check (3). Cleaning, inspecting, and repairing the power units (4) and calibrating the instrumentation (5) can be done only after the power units and instrumentation have been disassembled. Thus, activities 4 and 5 must follow activity 1 in the network. Following the installation of the new assembly (2) and after the instruments have been calibrated (5), a check of interfaces (6) and a check of the new assembly (7) can be made. The retrofit check (9) can be made after the assembly is checked (7) and the preparation for the retrofit check (3) has been completed. The assembly and test of power units (8) can be performed following the cleaning and maintenance of power units (4). The project is considered completed when all nine activities are completed. Since activities 6, 8, and 9 require the other activities to precede them, their completion signifies the end of the project. This is indicated on the network by having activities 6, 8, and 9 incident to node 6, the sink node for the project. The objective of this example is to illustrate the procedures for using Visual SLAM to model and simulate project planning networks.

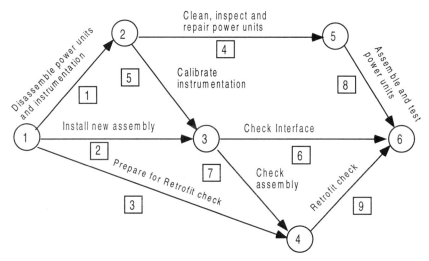

Figure 6-1 PERT network model of a retrofit project.

Table 6-1 Description of retrofit project activities.

Activity Number	Description	Mode	Minimum	Maximum	Average
1	Disassemble power units and instrumentation	3	1	5	3
2	Install new assembly	6	3	9	6
3	Prepare for retrofit check	13	10	19	14
4	Clean, inspect, and repair power units	9	3	12	8
5	Calibrate instrumentation	3	1	8	4
6	Check interfaces	9	8	16	11
7	Check assembly	7	4	13	8
8	Assemble and test power units	6	3	9	6
9	Retrofit check	3	1	8	4

Concepts Illustrated. Multiple runs are illustrated by this example. The ACCUMULATE node is used to model activity precedence relations. Activity start times are collected over multiple runs using a FIRST ARRIVE specification at COLCT nodes.

Visual SLAM Model. The Visual SLAM network model corresponding to the PERT network is shown in Figure 6-2. The Visual SLAM network is similar to the PERT network with the addition of: 1) the number of first and subsequent releases (equal to the number of incoming branches); and 2) a specification that FIRST ARRIVE statistics are to be collected after a node is released. When a single incoming activity releases the node, a COLCT node can be used directly. When more than one activity is required, an ACCUM node is also required.

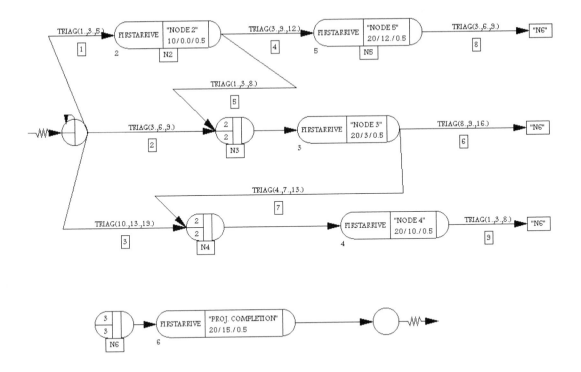

Figure 6-2 Visual SLAM network model of a PERT network.

In this Visual SLAM model, the CREATE node is only used to generate a single entity and, hence, no further specification is required (all default values are appropriate). Following the collection of statistics at the COLCT node after node N6, a run is completed. Four hundred runs are made as specified on the GEN statement. Statistics are not reset at the end of each run because the input for JJCLR on the INIT statement was NO.

The Visual SLAM statement model for this example is given in Figure 6-3. The coding of the statement model follows directly from the network model.

```
 1 GEN,"PRITSKER","PERT NETWORK",1/1/96,400;
 2 ;
 3 ;    PERFORM 400 ITERATIONS
 4 LIMITS,,,,1;
 5 REPORT,,,LAST;
 6 NETWORK;
 7    CREATE,,,,,3;
 8    ACTIVITY,1,TRIAG(1.,3.,5.),,"N2";       DISASSEMBLE
 9    ACTIVITY,2,TRIAG(3.,6.,9.),,"N3";       INSTALL NEW ASSEMBLY
10    ACTIVITY,3,TRIAG(10.,13.,19),,"N4";     PREPARE RETROFIT CHECK
11 N2:    COLCT,,FIRSTARRIVE,"NODE 2",10,0.0,0.5;
12    ACTIVITY,4,TRIAG(3.,9.,12.),,"N5";   CLEAN, INSPECT, REPAIR
13    ACTIVITY,5,TRIAG(1.,3.,8.),,"N3";        CALIBRATE
14 N3:    ACCUMULATE,2,2;
15    COLCT, , FIRSTARRIVE, "NODE 3", 20, 3, 0.5;
16    ACTIVITY,6, TRIAG(8.,9.,16.), ,"N6";     CHECK INTERFACES
17    ACTIVITY,7,TRIAG(4.,7.,13);              CHECK ASSEMBLY
18 N4:    ACCUM, 2, 2;
19    COLCT, , FIRSTARRIVE, "NODE 4", 20, 10., 0.5;
20    ACTIVITY,9,TRIAG(1.,3.,8.),,"N6";        RETROFIT CHECK
21 N5:    COLCT, , FIRSTARRIVE, "NODE 5", 20, 12., 0.5;
22    ACTIVITY,8,TRIAG(3.,6.,9.);              ASSEMBLY & TEST
23 N6:    ACCUM, 3, 3;
24    COLCT, , FIRSTARRIVE, "PROJ. COMPLETION", 20, 15., 0.5;
25    TERM;
26    END;
27 INIT, , , NO;
28 FIN;
```

Figure 6-3 Visual SLAM statement model for PERT network example.

Summary of Results. The final summary report for 400 independent simulations of the network is shown in Figure 6-4. The average time to complete the project is 20.78 time units with a standard deviation of 2.14 time units. By the central limit theorem, the average project duration is approximately normally distributed.

Since each of the 400 observations of the project completion time are performed in an independent manner, an estimate of the standard deviation of the average project completion time is 2.14 divided by 20 or 0.107. A 95% confidence interval on the average project completion time is 20.78±1.96*0.107 where 1.96 is the critical value of the normal distribution corresponding to a 95% confidence. The critical value for the normal distribution is used even though the estimate for the standard deviation is employed since the number of observations is large. The limits for the confidence interval are (20.57, 20.99) which indicates that the mean of the network model is expected to be in a narrow range. Specifically, the 95% confidence interval statement says that only one out of twenty confidence intervals calculated in the above manner would not contain the mean duration of the project network model.

```
            ** AweSim SUMMARY REPORT **

    Simulation Project : PERT NETWORK
    Modeler : PRITSKER
    Date : 1/1/1996

    Run number 400 of 400
    Current simulation time     : 21.719827
    Statistics cleared at time : 0.000000

           ** OBSERVED STATISTICS REPORT **

    Label    Mean    Standard   Number of     Minimum    Maximum
             Value   Deviation  Observations  Value      Value

    NODE 2   2.992   0.779         400          1.270      4.851
    NODE 3   7.451   1.300         400          4.456     11.984
    NODE 4  15.964   2.037         400         11.816     22.449
    NODE 5  11.023   2.041         400          5.562     15.713
    PROJ.   20.782   2.137         400         15.771     26.967
    COMPLETION
```

Figure 6-4 Visual SLAM summary report for 400 simulations of retrofit project.

The calculation of a tolerance interval is based on material presented in Section 17.7.2 (4,7). For this example, the assumptions required are satisfied. We compute with 95% confidence that at least 95% of the population of average completion times generated from the model should be in the tolerance interval (20.56, 21.00). For this case, the chi-square critical value is 353.75 for d =.05 with 399 degrees of freedom. We can also compute that the probability is at least 0.9025=(.95)(.95) that a sample of the project completion time generated from the model will be in the tolerance interval (16.33,25.23).

The average values for nodes 2, 3, 4, and 5 provide estimates of the average starting times for activities emanating from these nodes. Additional information concerning all nodes is available on the histograms obtained. The histogram for project completion is shown in Figure 6-5. From Figure 6-5, estimates of the probability that the project will be completed by a certain time can be made. Thus, it is estimated that the probability of the project being completed by 19 time units is 0.210; hence, the probability of the project taking more than 19 time units is 0.790. This provides an indication of the gross nature of PERT assumptions since the expected completion time as estimated using PERT techniques is 19 time units (2).

```
Observed Histogram Number 6
Label: PROJ. COMPLETION
Number of Observations: 400


Observed    Relative      Cumulative    Upper Cell
Frequency   Frequency     Frequency     Limit

     0      0.000         0.000         15.000
     0      0.000         0.000         15.500
     1      0.003         0.003         16.000
     3      0.007         0.010         16.500
     8      0.020         0.030         17.000
     6      0.015         0.045         17.500
    17      0.043         0.087         18.000
    27      0.068         0.155         18.500
    22      0.055         0.210         19.000
    35      0.087         0.297         19.500
    36      0.090         0.388         20.000
    36      0.090         0.477         20.500
    30      0.075         0.552         21.000
    33      0.083         0.635         21.500
    29      0.072         0.708         22.000
    33      0.083         0.790         22.500
    21      0.052         0.843         23.000
    20      0.050         0.892         23.500
    12      0.030         0.922         24.000
    13      0.033         0.955         24.500
     4      0.010         0.965         25.000
    14      0.035         1.000         INFINITY
```

Figure 6-5 Histogram of retrofit project completion time

6.4   BATCH NODE

The BATCH node is used to accumulate entities to a specified level and then to release a single entity which represents the batch. At a BATCH node, one or more batches of entities may be accumulated with the option to later unbatch and restore the individual members of the batch. This capability is useful for modeling pallets and transfer cars that accumulate a full load before moving.

The node is released when the sum of the values of an expression for all batch members is greater than or equal to a threshold. The expression to be summed is given the name ADDVAL. The threshold can be a constant value or an expression evaluated for the first entity of the batch. The batch may also be released upon the arrival of an entity with a negative value of ADDVAL. This allows the overriding of the threshold requirement. For example, if the threshold is 10 and the sum of the ATRIB[2] values is 7 for five entities waiting, then an entity arrival with ATRIB[2] < 0 releases a batch of 6 entities.

The entity released from the BATCH node has attributes which are a combination of the member entities. The combination of attributes is specified by a SAVE criterion. As part of the SAVE criterion, specific attributes of the batched entity may be defined to be the sum of the attributes of all individual entities forming the batch. A RETAIN field allows the modeler to save all the individual entities and their attributes that form the batch. If RETAIN is specified as YES, the individual entities are retained by Visual SLAM and the modeler can then retrieve these entities by sending the batched entity through an UNBATCH node.

A BATCH node can also be used to simultaneously sort groups of entities into multiple batches. An entity is placed in a batch (sorted) based on the value of an expression, SORTVAL, evaluated when the entity arrvies. A maximum of M activities are initiated at each release of a BATCH node.

As can be seen from the above description, the BATCH node performs many functions and is quite complex. The characteristics included with the BATCH node have been those found to be necessary when solving applied manufacturing and industrial problems. The symbol, statement and AweSim dialog box for the BATCH node are shown below.

BATCH,SORTVAL,THRESH,ADDVAL,
SAVE,{SUM, repeats),RETAIN,M;

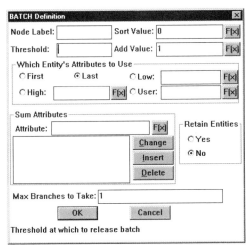

SORTVAL is the expression that specifies the batch for the arriving entity, that is, the value of SORTVAL is to be the same for entities in a batch. THRESH is the release threshold and can be a constant or an expression evaluated for the first arriving entity. Thus, if THRESH is specified as ATRIB[I], the Ith attribute of the first entity in a batch defines the threshold.

ADDVAL is the expression which contains the value to be summed. Thus, for entities arriving to the BATCH node which have the same value for SORTVAL, a sum is maintained of the values of ADDVAL. When this sum is greater than or equal to THRESH, a batched entity is formed and released from the BATCH node. A secondary use for ADDVAL is to cause the batch to be released when a negative number is given to the value of this attribute. For this case, the arriving entity with the negative value is included in the batch.

SAVE is used to specify a criterion for defining the attributes of the batched entity. The criterion specifies which entity in the batch should be used as a basis to define the attributes of the batched entity. The options for the criterion are:

> FIRST entity included in the batch;
> LAST entity included in the batch;
> Entity with the lowest value of an expression, LOW(expr);
> Entity with the highest value of an expression, HIGH(expr); and,
> A user written criterion, USER(expr), discussed in Chapter 9.

In addition to specifying this criterion, a list of attributes can be given. For each of the attributes in the list, the sum of the real attribute values of each entity included in the batch will be obtained, and the sum will be used as the value of the corresponding real attribute of the batched entity. For example, FIRST,{ATRIB[3],ATRIB[5]}, specifies that attribute 3 of the batched entity should be the sum of the attribute 3 values of every entity included in the batch and attribute 5 of the batched entity should be the sum of the values of attribute 5 of each entity included in the batch. All other attribute values for the batched entity would be taken from the first entity making up the batch.

RETAIN is a YES/NO field indicating whether the individual entities included in the batch should be maintained for future use. A YES specification allows the individual entities to be accessed at an UNBATCH node. If it is not necessary to retain the individual entities, then the field can be specified as NO. NO is the default for this field.

Because of the complexity of the BATCH node, three examples of its use are given below. Let us define a BATCH node that maintains batches where an entity's batch type is stored as the second integer attribute. A batch is formed when the sum of the values of attribute 3 for entities of the same type has a value which is 100 or greater. The individual entities making up the batch are not needed and the entity representing the batch should have the attributes of the first arriving entity of a batch except for attribute 4 which should be the sum of the values of attribute 4 of each individual entity.

The BATCH node and statement that accomplishes the above is

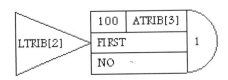

BATCH,LTRIB[2],100,ATRIB[3],FIRST,{ATRIB[4]},NO,1;

This statement defines a BATCH node which will maintain batches as sorted on the value of LTRIB[2]. When the sum of the values of ATRIB[3] for a batch reaches or exceeds 100, a batched entity will be released. This batched entity has the attributes of the FIRST entity forming the batch with the exception of ATRIB[4], which is the sum of all the ATRIB[4] values of entities in the batch. The attributes of the entities making up the batch are not retained since RETAIN is specified as NO. Since the M value is 1, at most one activity will be initiated with each release of a batch from this node.

The BATCH node and statement

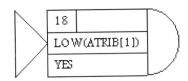

BATCH,,18,,LOW(ATRIB[1]),,YES;

maintains one batch (the default for SORTVAL). It is released when 18 entities arrive (the default for ADDVAL is to count each entity). The emanating entity will carry the attributes of the entity arriving with the lowest value of ATRIB[1].
All of the original entities will be saved for later unbatching.

As a third example of the BATCH node, consider

BATCH,,ATRIB[2],ATRIB[1],LAST,,NO;

which accumulates a batch until the sum of ATRIB[1] for all entities is greater than or equal to the value of ATRIB[2] of the first entity included in the batch. The batched entity will carry the attributes of the last entity included in the batch. The other entities included in the batch will not be retained.

6.5   UNBATCH NODE

The UNBATCH node is used to put the entities of a batch back in the network or to split an entity into multiple entities. The symbol, statement and AweSim dialog box for the UNBATCH node are shown below:

NCLONE   M   UNBATCH,NCLONE,M;

UNBATCH Definition   ☒

Node Label: [   ]

# of Clones: [   ] F[x]

Max Branches to Take: [1   ]

[OK]   [Cancel]

Number of clones of non-batched entity to make

where NCLONE is the number of copies of the arriving entity to be routed from the UNBATCH node. In this case, the UNBATCH node operates in the same fashion as a GOON node if NCLONE is 1. If NCLONE is defaulted, Visual SLAM determines whether or not the arriving entity was formed at a BATCH node. If so, each of the individual entities of the batch is released from the UNBATCH node, and the arriving entity to the UNBATCH node is destroyed.

If NCLONE is set by the modeler, it defines the number of identical entities to be released from the UNBATCH node. All attributes of such entities are set equal to the attributes of the arriving entity to the UNBATCH node. Note that the UNBATCH node can insert a large number of entities into the network. For example, if NCLONE is defined to be 50 and the M value for the UNBATCH node is 5, then up to 5 entities will be inserted into the network for each of the 50 entities to be split from the batched entity. Thus, up to 250 entities could be inserted into the network at this UNBATCH node.

Consider the following UNBATCH node.

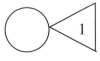

```
UNBATCH,,1;
```

If the arriving entity was formed at a BATCH node, the individual entities of the batch are restored. Otherwise, the entity is simply routed from the UNBATCH node. For the UNBATCH node shown above, at most, one activity branch is activated for each entity.

6.6   ILLUSTRATION 6-1.   BATCHING AND UNBATCHING

Consider the situation shown in Figure 6-6 involving metal parts as they complete a series of machining operations on one of two production lines. The parts are automatically loaded into one of five racks and processed through a washing unit to remove machine oil and dirt. Six parts of the same type produced on the same line are required to fill each rack before the rack enters the washer. After washing, parts are unloaded from the rack and are routed to other stations that are outside the model described in this illustration. The network model of this subsystem is shown in Figure 6-7. The statement model is shown in Figure 6-8.

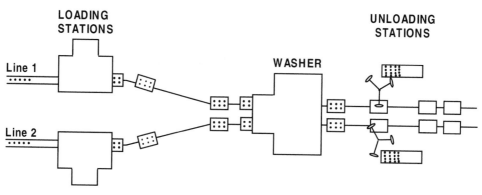

Figure 6-6   Schematic of batching and unbatching illustration.

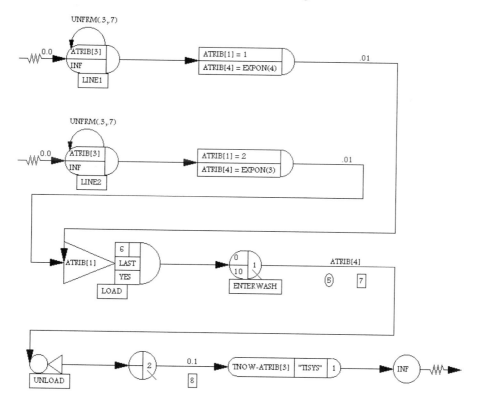

Figure 6-7 Network for batching and unbatching illustration.

The parts in this model arrive from one of two CREATE nodes with interarrival times specified by a uniform distribution between 0.3 time units and 0.7 time units. The entity representing a part is then assigned an ATRIB[1] value of 1 or 2 to identify the production line on which it was produced. A wash time for the part is then assigned to ATRIB[4]. Entities from both lines are routed to the BATCH node, LOAD, which sorts the entities into two groups according to the value in ATRIB[1]. Note that the loading time into the rack is included on the activities prior to the BATCH node. Each entity counts as one part from a particular line toward the release threshold of 6 parts needed to fill the rack. When the sixth part

```
;
; CREATE ENTITIES FROM LINE 1
;
            LINE1: CREATE,UNFRM(.3,.7),0.0,ATRIB(3),INF;
            ASSIGN,{{ATRIB[1],1},{ATRIB[4],EXPON(4)}};
            ACTIVITY,,0.1,,"LOAD";

;
; CREATE ENTITIES FROM LINE 2
;
            LINE2: CREATE,UNFRM(.3,.7),0.0,ATRIB[3],INF;
            ASSIGN,{{ATRIB[1],2},{ATRIB[4],EXPON(3)}};
            ACTIVITY,,0.1;

;
;   COMBINE 6 ENTITIES FROM THE SAME LINE
;
            LOAD: BATCH,ATRIB[1],6,1,LAST,{ATRIB[4]},YES;
            ENTERWASH: QUEUE,1,0,10,;
            ACTIVITY,7,ATRIB[4],,,5;
            UNLOAD: UNBATCH,,1;

;
;   PROCESS INDIVIDUAL ENTITIES
;
            QUEUE,2,0,INF,;
            ACTIVITY,8,0.1;
            COLCT,,TNOW-ATRIB[3],"TISYS";
             TERMINATE;
```

Figure 6-8 Statement model for batching and unbatching illustration.

from one of the lines arrives, a representative or batched entity is released from the node. The attributes of the batched entity are those of the LAST part entering the rack except for attribute 4 which is the sum of the wash times. The rack entity then enters a QUEUE node prior to being serviced in the washer which has a queue capacity of 10 racks. The washer can wash 5 racks at the same time and the wash time is taken as the fourth attribute of the rack entity which is the sum of the wash times of each part. After washing, the 6 entities are reestablished in the network at the UNBATCH node, UNLOAD, and the batched entity is automatically destroyed. In this model of the subsystem, the time through the subnetwork for each part is collected at the COLCT node since ATRIB[3] is the mark time established at the CREATE nodes for each part type.

6.7   SELECT NODE

SELECT nodes are points in the network where a decision regarding the routing of an entity is to be made and the decision concerns either QUEUE nodes or servers or both. To accomplish the routing at the SELECT node, the modeler chooses a *queue selection rule* (QSR) and/or a *server selection rule* (SSR). The rule establishes the decision process by which Visual SLAM will route entities when a decision point is reached. The decision points in the Visual SLAM network occur at the following times:

1.   An entity is to be routed to one of a set of parallel queues;

2.   A service activity has been completed and parallel queues exist that have entities waiting for the service activity. In this situation, a SELECT node is used to decide from which QUEUE node an entity should be taken; and

3.   An entity is to be routed to one of a set of non-identical idle servers.

The SELECT symbol is more complex than other Visual SLAM symbols in that the decision at the node can involve both a "looking ahead" and a "looking behind" capability. A look ahead capability is necessary to route entities to one of a set of parallel queues and to select from a set of parallel servers. These are decision types listed as 1 and 3 above. For the look-behind function, QUEUE nodes would precede the symbol and the SELECT node would perform the function listed as 2 above. A SELECT node can also perform both the look-behind and look-ahead functions. The symbol, statement and AweSim dialog box for the SELECT node are shown below.

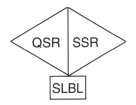

SLBL: SELECT,QSR,SSR,BLOCK or
BALK(NLBL),{QLBL,repeats};

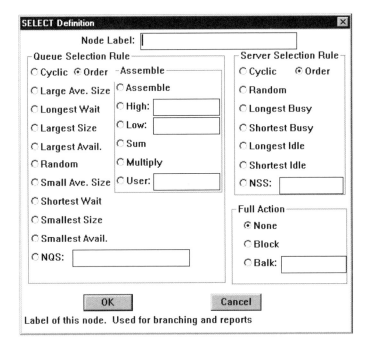

When the SELECT node is used for a single purpose, the field in the QSR or SSR rule that is not required should be defaulted. In the above statement, the QLBLs are the QUEUE node labels associated with the QSR rule. The QUEUE nodes could be before or after the SELECT node. The labels are not part of the SELECT node dialog box, since AweSim will add them to the SELECT node definition as the QUEUE nodes are connected to the SELECT node.

Five observations regarding the SELECT node are:

1. QUEUE nodes cannot be on both sides of a given SELECT node.

2. If service activities follow a SELECT node then QUEUE nodes must precede the SELECT node to hold entities when all the service activities are ongoing.

3. Balking and blocking occur at a SELECT node when all following QUEUE nodes are at their capacity and the BALK or BLOCK option is prescribed. The symbolism for this is shown below.

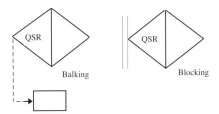

4. Whenever the look-behind capability is required, the preceding QUEUE nodes must refer to the SELECT node to transfer arriving entities.

5. A SELECT node always requires a node label.

The list of queue selection rules (QSR) is given in Table 6-2. The list of server selection rules (SSR) is given in Table 6-3.

Illustrations of the use of SELECT nodes follow.

1. Route entities to QUE1 or QUE2 based on the smallest number in queue (SNUM). The default server selection rule, ORDER, would be ignored in this case.

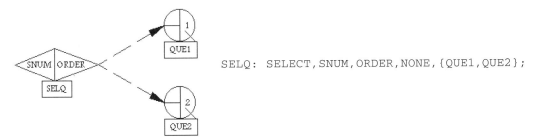

```
SELQ:  SELECT,SNUM,ORDER,NONE,{QUE1,QUE2};
```

This network segment could model the routing of customer entities to parallel queues before two airline ticket sellers.

Table 6-2 Priority rules associated with SELECT nodes for selecting from a set of queues.

Code	Definition
ORDER	Priority is given in a preferred order.
CYCLIC	Cyclic Priority - transfer to first available QUEUE node starting from the last QUEUE node that was selected.
RANDOM	Random Priority - assign an equal probability to each QUEUE node that has an entity in it.
LAVERAGE	Priority is given to the QUEUE node which has had the largest average number of entities in it to date.
SAVERAGE	Priority is given to the QUEUE node which has had the smallest average number of entitites in it to date.
LWAIT	Priority is given to the QUEUE node for which the waiting time of its first entity is the longest.
SWAIT	Priority is given to the QUEUE node for which the waiting time of its first entity is the shortest.
LNUM	Priority is given to the QUEUE node which has the current largest number of entities in the queue.
SNUM	Priority is given to the QUEUE node which has the current smallest number of entities in the queue.
LAVAIL	Priority is given to the QUEUE node which has the largest remaining unused capacity.
SAVAIL	Priority is given to the QUEUE node which has the smallest remaining unused capacity.
NQS(expr)	User written function to select a QUEUE node. The value of expr is an integer code to be used in function NQS. (See Chapter 9)
ASSEMBLE	All incoming queues must contribute one entity before a processor may begin service (this can be used to provide an "AND" logic operation). The resulting single entity gets its attributes from the entity in the first QUEUE listed.
HIGHASSEMBLE(expr)	Same as ASSEMBLE except the resulting single entity gets its attributes from the entity with the highest value of expr.
LOWASSEMBLE(expr)	Same as ASSEMBLE except the resulting single entity gets its attributes from the entity with the lowest value of expr.
SUMASSEMBLE	Same as ASSEMBLE except the resulting single entity gets its attributes by summing the numeric attributes of the entities. String attributes are those of the entity in the first QUEUE node.
MULTASSEMBLE	Same as ASSEMBLE except the resulting single entity gets its attributes by multiplying the numeric attributes of the entities. String attributes are those of the entity from the first QUEUE node.
USERASSEMBLE(expr)	Same as ASSEMBLE except the resulting single entity gets its attributes by calling the user-written function ASSEMBLE with integer code expr. (See Chapter 9).

Table 6-3 Priority rules for selecting from a set of servers at a SELECT node.

Code	Definition
ORDER	Select from free servers in a preferred order.
CYCLIC	Select servers in a cyclic manner. That is, select the next free server starting with the last server selected.
LBUSY	Select the server that has the largest amount of usage (busy time) to date.
SBUSY	Select the server which has the smallest amount of usage (busy time) to date.
LIDLE	Select the server who has been idle for the longest period of time.
SIDLE	Select the server who has been idle for the shortest period of time.
RANDOM	Select randomly from free servers according to preassigned probabilities.
NSS(expr)	User written function to select a server. The value of expr is an integer code to be used in function NSS. (See Chapter 9)

2. Select a server from servers 1, 2, and 3 to process entities waiting in queue, WAIT. It is preferred to use server I to server 2 and server 2 to server 3, that is, a preferred order for selecting servers is to be used. The default queue selection rule, ORDER, would be ignored in this case.

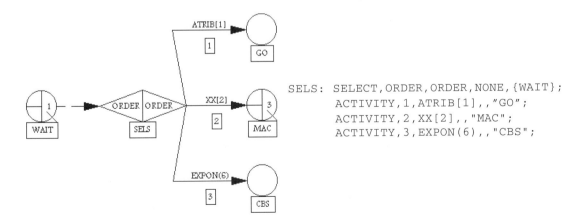

```
SELS:  SELECT,ORDER,ORDER,NONE,{WAIT};
       ACTIVITY,1,ATRIB[1],,"GO";
       ACTIVITY,2,XX[2],,"MAC";
       ACTIVITY,3,EXPON(6),,"CBS";
```

This network segment could represent three machines that can be used to process jobs waiting in QUEUE node WAIT. The processing time and the routing after processing is modeled as being machine dependent.

3. Illustrations 1 and 2 are combined below so that SELECT node SELS takes entities from QUEUE nodes QUE1 and QUE2 (rather than QUEUE node WAIT). A cyclic queue selection rule is used at SELECT node SELS.

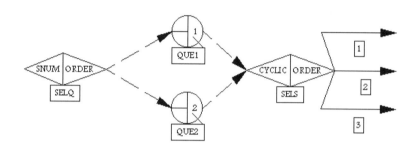

```
SELQ:   SELECT,SNUM,ORDER,,{QUE1,QUE2};
QUE1:   QUEUE,1,,,,{SELS};
QUE2:   QUEUE,2,,,,{SELS};
SELS:   SELECT,CYCLIC,ORDER,,{QUE1,QUE2};
```

In this network model, entities are routed by SELECT node SELQ to either QUE1 or QUE2 depending on which QUEUE node has fewer entities in it at the time of routing. If the queues have an equal number of entities in them, then QUE1 is selected as it is listed first. When an entity arrives to either QUEUE node and a server (activity 1, 2, or 3) is not busy, the entity is routed to the free server. If more than one server is free, the ORDER server selection rule associated with SELECT node SELS will select the first free server activity listed after the SELS SELECT node statement. Thus, the ORDER server selection rule gives priority to servers in the order they are listed in the statement model. The ORDER rule is the default for both queue selection at node SELQ and server selection at node SELS.

When a server becomes free and entities are waiting in both QUE1 and QUE2, SELECT node SELS uses the CYCLIC rule and takes an entity from the QUEUE node that was not selected when the last entity was routed to a server.

6.7.1 ASSEMBLY Queue Selection Rule

Six of the queue selection rules listed in Table 6-2 are ASSEMBLE rules. These rules differ from the other rules in that they involve the combining of two or more entities into an assembled entity. In this case the selection process requires that at least one entity be in each QUEUE node before any entity will be routed to a service activity. An air freight example of this assembly procedure is the requirement for both an aircraft entity and a cargo entity to be available before aircraft loading can begin. A network segment is shown for this situation where aircraft entities wait at QUEUE node ACFT, cargo entities wait at QUEUE node CARGO, and aircraft loading is modeled as activity 3.

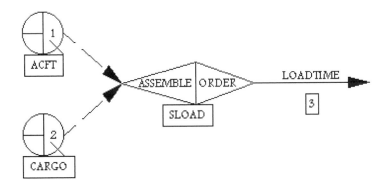

SELECT node SLOAD does not route an entity to service activity 3 until there is one entity in each QUEUE node. At the SELECT node, ASSEMBLE is prescribed as the QSR procedure. A SELECT node that employs an ASSEMBLE queue selection rule can assemble entities from two or more queues.

With the ASSEMBLE selection rule, the attributes of the assembled entity are those of the entity taken from the first QUEUE node listed. Other attribute-saving criteria, similar to those available at an ACCUMULATE node, are provided by the

HIGHASSEMBLE, LOWASSEMBLE, SUMASSEMBLE and MULTASSEMBLE selection rules. One additional criterion available at a SELECT node is USERASSEMBLE, in which the attributes are defined in a user-written function. (User functions are discussed in Chapter 9.)

As an example, consider the aircraft and cargo example presented previously. Suppose we desired to save the attributes of the aircraft. If aircraft entities are identified by a value of 1 in attribute 3 and cargo entities have a value of 2 in attribute 3, then specifying that the attributes of entities having a low value of attribute 3 will cause the aircraft entity's attributes to be saved. The statement for this case would be:

```
SLOAD:  SELECT,LOWASSEMBLE(ATRIB[3]),
        ORDER,NONE,{ACFT,CARGO};
```

6.8   EXAMPLE 6-2. A TRUCK HAULING SITUATION

The system to be modeled in this example consists of one bulldozer, four trucks, and two man-machine loaders (4, 5). The bulldozer stockpiles material for the loaders. Two piles of material must be stocked prior to the initiation of any load operation. The time for the bulldozer to stockpile material is Erlang distributed and consists of the sum of two exponential variables each with a mean of 4. (This corresponds to an Erlang variable with a mean of 8 and a variance of 32.) In addition to this material, a loader and an unloaded truck must be available before the loading operations can begin. Loading time is exponentially distributed with a mean time of 14 minutes for server 1 and 12 minutes for server 2.

After a truck is loaded, it is hauled, then dumped and must be returned before the truck is available for further loading. Hauling time is normally distributed. When loaded, the average hauling time is 22 minutes. When unloaded, the average time is 18 minutes. In both cases, the standard deviation is 3 minutes. Dumping time is uniformly distributed between 2 and 8 minutes. Following a loading operation, the loader must rest for a 5 minute period before he is available to begin loading again. A schematic diagram of the system is shown in Figure 6-9. The system is to be analyzed for 8 hours and all operations in progress at the end of 8 hours should be completed before terminating the operations for a run.

Concepts Illustrated. This example illustrates the use of the SELECT node for routing entities from multiple QUEUE nodes to multiple service ACTIVITY's. Additional concepts illustrated by this example include the use of the ACCUM node for the combining entities, the use of conditional branching for testing system status, the representation of several entity types by entities within the same model, and the ending of a simulation by completing processing of all entities in the system.

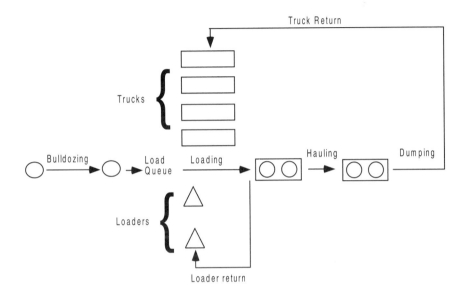

Figure 6-9   A truck hauling situation.

Visual SLAM Model. In this example, there are four distinct entities to be modeled. The first entity type is the pile of material created by the bulldozing operation. Since two piles must be combined to make one load, the entities representing piles of material must be combined two at a time to create a new entity representing a load. This accumulation of entities can be modeled with an ACCUM node that requires that two entities be combined for the first release and two entities be combined for subsequent releases. No attributes are used in this example, and, hence, no SAVE rule is required at the ACCUM node. Before the loading operation can begin, in addition to a load, there must also be an available truck and loader, each represented by separate entities. The loading operation can be performed by either of two non-identical servers.

This process can be modeled by employing separate QUEUE nodes for the trucks, loads, and loaders, in conjunction with a following SELECT node with two emanating servers. By specifying the ASSEMBLE and LIDLE (longest idle time) options for the queue and server selection rules, respectively, an entity is required in each queue before a service can be initiated, and available servers are selected based on longest idle time for each server. Following a loading operation, the entity is split and two entities are routed. One represents the truck and the other the loader. The entity representing the loader is delayed 5 minutes before being available to begin loading again. The consecutive activities of hauling, dumping, and return trip can be represented by serial ACTIVITY's with the last ACTIVITY returning the truck entity to the QUEUE node representing available trucks. The Visual SLAM network model of the system is depicted in   Figure 6-10.

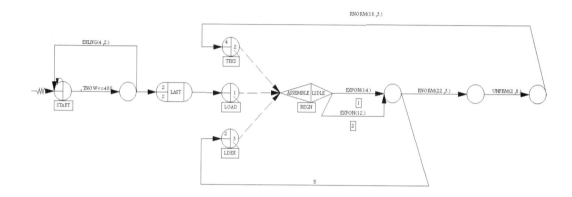

Figure 6-10   Visual SLAM network model of truck hauling system.

The Visual SLAM simulation statement listing for this example is shown in Figure 6-11. The network description begins with the CREATE statement (line 4) which creates the first entity at time 0. Thereafter, the time between entities is specified according to the Erlang distribution. The parameters for the Erlang distribution are: each exponential sample has a mean of 4 and there are to be 2 exponential samples. The entity continues through the conditional ACTIVITY (line 5) if TNOW is less than 480; otherwise the activity is not released and the entity is destroyed. This condition stops the creation of piles by the bulldozer after 480 minutes of operation. Since there is no INIT statement, an ending time for the simulation is not specified. In this situation, the run will end when all operations in progress at time 480 are completed since the arrival process was halted. Visual SLAM ends a run when the executive routine attempts to advance time and no events exist on the event calendar.

```
 1 GEN,"PRITSKER","TRUCK HAULING",1/1/96,1,,NO;
 2 LIMITS,,,,2;
 3 NETWORK;
 4 START: CREATE;                          CREATE LOAD ENTITIES
 5        ACT, , , TNOW<=480;              STOP IF AFTER 8 HOURS
 6        GOON;                            ELSE
 7        ACTIVITY,,ERLNG(4.,2.),,"START"; BRANCH BACK TO START
 8        ACTIVITY;                        AND CONTINUE
 9        ACCUM, 2, 2;                     ACCUMULATE TWO PILES
10 LOAD: QUEUE, 1,0, , , { BEGN };         QUEUE OF LOADS
11 TRKS: QUEUE, 2, 4, , , { BEGN };        QUEUE OF TRUCKS
12 LDER: QUEUE, 3, 2, , , { BEGN };        QUEUE OF LOADERS
13 BEGN: SELECT,ASSEMBLE,LIDLE,,{ LOAD, TRKS, LDER };
14        ACT, 1, EXPON(14.),,,, "LOADER1 TIME";
15        ACT, 2, EXPON(12.),,,, "LOADER2 TIME";
16        GOON;
17        ACT,,5,,"LDER";                  LOADER RESTING TIME
18        ACT,,RNORM(22.,3.);              TRUCK HAULING TIME
19        GOON;
20        ACT, , UNFRM(2.,8.);             TRUCK DUMPING TIME
21        GOON;
22        ACTIVITY,,RNORM(18.,3.),,"TRKS"; TRUCK RETURN TIME
23        END;
24  FIN;
```

Figure 6-11   Visual SLAM statement listing for truck hauling example.

Entities representing piles arrive at the ACCUM statement (line 9), where they are combined in pairs to form load transactions and continue to the LOAD QUEUE statement (line 10). The LOAD QUEUE is related to the TRKS QUEUE (line 11) and the LDER QUEUE (line 12), all of which have the statement labeled BEGN as a following SELECT node. The TRKS QUEUE represents the queue of waiting trucks which are stored in file. 2. There are initially four trucks in the queue. The LDER QUEUE represents the queue of waiting loaders which are stored in file 3. The queue is initialized to have two loaders in the queue at the beginning of the simulation. The SELECT statement labeled BEGN (line 13) employs the ASSEMBLE queue selection rule, LIDLE server selection rule, has neither balking nor blocking, and selects from the preceding QUEUE's labeled LOAD, TRKS, and LDER. Following the SELECT statement are two non-identical servers. The first server (line 14) representing loader 1 is assigned an activity number of 1 and has a service time which is exponentially distributed with a mean of 14 minutes. The second server (line 15) representing loader 2 is assigned an activity number of 2 and has a service time which is exponentially distributed with a mean of 12 minutes.

At the end of the loading operation, the entity arrives at the GOON statement (line 16). Following the GOON statement are two regular ACTIVITY's. The first ACTIVITY (line 17) representing the loader resting time has a duration of five minutes and routes the entity to the statement labeled LDER. The entity proceeding through the second ACTIVITY statement (line 18), representing the truck hauling operation, continues to a GOON statement (line 19). Next, the entity continues through the ACTIVITY statement (line 20) representing the dumping operation which ends at a GOON statement (line 21). The last ACTIVITY statement (line 22) models the return trip of the truck and routes the entity to the statement labeled TRKS.

In summarizing the Visual SLAM model for this example, it is interesting to note the representation of loaders as both service ACTIVITY's and entities queueing up at the LDER QUEUE. This dual representation is used to include the resting time for the loader. If the resting time requirement were omitted from the problem statement, the loaders need only be modeled by the service activities, and thus statements 12 and 17 could be deleted from the model.

Summary of Results. The Visual SLAM Summary Report for this example is shown in Figure 6-12. The first category of statistics is the file statistics for files 1, 2, and 3, and correspond to the queue of loads waiting for service, the queue of idle trucks, and the queue of available loaders, respectively. The second category of statistics is the service activity statistics representing the two loaders. A count of entities completing the two activities indicates that a total of 29 loads were processed through the model. This small number of observations suggest that considerable variation in both queue lengths and service activity utilizations can be expected between simulation runs employing different seed values.

```
** AweSim SUMMARY REPORT **

  Simulation Project : TRUCK HAULING
  Modeler : PRITSKER
  Date : 1/1/1996
  Scenario : EX72

  Run number 1 of 1
  Current simulation time   : 498.818250
  Statistics cleared at time : 0.000000

       ** FILE STATISTICS REPORT for scenario EX72 **

 File    Label or   Average Standard   Maximum  Current  Average
 Number  Input Loc. Length  Deviation  Length   Length   Wait Time

    1    QUEUE LOAD   0.663    0.959      3        0      11.402
    2    QUEUE TRKS   0.855    1.115      4        4      12.930
    3    QUEUE LDER   1.125    0.733      2        2      18.100
    0    Event Calendar 5.399  1.342      8        1      13.010

     ** SERVICE ACTIVITY STATISTICS REPORT for scenario EX72 **

 Activity  Label or      Server   Entity   Average     Standard
 Number    Input Loc.    Capacity Count    Utilization Deviation

    1      LOADER1 TIME     1       16      0.301       0.459
    2      LOADER2 TIME     1       13      0.283       0.450


 Activity  Current      Average    Maximum     Maximum
 Number    Utilization  Blockage   Idle Time   Busy Time
                                   or Servers  or Servers

    1         0         0.000       62.080      38.593
    2         0         0.000       63.779      36.204
```

Figure 6-12   Visual SLAM Summary Report for truck hauling example.

6.9   MATCH NODE

MATCH nodes in Visual SLAM are nodes that match entities residing in specified QUEUE nodes that have equal values of a specified expression. When each QUEUE node preceding a MATCH node has an entity with the specified common expression value, the MATCH node removes each entity from the corresponding QUEUE node.

For the MATCH node, there are nodes on both sides of the symbol and a node-to-node transfer is made when a match occurs. If there is no transfer node specified for a QUEUE node, the entity in that QUEUE node is destroyed after a match is made. The expression on which the match is based is specified within the MATCH node symbol. Only QUEUE nodes can precede MATCH nodes and the initial number in the QUEUE node must be zero. The symbol, statement and dialog box for the MATCH node are:

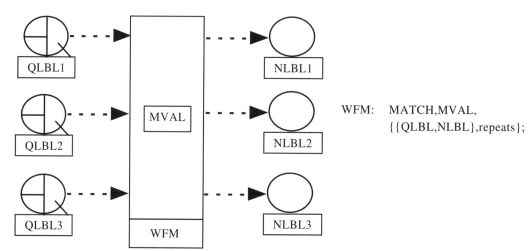

Illustrations of the use of MATCH nodes are shown below.

1. Hold entities in files 1 and 2 at QUEUE nodes TYP1 and TYP2, until there is an entity in each QUEUE node that has an attribute 3 value that is the same. Route both entities to ACCUMULATE node MAA and save the attribute set of the entity whose attribute 2 value is the largest.

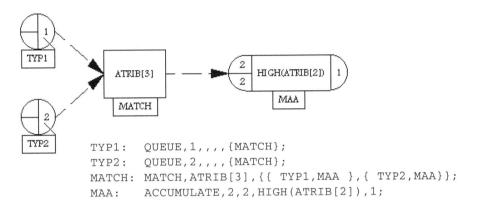

```
TYP1:   QUEUE,1,,,,{MATCH};
TYP2:   QUEUE,2,,,,{MATCH};
MATCH:  MATCH,ATRIB[3],{{ TYP1,MAA },{ TYP2,MAA}};
MAA:    ACCUMULATE,2,2,HIGH(ATRIB[2]),1;
```

This model segment could be used to represent an aircraft and crew where only a particular crew can be used with a given aircraft.

2. Hold a patient entity until his health records arrive. Route the patient to the queue before the doctor's office when both the patient and his records are available. Destroy the record entity. Patient identification is maintained as integer attribute 1.

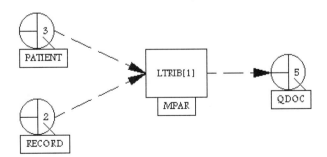

6.10 ILLUSTRATION 6-2. A MAIL ORDER CLOTHES MANUFACTURER

A clothes manufacturer supplies shirts and pants to a centralized distributor. The time to produce one dozen shirts is triangularly distributed with a minimum value of 11, maximum value of 22 and a modal value of 16. The time to produce one dozen pair of pants is also triangularly distributed with a minimum of 11, maximum of 22 and a most likely value of 19. After manufacturing the garments, they are transported by carts to packaging and the time for this transport is 7 minutes.

The time between the receipt of orders from the distributor is exponentially distributed with a mean of 30. Each order is made up of a combination of shirts and pants. From past purchases, the size of an order in terms of the number of dozen of pants and shirts is randomly distributed. The probability that an order is for 1, 2, 3, or 4 dozen of a product (either shirts or pants) is 0.6, 0.2, 0.15, and 0.05, respectively. Orders are filled as quickly as possible. When an order is filled, it is routed by a cart to a loading dock where it is packaged with other orders in a crate. A crate has a capacity of 112 cubic feet. Shirts are packaged in an 8 foot cubic box and pants in a 12 foot cubic box. A crate is considered loaded as soon as 100 cubic feet of its space or more has been filled. An evaluation of this rule is desired.

In order to buy insurance on the merchandise in a shipment, the dollar value of a crate and the number of crates shipped per week are desired. The dollar value for a dozen shirts is $60 and for a dozen pants is $102. Statistics are desired over five 8 hour days on the average time between the filling of a crate and the dollar value of the goods in a crate.

The Visual SLAM network model of the mail order clothes manufacturer is shown in Figure 6-13. In this model, clothes are manufactured throughout the day. In Figure 6-13, production of shirts and pants is modeled by two CREATE nodes with the time between creation as the production time for a dozen of the product. Each CREATE node is followed by an activity whose duration is 7 minutes representing the transport time. At QUEUE node Q2, entities representing a dozen shirts are stored in file 2. At QUEUE node Q4, entities representing a dozen pants are stored. These queues represent the inventory of shirts and pants.

When an order arrives, an entity representing a demand for one dozen shirts is placed in QUEUE node Q1. SELECT node ASM1 is used to assemble an order for a dozen shirts with an entity in node Q2 representing an inventory of a dozen shirts. The attributes of the order for a dozen shirts are saved by specifying that the entity with a high value of attribute 5 specifies which of the entity's attributes are to be saved.

The new entity is routed to BATCH node BAT1 where the entities are batched until the number of dozen of shirts in an order is reached. This counting of entities is modeled by specifying ATRIB[3] as the threshold value and not specifying an attribute defining an amount to batch toward the threshold value.

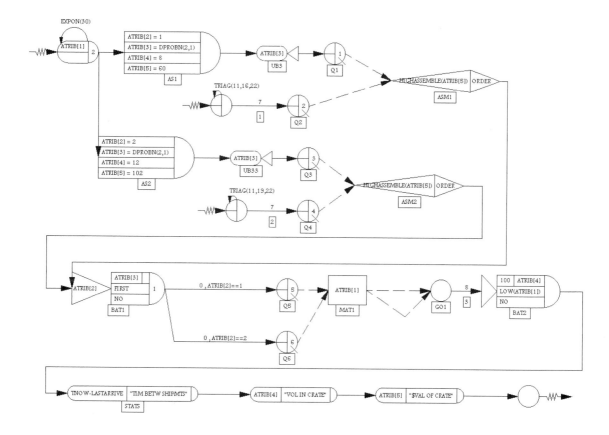

Figure 6-13 Network model of a mail order clothes manufacturer.

At ASSIGN node AS1, ATRIB[3] is assigned a value which represents the number of dozens of shirts requested on an order. Also assigned at node AS1 is a value of I to ATRIB[2] to indicate the product type (shirts), a value of 8 to ATRIB[4] which is the volume of a shirt box, and a value of $60 to ATRIB[5] which is the value of 1 dozen shirts. To summarize, the definitions of the attributes are given below:

Attribute	Definitions
1	Mark time of a receipt of an order.

2	Product type:	1 for shirts
		2 for pants
3	The number of dozens of product in the order.	
4	Volume of the product box.	
5	The value of the product.	

The receipt of an order for products is generated at a CREATE node with an exponentially distributed time between creations with a mean of 30. Attribute 1 is marked at the CREATE node and an M value of 2 is prescribed. This splits the order into a shirt entity and a pants entity. The shirt entity is sent to ASSIGN node AS1 and the pants entity is sent to ASSIGN node AS2. We will describe the routing of the shirts entity. From the ASSIGN node AS1, it is routed to an UNBATCH node where the entity is split into entities in accordance with the value of attribute 3. If four dozen shirts were requested on the order, the entity is split into four entities each of which is routed to QUEUE node Q1. A similar network section models the processing of an order entity for pants.

After a shirt order is assembled with shirts from inventory, the entity is routed to BATCH node BAT1 where shirt entities are combined into an entity representing all the shirts on a particular order. This is accomplished by batching on attribute 2 until a threshold defined by ATRIB[3] is reached. ATRIB[3] of the first entity of a new batch provides the number of dozens of shirts in the order. The save criterion specifies that the attributes of the batched entity are to be those of the first arriving entity except for attributes 4 and 5 whose values are the sum of these attributes of all entities included in the batch. This causes attribute 4 of the batched entity to be the sum of the volumes of the boxes and attribute 5 to be the dollar value of the product for the order.

When a batched entity representing the shirts for an order has been created, it is routed to QUEUE node Q5. Similarly, a batched entity representing the pants for the order is routed to QUEUE node Q6. MATCH node MAT1 causes the entities to wait until both the batched pants entity and the batched shirts entity from the same order are in the appropriate QUEUE nodes. When this occurs, they are both routed to GOON node GO1 and, after a transportation delay of eight minutes, are sent to BATCH node BAT2 where they are put into a crate. The batching continues until the volume attribute, ATRIB[4], exceeds the crate threshold of 100. In this way, a batched entity with the attributes of the entity with the lowest mark time is created. The value of all products in the crate is given by attribute 5 and the volume of all boxes by attribute 4. Statistics are then collected at three sequential COLCT nodes on the time between shipments, the dollar value of a crate, and the volume of boxes that have been put in a crate.

This model illustrates the use of the different types of Visual SLAM decision and logic nodes. A statement model corresponding to the network model of Figure 6-13 is shown in Figure 6-14.

```
GEN,"VASEK","CLOTHES MANUFACTURER",1/1/96;
LIMITS,1,1,,6;
;DEFINE PROBABILISTIC ASSIGNMENT OF NUMBER OF DOZENS IN EACH ORDER
ARRAY,1,4,{1,2,3,4};
ARRAY,2,4,{.6,.8,.95,1.};
NETWORK;
      CREATE,EXPON(30),0.0,ATRIB[1]2; CREATE ORDERS
      ACTIVITY,,,,"AS1";
      ACTIVITY,,,,"AS2";
AS1:  ASSIGN,{{ATRIB[1],TNOW},{ATRIB[2],1},
             {ATRIB[3],DPROBN(2,1)},{ATRIB[4],8},{ATRIB[5],60}};
      UNBATCH,ATRIB[3];
Q1:   QUEUE,1,0,,,{ASM1};
         CREATE,TRIAG(11,16,22),0.0; MANUFACTURE SHIRTS
           ACTIVITY,1,7;
Q2:   QUEUE,2,0,,,{ASM1};
ASM1: SELECT,HIGHASSEMBLE(ATRIB[5]),,,{Q1,Q2};
         ACTIVITY,,,,"BAT1";
AS2:  ASSIGN,{{ATRIB[1],TNOW},{ATRIB[2],2},
             {ATRIB[3],DPROBN(2,1)},{ATRIB[4],12},{ATRIB[5],102}};
      UNBATCH,ATRIB[3];
Q3:   QUEUE,3,0,,,{ASM2};
         CREATE,TRIAG(11,19,22),0.0; MANUFACTURE PANTS
           ACTIVITY,2,7;
Q4:   QUEUE,4,0,,,{ASM2};
ASM2: SELECT,ASSEMBLE,,,{Q3,Q4};
         ACTIVITY,,,,"BAT1";
BAT1: BATCH,ATRIB[2],ATRIB[3],1,FIRST,{ATRIB[4],ATRIB[5]};
         ACTIVITY,,,ATRIB[2]==1;
         ACTIVITY,,,ATRIB[2]==2,"Q6";
Q5:   QUEUE,5,0,,,{MAT1};
Q6:   QUEUE,6,0,,,{MAT1};
;
; MATCH THE SHIRT AND PANTS ON ORDER NUMBER
;
MAT1: MATCH,ATRIB[1],{{ Q5,GO1 },{ Q6,GO1 }};
GO1:  GOON;
         ACTIVITY,3,8;
;
; BATCH THE SHIRTS AND PANTS INTO A CRATE ENTITY
;
BAT2: BATCH,0,100,ATRIB[4],LOW(ATRIB[1]),{ATRIB[4],ATRIB[5]};
         COLCT,,TNOW-LASTARRIVE,"TIM BET SHIPMENTS",0,0.0,1.0;
         COLCT,,ATRIB[4],"VOL. IN CRATE",0,0.0,1.0;
         COLCT,,ATRIB[5],"$VALUE OF CRATE",0,0.0,1.0;
         TERMINATE;
         END;
INITIALIZE,0,2400;
FIN;
```

Figure 6-14 Statement model of a mail order clothes manufacturer.

6.11 SUMMARY OF SYMBOLS AND STATEMENTS

Table 6-5 presents the logic and decision nodes of Visual SLAM. The decision and logic nodes are used in conjunction with activities to model the grouping and control of entities. The SELECT node performs a decision function which routes entities to queues, from queues and to non-identical servers based on heuristic rules.

Table 6-5 Logic and decision nodes of Visual SLAM networks.

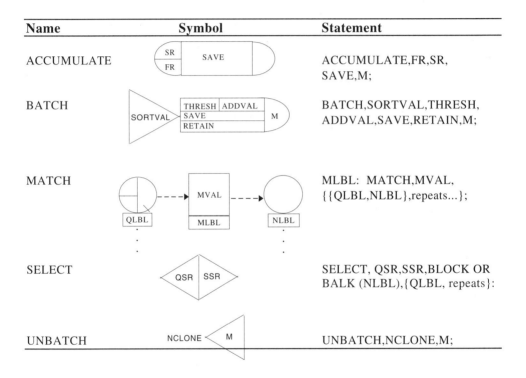

Name	Symbol	Statement
ACCUMULATE		ACCUMULATE,FR,SR, SAVE,M;
BATCH		BATCH,SORTVAL,THRESH, ADDVAL,SAVE,RETAIN,M;
MATCH		MLBL: MATCH,MVAL, {{QLBL,NLBL},repeats...};
SELECT		SELECT, QSR,SSR,BLOCK OR BALK (NLBL),{QLBL, repeats}:
UNBATCH		UNBATCH,NCLONE,M;

6.12 EXERCISES

6-1. In Visual SLAM, there are many ways to halt the flow of an entity through a network. Describe the node type or procedures you would use to stop and start the flow of an entity in each of the following situations:

a)   An entity called dinner cannot be served until the steak, potatoes, and salad are prepared.

b)   An entity called steak cannot be inserted into the oven until five minutes after the oven is turned on.

c)   The dessert, apple pie and ice cream, cannot be served until four people have completed eating.

d)   One of the diners requires that the steak be medium rare and that the salad dressing be blue cheese.

e)   The eating-of-dinner activity is not started until wine is poured for all diners.

6-2.   At a drive-in bank where there is only one teller, there is space for five waiting cars. If a customer arrives when the waiting line is full, the customer drives around the block and tries to join the waiting line again. The interarrival time between customer arrivals is exponentially distributed with a mean of 10. The time to drive around the block is normally distributed with a mean of 2 and a standard deviation of 0.5. The teller service time is uniformly distributed between and 6 and 12. When a customer arrives and can join the queue, it takes a negligible amount of time to become a member of the queue. Initially, no customers are waiting to be served and the teller is idle. Draw the Visual SLAM network associated with this situation which collects statistics on the customer's time in the queue, time in the system, and time between balks.

Embellishment: For this banking situation, cars depart from the teller into a street. The amount of time for a car to find a gap large enough to depart into the street is exponentially distributed with a mean of 3. The design of the drive-in bank parking lot only allows five cars to be waiting to enter the street. Modify your network to include this new feature.

6-3.   A server is stationed by a conveyor belt and the server can take items off the conveyor belt only if he is idle. Items arrive to the conveyor belt with the time between arrivals a constant 10 time units. Once the item is placed on the conveyor belt, it takes three time units for it to reach the service station. If the server is busy, the item continues on the conveyor belt and returns to the server in 9 time units. Service for the item is exponentially distributed with a mean of 2.5. When the server finishes working on an item, he places it on a second conveyor belt to be processed by a second server. The item spends five time units on the second conveyor belt before arriving at the second server. If the second server is busy, the item stays on the second conveyor belt for 12 time units before it is returned to the second server. The service time of the second server is normally distributed with a mean of 2.0 and a standard deviation of 1. After being served by the second server, the item departs the system. Draw a Visual SLAM network of this situation that collects information on the amount of time an item spends in the system and the number of items on each conveyor belt.

6-4.   Convert a PERT network with which you are familiar into a Visual SLAM network representation. For this Visual SLAM network, presume that there is a probability that some activities in the network will fail which would cause project failure. Redraw the Visual SLAM network to represent this situation.

6-5. Describe how an ACCUMULATE node of a Visual SLAM network can be used to represent the following logic operations: all preceding activities must be completed before successor activities can be started; any one of the preceding activities must be completed before the activity can be started; and three out of five of the preceding activities must be completed before the activity can be started (or, in general, a majority voting type of logic).

6-6. At an airline terminal, five ticket agents are employed and current practice is to allow queues to form before each agent. Time between arrivals to the agents is exponentially distributed with a mean of 5 minutes. Customers join the shortest queue at the time of their arrival. The service time for the ticket agents is uniformly distributed between 0.5 and 1.5 minutes. The queues of the ticket agents are not allowed to exceed two customers each. If the queues of all ticket agents are full, the customer goes directly to his gate to be served by a flight attendant. Develop the Visual SLAM network from which the total time a customer spends at the ticket agent windows, the utilization of the ticket agents, and the number of customers per minute that cannot gain service from the ticket agents can be determined.

Embellishments: (a) The airline has decided to change the procedures involved in processing customers by the ticket agents. A single line is formed and the customers are routed to the ticket agent that becomes free next. A tenth of a minute service time is added to the processing time of each ticket agent. Space available in the single line for waiting customers is ten. Develop the Visual SLAM network for this revised situation.

(b) It has been found that a subset of the customers purchasing tickets are taking a long period of time. By segregating ticket holders from non-ticket holders, improvements can be made in the processing of customers. To accomplish this segregation, four ticket agents are used for checking in customers and one agent is used for purchases. The time to check in a person is uniformly distributed between 0.2 and 1 minute and the time to purchase a ticket is exponentially distributed with a mean of 5 minutes. Assuming that 15 percent of the customers will be purchasing tickets, develop the Visual SLAM network for this situation. The time between all customer arrivals is exponentially distributed with a mean of 5 minutes.

6-7. For the model of a Mail Order Clothes Manufacturer given in Illustration 6-2, revise the model to include size as part of the order. For shirts, 30% are for size 15; 50% are for size 16; and 20% are for size 17. In addition, pants come in sizes 30, 32, 34 and 36. The probabilities of an order being for these sizes are 0.10, 0.20, 0.40, and 0. 30, respectively. Determine a production schedule or procedure for producing shirts and pants considering that it takes 2 minutes to setup to change to a new size. Establish an objective for determining a good production schedule.

6-8. In the model of Illustration 6-2 of the Mail Order Clothes Manufacturer, show how resources can be used to represent the production of shirts and pants to avoid the splitting of an order into entities representing 1 dozen units of product.

6-9. There are three stations on an assembly line and the service time at each station is exponentially distributed with a mean of 10. Items flow down the assembly line from server 1 to server 2 to server 3. A new unit is provided to server 1 every 15 time units. If any server has not completed processing its current unit within 15 minutes, the unit is diverted to one of two off-line servers who complete the remaining operations on the job diverted from the assembly line. One time unit is added to the remaining time of the operation that was not completed. Any following operations not performed are done so by the off-line servers in an exponentially distributed time with a mean of 16. Draw the Visual SLAM network to obtain statistics on the utilization of all servers, and the fraction of items diverted from each operation.

Embellishments: (a) Assume the assembly line is paced and that the movement of units can only occur at multiples of 15 minutes. (b) Allow one unit to be stored between each assembly line server. (c) If a server is available, route units back to the assembly line from the off-line servers.

6-10. Simulate the activities of the PERT network described below 400 times. Compute statistics and prepare a histogram on the time to reach each node of the network. Compare the results with the PERT calculations for the network.

Embellishment: (a) Based on the Visual SLAM simulation of a PERT network, develop a schedule of early start times and late start times for the activities in the network.

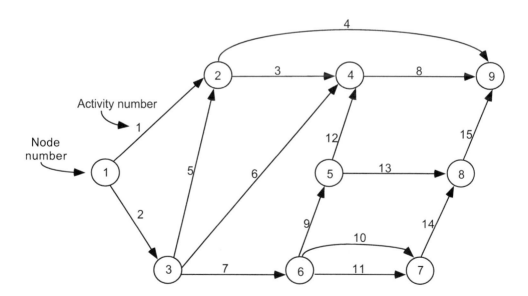

Activity Number	Start Node	End Node	Distribution Type	Mean	Variance
1	1	2	Lognormal	10	4.00
2	1	3	Exponential	6	36.00
3	2	4	Uniform	7	3.00
4	2	9	Gamma	14	21.00
5	3	2	Exponential	3	9.00
6	3	4	Uniform	13	5.33
7	3	6	Normal	5	1.00
8	4	9	Erlang	8	32.00
9	6	5	Constant	7	0.00
10	6	7	Normal	4	2.16
11	6	7	Normal	4	3.00
12	5	4	Normal	2	1.20
13	5	8	Normal	6	10.40
14	7	8	Normal	8	26.40
15	8	9	Normal	5	2.00

6-11. Consider a banking system involving two inside tellers and two drive-in tellers. Arrivals to the banking system are either for the drive-in tellers or for the inside tellers. The time between arrivals to the drive-in tellers is exponentially distributed with a mean of 0.75 minutes. The drive-in tellers have limited waiting space. Queueing space is available for only three cars waiting for the first teller and four cars waiting for the second teller. The first drive-in teller service time is normally distributed with a mean of 0.5 minutes and standard deviation of 0.25 minutes. The second drive-in teller service time is uniformly distributed between 0.2 and 1.0 minutes. If a car arrives when the queues of both drive-in tellers are full, the customer balks and seeks service from one of the inside bank tellers. However, the inside bank system opens one hour after the drive-in bank. Customers who directly seek the services of the inside tellers arrive through a different arrival process with the time between arrivals exponentially distributed with a mean of 0.5 minutes. However, they join the same queue as the balkers from the drive-in portion. A single queue is used for both inside tellers. A maximum of seven customers can wait in this single queue. Customers who arrive when there are seven in the inside queue balk and do not seek banking service. The service times for the two inside tellers are triangularly distributed between 0.1 and 1.2 minutes with a mode of 0.4 minutes. Simulate the operation of the bank for an 8 hour period.

6-12. Modify the bank teller operations described in Exercise 6-11 to model a credit inquiry on selected non-drive-in bank customers. A credit inquiry is performed by the bank manager on new customers. Ten percent of the non-drive-in customers are in this category. The bank manager obtains the necessary information on the customer and initiates the inquiry which takes between 2 and 5 minutes, uniformly distributed. The time for a credit inquiry is exponentially distributed with a mean of 5 minutes during which time the customer waits in a separate room. The manager processes other customers during the time the credit inquiry is being performed, and there is no limit to the number of simultaneous credit inquiries that can be done. When the credit inquiry is completed, the customer for which the credit inquiry was made is served again by the manager and is given preference over customers who have not seen the manager. The manager completes any information gathering task before he issues the credit inquiry which takes 1 minute. Five percent of the credit inquiries result in a negative response and the customer is not routed to the tellers. The time to give a negative response is exponential with a mean of 10 minutes. Embellishment: Model the manager in the case where the rule is that two inquiries are made for each customer requiring an inquiry. Each inquiry has a 0.05 negative response probability.

6-13. Kits consist of two parts, Part A and Part B. A kit arrives to a cleaning and assembly station every 10 minutes. The station attempts to process each kit in 60 minutes. Functions of the station are to disassemble the kit into its two parts which takes eight minutes on the average and is exponentially distributed. Each part is then sent to a cleaning station. The time to clean Part A is normally distributed with a mean of 12 and a standard deviation of 2. There is only one cleaning machine for Part A. The time to clean Part B is uniformly distributed between 20 and 28 minutes and there are two cleaning machines for Part B. Inspection and assembly are done at the same time. There are two expert assemblers and one trainee. From past analysis it is known that Part B holds up the reassembling of the kit, and a procedure that specifies that if Part type B is within 10 minutes of the due date it should be assembled by one of the expert assemblers. When a choice exists between an expert assembler and the trainee, the expert assembler is used. The time to perform the assembly operation is triangularly distributed for the most expert of the assemblers with a modal value of 25 minutes, minimum of 16 minutes and a maximum of 40 minutes. The second expert assembler takes 1.1 times the time of the first expert assembler. When a choice exists, the faster assembler is used. The trainee assembler takes 1.25 of the time of the most expert assembler. Assume that Part A and Part B do not have to be reassembled from the same kit in which they arrived.

Embellishment: Change the model to require that each Part A is assembled with the Part B of the kit from which they were disassembled.

6-14. An indexed rotary table serves eight machining centers. A part enters the table for Operation 1, then is rotated in turn through all eight operations before being unloaded. The table can rotate only when all eight machines have finished their current operation. Suppose that processing time on each machine is uniformly distributed between 3 and 6 minutes, and that indexing (rotation) takes one minute. Model the rotary table to determine the utilization of each machine center in a 50-part production run. Estimate the length of the production run. Assume that the simulation starts at time 8 minutes with each machine center ready to work on an operation.

Embellishment: Build two different models of the rotary table.

6-15. Develop a 99.7 percent confidence interval for the project completion time in the PERT model, Example 6-1. Compute an interval such that with 90 percent confidence at least 80 percent of the population of average completion times are in the interval.

6.13 REFERENCES

1. Archibald, R.D. and R.L. Villoria, *Network-Based Management Systems (PERT/CPM),* John Wiley, 1968.

2. MacCrimmon, K.R. and C.A. Ryavec, "An Analytical Study of the PERT Assumptions," *Operations Research* , Vol. 12, 1964, pp. 16-38.

3. Moder, J.J. and C.R. Phillips, *Project Management with CPM and PERT,* Second Edition, Van Nostrand-Reinhold, 1970.

4. Pritsker, A.A.B., *Introduction to Simulation and SLAM II,* Fourth Edition, Systems Publishing and John Wiley, 1995.

5. Pritsker, A.A.B., *Modeling and Analysis Using Q-Gert Networks,* Second Edition, Halsted Press and Pritsker & Associates, 1979.

6. Weist, J. and F. Levy, *Management Guide to PERT-CPM,* Prentice-Hall, 1969.

7. Wilson, J.R., "Statistical Aspects of Simulation," Proceedings, IFORS, 1984, pp. 825-841.

CHAPTER 7

Interface, Find and Subnetwork Nodes

7.1   INTRODUCTION

Modern day computing involves the integration of computers, software programs and models. This chapter presents Visual SLAM's capabilities to read inputs from files, spreadsheets and databases and to write outputs to files. An interface to allow entities to be passed into a network model from discrete-event and continuous models is the ENTER node. The passing of an entity from the network to discrete event code is accomplished through the use of an EVENT node. The searching of a network file and the capability to change the attributes of entities in the file or to remove entities from the file is accomplished through the FINDAR node. The monitoring of Visual SLAM values computed from expressions to detect crossings of threshold values is accomplished at DETECT nodes. The crossing of a threshold causes an entity to be created at the DETECT node from which it is routed into the network. Hierarchical network models are built through the use of Visual SLAM subnetworks which route entities from a calling network to a subnetwork. The calling network can be the main network or a subnetwork.

The network capabilities presented in this chapter build on the Visual SLAM network nodes and activities previously presented. The READ, WRITE, and FINDAR nodes are typically used to perform a function not necessarily related to the arriving entity. In such situations, entities representing messages are routed to these nodes. In some cases, the entities that model system elements such as parts, transactions and customers are used to represent both the message and the system element. The ENTER and EVENT nodes represent interface nodes to alternate modeling perspectives. Descriptions of the use of the ENTER and EVENT nodes are given in Chapter 9 where the details of augmenting network models with user code is presented. The DETECT node is used to monitor Visual SLAM values and to detect the occurrence of state events. When a state event is detected, an entity representing the occurrence of the event is entered into the network.

Visual SLAM subnetworks are used for the following purposes: to reuse network sections in different locations within a large network model; to build a network section for use by other modelers; and to provide an object-oriented network capability. A Visual SLAM subnetwork is an object class with each subnetwork being an instance of the object class, that is, an object. For example, the processing of parts at different machines that perform similarly can be modeled as a subnetwork. Each use of the subnetwork for a different machine defines an instance of the subnetwork with the specific machine model defined by Visual SLAM elements and by parameters defining the subnetwork instance. A CALLVSN node is used to define an instance of the subnetwork and to pass parameters into the subnetwork object. Within the subnetwork, each entity may have additional attributes in addition to its standard attributes. Furthermore, local variables that pertain to each subnetwork instance are made available.

The control statements that define the characteristics for a network are also used to define characteristics for a subnetwork. An entity may enter a subnetwork at different locations which are defined as ENTERVSN nodes. RETURNVSN nodes are used to return an entity to its calling network. At the RETURNVSN node, a return value ERETURN can be assigned as an entity attribute and an exit number can be used to prescribe a routing in the calling network. The concept of a subnetwork within Visual SLAM is a graphical version of a procedure in C or a method in Visual Basic. Based on its graphic portrayal, it is referred to as a visual subnetwork and abbreviated VSN.

7.2   READ NODE

The READ node is used to read one or more values from an external file. The options available for the format code are given in Table 7-1. The format is defined as is done for the C function scanf where the general format specifier with optional items between brackets is %[width][.][precision]format-code or \code. If the format is not specified, the READ node uses a space delimited standard format for the variables to be read.

Table 7-1 READ and WRITE Formats

Code	Description
%c	Character
%s	String of characters
%d	Signed decimal integers
%ld	Signed long integers
%u	Unsigned integers
%f	Floating point (real)
%lf	Long floating point (double)
\b	backspace
\f	form feed
\n	newline
\r	carriage return
\t	horizontal tab

The first entity arrival to a READ node opens the file to be read. A REOPEN field, if specified as YES, will reopen the file between runs to repeat the input data for subsequent runs. A STORVAR field is used to have Visual SLAM count and return the number of values actually read in the variable specified for the STORVAR field. The symbol, statement and AweSim dialog box for the READ node are shown below.

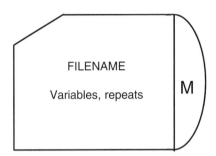

READ,"FILE",REOPEN,STORVAR,"FORMAT",{VAR,repeats},M:

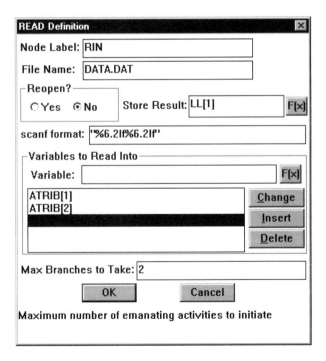

The following example is a READ node which will read the variables ATRIB[1] and ATRIB[2] from the file DATA.DAT each time an entity arrives to node RIN. The input is formatted in two columns with the width of each column being six characters and having two digits following the decimal point. The values are long floating (lf) point and the format specification is %6.2lf%6.2lf. The number of values read will be stored in the global variable LL[1]. As long as LL[1] is not zero, an entity will be sent back to read the next line as the M−number is 2.

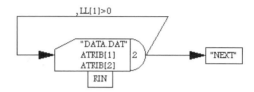

```
RIN:
    READ,"DATA.DAT",,LL[1],"%6.2lf%6.2lf",{ATRIB[1],ATRIB[2]},2;
        ACTIVITY,,,LL[1]>0,"RIN";
        ACTIVITY,,,,"NEXT";
```

7.3   WRITE NODE

The WRITE node is used to write one or more values to an external file. The format is defined as for the C function printf. The options available are given in Table 7-1. If the format is unspecified, the WRITE node uses a space-delimited format for the variables to be written. The file is created by the first arrival to the WRITE node. A FLUSH field, if specified as YES, flushes the values to be written to the disk after each release of the WRITE node. The default value is NO which waits to write the values recorded until the end of a run. This is faster, but output may be lost if there is an execution error which aborts the simulation run prematurely.

The symbol, statement and AweSim dialog box for the WRITE node are shown below.

WRITE,"FILE",FLUSH,"FORMAT",{VALUE,repeats},M ;

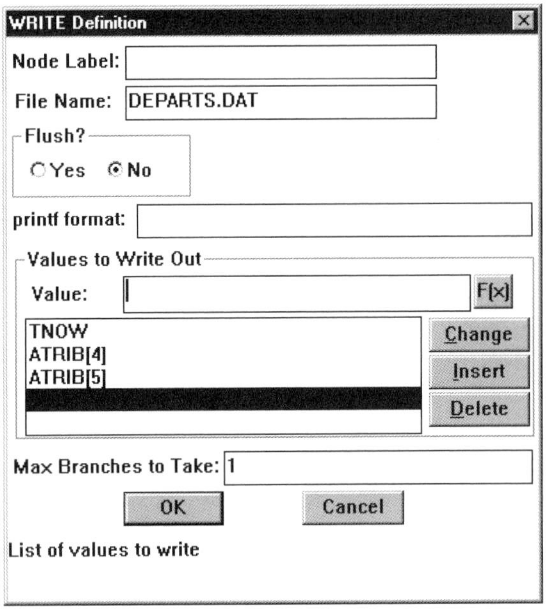
WRITE Definition
Node Label:
File Name: DEPARTS.DAT
Flush?
Yes No
printf format:
Values to Write Out
Value:
F[x]
TNOW
ATRIB[4]
ATRIB[5]
Change
Insert
Delete
Max Branches to Take: 1
OK
Cancel
List of values to write

An example of the WRITE node to create a three-column list in the file DEPARTS.DAT is given below. Each entity arrival to the WRITE node causes the variables TNOW, ATRIB[4] and ATRIB[5] to be written to the output file, DEPARTS.DAT. The default format is used which creates space-delimited columns.

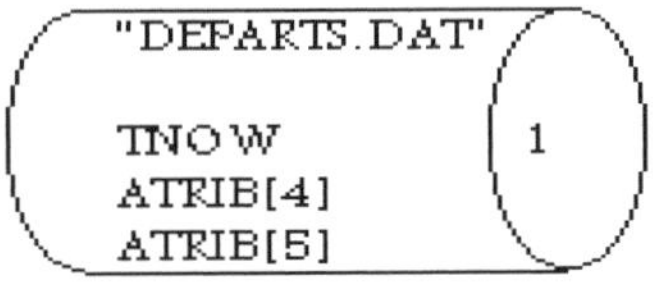
"DEPARTS.DAT"
TNOW
ATRIB[4]
ATRIB[5]
1

```
WRITE,"DEPARTS.DAT",,{TNOW,ATRIB[4],ATRIB[5]},1;
```

7.3.1   Illustration 7-1. Using the WRITE Node in Conjunction with Data Analysis

In this illustration, a single server system is analyzed using a WRITE node to obtain a table with the following 4 columns: entity number, arrival time, wait time and system time. The network that produces this table is shown in Figure 7-1. The time between arrivals of entities is exponentially distributed with a mean of 1. ATRIB[0] is set to the arrival time of the entity. The entity waits for the server in an AWAIT node. When the server is allocated to the entity, its wait time XX[0] is computed as TNOW-ATRIB[0] at an ASSIGN node. Activity 1 is used to model the service time which is exponentially distributed with a mean of 0.9. After service is completed, the server is freed and the system time is computed as XX[1]. The entity number (ENUM), arrival time (ATRIB[0]), wait time (XX[0]) and system time (XX[1]) are written to file TSE.dat using a WRITE node. The entity is then terminated from the network.

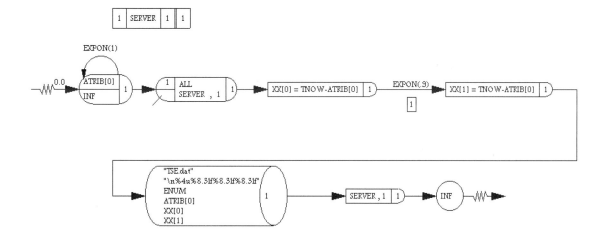

Figure 7-1 Network for recording output values.

At the WRITE node, the format \n%4u%8.3lf%8.3lf%8.3lf is used for the 4 variables. After the simulation of the network is performed, Table TSE.dat can be accessed from Excel and an Excel spreadsheet is automatically prepared by opening TSE.dat which is in the Visual SLAM project\scenario directory under the project and scenario names prescribed by the modeler. With the table as a spreadsheet, Excel functions for statistical calculations and charting can be used to analyze and display the data.

The network model was simulated for 300 time units with a PRIORITY control statement that specifies that entities wait in File 1 on a first-in/first-out (FIFO) basis. In this run, 283 entities were processed in the 300 time units. The Excel statistical function CORREL was then used to calculate the correlation coefficient between the wait time and system time for the 283 arrivals. As expected, the correlation coefficient is high, 0.979, as the wait time is part of the system time. The autocorrelation coefficient between successive wait times was then calculated in the same manner by identifying rows 1-282 of the wait time column as the first data set and rows 2-283 as the second data set for function CORREL. The autocorrelation coefficient for the one run is 0.962. Again, a high correlation is expected since the second of two entities incurs all the waiting time of the first entity since its arrival to the queue. The autocorrelation coefficient for the system time of two successive entities is 0.963.

Charts graphing the values that show these correlations were then prepared using the chart capabilities of Excel. Figure 7-2 is a scatter plot where each point is for an entity and represents its waiting time and system time. From the scatter plot, it is seen that higher values of waiting time results in higher values of system time. Figure 7-3 shows the system time for an entity plotted at its arrival time. The entity arrival times are locations on the x-axis at which a square symbol is plotted with the height of the diamond symbol representing the entity's system time. This illustration demonstrates the ease with which outputs from a Visual SLAM model can be transferred to Excel and used to analyze model behavior.

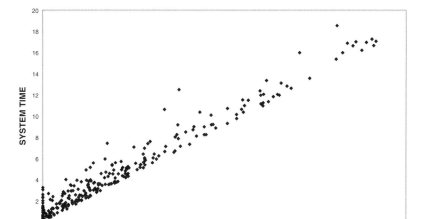

Figure 7-2 Scatter plot where each point is for an entity and represents its
waiting time and system time.

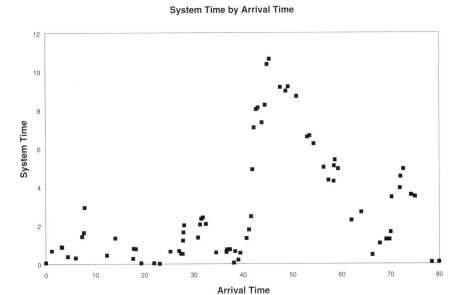

Figure 7-3 System time plotted at arrival time.

7.4   EVENT NODE

The symbol, input statement and the AweSim dialog box for the EVENT node are shown below.

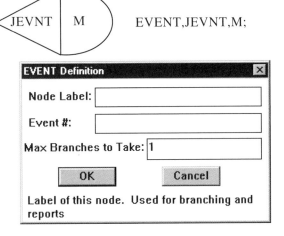

The EVENT node is included in a network model to interface the network portion of a model with event coding written by the modeler. The EVENT node causes function EVENT to be called every time an entity arrives at the EVENT node. The event #, JEVNT, specifies the event code to be executed, and M specifies the maximum number of emanating activities to be taken following the processing of the EVENT node. Since the logic associated with the EVENT node is coded by the modeler, complete modeling flexibility is obtained. Thus, if the modeler is faced with an operation for which a standard network node is not provided, the modeler can employ the EVENT node to perform the specialized logic required.

The procedure for coding an event invoked by an EVENT node is identical to the procedure for coding any C or Visual Basic function. Function EVENT maps the event code JEVNT onto the appropriate event function containing the coding for the event logic. In coding the event logic, the modeler has access to the Visual SLAM functions provided for performing commonly encountered activities such as random sampling, file manipulation, and data collection. Procedures for coding function EVENT along with examples are given in Chapter 9.

7.5   ENTER NODE

The ENTER node is provided to permit the modeler to insert selectively an entity into the network from a user-written function. The symbol, input statement and AweSim dialog box for the ENTER node are shown below.

NUM   M   ENTER,NUM,M;

ENTER Definition

Node Label: |

Enter #:

Max Branches to Take: 1

OK   Cancel

Label of this node. Used for branching and reports

Each ENTER node has a unique user-assigned Enter #, NUM, and an M –number which specifies the maximum number of emanating activities to be taken at each release of the node. The ENTER node is released following a return from a user-written ENTER function.

The statement format for the ENTER node consists of the node type ENTER followed by the numeric code NUM and the M value separated by commas. The ENTER node can be released by entity arrivals to the node as well as by calls to function ENTER which is discussed in Section 9.3.

7.6   DETECT NODE

A DETECT node is used in a network to create an entity based on system conditions. When the conditions are realized, the DETECT node is released and an entity with all attribute values equal to 0 or blank is routed from the DETECT node in accordance with the M number of the DETECT node. The symbol for the DETECT node is given below.

| VALUE | XDIR | THRESH | TOL | M |

When a DETECT node is included in the network model, it is released whenever the crossing expression, VALUE, crosses a threshold THRESH in the direction specified by XDIR. The value of TOL is used for continuous variables as described in Chapter 10.

The DETECT node is also released whenever an entity arrives to it. A maximum of M emanating activities are initiated at each release. The statement format and AweSim dialog box for the DETECT node are as follows:

DETECT, VALUE, XDIR, THRESH, TOL, M;

where

VALUE specifies the crossing variable and can be any Visual SLAM global expression;

XDIR is the crossing direction and can be specified as NEGATIVE, POSITIVE, or EITHER;

THRESH is a Visual SLAM expression representing the threshold; and

TOL is a numeric value which specifies the tolerance within which the crossing is to be detected (for continuous variables only).

```
┌─────────────────────────────────────────────────────────┐
│ DETECT Definition                                    [×] │
├─────────────────────────────────────────────────────────┤
│ Node Label: |                                            │
│                                                          │
│ Value:          [                              ]  [F(x)] │
│                                                          │
│ Threshold:      [                              ]  [F(x)] │
│                                                          │
│ Tolerance:      [INF                           ]         │
│ ┌─ Crossing Direction ──────────────────────────────┐   │
│ │   ○ Positive       ○ Negative       ⊙ Either      │   │
│ └───────────────────────────────────────────────────┘   │
│                                                          │
│ Max Branches to Take: [1                          ]      │
│         [    OK    ]        [  Cancel  ]                 │
│ Label of this node.  Used for branching and reports      │
└─────────────────────────────────────────────────────────┘
```

To illustrate the use of DETECT nodes, consider the following network where the time between arrivals to a machine is adjusted based on the number of entities waiting for processing. The top network segment begins with a CREATE node with a time between arrivals sampled from a uniform distribution with a lower limit of XX[1] and an upper limit of XX[2]. Initial values of XX[1] and XX[2] are 6 and 12 respectively. The entities created are sent to an AWAIT node where they wait in file 1 for one unit of a machine. When the number of entities in file 1 reaches 20 or more then the time between entity arrivals is increased by changing the parameters of the uniform distribution to 16 and 22. This is accomplished by first detecting the need for the change at a DETECT node as shown in the middle network. The DETECT node monitors NNQ(1) until it crosses the threshold of 20 in the positive direction. When this occurs, an entity is created and routed to an ASSIGN node to make the required changes. This entity is then terminated.

When the number in the queue becomes 5 or less, then the values of the XX variables are reestablished at their original values. This is shown in the bottom network where a DETECT node is used to monitor NNQ(1) for a crossing of the threshold 5 in the negative direction. When this occurs, an entity is sent to the ASSIGN node where XX[1] is reset to 6 and XX[2] is reset to 12. The entity created at the DETECT node is then terminated. The two DETECT nodes continue in operation throughout the entire simulation and each time that there is a crossing, the values of XX[1] and XX[2] are changed accordingly.

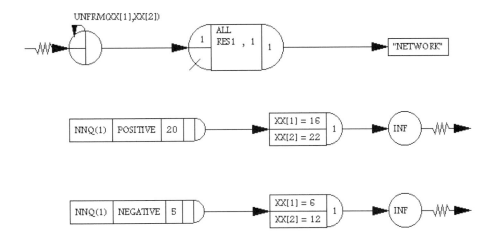

7.7   FINDAR NODE

FINDAR nodes search for an entity or entities in a FILE for which a CONDITION is satisfied. When an entity is found for which the condition is true, assignments can be made to Visual SLAM variables including the attributes of the entity found in the file except for its ranking attribute. The entity can also be removed from the file and scheduled to arrive to a labeled node (ROUTENODE) in the network. When an entity is removed and routed, the assignments specified at the FINDAR node are made to the removed entity.

The search of the file can be specified to START at any entity in the file by specifying its rank in the file. The search can be either in the forward (F) or backward (B) direction where a forward search starts with an entity closer to the beginning of the file and moves to an entity with a higher rank number. (An entity with rank 1 is the first entity in the file.) A backward search starts with an entity of higher rank number and moves to an entity with lower rank number. The number (NUMB) of entities for which the search condition is to be satisfied is also specified and, if desired, a variable can be specified to store the number of entities found (FOUND) which satisfies the condition. The symbol, statement and AweSim dialog box for the FINDAR node are shown below.

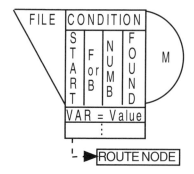

FINDAR, FILE, CONDITION, START, DIRECTION, NUMBER, ROUTENODE,
{{VAR, Value}, repeats}, MAXTAKE;

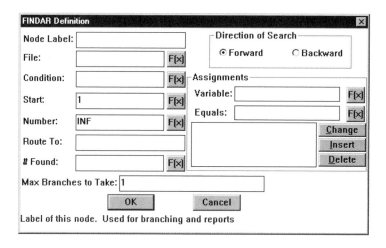

If a condition is not specified then each entity in the file will be assigned the values specified and be routed in accordance with the ROUTENODE. *Attribute references in a condition specification always reference the attributes of the entity in the file being searched not the entity arriving to the FINDAR node.* This includes ENUM, ETYPE and ERETURN attributes.

The default for the START and DIRECTION is to begin with the entity of rank 1 and move in the forward direction to the last entity in the file. The default for the NUMBER of entities to be considered for assignment and routing is to consider all entities, that is, INF. The default for the variable for storing the number of entities FOUND that meets the condition is to not record the number. The default for the ROUTENODE is not to remove the entity but only to change the attributes as specified by the assignments. Three uses of the FINDAR node are given below.

1. Find the first entity whose LTRIB[1] value exceeds 100 in file 3 by searching file 3 from the highest priority entity in the file. When an entity is found that satisfies the condition, increase its ATRIB[2] value by 20. Set the variable LL[4] to 1 if there was an entity that met the prescribed condition. The statement and node symbol to perform the above function are shown below.

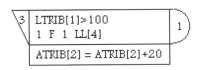

FINDAR, 3, LTRIB[1] > 100, 1, FORWARD, 1, , {ATRIB[2], ATRIB[2] + 20.}, LL[4], 1;

2. At the end of each hour, remove up to 3 customers who have waited for more than 3/4 of an hour and route them to a location to receive special processing. The customer's arrival time is maintained in ATRIB[2] and customers wait in file 1. Count the number of customers removed from file 1 who were routed for special processing. The network segment and statements for this situation are shown below.

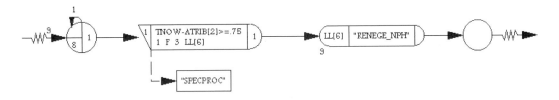

CREATE, 1, 9, , 8, 1;
FINDAR, 1, TNOW-ATRIB[2] > = .75, 1, FORWARD, 3, "SPECPROC", LL[6], 1;
COLCT, 9, LL[6], "RENEGE_NPH";
TERM;

In the above network segment, the CREATE node releases an entity for the first time at time 9 and every hour thereafter until 8 more timing entities are routed to the FINDAR node. At the FINDAR node, file 1 is searched starting with the highest ranking entity. The search continues until 3 entities are found such that the current time minus the arrival time is greater than or equal to .75 hours As soon as 3 such entities are found the search is completed. When an entity is found that has waited for more than .75 hours, it is routed to node "SPECPROC". The number of entities found is stored in the global variable LL[6]. Following the completion of the search, the timing entity is routed to a COLCT node which has a collect number of 9. The value of LL[6] is then collected with identifier "RENEGE_NPH" to provide information on the number of entities that reneged from the file per hour of operation. The timing entity is then terminated. The special processing node is not shown.

3. It is desired to empty a queue at the end of the day. The FINDAR node and its statement are shown below.

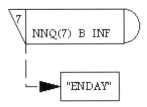

FINDAR, 7, , NNQ(7), BACKWARD, INF, "ENDAY";

This node searches file 7 starting with the last entity in the file and moves backward toward the front of the file. All entities in the file are removed as no condition is specified. Each of the entities is routed to node "ENDAY".

7.8   EXAMPLE 7-1. RENEGING FROM A QUEUE

This example models customers arriving to a queue and leaving a queue after a prescribed period of time. The time between customer arrivals is exponentially distributed with a mean of 20 minutes. The service time for customers is uniformly distributed between 15 and 25 minutes. Customers will only wait for service if the waiting time is less than a renege time which is lognormally distributed with a mean of 10 minutes and a standard deviation of 2 minutes. It is desired to estimate the time in the system for those customers served, the percent of customers that renege and the length of the waiting line.

Concepts Illustrated. The use of the FINDAR node to locate an entity in a queue is illustrated. The Visual SLAM procedure for assigning entity numbers, ENUM, as an attribute of an entity is described.

Visual SLAM Model. The network model is shown in Figure 7-4. Customer entities arrive to the system with the time between arrivals being exponentially distributed with a mean of 20. LTRIB[0] is assigned the entity number given to the entity by Visual SLAM. The entity and a clone of the entity are sent to QUEUE node RQ and to ASSIGN node REAS. The entity sent to the QUEUE node retains the entity number assigned by Visual SLAM. The entity sent to node REAS is given the next entity number which in this case is ENUM + 1 since no new entities were created during the interval of time until the clone was made.

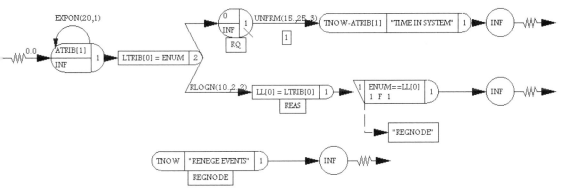

Figure 7-11 Visual SLAM network model of customers arriving and reneging from a queue

The determination of which entity receives the new entity number is based on the location of the activity in the network. The first activity taken retains the entity number of the originally created entity. At this point, the two entities are moving through the model in a competitive fashion. If the entity routed to the QUEUE node is still in the queue when the clone entity reaches the FINDAR node with label FENTR, then the queue will be searched for the entity and removed and routed to COLCT node REGNODE as specified by the FINDAR node. If the entity starts service and is out of QUEUE node RQ, then the FINDAR node will not be able to find the entity in the queue and no further action is taken.

If the entity does not renege, it is served at activity 1 and statistics are collected on its time in the system at a COLCT node. At the FINDAR node, a search is made of file 1 for an entity whose ENUM attribute is equal to LL[0]. LL[0] is assigned the value of LTRIB[0] of the cloned entity prior to its arrival to the FINDAR node. This is necessary because the condition statement of the FINDAR node always references attribute values of entities for which the search is being performed, that is, entities residing in the file of the QUEUE node. If an entity is found with the appropriate entity number, ENUM, the entity is removed from file 1 and routed to node REGNODE where the time to renege is calculated.

Summary of Results. The summary report for this example is shown in Figure 7-5. The model was run for 10,000 time units during which time 205 out of 535 entities reneged. Over 40% of the arriving customers leave the queue because the mean time to renege is small compared to the service time, that is, the mean time to renege is 10 time units and the mean service time is 20 time units. This is reflected in the 54% utilization of activity 2, the low average length of entities in the queue, 0.28, and the low average waiting time in the queue, 5.26 minutes. In such a system, it is usually necessary to try to change the characteristics of the customer in order to improve system performance. Examples of ways to change customer behavior are to install a television set to keep the customers busy while waiting and to display which customer is next if the customers are not in an organized line.

In this example the mean time between arrivals is equal to the mean service time. This would normally produce an unstable system. However when customers renege, the effective arrival rate is reduced by customers leaving the system and the arrival rate of those customers served is decreased.

```
              ** AweSim SUMMARY REPORT **

   Simulation Project : RENEGING
   Modeler : PRITSKER
   Date : 9/5/1996
   Scenario : EX71

   Run number 1 of 1
   Current simulation time    : 10000.000000
   Statistics cleared at time : 0.000000

         ** OBSERVED STATISTICS REPORT for scenario EX71 **

   Label              Mean      Standard   Number of   Minimum    Maximum
                      Value     Deviation  Observations Value      Value

   TIME IN SYSTEM   22.257      4.950          330      15.026     37.114
   RENEGE EVENT   4956.079   3090.969          205      55.098   9943.896

            ** FILE STATISTICS REPORT for scenario EX71 **

   File    Label of     Average  Standard  Maximum  Current  Average
   Number Input Location Length  Deviation  Length  Length  Wait Time
   1    QUEUE  RQ        0.282    0.592      6        0       5.257
   0    Event Calendar   3.189    1.067      9        4      19.671

          ** ACTIVITY STATISTICS REPORT for scenario EX71 **

   Activity Label   Average    Standard  Entity  Maximum     Current
   Number           Utilization Deviation Count Utilization Utilization

   2  Renege Time  0.536       0.734      535       6           1

         ** SERVICE ACTIVITY STATISTICS REPORT for scenario EX71 **

   Activity       Label      Server    Entity    Average    Standard
    Number                   Capacity  Count   Utilization Deviation

      1   Service Time         1        330      0.653       0.476

   Activity   Current    Average    Maximum     Maximum
    Number   Utilization Blockage   Idle Time   Busy Time
                                    or Servers  or Servers

      1          1       0.000      94.789      155.274
```

Figure 7-5 Summary Report for Visual SLAM model of customers arriving and
reneging from a queue.

7.9   VISUAL SUBNETWORKS

In Visual SLAM, a subnetwork consists of Visual SLAM network nodes and branches. The subnetwork is an object within Visual SLAM with each instance of the object maintaining its own set of subnetwork variables, entity attributes, parameters and control statements. In addition, all information prescribed for the main network (for which there can only be one) is accessible within the subnetwork Because of the object nature of a subnetwork, it is referred to as a visual subnetwork or VSN. Before describing the syntax and semantics associated with VSNs, a brief overview of the procedures for using VSNs within Visual SLAM is given.

To invoke a VSN, an entity is routed to a CALLVSN node in the calling network. At the CALLVSN node, the VSN is identified by name and the instance for which the VSN is to be invoked is prescribed. VSNs may have multiple enter and exit locations which are specified at the CALLVSN node. A list of parameters used in the subnetwork are also specified and passed to the VSN. Table 7-2 provides a list of Visual SLAM network elements and locations which can be represented by parameters. In general, parameters are allowed throughout the subnetwork where expressions may be specified for variables and values. The CALLVSN node can be in the main network or in a VSN.

Table 7-2 List of Eligible Locations for Parameter Specification to a VSN

Network Element	Parameter Specification Permitted
RESOURCE Block	Resource Capacity (CAP)
ACTIVITY	Activity time (Duration)
	Probability (PROB)
	Condition (variables or values in COND)
ALTER Node	Capacity Change (CC)
ASSIGN Node	Variables (VAR)
	Values (VALUE)
AWAIT Node	File number (IFL)
	Number of Resource Units Requested (UR)
FREE Node	Number of Units to FREE (UF)
PREEMPT Node	File (IFL)
	Priority Attribute (PR)
	Time Remaining Attribute (NATR)
QUEUE Node	File Number (IFL)
TERMINATE Node	Termination Count (TC)

The VSN is built in the same manner as a Visual SLAM network. The entity that invokes the VSN by arriving to a CALLVSN node is passed to the VSN at an ENTERVSN node which is identified in the CALLVSN specification. The entity then proceeds to move through the subnetwork in the same manner as it would through any Visual SLAM set of nodes and branches. The attributes of the entity are directly accessible within the subnetwork as are resources, files and other information that is prescribed in the main network. In addition, local attributes and variables are defined for the subnetwork through a LIMITSVSN control statement. Other control statements that can be specified for a subnetwork are: EQUIVALENCE, INTLC, MONTR, PRIORITY, RECORD, SEEDS, SEVNT, TIMST and DOCOLCT. These control statements have the same form as the control statements for the main Visual SLAM network.

The first time a VSN is called for a particular instance, the control statements are interpreted for that instance, for example, the values on the LIMITVSN statement and initial conditions prescribed on the INTLC statement. Also established at the first call to a VSN are specifications for RESOURCE or GATE BLOCKS defined by subnetwork parameters. For example, a RESOURCE capacity or a RESOURCE file number. In object terminology, this is referred to as "instantiation".

At each call to the VSN, the INSTANCE name identifies the resources, groups and gates to be used to process the entity arriving to the VSN. For example, if there is a resource defined for a VSN with the name COMPUTER and the CALLVSN node has specified an instance named "CPU1", then wherever the name COMPUTER appears in the VSN, the resource CPU1 will be used. If, at another CALLVSN node, the instance name is prescribed as "CPU2", then the resource name COMPUTER will be interpreted as resource CPU2. The VSN should be viewed as a separate subnetwork for each call with a different instance name. The instance specifies the file numbers at AWAIT, QUEUE and PREEMPT nodes; ACTIVITY numbers; and COLCT node numbers. Thus, when a call is made with instance name CPU1, the file numbers are technically CPU1:1, and CPU1:2; activity numbers are CPU1:1, CPU1:2 and so on. When the VSN is called with instance name CPU2, then the file numbers become CPU2:1, and CPU2:2 and so on. This object oriented view of subnetworks provides a powerful capability to use subnetworks in different locations within a model and to employ the same subnetwork for different resources, gates, files, activities and data collections. The observations and statistics for network elements in a VSN are stored in the AweSim database. Statistical reports for each instance of the VSN are included with a summary report.

In building a VSN, two new node types, ENTERVSN and RETURNVSN, are used and an ENDVSN statement is employed to indicate the end of the statements for a VSN.

7.9.1 VSN Block

The VSN block indicates the beginning of a VSN, identifies the name of the VSN, and the types, names and descriptions of all parameters used in the VSN. The symbol, syntax and dialog box for the VSN BLOCK are shown below:

VSNNAME		PNAME, PTYPE, PDESC	repeats …

VSN, VSNNAME,{ {PNAME, PTYPE, PDESC}, repeats};

VSNNAME	Name of the VSN (string). Required.
PNAME	Name for parameter. Used throughout the VSN for the parameter value. Default is PP[I] where I is determined by input order.
PTYPE	Type of parameter expected (longval, longref, doubleval, doubleref, stringval, stringref). Required.
PDESC	Description of parameter(string). Optional.

The parameter types, longval, doubleval, and stringval, are all passed by value and may not be changed in the VSN. The parameter types, longref, doubleref, and stringref, are all passed by reference and may not be constants in the calling network. If a member of an array is passed by using PNAME[I] then the remainder of the array is passed.

7.9.2 VSN Control Statements

Control statements for a VSN are used for the same purpose as in the main network (see Section 5.13 and Chapter 8). Differences are the use of a SUBNETWORK statement and an ENDVSN statement to identify the beginning and ending of the statements for a VSN; and a LIMITVSN statement to set the maximum index for subnetwork attributes for an entity and the maximum index for subnetwork variables for each instance of the VSN.

The SUBNETWORK control statement shown below has the same syntax and purpose as a NETWORK statement.

SUBNETWORK, option, FILENAME;

where the option field can be {READ, SAVE, LOAD}.

The default for the option field is READ which decodes the network statements without saving their translation. To store a decoded network, the SAVE option is selected and a file name is given in the file field. Thus, the statement

SUBNETWORK,SAVE,NET.DAT;

causes the decoded subnetwork to be written in binary form to the file NET.DAT. In future uses of the network, the statement

SUBNETWORK,LOAD, NET.DAT;

causes the decoded subnetwork to be used. This saves the computer time necessary to decode a large set of subnetwork statements. When the option is specified as LOAD, no subnetwork statements follow the SUBNETWORK statement.

A new control statement, LIMITSVSN, defines the larget index for subnetwork specific attributes and variables using the following syntax and AweSim dialog box:

LIMITSVSN, MXXXINST,MXLLINST,MXSZINST,MXANTRIB,MXLNATRIB,MXSNATRIB;

where   MXXXINST is the largest index for XXINST variables (doubles);
MXLLINST is the largest index for LLINST variables (longs);
MXSZINST is the largest index for SZINST variables (strings);
MXANTRIB is the largest index for ANTRIB values (doubles);
MXLNTRIB is the largest index for LNTRIB values (longs);
MXSNTRIB is the largest index for SNTRIB values (strings).

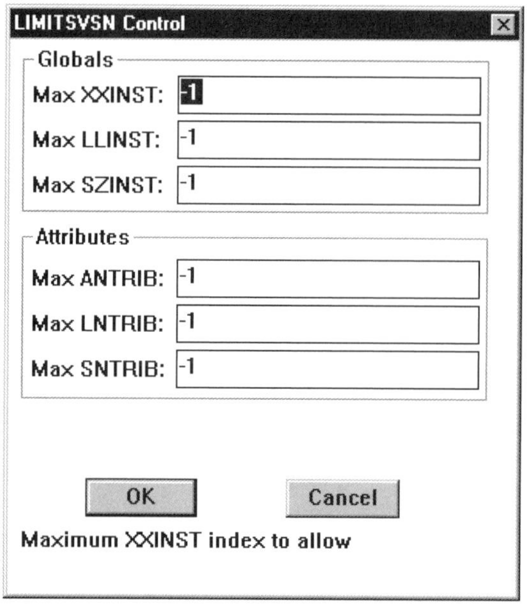

The following control statements are valid for a VSN and follow the SUBNETWORK statement: DOCOLCT, EQUIVALENCE, INTLC, LIMITSVSN, MONTR, PRIORITY, RECORD, SEEDS, SEVNT, TIMST. The AweSim dialog box for inserting control statements for subnetworks is shown below.

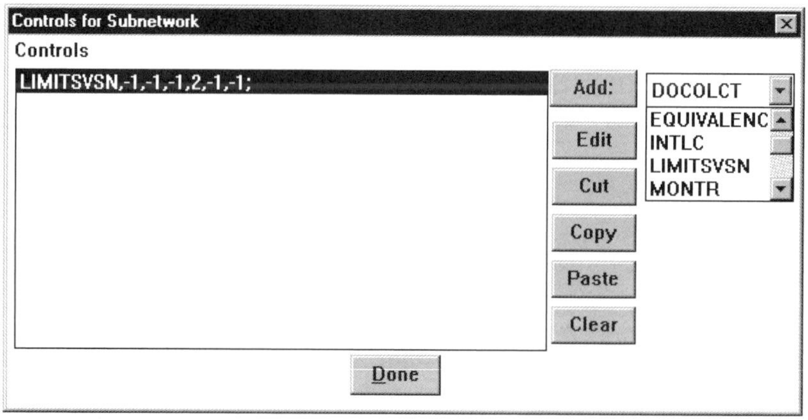

7.9.3 Building Subnetworks

The building of a VSN starts with a ENTERVSN node. An entity arriving to a CALLVSN node is transferred to the VSN at the ENTERVSN node specified its name. The syntax, symbol and AweSim dialog box for the ENTERVSN node are given below.

ENTERVSN, NAME,M;

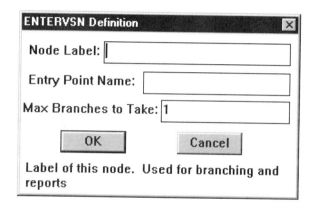

If the NAME is defaulted (blank) then this ENTERVSN node is the default starting node of the VSN.

Following the ENTERVSN node are standard Visual SLAM nodes and branches to model an entity's path in the VSN. The entity is returned to the CALLVSN node when it arrives to a RETURNVSN node.

The RETURNVSN node passes the entity back from the VSN with its new ERETURN value which is an attribute of the entity. ERETURN provides a value for an entity obtained during its last sojourn in a VSN. The EXIT # specifies a node to which the entity is to be routed from the calling node. The route node is defined on the CALLVSN node. If the EXIT # is 1 or is not specified then the entity branches in a normal fashion from the CALLVSN node employing its M-number.

The syntax, symbol and AweSim dialog box for the RETURNVSN node are shown below:

RETURNVSN, ERETURN, EXIT#;

```
┌─────────────────────────────────────────────┐
│ RETURNVSN Definition                    [X]  │
│                                              │
│  Node Label: │                            │  │
│                                              │
│  Return Value: │0.0                    │ F(x)│
│                                              │
│  Exit #:        │1                        │  │
│                                              │
│       ┌──────────┐      ┌──────────┐         │
│       │    OK    │      │  Cancel  │         │
│       └──────────┘      └──────────┘         │
│  Label of this node.  Used for branching and │
│  reports                                     │
└─────────────────────────────────────────────┘
```

In building VSNs, use can be made of the VSN variables which are listed below.

PP[I]	Default values of parameter I if PNAME[I] is not specified
LNTRIB[I]	Long attribute value for entity in VSN
ANTRIB[I]	Double attribute value for entity in VSN
SNTRIB[I]	String attribute value for entity in VSN
LLINST[I]	Long local variable for VSN instance
XXINST[I]	Double local variable for VSN instance
SZINST[I]	String local variable for VSN instance
INSTNAME	Name of the current instance in VSN
SIZE(PARRAY)	Provides the number of elements in a parameter array, PARRAY, passed by reference

The name and values of parameters, PP[I], are specified at the CALLVSN node. The three vectors LNTRIB, ANTRIB, and SNTRIB are VSN versions of the attribute vectors associated with an entity. These vectors allow a VSN to be developed based on attributes that are local to the subnetwork. Attributes from the main network for an entity are also available in their normal form for use in a VSN. LLINST, XXINST and SZINST correspond to the LL, XX and SZ vectors in the main network. Values for these variables within a VSN are dependent on the instance for which the VSN is used. The name of the instance of the VSN object that is current is INSTNAME. The number of elements in a parameter array PARRAY passed by reference can be obtained through use of the function SIZE.

In building a VSN, only resources, files, labels, user code numbers and event numbers defined in the VSN or the main program may be referenced. If there is a conflict, that is, the same label, code number, or name is used in both the VSN and the main network then Visual SLAM will use the label, code number or name that is employed in the VSN. In all cases it is assumed that the VSN model accesses VSN elements first and then searches the main network for elements not found. With this assumption, COLCT node numbers,

RECORD statement numbers, and TIMST statement numbers may be the same as the corresponding numbers used in the main network or in other VSNs.

In building the VSN, the following restrictions regarding nodes and statements for use within VSNs are imposed:

1. CREATE and ENTER nodes may not be used in subnetworks.
2. Created entities at DETECT nodes and SEVNT statements may not be routed to a RETURNVSN node.
3. ACCUMULATE nodes may be used but the SAVE field is used to specify which entity's context is used. The context of an entity relates to its main network attributes and its VSN attributes. The latter set of attributes are not required to be the same for an entity routed to different VSNs.
4. BATCH nodes may be used but if RETAIN is specified the resulting batched entity may only be unbatched in the same subnetwork or the main network.
5. MATCH and SELECT nodes may not reference QUEUE nodes outside a VSN.

The reporting of messages for a VSN is accomplished by concatenating the name of a Visual SLAM element with a called VSN name and the instance for the called VSN. For example, an arrival to an AWAIT node in a VSN with name LINE1 in the instance DRILL would be shown on a trace report as LINE1 DRILL: AWAIT. Resource statistics for this instance would be entitled RESOURCE STATISTICS REPORT for LINE1 DRILL.

7.9.4 CALLVSN Node

The CALLVSN node is used to invoke a VSN. An entity that arrives to the CALLVSN node is transferred to the subnetwork with name VSNNAME. The name of the instance of the subnetwork object is specified as INSTANCE. If INSTANCE is not specified, then the VSN is processed as the "blank" instance. The names or values of the parameters for use in the VSN are listed at the CALLVSN node as P1, P2 ,and so on. The M-number for the CALLVSN node is then specified and this exit from the VSN back to the calling network is defined as EXIT 1.

To allow for alternate enter locations and exit locations from the VSN, the CALLVSN node provides the name of a ENTERVSN node where the entity is to start its route through the VSN. If no ENTERNAME is specified, the entity starts at an ENTERVSN node without a name, typically, the first node following the VSN statement. Alternative nodes in the calling network may be specified at the CALLVSN node to allow for the routing of the entity upon leaving a VSN. These exit locations are specified by assigning an exit number that is greater than 1 and a corresponding label for a node in the calling network. An exit number is given on each RETURNVSN node in the VSN which is then decoded at the CALLVSN node. The syntax, symbol and AweSim dialog box for the CALLVSN node are presented below.

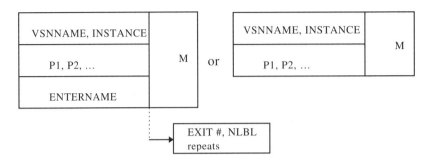

CALLVSN, VSNNAME, INSTANCE, {P1, P2,…},M,ENTERNAME, {{EXIT #, NLBL}, repeats};

where   VSNNAME is the name of the visual subnetwork to call (string expr);
INSTANCE is the name of the instance of the visual subnetwork to call;
P1 is parameter 1 (any type);
P2 is parameter 2 (any type) and so on;
M is the maxtake for normal exit which is defined as EXIT 1;
ENTERNAME is the name of the ENTERVSN node within the VSN; and
EXIT # is the exit number; and
NLBL is the node label corresponding to EXIT #.

7.10   ILLUSTRATIONS OF SUBNETWORK CAPABILITIES

In this section, we present illustrations of the use of subnetworks. Both network and statement models are presented.

7.10.1 Illustration 7-2.   Using a VSN from Multiple Locations

The VSN shown below is used to demonstrate the basic capabilities and concepts related to subnetworks. The VSN block provides a name, COMPRES, a computer resource for the subnetwork. COMPRES is used to make a computer resource available at different locations in a calling network. The parameters of COMPRES are COMPCAP, a computer resource capacity, and PROCTIME, a processing time for the computer activity.

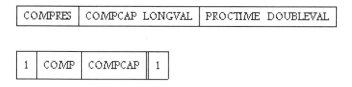

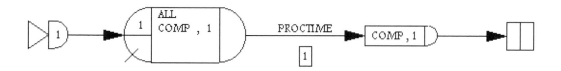

```
SUBNETWORK;
VSN, COMPRES, {{COMPCAP, LONGVAL, computer capacity},
      {PROCTIME, DOUBLEVALUE, processing time}};
RESOURCE, 1, COMP, COMPCAP, {1};
ENTERVSN, , 1;
AWAIT, 1, {{COMP, 1 }};
ACTIVITY, 1, PROCTIME;
FREE, {{COMP, 1}};
RETURNVSN;
```

The RESOURCE block in the VSN specifies the label for resource 1 as COMP which has a capacity as defined by Parameter 1, that is, COMPCAP. The value of COMPCAP on the RESOURCE block for the instance CPU is set on the first call to VSN COMPRES through the process of instantiation. Entities that are passed to the subnetwork wait in file 1 for resource COMP. The next statement is an ENTERVSN statement which is the start of the path of the entity in the subnetwork. Next the entity waits at an AWAIT node in file 1 for one unit of the resource COMP. When the entity is allocated the resource, it proceeds to activity 1 where Parameter 2, PROCTIME, provides a value for the processing time. Following the processing time activity, resource COMP is freed at a FREE node and the entity is returned from the VSN by the RETURNVSN node.

The VSN is called from the main network or a subnetwork when an entity arrives to a CALLVSN node. An example of a calling network with two calls to the VSN COMPRES from nodes CALL1 and CALL2 is shown below.

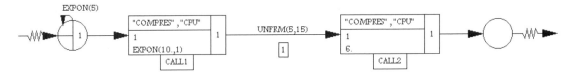

```
NETWORK;
CREATE, EXPON (5), , , , 1;
CALL1: CALLVSN, "COMPRES", "CPU", {1, EXPON(10., 1}, 1;
        ACTIVITY, 1, UNFRM (5,15), , , , "THINKTIME";
CALL2: CALLVSN, "COMPRES", "CPU", { 1, 6. }, 1;
TERM;
```

At both CALLVSN nodes, the resource is identified as CPU which provides an instance of the VSN whose name is COMPRES. At node CALL1, the processing time is specified as EXPON(10.,1) and at node CALL2 the processing time is specified as 6. In this illustration, the entities arriving to the CALLVSN nodes both wait in file 1 for resource COMP with instance CPU in accordance with the priority rule for file 1. The processing time is taken as parameter 2 of the VSN. The resource capacity, COMPCAP, is taken from parameter 1. Since the use of the VSN is for the same instance of the resource, the capacity could have been set as 1 in the resource block and not passed as a parameter. Also, the instance name could have been left as blanks in which case we refer to it as the "blank instance". Since no special exit numbers are prescribed, the entity is returned to the CALLVSN node from which it came and normal branching from the CALLVSN node occurs.

7.10.2 Illustration 7-3. Using a VSN for Multiple Resources

In this illustration, the VSN of Illustration 7-2 is used to represent 2 resources, CPU1 and CPU2. The CALLVSN statements CALL3: and CALL4: illustrate this capability by specifying the instance of the subnetwork as CPU1 and CPU2, respectively. These statements and the main network are shown below.

CALL3: CALLVSN, "COMPRES", "CPU1", { 1, EXPON (10., 1) }, 1;
CALL4: CALLVSN, "COMPRES", "CPU2", {1, 6. }, 1;

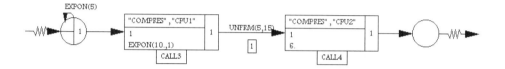

Parameter 1 at both CALLVSN nodes indicates a capacity of 1. Parameter 2 specifies the same processing times as were used in Illustration 7-1. Entities wait in file 1 but in a different instance of file 1. Statistics for file 1 would be collected separately for entities waiting for CPU1 from those waiting for CPU2.

If CPU2 has a capacity of 2 then parameter 1 at the CALL4 node would be changed to a 2. Since there are 2 instances of the VSN COMPRES, the resource capacity COMPCAP is set on the first call of VSN COMPRES for each instance.

7.10.3 Illustration 7-4. Using a VSN With Multiple Queues

If it is desired to have separate queues for entities waiting for the resource COMP described in Illustration 7-2, then a third parameter would be added to the VSN statement as follows: {FILENO, longval, "file number"}. The file number parameter would be used in the AWAIT nodes in the VSN, that is, AWAIT, FILENO, {{COMP, 1}};. If the entities waiting in file 2 are to receive preference when the CPU becomes free, the RESOURCE block in the VSN should be changed to

RESOURCE, 1, "COMP", COMPCAP, 2, 1;

The CALLVSN statement replacing CALL2 of Illustration 7-2 is renamed as CALL5 and is shown below:

CALL5: CALLVSN, "COMPRES", "CPU", { 1, 6., 2 }, 1;

These changes separate entities into two files while waiting for the same resource and give preference to entities waiting in file 2.

7.10.4   Illustration 7-5.   Use of Attributes in a VSN

Suppose that an entity is reprocessed within the subnetwork of Illustration 7-2 on a probabilistic basis and it is desired to limit the number of times an entity is processed by CPU1 to 3 and by CPU2 to 6.   To accomplish this, we use subnetwork attributes. This requires a LIMITSVSN statement for the subnetwork to provide LNTRIB and ANTRIB attributes for each entity. LNTRIB[1] is used to count the number of times the entity has been processed, ANTRIB[0] is set to the next processing time and ANTRIB[1] is used to sum the processing times for an entity. For the subnetwork, the following LIMITSVSN control statement is added to specify a maximum index of 1 for variables ANTRIB and LNTRIB.

LIMITSVSN, , , ,1,1;

The VSN including the changes described in the previous illustrations is presented in Figures 7-6 and 7-7. A change is made in the definition of parameter 2 to pass the average processing time so that the processing times can be generated in the VSN. A fourth parameter, MAXTIMES, is added as the maximum number of times reprocessing is allowed for each call to the VSN. In the VSN, MAXTIMES takes on the values specified by parameter 4 and is maintained for each instance of the VSN. At the RETURNVSN node, the sum of the processing times is set as the ERETURN attribute of the entity.

For this VSN, suppose it is desired to return to node ABNORM in the main network if an entity is processed MAXTIMES before processing is completed and to have a normal return to the calling node if processing is completed in less than MAXTIMES. The CALLVSN node in the main network would be as shown below.

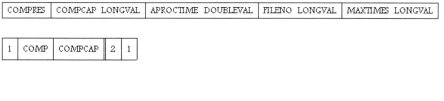

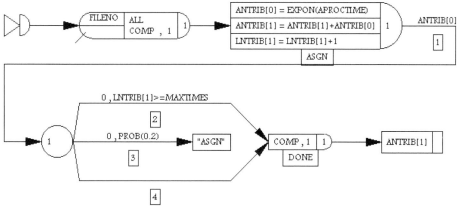

Figure 7-6 Subnetwork model for Illustration 7-4.

```
        VSN, "COMPRES", {{ COMPCAP, LONGVAL, computer capacity },
                { APROCTIME, DOUBLEVALUE, average processing time},
                { FILENO, LONGVAL, file number },
                { MAXTIMES, LONGVAL, maximum reprocessing}}};
        LIMITSVSN, , , , 1, 1;
        RESOURCE, 1, COMP, COMPCAP, {2,1};
        ENTERVSN;
        AWAIT, FILENO, {{ COMP, 1 }};
ASGN:   ASSIGN{ANTRIB[0], EXPON (APROCTIME) },
                {LNTRIB[1], LNTRIB[1] +1},
                {ANTRIB[1], ANTRIB[1] + ANTRIB[0] }};
        ACT, 1, ATRIB[0];
        GOON, 1
                ACT, 2, , LNTRIB[1] >= MAXTIMES, "DONE";
                ACT, 3, , PROB (0.2), "ASGN";
                ACT, 4;
DONE:   FREE, {{ COMP, 1 }};
        RETURNVSN, ANTRIB[1];
```

Figure 7-7 Statement model for Illustration 7-4

At this CALLVSN node, EXIT#2 is prescribed which routes the returning entity to a node with label ABNORM in the main network. In the VSN, the RETURNVSN statements return the total processing time for an entity as its ERETURN attribute and specifies either EXIT 1 or EXIT 2 to the CALLVSN node.

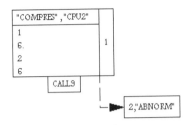

In the VSN COMPRES statement model of Figure 7-7, the following changes to the last part of the VSN are required.

CALL9:CALLVSN,"COMPRES","CPU2",
1,6.0,2,6},1,,{{2,"ABNORM"}};

```
GOON, 1;
     ACT, 2, , LNTRIB[1] >=MAXTIMES, "AB"
     ACT, 3, , PROB(0.2), "ASGN";
     ACT 4;
; Entity returned for normal exit
DONE: FREE, {{ COMP, 1 }};
     RETURNVSN, ANTRIB[1], 1;
; Entity returned to EXIT 2
AB: FREE, {{ COMP, 1 }};
     RETURNVSN, ANTRIB[1], 2;
```

7.11 EXAMPLE 7-2. JOBSHOP PRODUCTION

Schriber (2) describes a production shop (job shop) that is comprised of six different groups of machines. Each group consists of identical machines as described in Table 7-3. Three different types of jobs move through the production shop. These job types are designated as Type 1, Type 2 and Type 3. Each job type requires that operations be performed at specified kinds of machines in a specified sequence. All operation times are exponentially distributed. The visitation sequences and mean operation times are given in Table 7-4. At each machine group, the jobs are processed in a first-in, first-out order independent of job type.

Table 7-3 Machine group information for Example 7-2.

Machine Group Number	Kind of Machine in Group	Number of Machines in Group
1	CASTER	14
2	LATHE	5
3	PLANER	4
4	DRILL	8
5	SHAPER	16
6	POLISHER	4

Table 7-4 Job visitation sequences and mean operation time for Example 7-2.

Job Type	Machine Visitation Sequence	Mean Operation Time (Minutes)
1	CASTER	125
	PLANER	35
	LATHE	20
	POLISHER	60
2	SHAPER	105
	DRILL	90
	LATHE	65
	CASTER	235
	SHAPER	250
3	DRILL	50
	PLANER	30
	POLISHER	25

Jobs arrive at the shop with exponential interarrival times with a mean of 9.6 minutes. Twenty-four percent of the jobs are of Type 1, 44 percent are of Type 2 and the rest are of Type 3. The type of arriving job is independent of the job type of the preceding arrival. It is desired to simulate the production shop over a five week period assuming the shop is in operation for 40 hours a week to estimate: 1) the job residence time in the shop for each job type; 2) the utilization of the machines; and 3) the statistics for the queue length for each machine group.

Concepts Illustrated. The subnetwork capability of Visual SLAM is demonstrated in this example to provide a general jobshop modeling capability. It illustrates how subnetworks can decompose a modeling project. The jobshop model is data driven to allow the number of machine groups, the number of machines in a group, the number of types of jobs processed by the jobshop, the visitation sequence for each type of job and the operation times for each job at each machine group to be input as data.

Visual SLAM Model.   The model of the jobshop consists of a main network and a subnetwork. The subnetwork represents all machine groups and is given the name MACHGR. The instances of the subnetwork object are the machine group names with their corresponding numbers: 1. CASTER; 2. LATHE; 3. PLANER; 4. DRILL; 5. SHAPER; and 6. POLISHER. These names are maintained in the global string variable SZ[·] with the argument being the number specified in the preceding list. The parameters of the subnetwork are the number of machines for each resource and the operation times of a job on one of the machines in a machine group. When a job entity is routed to the subnetwork by a CALLVSN node in the main network, the instance name establishes a subnetwork object for the job entity with respect to a particular machine group The parameters provide the number of machines in the machine group and the mean operation time for the job entity at a machine of the machine group. The VSN is named MACHGR and is shown in Figure 7-8. There is one resource in the VSN with a resource label of MACHINE. The name of the capacity of the resource is NUMMACH. For each instance of the VSN, job entities wait in file 1 for one unit of resource MACHINE, that is, there is a file 1 for the CASTER machine group, a file 1 for the LATHE machine group and so on.

The processing of the job entity at the machine group involves waiting for one machine of the machine group defined by the instance prescribed at the CALLVSN node of the main network. When the machine is allocated, the entity is processed by activity 1 of the subnetwork with the mean time prescribed by parameter 2. After processing, the entity is routed to a FREE node which releases the resource allocated to it and the entity is returned to the calling network at a RETURNVSN node. This completes the description of the subnetwork.

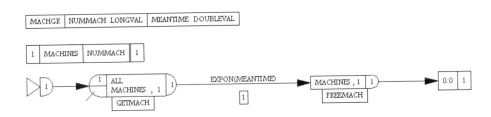

Figure 7-8 Subnetwork for jobshop model.

The main network for the jobshop model is shown in Figure 7-9. Job entities are created at CREATE node BEGIN with an exponential time between arrivals of 9.6 minutes. The job entity's arrival time is stored in ATRIB[1]. The job entity is routed to an ASSIGN node where its job type is obtained as a sample from a discrete distribution whose job numbers are presecribed in Row 7 of ARRAY which is part of the input data. The probabilities associated with the job type as being classified as either 1, 2 or 3 are stored in ARRAY row 8 as .24, .68 and 1. The input data for this example is shown in Figure 7-10.

The job entity is then routed to ASSIGN node NEXT_STEP where the jobstep for the entity is indexed by 1. JOBTYPE and JOBSTEP are attributes of the job entity and are equivalenced to LTRIB[1] and LTRIB[2] as shown in Figure 7-10.

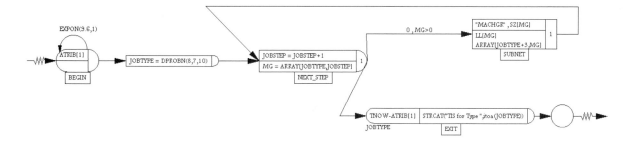

Figure 7-9 Main network for jobshop model.

The third attribute of the job entity is MG, the machine group number, and it is equivalenced to LTRIB[3]. The machine group number is taken from row JOBTYPE and column JOBSTEP of ARRAY. In Figure 7-10 the sequence numbers prescribed by the machine visitation sequence presented in Table 7-4 are included in the first three rows of ARRAY.

If MG is greater than 0, the job entity is to visit another machine group and it is routed to the CALLVSN node SUBNET where VSN MACHGR is called for instance SZ[MG]. The string for a machine group name is defined in an INTLC statement shown in Figure 7-10. The parameters passed to the subnetwork are obtained from the global variables LL[MG] also defined in the INTLC statements shown in Figure 7-10 and from ARRAY rows 4, 5 and 6 (JOBTYPE + 3) in column MG.

After the job entity returns from VSN MACHGR, it is routed back to ASSIGN node NEXT_STEP to be given its next machine group assignment. If the next machine group is 0, the job entity has completed its visitation sequence and is routed to a COLCT node with COLCT number JOBTYPE where time-in-system statistics are collected by job type. The utilization of machines in each machine group is obtained from each resource represented by the 6 instances of the subnetwork object. In the statement model for the subnetwork, a TIMST statement is used to compute the percent utilization of machines in each group by collecting statistics of the number of units in use divided by the number of machines in the subgroup multiplied by 100. The label for time-persistent statistics reported within a subnetwork includes the variable INSTNAME, the instance name passed by the CALLVSN node. Through the use of a subnetwork, the modeling of the routing of an entity has been separated from the modeling of the resources used to process the entity.

```
Control statements:
    1 GEN,"PRITSKER","JOBSHOP",10/3/96,1,YES,YES;
    2 LIMITS,,6,6,1,3;
    4 EQUIVALENCE,{{JOBTYPE,LTRIB[1]},{JOBSTEP,LTRIB[2]}};
    5 EQUIVALENCE,{{MG,LTRIB[3]}};
    7 ARRAY,1,6,{1,3,2,6,0}; Machine Sequence, Type 1
    8 ARRAY,2,6,{5,4,2,0}; Machine Sequence, Type 2
    9 ARRAY,3,6,{1,5,4,3,6,0}; Machine Sequence, Type 3
   10 ARRAY,4,6,{ 125, 20, 35, 0, 0, 60 }; Mean Times, Type 1
   11 ARRAY,5,6,{ 0, 65, 0, 90, 105, 0 }; Mean Times, Type 2
   12 ARRAY,6,6,{ 235, 0, 30, 50, 250, 25 }; Mean Times, Type 3
   13 ARRAY,7,3,{ 1, 2, 3 }; JOBTYPE
   14 ARRAY,8,3,{ .24, .68, 1. }; Cumulative Probability Of Being Job Type
   15 ;
   16 INTLC,{{SZ[1],"CASTER"},{SZ[2],"LATHE"},{SZ[3],"PLANER"}};
                INSTANCE NAMES
   17 INTLC,{{SZ[4],"DRILL"},{SZ[5],"SHAPER"},{SZ[6],"POLISHER"}};
   18 INTLC,{{LL[1],14},{LL[2],5},{LL[3],4}}; INSTANCE NUMBER OF MACHINES
   19 INTLC,{{LL[4],8},{LL[5],16},{LL[6],4}};
   21 INITIALIZE,0,12000,YES;
   22 ;
   23 NETWORK;
   24 FIN;
Network statements:
    2 BEGIN: CREATE,EXPON(9.6,1),,ATRIB[1];
    3        ACTIVITY;
    4        ASSIGN,{ { JOBTYPE, DPROBN(8,7,10) } };
    5        ACTIVITY;
    6 NEXT_STEP: ASSIGN,{{JOBSTEP,JOBSTEP+1},
         {MG,ARRAY[JOBTYPE,JOBSTEP]}},1;
    7 ACTIVITY,,0,MG>0;
    8 ACTIVITY,,,,"EXIT";
    9 SUBNET: CALLVSN,"MACHGR",SZ[MG],{LL[MG],ARRAY[JOBTYPE+3,MG]},1;
   10 ACTIVITY,,,,"NEXT_STEP";
   11 EXIT: COLCT,JOBTYPE,TNOW-ATRIB[1],STRCAT("TIS for Type",itoa(JOBTYPE));
   12 ACTIVITY;
   13 TERMINATE;
   14 ;

Subnetwork statements:
    1 VSN,MACHGR,{{NUMMACH,LONGVAL,Number of machines},
                 {MEANTIME,DOUBLEVAL,Mean operation time}};
    2 RESOURCE,1,MACHINE,NUMMACH,{1};
    3 LIMITSVSN,-1,-1,-1,2,-1,-1;
    4 TIMST,1,100.*NRUSE(1)/(NRUSE(1)+NNRSC(1)),STRCAT
                 ("%Util: ",INSTNAME);
    5 ENTERVSN,,1;
    6 ACTIVITY;
    7 GETMACH: AWAIT,1,{{MACHINE,1}},ALL,,NONE,1;
    8 ACTIVITY,1,EXPON(MEANTIME),,,,STRCAT(INSTNAME," PROCESSING");
    9 FREEMACH: FREE,{{MACHINE,1}},,1;
   10 ACTIVITY;
   11 RETURNVSN,0.0,1;
```

Figure 7-10 Statement model for jobshop model.

Analysis of Results. The desired outputs for the production shop are presented in Table 7-5. From the table, the estimated mean times in the shop for job types 1, 2 and 3 respectively are 262 minutes, 285 minutes and 583 minutes. These times are close to the sum of the machine processing times for each type which are 240, 260 and 589 minutes.

Table 7-5 Output statistics for Example 7-2.

```
** OBSERVED STATISTICS REPORT for scenario EX72 **
```

Label	Mean Value	Standard Deviation	Number of Observations	Minimum Value	Maximum Value
TIS for Type 1	262.155	145.796	317	36.663	862.048
TIS for Type 2	284.792	151.509	582	12.125	887.512
TIS for Type 3	583.052	310.079	405	112.665	1752.194

Resource Label	Average Util.	Standard Deviation	Current Util.	Capacity	
SHAPER	12.950	3.102	14	16	

	File Average Length	Standard Deviation	Maximum Length	Current Length	Average Wait Time
	1.012	2.245	12	0	11.995

Resource Label	Average Util.	Standard Deviation	Current Util.	Capacity	
CASTER	10.717	2.777	4	14	

	File Average Length	Standard Deviation	Maximum Length	Current Length	Average Wait Time
	0.721	1.688	9	0	11.599

Resource Label	Average Util.	Standard Deviation	Current Util.	Capacity	
DRILL	6.033	2.004	3	8	

	File Average Length	Standard Deviation	Maximum Length	Current Length	Average Wait Time
	0.786	1.634	10	0	9.456

Resource Label	Average Util.	Standard Deviation	Current Util.	Capacity	
PLANER	1.901	1.213	2	4	

	File Average Length	Standard Deviation	Maximum Length	Current Length	Average Wait Time
	0.062	0.349	5	0	1.011

Resource Label	Average Util.	Standard Deviation	Current Util.	Capacity	
LATHE	3.604	1.472	5	5	

	File Average Length	Standard Deviation	Maximum Length	Current Length	Average Wait Time
	0.881	2.008	15	2	11.625

Resource Label	Average Util.	Standard Deviation	Current Util.	Capacity	
POLISHER	2.408	1.288	4	4	

	File Average Length	Standard Deviation	Maximum Length	Current Length	Average Wait Time
	0.345	0.992	9	1	5.688

This indicates that there is only a small amount of queueing occurring in the jobshop. This is confirmed by examining the values in Table 7-5 for the number waiting before each machine group and the waiting time per job in a queue.

The Observed Statistics part of Table 7-5 shows that there were 317 jobs of type 1, 582 jobs of type 2 and 405 jobs of type 3 that completed processing. In comparing the percentages of type jobs observed to the percentages input to the model we have: (24.3 vs. 24%), (44.6 vs. 44%) and (31.1 vs 32%). The observed number of jobs that arrived during the 12,000 minute simulation is the sum of those that finished, 1,304, and the jobs that are still in the system. By adding up the number of jobs in activity 1 for each machine group and the number in the files for each machine group, there are 35 jobs currently in the sytem. Thus, 1,339 jobs arrived during the 12,000 minute simulation.

With jobs arriving every 9.6 minutes, the expected number of job arrivals in 12,000 minutes is 1,250. Since the job arrivals are exponentially distributed, the number of arrivals is Poisson distributed. The variance of the number of arrivals for a Poisson distribution is equal to the mean of the Poisson distribution. Thus, the standard deviation is the square root of 1,250 or approximately 35. Since the mean of the Poisson distribution is large, the normal distribution is a good approximation and the observed number of arrivals, 1,339, is within a three standard deviation limit which includes 99.7% of the distribution values. Thus, the number of job arrivals, although within reason, is large compared to the expected number of arrivals. With the larger number of arrivals, the time in the system is expected to be larger and the waiting times longer. Since the resource utilization and waiting time for this one run are small, the observation that the production shop is underutilized is a reasonable conclusion. To confirm this conclusion, additional runs should be made and a clearing of statistics should be considered as there is an initial period of the simulation in which entities find no queues before the machines. However, based on the results obtained, there are many periods where this occurs during the 12,000 minute simulation run.

7.12 ILLUSTRATION 7-6. A MANUFACTURING CELL MODEL USING A SUBNETWORK

This illustration provides an example of the use of a subnetwork to model the flow of an entity (a part) through a manufacturing cell consisting of three machines: DRILL, DEBUR and POLISH. A general MACHINE subnetwork is used to model the three machines and their work-in-process (WIP) areas. The illustration demonstrates the blocking of a ma-chine due to the unavailability of space in the WIP area of the next machine on the entity's route. It also provides a general model of a manufacturing cell which employs group technology concepts. The logic to model blocking is included in the subnetwork model.

The area before the DRILL is referred to as DRILLWIP which has a capacity for five entities. Similarly, the area before the debur machine is referred to as DEBURWIP and has a capacity of three entities, and the area before the polish machine is referred to as POLISHWIP and it has a capacity of two entities. An entity that arrives to the manufacturing cell and finds the DRILLWIP area full, that is, there are already five entities waiting, is subcontracted and the time of subcontracting is to be recorded.

The routing of each entity is processed first by the drill then by the debur machine and the last operation is polishing. Within the manufacturing cell, part entities cannot leave a machine until a space is available in the WIP area for the next machine in its routing. Following the polishing operation, the entity is to be routed to node GO2 for statistics collection and analysis which is not modeled in this illustration.

The model of the manufacturirng cell involves three machines and three machine WIP areas. The machine WIP areas are modeled as resources and defined in the main network presented in Figure 7-11a. The RESOURCE blocks for these WIP resources shows the capacity of the WIP areas as 5, 3, and 2 entities respectively and that waiting for a space in a WIP is done in files 101, 102 and 103 respectively.

The main network begins with a CREATE node and then moves through three CALLVSN nodes representing the routing of the entity. Following the third CALLVSN node, the entity is routed to node GO2 for further processing in the main network. In addition, WRITE node SUBC records the time that each entity is subcontracted because the DRILLWIP is full. At each CALLVSN node, the instance of the VSN is shown following the name of the VSN which is MACHINE. The instance names are shown as DRILL, DEBUR and POLISH. The parameters for VSN MACHINE are:

PROCTIME, the processing time on the machine;

INWIP, the name of the WIP area resource for the machine;

INFILE, the file number of the WIP area resource for the machine;

OUTWIP, the name of the next WIP area resource for the entity;

OUTFILE, the file number associated with the next WIP area resource for the entity; and

FIRST, an indicator to specify if the MACHINE is the first in the routing for the entity.

In the first CALLVSN node for a VSN MACHINE, the DRILL is specified as the instance of the object MACHINE for which the VSN is being called. The parameter specification indicates that the processing time on the drill is normally distributed with a mean of 2 and a standard deviation of 0.1, the input WIP area is the DRILLWIP for which entities wait in file 101. The output WIP area is the DEBURWIP whose file number is 102. Since the DRILL instance is the first call to the subnetwork, that is, it is the first machine on the routing for the entity, the parameter FIRST is set to 1. An exit is defined as EXIT#2 with label SUBC which causes an entity upon return from the VSN with an EXIT#2 set to 2 to be subcontracted at node SUBC. The descriptions of the other CALLVSN nodes are similar to the above.

In the VSN, presented in Figure 7-11b, a resource is defined as MACHRES which will take on values in accordance with the instance for which the VSN is called. The capacity of each of the MACHRES resources is 1 and entities waiting for MACHRES wait in file 1. The first node in the VSN is an ENTERVSN node. If FIRST equals 1, the branch to GOON node GOSUB is taken where it is determined whether there is space in the input WIP of the first machine, that is, DRILLWIP. If no space is available, NNRSC(INWIP) equals 0 and a branch is taken to the RETURNVSN node RET2. The value of TNOW is assigned as the ERETURN attribute of the entity which is recorded at WRITE node SUBC in the calling network.

If the entity can obtain a space in the WIP of the machine to which it was routed, it does so at node GETSP and then moves on to node GETMACH where it waits in file 1 for the MACHINE resource. Note that file 1 represents three separate files, one for each instance of the VSN object corresponding to the DRILL, DEBUR, and POLISH machines. When the entity leaves file 1 by acquiring the appropriate machine, it frees up a space in the WIP of that machine. The processing time on the machine is performed in activity 1. Following processing, it is determined if the output WIP for the machine, that just completed processing, has a space available. For this illustration, the output WIP of a machine is the input WIP of the next machine in the entity's routing. First, it is determined if there is an output machine by testing OUTWIP being equal to a zero. If this is not the case, the entity is routed to node GETOUT where it requests a space in the WIP of the next machine in its routing. The entity is then routed to node FREEMACH to free the machine on which processing just occurred. If the entity was at the end of its route of machines, that is, it has just finished the polishing operation, it is directly sent to the node FREEMACH. The entity is then routed to a RETURNVSN node to make a normal exit from the CALLVSN node. This completes the description of the VSN.

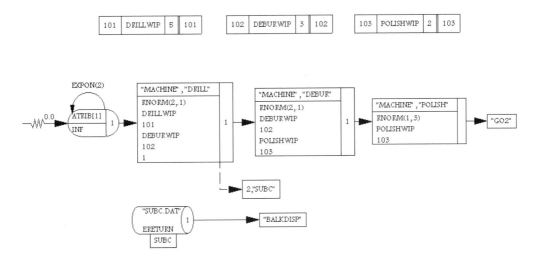

Figure 7-11a Main network model for Illustration 7-6

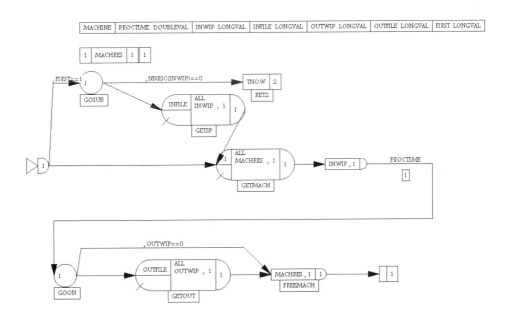

Figure 7-11b Subnetwork model for Illustation 7-6.

Figure 7-11 Network model for Illlustation 7-6.

The statement model is given in Figure 7-12.

```
NETWORK;
     RESOURCE,101,DRILLWIP,5,{101};
     RESOURCE,102,DEBURWIP,3,{102};
     RESOURCE,103,POLISHWIP,2,{103};

     CREATE,EXPON(2),,ATRIB[1];
     CALLVSN,"MACHINE","DRILL",{RNORM(2,0.1),DRILLWIP,101,
                     DEBURWIP,102,1},1,,{{2,"SUBC"}};
     CALLVSN,"MACHINE","DEBUR",{RNORM(2,.1),DEBURWIP,102,
                     POLISHWIP,103},1;
     CALLVSN,"MACHINE","POLISH",{RNORM(1,.3),POLISHWIP,103},1;
          ACTIVITY,,,,"GO2";
  SUBC: WRITE,"SUBC.DAT",NO,,{ERETURN},1;
          ACTIVITY,,,,"BALKDISP";
;
     VSN,MACHINE,{{PROCTIME,DOUBLEVAL,processing time},
          {INWIP,LONGVAL,input WIP resource},
          {INFILE,LONGVAL,input WIP file},
          {OUTWIP,LONGVAL,output WIP resource},
          {OUTFILE,LONGVAL,output WIP file},
          {FIRST,LONGVAL,flag for first machine}};
     RESOURCE,1,MACHRES,1,{1};
     ENTERVSN,,1;
          ACTIVITY,,,FIRST==1;
          ACTIVITY,,,,"GETMACH";
GOSUB: GOON,1;
          ACTIVITY,,,NNRSC(INWIP)==0;
          ACTIVITY,,,,"GETSP";
RET2: RETURNVSN,TNOW,2;
GETSP: AWAIT,INFILE,{{INWIP,1}},ALL,,NONE,1;
GETMACH: AWAIT,1,{{MACHRES,1}},ALL,,NONE,1;
     FREE,{{INWIP,1}};
          ACTIVITY,1,PROCTIME;
 GOON: GOON,1;
          ACTIVITY,,,OUTWIP==0, "FREEMACH";
          ACTIVITY,,,,"GETOUT";
GETOUT: AWAIT,OUTFILE,{{OUTWIP,1}},ALL,,NONE,1;
          ACTIVITY,,,,"FREEMACH";
FREEMACH: FREE,{{MACHRES,1}},1;
     RETURNVSN,,1;
```

Figure 7-12 Visual SLAM Statement Model for Manufacturing Cell, Illustration 7-5

This illustration was for three machines in a series but could easily be adapted to a jobshop environment by branching probabilistically or conditionally in the main network from CALLVSN node to CALLVSN node. In addition, there could be multiple copies of each machine in the subnetwork by including a machine capacity as a parameter in the VSN.

7.13   ILLUSTRATION 7-7. ALTERNATE MODEL FOR A MANUFACTURING CELL

The problem statement for Illustration 7-7 is the same as the one given for Illustration 7.6. An alternate VSN with the name QMACHINE is developed which includes both the machine resource and its WIP resource in the VSN. Four parameters are provided to the VSN which are the processing time, PROCTIME; the input queue capacity, INQCAP; the output machine, OUTMACH; and the output queue capacity, OUTQCAP. The machine for which the entity is being routed is passed to the subnetwork as an instance of the VSN. The main network is shown in Figure 7-13a and is similar to the main network developed for Illustration 7-6. In this case, four CALLVSN nodes are used. The first CALLVSN node has an ENTERVSN node of ARRIVE. The processing time parameter is set to 0 to indicate that this CALLVSN node is to be used as a call to the VSN for the first machine in the routing of the entity. The call is used to establish if the entity can enter the WIP of the first machine, and if it can, to seize a space in the input queue of the first machine, that is, the DRILL. The three other CALLVSN nodes have an ENTERVSN node with the name PROCESS which is used to process the entity through the instance of the VSN corresponding to the machine specified for the instance.

In Figure 7-13b, the VSN is presented and starts with two resources being defined as the MACHINE resource, MACHRES, and the input queue, INPUTQ, for that resource, that is, its WIP. Since the network is called for three different instances, that is, DRILL, DEBUR, and POLISH, the two RESOURCE blocks identify 6 resources for the VSN. For machine resource, MACHRES, the capacity is always 1, that is, the problem specification states that there is only 1 drill, 1 debur and 1 polish machine. If there were a different number of machines for each instance, then the resource capacity would need to be a parameter that is specified to the VSN. This is the case for the input WIP and the parameter INQCAP is established as parameter 2 in the CALLVSN nodes.

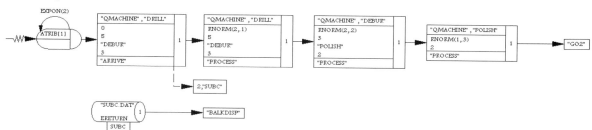

Figure 7-13a Main network model.

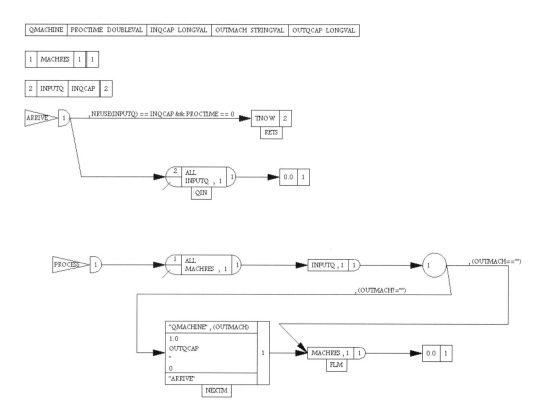

Figure 7-13b Subnetwork model.

Figure 7-13 Network model for Illustration 7-7.

From ENTERVSN node ARRIVE, the entity exits the VSN at node RETS which passes the entity back to the calling network to be routed through EXIT#2 of the CALLVSN node. The other exit from the ARRIVE ENTERVSN node routes the entity after it has acquired a space in the desired WIP of the machine to make a normal exit from the CALLVSN node.

At the PROCESS ENTERVSN node, the entity waits in file 1 for the appropriate machine resource MACHRES. When it is allocated, the entity frees up a space in the INPUTQ resource and is then processed at activity 1. If there is another machine on its routing, the entity is branched to node NEXTM which is a CALLVSN node. At this CALLVSN node the entity is put back into the VSN at the ARRIVE ENTERVSN node to acquire an input space in the following WIP area. If no space is available, the entity waits in file 2 for a space to become available. When a space in the next WIP area becomes available, the entity is taken from file 2 and makes a normal exit from the VSN. In this case, the CALLVSN node was in the subnetwork and the entity is passed back to the CALLVSN node NEXTM and branches normally from the node to FREE node FLM where it frees its last machine resource. If this is the last machine in an entity's route, node FLM is always released as there is no following machine. Following FREE node FLM, a normal exit is made from the VSN which places the entity back in the main network. The statement model for Illustration 7-7 is presented in Figure 7-14.

```
;Illustration 7-7  Alternate Subnetwork to Illustration 7-6
;Main Network
NETWORK;
CREATE, EXPON(2), , ATRIB[1];
CALLVSN, "QMACHINE", "DRILL", {0, 5, "DEBUR", 3}, 1, "ARRIVE", {2 "SUBC"};
CALLVSN, "QMACHINE", "DRILL", {RNORM(2,.1), 5, "DEBUR", 3}, 1, "PROCESS";
CALLVSN, "QMACHINE", "DEBUR", {RNORM(2, .2), 3, "POLISH", 2}, 1, "PROCESS";
CALLVSN, "QMACHINE", "POLISH", {RNORM(1, .3), 2} , 1, "PROCESS";
ACT,,,,"GO2";
SUBC: WRITE, SUBC.DAT, , {ERETURN}, 1;
   ACT, , , , "BALKDISP";

SUBNETWORK;
;VSN Block
VSN, "QMACHINE",
   {PROCTIME, DOUBLEVAL, processing time},
   {INQCAP, LONGVAL, input queue capacity},
   {OUTMACH, STRINGVAL, output machine},
   {OUTQCAP, LONGVAL, output machine q capacity}
   };
RESOURCE, 1, MACHRES, 1, {1};
RESOURCE, 2, INPUTQ, INQCAP, {2};
ENTERVSN, ARRIVE, 1;
   ACT, , , NRUSE(INPUTQ) = = INQCAP&& PROCTIME = = 0, "RETS";
   ACT, , , , "QIN",
RETS: RETURNVSN, TNOW, 2;
;Get space in next WIP area
QIN: AWAIT, 2, {{INPUTQ, 1}};
   RETURNVSN, , 1;
; Start PROCESS after space in WIP is allocated
ENTERVSN, PROCESS, 1;
   AWAIT, 1, {{MACHRES, 1}};
   FREE, {{INPUTQ, 1};
     ACT, 1, PROCTIME;
   GOON, 1;
     ACT, , , OUTMACH != "", "NEXTM";
     ACT, , , OUTMACH == "", "FLM";
NEXTM: CALLVSN, "QMACHINE", OUTMACH, {1.0, OUTQCAP, "", 0}, 1, "ARRIVE";
           ACT, , , , "FLM";
FLM: FREE, {{MACHRES, 1}};
     RETURNVSN, , 1;
```

Figure 7-14 Statements for Alternate Machine Model, Illustration 7-7.

7.14 CHAPTER SUMMARY

This chapter presents the concepts and illustrations of interface nodes; a find entities, assign attributes and remove entities from files node and visual subnetwork nodes. A summary listing of nodes and statements is given in Table 7-6.

Table 7-6 Interface, find and subnetwork node summary.

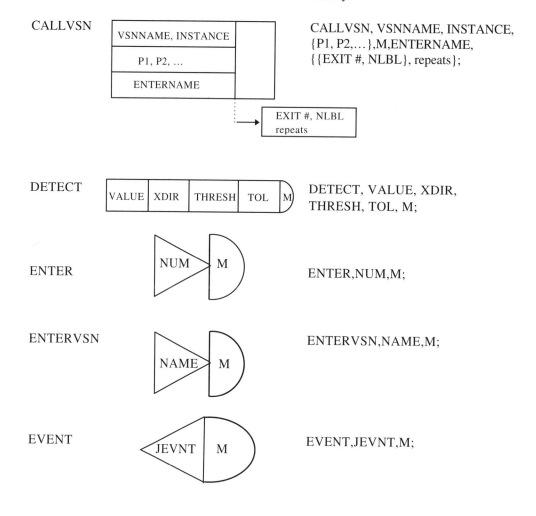

CALLVSN, VSNNAME, INSTANCE,
{P1, P2,...},M,ENTERNAME,
{{EXIT #, NLBL}, repeats};

DETECT, VALUE, XDIR,
THRESH, TOL, M;

ENTER,NUM,M;

ENTERVSN,NAME,M;

EVENT,JEVNT,M;

Table 7-6 Interface, find and subnetwork node summary (continued).

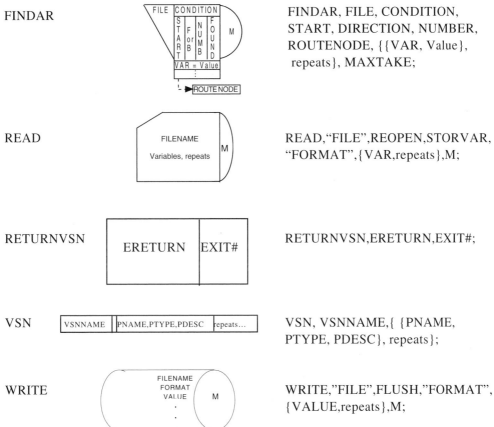

FINDAR

FINDAR, FILE, CONDITION, START, DIRECTION, NUMBER, ROUTENODE, {{VAR, Value}, repeats}, MAXTAKE;

READ

READ,"FILE",REOPEN,STORVAR, "FORMAT",{VAR,repeats},M;

RETURNVSN

RETURNVSN,ERETURN,EXIT#;

VSN

VSN, VSNNAME,{ {PNAME, PTYPE, PDESC}, repeats};

WRITE

WRITE,"FILE",FLUSH,"FORMAT", {VALUE,repeats},M;

7.15 EXERCISES

7-1.   Write the set of statements that reads in the following information into a network model: (a) The values of ATRIB[0] ATRIB[1] and LTRIB[0] from file ATTRIBUTES.DAT which has the above three values stored in sequence for 1,000 entities. The format is %6.2lf%6.2lf%6ld for the three attributes.   (b) Perform the reading task described in (a) when the three attribute values are stored in a database table with the name ND.

7-2. Prepare a WRITE node statement for the following situations: (a) Write out the values of the number in file 1, the number of units of resource 2 in use and the number of entities in activity 3 to a database table. (b) Write out the values of current simulated time, the first real attribute and the first integer attribute of the current entity to the file TRACE.DAT.

7-3. Build a Visual SLAM model of a banking situation in which there is a single line waiting for service from tellers. The arrival rate of customers is exponentially distributed with a mean time between time arrivals of 5 minutes. The service time of the teller is uniformly distributed between 5 and 10 minutes. If the length of the line reaches 3, then the server works faster and the service time is reduced to half its normal value. If the line reaches a length of 8, then customers do not join the line. When the line reaches a length of 6, the mean arrival rate decreases and the time between arrivals becomes 8 minutes. Run the model to determine the number of customers served in an 8 hour day. Collect statistics on the number of customers that balk from the system, the utilization of the server, the average length of the waiting line and the waiting time and total time in the system for a customer.

7-4. At a grocery store checkout line, there are typically 3 cashiers. Customers arrive to the cashiers with an exponential time between arrival with a mean of 4 minutes. One of the cashiers is dedicated to express service for customers with less than 12 items. The number of items that a customer has is Poisson distributed with a mean of 18. The service time by a cashier is dependent on the number of items that a customer is purchasing. For each item, the time to process an item is 15 seconds plus or minus 5 seconds. If the total number of customers waiting for the 3 cashiers is greater than 9, a fourth cashier station is opened. Three customers from the line of cashier 2 move over to the new cashier's station. The additional cashier is taken off the line when the total number of customers waiting for any cashier is 0. Model and simulate this situation for an 8 hour day.

7-5. In simulation models, it often occurs that there are many types of entities that are modeled. For each type of entity it is normally desired to collect statistics on the time spent in the system. Given that entities have been given an attribute which describes their type, that is, ETYPE, develop a VSN which collects time in the system for each entity type using a single CALLVSN node in the main network. The label for the COLCT node should be TIS-TYPE-# where # is the entity type number.

7-6. In project planning network analysis, precedence networks are defined with activity durations at the nodes. The branches are used to indicate precedence among the activities. Using subnetworks, convert the project planning example of Chapter 6 to a precedence network.

7-7. Build a Visual SLAM model of the following job shop situation. The job shop consists of six machines with each machine performing a different operation. The estimated processing time for each machine is 20 minutes on the average with an exponential distribution. Jobs arrive to the shop with interarrival times being exponentially distributed with a mean of 25 minutes. Each job consists of a set of operations to be performed on the machines in the job shop. The number of operations per job is Poisson distributed with a mean of 4. The routing of a job through the machines is determined by random assignment.

7-8.   Build a Visual SLAM subnetwork that models the following conveyor movement. The conveyor can hold eight parts. Parts are loaded on the conveyor at segment 1 and taken off the conveyor at segment 8. The time to load the conveyor is 2 minutes and the time to unload the conveyor is 1 minute. The conveyor is a gravity feed conveyor so that the parts move on the conveyor as long as there is not a part on the following section. The time to move on each section is 1/10th of a minute. If a part is on the following section then the part is blocked from moving on to that section. In a plant, there are 3 conveyors that have conveyors as described above. Demonstrate how the conveyor VSN can be used at the 3 locations in a model of the plant.

7-9.   Perform additional simulation runs for Example 7-2 and analyze the results. Make a comparison with the results presented in the example.

Embellishments: (a) Employ the shortest processing time rule for ordering jobs waiting before each machine group. Compare the output values with the first-in, first-out rule used in the example; (b) Give priority to jobs on the following basis: Type 3 is to have the highest priority, then Type 2 and then Type 1; (c) Change the mean arrival time to 9 minutes and evaluate system performance; (d) Change the model to include Type 4 jobs that visit 4 machines in the following order: CASTER, LATHE, PLANER and POLISHER with operation times of 150, 40, 30 and 75 minutes respectively. The interarrival time of jobs is 9 minutes and the probability of each job type is 10%, 44%, 32% and 14% for Types 1, 2, 3 and 4, respectively.

7-10.   For the job shop model of Example 7-2, revise the model so that jobs cannot proceed to the next machine group on its routing unless one of the machines of the machine group is idle. Simulate the model and compare results with those obtained from running Example 7-2 for 10 runs.

7.16 REFERENCES

1.   Pritsker, A. A. B., *Introduction to Simulation and SLAM II*, Fourth Edition, John Wiley and Systems Publishing Corporation, 1995.

2.   Schriber, T., *Simulation Using GPSS*, John Wiley, 1974.

CHAPTER 8

Visual SLAM Processor, Inputs and Outputs

8.1   INTRODUCTION

In this chapter, we discuss the use of the Visual SLAM simulation program to simulate network models. We begin by presenting an overview of the network simulation procedure employed by the Visual SLAM processor. This is followed by a detailed description of the input statements used in constructing network models, the control statements used when performing experiments with the Visual SLAM processor, and the standard output reports obtained from a Visual SLAM simulation. A Visual SLAM Quick Reference Manual is available that covers material from this chapter and the complete syntax and semantics of the language (1). With AweSim, described in Chapter 14, a graphical user interface is provided to facilitate the input and output activities associated with Visual SLAM. AweSim also includes an Interactive Execution Environment used to debug and verify model operations (2). These programs provide standard procedures for Applications Programming Interfaces (API) so that spreadsheet and statistical programs can easily be used with Visual SLAM.

8.2   NETWORK ANALYSIS

The network modeling approach consists of modeling a system as a set of entities which flow through a network of nodes and activities. As entities flow through a network, they occupy servers; advance time; await, seize and free resources; open and close gates; queue up in files; change variable values; and, in general, cause changes in the state of the system. A fundamental observation is that these changes can only occur at the time of arrival of an entity to a node. The Visual SLAM processor generates a complete portrayal of the changes in state of a network model by processing in a time-ordered sequence the events representing the arrival of an entity to a node.

The mechanism employed for maintaining the time-ordered sequence of entity arrival events is the event calendar. The event calendar consists of a list of entity arrival events, each characterized by an "event time" and an "end node". The event time specifies the time at which the entity arrival is to occur. The end node specifies the node to which the entity is to arrive. The events on the event calendar are ranked low-value-first (LVF) based on their event time.

The next-event processing logic employed by Visual SLAM for simulating networks is depicted in Figure 8-1. The processor begins by interpreting the Visual SLAM statements. This is followed by an initialization phase which is completed prior to the start of the simulation. During this initialization phase, the processor places on the event calendar an entity arrival event to occur at each CREATE node at the time of the first release of the node. Also, entities initially in QUEUE nodes are created and end-of-service activity events are scheduled where appropriate. Therefore, the event calendar will initially contain one arrival event corresponding to each CREATE node and one arrival event representing an end-of-activity for each busy server in the network.

The execution phase of a simulation begins by selecting the first event on the calendar. The processor advances the current simulated time, TNOW, to the event time corresponding to this event. It processes the event by performing all appropriate actions based on the decision logic associated with the node type to which the entity is arriving. For example, if the entity is arriving to an AWAIT node, the decision logic involved with realizing the event consists of testing to determine if the required level of resource is available; if yes, the entity seizes the desired units of resource and exits the node; otherwise, the entity is placed in the specified file and awaits the required resource. Although the decision logic is different for each node, the logic will result in one of three possible outcomes for the arriving entity:

1. The entity will be routed to another node;
2. The entity will be destroyed at the node; or
3. The entity will be delayed at the node based on the state of the system.

The routing of an entity from a node involves a test for activities emanating from the node. If there are no emanating activities or a sequential node, the entity is destroyed. When there are emanating activities, as many as M activities are selected in accordance with the probability or conditions associated with each activity where M is the M-number associated with the node. If an activity is selected, the entity or its clone with a new entity number is routed to the end node of the activity at the current time, TNOW, plus the duration of the activity.

After all events have been scheduled, the Visual SLAM processor tests for one of the following end-of-simulation conditions:

1. TNOW is greater than or equal to the user specified ending time of the simulation;
2. There are no events on the event calendar; or
3. A TERMINATE node has been released.

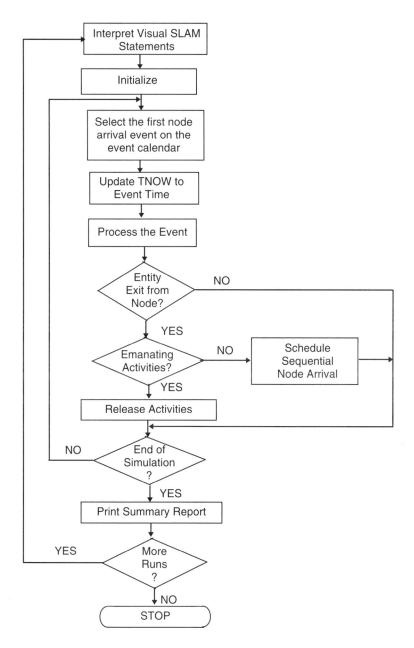

Figure 8-1 Visual SLAM next event processing logic for network simulations.

If none of the end of simulation conditions are satisfied, the Visual SLAM processor selects the next arrival event on the event calendar and continues. When a simulation run is ended, statistics are calculated and the Visual SLAM Summary Report is printed. A test is then made to determine if additional simulation runs are to be executed. If more runs remain, the next run is initiated. If all simulation runs have been completed, execution by the Visual SLAM processor is stopped and control is returned to the operating system.

The next event logic described above is well defined except when two or more arrival events are scheduled to occur at the same instant in time. To illustrate the problem, consider the case where we have a gate named DOOR which is currently open, and entities are scheduled to arrive at precisely the same time to the following statements:

	Statement 1	*Statement 2*
	AWAIT,1,DOOR;	CLOSE,DOOR;

If statement 1 is processed before statement 2, the gate DOOR will be open and the entity will exit the AWAIT node. However, if statement 2 is processed before statement 1, the entity arriving at statement 1 will be delayed at the AWAIT node because the gate DOOR was just closed. Therefore, the order in which simultaneous events are processed can affect the results of the simulation.

In describing the node arrival tie-breaking rules employed by Visual SLAM, it is convenient to classify all events on the event calendar as either "current events" or "future events." Current events are those events which are scheduled to occur at the current simulation time (TNOW), whereas future events are those events which are scheduled to occur at some simulated time in the future (not at TNOW). The reason for conceptually distinguishing between current and future events is that different tie-breaking procedures are employed depending upon whether the event is initially scheduled as a current event or as a future event.

The scheduling of an arrival event as a current event results from scheduling either a sequential node arrival or an end of activity node arrival where the activity has a duration of zero. In either case, the time at which the event is to occur is the current simulation time (TNOW). The scheduling procedure employed by Visual SLAM is always to place current events at the top of the event calendar, regardless of other events on the calendar. Therefore, current events are scheduled onto the calendar on a last-in, first-out (LIFO) basis. In the case where several zero duration activities emanate from a single node, the arrival events corresponding to the end of the activities are placed at the front of the calendar in the order that the activities appear in the statement model; that is, the first event would correspond to the first zero duration activity, the second event would correspond to the second zero duration activity, and so on. The ordering is based on the graphical location of the activities in the network. The topmost activity emanating from a node would be the first one processed, and so on.

Since the only mechanism for advancing time in a Visual SLAM network model is the activity, the scheduling of a future event necessarily corresponds to the arrival event resulting from an end of activity of nonzero duration. The tie-breaking procedure for scheduling future events employs a secondary ranking procedure which is defaulted to first-in, first-out (FIFO). The secondary ranking can be specified by the modeler (see Section 8.5.3) to be FIFO; LIFO; LVF(expr), low-value-first based on an expression; or HVF(expr), high-value-first based on an expression. In the case of the LVF or HVF secondary ranking, ties can still exist and they are broken using the FIFO rule.

At this point, the reader may be questioning the rationale of scheduling current events using LIFO as the tie-breaking rule while scheduling future events using a user specified tie-breaking rule. Why not just use one rule and avoid distinguishing between current and future events? The reason is that the LIFO rule is not only considerably more efficient in terms of computer execution time for scheduling current events, but it moves one entity at a time as far through the network as possible until it is either destroyed, delayed by the status of the system, or encounters a time delay. A FIFO rule would advance one entity one node, then advance the next entity one node, and so on. The advantage of the LIFO flow pattern will become apparent when the reader encounters traces of entity flow (the TRACE option is discussed in Section 8.5.9).

8.3   GENERAL FORMAT CONVENTIONS

Input statements are read by the Visual SLAM processor from an input file. This input file is generated by the AweSim network and control builders and is reported prior to the simulation run (Section 8.7.1). Each input statement is uniquely defined by the first three letters of the statement name. Each field in the statement is separated by a comma [,],and the semi-colon character [;] is used to denote the end of a statement. Braces, {}, are used to enclose compound fields and repeated fields. A few statements, such as the ASSIGN node definition, have fields which are compound and repeatable. An ASSIGN node with one assignment would be defined as follows:

ASSIGN,{ATRIB[1],1},1;

An example with two assignments would be:

ASSIGN,{{ATRIB[1],1},{ATRIB[2],TNOW}};

A field in a statement can be defaulted by simply omitting the entry while including the terminator. For example, an activity with zero duration, no branching condition, and an end node labeled EXIT can be specified by defaulting the number, duration and condition fields as follows:

ACTIVITY,,,,"EXIT";

Also, if a statement is terminated with remaining fields unspecified, the remaining fields take on their default values. For example, an ACTIVITY of duration 1, unconditionally taken, with an end node as the sequential node can be specified by defaulting all but the first two fields as follows:

ACTIVITY,,1;

The end node for this activity is assumed to be the next node statement encountered.

Input statements are read using a free format which permits a statement to be spaced across a line or over several lines. One restriction is that a field may not be split between lines. A continuation of a statement to the next line is assumed if the last non-blank character of the statement is a comma[,]. If the last non-blank character is any other character, an end of statement is assumed. However, the preferred method for ending a statement is the explicit use of the statement terminator [;] which permits the inclusion of comments following the terminator. All blanks are ignored, except within alphanumeric fields, and therefore can be freely employed to improve the readability of statements.

For example, the following ACTIVITY statement:

ACTIVITY,,10,ATRIB(1)==1&&TNOW<100,"LOOP";

can be spaced over three lines as follows:

ACTIVITY,,10,
        ATRIB(1)==1&&TNOW<100,
                              "LOOP";

However, it should be noted that the three lines would require a longer processing time than that required for the single line.

Numeric data can be entered as whole numbers (integers) or numbers with a fractional part (decimal numbers), and may be signed or unsigned. In addition, extremely large or extremely small numbers can be entered in scientific notation using an E format. For example, the number ten can be entered as 10 or 10. or + 10. or 1.E + 1 or 1E1 or 100E - 1. If a decimal number is entered in a field specified to be integer, the fractional part is dropped. Likewise if an integer is entered in a field specified to be decimal, its decimal equivalent is used. Therefore, the Visual SLAM input processor does not distinguish between 1. and 1 regardless of the field type specified.

8.4   NETWORK STATEMENT FORMATS

The network statements are preceded by a NETWORK statement and followed by an ENDNETWORK statement. The NETWORK statement consists of the characters NET entered anywhere on a line and denotes to the Visual SLAM processor that the lines to follow are network statements. The NETWORK statement and dialog box are shown below:

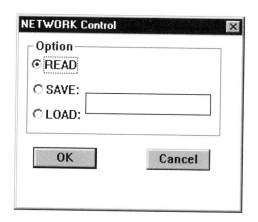

NETWORK,Option,File;

To store a decoded network, the SAVE option is selected and a file name is given in the file field. Thus, the statement

       NETWORK,SAVE,NET.DAT;

causes the decoded network to be written in binary form to the file NET.DAT. In future uses of the network, the statement

       NETWORK,LOAD, NET.DAT;

causes the decoded network to be used. This saves the computer time necessary to decode a large set of network statements. When the option is specified as LOAD, no network statements follow the NETWORK statement.

   The default for the option field assumes that a network is to be read. The ENDNETWORK statement consists of the characters END and denotes an end to all network statements. The ENDNETWORK statement is automatically inserted by AweSim when network input is translated. A list of network statements is presented in Table 8-1 which includes the default values for each field.

   Some of the features of the network input statements require further explanation. The overall design is intended to increase the readability of the statements without encumbering the user with extraneous information requirements. This goal led to the use of six delimiters to separate values:

   1.   Commas are used to separate fields.
   2.   Curly braces are used to enclose repeatable fields.
   3.   Fields which are constant strings are enclosed in double quotes.
   4.   Parentheses are used to enclose function arguments as in EXPON(1).
   5.   Square brackets are used to enclose subscripts, as in XX[2].
   6.   A semicolon is used to end a statement.

With these delimiters, efficient input statement preparation has been obtained. The examples demonstrate this point. As with any simulation language, it does require using the language to feel comfortable with the wide range of alternatives.

   Another aspect of the input statements is that all node types have been given verbs as names. This corresponds to the modeling approach which requires decisions and logical functions to be performed at the nodes of the network.

Table 8-1   Visual SLAM network statement types.

Statement Form	Statement Defaults (ND is no default)
Nodes	
ACCUM,FR,SR,SAVE,M;	ACCUM,1,1,LAST,∞;
ALTER,RES,CC,M;	ALTER,ND,ND, ∞;
ASSIGN,{{VAR,VALUE},repeats},	ASSIGN,{ND},∞;
AWAIT,IFL,{{RESORGATE,UR},repeats},	AWAIT,first IFL in RESORGATE list,
RULE,QC,FULLCOND,M;	{ND,1}, ALL, ∞, none, ∞;
BATCH,SORTVAL,THRESH,ADDVAL,	BATCH,none,ND, 1,
SAVE,{SUM,repeats},RETAIN,M;	LAST,{none}, NO, ∞;
CLOSE,GATE,M;	CLOSE,ND, ∞;
COLCT,N,VAR,"ID",	COLCT,ordered,ND,blanks,
NCEL,HLOW,HWID,M;	no histogram,0.0,1.0, ∞;
CREATE,TBC,TF,MV,MC,M;	CREATE, ∞,0.,no marking, ∞, ∞;
DETECT,XVAR,XDIR,VALUE,XTOL,M;	DETECT,ND,EITHER,ND,0, ∞;
ENTER,NUM,M;	ENTER,ND, ∞;
EVENT,JEVNT,M;	EVENT,ND, ∞;
FINDAR,FILE,COND,STRT,DIR,NUM,	FINDAR,ND,TRUE,FORWARD,
RNODE,{{VAR,VALUE}, repeats}, FOUND,M;	ALL, none, {none}, none, ∞;
FREE,{{RES,UF},repeats},M;	FREE,{ND,1}, ∞;
GOON,M;	GOON, ∞;
MATCH,MVAL,{{QLBL,NLBL},repeats};	MATCH,ND,{ND,no routing};
OPEN,GATE,M;	OPEN,ND, ∞;
PREEMPT,IFL,PR,RES,SNLBL,	PREEMPT,ND,no priority,ND, node of
REMTIME,M;	preemption, none, ∞;
QUEUE,IFL,IQ,QC,BLOCK or	QUEUE,ND,0, ∞, none,{none};
BALK(NLBL),{SLBL,repeats};	
READ,"FILE",REOPEN,STATVAR,	READ,ND,NO,no return,
"FORMAT",{VAR,repeats},M;	standard format,{ND}, ∞;
SELECT,QSR,SSR,FULLCOND,{QLBL,repeats};	SELECT,ORDER,ORDER,none,{ND};
TERMINATE,TC;	TERMINATE, ∞;
UNBATCH,NCLONE,M;	UNBATCH,0, ∞;
WRITE,"FILE",FLUSH,"FORMAT",	WRITE,ND,NO,standard format,{ND}, ∞;
{VAL,repeats},M;	
Blocks	
GATE,NUM,GLBL,INITSTAT,{IFL,repeats};	GATE,ordered,ND,OPEN,{ND} ∞;
GROUP,NUM,LABEL,{RESNUM, repeats},RULE;	GROUP,ordered,ND,ND,ORDER;
RESOURCE,NUM,RLBL,CAP,{IFL,repeats};	RESOURCE, ordered,ND,1,{ND};
VSN,NAME,{{PNAME,PTYPE,PDESC},repeats};	VSN,ND{none};
Activity	
ACTIVITY,A,duration,PROB (or) COND,	ACTIVITY,no ACT#number,0.0,
NLBL,NSERVERS, "ID";	PROB(1.0), next node,1,blank;
Subnetwork Nodes	
CALLVSN,NAME,INSTANCE, {PARAM,repeats},	CALLVSN,ND,ND {none}, ∞,
M,ENTER,{{EXIT#,NLBL}, repeats},	blank, this node;
ENTERVSN,NAME,M;	ENTERVSN, blank, ∞;
RETURNVSN,ERETURN,EXIT#;	RETURNVSN, none, none;

8.5   SIMULATION CONTROL STATEMENTS

In this section, we describe control statement types which are used in Visual SLAM simulations. A list of the statement types is presented in Table 8-2 in alphabetical order.

The control statement types related to network processing are described in the order of their most frequent use. The EQUIVALENCE and ARRAY statements were described in Chapter 5. The CONTINUOUS statement is used to define continuous variables and their evaluation procedures. The statement is described in Chapter 10. The SEVNT statement is used to specify state events which are events specified as the crossing of a threshold value by a variable. This statement is described in Chapter 12.

Table 8-2   VISUAL SLAM control statements.

Statement Form

ARRAY,IROW,NELEMENTS,{initial value,repeats};
CONTINUOUS,NNEQD,NNEQS,DTMIN,DTMAX,DTSAV,ERRCHK,AAERR,RRERR;
DOCOLCT,NCOLCT, "TABLENAME", "VARIABLE";
ENTRY,IFILE,NLBL,{attribute value, repeats};
EQUIVALENCE,{{NAME,VAR},repeats};
FIN:
GEN,NAME,PROJECT,DATE,NNRNS,EXECUTE,WARN,MXERR;
INITIALIZE,TTBEG,TTFIN,CLEAR,UPTO;
INTLC,{{VAR,VALUE},repeats};
LIMITS,MXX,MLL,MSZ,MATRIB,MLTRIB,MSTRIB,MNTRY;
MONTR,Option,TFRST,TSEC,{Trace expression,repeats};
NETWORK,Option,File;
PRIORITY,{{IFILE,ranking},repeats};
RECORD,RECORD#,"FILENAME",INDVAR,INDID,{Outputto},INDPF,
   START,END,INTVL,{{DEPVAREXPR,"DEPID",DEPPF},repeats};
REPORT,WIDTH,ECHO,SUMMARY,{{REPNAME,PRECISION},repeats};
SEEDS,{{ISEED,IS,R},repeats};
SEVNT,JEVNT,EXPR,XDIR,THRESH,TOL;
SIMULATE;
TIMST,STAT#,EXPR,"ID",#CELLS,LOWER,WIDTH;

8.5.1   GEN Statement

The GEN statement provides general information about a simulation in the format shown below.

GEN,NAME,PROJECT,DATE,NNRNS,EXECUTE,WARN,MXERR;

It is created by the following AweSim dialog box.

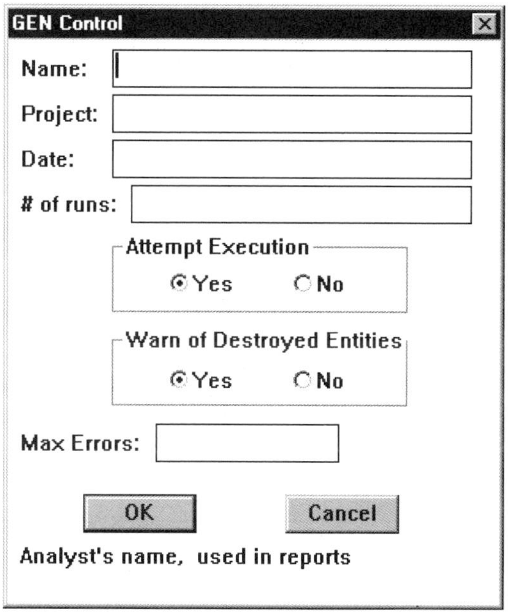

The GEN statement should be the first statement in any set of Visual SLAM control statements. Included on the GEN statement are: the analyst's name, a project identifier, date, number of simulation runs, and execution options. The NAME, PROJECT, and DATE are alphanumeric and are used for output reports to identify the analyst and the project. Recall that blanks are significant within alphanumeric fields. The Visual SLAM variable NNRNS is entered as an integer, has a default value of 1 and denotes the number of simulation runs to be made. The next three fields correspond to the following options:

EXECUTE If yes, execution is attempted if no input errors are detected. If specified as no, execution is not attempted.

WARN   If yes, a warning message is printed when an entity is destroyed before reaching a TERMINATE node; otherwise the printing is omitted.

MXERR   The number of execution errors allowed before the simulation is halted. The default is 1.

8.5.2   LIMITS Statement

The format of the LIMITS statement and its AweSim dialog box are shown below.

LIMITS,MXX,MLL,MSZ,MATRIB,MLTRIB,MSTRIB,MNTRY;

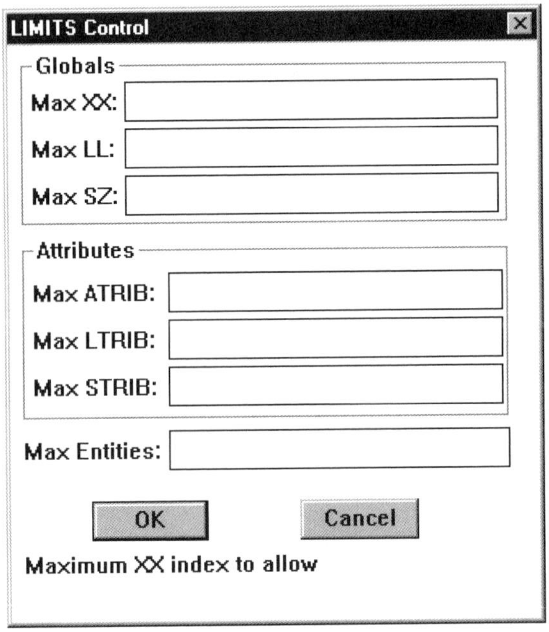

The second statement in a set of Visual SLAM controls is normally the LIMITS statement. The LIMITS statement is used to specify integer limits on the largest global variable numbers used, the largest number of attributes per entity, and the maximum number of concurrent entries in all files (MNTRY). The MXX, MLL and MSZ fields define the number of XX, LL, and SZ global variables (Table 5-1) used in the model. The MATRIB, MLTRIB and MSTRIB fields specify the largest index used for attributes of various types (ATRIB, LTRIB, STRIB) and MNTRY puts an upper limit on the number of entities that can exist in the model at one time. Although MNTRY may be defaulted, which allows all storage space available on the computer to be used, defining a limit is recommended in case a large number of entities is created in error.

8.5.3   PRIORITY Statement

The format of the PRIORITY statement and its AweSim dialog box are shown below.

PRIORITY,{{FILE, ranking},repeats};

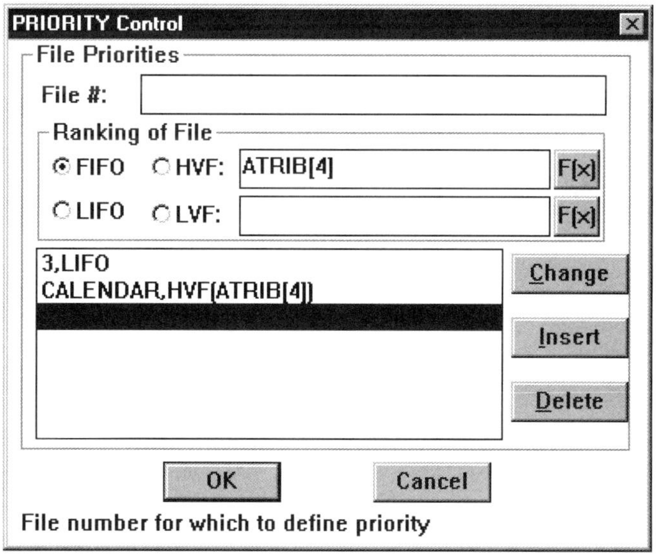

The PRIORITY statement is used to specify the criterion for ranking entities within a file. There are four possible specifications for the criterion:

FIFO	Entries are ranked based on their order of insertion in the file with early insertion given priority. This is a first-in, first-out ranking criterion.
LIFO	Entries are ranked based on their time of insertion with late insertions given priority. This is a last-in, first-out ranking criterion.
HVF(expr)	The entries are ranked high-value-first based on the value of an expression.
LVF(expr)	The entries are ranked low-value-first based on the value of an expression.

The default for the criterion for all files is FIFO, therefore a PRIORITY statement for a file need be included only if the file is ranked LIFO, HVF(expr), or LVF(expr). A file ranking is specified by entering the file number and the file ranking. The rankings for different files can be specified on a single PRIORITY statement by repeated insertions.

The PRIORITY statement can also be used to specify the secondary ranking procedure for breaking ties between simultaneous node arrivals which are scheduled as future events by specifying the file number (File#) with the alphanumeric characters CALENDAR denoting the event calendar. The event code can be used as the attribute specification by inserting the characters ETYPE for the attribute number. The following statement specifies that file 3 is to be ranked on a LIFO basis and the tie-breaking rule for events is high-value-first based on attribute 4:

PRIORITY,{{3,LIFO},{CALENDAR,HVF(ATRIB[4])}};

If the secondary ranking for the event calendar is to be low-value-first based on the event code, the statement would be:

PRIORITY,{{3,LIFO},{CALENDAR,LVF(NNVNT)}};

8.5.4   TIMST Statement

The format for the TIMST statement is shown below and its AweSim dialog box on the next page.

TIMST,STAT#,EXPR,"ID",#CELLS,LOWER,WIDTH;

The TIMST statement is normally employed to initiate the automatic collection of time-persistent statistics on the global variables XX[N] and LL[N] or on the state or derivative variables SS[N] and DD[N]. To employ the TIMST statement to initiate statistics on the indexed variable XX[N] where N is an integer, the user simply enters XX[N] in the variable field and provides an alphanumeric identifier (ID) which is to be used in displaying the statistics in the Visual SLAM Summary Report.

An example of the TIMST statement to collect statistics on the global variable XX[1] defined to be the number of entities currently in the network is shown below.

TIMST,1,XX[1],"NUMBER IN SYSTEM";

Histograms can also be obtained on the fraction of time that the expression EXPR was within a range of values. The number of cells in the histogram and the width of each cell is specified by #CELLS, LOWER and WIDTH as discussed in Section 5.12. The statement TIMST, 2,NNQ[1], "QUEUE LENGTH", 10,0,1; specifies that statistics and a histogram are to be obtained with the histogram presenting the amount of time the queue length is 0, 1, 2, ...,9.

8.5.5   SEEDS Statement

The format and AweSim dialog box for the SEEDS statement are shown below.

SEEDS,{{SEED,STREAM,REINIT},repeats};

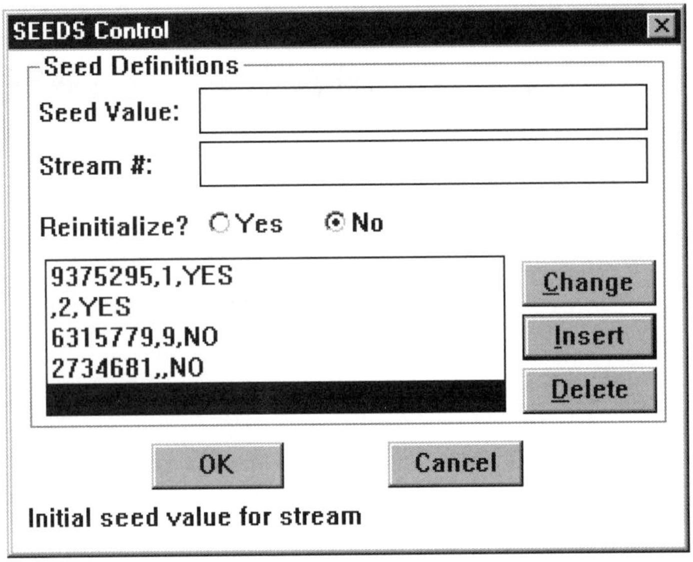

The purpose of the SEEDS statement is to permit the user to specify the starting unnormalized random number seed for any of the 100 random number streams available within Visual SLAM and to control the reinitialization of streams for multiple simulation runs. The seeds are entered as integers followed by the stream number of the seed and the reinitialization flag.   If the stream number is not specified, then stream numbers are assigned based on the position of the seed in the SEEDS statement list. The first seed is for stream 1, the second for stream 2, and so on. The reinitialization of each stream is controlled by specifying YES or NO after the seed value and stream number. If the subfield is not included, the default case is assumed and the seed values are not reinitialized. If the SEEDS input statement is not included, the Visual SLAM processor uses default seed values.

An example of the SEEDS input statement is shown below:

SEEDS,{{9375295,1,YES},{,2,YES},{6315779,9,},{2734681,,}};

This statement initializes the seed for stream 1 to 9375295 and specifies that this value be used as the first value for each run. The empty field specifies that the default value should be used for stream 2 and that it should be the first value for each run. The seed value for stream 9 is 6315779 and it is not to be reinitialized on subsequent runs. The seed value for stream 10 is 2734681 and is not to be reinitialized. If antithetic random numbers are desired for a run then a negative seed value is used. The sequence of random numbers generated will be the complement of the numbers generated from the use of a positive value of the seed. The function XRN(IS) can be used to access the value of the last random number generated from stream IS.

8.5.6   INTLC Statement

The format and AweSim dialog box for the INTLC statement are shown below.

INTLC,{{VAR, value},repeats};

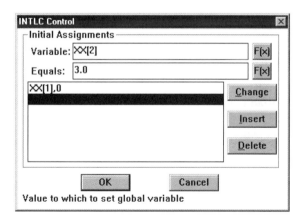

The INTLC statement is used to assign initial values to the Visual SLAM global variables XX[N], LL[N], SZ[N], ARRAY[N,N], SS[N], or DD[N] where N is an integer. Multiple initial values can be specified on the statement by specifying each assignment and inserting it into the list. An example is:

INTLC,{{XX[1],0},{XX[2],3.0}};

8.5.7   INITIALIZE Statement

The format and AweSim dialog box for the INITIALIZE statement are shown below.

INITIALIZE,TTBEG,TTFIN,CLEAR,UPTO;

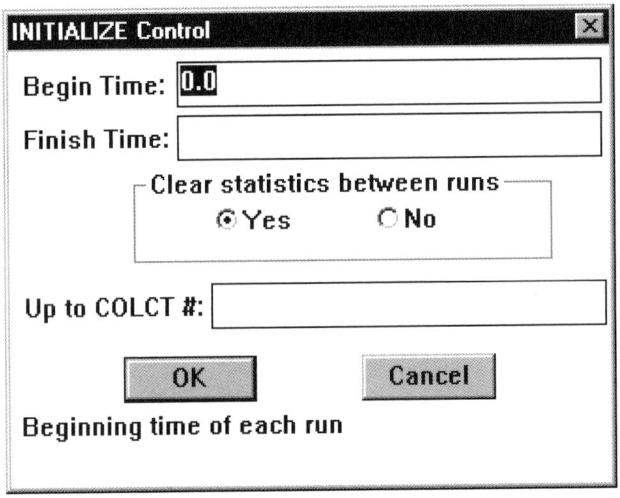

The INITIALIZE statement is used to specify the beginning time (TTBEG) and ending time (TTFIN) for a simulation, and initialization options for clearing statistics. If CLEAR is specified as YES (the default), UPTO specifies the number of the collect variable up to which clearing is to be performed. If CLEAR is specified as NO, UPTO specifies the collect variable number up to which clearing is not to be performed. The default value for UPTO is that CLEAR applies to all collect variables.

8.5.8   ENTRY Statement

The format and AweSim dialog box for the ENTRY statement are shown below:

ENTRY,FILE,NLBL,{attribute values, repeats};

```
┌─────────────────────────────────────────────────────────────────┐
│ ENTRY Control                                              [×]    │
│                                                                   │
│   File: │1│          Net Node Label: │                    │      │
│  ┌─ Entry Definitions ──────────────────────────────────────┐    │
│  │ Attribute Values: │                        │ │F(x)│       │    │
│  │ ┌──────────────────────────────────────┐  ┌────────────┐ │    │
│  │ │ 0                                    │  │  Change    │ │    │
│  │ │ 20.                                  │  ├────────────┤ │    │
│  │ │ 3.5                                  │  │  Insert    │ │    │
│  │ │ 4                                    │  ├────────────┤ │    │
│  │ │                                      │  │  Delete    │ │    │
│  │ └──────────────────────────────────────┘  └────────────┘ │    │
│  │                                                          │    │
│        ┌──────────┐              ┌──────────┐                     │
│        │   OK     │              │  Cancel  │                     │
│        └──────────┘              └──────────┘                     │
│   List of initial attribute values                                │
└─────────────────────────────────────────────────────────────────┘
```

The ENTRY statement is used to place an entity into a file or release it from a node at the beginning of a simulation run. An entity is specified by entering the file number (FILE) or the node label (NLBL) followed by the attributes of the entity separated by commas. The ordering of the attributes is ATRIB[0], ATRIB[1],..., ATRIB[MATRIB], LTRIB[0], LTRIB[1],..., LTRIB[MLTRIB], STRIB[0], STRIB[1],..., STRIB[MSTRIB]. That is, the number of real-valued attributes as specified on the LIMITS statement is defined, followed by the number of integer-valued attributes, followed by the string attributes. Any unspecified attribute value is defaulted to zero (for ATRIB or LTRIB) or to blank (for STRIB). If the file is associated with a QUEUE or AWAIT node, the entity is processed as an arrival to the node at the beginning of the simulation. Examples of ENTRY statements are shown below.

ENTRY,1,,{0,20.,3.5,4};   Inserts an entity into file 1 with ATRIB[0] = 0, ATRIB[1] = 20., ATRIB[2] = 3.5 and ATRIB[3] = 4.

ENTRY,,"VLDZ";   Schedules an entity arrival to node labeled VLDZ with all attribute values defaulted.

ENTRY statements apply only to a single run and would need to be repeated (after the SIMULATE statement) if used with multiple runs.

8.5.9   MONTR Statement

The format and AweSim dialog box for the MONTR statement are shown below.

MONTR,Option,TFRST,TSEC,{Trace Expression, repeats};

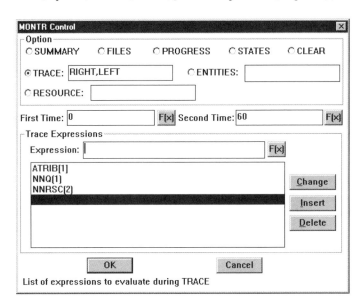

The MONTR statement is used to monitor selected intermediate simulation results. The MONTR statement can also be used to clear statistical arrays after a "warm up" period in order to reduce any bias that is due to initial starting conditions. The values on the MONTR statement consist of the MONTR option, the time for the first execution of the option (TFRST), and a time for the successive executions or the completion of the option (TSEC). The times TFRST and TSEC default to TTBEG and infinity, respectively. If TSEC is defaulted, the MONTR option is executed only at time TFRST. However, if TSEC is specified, the MONTR option is executed at time TFRST and, except for the TRACE, ENTITIES, and RESOURCE option, every TSEC time units thereafter. For the other options, TSEC specifies the stopping time. There are eight MONTR options available:

PROGRESS	Writes a "simulation continuing" message.
SUMMARY	Causes a Visual SLAM Summary Report to be printed.
FILES	Causes a listing of all entries in the files to be printed.

STATES   Causes SS[N] and DD[N] to be printed.

CLEAR   Causes all statistical arrays to be cleared.

TRACE   Causes the starting and stopping of detailed tracing of
                                each entity as it moves through the network. The trace
                                will start at time TFRST and end at TSEC. A list of
                                nodes can be provided with the TRACE option as
        follows: TRACE (nodelist). This causes an output only
        when one of the nodes in the list is processed. Also for
        the TRACE option, a list of variables to print with the
        trace may be defined.

ENTITY(enum,...)   Causes a trace record to be printed when any of the listed
        entities are processed. The listed entities are identified
        by their entity number, enum.

RESOURCE(rnum,...)   Causes a trace record to be printed when a status change
                                occurs for any of the listed resources. The listed
        resources are identified by their resource number, rnum.
        If the list is omitted, all resources are traced.

Below are examples of the MONTR statement:

Statement	*Description*
MONTR ,SUMRY,200., l00. ;	Print a summary report at TNOW= 200 and every 100 time units thereafter
MONTR,CLEAR,500;	Clear STATISTICS at TNOW= 500
MONTR,TRACE(RIGHT ,LEFT), 0,10,{ATRIB[1],NNQ(1), NNRSC(2)};	From time 0 to 10, trace events associated with the nodes labeled RIGHT and LEFT. Print the values of ATRIB [1] of each entity, the number in file l, and the availability of resource 2 with each trace message.

MONTR statements apply only to a single run and must be restated for each run.

8.5.10 RECORD Statement

The RECORD statement provides the information required to record data for plots and tables. This includes an explicit specification for a plot number, IPLOT, or an implicit value determined by the order in which the RECORD statement appears. Also provided on the RECORD statement are definitions for the independent variable, the dependent variables, the storage medium, and detailed specifications concerning the type and time interval for the output reports.

The format and AweSim dialog box of the RECORD statement are:

RECORD,RECORD#,"FILENAME",INDVAR,"INDID",{Outputto},INDPF,
    START, END,INTVL,{{DEPVAREXPR,"DEPID",DEPPF},repeats};

The definitions of the fields are listed below.

Variable	Definition	Default
RECORD#	Record number.	next sequential index
FILENAME	Name of the external file for saving data. If multiple save formats are specified, then only the base name of the file is used, and extensions are based on the format.	OUT1.PLT
INDVAR	Independent variable expression.	error
"INDID"	Label for the independent variable, used for a column header.	blanks
Outputto	One or more output formats: AWESIM - format for AweSim plots TABLE - tabular report of data points COMMA - comma delimited format for import into most spreadsheet packages. EXCEL - EXCEL spreadsheet file format. Database - DBASE file format. USER - format defined by user-written function.	AWESIM
INDPF	Format for printing independent variable in TABLE and COMMA formats. Refer to printf formats in a C reference.	use standard format for expression type
START	Time to start recording plot data.	TTBEG
END	Time to stop recording plot data.	TTFIN
INTVL	Interval between data record times. If data will be recorded from user code through function GPLOT, START should be greater than END.	when variable value changes
DEPVAREXPR	Dependent variable expression	error
"DEPID"	Label for the dependent variable, used for column header.	blanks
DEPPF	Format for printing dependent variable in TABLE and COMMA formats. Refer to printf formats in a C reference.	use standard format for expression type

Examples of RECORD definitions are shown below.

RECORD,,,TNOW,"TIME",,,,,,{NNQ(1),,};   Creates an AweSim plot of the variable NNQ(1) from the beginning to the end of the simulation run. Data is recorded whenever the length of file 1 changes.

RECORD,1,"SPLOT",SS[1],"X POSITION", {AWESIM,TABLE},,,,{SS(2), "Y POSITION",,};   Creates an AweSim plot and a table of SS(2) plotted against SS(1) from the beginning to the end of the simulation run. Data is recorded at the step times defined by the CONTINUOUS statement. Data will be saved in the files SPLOT.PLT and SPLOT.TAB.

8.5.11   REPORT Statement

The REPORT statement is used to set the report width, control the number of reports generated, and define the precision with which real numbers are reported. The format and AweSim dialog box for the REPORT statement are shown below.

REPORT,WIDTH,ECHO,INT,SUMMARY,{{REPNAME,PRECISION},repeats};

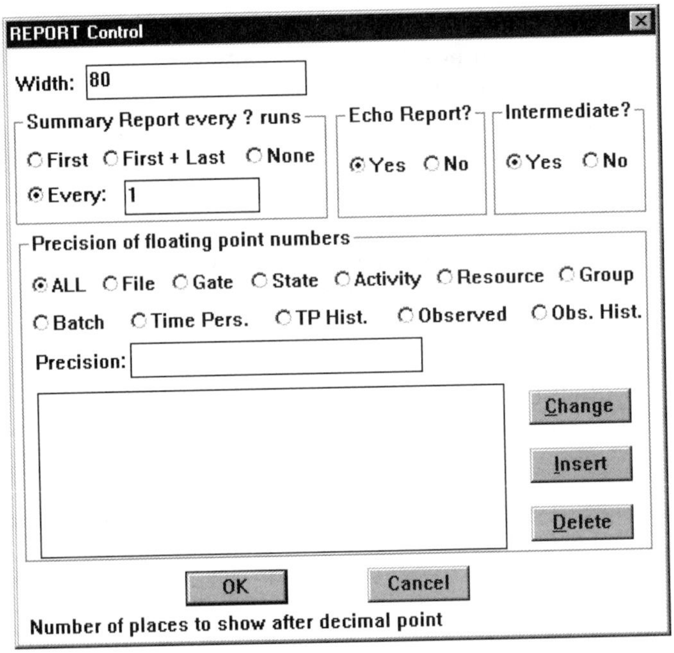

The default values for each field are displayed in the dialog box.

Examples of the REPORT statement are:

REPORT,,YES,,FIRST,{{FILE,4},{ACTIVITY,4}}; Writes an echo report and a summary report only on the first run. Reports file statistics and activity statistics to the fourth decimal place.

REPORT,72,NO,NO,EVERY(10); Writes a 72-column summary report every 10th run starting with run 10. No echo report and no intermediate report are written. Precision for all outputs is defaulted to 3 decimal places.

8.5.12   DOCOLCT Statement

The format and AweSim dialog box for the DOCOLCT statement are shown below.

DOCOLCT,NCOLCT,"TABLENAME","VARIABLE";

The DOCOLCT statement is used to save the individual observations at a COLCT node with statistic number NCOLCT, to an AweSim database file, TABLENAME.dbf. Within the database file, observations from COLCT node number NCOLCT are stored in a column named VARIABLE. The data can then be retrieved and analyzed, using standard database tools.

8.5.13   SIMULATE Statement

The SIMULATE statement consists of a single field as shown below.

SIMULATE;

The SIMULATE statement is used when making multiple simulation runs. One simulation run is executed for the statements preceding the SIMULATE statement. Following each SIMULATE statement, the user can insert any updates such as new random number seeds using the SEEDS statement, new ENTRY statements, or new initial values for the global variables such as XX[N] using the INTLC statements. If only one simulation run is being made (NNRNS=1), or multiple runs are being made (NNRNS>1) with the same starting conditions, the SIMULATE statement is not required. Recall, however, that ENTRY and MONTR statements only apply for one run.

8.5.14   FIN Statement

The FIN statement consists of a single field as shown below.

FIN;

The FIN statement denotes the end to all Visual SLAM input statements. The FIN statement causes the execution of all remaining simulation runs.

This completes the description of network statements and control statements for executing network models. The description of other control statements that relate to discrete, continuous, and combined models is given in later chapters.

8.6   PROGRAM SETUP FOR NETWORK MODELS

The control statements in a simulation input file can be in any order, except that a component must be defined before it is used. If the variable ATRIB[1] is a trace variable on a MONTR statement, for example, the LIMITS statement defining the number of attributes being used must precede the MONTR statement. Also, a set of control statements must end with a SIMULATE or FIN statement.

8.7   VISUAL SLAM OUTPUT REPORTS

The purpose of this section is to describe the output reports which are generated by the Visual SLAM processor. The output reports include the input listing, echo report, intermediate report, and Visual SLAM summary report. A description of each report is given in the following sections. Since the data for each report is available in the AweSim database and in accessible files, customized reports can easily be developed using Crystal Report capabilities or by developing a Visual Basic Report Wizard.

8.7.1   Statement Listing and Input Error Messages

The Visual SLAM processor interprets each input statement and performs extensive checks for possible input errors. If the variable IECHO on the REPORT statement is specified as YES or defaulted, the processor prints out a listing of the input statements. Each statement is assigned a line number and, if an input error is detected, an error message is printed immediately following the statement where the error occurred.

Each item of data in a statement following the statement type counts as a field. Fields are counted left to right. For example, the following statement with field numbers shown circled over the statement would result in the message "Incorrect type of function argument. Field: 3, at or near)".

The incorrect field in this contains "85" which is not a valid entry for a probability.

All input errors are treated as fatal errors in Visual SLAM; that is, no execution is attempted if one or more input errors are detected.

8.7.2   Intermediate Report

The Visual SLAM Intermediate Report begins with a summary of the simulation model as interpreted by the Visual SLAM processor. This report is particularly useful during the debugging and verification phases of the simulation model development process. This Echo Report is followed by the Trace Report, if any.

The Trace Report is initiated by the MONTR statements using the TRACE option and causes a report summarizing each entity arrival event to be printed during execution of the simulation. The Trace Report generates a detailed account of the progress of a simulation by printing for each entity arrival event, the event time, the node label and type to which the entity is arriving, the input line number, and any variable values selected by the modeler. In addition, a summary of all regular activities which emanate from the node is printed denoting if the activity was scheduled, the duration of the activity, and the input line number for the activity. An illustration of a trace report is given in Figure 4-9.

8.7.3   Visual SLAM Summary Report

The Visual SLAM summary report displays the statistical results for the simulation and is automatically printed at the end of each simulation run. The report consists of a general section followed by the statistical results for the simulation categorized by type. The output statistics provided by the report are defined in Figure 8-2 and Table 8-3. The first category of statistics is for variables based on discrete observations and includes the statistics collected within network models by the COLCT statement. The second category of statistics is for time-persistent variables. This is followed by statistics on files and the event calendar. The next two categories correspond to statistics collected on regular and service activities, respectively. The next category of statistics is for resource and gate statistics. The last category of statistics is for BATCH nodes and is followed by the printout of histograms. A Visual SLAM Summary Report includes only those categories of statistics which are applicable to the particular simulation, and therefore may include none, some or all of the above categories.

```
                      ** AweSim SUMMARY REPORT **
                         Time/Date Stamp

      Simulation Project :  A1
      Modeler :  A2
      Date :  A3
      Scenario :  A4
      Run number A5 of A6
      Current simulation time    :  A7
      Statistics cleared at time :  A8

                ** OBSERVED STATISTICS REPORT for scenario A4 **

   Label      Mean        Standard      Number of    Minimum     Maximum
              Value       Deviation     Observations Value       Value

    B1        B2            B3             B4           B5          B6

                ** TIME-PERSISTENT STATISTICS REPORT for scenario A4 **

   Label    Mean     Standard   Minimum     Maximum    Time       Current
            Value    Deviation  Value       Value      Interval   Value

    C1      C2       C3         C4          C5         C6         C7


                ** FILE STATISTICS REPORT for scenario A4 **

   File     Label or    Average   Standard   Maximum   Current    Average
   Number   Input Loc.  Length    Dev.       Length    Length     Wait Time

    D1       D2          D3        D4         D5        D6         D7


                ** ACTIVITY STATISTICS REPORT for scenario A4 **

   Activity Label or   Average    Standard  Entity    Maximum     Current
   Number   Input Loc. Util.      Dev.      Count     Util.       Util.

    E1       E2          E3         E4        E5        E6          E7


                ** SERVICE ACTIVITY STATISTICS REPORT for scenario A4 **

   Activity Label or   Server    Entity   Average    Standard    Current
   Number   Input Loc. Capacity  Count    Util.      Dev.        Util.

    F1       F2          F3         F4       F5        F6          F7
```

Figure 8-2 Definition of Visual SLAM output statistics corresponding to Table 8-3.

Activity Number	Average Blockage	Maximum Idle Time or Servers	Maximum Busy Time or Servers
F1	F8	F9	F10

** RESOURCE STATISTICS REPORT for scenario A4 **

Resource Number	Resource Label	Average Util.	Standard Dev.	Current Util.	Maximum Util.	Current Capacity
G1	G2	G3	G4	G5	G6	G7

Resource Number	Average Available	Current Available	Minimum Available	Maximum Available
G1	G8	G9	G10	G11

** GROUP STATISTICS REPORT for scenario A4 **

Group Number	Group Label	Average Util.	Standard Dev.	Current Util.	Maximum Util.	Current Capacity
H1	H2	H3	H4	H5	H6	H7

Group Number	Average Available	Current Available	Minimum Available	Maximum Available
H1	H8	H9	H10	H11

** GATE STATISTICS REPORT for scenario A4 **

Gate Number	Gate Label	Current Status	Percent of Time Open
I1	I2	I3	I4

** BATCH STATISTICS REPORT for scenario A4 **

Batch Node	Average Number Waiting	Maximum Number Waiting	Current Number Waiting	Average Waiting Time
J1	J2	J3	J4	J5

Figure 8-2 (continued)

Table 8-3 Definition of output statistics corresponding to Figure 8-2.

General Section

A1	The project title from the GEN statement
A2	The analyst name from the GEN statement
A3	The date from the GEN statement
A4	The AweSim Scenario name
A5	The number of the simulation run
A6	The number of simulation runs to be made
A7	The current value of TNOW
A8	Time at which all statistical arrays were last cleared

Statistics for Variables Based on Observation

B1	The first 16 characters of the statistics label
B2	The arithmetic mean of the observations
B3	The standard deviation of the observations
B4	The number of observations
B5	The minimum value over all observations
B6	The maximum value over all observations

Statistics for Time-Persistent Variables

C1	The label for the variable
C2	The average value of the variable over time
C3	The standard deviation over time
C4	The minimum value of the variable over time
C5	The maximum value of the variable over time
C6	The time interval over which the statistics are accumulated
C7	The current value of the variable

Table 8.3   (Continued)

File Statistics

    D1   The file number or event calendar

    D2   The network symbol label or input line number associated with the file

    D3   The average number of entities in the file over time

    D4   The standard deviation of the number of entities in the file over time

    D5   The maximum number of entities in the file at any one time

    D6   The current number of entities in the file

    D7   The average waiting time of all entities that arrived to the file including those that did not wait

Regular Activity Statistics

    E1   The activity index number for the activity

    E2   The identifying label or input line number of the activity definition

    E3   The average number of entities in the activity

    E4   The standard deviation of the number of entities in the activity

    E5   The number of entities which have completed the activity

    E6   The maximum number of entities in the activity at any one time

    E7   The number of entities currently in the activity

Service Activity Statistics

    F1   The activity number for the activity. A zero if a number is not assigned.

    F2   Statistics are listed in the same order as the input statements.

    F3   The identifying label or input line number of the activity definition.

    F4   The number of parallel identical servers represented by the activity.

    F5   If the service activity is assigned an activity index number, the number of entities completing service; otherwise no value is printed.

    F6   The average number of entities in service over time. If the capacity of the server is 1, this corresponds to the fraction of time the server is busy.

    F7   The standard deviation of the number of entities in service over time.

    F8   The current number of entities in service.

    F9   The average number of servers blocked over time. If the capacity of the server is 1, this corresponds to the fraction of time blocked.

Table 8.3   (Continued)

F10	If the capacity of the server is 1, this value specifies the maximum idle time of the server. If the capacity of the server is greater than 1, this value specifies the maximum number of idle servers.
F11	Maximum busy time for a single server or maximum number of busy servers.

Resource Statistics

G1	The resource number
G2	The resource label as specified on the RESOURCE block
G3	The average utilization of the resource over time
G4	The standard deviation of the resource utilization over time
G5	The current number of units of resource in use
G6	The maximum number of units of resource available at any one time
G7	The current capacity of the resource
G8	The average availability of the resource over time
G9	The current number of units of resource available
G10	The minimum number of units of resource available at any one time
G11	The maximum number of units of resource utilized at any one time

Group Statistics

H1	The group number
H2	The group label as specified on the group block
H3	The average utilization of the group over time
H4	The standard deviation of the group utilization over time
H5	The current number of units of group in use
H6	The maximum number of units of group available at any one time
H7	The current capacity of the group
H8	The average availability of the group over time
H9	The current number of units of group available
H10	The minimum number of units of group available at any one time
H11	The maximum number of units of group utilized at any one time

Table 8.3   (Concluded)

Gate Statistics

I1	The gate number
I2	The gate label as specified on the GATE block
I3	The current status of the gate
I4	The percentage of time the gate was opened

Batch Statistics

J1	The label or input line number of the BATCH node
J2	The average number of entities waiting to be batched
J3	The maximum number of entities waiting to be batched
J4	The current number of entities waiting to be batched
J5	The average time spent waiting to be batched

8.7.4   Multiple Run Summary Report

The Visual SLAM multiple run summary report displays the average of averages for each statistic reported on the individual summary report for each run.   The maximum average value, minimum average value, standard error and standard deviation of the averages are also included.

8.8   CHAPTER SUMMARY

This chapter describes the input statements and output reports associated with Visual SLAM network models and the overall processing logic for simulating Visual SLAM networks.

8.9   EXERCISES

8-1.   Obtain a trace for Example 5-3 from which you can determine if the operation time of jobs preempted is equal to the remaining processing time on the operation from which they were preempted.

8-2.   In the following input statements, detect at least eight errors.

```
        GEN,"EXERCISE 8-2",ERRORS,JULY/18/1995,2;
    LIMITS,,,,1;
    PRIORITY,{3,HVT(2)};
    INTLC,{XX[1],2.0};
    NETWORK;
        CREATE,UNIFORM(XX[1],10.);
        AWAIT,1,TELLER;
            ACT,,EXPON (4.0);
        FREE,TELLER;
        TERM;
    INIT,0,100;
    SIMULATE;
    INTLC,{XX(1),4.0};
    FIN;
```

8-3.   Prepare the input data for Illustration 4-2 in Section 4.10.2 to make 5 runs with each run lasting 1000 time units. On the second run, the mean and standard deviation for the normal distribution should be changed to 0.0 and 2.0. No additional changes are required on the third run. On the fourth run, the ranking at QUEUE node QOFS should be changed to last-in, first-out. No additional changes are required for run number 5.

8-4.   The thief of Baghdad has been placed in a dungeon with three doors. One door leads to freedom, one door leads to a long tunnel, and a third door leads to a short tunnel. The tunnels return the thief to the dungeon. If the thief returns to the dungeon, he attempts to gain his freedom again but his past experiences do not help him in selecting the door that leads to freedom, that is, we assume a Markov thief. The thief's probabilities of selecting the doors are: 0.30 to freedom; 0.20 to the short tunnel; and 0.50 to the long tunnel. Draw the network and prepare the data input for 1000 runs using the following information: P_F=0.3, P_S=0.2, P_L=0.5, the time in the short tunnel is exponentially distributed with a mean of 3, and the time in the long tunnel is lognormally distributed with a mean of 6 and a standard deviation of 2.

Suppose the thief's remaining time to live is normally distributed with a mean of 10 and a standard deviation of 2. Redraw the network and redo the data input in order to ascertain the probability that the thief reaches freedom before he dies based on 1000 simulations of the network.

8-5.   For the following network, describe the chronological sequence of node arrival events if the secondary ranking for future events is FIFO.

Embellishment: Repeat the exercise with the secondary ranking for future events as LIFO.

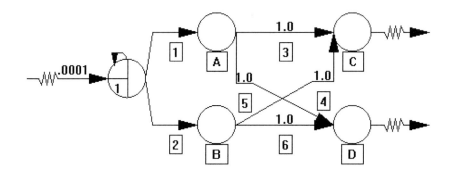

8-6.   Prepare the Visual SLAM input statements for Exercise 8-5 to make two runs. The secondary ranking for future events should be FIFO on the first run and LIFO on the second run. Obtain a TRACE report on both runs.

8-7.   Perform a simulation of a queueing situation using Visual SLAM and discuss the meaning of each output statistic that is given on the Visual SLAM summary report.

8. 10 REFERENCES

1.   *VISUAL SLAM Quick Reference Manual*, Pritsker Corporation, 1996.

2.   *AweSim User's Guide*, Pritsker Corporation, 1996.

Network Modeling With Visual Basic Inserts

9.1   INTRODUCTION

In this chapter, we describe the procedures for constructing network models with user-written Visual Basic inserts. We begin by describing the EVENT and ENTER nodes which provide the key interface points between the network model and user code. The support subprograms of Visual SLAM for performing file manipulations and setting attribute values and activity durations are presented. We next describe a set of Visual SLAM provided functions which allow the modeler to change the status of the network elements by allocating and freeing units of resources, altering resource capacities, opening and closing gates, stopping activities and specifying selection rules from user-written subprograms.

Before describing user-written inserts, a brief discussion of Visual SLAM objects and their methods and properties as related to network inserts is presented.

9.1.1   Visual SLAM Objects

Visual SLAM provides a means to understand and build a model from distinct objects. An object can be anything: a button, a form, a control, a network element, a file and so on (1). For objects, you need to know how to use them, not how they do their function. For example, a CREATE node is an object that creates entities and causes them to be routed into the network. What is important is that the CREATE node carries out its functions, not the code that underlies the CREATE node.

In this chapter, the object classes of Visual SLAM networks are summarized to allow their use in user inserts written in Visual Basic. The Visual Basic programmer will be able to use these concepts to build new Visual SLAM interfaces quickly, to define new object classes and to integrate with other applications. Integration can be accomplished through object linking and embedding, custom controls and Visual SLAM's database architecture.

As discussed above, a node is an object. All nodes taken as a group are referred to as an object class. In Visual SLAM, this object class is referenced by the name VSNODE. Where you need to access the properties or use the methods associated with a specific node then an object with a name must be defined as an instance of this object class. For user inserts, this establishing of an object has been simplified by creating a global Visual SLAM object class named VSLAM. An instance of VSLAM named VS is provided automatically in the Visual Basic public subroutine CONNECT. Thus many references to methods and properties of objects in user inserts have the prefix VS. For example, VS.TNOW is the current time. Since VS is the only object that is provided by Visual SLAM, it has been capitalized. When objects are obtained in examples of user code in this book either lower case names or combinations of upper and lower case names are used to help differentiate between objects and object classes. Both methods and properties of objects are referenced in Visual Basic and, hence in Visual SLAM, in the following manner:

> object.method
> object.property

The methods and properties associated with objects is provided throughout this chapter and in Chapter 11VB. In AweSim, the object browser of Visual Basic provides a complete list of Visual SLAM object classes and the methods and properties of objects. This list is provided under project "Ss_vb-Visual SLAM OLE interface". On-line Help is provided on Visual SLAM syntax for objects.

In this chapter, most references are to VS, the instance of the global object VSLAM. However, arguments to some of the methods require instances of the following Visual SLAM object classes:

Name	Object Class
VSFILE	Visual SLAM Files
VSENTITY	Entities
VSENTRY	Placeholders including predecessor and successor pointers of entries in a file
VSNODE	Network Nodes
VSACT	Network Activities
VSACTSTA	Network Activity Statistics
VSRES	Network Resources
VSGATE	Network Gates

9.2   FUNCTION EVENT

The symbol, input statement and the AweSim dialog box for the EVENT node were described in Section 7.4. For convenience, the symbol and statement are shown below:

EVENT,JEVNT,M;

The EVENT node is included in a network model to interface the network portion of a model with event coding written by the modeler. The EVENT node causes subroutine EVENT to be called every time an entity arrives to the EVENT node. Subroutine EVENT maps the event code JEVNT onto the appropriate event function containing the coding for the event logic. In coding the event logic, the modeler has access to the Visual SLAM functions provided for performing commonly encountered activities such as random sampling, file manipulation and data collection.

The general form for subroutine EVENT is shown below.

```
Public Sub EVENT(I As Long, Ent As VSENTITY)
   Select Case I
     Case 1
         Code for event node 1
     Case 2
         Code for event node 2
   End Select
End Sub
```

The argument I is the event code that is defined for the EVENT node, that is, JEVNT. This code is used to determine which node has had an entity arrive to it. The argument Ent is an object of type VSENTITY. This object holds the properties of the entity arriving to the EVENT node which are referenced as follows.

(Note that in Visual Basic, parentheses ( ) are used for indices of variables instead of brackets [ ]):

Properties	Description
ATRIB(Index) As Double	Real attribute values
LTRIB(Index) As Long	Long integer attribute values
STRIB(Index) As String	String attribute values(STRIB)
Type As Integer	Entity type attribute ETYPE
Number As Long	Unique integer number given to entity
Time As Double	Time scheduled for or remaining time
ERETURN As Double	Value returned from subnetwork
ANTRIB As Double	Real subnetwork attribute values
LNTRIB As Double	Integer subnetwork attribute values
SNTRIB As Double	String subnetwork attribute values

The EVENT routine is written by the user and normally consists of a Select Case statement indexed on the event code JEVNT causing a transfer to the appropriate statement where the logic associated with the EVENT node is written. In many cases, the logic for each EVENT node is written in a separate function to facilitate the identification of the logic and the documentation of the code associated with an EVENT node. An example of EVENT is shown below for a simulation model with two EVENT nodes consisting of a start of lunch break coded in function LUNCH and assigned event code 1, and an end-of-lunch break coded in function ELUNCH and assigned event code 2.

```
Public Sub EVENT(JEVNT As Integer,worker As VSENTITY)

        Select Case JEVNT
        Case 1
           Call SLUNCH(worker)
        Case 2
           Call ELUNCH(worker)
        End Select
        End Sub
```

The entity worker is the entity that arrived to the EVENT node.

9.2.1   Accessing Variable and Attribute Values

Visual SLAM variables may be accessed in Visual Basic code by using the general simulator object VSLAM. This object's name, VS, is created by AweSim's CONNECT routine and destroyed by the AweSim DISCONNECT routine. It is used to reference the support subprograms described in this chapter and to reference the global variables which are its properties. These properties include:

LL(Index) As Long	Global long integer variables
XX(Index) As Double	Global real variables
SZ(Index) As String	Global string variables
Array(Row,Column) As Double	Global ARRAY variable
MSTOP As Integer	May be set to -1 to stop a run
TNOW as Double	Current simulated time

Entity attributes may be accessed in Visual Basic code by using a VSENTITY object passed to the user-written function. For example, the assignment of TNOW to the second real attribute of the entity referenced by the object User can be made by this statement:

User.ATRIB(2) = VS.TNOW

9.2.2   Accessing Network Values

The logic at an EVENT node may involve testing the status or changing the value of variables associated with the network portion of the model. In function EVENT, values of network related variables can be obtained using the Visual SLAM functions listed in Table 9-l.

On a Visual SLAM network, ARRAY is a two-dimensional table for global values. The values in ARRAY can be accessed and changed in event routines by using the Array property of the VSLAM object.

Table 9-1 Functions for accessing the status of an activity, gate or resource.

Function	Definition
VS.NNACT(I)	Number of active entities in activity I at current time
VS.NNCNT(I)	The number of entities that have completed activity I
VS.NNGAT(I)	Status of gate number I at current time:
	True → open, False → closed
VS.NRUSE(I)	Current number of resource type I in use
VS.NNRSC(I)	Current number of resource type I available
VS.NNBLK(I,IFILE)	Number of entities in activity I blocked by file IFILE

On a Visual SLAM network, ARRAY is a two-dimensional table for global values. The values in ARRAY can be accessed and changed in event routines by using the Array property of the VSLAM object. The statement X2=VS.Array(3,4) sets X2 equal to the value of the fourth cell in the third row of ARRAY. To put the value 10 into the seventh cell of row 1, the following statement would be used.

VS.Array(1,7)=10.

9.3   ENTER FUNCTION

The ENTER node, described in Section 7.5, allows the modeler to insert selectively an entity into the network from a user-written function. For convenience, the symbol and the input statement for the ENTER node are shown below.

ENTER,NUM,M;

The ENTER node is released following a return from a user-written function in which a call is made to the function

VS.ENTER (NUM As Integer,Ent As VSENTITY) As Integer

The argument NUM is the numeric code of the ENTER node to be released and Ent is the object referencing the entity to arrive at the ENTER node. This entity is often a new entity created using the function

VS.DefineEntity(EntType As Integer) As VSENTITY

The function DefineEntity returns the object referencing the new VSENTITY object and initializes its type and attributes. The following statements, for example, would create a new entity, set its first real attribute equal to the current simulation time, and route it from ENTER node 1.

```
Dim ENew As VSENTITY          ' Declare an entity object
ENew = VS.DefineEntity(0)      ' Create an entity
ENew.ATRIB(1) = VS.TNOW        '  Define ATRIB[1]
VS.ENTER 1,ENew                '  Insert at ENTER node 1
```

9.4   FILE MANIPULATIONS

A file provides the mechanism for storing the attributes of an entity in a prescribed ranking with respect to other entities in the file. In network models, files are used to maintain entities waiting at QUEUE, AWAIT and PREEMPT nodes.

Associated with a file is a ranking criterion which specifies the procedure for ordering entities within the file. Thus, each entity in a file has a rank which specifies its position in the file relative to the other members in the file. A rank of one denotes that the entity is the first entry in the file. Possible ranking criterion for files are: first-in, first-out (FIFO); last-in, first-out (LIFO); high-value-first (HVF) based on an expression; and low-value-first (LVF) based on an expression. The ranking criterion for entries in a file is assumed to be FIFO unless otherwise specified using the PRIORITY statement described in Chapter 8.

In Visual SLAM, files are distinguished by integer numbers assigned to the files by the user. Visual SLAM automatically collects statistics on each file and provides the function NNQ(IFILE) which returns the number of entries in file IFILE. For example, NNQ(2) denotes the number of entries in file 2.

The modeler can, when referencing files associated with network nodes, employ any of the file manipulation routines which are available in discrete event simulations.

9.4.1   Filing an Entity, FILEM

An entity can be inserted into a file by making a call to the Visual SLAM function **VS.FILEM(IFILE As Integer, Ent As VSENTITY) As VSENTRY**. This function files the entity referenced by the object **Ent** into file number **IFILE**. FILEM returns the placeholder of the entity in the file.   The placeholder is a VSENTRY object, Ntry, which maintains the entity's position in the file. The rank of Ntry in the file is determined by Visual SLAM based upon the priority specified by the user.   As noted earlier, if no priority is specified, then a first-in, first-out ranking is assumed.   As an example of the use of function FILEM, the following statements cause an entity with its first attribute set equal to the current simulation time to be inserted into file 1.

Ent.ATRIB(1) = VS.TNOW   **' Define ATRIB[1] of the current entity**
Set Ntry = VS.FILEM (1, Ent)   **' File the current entity in file 1**

It is possible to access the attributes of a file entry through its VSENTRY object using the Entity property of that object.   The first integer attribute of the entry inserted into file 1 in the above example would be referenced as **Ntry.Entity. ATRIB (1)** (Section 11.5.4).

9.4.2   Removing an Entity, RMOVE

An entity can be inserted into a file by making a call to the Visual SLAM function **VS.RMOVE (IFILE As Integer, Rank As Long) As VSENTITY**.   This function removes the entry with rank **Rank** from file number **IFILE** and returns the object referencing the removed entity.   As an example of the use of function RMOVE, the following statement removes the last entry in file 1 and assigns its object to the ENTITY variable Ent.

   Set Ent = VS.RMOVE(1, NNQ(1))

As a second example, the following statements cause the second entry in file 3 to be removed and its entity object set to Old.

   Dim Old As VSENTITY   **' Declare an entity object**

Set Old = VS.RMOVE(3, 2)   ' Remove the second entry from file 3

An entity removed from a file could be inserted into another file using function FILEM or inserted into the network using function ENTER. The entity could also be terminated and the memory it occupied released for reuse using the function **EntObj.Terminate**(). The entity object should be set to Nothing after this function call. To destroy the object removed from file 3 in the preceding example, the following statements would be used:

Old.Terminate
Set Old = Nothing

9.5   USER FUNCTION USERF

Visual SLAM provides the function **USERF (IFN As Long, Ent As VSENTITY) As Double** to assign values to Visual SLAM variables using Visual Basic code. The argument IFN is a code established by the user and is referred to as a user function number. The name USERF can be used in a network in locations that allow a Visual SLAM variable to be an option. It is most frequently used in the following two situations:

1. An entity passes through an ASSIGN node and one of the assignments is to be made in USERF; and
2. A duration for an activity is specified as USERF.

The entity object Ent references to the entity currently being processed at the network location. The function USERF allows a modeler to make programming inserts into the network model. In the programming insert, the user can employ all Visual Basic coding procedures and the Visual SLAM functions described above and in Chapter 11VB.

As an example of the uses of function USERF, consider the following single-server, single-queue network.

In this network, user function 1 is used to assign a value to attribute 1 at the ASSIGN node, and user function 2 is used to specify the duration of the service time of activity 2. ATRIB[1] is the duration of activity 1, representing the entity's travel to the QUEUE node. In this example, we will make this time a function of the number of remaining spaces in the QUEUE node, that is, 5-NNQ(1). If ATRIB[1] was used only as the duration of the activity then user function 1 could have been specified for the activity. Here we illustrate a concept and demonstrate the use of function USERF to assign an attribute value. If future decisions were made based on the value of ATRIB[1] then the model as depicted would be required.

The service time for activity 1 will also be made a function of the number of entities waiting for service. The general form for writing function USERF is shown below.

```
Public Function USERF(IFN As Long,CurEnt As VSENTITY) As Double

  Select Case IFN
  Case 1
    Set USERF as the time to travel to the QUEUE node
  Case 2
    Set USERF as service time, a function of NNQ(1)

  End Select
End Function
```

This example illustrates how IFN, the user function number, is decoded to allow different user functions to be employed throughout the network model. User function 1 only requires USERF to return 5-NNQ(1). When a return is made, Visual SLAM assigns the value of USERF to ATRIB(1). For user function 2, we require knowledge of how service time varies as a function of the number of entities in the QUEUE node. For illustrative purposes, we will assume an exponential service time whose mean decreases as the number in the queue is increased to a value of 3. When there are more than 3 in the queue, the mean service time increases. A table of mean service time as a function of the number in the queue is shown below.

Number in Queue	Mean Service Time
0	10.
1	9.
2	8.
3	7.
4	9.
5	10.

The specific coding for function USERF(IFN) for this situation would be:

```
Public Function USERF(IFN As Long,CurEnt As VSENTITY) As Double

Dim AVEST As Double
Select Case IFN
     Case 1
         USERF = 5 - VS.NNQ(1)
     Case 2
         If VS.NNQ(1) <=3 Then
           AVEST = 10-VS.NNQ(1)
         Else
           AVEST = 5 + VS.NNQ(1)
         End if
         USERF = VS.EXPON AVEST,1
End Select
End Function
```

The Select statement passes control to Case 1 if IFN is 1, Case 2 otherwise. At Case 1, USERF is established as the value to be assigned when user function 1 is invoked. At Case 2, the average service time is calculated based on the above table. The return value is then set equal to a sample from an exponential distribution using AVEST as the average service time and employing stream number 1. Note that the stream number must be given in function EXPON since direct coding is being employed.

This example illustrates the flexibility available by allowing program inserts to set Visual SLAM variables in network models. For this example it was not neessary to access the attributes of the current entity project, CurEnt. The following statement would provide the value of attribute 1:

Attribute1 = CurEnt.ATRIB (1)

9.6   EXAMPLE 9-1. DRIVE-IN BANK WITH JOCKEYING

A drive-in bank has two windows, each manned by a teller and each with a separate drive-in lane. The drive-in lanes are adjacent. From previous observations, it has been determined that the time interval between customer arrivals during rush hours is exponentially distributed with a mean time between arrivals of 0.5 time units. Congestion occurs only during rush hours, and only this period is to be analyzed. The service time is normally distributed for each teller with a mean service time of one time unit and a standard deviation of 0.3 time units. It has also been shown that customers have a preference for lane 1 if neither teller is busy or if the waiting lines are equal. At all other times, however, a customer chooses the shortest line. After entering the system, a customer does not leave until served. However, the last customer in a lane may change lanes if there is a difference of two customers between the two lanes. Because of parking space limitations only three cars can wait in each lane. These cars, plus the car of the customer being serviced by each teller, allow a maximum of eight cars in the system. If the system is full when a customer arrives, the customer balks and is lost to the system.

The initial conditions are as follows:

1.   Both drive-in tellers are busy. The initial service time for each teller is normally distributed with a mean of one time unit and a standard deviation of 0.3 time units.
2.   The first customer is scheduled to arrive at 0.1 time units.
3.   Two customers are waiting in each queue.

The objective is to develop a simulation model that can be used to analyze the banking situation in terms of the following statistics:

1.   Teller utilization = $\dfrac{\text{total time performing service}}{\text{total simulation time}}$
2.   Time-integrated average number of customers in the system.
3.   Time between departures from the drive-in windows.
4.   Average time a customer is in the system.
5.   Average number of customers in each queue.
6.   Percent of arriving customers who balk.
7.   Number of times cars jockey.

The system is to be simulated for 1000 time units.

Concepts Illustrated. This example illustrates user-written code to augment the modeling concepts in a network model. Two key concepts which are specifically illustrated by this example are: 1) the use of the EVENT node to model jockeying; and 2) the referencing of a common file number between the network and discrete event portions of a model. In addition, this example illustrates balking from a SELECT node.

Visual SLAM Model. The drive-in bank example is amenable to modeling with network concepts. However, we will represent the drive-in bank system as a network model with the jockeying of cars modeled using an EVENT node. Since jockeying can occur only when a teller completes service on a customer, the EVENT node for processing the jockeying of cars between lanes will be executed following the end-of-service for each entity in the system.

The network model for this example is depicted in Figure 9-1. Arriving cars are created by the CREATE node which marks current time as ATRIB[1]. The first entity is created at time 0.1, and the time between car arrivals is exponentially distributed with a mean of 0.5 time units. The SELECT node routes each entity to either the LEFT or RIGHT QUEUE node based on the smallest number in the queue rule (SNUM). The LEFT QUEUE node initially contains two entities and permits a maximum of three waiting entities which are stored in file 1. The LEFT QUEUE is followed by an ACTIVITY representing teller 1 which is prescribed as activity number 1. The duration of the activity is normally distributed with a mean of 1.0 and a standard deviation of 0.3. The ACTIVITY routes the entity to an EVENT node whose event code is 1. The RIGHT QUEUE node also initially contains two entities and permits a maximum of three waiting entities which are stored in file 2. The ACTIVITY following the RIGHT QUEUE node is assigned activity number 2, is normally distributed, and routes the entities to the EVENT node with event code 2. This ACTIVITY represents the service by teller 2.

At the EVENT nodes, Visual SLAM calls the user-coded function EVENT (JEVNT,Cur) with JEVNT set equal to 1 or 2 to process the discrete event logic associated with the node, and Cur set to the VSENTITY object of the car about to leave the system. The jockeying event logic is coded directly in function EVENT as depicted in Figure 9-2.

In function EVENT, the variables NumInLane1 and NumInLane2 are computed as the number of cars in lane 1 (LEFT) and lane 2 (RIGHT), respectively. Note that the number in each lane is calculated to include the customer in service, if any. At Case 1, jockeying from the RIGHT lane to the LEFT lane is investigated. If the number of cars in the RIGHT lane exceeds the number in the LEFT lane by two, then the last entity in file 2 (whose rank is NNQ(2)) is removed from the RIGHT QUEUE node by a call to RMOVE with IFILE = 2 and is scheduled to arrive at the LEFT QUEUE node at the current simulated time by a call to function FILEM with IFILE = 1.

At Case 2, if the number of cars in the LEFT lane exceeds the number in the RIGHT lane by two, the reverse jockeying procedure is executed. If the lanes do not differ by two cars, then a return from function EVENT is made without a car jockeying.

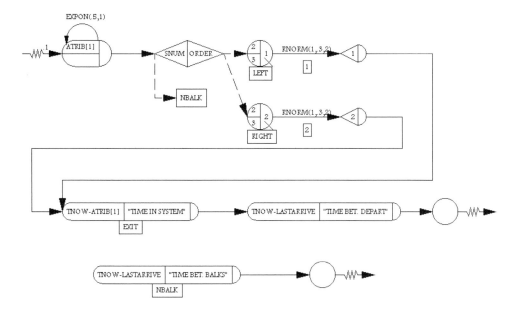

Figure 9-1 Network model of a drive-in bank.

```
Public Sub EVENT(Code As Long, CurEnt As VSENTITY)
    Dim NumInLane1 As Long
    Dim NumInLane2 As Long
    Dim Jockey As VSENTITY
    ' compute the number in each lane
    NumInLane1 = VS.NNQ(1) + VS.NNACT(1)
    NumInLane2 = VS.NNQ(2) + VS.NNACT(2)
    Select Case Code
        Case 1 ' arrive to event node 1
            ' entity leaving lane 1,  see if lane 2 should jockey
            If NumInLane2 >= NumInLane1 + 2 Then
                Set Jockey = VS.RMOVE(2, VS.NNQ(2))
                VS.FILEM 1, Jockey
            End If
        Case 2 ' arrive to event node 2
            ' entity leaving lane 2,  see if lane 1 should jockey
            If NumInLane1 >= (NumInLane2 + 2) Then
                Set Jockey = VS.RMOVE(1, VS.NNQ(1))
                VS.FILEM 2, Jockey
            End If
        Case Else
            VS.Error 1, "Unknown event code"
    End Select
End Sub
```

Figure 9-2 Function EVENT for model of the drive-in bank.

Following execution of the EVENT node, the entity that arrived to the EVENT node is again the current entity object as CurEnt was not altered in the EVENT function. CurEnt is routed from the EVENT node using standard network procedures. This entity continues to the COLCT node EXIT where interval statistics are collected using the mark time in ATRIB[1] as a reference. The results are displayed using the identifier TIME IN SYSTEM. A second COLCT node collects statistics on the time between departures and displays the results using the identifier TIME BET. DEPART. The entities are then terminated. The input statements for the model are shown in Figure 9-3.

```
GEN,"PRITSKER","DRIVE IN BANK",1/1/1996,1;
    LIMITS,-1,-1,-1,2,-1,-1;
    TIMST,1,NNQ(1)+NNACT(1)+NNQ(2)+NNACT(2),"NO. OF CUST";
    SEEDS,{ { 4367651, 1 }, { 6121137, 2 } };
    NETWORK;
        CREATE,EXPON(.5,1),.1,ATRIB[1];
        ACTIVITY;
        SELECT,SNUM, ,BALK(NBALK),{LEFT,RIGHT};
    LEFT: QUEUE,1,2,3;
        ACT,1,RNORM(1,.3,2), , , ,"TELLER 1";
        EVENT,1;
        ACT, , , ,"EXIT";
    RIGHT: QUEUE,2,2,3;
        ACT,2,RNORM(1,.3,2), , , ,"TELLER 2";
        EVENT,2;
        ACTIVITY, , , ,"EXIT";
     EXIT: COLCT, ,TNOW-ATRIB[1],"TIME IN SYSTEM";
        ACTIVITY;
        COLCT, ,TNOW-LASTARRIVE,"TIME BET. DEPART";
        ACTIVITY;
        TERM;
    NBALK: COLCT, ,TNOW-LASTARRIVE,"TIME BET. BALKS";
        ACTIVITY;
        TERM;
        END;
    INIT,0,1000;
    FIN;
```

Figure 9-3 Input statements for model of the drive-in bank.

The control statements for this model include GEN, LIMITS, TIMST, SEEDS, INIT and FIN statements. The GEN, LIMITS, INIT and FIN statement are in standard form. The TIMST statement is employed to obtain statistics on the number of customers in the drive-in bank system. The SEEDS control statement sets the initial seed value for stream number 1 to be 4367651 and the initial seed value for stream number 2 to be 6121137.

Summary of Results. The results for this example are summarized by the Visual SLAM summary report shown in Figure 9-4. Statistics for variables based on observations are given first with the identifiers specified at the COLCT nodes. For this example, observation statistics were collected on the time in the system for each customer and the time between departures of customers. From the summary report, it is seen that 1854 customers were served and the average time in the system was 2.317 minutes. Also customers leave the bank every 0.54 minutes on the average.

```
            ** AweSim SUMMARY REPORT **
  Simulation Project : DRIVE IN BANK
  Modeler : PRITSKER
  Date : 1/1/1996
  Scenario : EX91

  Run number 1 of 1
  Current simulation time    : 1000.000000
  Statistics cleared at time : 0.000000
```

```
         ** OBSERVED STATISTICS REPORT for scenario EX91 **
```

Label	Mean Value	Standard Deviation	Number of Observations	Minimum Value	Maximum Value
TIME IN SYSTEM	2.317	1.018	1854	0.304	5.068
TIME BET. DEPART	0.539	0.361	1853	0.000	3.004
TIME BET. BALKS	6.982	13.152	142	0.014	70.818

```
      ** TIME-PERSISTENT STATISTICS REPORT for scenario EX91 **
```

Label	Mean Value	Standard Deviation	Minimum Value	Maximum Value	Time Interval	Current Value
NO. OF CUST	4.312	2.154	0.000	8.000	1000.000	7.000

```
         ** FILE STATISTICS REPORT for scenario EX91 **
```

File Number	Label or Input Location	Average Length	Standard Deviation	Maximum Length	Current Length	Average Wait Time
1	QUEUE LEFT	1.311	1.033	3	3	1.109
2	QUEUE RIGHT	1.148	0.993	3	2	1.231
0	Event Calendar	3.853	0.432	5	4	0.935

```
      ** SERVICE ACTIVITY STATISTICS REPORT for scenario EX91 **
```

Activity Number	Label or Input Location	Server Capacity	Entity Count	Average Utilization	Standard Deviation	Current Utilization
1	TELLER 1	1	942	0.939	0.239	1
2	TELLER 2	1	912	0.914	0.280	1

Activity Number	Average Blockage	Maximum Idle Time or Servers	Maximum Busy Time or Servers
1	0.000	2.202	84.843
2	0.000	4.095	71.472

Figure 9-4 Visual SLAM summary report for drive-in bank.

The second category of statistics for this example is for time-persistent variables. The results show the average number of customers in the system is 4.312.

The third category of statistics relate to the number of customers waiting in line for teller 1 and teller 2, respectively. The results show that there was an average of 1.311 customers waiting in file 1 for service by teller 1 and an average of 1.148 customers waiting in file 2 for service by teller 2. The final category of statistics for this example is service activity statistics. The results show that teller 1 was busy 93.9 percent of the time while teller 2 was busy 91.4 percent of the time. The slightly longer length of the waiting line and higher utilization for teller 1 as compared to teller 2 is because of the preference by customers for teller 1 when both waiting lines are equal. This information could be used by bank management for assigning tellers to windows.

9.7   SAMPLING FROM PROBABILITY DISTRIBUTIONS

An important aspect of many systems of interest is the stochastic nature of one or more elements in the system. For example, in queueing systems the arrival times and service times are usually not known with certainty but are depicted as random variables. Therefore, in order to build models of such systems, the simulation programmer needs to be able to sample from commonly encountered distributions such as the exponential, normal, and beta as well as from user-defined distributions. Visual SLAM provides Visual Basic function statements for this purpose. A list of such functions is summarized in Table 9-1. Note that the functional names are the same as those employed in network models except for DPROB and the parameter specifications are identical to those specified in Chapter 5. The reader should note that these are Visual Basic functions, and all arguments must be specified with the correct type of variable (Integer or Double). In particular, the stream parameter cannot be defaulted as in the case of network statements.

Table 9-1 Function statements to obtain random samples.

Function	Descriptions‡
BETA(Theta As Double, Phi As Double, Stream As Integer) As Double	Returns a sample from a beta distribution with parameters Theta and Phi using random number stream Stream.
DPROB (CumProbs As Double Reference, Values As Double Reference, NumVals As Integer, Stream As Integer)	Returns a sample from a user-defined discrete probability distribution with cumulative probabilities in the array CumProbs and associated values in the array Values. NumVals values are defined, and random number stream Stream is used.
DRAND(Stream As Integer) As Double	Returns a random number uniformly distributed between 0 and 1 using random number stream Stream.
ERLNG(Mean As Double, XK As Integer, Stream As Integer) As Double	Returns a sample from an Erlang distribution which is the sum of XK exponential samples each with mean Mean using random number stream Stream.
EXPON(Mean As Double, Stream As Integer) As Double	Returns a sample from an exponential distribution with mean Mean using random number stream Stream.
GAMA(Beta As Double, Alpha As Double, Stream As Integer) As Double	Returns a sample from a gamma distribution with parameters Beta and Alpha using random number stream Stream.
GETSEED(Stream As Integer) As Long	Returns the current seed value for random number stream Stream.
NPSSN(Mean As Double, Stream As Integer) As Long	Returns a sample from a Poisson distribution with mean Mean using random number stream Stream.
RLOGN(Mean As Double, StdDev As Double, Stream As Integer) As Double	Returns a sample from a lognormal distribution with mean Mean and standard deviation StdDev using random number stream Stream.
RNORM(Mean As Double, StdDev As Double StdDev, Stream As Integer) As Double	Returns a sample from a normal distribution with mean Mean and standard deviation StdDev using random number stream Stream.
TRIAG(Low As Double, Mode As Double, Hi As Double, Stream as Integer) As Double	Returns a sample from a triangular distribution in the interval Low to Hi with mode Mode using random number stream Stream.
UNFRM(Low As Double, Hi As Double, Stream As Integer) As Double	Returns a sample from a uniform distribution in the interval Low to Hi using random number stream Stream.
WEIBL(Alpha, As Double, Beta As Double, Stream As Integer) As Double	Returns a sample from a Weibull distribution with scale parameter Alpha and shape parameter Beta using random number stream Stream.
XRN(Stream As Integer) As Double	Returns the last normalized random sample obtained from stream Stream.

‡ See Chapter 16 for the equations of the distribution functions associated with the random variables, the definitions of the arguments and their calculation.

9.8   USER-WRITTEN INITIALIZATION AND POST-RUN PROCESSING ROUTINES: FUNCTIONS INTLC AND OTPUT

At the beginning of each simulation run, the Visual SLAM processor calls function INTLC to enable the modeler to set initial conditions and to schedule initial events. All the functions included within Visual SLAM can be used at this time. Function OTPUT is called at the end of each simulation run and is used for end-of-run processing such as clearing out files and printing special results for the simulation run. INTLC and OTPUT should return True if the current run (for INTLC) or the next run (for OTPUT) should be performed. If False (0) is returned, the simulation will be stopped. Visual SLAM provides many functions to access all variables and statistics collected during a run. These functions are described in detail in Chapter 11VB.

9.9   CHANGING THE STATUS OF A RESOURCE

Visual SLAM provides the modeler with functions which free a specified number of units of a resource, alter the capacity of a resource by a specified amount, and support complex resource allocation decisions. Before describing these functions, the method for referencing a resource needs to be established.

In network statements, resources are referenced by either the resource name or number. In the resource functions, a resource must be referenced by its number. Recall from Chapter 5 that if a resource number is not specified, the Visual SLAM processor automatically numbers the resources in the order in which the RESOURCE blocks are inputted to the Visual SLAM processor. The first resource is assigned number 1, the second resource is assigned number 2, and so on. For example, consider the following set of RESOURCE blocks included in the network portion of a model.

RESOURCE,,TUG,2,{1,2};
RESOURCE,,BERTH,3,{3};
RESOURCE,,CREW,,{4};

The processor would assign the TUGs as resource number 1, the BERTHs as resource number 2, and the CREW as resource number 3. When changing the status of a resource from within a discrete event, the resource number is included as an argument to the appropriate function to distinguish between resource types.

9.9.1   Freeing Resources: Function FREE

FREE(Res As Integer, Units As Integer) As Integer releases Units units of resource number Res. It returns True if no error was encountered, False otherwise. The freed units of the resource are made available to waiting entities according to the order of the file numbers specified in the RESOURCE statement included in the network model. For the RESOURCE blocks depicted above, the Visual Basic statement

VS.FREE 1,2

would release 2 units of the resource TUG. These tugs are made available to entities waiting in file 1. If both tugs are not used, then file 2 would be interrogated to determine if an entity was waiting for the use of a tug. The execution of the statement **VS.FREE 1,2** is identical to the execution of the following network statement.

FREE,{TUG,2};

9.9.2   Altering Resource Capacities: Function ALTER

ALTER(Res As Integer, Units As Integer) As Integer changes the capacity of resource number Res by Units units. It returns True if no error was encountered, False otherwise. In the case where the capacity of the resource is decreased below current utilization, the excess capacity is destroyed as it becomes freed. The capacity can be reduced to a minimum of zero with additional reduction requests having no effect. Assuming the RESOURCE blocks depicted earlier, the following Visual Basic statement would reduce the number of tugs by 1.

VS.ALTER 1,-1

This statement produces the same effect as the execution of the following network statement.

ALTER,TUG,−1;

9.10 USER-WRITTEN RESOURCE ALLOCATION PROCEDURES:
FUNCTIONS ALLOC AND SEIZE

AWAIT nodes are used to store entities waiting for resources. When an AWAIT node description includes a resource name, an entity cannot pass through the AWAIT node until a specified number of units of that resource are available. When this condition occurs, the proper number of resources of that type are "seized" (set busy) and the entity proceeds from the AWAIT node. When the modeler specifies ALLOC(Code) as the resource allocation rule, the function **ALLOC(Code As Integer, First As VSENTRY) As VSENTRY** is called by Visual SLAM when an entity arrives to the AWAIT node. The argument First is the placeholder of the first entity in the file currently being polled by ALLOC. ALLOC is also called when the file associated with that AWAIT node is polled as the result of a newly available or freed resource. The VSENTRY object type was discussed in Section 9.4.1.

Function ALLOC is coded to determine which, if any, entity in the file can proceed. If it is determined that an entity should proceed from the AWAIT node, the user will seize the appropriate resources (discussed below). The return value is the placeholder of the entity to be removed from the AWAIT node file for processing in the network. If, as normally happens, the first entity in the file should proceed, the return value would be the argument First. If no allocation is possible, the returned placeholder should be set to Nothing.

When the resources to be allocated at an AWAIT node are determined by the user in function ALLOC, the required number of units of the required resources are seized through a call to the function **SEIZE(Resource As Integer, Units As Integer) As Integer** where Resource is the numeric code for the resource type and Units is the number of units to be seized. Function SEIZE then sets Units of resource type Resource busy and updates the statistics for that resource. The function returns True if no error was encountered, False otherwise. For example, the statement **VS.SEIZE 3,2** sets busy 2 units of resource type 3. Before invoking function SEIZE, the user must test to determine if 2 units of resource type 3 are available. Through the use of functions ALLOC and SEIZE, complex resource allocation rules can be included in simulation models. A resource allocated in function ALLOC may not be preempted.

9.10.1 Illustration 9-1. Joint and Alternative Resource Requirements

Consider a situation in which there are two operators who are modeled as resources. The resource names are OP1 and OP2. The resource blocks for defining these operators and the files at which they are allocated are shown below.

> RESOURCE,1,OP1,1,{1,2};
> RESOURCE,2,OP2,1,{1,2};

From the resource block definition we see there is one unit of each resource and that resources OP1 and OP2 are allocated at either files 1 and 2. The numeric code for resource OP1 is 1 and the numeric code for resource OP2 is 2.

In the network model, suppose we require that activity 1 be performed by both OP1 and OP2. Although this does not require a function ALLOC, the use of ALLOC is illustrated by coding a standard Visual SLAM allocation rule. The network statements for the AWAIT node and ACTIVITY are listed below.

> AWAIT,1,,ALLOC(1);
> ACT,1,10;

These network statements show that an entity arriving to the AWAIT node will pass through file 1 to ACTIVITY 1 if allocation rule 1 indicates that resources are available to work on the arriving entity. The code for allocation case 1 is shown below. Note that a new arrival to the AWAIT node is placed in the file while resource allocation is being processed.

```
Select Case Rule

    Case 1
        If VS.NNRSC(1)>0 And VS.NNRSC(2)>0 Then
            VS.SEIZE 1,1
            VS.SEIZE 2,1
            Set ALLOC = First
        Else
            Set ALLOC = Nothing
```

In the above code, a switch on the allocation rule code is made as we will have two allocation codes associated with this illustration. At Case 1 both resource 1 (OP1) and resource 2 (OP2) are required or no allocation can be made. NNRSC(I) is the current number of resources available for resource I. If the condition in case 1 is satisfied, then both resources are available. Function SEIZE is then called twice to allocate resource 1 and resource 2. Since the first entity in the AWAIT node file is the one which should be released when the resources are available, function ALLOC returns the VSENTRY object of the first entity which was provided as the input argument First. If either of the resources are unavailable, function ALLOC returns Nothing and no allocation is made.

Consider now a second allocation function represented by the following statements.

> AWAIT,2,,ALLOC(2),3,BALK(OUT);
> ACT,5,22;

The above code indicates that arriving entities to the AWAIT node will wait in file 2 which has a queue capacity of 3. If an entity arrives with three units already in file 2 it will balk to a node labeled **OUT**. When an entity arrives to file 2 and it is empty, the entity is placed in the file and function ALLOC is invoked with a request to use allocation case 2. Allocation case 2 will be coded to have either resource 1 or resource 2 assigned to an entity.

Function ALLOC, which includes both allocation case 1 and allocation case 2, is shown below. For case 2, function ALLOC is entered with Code=2.

```
Public Function ALLOC(Code As Long, First As VSENTRY) As VSENTRY
'*****************************************************
'* Illustration of seizing two resources jointly (the
'* ALL allocation rule) or alternatively (the OR
'* allocation rule).
'*****************************************************
Dim Current As VSENTITY

Select Case Code
  Case 1    ' Need both resource type 1 and resource type 2
    If VS.NNRSC(1) > 0 And VS.NNRSC(2) > 0 Then
        VS.SEIZE 1, 1
        VS.SEIZE 2, 1
    ___ Set ALLOC = First
    Else
        Set ALLOC = Nothing
    End If
  Case 2 'If resource type 1 is available, seize it
    If VS.NNRSC(1) > 0 Then
        VS.SEIZE 1, 1
        First.Entity.LTRIB(1) = 1
        Set ALLOC = First
    ElseIf VS.NNRSC(2) > 0 Then ' Otherwise try for resource type 2
        VS.SEIZE 2, 1
        First.Entity.LTRIB(1) = 2
        Set ALLOC = First
    Else
        Set ALLOC = Nothing ' Otherwise no allocation
    End If
  End Select
End Function
```

Now a test is made to see if resource 1 is available. If it is, function **SEIZE** is called to seize one unit of resource 1. LTRIB[1] is set to 1 to indicate that the current entity is to be processed by resource 1, and the VSENTRY object for the first entity in the AWAIT node file is returned. If resource 1 is not available but resource 2 is, then resource 2 is allocated, LTRIB[1] is set to 2. Note that a preferred choice for resource 1 over resource 2 when both are available is coded directly into allocation case 2. It should be clear how the coding could be changed to make resource 2 the preferred resource.

9.10.2   Illustration 9-2.   Assembling Resources in the Truck Hauling Situation

This illustration demonstrates how function ALLOC can be used to provide an assembly capability for resources. The truck hauling situation modeled in Example 6-2 is used to demonstrate this capability. In that example, a SELECT node with the assembly queue selection rule is used to assemble a truck, a load and a loader. The use of a loader as both a service activity and as an entity to be assembled was required to model the situation in Chapter 6.

In the network shown below, an AWAIT node is used to queue loads that wait for both a truck and a loader. Trucks and loaders are modeled as resources with the labels TRUCKS, LOADER1 and LOADER2 which have resource numbers 1,   2 and 3 respectively. In function ALLOC, a check is made to determine if both a truck and a loader are available. If available, they are allocated and a load continues through the network. Function ALLOC is shown below.   It is a combination of the "ALL" and "ONE" allocation rules, since it allocates a truck resource and one of the loader resources.

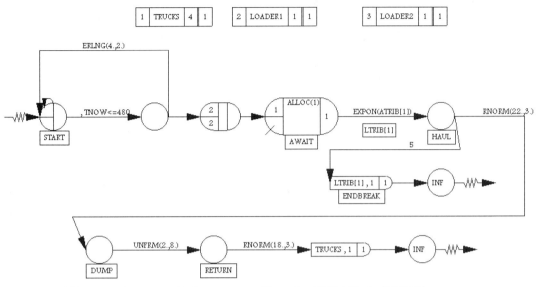

```
Public Function ALLOC(Code As Long, First As VSENTRY) As VSENTRY
Dim LOADER As Integer, TEST As Integer
Dim Time As Double

Set ALLOC = Nothing                 'Initialize entry to return
LOADER = 0                          'and which loader to seize
If VS.NNRSC(1) > 0 Then             'If there is a truck,
TEST = VS.NNRSC(2) + VS.NNRSC(3)         ' Case is a function of
  Select Case TEST                       ' available loader resources.
    Case 0
      Exit Function                 'Case 0:  No loader available
    Case 1                          'Case 1:  One loader available
      If VS.NNRSC(2) > 0 Then
        LOADER = 2                  '  LOADER1 is available
        Time = 14#                  '  Assign resource type & time
      Else
        LOADER = 3                  '  LOADER2 is available
        Time = 12#
      End If
    Case 2                          'Case 2: Both are available.
      If (VS.RRTLC(2) <= VS.RRTLC(3)) Then
        LOADER = 2                  '    If resource 2 became available
        Time = 14#                  '    first, resource type is 2 and
      Else                          '    mean service time is 14. Else,
        LOADER = 3                  '    resource type is 3 and mean
        Time = 12#                  '    service time is 12.
      End If
  End Select
  If (LOADER > 0) Then              ' If a loader has been found,
    VS.SEIZE 1, 1                   ' Seize a truck and a loader.
    VS.SEIZE LOADER, 1
    First.Entity.ATRIB(1) = Time    'Entity attributes hold mean
    First.Entity.LTRIB(1) = LOADER  'loading time and the resource
    Set ALLOC = First                    'type to be freed.
  End If
End If
End Function
```

The return value in ALLOC is first set to null and the loader resource to be seized is set to zero. If no trucks are available (NNRSC(1) is zero), no further action is taken. If a truck is available, the loader resources are evaluated. Four cases are provided for: (1) no loader is available, (2) only LOADER1 is available, (3) only LOADER2 is available and (4) both are available. If a loader is available the resource type, LOADER, and the mean service time, TIME, are assigned. If both loader resources are available, we wish to assign the one which has been available the longest. The function RRTLC (described in Section 11.9) returns the time at which the resource status was changed to "available", so if both loaders are idle, the resource with the earliest value of RRTLC is chosen. When a LOADER resource can be assigned, it is seized in addition to one unit of the TRUCKS resource. The first load entity at the AWAIT node is accessed using the Entity property of the VSENTRY object in order to set ATRIB[1] of the load entity to mean service time and LTRIB[1] to the loader resource type so that the correct resource will later be released.

In the network model, the activity number for the loading activity is defined to be LTRIB[1] so that separate statistics will be reported depending on the loader assigned at the AWAIT node. Following the loading activity, an entity representing the loader is routed to a FREE node after a five minute break. A second entity representing a loaded truck is sent over hauling, dumping and truck return activities after which a TRUCKS resource is freed. Utilization statistics for the two loader resources will include both time spent loading a truck and break time. The percentage of time actually spent loading will be reported by the utilization statistics for activities 2 and 3.

9.11   CHANGING THE STATUS OF A GATE

Visual SLAM provides the capability to open and close gates using Visual Basic functions. A gate must be referenced by its gate number. If the gate number is defaulted, it is automatically assigned by Visual SLAM to each gate in the order that the GATE blocks are input to the Visual SLAM processor. For example, consider the following set of GATE blocks included in the network portion of a model:

```
GATE,,DOOR1 ,OPEN,4;
GATE,,DOOR2,CLOSED,5;
```

The processor would assign DOOR1 as gate number 1 and DOOR2 as gate number 2.

9.11.1   Opening a Gate: Function OPEN

The function **OPEN(Gate As Integer) As Integer** opens gate number Gate and releases all waiting entities in the AWAIT files specified in the GATE block. For the GATE blocks depicted above, the following statement would open DOOR2:

VS.OPEN 2

This statement is equivalent to the following network statement.

OPEN,DOOR2;

Function OPEN returns True if no error was encountered, False otherwise.

9.11.2   Closing a Gate: Function CLOSX

The function **CLOSX(Gate As Integer) As Integer** closes gate number Gate. For the GATE blocks depicted above, the following statement would close DOOR1.

VS.CLOSX 1

This statement is equivalent to the following network statement.

CLOSE,DOOR1;

Function CLOSX returns True if no error was encountered, False otherwise.

9.12   USER-WRITTEN SELECT NODE FUNCTIONS

In a network model, SELECT nodes are used to route an entity to one of a set of parallel QUEUE nodes or to select an entity from a set of parallel queues for processing by a server. The Visual SLAM standard queue selection rules and server selection rules are presented in Tables 7-2 and 7-3. The USER queue selection or server selection rule allows user-written logic to determine a selection criterion. Further, the USERASSEMBLE queue selection rule provides that the attributes of the assembled entity are assigned in a user-written Visual Basic function.

9.12.1   User-Written QUEUE Selection: NQS

When the queue selection rule at a SELECT node is specified as **NQS(expr)**, the function **NQS(Code As Integer, Current As VSENTITY, Node As VSNODE) As Long** is called with Code equal to the evaluated expression, Current equal to the entity object being processed at the SELECT node, and Node equal to the object referencing the SELECT node description. The properties of a VSNODE object include the following information about the node.

Line As Long	Input line number from network
File As String	Input file name from network
Next as VSNODE	Next node if no following activities
Label As String	Node label
NumFile as Integer	Number of files defined at node
FileN As VSFILE	Nth file defined at node
NumAct As Integer	Number of activities following node
ActN As VSACT	Nth activity following node
NumQueue As Integer	Number of QUEUEs following SELECT node
QueueN As VSNODE	Nth QUEUE following select node

The Visual SLAM user writes the function NQS to execute the desired queue selection logic and returns the file number of the selected QUEUE. When queue selection is done by the user, it is the user's responsibility to insure that a feasible choice is made, that is, an entity must be able to be routed to the QUEUE node or taken from the QUEUE node. Whenever there are no feasible choices, the user should return zero to indicate that no QUEUE node was selected.

The network segment and its corresponding statement model shown on the next page will be used to illustrate how to code function NQS. At SELECT node SSS, arriving entities are to be routed to QUEUE nodes Q1, Q2, and Q3 based on the value of LL[1]. In a section of the model not shown, the modeler has specified the value of LL[1] to be 1, 2 or 3. Queue selection function with Case 1 will be used to make this selection and NQS(1) is specified as the queue selection rule for SELECT node SSS. In function NQS, a transfer to Case 1 is made when the queue selection code number is 1. At case 1, the value to return, NQS, is set equal to LL[1] to indicate that the QUEUE node with the file number LL[1] is to be selected for the arriving entity. In this situation, no check is made on the feasibility of routing the arriving entity to the prescribed QUEUE node as all three QUEUE nodes have unlimited capacity.

At SELECT node SEL, queue selection function 2 is prescribed for selecting entities from Q1 or Q2 when either activity 1, 2 or 3 is completed. The coding for queue selection function 2 is shown in function NQS starting at Case 2. First it is determined whether an entity is waiting for the service activities following SELECT node SEL. Thus, if the number in Q1 and the number in Q2 are 0, a value of 0 is assigned to NQS to indicate to Visual SLAM that the server should be set to idle status. Next, if no entity exists in either queue, the other queue is selected. When entities are available in both queues, the queue selection rule is to select an entity from the longer queue.

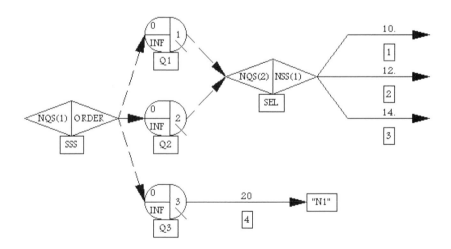

```
SSS: SELECT,NQS(1),,,{Q1,Q2,Q3};
Q1:  QUEUE,1,0,,,{SEL};
Q2:  QUEUE,2,0,,,{SEL};
Q3:  QUEUE,3,0;
     ACT,4,20, ,N1; N1 NOT SHOWN
SEL: SELECT,NQS(2),NSS(1),,{Q1 ,Q2};
     ACT, 1 , 10;
     ACT,2, 12;
     ACT,3, 14; ,

Public Function NQS(Code As Long,User As VSENTITY, _
                   Node As VSNODE) As Long
'*****************************************************
'* User-coded QUEUE selection rules 1 and 2
'*****************************************************
  NQS = 0

  Select Case Code
     Case 1
        NQS = VS.LL(1)
        Exit Function
     Case 2
        If VS.NNQ(1) <> 0 Or VS.NNQ(2) <> 0 Then
           If VS.NNQ(1)= 0 Then
              NQS = 2
           Else If VS.NNQ(2) = 0 Then
              NQS = 1
           Else
             If VS.NNQ(1)>=VS.NNQ(2) Then
              NQS = 1
             Else
              NQS=2
             End If
           End If
         End If
     End Select
End Function
```

As seen from this discussion, the coding of function NQS permits complex queue selection rules to be included in a Visual SLAM network.

9.12.2   User-Written Server Selection: NSS

When the server selection rule at a SELECT node is specified as NSS(expr), function **NSS(Code As Integer, Current As VSENTITY, Node As VSNODE) As**

Long is called with Code equal to the evaluated expression, Current equal to the entity object being processed at the SELECT node, and Node equal to the SELECT node object.

Function NSS is called when an entity arrives to an empty QUEUE node associated with the SELECT node whose server selection rule is NSS(Code) where the index Code is used to select the appropriate portion of the code for the SELECT node. In function NSS, an activity number is to be returned to indicate the service activity selected. If all servers following the SELECT node are busy, NSS should return zero, in which case the newly arriving entity will be placed in the QUEUE node to which it arrived. The service activity numbers following the SELECT node are known to the user as they are associated with the activity statements following the SELECT node in the network input statements. When a value is returned from NSS, Visual SLAM takes the appropriate action of either putting the arriving entity into a QUEUE node or making the selected service activity busy by scheduling the start of the activity.

The example used in the section on function NQS will be continued in this section. The appropriate portions of the statement model to illustrate function NSS are:

```
SEL:    SELECT,NQS(2),NSS(1),,{Q1 ,Q2};
        ACT,1 ,10;
        ACT,2, 12;
        ACT,3, 14;
```

When an entity arrives to either QUEUE node Q1 or Q2 and there are no entities waiting at the time of arrival, function NSS with an argument of 1 is called in order to determine if server 1, 2, or 3 can process the arriving entity. If all three servers are busy, then the arriving entity is put into the appropriate file. If only one server is free, that server is selected for processing the entity. If more than one server is free, a selection rule is coded in function NSS. The coding for function NSS is shown on the next page.

In NSS, only one server selection function is indicated and only the code is given for server selection function 1. First, the selected server number NSS is set to 0 to indicate that a server could not be selected. In the middle part of the function, each service activity status is tested and if a server is available, the service activity number is stored in the vector NSER(J) where J is an index for available servers. If no servers are available, J is zero and a return is made with NSS remaining zero.

```
Public Function NSS(Code As Long, Current As VSENTITY, _
                    Node As VSNODE) As Long
'*********************************************************
'* User-written random selection rule: 3 servers
'*********************************************************
Dim NSER(3) As Integer
Dim i, j, NR As Integer
Dim XJ As Double

NSS = 0
j = 0
For i = 1 To 3
   If VS.NNACT(1) = 0 Then    'Store the number of up to
      NSER(j) = i             '3 available servers in the
      j = j + 1               'NSER aray
   End If
Next i

If j > 0 Then                 'If a server is available,
   XJ = j                     'randomly select a server between
   NR = Int(VS.UNFRM(1#, XJ, 1)) - 1    '1 and j
   NSS = NSER(NR)
End If

End Function
```

If one or more servers are available, then an integer is selected from 1 to the number of available servers. Note that XJ is set equal to j + 1 and a number drawn between 1 and XJ. By using the integer variable NR, these values will be truncated down to the next lowest integer so that an integer from 1 to j will be obtained as the value of NR. In this way, each integer has an equal likelihood of being selected. The selected server activity number, NSS, is then obtained from the NRth location of the vector NSER.

The code shown for function NSS is equivalent to selecting randomly from among the available service activities. It is equivalent to the standard priority rule RAN with an equal probability assigned to each of the servers following the SELECT node.

9.12.3   User-Written Attribute Save Criteria: ASSEMBLE

When the queue selection rule at a SELECT node is specified as USERASSEMBLE(expr), function **ASSEMBLE(Code As Long, Node As**

VSNODE) As VSENTITY is called with Code equal to the evaluated expression and Node equal to the pointer to the SELECT node description. The function is written to create the assembled entity and return its pointer. The first entity in each of the QUEUE nodes preceding the SELECT node will be removed and destroyed. The following example saves attributes from entities being assembled from QUEUE node file 1 and QUEUE node file 2. The first and third attributes of the assembled entity will be taken from the first entity in file 1, while the second and fourth attributes will be taken from the first entity in file 2. The function MMFE, described in Chapter 11VB, is used to obtain the placeholder of the first entity in a file.

```
Public Function ASSEMBLE(Code As Long,Node As VSNODE) As VSENTITY
'*************************************************************
'* Function to set attributes from entities assembled
'* at a SELECT node whose Queue Selection Rule is
'* USERASSEMBLE(1).
'*
'* Input parameter Code is not used, since there is only
'* one user-written assembly function, and input parameter
'* Node is not used, since we know that the entities to
'* be assembled are in QUEUE node files 1 and 2.
'*************************************************************/

    Dim ENew As VSENTITY
    Dim One As VSENTITY
    Dim Two As VSENTITY

    'Define the first entity in each file and
    'the new entity to be assembled.

    Set ENew = VS.DefineEntity(0)
    Set One = VS.MMFE(1).Entity
    Set Two = VS.MMFE(2).Entity

    'The new entity will have its first and third attributes
    'taken from the first entity in File 1.  Its second and
    'fourth attributes are taken from the first entity in
    'File 2.

    ENew.ATRIB(1) = One.ATRIB(1)
    ENew.ATRIB(2) = Two.ATRIB(2)
    ENew.ATRIB(3) = One.ATRIB(3)
    ENew.ATRIB(4) = Two.ATRIB(4)

      Set ASSEMBLE = ENew
      Set One = Nothing
      Set Two = Nothing
    End Function
```

9.13   SAVING BATCHED ATTRIBUTES: BATCHSAVE

The user-written subroutine **BATCHSAVE(Code As Long, Form As VSENTITY, Add As VSENTITY)** is called when an entity is being added to a batch and the attribute save criterion at the BATCH node is USER(expr). The arguments to BATCHSAVE are the evaluted expression (Code), the object referencing the forming batched entity (Form) and the object referencing the entity being added to the batch (Add). The function is written to update the attributes which will belong to the batched entity when the batch is released. A simple example follows.

```
Public Sub BATCHSAVE(Code as Long,Form As VSENTITY,Add As VSENTITY)
'*****************************************************************
'* Function to make the third attribute of a batched
'* entity equal to the sum of twice the second attribute
'* of each member of the batch.
'*
'* Input parameter Code is not used, since there is only
'* one BATCH node with USER as the attribute save rule.
'*****************************************************************
   Form.ATRIB(3) = Form.ATRIB(3) + 2.0*Add.ATRIB(2)
   End Sub
```

9.14   STOPPING AN ACTIVITY: STOPA(Code As Integer) As Integer

In complex systems, the length of a specific activity may not be known *a priori* but may depend upon the dynamics of the system. For example, in a queueing system the service rate may be a function of the number of entities waiting for the server and thus may change over time. Therefore the duration of the activity is unknown at the start time of the activity and is affected by future arrivals. One way of modeling an indefinite activity duration using network concepts is to specify the activity duration as keyed to STOPA(NTC). This allows the modeler to stop selectively a specific entity undergoing an activity without stopping the other entities undergoing the same activity.

To stop an activity for a network entity from user-written code, the modeler must specify the duration of the activity in the network model as STOPA(NTC) where NTC is a positive integer which is user-assigned as an entity code to distinguish the entity from other entities in the same activity or elsewhere in the network. If NTC is specified as a real value it is truncated to the nearest integer. The value of NTC can be specified as a number, a Visual SLAM variable, a Visual SLAM random variable or by an expression. By specifying the entity code as an attribute of the entity or as a random variable, the modeler can assign different entity codes to entities within the same activity. The activity statement

ACT,,STOPA(1);

specifies that all entities in the activity are to be assigned entity code l. The statement

ACT,,STOPA(ATRIB[3]);

specifies that the third attribute of each entity is to be assigned as the entity code.

The mechanism for stopping the activity for a network entity from C code is to call function STOPA. A call to function STOPA(NTC) causes an end of activity to occur for every entity with entity code NTC that is being processed by an activity whose duration is specified as STOPA. For example, execution of the statement **Call VS.STOPA(1)** causes all activities to be completed whose duration was specified as STOPA(1).

Since the execution of the **Call VS.STOPA(NTC)** statement causes the end of an activity to occur for each entity with entity code NTC, there may be none, one, or several activities ended by a call to STOPA(NTC). For each activity that is ended, the end-of-activity event for the entity in the activity is placed at the top of the event calendar to be processed immediately following the return from the discrete event. If more than one activity is stopped in this manner, then the end-of-activity event for each entity is processed following the return to Visual SLAM in the order in which the activities were started. If no entities are currently keyed to STOPA(NTC), then execution of a call to STOPA(NTC) has no effect.

9.15   EXAMPLE 9-2. PSYCHIATRIC WARD

Clients of a psychiatric ward arrive at the rate of two per day. Each client is given a test and the test scores are uniformly distributed between 30 and 44. When the ward is full, clients are not admitted if their score is greater than 41. The ward has space for 25 patients. A patient's test score is estimated to change daily in a uniform manner in the range from -0.2 to 1.2. When a patient's test score reaches 48, the patient is discharged from the ward. If a potential patient arrives to the ward and the ward is full, a current patient will be bumped from the ward if a test score higher than 47 has been achieved. Initially there are 18 patients in the ward and their test scores range from 30 to 44. The objective is to simulate the operation of the ward for 1000 days to determine the average time in the system for each patient, the ward utilization, the number of clients balking and number of patients bumped.

Concepts Illustrated. This example illustrates the use of the EVENT node, function EVENT, ENTER node, function ENTER, the STOPA duration specification and function STOPA. This example also illustrates the use of the functions USERF and INTLC.

Visual SLAM Model. In this problem, the discharge from the system for each patient in the ward cannot be scheduled in advance. The test scores for each patient and the ranking of patients based on test scores change daily. This process can be modeled using Visual SLAM by representing patients in the ward as entities in an ACTIVITY with a duration specified as STOPA(II) where II denotes the space or bed number in the ward. The test scores for patients in each of the twenty-five spaces is maintained in the Visual SLAM variable XX[II]. If space number II is not occupied, then XX[II] is set equal to 0.

The network portion of the model is depicted in Figure 9-5. Entities which represent clients seeking admittance to the ward are created at the CREATE node with the current time marked as ATRIB[1] and the time between entities exponentially distributed with mean of 0.5 day. The entities proceed to the ASSIGN node where the initial test score is assigned as ATRIB[2] of the entity.

The M-number for the ASSIGN node is specified as 1, thus a maximum of one of the three emanating ACTIVITY's will be taken. If the ward is full (the number of active entities in the ACTIVITY with index number 1 is 25) and the test score for this client (ATRIB[2]) is greater than 41, then the entity is routed to the COLCT node labeled BALK. If this ACTIVITY is not taken and the ward is full, then the entity is routed to the EVENT node labeled BUMP. If neither of these ACTIVITY's is taken, then the entity is routed to the ASSIGN node labeled WARD.

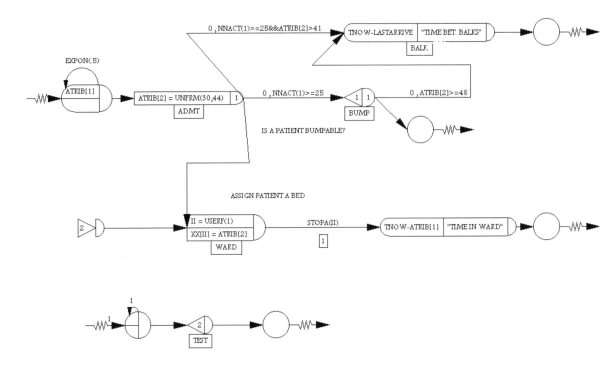

Figure 9-5 Network model of psychiatric ward example.

Consider the entities which arrive to the COLCT node BALK. At each entity arrival to the node, statistics are collected on the time between entity arrivals with the results displayed using the identifier TIME BET. BALKS. The entities are then terminated from the system. No terminate count is used so that the entity is destroyed, but no end of run will occur because of it.

Next, consider the entities which are routed to the EVENT node BUMP, which represents a client attempting to bump one of the patients currently on the ward. Determining if a patient can be bumped is a complex decision. Based on the current test scores of the patients in the ward, a new client is not admitted or a patient is bumped (discharged). In the former case, the client entity is assigned an ATRIB[2] value equal to 48. A return to the EVENT node then causes the entity to be routed to the node BALK based on the condition that ATRIB[2] >= 48 on the activity emanating from node BUMP. In the latter case, the client entity enters into the network through ENTER node 2 to arrive at the ASSIGN node WARD. Before describing the code for event 1, we will complete our description of the network portion of the model.

The entities, which are routed to the ASSIGN node WARD, represent clients who are to be assigned an available space in the ward. At the ASSIGN node, the index variable II is set equal to the value computed in the user-coded function USERF(I) with I = 1. The coding for function USERF is shown in Figure 9-6 and it returns the value of USERF as the smallest index J for which XX[J] is equal to zero. An XX[J]=0 indicates that space J is available. Since entities should only arrive to the ASSIGN node WARD when at least one space is available, a call is made to function VS.Error to cause an error exit from Visual SLAM if all spaces are full. Following the assignment of the first available space number to II, we set XX[II] to the initial test score for this patient.

```
Public Function USERF(Code As Long, Cur As VSENTITY) As Double
    Dim i As Integer
    USERF = 0#

    Select Case Code
        Case 1 ' return bed for new patient
            For i = 1 To NUMBEDS
                If VS.XX(i) <= 0# Then
                    ' idle bed
                    USERF = CDbl(i)
                    Exit Function
                End If
            Next i
            If i > NUMBEDS Then
                VS.Error 3, "No empty bed found"
                VS.MStop = -1
            End If
        Case Else
            VS.Error 2, "Unknown userf code"
    End Select
End Function
```

Figure 9-6 Function USERF for psychiatric ward example.

The ACTIVITY following the ASSIGN node WARD represents the duration for which the patient remains in the ward. The duration for the ACTIVITY is specified to be STOPA(II) denoting that the duration is to be terminated by a call to function STOPA(NTC) with NTC equal to space number II of the patient who is to leave the ward. In this manner, each patient can be selectively discharged from the ward by specifying NTC as the space number for the patient. Following discharge from the ward, interval statistics on the time in system are collected at the COLCT node using the mark time in ATRIB[1] as a reference time. The identifier is TIME IN WARD. The entity is then terminated. A disjoint network is used to create an entity every day which arrives at EVENT node TEST that initiates the testing event for the model. The input statements for this example are shown in Figure 9-7.

```
      GEN,"PRITSKER","PSYCHIATRIC WARD",1/1/1996,1;
      LIMITS,25,-1,-1,2,-1,-1;
      NETWORK;
           CREATE,EXPON(.5), ,ATRIB[1];                 PATIENT ARRIVALS
      ADMT: ASSIGN,{ { ATRIB[2], UNFRM(30,44) } },1;   ASSIGN SCORE
           ACTIVITY, ,0,NNACT(1)>=25&&ATRIB[2]>41;       NO BED
           ACTIVITY, ,0,NNACT(1)>=25,"BUMP";            TRY TO BUMP
           ACTIVITY, , , ,"WARD";                       BED AVAILABLE
      BALK: COLCT, ,TNOW-LASTARRIVE,"TIME BET. BALKS";COLLECT BALK STATS
           TERM;
;
; IS A PATIENT BUMPABLE?
;
  BUMP: EVENT,1;
           ACTIVITY, ,0,ATRIB[2]>=48,"BALK";        PATIENT BALKS
           ACT;
           TERM;
;
;  ASSIGN A PATIENT A BED
           ENTER,2;
      WARD: ASSIGN,{ { II, USERF(1) }, { XX[II], ATRIB[2] } };
           ACT,1,STOPA(II),,,,"IN WARD";      WAIT FOR CALL TO STOPA
           COLCT, ,TNOW-ATRIB[1],"TIME IN WARD";
           TERM;
;
           CREATE,1,1;
      TEST: EVENT,2; DAILY RETEST OF OCCUPIED BEDS
           TERM;
           END;
      INITIALIZE,0,500;
      FIN;
```

Figure 9-7 Statement model for psychiatric ward example.

There are two events that are coded outside of the network model. The first event is initiated by an entity arrival to the EVENT node BUMP and is coded in subroutine BUMP. The second event processes the daily changes in the patients' test scores and discharges patients as necessary. The logic for this event is coded in subroutine TEST. Subroutine EVENT which maps the event code onto the appropriate event subroutine is shown in Figure 9-8.

```
Public Sub EVENT(Code As Long, Ent As VSENTITY)
Select Case Code
     Case 1 ' arrive to event node 1 - bump
        Call BUMP(Ent)
     Case 2 ' arrive to event node 2 - test
        Call TEST(Ent)
     Case Else
        VS.Error 1, "Unknown event code"
   End Select
End Sub
```

Figure 9-8 Subroutine EVENT for psychiatric ward example.

Subroutine BUMP contains the processing logic for the EVENT node BUMP and is depicted in Figure 9-9. Subroutine BUMP is only called when a new client arrives. It uses user-defined global variables BUMP_THRESHOLD (initialized to 47), NUMBEDS (initialized to 25), and WELL_THRESHOLD (initialized to 48). Initially, the variable dBest is set to BUMP_THRESHOLD, and the variable iBest is set to 0. The For loop then searches the current test scores of patients and sets iBest equal to the index of the patient with the largest test score greater than 47. If no patient has a score greater than BUMP_THRESHOLD, ATRIB[2] is set to WELL_THRESHOLD to represent the departure of the new client. If a patient can be bumped, an entity is entered into the network at ENTER node 2 and the bumped patient is discharged from the ward by setting the test score for space iBest to 0, that is, XX(iBest)=0.0, and calling function STOPA(iBest). Note that in the latter case, the order in which the function calls are executed is important. The call to function VS.ENTER 2,eNew is executed first and causes an entity arrival to the ENTER node to be scheduled at the top of the calendar. This is followed by the call to function STOPA(iBest) which causes the end-of-activity event for the patient with entity code iBest to be scheduled at the top of the event calendar. Therefore upon the return to Visual SLAM, the end-of-activity event will be processed prior to the entity arrival to ENTER node 2.

```
Public Sub BUMP(CurEnt As VSENTITY)
    Dim i As Integer
    Dim iBest As Integer
    Dim dBest As Double
    Dim eNew As VSENTITY
 'check to see if any patients have scores above the threshold
    iBest = 0
    dBest = BUMP_THRESHOLD
    For i = 1 To NUMBEDS
       If VS.XX(i) > dBest Then
          iBest = i
        dBest = VS.XX(i)
     End If
   Next i

If iBest Then
    ' found one to bump
    Set eNew = CurEnt.Clone(0)
    If IsObject(eNew) Then
    ' empty bed and stop processing
      VS.XX(iBest) = 0#
    VS.ENTER 2, eNew ' put new patient into network
    VS.STOPA (iBest)
    End If
Else
    ' mark this entity so it will balk
    CurEnt.ATRIB(2) = WELL_THRESHOLD
End If
End Sub
```

Figure 9-9 Subroutine BUMP for psychiatric ward example.

The coding for subroutine TEST which processes the daily changes in each patient's test score is depicted in Figure 9-10. The processing is performed in the For loop which changes each patient's score by adding a uniform sample between -0.2 and 1.2 using stream 1 to their current score. Those patients with test scores exceeding 48.0 are discharged from the ward by calling STOPA(i) and setting XX(i)=0.0 where i is the space number occupied by a discharged patient.

```
' daily update patient scores and see if patient is well enough to
' leave.  if well enough, stop processing
Public Sub TEST(Ent As VSENTITY)
   Dim i As Integer
For i = 1 To NUMBEDS
      If VS.XX(i) > 0# Then
         ' is a patient in this bed
         VS.XX(i) = VS.XX(i) + VS.UNFRM(-0.2, 1.2, 1)
         If VS.XX(i) >= WELL_THRESHOLD Then
            VS.STOPA (i)
            VS.XX(i) = 0#
         End If
      End If
   Next i
End Sub
```

Figure 9-10 Subroutine TEST for psychiatric ward example.

The initial conditions for the simulation are established in function INTLC which is shown in Figure 9-11. This function inserts the initial 18 patients into the network through ENTER node 2.

```
Const NUMBEDS As Integer = 25
Const BUMP_THRESHOLD As Double = 47#
Const WELL_THRESHOLD As Double = 48#
Const INIT_PATIENTS As Integer = 18

Public Function INTLC(Run As Long) As Long
   Dim eNew As VSENTITY
   Dim i, j As Integer

   INTLC = True

   ' create initial patients
   For i = 1 To INIT_PATIENTS
      Set eNew = VS.DefineEntity(0)
      eNew.ATRIB(1) = VS.Time
      eNew.ATRIB(2) = VS.UNFRM(30#, 44#, 1)

      VS.ENTER 2, eNew
   Next i
End Function
```

Figure 9-11 Constants and Function INTLC for psychiatric ward example.

Summary of Results. The Visual SLAM Summary Report shown in Figure 9-12 displays statistics for the time in the ward for each patient, the time between balks from the system and the utilization of the twenty-five spaces in the ward. The results show that on the average 24.8 of the 25 available spaces in the ward are utilized and that over half of the patients seeking admittance to the ward balked from the system as the result of the lack of space on the ward. These results clearly indicate the need for additional space for patients. Additional runs should be made with increased spaces available to determine the number of spaces that should be added. Cost information should also be added to the model to access the worth of proposed new additions. If space cannot be added then research on new patient-improvement procedures and on the criterion for discharge should be initiated.

```
            ** AweSim SUMMARY REPORT **

   Simulation Project : PSYCHIATRIC WARD
   Modeler : PRITSKER
   Date : 1/1/1996
   Scenario : EX92

   Run number 1 of 1
   Current simulation time    : 500.000000
   Statistics cleared at time : 0.000000

          ** OBSERVED STATISTICS REPORT for scenario EX92 **

   Label              Mean        Standard    Number of       Minimum      Maximum
                      Value       Deviation   Observations    Value        Value

   TIME BET. BALKS  0.892         1.286          556          0.000        11.895
   TIME IN WARD    22.975         8.004          526          5.112        45.060

          ** ACTIVITY STATISTICS REPORT for scenario EX92 **

   Activity Label or      Average    Standard Entity   Maximum     Current
   Number   Input Location Utilization Deviation Count  Utilization Utilization

      1         IN WARD     24.838      0.593    526       25          25
```

Figure 9-12 Visual SLAM summary report for psychiatric ward example.

9.16 CHAPTER SUMMARY

   This chapter has provided many capabilities for inserting user-written logic directly into a network model. These user-written inserts increase the flexibility of the network-oriented world view. The EVENT node provides a general capability to include a node in the network to perform logic functions and attribute assignments limited only by the programming capabilities of the modeler. The ENTER node allows entities to be inserted in the network based on logic written in event routines.

A discussion of filing and removing entities waiting at QUEUE nodes or AWAIT nodes is given. A large complement of functions is described for extending the logical capabilities provided by Visual SLAM's routing, selection and resource allocation methods. In addition, advanced procedures for allocating resources to entities and for stopping activities based on external conditions is described. An example illustrating the jockeying of entities from one queue to another is presented. A second example illustrates the activity scanning features associated with the STOPA specification as well as user-written modeling features associated with EVENT, ENTER, and USERF functions.

9.17   EXERCISES

9-1. In Example 5-2, add the feature that if there are more than three jobs to be processed by the machine tool when it breaks down, all jobs except the last three to arrive are routed to a subcontractor. The job in progress is also routed to the subcontractor.

9-2. For Example 5-2, redevelop the model to include the possibility that the repairman process breaks down and a delay of three hours is incurred in order to get a spare part for the repair process. The time between repair process breakdowns is exponentially distributed with a mean of 100 hours. If the repair breakdown occurs when the repair process is not active, no action is taken.

9-3. Model and analyze the admitting process of a hospital as described below. The following three types of patients are processed by the admitting function:

Type 1.   Those patients who are admitted and have previously completed their pre-admission forms and tests;

Type 2.   Those patients who seek admission but have not completed pre-admission; and

Type 3.   Those who are only coming in for pre-admission testing and information gathering.

Service times in the admitting office vary according to patient type as given in the following table.

Patient Types and Service Times

Patient Type	Relative Frequency	Mean Time to Admit
1	0.90 before 10:00 A.M.	15 minutes
	0.50 after 10:00 A.M.	
2	0.10 always	40 minutes
3	0 before 10:00 A.M.	30 minutes
	0.40 after 10:00 A.M.	

Note: All of the above times are normally distributed
with $\sigma = 0.1\mu$ (min. = 0.0).

On arrival to admitting, a person waits in line if the two admitting officers are busy. When idle, an admitting officer selects a patient who is to be admitted before those who are only to be pre-admitted. In addition, Type 1 patients are given highest priority. After filling out various forms in the admitting office, Type 1 patients are taken to their floor by an orderly while Type 2 and 3 patients walk to the laboratory for blood and urine tests. Three orderlies are available to escort patients to the nursing units. Patients are not allowed to go to their floor by themselves as a matter of policy. If all orderlies are busy, patients wait in the lobby. Once patients have been escorted to a floor, they are considered beyond the admitting process. It takes the orderly 3 time units to return to the admitting room. Those patients who must go to the lab are always ambulatory, and as a result require no escorts. After arriving in the lab, they wait in line at the registration desk. After registration, they go to the lab waiting room until they are called on by one of two lab technicians. After the samples are drawn, they walk back to the admitting office if they are to be admitted or leave if only pre-admission has been scheduled. Upon return to admitting, they are processed as normal Type 1 patients. The admitting office is open from 7:00 A.M. until 5:00 P.M. However, no pre-admissions (Type 3) are scheduled until 10:00 A.M. because of the heavy morning workload in the lab. At 4:00 P.M., incoming admissions are sent to the outpatient desk for processing. However, Type 2 patients returning from the lab are accepted until 5:00 P.M. which is the time both admitting officers go home and the office is closed. Analyze the above system for 10 days. It is of interest to determine the time in the system, that is, the time from arrival until on a floor (Type 1 and 2) or exit from the lab (Type 3). Also, determine the time between arrivals to the laboratory. Assume all patient queues are infinite and FIFO ranked except where noted. Activity times are specified below.

Activity Times (all times in minutes)

Explanation	Distribution: Parameters
time between arrivals to admitting office, t_1	exponential: mean = 15
travel time between admitting and floor, t_2	uniform: min = 3, max = 8
travel time between admitting and lab or lab and admitting, t_3	uniform: min = 2, max = 5
service time at lab registration desk, t_4	Erlang-3: mean = 4.5, k = 3
time spent drawing lab specimen, t_5	Erlang-2: mean = 5, k = 2
time for orderly to return from floor to admitting desk, t_6	constant: 3

9-4.   There are three stations on an assembly line and the service time at each station is exponentially distributed with a mean of 10. Items flow down the assembly line from server 1 to server 2 to server 3. A new unit is provided to server 1 every 15 time units. If any server has not completed processing its current unit within 15 minutes, the unit is diverted to one of two off-line servers who complete the remaining operations on the job diverted from the assembly line. One time unit is added to the remaining time of the operation that was not completed. Any following operations not performed are done so by the off-line servers in an exponentially distributed time with a mean of 16. Obtain statistics on the utilization of all servers, and the fraction of items diverted from each operation.

Embellishments: (a) Assume the assembly line is paced and that the movement of units can only occur at multiples of 15 minutes.   (b) Allow one unit to be stored between each assembly line server.   (c) If a server is available, route units back to the assembly line from the off-line servers.

9-5.   A conveyor system involves five servers stationed along a conveyor belt. Items to be processed by the servers arrive at the first server at a constant rate of four per minute. Service time for each server is 1 minute, and is exponentially distributed. No storage is provided before each server; therefore, the server must be idle to remove the item from the conveyor belt. If the first server is idle, the item is processed by that server. At the end-of-service time, the item is removed from the system. If the first server is busy when the item arrives, it continues down the conveyor belt until it arrives at the second server. The delay time between servers is 1 minute. If an item encounters a situation in which all servers are busy, it is recycled to the first server with a time delay of 5 minutes. Simulate the above conveyor system for 100 time units to determine statistics concerning the time spent in the system by an item, the percentage of time each server is busy and the number of items in the conveyor system.

Embellishments: (a) Repeat the simulation with a time delay of 2 minutes between servers. Is there an effect on the utilization of the servers because of a change in the time delay between servers, that is, the speed of the conveyor?   (b) Evaluate the situation in which the last server has sufficient space for storage so that all items passing servers 1, 2, 3, and 4 are processed by server 5. Simulate this situation.

(c) Assess the increased performance obtained by allowing a one item buffer before each server. Based on the results of this study, specify how you would allocate ten buffer spaces to the five servers. (d) Discuss how you would evaluate the tradeoffs involved between reducing the number of servers in the conveyor system versus increasing the buffer size associated with each server.

9-6.   Let the storage space before each server for the conveyor system described in Exercise 9-5 be two units. When storage exists before each server of a conveyor system, decisions regarding the removal of items must be established. Propose decision rules for determining whether items should be removed from the conveyor belt and placed in storage before a particular server. Simulate the decision rules to obtain the statistics requested in Exercise 9-5.

9-7.   Simulate the following resource constrained PERT network to evaluate a set of dispatching rules for determining the order in which to perform activities when the resources available are insufficient to perform all the activities that have been released. The following statistics are to be recorded based on 100 simulations of the network for each dispatching rule.

   1.   Average time at which each node is realized.
   2.   Minimum time at which each node is realized.
   3.   Maximum time at which each node is realized.
   4.   Standard deviation of the time each node is realized.
   5.   Histograms of the time to realize nodes.
   6.   Percentage of the simulation runs in which an activity was on a critical path (a criticality index).
   7.   Network completion time distribution.
   8.   Utilization of each resource type.

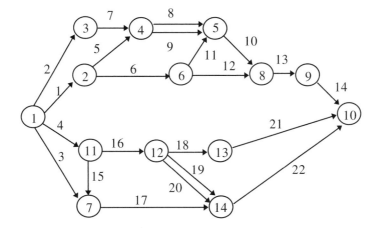

Parameters of Activities of the Network for Exercise 9-7

Activity Number	Distribution	Mean Time	Variance	Requirement for Resource Type			
				1	2	3	4
1	Lognormal	7	2	2	0	1	3
2	Constant	3	0	2	0	1	1
3	Constant	10	0	0	2	0	0
4	Constant	5	0	1	1	1	1
5	Dummy	0	0	0	0	0	0
6	Constant	5	0	2	0	3	2
7	Uniform	3	1/3	1	0	2	3
8	Gamma	8	6	3	0	0	1
9	Constant	3	0	1	0	0	0
10	Constant	5	0	2	0	1	3
11	Dummy	0	0	0	0	0	0
12	Constant	2	0	2	1	2	2
13	Constant	6	0	1	1	0	0
14	Constant	10	0	0	0	0	0
15	Exponential	10	0	1	1	1	0
16	Constant	3	0	1	1	2	0
17	Constant	5	0	0	1	1	1
18	Constant	2	0	0	1	0	3
19	Normal	5	4	1	0	0	2
20	Constant	1	0	1	1	0	0
21	Constant	15	0	0	1	2	0
22	Constant	5	0	0	1	0	0

Resource Availability and Types

Type	Description	Availability
1	Systems analyst	3
2	Marketing personnel	2
3	Maintenance personnel	3
4	Engineering personnel	3

9-8. A multiprocessor computing system is composed of two processors (CPUs) sharing a common memory (CM) of 131 pages, four disk drives, each of which can be accessed by either processor, and a single data channel. A schematic diagram of the system is shown below.

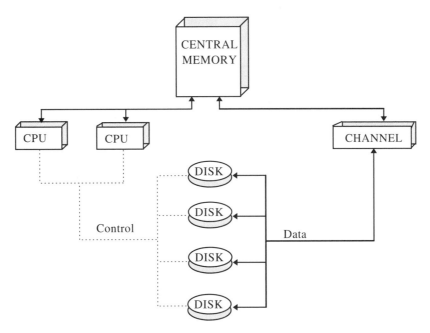

Schematic Diagram of a Multiprocessor Computing System

Jobs arrive to the system at an average rate of 12 jobs per minute in accordance with a Poisson distribution. Total CPU time for a job follows a normal distribution with a mean of 10 seconds and a standard deviation of 3 seconds. The CPU processing time consists of bursts, each of which is followed by an I/O requirement. Each burst follows a negative exponential distribution whose mean is equal to the reciprocal of the average I/O rate of a job. The average I/O rate per job varies uniformly from 2 to 10. I/O operations are assigned to a specific disk upon arrival.

Jobs arriving to the system are assigned a priority which is inversely related to their memory requirements. The CM requirements for a job are distributed uniformly between 20 and 60 pages. Once memory has been allocated to a job it begins execution on any available CPU. Upon issuing an I/O request, the job can continue using the CPU as long as only one I/O request is outstanding. Thus, if an I/O request is made and the job has an I/O request pending, the CPU is relinquished and the I/O request is queued. Following completion of a nonpending I/O request, CPU operations on the job can be reinitiated if a CPU is available.

After a CPU burst, an I/O request is automatically made on the disk assigned to the job, that is, direct access to the disks from the CPUs is made. The seek time to locate the proper position on any disk is assumed to be uniformly distributed between 0. and .075 seconds. Only one seek operation per disk can be performed at a time. Following the seek operation, a data transfer through the data channel is made. The transfer time is equal to .001*(2.5+U) where U is uniformly distributed between 0 and 25. After the transfer, the I/O request is considered satisfied.

Simulate the computing system to determine the residence time of jobs processed by the system, and the utilization statistics for the four disks, the input/output channel, and the two processors (CPUs). Also, the average use of memory is to be obtained. Statistics on the number of jobs waiting for a resource and the waiting time of jobs are also desired. The simulation is to be run for 12,000 seconds.

9-9.   A machine tool processes two different types of parts. The time between arrivals of Type 1 parts is triangularly distributed with a mode of 30 minutes, a minimum of 20 minutes, and a maximum of 50 minutes. The interarrival time of Type 2 parts is a sample from a triangular distribution with a mode of 50 minutes, a minimum of 35 minutes, and a maximum of 60 minutes. Processing time for Type 1 parts is exponentially distributed with a mean of 20 minutes. For Type 2 parts processing time is a sample from a uniform distribution with a minimum of 15 minutes and a maximum of 20 minutes. Processing time includes an inspection of the completed part. Fifteen percent of the parts fail inspection and return to the end of the queue of parts awaiting processing. Assume that parts which fail inspection have a rework time equal to 90% of the previous processing time.

Include in the model a cart that transports parts from arrival to the processing area. Once the parts have passed inspection the same cart transports the finished product to the packaging area. No cart is required if a part requires reprocessing. The cart transports four parts at a time to the processing area. All transport times are 5 minutes. A packaged product includes one of each type of part. The packaging time is exponentially distributed for each of the two products with a mean of 20 minutes. There is only one cart and it is freed immediately after transporting the products. In addition, if more than three parts are waiting for the machine at a scheduled maintenance time, remove all but the first 3 parts for subcontracting. Make the probability of failing inspection 10 percent for Type 1 parts and 13% for Type 2 parts. Model and analyze this situation for 2400 minutes collecting utilization statistics and time spent in the system by a part.

Embellishment: Using the following data, replace the constant 5-minute travel time with the actual time that it takes for the cart to travel between stations. Assume that the cart remains at the station where it was last stopped until it is needed elsewhere. The cart travels at the rate of 100 feet per minute. The distances between the arrival and the machining areas is 45 feet and between the machining and packaging areas is 55 feet.

9.18 REFERENCES

1.   Norton, P., H. Davis and P. Davis, *Peter Norton's Guide to Visual Basic™ 4 for Windows® 95*, Fourth Edition, Sams Publishing, 1995.

2.   Pritsker, A.A.B., *Introduction to Simulation and SLAM II*, Fourth Edition, Systems Publishing and John Wiley, 1995.

CHAPTER 9C

Network Modeling With C Inserts

9.1   INTRODUCTION

In this chapter, we describe the procedures for constructing network models with user-written C inserts. We begin by describing the EVENT and ENTER nodes which provide the key interface points between the network model and user code. The support subprograms of Visual SLAM for performing file manipulations and setting attribute values and activity durations are presented. We next describe a set of Visual SLAM provided functions which allow the modeler to change the status of the network elements by allocating and freeing units of resources, altering resource capacities, opening and closing gates, stopping activities and specifying selection rules from user-written subprograms.

9.1.1   Visual SLAM Structures and Variable Types

To allow the modeler nearly unlimited flexibility in affecting a simulation from user-written C code, access is given to the data structures of Visual SLAM. Two types of structures in particular, ENTITY and ENTRY, are important in writing the user inserts described in this chapter. The ENTITY* variable type is a pointer to a structure which holds an entity's attributes. The ENTITY* pointer of the current entity is passed into most user-written C functions so that information about the entity may be used or that the entity may be acted upon. Access to entity attributes is described in the following section.

The ENTRY* variable type is a pointer to a structure which holds a file entry's "placeholder" information. While an entity is waiting in a Visual SLAM file, it holds a position (known as rank) in that file. If the entity is not the only entry in the file, it will have a predecessor entry and/or a successor entry.

Structure and variable definitions and function prototypes may be found in the header file vslam.h which is included in each file containing user inserts for a Visual SLAM model. In addition to the ENTITY* and ENTRY* pointer variables, variable types defined in vslam.h include UINT (unsigned integer), ULONG(unsigned long), and BOOL(integer, equal to either 1 or 0). For use with BOOL functions, vslam.h defines the word TRUE to be 1 and FALSE to be 0.

9.2   FUNCTION EVENT

The symbol, input statement and the AweSim dialog box for the EVENT node were described in Section 7.4. For convenience, the symbol and statement are shown below:

EVENT,JEVNT;M

The EVENT node is included in a network model to interface the network portion of a model with event coding written by the modeler. The EVENT node causes function EVENT to be called every time an entity arrives to the EVENT node.

Function EVENT maps the event code JEVNT onto the appropriate event function containing the coding for the event logic. In coding the event logic, the modeler has access to the Visual SLAM functions provided for performing commonly encountered activities such as random sampling, file manipulation and data collection.

The general form for function EVENT is shown below.

```
void EVENT(int I, ENTITY *peCurrent)
{
  switch (I)      {
    case 1:  Code for event node 1
          break;
    case 2:   Code for event node 2
          break;
  }
}
```

The argument I is the event code that is defined for the EVENT node, that is, JEVNT. This code is used to determine which node has had an entity arrive to it. The argument peCurrent is a pointer to a structure of type ENTITY which holds the attributes of the entity which has arrived to the EVENT node.

The EVENT function is written by the user and normally consists of a switch statement indexed on the event code I causing a transfer to the appropriate statement where the logic associated with the EVENT node is written. In many cases, the logic for each EVENT node is written in a separate function to facilitate the identification of the logic and the documentation of the code associated with an EVENT node. An example of function EVENT is shown below for a simulation model with two EVENT nodes consisting of a lunch break coded in function LUNCH and assigned event code 1, and an end-of-lunch break coded in function ELUNCH and assigned event code 2.

```
void EVENT(int I, ENTITY *worker)
  switch (I)        {
  {
      case 1: LUNCH(worker);
              break;
      case 2: ELUNCH(worker);
              break;
  }
}
```

9.2.1   Accessing Attribute Values

Entity attributes may be accessed in C code by using the pointer to the ENTITY structure passed to the user-written function. This structure holds the attributes of the entity which has arrived to the EVENT node, referenced as follows:

```
int    iType;              /*entity type attribute, ETYPE */
UINT uiNumber;             /* unique integer number for entity, ENUM    */
double *ATRIB;             /* real attribute values    */
long   * LTRIB;            /* long attribute values    */
char  **STRIB;             /* string attribute values  */
double *ANTRIB             /* real subnetwork attribute values  */
long *LNTRIB               /* long integer subnetwork attribute values  */
char **SNTRIB              /* string subnetwork attribute values  */
double ERETURN             /* value returned from subnetwork   */
STIME  tTime;              /* time scheduled for or remaining time  */
```

For example, the assignment of TNOW to the second real attribute of the entity whose pointer is peUser can be made by this statement:

$$peUser\text{->}ATRIB[2] = TNOW;$$

9.2.2   Accessing Network Values

The logic at an EVENT node may involve testing the status or changing the value of variables associated with the network portion of the model. In function EVENT, values of network related variables can be obtained using the Visual SLAM functions listed in Table 9-1.

Table 9-1 Functions for accessing the status of an activity, gate or resource.

Function	Definition
UINT NNACT(I)	Number of active entities in activity I at current time
UINT NNCNT(I)	The number of entities that have completed activity I
BOOL NNGAT(I)	Status of gate number I at current time:
	TRUE → open, FALSE → closed
int NRUSE(I)	Current number of resource type I in use
int NNRSC(I)	Current number of resource type I available
UINT NNBLK(I,IFILE)	Number of entities in activity I blocked by file IFILE

On a Visual SLAM network, ARRAY is a two dimensional table for global values. The values in ARRAY can be accessed and changed in event routines by using Visual SLAM provided functions. Table 9-2 provides the definitions for functions GETARY, PUTARY and SETARY for storing and retrieving values from ARRAY.

Table 9-2   Functions for storing and retrieving values from the Visual SLAM global table ARRAY.

Function	Definition
double GETARY(UINT uiRow, UINT uiCol)	Returns the value of row uiRow, column uiCol from the global table, ARRAY.
BOOL PUTARY(UINT uiRow, UINT uiCol, double dValue)	Sets the value of row uiRow, column uiCol of the global table, ARRAY, to dValue. If the array row specified does not contain enough columns or does not exist, it is created. The return value is TRUE if the column/row already existed.
BOOL SETARY(UINT uiRow, double*adValue, UINT uiNumCols)	Sets the values of row uiRow of the global table, ARRAY, to the values passed in array adValue. If the ARRAY row specified does not contain enough columns or does not exist, it is created. The return value is TRUE if the columns/row already existed.

The statement X2=GETARY(3,4); sets X2 equal to the value of the fourth cell in the third row of ARRAY. To put the value 10 into the seventh cell of row 1, the following statement would be used.

PUTARY(1,7,10.0);

If it is desired to set all the values in row 2 of ARRAY and there are three cells in this row then the following statements could be used.

```
double VALUE[3];
VALUE[1] = 100;
VALUE[2] = 200;
VALUE[3] = 300;
SETARY(2,VALUE);
```

9.3   ENTER FUNCTION

The ENTER node, described in Section 7.5, allows the modeler to insert selectively an entity into the network from a user-written function. For convenience, the symbol and the input statement for the ENTER node are shown below.

ENTER,NUM,M;

The ENTER node is released following a return from a user-written function in which a call is made to function ENTER whose prototype is

BOOL ENTER (UINT NUM, ENTITY *peEnt);

The argument NUM is the numeric code of the ENTER node to be released and peEnt is the pointer to the entity to arrive at the ENTER node. This entity is often a new entity, created using the function su_entnew whose prototype is

ENTITY *su_entnew(int iType, double *pdAttrib, long *plLttrib, char **aszSttrib);

The function su_entnew returns a pointer to a new ENTITY structure and initializes its type and attributes. The following statements, for example, would create a new entity, set its first attribute equal to the current simulation time, and route it from ENTER node 1.

```
ENTITY *peNew;                            /* Declare an entity pointer */
peNew = su_entnew(0,NULL,NULL,NULL);      /* Create an entity          */
peNew->ATRIB[1] = TNOW;                   /* Define ATRIB[1]           */
ENTER(1,peNew);                           /* Insert at ENTER node 1    */
```

9.4   FILE MANIPULATIONS

A file provides the mechanism for storing the attributes of an entity in a prescribed ranking with respect to other entities in the file. In network models, files are used to maintain entities waiting at QUEUE, AWAIT and PREEMPT nodes.

Associated with a file is a ranking criterion which specifies the procedure for ordering entities within the file. Thus, each entity in a file has a rank which specifies its position in the file relative to the other members in the file. A rank of one denotes that the entity is the first entry in the file. Possible ranking criterion for files are: first-in, first-out (FIFO); last-in, first-out (LIFO); high-value-first (HVF) based on an expression; and low-value-first (LVF) based on an expression. The ranking criterion for entries in a file is assumed to be FIFO unless otherwise specified using the PRIORITY statement described in Chapter 8.

In Visual SLAM, files are distinguished by integer numbers assigned to the files by the user. Visual SLAM automatically collects statistics on each file and provides the function NNQ(IFILE) which returns the number of entries in file IFILE. For example, NNQ(2) denotes the number of entries in file 2.

The modeler can, when referencing files associated with network nodes, employ any of the file manipulation routines which are available in discrete event simulations.

9.4.1   Filing an Entity, FILEM

A call to function FILEM, whose prototype is **ENTRY*FILEM(UINT IFILE,ENTITY*peEnt);** files the entity pointed to by **peEnt** into file number **IFILE**. FILEM returns the placeholder of the entity in the file where the placeholder is a pointer, Ntry, to the ENTRY structure which maintains the entity's position in the file. The rank of Ntry in the file is determined by Visual SLAM based upon the priority specified by the user. As noted earlier, if no priority is specified, then a first-in, first-out ranking is assumed. As an example of the use of function FILEM, the following statements cause an entity with its first attribute set equal to the current simulation time to be inserted into file 1.

peEnt->ATRIB[1] = TNOW;   /* **Define ATRIB[1] of the current entity** */
Ntry = FILEM (1, peEnt);   /* **File the current entity in file 1** */

To access the attributes of a file entry, the function **ENTITY *su_sfnentity (ENTRY *Ntry)** would be used to return the ENTITY* pointer to the file entry.

9.4.2   Removing an Entity, RMOVE

A call to function RMOVE, whose prototype is **ENTITY*RMOVE(UINT IFILE,ULONG ulRank);** removes the entry with rank **ulRank** from file number **IFILE.** and returns the pointer to the removed entity. As an example of the use of function RMOVE, the following statement removes the last entry in file 1 and places its pointer in the variable peEnt.

     peEnt = RMOVE(1, NNQ(1));

As a second example, the following statements cause the second entry in file 3 to be removed and its pointer set to peOld.

     ENTITY *peOld;   /* **Declare an entity pointer** */
     peOld = RMOVE(3, 2);   /* **Remove the second entry from file 3** */

An entity removed from a file could be inserted into another file using function FILEM or inserted into the network using function ENTER. The entity could also be destroyed and the memory it occupied released for reuse using function su_entterminate whose prototype is

     void su_entterminate (ENTITY *peUser);

where peUser is the pointer to the entity to be destroyed.

9.5   USER FUNCTION USERF

Visual SLAM provides the function **double USERF (int IFN, ENTITY *peEnt);** to assign values to Visual SLAM variables using C code. The argument IFN is a code established by the user and is referred to as a user function number. The name USERF can be used in a network in locations that allow a Visual SLAM variable to be an option. It is most frequently used in the following two situations:

1. An entity passes through an ASSIGN node and one of the assignments is to be made in USERF; and
2. A duration for an activity is specified as USERF.

The entity pointer peEnt points to the entity currently being processed at the network location. The function USERF allows a modeler to make programming inserts into the network model. In the programming insert, the user can employ all C coding procedures and the Visual SLAM functions described above and in Chapter 11C.

As an example of the uses of function USERF, consider the following single-server, single-queue network.

In this network, user function 1 is used to assign a value to attribute 1 at the ASSIGN node, and user function 2 is used to specify the duration of the service time of activity 2. ATRIB[1] is the duration of activity 1 representing the entity's travel to the QUEUE node. In this example, we will make this time a function of the number of remaining spaces in the QUEUE node, that is, 5-NNQ(1). If ATRIB[1] was used only as the duration of the activity then user function 1 could have been specified for the activity. Here we illustrate a concept and demonstrate the use of function USERF to assign an attribute value. If future decisions were made based on the value of ATRIB[1] then the model as depicted would be required.

The service time for activity 2 will also be made a function of the number of entities waiting for service. The general form for writing function USERF is shown below.

```
double USERF(int IFN, ENTITY *peCur);
{
    double dReturn;
     switch (IFN)
     {
         case 1:   set dReturn as the time to travel to
                   the QUEUE node
                   break;
         case 2:   set dReturn as service time, a function
                   of NNQ(1)
                   break;
     }
    return dReturn;
}
```

This example illustrates how IFN, the user function number, is decoded to allow different user functions to be employed throughout the network model. User function 1 only requires USERF to return 5-NNQ(1). When a return is made, Visual SLAM assigns the value of USERF to ATRIB[1]. For user function 2, we require knowledge of how service time varies as a function of the number of entities in the QUEUE node. For illustrative purposes, we will assume an exponential service time whose mean decreases as the number in the queue is increased to a value of 3. When there are more than 3 in the queue, the mean service time increases. A table of mean service time as a function of the number in the queue is shown below.

Number in Queue	Mean Service Time
0	10.
1	9.
2	8.
3	7.
4	9.
5	10.

The specific coding for function USERF(IFN) for this situation would be:

```
double USERF (int IFN, ENTITY *peCur);
{
    double dReturn, AVEST, XNINQ;

    switch (IFN)              {
        case 1:  dReturn = 5 - NNQ(1);
                 break;
        case 2: XNINQ = (float)NNQ(1);
                if (NNQ (1) <= 3) AVEST = 10.-XNINQ;
                if (NNQ (1) > 3) AVEST = 5.+XNINQ;
                dReturn = EXPON (AVEST, 1);
                break;
    }
    return dReturn;
}
```

The switch statement passes control to case 1 if IFN is 1, case 2 otherwise. At case 1, dReturn is established as the value to be assigned when user function 1 is invoked. At case 2, the average service time is calculated based on the above table. The value of dReturn is then set equal to a sample from an exponential distribution using AVEST as the average service time and employing stream number 1. Note that the stream number must be given in function EXPON since direct coding is being employed.

This example illustrates the flexibility available by allowing program inserts to set Visual SLAM variables in network models. For this example it was not necessary to access the attributes of the current entity, peCur. The following statement would provide the value of attribute 1:

Attribute1=peCur –>ATRIB [1];

9.6   EXAMPLE 9-1. DRIVE-IN BANK WITH JOCKEYING

A drive-in bank has two windows, each manned by a teller and each with a separate drive-in lane. The drive-in lanes are adjacent. From previous observations, it has been determined that the time interval between customer arrivals during rush hours is exponentially distributed with a mean time between arrivals of 0.5 time units. Congestion occurs only during rush hours, and only this period is to be analyzed. The service time is normally distributed for each teller with a mean service time of one time unit and a standard deviation of 0.3 time units. It has also been shown that customers have a preference for lane 1 if neither teller is busy or if the waiting lines are equal. At all other times, however, a customer chooses the shortest line. After entering the system, a customer does not leave until served. However, the last customer in a lane may change lanes if there is a difference of two customers between the two lanes. Because of parking space limitations only three cars can wait in each lane. These cars, plus the car of the customer being serviced by each teller, allow a maximum of eight cars in the system. If the system is full when a customer arrives, the customer balks and is lost to the system.

The initial conditions are as follows:
1. Both drive-in tellers are busy. The initial service time for each teller is normally distributed with a mean of one time unit and a standard deviation of 0.3 time units.
2. The first customer is scheduled to arrive at 0.1 time units.
3. Two customers are waiting in each queue.

The objective is to develop a simulation model that can be used to analyze the banking situation in terms of the following statistics:
1. Teller utilization = $\dfrac{\text{total time performing service}}{\text{total simulation time}}$
2. Time-integrated average number of customers in the system.
3. Time between departures from the drive-in windows.
4. Average time a customer is in the system.
5. Average number of customers in each queue.
6. Percent of arriving customers who balk.
7. Number of times cars jockey.

The system is to be simulated for 1000 time units.

Concepts Illustrated. This example illustrates user-written code to augment the modeling concepts in a network model. Two key concepts which are specifically illustrated by this example are: 1) the use of the EVENT node to model jockeying; and 2) the referencing of a common file number between the network and discrete event portions of a model. In addition, this example illustrates balking from a SELECT node.

Visual SLAM Model. The drive-in bank example is amenable to modeling with network concepts. However, we will represent the drive-in bank system as a network model with the jockeying of cars modeled using an EVENT node. Since jockeying can occur only when a teller completes service on a customer, the EVENT node for processing the jockeying of cars between lanes will be executed following the end-of-service for each entity in the system.

The network model for this example is depicted in Figure 9-1. Arriving cars are created by the CREATE node which marks current time as ATRIB[1]. The first entity is created at time 0.1, and the time between car arrivals is exponentially distributed with a mean of 0.5 time units. The SELECT node routes each entity to either the LEFT or RIGHT QUEUE node based on the smallest number in the queue rule (SNUM). The LEFT QUEUE node initially contains two entities and permits a maximum of three waiting entities which are stored in file 1. The LEFT QUEUE is followed by an ACTIVITY representing teller 1 which is prescribed as activity number 1. The duration of the activity is normally distributed with a mean of 1.0 and a standard deviation of 0.3. The ACTIVITY routes the entity to an EVENT node whose event code is 1. The RIGHT QUEUE node also initially contains two entities and permits a maximum of three waiting entities which are stored in file 2. The ACTIVITY following the RIGHT QUEUE node is assigned activity number 2, is normally distributed, and routes the entities to the EVENT node with event code 2. This ACTIVITY represents the service by teller 2.

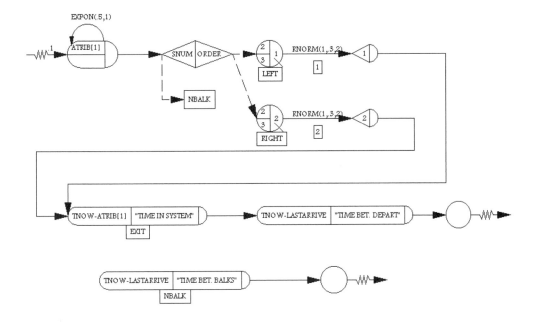

Figure 9-1 Network model of drive-in bank.

At the EVENT nodes, Visual SLAM calls the user-coded function EVENT (JEVNT,peCur) with JEVNT set equal to 1 or 2 to process the discrete event logic associated with the node, and peCur set to the ENTITY structure pointer of the car about to leave the system. The jockeying event logic is coded directly in function EVENT as depicted in Figure 9-2.

In function EVENT, the variables NumInLane1 and NumInLane2 are computed as the number of cars in lane 1 (LEFT) and lane 2 (RIGHT), respectively. Note that the number in each lane is calculated to include the customer in service, if any. At case 1, jockeying from the RIGHT lane to the LEFT lane is investigated. If the number of cars in the RIGHT lane exceeds the number in the LEFT lane by two, then the last entity in file 2 (whose rank is NNQ(2)) is removed from the RIGHT QUEUE node by a call to RMOVE with IFILE = 2 and is scheduled to arrive at the LEFT QUEUE node at the current simulated time by a call to function FILEM with IFILE = 1. This completes the code for jockeying and is followed by a break statement.

```
#include "vslam.h"

void SWFUNC EVENT(int iCode, ENTITY * peCurEnt)
{
    int NumInLane1,NumInLane2;
    ENTITY * peJockey;

    /* compute the number in each lane */
    NumInLane1  = NNQ(1) + NNACT(1);
    NumInLane2  = NNQ(2) + NNACT(2);

    switch (iCode)                                  {
       case 1: /* arrive to event node 1 */
    /* entity leaving lane 1,  see if lane 2 should jockey */
          if (NumInLane2 >= (NumInLane1 + 2))        {
             peJockey = RMOVE(2,NNQ(2));
             FILEM(1,peJockey);
          }
       break;
       case 2: /* arrive to event node 2 */
    /* entity leaving lane 2,  see if lane 1 should jockey */
          if (NumInLane1 >= (NumInLane2 + 2))        {
             peJockey = RMOVE(1,NNQ(1));
             FILEM(2,peJockey);
          }
       break;
       default:
          su_error(1,"Unknown event code");
       break;
    }
}
```

Figure 9-2 Function EVENT for model of the drive-in bank.

At case 2, if the number of cars in the LEFT lane exceeds the number in the RIGHT lane by two, the reverse jockeying procedure is executed. If the lanes do not differ by two cars, then a return from function EVENT is made without a car jockeying.

Following execution of the EVENT node, the entity that arrived to the EVENT node is routed from the EVENT node, as the current entity was not altered. This entity continues to the COLCT node EXIT where interval statistics are collected using the mark time in ATRIB[1] as a reference. The results are displayed using the identifier TIME IN SYSTEM. A second COLCT node collects statistics on the time between departures and displays the results using the identifier TIME

BET. DEPART. The entities are then terminated. The input statements for the model are shown in Figure 9-3.

```
GEN,"PRITSKER","DRIVE IN BANK",1/1/1996,1;
LIMITS,-1,-1,-1,2,-1,-1;
TIMST,1,NNQ(1)+NNACT(1)+NNQ(2)+NNACT(2),"NO. OF CUST";
SEEDS,{ { 4367651, 1 }, { 6121137, 2 } };
NETWORK;
        CREATE,EXPON(.5,1),.1,ATRIB[1];
        ACTIVITY;
        SELECT,SNUM, ,BALK(NBALK),{LEFT,RIGHT};
LEFT: QUEUE,1,2,3;
        ACT,1,RNORM(1,.3,2), , , ,"TELLER 1";
        EVENT,1;
        ACT, , , ,"EXIT";
EXIT: COLCT, ,TNOW-ATRIB[1],"TIME IN SYSTEM";
        ACTIVITY;
        COLCT, ,TNOW-LASTARRIVE,"TIME BET. DEPART";
        ACTIVITY;
        TERM;
RIGHT: QUEUE,2,2,3;
        ACT,2,RNORM(1,.3,2), , , ,"TELLER 2";
        EVENT,2;
        ACTIVITY, , , ,"EXIT";
NBALK: COLCT, ,TNOW-LASTARRIVE,"TIME BET. BALKS";
        ACTIVITY;
        TERM;
        END;
INIT,0,1000;
FIN;
```

Figure 9-3 Input statements for model of the drive-in bank.

The control statements for this model include GEN, LIMITS, TIMST, SEEDS, INIT and FIN statements. The GEN, LIMITS, INIT and FIN statement are in standard form. The TIMST statement is employed to obtain statistics on the number of customers in the drive-in bank system. The SEEDS control statement sets the initial seed value for stream number 1 to be 4367651 and the initial seed value for stream number 2 to be 6121137.

Summary of Results. The results for this example are summarized by the Visual SLAM summary report shown in Figure 9-4. Statistics for variables based on observations are given first with the identifiers specified at the COLCT nodes. For this example, observation statistics were collected on the time in the system for each customer and the time between departures of customers. From the summary report, it is seen that 1854 customers were served and the average time in the system was 2.317 minutes. Also customers leave the bank every 0.54 minutes on the average.

```
                    ** AweSim SUMMARY REPORT **

             Simulation Project : DRIVE IN BANK
                    Modeler : PRITSKER
                    Date : 1/1/1996
                    Scenario : EX91

                    Run number 1 of 1
                    Current simulation time   : 1000.000000
                    Statistics cleared at time : 0.000000

          ** OBSERVED STATISTICS REPORT for scenario EX91 **

Label             Mean      Standard   Number of    Minimum     Maximum
                  Value     Deviation  Observations  Value      Value

TIME IN SYSTEM    2.317      1.018       1854        0.304       5.068
TIME BET. DEPART  0.539      0.361       1853        0.000       3.004
TIME BET. BALKS   6.982     13.152        142        0.014      70.818

        ** TIME-PERSISTENT STATISTICS REPORT for scenario EX91 **

Label          Mean   Standard    Minimum    Maximum      Time        Current
               Value  Deviation   Value      Value        Interval    Value

NO. OF CUST    4.312  2.154       0.000      8.000        1000.000     7.000

            ** FILE STATISTICS REPORT for scenario EX91 **

File     Label or      Average    Standard   Maximum  Current   Average
Number   Input Location Length    Deviation  Length   Length    Wait Time

  1 QUEUE    LEFT        1.311      1.033       3        3       1.109
  2 QUEUE    RIGHT       1.148      0.993       3        2       1.231
  0 Event Calendar       3.853      0.432       5        4       0.935

        ** SERVICE ACTIVITY STATISTICS REPORT for scenario EX91 **

Activity  Label or       Server   Entity  Average     Standard   Current
Number    Input Location Capacity Count   Utilization Deviation  Utilization

   1       TELLER 1        1        942     0.939       0.239        1
   2       TELLER 2        1        912     0.914       0.280        1

Activity  Average     Maximum      Maximum
Number    Blockage    Idle Time    Busy Time
                      or Servers   or Servers

   1       0.000       2.202        84.843
   2       0.000       4.095        71.472
```

Figure 9-4 Visual SLAM summary report for drive-in bank.

The second category of statistics for this example is for time-persistent variables. The results show the average number of customers in the system is 4.312.

The third category of statistics relate to the number of customers waiting in line for teller 1 and teller 2, respectively. The results show that there was an average of 1.311 customers waiting in file 1 for service by teller 1 and an average of 1.148 customers waiting in file 2 for service by teller 2. The final category of statistics for this example is service activity statistics. The results show that teller 1 was busy 93.9 percent of the time while teller 2 was busy 91.4 percent of the time. The slightly longer length of the waiting line and higher utilization for teller 1 as compared to teller 2 is because of the preference by customers for teller 1 when both waiting lines are equal. This information could be used by bank management for assigning tellers to windows.

9.7   SAMPLING FROM PROBABILITY DISTRIBUTIONS

An important aspect of many systems of interest is the stochastic nature of one or more elements in the system. For example, in queueing systems the arrival times and service times are usually not known with certainty but are depicted as random variables. Therefore, in order to build models of such systems, the simulation programmer needs to be able to sample from commonly encountered distributions such as the exponential, normal, and beta as well as from user-defined distributions. Visual SLAM provides C function statements for this purpose. A list of such functions is summarized in Table 9-1. Note that the functional names are the same as those employed in network models except for DPROB and the parameter specifications are identical to those specified in Chapter 5. The reader should note that these are C functions, and all arguments must be specified with the correct type of variable (int or double). In particular, the stream parameter cannot be defaulted as in the case of network statements.

Table 9-1 Function statements to obtain random samples.

Function	Descriptions‡
double BETA(double dTheta, double dPhi, int iStream)	Returns a sample from a beta distribution with parameters dTheta and dPhi using random number stream iStream.
double DPROB(double*adCumProb, double*adValue, int iNum, int iStream)	Returns a sample from a user-defined discrete probability distribution with cumulative probabilities in the array adCumProb and associated values in the array adValue. iNum values are defined and random number stream iStream is used.
double DRAND(int iStream)	Returns a random number uniformly distributed between 0 and 1 using random number stream iStream.
double ERLNG(double dMean, int iXK, int iStream)	Returns a sample from an Erlang distribution which is the sum of iXK exponential samples each with mean dMean using random number stream iStream.
double EXPON(double dMean, int iStream)	Returns a sample from an exponential distribution with mean dMean using random number stream iStream.
double GAMA(double dBeta, double dAlpha, int iStream)	Returns a sample from a gamma distribution with parameters dBeta and dAlpha using random number stream iStream.
long INTRN(int iStream)	Returns the current seed value for random number stream iStream.
long NPSSN(double dMean, int iStream)	Returns a sample from a Poisson distribution with mean dMean using random number stream iStream.
double RLOGN(double dMean, double dStdDev, int iStream)	Returns a sample from a lognormal distribution with mean dMean and standard deviation dStdDev using random number stream iStream.
double RNORM(double dMean, double dStdDev, int iStream)	Returns a sample from a normal distribution with mean dMean and standard deviation dStdDev using random number stream iStream.
double TRIAG(double dLow, double dMode, double dHi, int iStream)	Returns a sample from a triangular distribution in the interval dLow to dHi with mode dMode using random number stream iStream.
double UNFRM(double dLow, double dHi, int iStream)	Returns a sample from a uniform distribution in the interval dLow to dHi using random number stream iStream.
double WEIBL(double dAlpha, double dBeta, int iStream)	Returns a sample from a Weibull distribution with scale parameter dAlpha and shape parameter dBeta using random number stream iStream.
double XRN(iStream)	Returns the last normalized random sample obtained from stream iStream.

‡ See Chapter 16 for the equations of the distribution functions associated with the random variables, the definitions of the arguments and their calculation.

Function DPROB allows the user to obtain a sample from a user-defined discrete distribution (a probability mass function). The user must convert the probability mass function into a cumulative distribution. Two user arrays are required to describe this distribution: the first for the potential values of the random variable and the second for the associated cumulative probabilities. The arguments of function DPROB are: the user array name for the cumulative probabilities (adCumProb), the user array name for the associated values (adValue), the number of values (iNum) contained in adCumProb and adValue and the random stream number (iStream).

As an example of the use of Function DPROB, consider the following probability mass function for the random variable Z:

Z	f (Z)
3	.1
4	.4
5	.5

First, the probability mass function is converted to a cumulative distribution. We define the cumulative distribution using arrays Z[I] and FZ[I] as follows:

I	Z[I]	FZ[I]
0	3	.1
1	4	.5
2	5	1.0

These values can be conveniently assigned to the arrays by an array declaration statement in the function calling function DPROB or can be read from input records. The following statement draws a sample, ZSAMP, from the desired probability mass function using random stream number 1.

$$ZSAMP = DPROB(FZ,Z,3,1);$$

Function DPROB differs from the network discrete probability function, DPROBN, in that for DPROBN, rows of the Visual SLAM variable ARRAY are specified as the first two arguments.

9.8   USER-WRITTEN INITIALIZATION AND POST-RUN PROCESSING ROUTINES: FUNCTIONS INTLC AND OTPUT

At the beginning of each simulation run, the Visual SLAM processor calls function INTLC to enable the modeler to set initial conditions and to schedule initial events. All the functions included within Visual SLAM can be used at this time. Function OTPUT is called at the end of each simulation run and is used for end-of-run processing such as clearing out files and printing special results for the simulation run. INTLC and OTPUT are of type BOOL and should return TRUE if the current run (for INTLC) or the next run (for OTPUT) should be performed. If FALSE (0) is returned, the simulation will be stopped. Visual SLAM provides many functions to access all variables and statistics collected during a run. These functions are described in detail in Chapter 11C.

9.9   CHANGING THE STATUS OF A RESOURCE

Visual SLAM provides the modeler with functions which free a specified number of units of a resource, alter the capacity of a resource by a specified amount, and support complex resource allocation decisions. Before describing these functions, the method for referencing a resource needs to be established.

In network statements, resources are referenced by either the resource name or number. In the resource functions, a resource must be referenced by its number. Recall from Chapter 5 that if a resource number is not specified, the Visual SLAM processor automatically numbers the resources in the order in which the RESOURCE blocks are inputted to the Visual SLAM processor. The first resource is assigned number 1, the second resource is assigned number 2, and so on. For example, consider the following set of RESOURCE blocks included in the network portion of a model.

```
RESOURCE,,TUG,2,{1,2};
RESOURCE,,BERTH,3,{3};
RESOURCE,,CREW,,{4};
```

The processor would assign the TUGs as resource number 1, the BERTHs as resource number 2, and the CREW as resource number 3. When changing the status of a resource from within a discrete event, the resource number is included as an argument to the appropriate function to distinguish between resource types.

9.9.1 Freeing Resources: Function FREE

BOOL FREE(UINT uiRes, int iUnits) releases iUnits units of resource number uiRes. The freed units of the resource are made available to waiting entities according to the order of the file numbers specified in the RESOURCE statement included in the network model. For the RESOURCE blocks depicted above, the statement

    FREE(1,2);

would release 2 units of the resource TUG. These tugs are made available to entities waiting in file 1. If both tugs are not used, then file 2 would be interrogated to determine if an entity was waiting for the use of a tug. The execution of the statement FREE(1,2); is identical to the execution of the following network statement.

    FREE,{TUG,2};

9.9.2 Altering Resource Capacities: Function ALTER

BOOL ALTER(UINT uiRes, int iUnits) changes the capacity of resource number uiRes by iUnits units. In the case where the capacity of the resource is decreased below current utilization, the excess capacity is destroyed as it becomes freed. The capacity can be reduced to a minimum of zero with additional reduction requests having no effect. Assuming the RESOURCE blocks depicted earlier, the following statement would reduce the number of tugs by 1.

    ALTER(1,-1);

This statement produces the same effect as the execution of the following network statement.

ALTER,TUG,–1;

9.10   USER-WRITTEN RESOURCE ALLOCATION PROCEDURES: FUNCTIONS ALLOC AND SEIZE

AWAIT nodes are used to store entities waiting for resources. When an AWAIT node description includes a resource name, an entity cannot pass through the AWAIT node until a specified number of units of that resource are available. When this condition occurs, the proper number of resources of that type are "seized" (set busy) and the entity proceeds from the AWAIT node. When the modeler specifies ALLOC(iCode) as the resource allocation rule, the function **ENTRY *ALLOC(int iCode, SFILNODE * peFirst)** is called by Visual SLAM when an entity arrives to the AWAIT node. The argument peFirst is the placeholder of the first entity in the file currently being polled by ALLOC. ALLOC is also called when the file associated with that AWAIT node is polled as the result of a newly available or freed resource. The ENTRY* pointer type is discussed in Section 9.4.1.

Function ALLOC is coded to determine which, if any, entity in the file can proceed. If it is determined that an entity should proceed from the AWAIT node, the user will seize the appropriate resources (discussed below). The return value is the placeholder of the entity to be removed from the AWAIT node file for processing in the network. If, as normally happens, the first entity in the file should proceed, the return value would be the argument peFirst. If no allocation is possible, NULL should be returned.

When the resources to be allocated at an AWAIT node are determined by the user in function ALLOC, the required number of units of the required resources are seized through a call to **BOOL SEIZE(UINT uiRes, UINT uiUnits)** where **uiRes** is the numeric code for the resource type and uiUnits is the number of units to be seized. Function SEIZE then sets uiUnits of resource type uiRes busy and updates the statistics for that resource. For example, the statement **SEIZE(3,2);** sets busy 2 units of resource type 3. Before invoking function SEIZE, the user must test to determine if 2 units of resource type 3 are available. Through the use of functions ALLOC and SEIZE, complex resource allocation rules can be included in simulation models. A resource allocated in function ALLOC may not be preempted.

9.10.1   Illustration 9-1. Joint and Alternative Resource Requirements

Consider a situation in which there are two operators who are modeled as resources. The resource names are OP1 and OP2. The resource blocks for defining these operators and the files at which they are allocated are shown below.

> RESOURCE,1,OP1,1,{1,2};
> RESOURCE,2,OP2,1,{1,2);

From the resource block definition we see there is one unit of each resource and that resources OP1and OP2 are allocated at files 1 and 2. The numeric code for resource OP1 is 1 and the numeric code for resource OP2 is 2.

In the network model, suppose we require that activity 1 be performed by both OP1 and OP2. Although this does not require a function ALLOC, the use of ALLOC is illustrated by coding a standard Visual SLAM allocation rule. The network statements for the AWAIT node and ACTIVITY are listed below.

> AWAIT,1,,ALLOC(1);
> ACT,1,10;

These network statements show that an entity arriving to the AWAIT node will pass through file 1 to ACTIVITY 1 if allocation rule 1 indicates that resources are available to work on the arriving entity. The code for allocation case 1 is shown below. Note that a new arrival to the AWAIT node is placed in the file while resource allocation is being processed.

```
switch(iRule)
 {
   case 1: if(NNRSC(1)>0 && NNRSC(2)>0)
            {
             SEIZE(1,1);
             SEIZE(2,1);
             return(First);
            }
            else
             return (NULL);
```

In the above code, a switch on the allocation rule code is made as we will have two allocation codes associated with this illustration. At case 1 both resource 1 (OP1) and resource 2 (OP2) are required or no allocation can be made. NNRSC(I) is the current number of resources available for resource I. If the condition in case 1 is satisfied, then both resources are available. Function SEIZE is then called twice to allocate resource 1 and resource 2. Since the first entity in the AWAIT node file is the one which should be released when the resources are available, function ALLOC returns the ENTRY pointer to the first entity which was provided as the input argument First. If either of the resources are unavailable, function ALLOC returns a NULL pointer and no allocation is made.

Consider now a second allocation function represented by the following statements.

AWAIT,2,,ALLOC(2),3,BALK(OUT);
ACT,5,22;

The above code indicates that arriving entities to the AWAIT node will wait in file 2 which has a queue capacity of 3. If an entity arrives with three units already in file 2 it will balk to a node labeled OUT. When an entity arrives to file 2 and it is empty, the entity is placed in the file and function ALLOC is invoked with a request to use allocation case 2. Allocation case 2 will be coded to have either resource 1 or resource 2 assigned to an entity.

Function ALLOC, which includes both allocation case 1 and allocation case 2, is shown below. For case 2, function ALLOC is entered with iRule=2. At case 2, an ENTITY pointer is set equal to the pointer to the first entity in the AWAIT node file, since we will need to set one of this entity's attributes.

Now a test is made to see if resource 1 is available. If it is, function SEIZE is called to seize one unit of resource 1. LTRIB[1] is set to 1 to indicate that the current entity is to be processed by resource 1, and the ENTRY pointer to the first entity in the AWAIT node file is returned. If resource 1 is not available but resource 2 is, then resource 2 is allocated and LTRIB[1] is set to 2. Note that a preferred choice for resource 1 over resource 2 when both are available is coded directly into allocation case 2. It should be clear how the coding could be changed to make resource 2 the preferred resource.

```
#include "vslam.h"
ENTRY *ALLOC(int iRule, ENTRY * First)
/****************************************************
 * Illustration of seizing two resources jointly
 * or alternatively.
 ***************************************************/
{
 ENTITY *peCurrent;

 switch(iRule)  {
 case 1: if(NNRSC(1)>0 && NNRSC(2)>0)     {
            SEIZE(1,1);    /*Rule 1: Seize both resources       */
            SEIZE(2,1);        return(First);
                       /* and return pointer to first entity    */
          }              /* in AWAIT node file                  */
          else           /* If both resources are not available, */
          return (NULL); /* return NULL pointer                 */

 case 2: peCurrent = su_sfnentity(First); /*Rule 2: Seize oneofthem */
           if(NNRSC(1)>0)                {
              SEIZE(1,1);
              peCurrent -> LTRIB[1]=1;
              return(First);
           }
           else if (NNRSC(2)>0)          {
                SEIZE(2,1);
                peCurrent -> LTRIB[1]=2;
                return (First);
           }
                else
                return (NULL);
     }
  }
```

9.10.2 Illustration 9-2. Assembling Resources in the Truck Hauling Situation

This illustration demonstrates how function ALLOC can be used to provide an assembly capability for resources. The truck hauling situation modeled in Example 6-2 is used to demonstrate this capability. In that example, a SELECT node with the assembly queue selection rule is used to assemble a truck, a load and a loader. The use of a loader as both a service activity and as an entity to be assembled was required to model the situation in Chapter 6.

In the network shown below, an AWAIT node is used to queue loads that wait for both a truck and a loader. Trucks and loaders are modeled as resources with the labels TRUCKS, LOADER1 and LOADER2 which have resource numbers 1, 2 and 3, respectively. In function ALLOC, a check is made to determine if both a truck and a loader are available. If available, they are allocated and a load continues through the network. Function ALLOC is shown below. It is a combination of the "ALL" and "ONE" allocation rules, since it allocates a truck resource and one of the loader resources.

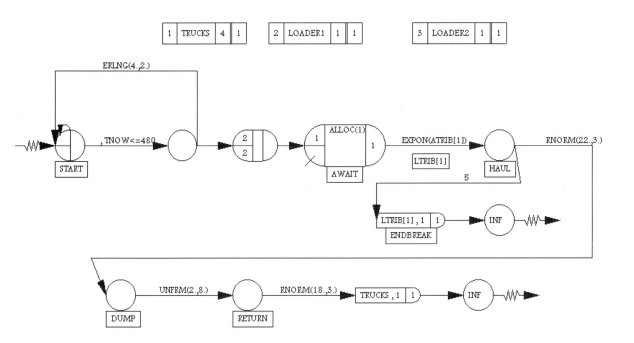

```c
#include "vslam.h"
ENTRY * SWFUNC ALLOC(int iRule,ENTRY*First)
{
 ENTRY* pReturn;
 ENTITY* peCurrent;

 int LOADER, CASE;
 double TIME;
 pReturn = NULL;                        /*Initialize entry to return  */
 LOADER=0;                              /* and which loader to seize   */
 if(NNRSC(1) > 0)                       /*If there is a truck,         */
 {
CASE = NNRSC(2)+NNRSC(3);               /*CASE is a function of        */
   switch (CASE)                        /* available loader resources  */
{
   case 0:  break;                      /*case 0:  No loader available */
   case 1:                              /*case 1:  One loader available*/
      if (NNRSC(2) > 0)    {
         LOADER = 2;                     /*  Resource type is 2         */
         TIME = 14.;                     /* Mean service time is 14     */
      }
      else                 {
         LOADER = 3;                     /* Resource type is 3          */
         TIME = 12.;                     /* Mean service time is 12     */
      }
      break;
   case 2:                              /*case 2:  Both are available. */
      if (RRTLC(2)<=RRTLC(3))           /*  If resource 2 became       */
      {                                 /*  available first,           */
         LOADER = 2;                     /*  resource type is 2 and     */
         TIME = 14.;                     /*  mean service time is 14.   */
      }
      else                             /*  Otherwise,                 */
      {
         LOADER = 3;                     /*  resource type is 3 and     */
         TIME = 12.;                     /*  mean service time is 12.   */
      }
      break;

   default:
      su_error(1,"No matching case in ALLOC.");
   }                                    /*End of switch               */

   if (LOADER > 0)                      /*If a loader has been found,  */
   {
     SEIZE(1,1);                        /* seize a truck and a loader. */
     SEIZE(LOADER,1);
     peCurrent = su_sfnentity(First);/*Get pointer to load and       */
     peCurrent->ATRIB[1] = TIME;     /*assign mean service time for */
     peCurrent->LTRIB[1] = LOADER;   /*the loading activity and     */
     pReturn = First;                /*resource type to be freed    */
   }
 }                 /*End of leading if, when a truck is available*/
 return pReturn;
}
```

The return value in ALLOC is first set to null and the loader resource to be seized is set to zero. If no trucks are available (NNRSC(1) is zero), no further action is taken. If a truck is available, the loader resources are evaluated. Four cases are provided for: (1) no loader is available, (2) only LOADER1 is available, (3) only LOADER2 is available and (4) both are available. If a loader is available, the resource type, LOADER, and the mean service time, TIME, are assigned. If both loader resources are available, we wish to assign the one which has been available the longest. The function RRTLC (described in Section 11.9) returns the time at which the resource status was changed to "available", so if both loaders are idle, the resource with the earliest value of RRTLC is chosen. When a LOADER resource can be assigned, it is seized in addition to one unit of the TRUCKS resource. The pointer of the first load entity at the AWAIT node is obtained using the function su_sfnentity and is used to set ATRIB[1] of the load entity to mean service time and LTRIB[1] to the loader resource type so that the correct resource will later be released.

In the network model, the activity number for the loading activity is defined to be LTRIB[1] so that separate statistics will be reported depending on the loader assigned at the AWAIT node. Following the loading activity, an entity representing the loader is routed to a FREE node after a five minute break. A second entity representing a loaded truck is sent over hauling, dumping and truck return activities after which a TRUCKS resource is freed. Utilization statistics for the two loader resources will include both time spent loading a truck and break time. The percentage of time actually spent loading will be reported by the utilization statistics for activities 2 and 3.

9.11   CHANGING THE STATUS OF A GATE

Visual SLAM provides the capability to open and close gates using C functions. A gate must be referenced by its gate number. If the gate number is defaulted, it is automatically assigned by Visual SLAM to each gate in the order that the GATE blocks are inputted to the Visual SLAM processor. For example, consider the following set of GATE blocks included in the network portion of a model:

GATE,,DOOR1,OPEN,4;
GATE,,DOOR2,CLOSED,5;

The processor would assign DOOR1 as gate number 1 and DOOR2 as gate number 2.

9.11.1   Opening a Gate: Function OPEN

BOOL OPEN(UINT uiGate) opens gate number uiGate and releases all waiting entities in the AWAIT files specified in the GATE block. For the GATE blocks depicted above, the following statement would open DOOR2:

OPEN(2);

This statement is equivalent to the following network statement.

OPEN,DOOR2;

Function OPEN returns TRUE if no error was encountered, FALSE otherwise.

9.11.2   Closing a Gate: Function CLOSX

BOOL CLOSX(UINT uiGate) closes gate number uiGate. For the GATE blocks depicted above, the following statement would close DOOR1.

CLOSX(1);

This statement is equivalent to the following network statement.

CLOSE,DOOR1;

Function CLOSX returns TRUE if no error was encountered, FALSE otherwise.

9.12   USER-WRITTEN SELECT NODE FUNCTIONS

In a network model, SELECT nodes are used to route an entity to one of a set of parallel QUEUE nodes or to select an entity from a set of parallel queues for processing by a server. The Visual SLAM standard queue selection rules and server selection rules are presented in Tables 7-2 and 7-3. The USER queue selection or server selection rule allows user-written logic to determine a selection criterion. Further, the USERASSEMBLE queue selection rule provides that the attributes of the assembled entity are assigned in a user-written C function.

9.12.1   User-Written QUEUE Selection, NQS

When the queue selection rule at a SELECT node is specified as NQS(expr), the function **UINT NQS(int iCode, ENTITY *peCur, SN_NODE *pNode)** is called with iCode equal to the evaluated expression, peCur equal to the pointer to the entity being processed at the SELECT node, and pNode equal to the pointer to the SELECT node description.

The Visual SLAM user writes the function NQS to execute the desired queue selection logic and returns the file number of the selected QUEUE. When queue selection is done by the user, it is the user's responsibility to insure that a feasible choice is made, that is, an entity must be able to be routed to the QUEUE node or taken from the QUEUE node. Whenever there are no feasible choices, the user should return zero to indicate that no QUEUE node was selected.

The network segment and its corresponding statement model shown below illustrate how to code function NQS. At SELECT node SSS, arriving entities are to be routed to QUEUE nodes Q1, Q2, and Q3 based on the value of LL[1]. In a section of the model not shown, the modeler has specified the value of LL[1] to be 1, 2 or 3. Queue selection function 1 will be used to make this selection and NQS(1) is specified as the queue selection rule for SELECT node SSS. In function NQS, shown following the network segment, a transfer to case 1 is made when the queue selection code number is 1. At case 1, the value to return, iReturn, is set equal to LL[1] to indicate that the QUEUE node with the file number LL[1] is to be selected for the arriving entity. In this situation, no check is made on the feasibility of routing the arriving entity to the prescribed QUEUE node as all three QUEUE nodes have unlimited capacity.

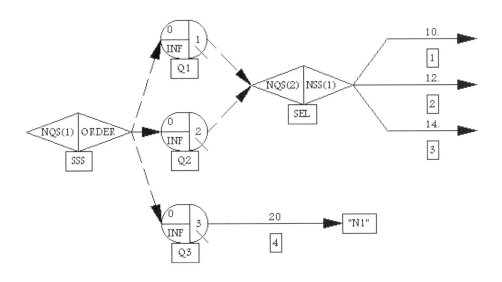

```
SSS:   SELECT,NQS(1),,,{Q1,Q2,Q3};
Q1:    QUEUE,1,0,,,{SEL};
Q2:    QUEUE,2,0,,,{SEL};
Q3:    QUEUE,3,0;
       ACT,4,20, ,N1;     N1 NOT SHOWN
SEL:   SELECT,NQS(2),NSS(1),,{Q1 ,Q2};
       ACT, 1 , 10;
       ACT,2, 12;
       ACT,3, 14; ,
```

At SELECT node SEL, queue selection function 2 is prescribed for selecting entities from Q1 or Q2 when either activity 1, 2 or 3 is completed. The coding for queue selection function 2 is shown in function NQS starting at case 2. First it is determined whether an entity is waiting for the service activities following SELECT node SEL. Thus, if the number in Q1 and the number in Q2 are 0, a value of 0 is assigned to NQS to indicate to Visual SLAM that the server should be set to idle status. Next, if no entity exists in either queue, the other queue is selected. When entities are available in both queues, the queue selection rule is to select an entity from the longer queue.

```
#include "vslam.h"
UINT NQS(int iCode,ENTITY *peCur, SN_NODE *pNode)
/*******************************************************
 * User-coded QUEUE selection rules 1 and 2
 ******************************************************/
{
  UINT iReturn;

  switch(iCode)                    {
    case 1:  iReturn= LL[1];
             break;

    case 2:  iReturn= 0;
             if (NNQ(1)==0 && NNQ(2)==0) break;
             if (NNQ(1)==0)
             { iReturn = 2; /* Select Queue 2 if 1 is empty*/
               break;
             }
             else if (NNQ(2)==0)
             {  iReturn = 1;        /* Select Queue 1 if 2 is empty */
               break;
             }
             else            /* If both are occupied, select the*/
             {if(NNQ(1)>=NNQ(2))  /* longer one */
               iReturn = 1;
              else
               iReturn = 2;
             }
  }
  return (iReturn);
 }
```

As seen from this discussion, the coding of function NQS permits complex queue selection rules to be included in a Visual SLAM network. The information about a node which can be returned using the pNode pointer is given in Table 9-2.

Table 9-2 Functions returning node information.

Function	Descriptions
UINT su_nodenumfile (SN_NODE*pnNode)	Returns the number of files associated with a node.
SIM_FILE*su_nodefile (SN_NODE*pnNode,UINT uiOff)	Returns the pointer to the file associated with the node located at pnNode and offset by uiOff.
char*su_nodelabel (SN_NODE*pnNode)	Returns the node label given the pointer to the node.
SN_NODE*su_nodenext (SN_NODE*pnNode)	Given a node pointer, returns the pointer to the next node. If an activity follows the node, NULL is returned.
UINT su_nodenumact (SN_NODE*pnNode)	Given a node pointer, returns the number of activities emanating from the node.
SN_ACT*su_nodeact (SN_NODE*pnNode,UINT uiOff)	Given a node pointer, returns the pointer to the activity emanating from the node which is offset by uiOff.
int su_nodetype (SN_NODE*pnNode)	Returns a node type given the pointer to the node. Refer to the header file vslam.h for the node type associated with a given integer.
UINT su_selnumq (SN_NODE*pnNode)	Given a pointer to a SELECT node, returns the number of associated QUEUE nodes.
SN_NODE*su_selqueue (SN_NODE*pnNode,UINT uiOff)	Given a pointer to a SELECT node, returns the pointer to the associated QUEUE node offset in the list by uiOff.

9.12.2 User-Written Server Selection, NSS

When the server selection rule at a SELECT node is specified as NSS(expr), the function **UINT NSS(int iCode, ENTITY *peCur, SN_NODE *pNode)** is called with iCode equal to the evaluated expression, peCur equal to the pointer to the entity being processed at the SELECT node, and pNode equal to the pointer to the SELECT node description. Information about a node given its SN_NODE pointer is listed in Table 9-2.

Function NSS is called when an entity arrives to an empty QUEUE node associated with the SELECT node whose server selection rule is NSS(I) where the index I is the iCode value for the SELECT node. In function NSS, an activity number is to be returned to indicate the service activity selected. If all servers following the SELECT node are busy, NSS should return zero, in which case the newly arriving entity will be placed in the QUEUE node to which it arrived. The service activity numbers following the SELECT node are known to the user as they are associated with the activity statements following the SELECT node in the network input statements. When a value is returned from NSS, Visual SLAM takes the appropriate action of either putting the arriving entity into a QUEUE node or making the selected service activity busy by scheduling the start of the activity.

The example used in the section on function NQS will be continued in this section. The appropriate portions of the statement model to illustrate function NSS are:

```
SEL:    SELECT,NQS(2),NSS(1),,{Q1 ,Q2};
        ACT,1 ,10;
        ACT,2, 12;
        ACT,3, 14;
```

When an entity arrives to either QUEUE node Q1 or Q2 and there are no entities waiting at the time of arrival, function NSS with an argument of 1 is called in order to determine if server 1, 2 or 3 can process the arriving entity. If all three servers are busy, then the arriving entity is put into the appropriate file. If only one server is free, that server is selected for processing the entity. If more than one server is free, a selection rule is coded in function NSS. The coding for function NSS is shown below.

In NSS, only one server selection function is indicated and only the code is given for server selection function 1. First, the selected server number iReturn is set to 0 to indicate that a server could not be selected. In the middle part of the function, each service activity status is tested and if a server is available, the service activity number is stored in the vector NSER(J) where J is an index for available servers. If no servers are available, J is zero and a return is made with iReturn.

```
#include "vslam.h"
UINT NSS(int iCode, ENTITY *peCur, SN_NODE *pNode)
/*****************************************************
 * User-written random server selection rule: 3 servers
 *****************************************************/
{
 int NSER[3];
 int i,J,NR,iReturn;
 float XJ;

 iReturn = 0;                 /* Initialize return value */
 J = 0;
 for (i=1; i<=3; i++)
    { if (NNACT(i)==0)        /* For each available server,*/
      {
        NSER[J]=i;            /* save the activity number  */
        J++;                  /* and count how many are saved */
      }
    }
 if (J>0)                     /* If there are available servers, */
   {
     XJ = (float)J;
     NR = (int)UNFRM(1.,XJ,1)-1; /* take a random draw and  */
     iReturn = NSER[NR];      /* return NSER[0],NSER[1] or NSER[2]*/
   }
 return(iReturn);
}
```

If one or more servers are available, then an integer is selected from 1 to the number of available servers. Note that XJ is set equal to J + 1 and a number drawn between 1 and XJ. By using the integer variable NR, these values will be truncated down to the next lowest integer so that an integer from 1 to J will be obtained as the value of NR. In this way, each integer has an equal likelihood of being selected. The selected server activity number, iReturn, is then obtained from the NRth location of the vector NSER.

The code shown for function NSS is equivalent to selecting randomly from among the available service activities. It is equivalent to the standard priority rule RAN with an equal probability assigned to each of the servers following the SELECT node.

9.12.3   User-Written Attribute Save Criteria, ASSEMBLE

When the queue selection rule at a SELECT node is specified as USERASSEMBLE(expr), the function **ENTITY*(int iCode,SN_NODE *pNode)** is called with iCode equal to the evaluated expression and pNode equal to the pointer to the SELECT node description. The function is written to create the assembled entity and return its pointer. The first entity in each of the QUEUE nodes preceding the SELECT node will be removed and destroyed. The following example saves attributes from entities being assembled from QUEUE node file 1 and QUEUE node file 2. The first and third attributes of the assembled entity will be taken from the first entity in file 1, while the second and fourth attributes will be taken from the first entity in file 2. The function MMFE, described in Chapter 11C, is used to obtain the placeholder of the first entity in a file.

```
#include "vslam.h"
ENTITY*ASSEMBLE(int iCode,SN_NODE*pNode)
/****************************************************************
 * Function to set attributes from entities assembled at a SELECT node
 * whose Queue Selection Rule is USERASSEMBLE(1).  Input parameter
 * iCode is not used, since there is only one user-written assembly

 * function, and input parameter pNode is not used, since we know that
 * the entities to be assembled are in QUEUE node files 1 and 2.
 ****************************************************************/
{
    ENTITY*peNew,*peOne,*peTwo;
/*
    Define pointers to the first entity in each file and to the new
    entity to be assembled.
*/
    peNew = su_entnew(0,NULL,NULL,NULL);
    peOne = su_sfnentity(MMFE(1));
    peTwo = su_sfnentity(MMFE(2));
/*
    Assign first and third attributes from the first entity in File 1,
   second and  fourth attributes from the first entity in File 2.
*/
    peNew->ATRIB[1] = peOne->ATRIB[1];
    peNew->ATRIB[2] = peTwo->ATRIB[2];
    peNew->ATRIB[3] = peOne->ATRIB[3];
    peNew->ATRIB[4] = peTwo->ATRIB[4];
    return(peNew);
}
```

9.13 Saving Batched Attributes, BATCHSAVE

The function **void BATCHSAVE(int iCode, ENTITY *peForm, ENTITY *peAdd);** is called when an entity is being added to a batch and the attribute save criterion at the BATCH node is USER(expr). The arguments to BATCHSAVE are the evaluted expression (iCode), the pointer to the forming batched entity (peForm) and the pointer to the entity being added to the batch (peAdd). The function is written to update the attributes which will belong to the batched entity when the batch is released. A simple example follows.

```
#include "vslam.h"
void BATCHSAVE(int iCode,ENTITY*peForm,ENTITY*peAdd)
/********************************************************
 * Function to make the third attribute of a batched
 * entity equal to the sum of twice the second attribute
 * of each member of the batch.
 *
 * Input parameter iCode is not used, since there is only
 * one BATCH node with USER as the attribute save rule.
 ********************************************************/
{
   peForm->ATRIB[3] = peForm->ATRIB[3]
                           + 2.0*peAdd->ATRIB[2];
   return;
}
```

9.14 STOPPING AN ACTIVITY: FUNCTION STOPA

In complex systems, the length of a specific activity may not be known *a priori* but may depend upon the dynamics of the system. For example, in a queueing system the service rate may be a function of the number of entities waiting for the server and thus may change over time. Therefore the duration of the activity is unknown at the start time of the activity and is affected by future arrivals. One way of modeling an indefinite activity duration using network concepts is to specify the activity duration as keyed to STOPA(NTC). This allows the modeler to stop selectively a specific entity undergoing an activity without stopping the other entities undergoing the same activity.

To stop an activity for a network entity from user-written code, the modeler must specify the duration of the activity in the network model as STOPA(NTC) where

NTC is a positive integer which is user-assigned as an entity code to distinguish the entity from other entities in the same activity or elsewhere in the network. If NTC is specified as a real value it is truncated to the nearest integer. The value of NTC can be specified as a number, a Visual SLAM variable, a Visual SLAM random variable or by an expression. By specifying the entity code as an attribute of the entity or as a random variable, the modeler can assign different entity codes to entities within the same activity. The activity statement

    ACT,,STOPA(1);

specifies that all entities in the activity are to be assigned entity code l. The statement

    ACT,,STOPA(ATRIB[3]);

specifies that the third attribute of each entity is to be assigned as the entity code.

The mechanism for stopping the activity for a network entity from C code is to call function STOPA whose prototype is **BOOL STOPA(int NTC);** A call to function STOPA(NTC) causes an end of activity to occur for every entity with entity code NTC that is being processed by an activity whose duration is specified as STOPA. For example, execution of the statement STOPA(1); causes all activities to be completed whose duration was specified as STOPA(1).

Since the execution of the STOPA(NTC); statement causes the end of an activity to occur for each entity with entity code NTC, there may be none, one, or several activities ended by a call to STOPA(NTC). For each activity that is ended, the end-of-activity event for the entity in the activity is placed at the top of the event calendar to be processed immediately following the return from the discrete event. If more than one activity is stopped in this manner, then the end-of-activity event for each entity is processed following the return to Visual SLAM in the order in which the activities were started. If no entities are currently keyed to STOPA(NTC), then execution of a call to STOPA(NTC) has no effect.

9.15   EXAMPLE 9-2. PSYCHIATRIC WARD

Clients of a psychiatric ward arrive at the rate of two per day. Each client is given a test and the test scores are uniformly distributed between 30 and 44. When the ward is full, clients are not admitted if their score is greater than 41. The ward has space for 25 patients. A patient's test score is estimated to change daily in a uniform manner in the range from -0.2 to 1.2. When a patient's test score reaches 48, the patient is discharged from the ward. If a potential patient arrives to the ward and the ward is full, a current patient will be bumped from the ward if a test score higher than 47 has been achieved. Initially there are 18 patients in the ward and their test scores range from 30 to 44. The objective is to simulate the operation of the ward for 1000 days to determine the average time in the system for each patient, the ward utilization, the number of clients balking and number of patients bumped.

Concepts Illustrated. This example illustrates the use of the EVENT node, function EVENT, ENTER node, function ENTER, the STOPA duration specification and function STOPA. This example also illustrates the use of the functions USERF and INTLC.

Visual SLAM Model. In this problem, the discharge from the system for each patient in the ward cannot be scheduled in advance. The test scores for each patient and the ranking of patients based on test scores change daily. This process can be modeled using Visual SLAM by representing patients in the ward as entities in an ACTIVITY with a duration specified as STOPA(II) where II denotes the space or bed number in the ward. The test scores for patients in each of the twenty-five spaces is maintained in the Visual SLAM variable XX[II]. If space number II is not occupied, then XX[II] is set equal to 0.

The network portion of the model is depicted in Figure 9-5. Entities which represent clients seeking admittance to the ward are created at the CREATE node with the current time marked as ATRIB[1] and the time between entities exponentially distributed with mean of 0.5 day. The entities proceed to the ASSIGN node where the initial test score is assigned as ATRIB[2] of the entity.

The M-number for the ASSIGN node is specified as 1, thus a maximum of one of the three emanating ACTIVITY's will be taken. If the ward is full (the number of active entities in the ACTIVITY with index number 1 is 25) and the test score for this client (ATRIB[2]) is greater than 41, then the entity is routed to the COLCT node labeled BALK. If this ACTIVITY is not taken and the ward is full, then the entity is routed to the EVENT node labeled BUMP. If neither of these ACTIVITY's is taken, then the entity is routed to the ASSIGN node labeled WARD.

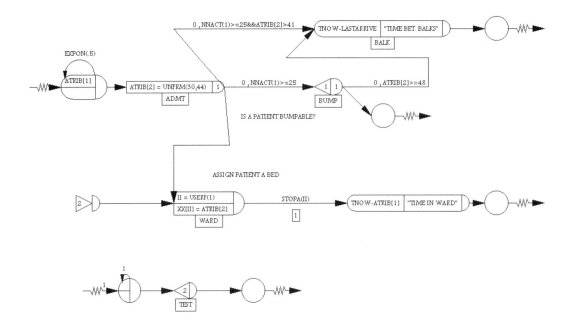

Figure 9-5 Network model of psychiatric ward example.

Consider the entities which arrive to the COLCT node BALK. At each entity arrival to the node, statistics are collected on the time between entity arrivals with the results displayed using the identifier TIME BET. BALKS. The entities are then terminated from the system. No terminate count is used so that the entity is destroyed, but no end of run will occur because of it.

Next, consider the entities which are routed to the EVENT node BUMP, which represents a client attempting to bump one of the patients currently on the ward. Determining if a patient can be bumped is a complex decision. Based on the current test scores of the patients in the ward, a new client is not admitted or a patient is bumped (discharged). In the former case, the client entity is assigned an ATRIB[2] value equal to 48. A return to the EVENT node then causes the entity to be routed to the node BALK based on the condition that ATRIB[2] > = 48 on the activity emanating from node BUMP. In the latter case, the client entity enters into the network through ENTER node 2 to arrive at the ASSIGN node WARD. Before describing the code for event 1, we will complete our description of the network portion of the model.

The entities, which are routed to the ASSIGN node WARD, represent clients who are to be assigned an available space in the ward. At the ASSIGN node, the index variable II is set equal to the value computed in the user-coded function USERF(I) with I = 1. The coding for function USERF is shown in Figure 9-6 and it returns the value of USERF as the smallest index J for which XX[J] is equal to zero. An XX[J]=0 indicates that space J is available. Since entities should only arrive to the ASSIGN node WARD when at least one space is available, a call is made to function su_error to cause an error exit from Visual SLAM if all spaces are full. Following the assignment of the first available space number to II, we set XX[II] to the initial test score for this patient.

The ACTIVITY following the ASSIGN node WARD represents the duration for which the patient remains in the ward. The duration for the ACTIVITY is specified to be STOPA(II) denoting that the duration is to be terminated by a call to function STOPA(NTC) with NTC equal to space number II of the patient who is to leave the ward. In this manner, each patient can be selectively discharged from the ward by specifying NTC as the space number for the patient. Following discharge from the ward, interval statistics on the time in system are collected at the COLCT node using the mark time in ATRIB[1] as a reference time. The identifier is TIME IN WARD. The entity is then terminated. A disjoint network is used to create an entity every day which arrives at EVENT node TEST that initiates the testing event for the model. The input statements for this example are shown in Figure 9-7.

```
double SWFUNC USERF(int iCode, ENTITY * peCur)
{  double dReturn = 0.0;
   int i;
   switch (iCode)                              {
      case 1: /* return bed for new patient */
         for (i=1; i <= NUMBEDS; I++)          {
            if (XX[i] <= 0.0)                   {
               /* idle bed */
               dReturn = (double) i;
               break;
            }
         }
         if (i > NUMBEDS)                       {
            su_error(3,"No empty bed found");
            MSTOP = -1;
         }
      break;
      default:
         su_error(2,"Unknown userf code");
      break;
   }
   return(dReturn);
}
```

Figure 9-6 Function USERF for psychiatric ward example.

```
        GEN,"PRITSKER","PSYCHIATRIC WARD",1/1/1996,1;
        LIMITS,25,-1,-1,2,-1,-1;
        NETWORK;
              CREATE,EXPON(.5), ,ATRIB[1];              PATIENT ARRIVALS
        ADMT: ASSIGN,{ { ATRIB[2], UNFRM(30,44) } },1;  ASSIGN SCORE
              ACTIVITY, ,0,NNACT(1)>=25&&ATRIB[2]>41;   NO BED
              ACTIVITY, ,0,NNACT(1)>=25,"BUMP";         TRY TO BUMP
              ACTIVITY, , , ,"WARD";                    BED AVAILABLE
        BALK: COLCT,,TNOW-LASTARRIVE,
                    "TIME BET. BALKS";              COLLECT BALK STATS
              TERM;
;
        BUMP: EVENT,1;                          IS A PATIENT BUMPABLE?
              ACTIVITY, ,0,ATRIB [2]>=48, "BALK";
        PATIENT BALKS
              ACT;
              TERM;
;
              ENTER,2;                          ASSIGN A PATIENT A BED
        WARD: ASSIGN,{ { II, USERF(1) }, { XX[II], ATRIB[2] } };
              ACT,1,STOPA(II),,,,"IN WARD"; WAIT FOR CALL TO STOPA
              COLCT, ,TNOW-ATRIB[1],"TIME IN WARD";
              TERM;
;
              CREATE,1,1;
        TEST: EVENT,2;              DAILY RETEST OF OCCUPIED BEDS
              TERM;
              END;
        INITIALIZE,0,500;
        FIN;
```

Figure 9-7 Statement model for psychiatric ward example.

There are two events that are coded outside of the network model. The first event is initiated by an entity arrival to the EVENT node BUMP and is coded in function BUMP. The second event processes the daily changes in the patients' test scores and discharges patients as necessary. The logic for this event is coded in function TEST. Function EVENT which maps the event code onto the appropriate event function is shown in Figure 9-8.

```
void SWFUNC EVENT(int iCode, ENTITY * peCurrent)
{
   switch (iCode)                    {
      case 1: /* arrive to event node 1 - bump */
         BUMP(peCurrent);
      break;
      case 2: /* arrive to event node 2 - test */
         TEST(peCurrent);
      break;
      default:
         su_error(1,"Unknown event code");
      break;
   }
}
```

Figure 9-8 Function EVENT for psychiatric ward example.

Function BUMP contains the processing logic for the EVENT node BUMP and is depicted in Figure 9-9. Function BUMP is only called when a new client arrives. It uses user-defined global variables BUMP_THRESHOLD (initialized to 47), NUMBEDS (initialized to 25), and WELL_THRESHOLD (initialized to 48). Initially, the variable dBest is set to BUMP_THRESHOLD, and the variable iBest is set to 0. The for loop then searches the current test scores of patients and sets iBest equal to the index of the patient with the largest test score greater than 47. If no patient has a score greater than BUMP_THRESHOLD, ATRIB[2] is set to WELL_THRESHOLD to represent the departure of the new client. A return from function BUMP is then made. If a patient can be bumped, an entity is entered into the network at ENTER node 2 and the bumped patient is discharged from the ward by setting the test score for space iBest to 0, that is, XX[iBest]=0.0, and calling function STOPA(iBest). Note that in the latter case, the order in which the function calls are executed is important. The call to function ENTER(2,peNew) is executed first and causes an entity arrival to the ENTER node to be scheduled at the top of the calendar. This is followed by the call to function STOPA(iBest) which causes the end-of-activity event for the patient with entity code iBest to be scheduled at the top of the event calendar. Therefore upon the return to Visual SLAM, the end-of-activity event will be processed prior to the entity arrival to ENTER node 2.

```c
static void BUMP(ENTITY * peCurrent)
{
    int i;
    int iBest;
    double dBest;
    ENTITY * peNew;
/* check to see if any patients have scores above the threshold */
    iBest = 0;
    dBest = BUMP_THRESHOLD;
    for (i=1; i <= NUMBEDS; I++)    {
        if (XX[i] > dBest)          {
            iBest = i;
            dBest = XX[i];
        }
    }
    if (iBest)                      {
        /* found one to bump */
        peNew = su_entclone(peCurrent,0);
        if (peNew)                  {
            /* empty bed and stop processing */
            XX[iBest] = 0.0;
            ENTER(2,peNew); /* put new patient into network */
            STOPA(iBest);
        }
    }
    else                            {
        /* mark this entity so it will balk */
        peCurrent->ATRIB[2] = WELL_THRESHOLD;
    }
}
```

Figure 9-9 Function BUMP for psychiatric ward example.

The coding for function TEST which processes the daily changes in each patient's test score is depicted in Figure 9-10. The processing is performed in the "for loop" which changes each patient's score by adding a uniform sample between -0.2 and 1.2 using stream 1 to their current score. Those patients with test scores exceeding 48.0 are discharged from the ward by calling STOPA(i) and setting XX[i]=0.0 where i is the space number occupied by a discharged patient.

The initial conditions for the simulation are established in function INTLC which is shown in Figure 9-11. This function inserts the initial 18 patients into the network through ENTER node 2.

```
static void TEST(ENTITY * peCurrent)
/* daily update patient scores and see if patient is well enough
   to leave.  if well enough, stop processing */
{
    int i;
    for (i=1; i <= NUMBEDS; I++)               {
        if (XX[i] > 0.0)                       {
            /* is a patient in this bed */
            XX[i] += UNFRM(-0.2, 1.2, 1);
            if (XX[i] >= WELL_THRESHOLD)       {
                STOPA(i);
                XX[i] = 0.0;
            }
        }
    }
}
```

Figure 9-10 Function TEST for psychiatric ward example.

```
#include "vslam.h"
#define NUMBEDS 25
#define BUMP_THRESHOLD 47.0
#define WELL_THRESHOLD 48.0
#define INIT_PATIENTS 18
BOOL SWFUNC INTLC(UINT uiRun)
{
    BOOL bReturn = TRUE;
    ENTITY * peNew;
    int i;
    /* create initial patients */
    for (i=0; i < INIT_PATIENTS; I++)          {
        peNew = su_entnew(0,NULL,NULL,NULL);
        peNew->ATRIB[1] = TNOW;
        peNew->ATRIB[2] = UNFRM(30.0,44.0,1);
        ENTER(2,peNew);
    }
    return(bReturn);
}
```

Figure 9-11 Function INTLC and constants for psychiatric ward example.

Summary of Results. The Visual SLAM Summary Report shown in Figure 9-12 displays statistics for the time in the ward for each patient, the time between balks from the system and the utilization of the twenty-five spaces in the ward. The results show that on the average 24.8 of the 25 available spaces in the ward are utilized and that over half of the patients seeking admittance to the ward balked from the system as the result of the lack of space on the ward. These results clearly indicate the need for additional space for patients. Additional runs should be made with increased spaces available to determine the number of spaces that should be added. Cost information should also be added to the model to access the worth of proposed new additions. If space cannot be added then research on new patient-improvement procedures and on the criterion for discharge should be initiated.

```
               ** AweSim SUMMARY REPORT **

  Simulation Project : PSYCHIATRIC WARD
  Modeler : PRITSKER
  Date : 1/1/1996
  Scenario : EX92

  Run number 1 of 1
  Current simulation time    : 500.000000
  Statistics cleared at time : 0.000000


          ** OBSERVED STATISTICS REPORT for scenario EX92 **

Label              Mean    Standard   Number of    Minimum   Maximum
                   Value   Deviation  Observations Value     Value

TIME BET. BALKS    0.892   1.286        556        0.000     11.895
TIME IN WARD      22.975   8.004        526        5.112     45.060


          ** ACTIVITY STATISTICS REPORT for scenario EX92 **

Activity  Label or       Average     Standard Entity Maximum     Current
Number    Input Location Utilization Deviation Count Utilization Utilization

   1         IN WARD      24.838       0.593    526      25          25
```

Figure 9-12 Visual SLAM summary report for psychiatric ward example.

9.16   CHAPTER SUMMARY

This chapter has provided many capabilities for inserting user-written logic directly into a network model. These user-written inserts increase the flexibility of the network-oriented world view. The EVENT node provides a general capability to include a node in the network to perform logic functions and attribute assignments limited only by the programming capabilities of the modeler. The ENTER node allows entities to be inserted in the network based on logic written in event routines.

A discussion of filing and removing entities waiting at QUEUE nodes or AWAIT nodes is given. A large complement of functions is described for extending the logical capabilities provided by Visual SLAM's routing, selection and resource allocation methods. In addition, advanced procedures for allocating resources to entities and for stopping activities based on external conditions is described. An example illustrating the jockeying of entities from one queue to another is presented. A second example illustrates the activity scanning features associated with the STOPA specification as well as user-written modeling features associated with EVENT, ENTER and USERF functions.

9.17   EXERCISES

9-1.   In Example 6-2, add the feature that if there are more than three jobs to be processed by the machine tool when it breaks down, all jobs except the last three to arrive are routed to a subcontractor. The job in progress is also routed to the subcontractor.

9-2.   For Example 6-2, redevelop the model to include the possibility that the repairman process breaks down and a delay of three hours is incurred in order to get a spare part for the repair process. The time between repair process breakdowns is exponentially distributed with a mean of 100 hours. If the repair breakdown occurs when the repair process is not active, no action is taken.

9-3.   Model and analyze the admitting process of a hospital as described below. The following three types of patients are processed by the admitting function:

      Type 1.   Those patients who are admitted and have previously completed their pre-admission forms and tests;

      Type 2.   Those patients who seek admission but have not completed pre-admission; and

Type 3.   Those who are only coming in for pre-admission testing and information gathering.

Service times in the admitting office vary according to patient type as given below.

Patient Types and Service Times

Patient Type	Relative Frequency	Mean Time to Admit
1	0.90 before 10:00 A.M.	15 minutes
	0.50 after 10:00 A.M.	
2	0.10 always	40 minutes
3	0 before 10:00 A.M.	30 minutes
	0.40 after 10:00 A.M.	

Note: All of the above times are normally distributed with $\sigma = 0.1\mu$ (min. = 0.0).

On arrival to admitting, a person waits in line if the two admitting officers are busy. When idle, an admitting officer selects a patient who is to be admitted before those who are only to be pre-admitted. In addition, Type 1 patients are given highest priority. After filling out various forms in the admitting office, Type 1 patients are taken to their floor by an orderly while Type 2 and 3 patients walk to the laboratory for blood and urine tests. Three orderlies are available to escort patients to the nursing units. Patients are not allowed to go to their floor by themselves as a matter of policy. If all orderlies are busy, patients wait in the lobby. Once patients have been escorted to a floor, they are considered beyond the admitting process. It takes the orderly 3 time units to return to the admitting room. Those patients who must go to the lab are always ambulatory, and as a result require no escorts. After arriving in the lab, they wait in line at the registration desk. After registration, they go to the lab waiting room until they are called on by one of two lab technicians. After the samples are drawn, they walk back to the admitting office if they are to be admitted or leave if only pre-admission has been scheduled. Upon return to admitting, they are processed as normal Type 1 patients. The admitting office is open from 7:00 A.M. until 5:00 P.M. However, no pre-admissions (Type 3) are scheduled until 10:00 A.M. because of the heavy morning workload in the lab. At 4:00 P.M., incoming admissions are sent to the outpatient desk for processing. However, Type 2 patients returning from the lab are accepted until 5:00 P.M. which is the time both admitting officers go home and the office is closed. Analyze the above system for 10 days. It is of interest to determine the time in the system, that is, the time from arrival until on a floor (Type 1 and 2) or exit from the lab (Type 3). Also, determine the time between arrivals to the laboratory. Assume all patient queues are infinite and FIFO ranked except where noted. Activity times are specified below.

Activity Times (all times in minutes)

Explanation	Distribution: Parameters
time between arrivals to admitting office, t_1	exponential: mean = 15
travel time between admitting and floor, t_2	uniform: min = 3, max = 8
travel time between admitting and lab or lab and admitting, t_3	uniform: min = 2, max = 5
service time at lab registration desk, t_4	Erlang-3: mean = 4.5, k = 3
time spent drawing lab specimen, t_5	Erlang-2: mean = 5, k = 2
time for orderly to return from floor to admitting desk, t_6	constant: 3

9-4. There are three stations on an assembly line and the service time at each station is exponentially distributed with a mean of 10. Items flow down the assembly line from server 1 to server 2 to server 3. A new unit is provided to server 1 every 15 time units. If any server has not completed processing its current unit within 15 minutes, the unit is diverted to one of two off-line servers who complete the remaining operations on the job diverted from the assembly line. One time unit is added to the remaining time of the operation that was not completed. Any following operations not performed are done by the off-line servers in an exponentially distributed time with a mean of 16. Obtain statistics on the utilization of all servers and the fraction of items diverted from each operation.

Embellishments: (a) Assume the assembly line is paced and that the movement of units can only occur at multiples of 15 minutes. (b) Allow one unit to be stored between each assembly line server. (c) If a server is available, route units back to the assembly line from the off-line servers.

9-5. A conveyor system involves five servers stationed along a conveyor belt. Items to be processed by the servers arrive at the first server at a constant rate of four per minute. Service time for each server is 1 minute, and is exponentially distributed. No storage is provided before each server; therefore, the server must be idle to remove the item from the conveyor belt. If the first server is idle, the item is processed by that server. At the end-of-service time, the item is removed from the system. If the first server is busy when the item arrives, it continues down the conveyor belt until it arrives at the second server. The delay time between servers is 1 minute. If an item encounters a situation in which all servers are busy, it is recycled to the first server with a time delay of 5 minutes. Simulate the above conveyor system for 100 time units to determine statistics concerning the time spent in the system by an item, the percentage of time each server is busy and the number of items in the conveyor system.

Embellishments: (a) Repeat the simulation with a time delay of 2 minutes between servers. Is there an effect on the utilization of the servers because of a change in the time delay between servers, that is, the speed of the conveyor? (b) Evaluate the situation in which the last server has sufficient space for storage so that all items passing servers 1, 2, 3, and 4 are processed by server 5. Simulate this situation. (c) Assess the increased performance obtained by allowing a one item buffer before each server. Based on the results of this study, specify how you would allocate ten buffer spaces to the five servers. (d) Discuss how you would evaluate the tradeoffs involved between reducing the number of servers in the conveyor system versus increasing the buffer size associated with each server.

9-6. Let the storage space before each server for the conveyor system described in Exercise 9-5 be two units. When storage exists before each server of a conveyor system, decisions regarding the removal of items must be established. Propose decision rules for determining whether items should be removed from the conveyor belt and placed in storage before a particular server. Simulate the decision rules to obtain the statistics requested in Exercise 9-5.

9-7. Simulate the following resource constrained PERT network to evaluate a set of dispatching rules for determining the order in which to perform activities when the resources available are insufficient to perform all the activities that have been released. The following statistics are to be recorded based on 100 simulations of the network for each dispatching rule.

1. Average time at which each node is realized.
2. Minimum time at which each node is realized.
3. Maximum time at which each node is realized.
4. Standard deviation of the time each node is realized.
5. Histograms of the time to realize nodes.
6. Percentage of the simulation runs in which an activity was on a critical path (a criticality index).
7. Network completion time distribution.
8. Utilization of each resource type.

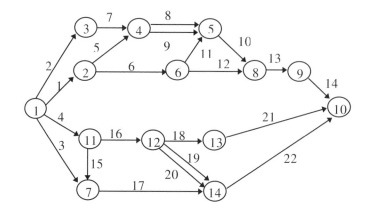

Parameters of Activities of the Network for Exercise 9-7

Activity Number	Distribution	Mean Time	Variance	Requirement for Resource Type			
				1	2	3	4
1	Lognormal	7	2	2	0	1	3
2	Constant	3	0	2	0	1	1
3	Constant	10	0	0	2	0	0
4	Constant	5	0	1	1	1	1
5	Dummy	0	0	0	0	0	0
6	Constant	5	0	2	0	3	2
7	Uniform	3	1/3	1	0	2	3
8	Gamma	8	6	3	0	0	1
9	Constant	3	0	1	0	0	0
10	Constant	5	0	2	0	1	3
11	Dummy	0	0	0	0	0	0
12	Constant	2	0	2	1	2	2
13	Constant	6	0	1	1	0	0
14	Constant	10	0	0	0	0	0
15	Exponential	10	0	1	1	1	0
16	Constant	3	0	1	1	2	0
17	Constant	5	0	0	1	1	1
18	Constant	2	0	0	1	0	3
19	Normal	5	4	1	0	0	2
20	Constant	1	0	1	1	0	0
21	Constant	15	0	0	1	2	0
22	Constant	5	0	0	1	0	0

Resource Availability and Types

Type	Description	Availability
1	Systems analyst	3
2	Marketing personnel	2
3	Maintenance personnel	3
4	Engineering personnel	3

9-8. A multiprocessor computing system is composed of two processors (CPUs) sharing a common memory (CM) of 131 pages, four disk drives, each of which can be accessed by either processor, and a single data channel. A schematic diagram of the system is shown below.

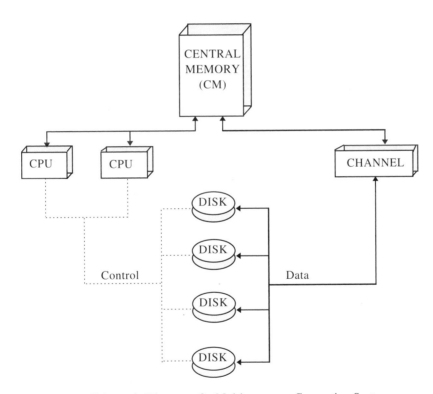

Schematic Diagram of a Multiprocessor Computing System

Jobs arrive to the system at an average rate of 12 jobs per minute in accordance with a Poisson distribution. Total CPU time for a job follows a normal distribution with a mean of 10 seconds and a standard deviation of 3 seconds. The CPU processing time consists of bursts, each of which is followed by an I/O requirement. Each burst follows a negative exponential distribution whose mean is equal to the reciprocal of the average I/O rate of a job. The average I/O rate per job varies uniformly from 2 to 10. I/O operations are assigned to a specific disk upon arrival.

Jobs arriving to the system are assigned a priority which is inversely related to their memory requirements. The CM requirements for a job are distributed uniformly between 20 and 60 pages. Once memory has been allocated to a job it begins execution on any available CPU. Upon issuing an I/O request, the job can continue using the CPU as long as only one I/O request is outstanding. Thus, if an I/O request is made and the job has an I/O request pending, the CPU is relinquished and the I/O request is queued. Following completion of a nonpending I/O request, CPU operations on the job can be reinitiated if a CPU is available.

After a CPU burst, an I/O request is automatically made on the disk assigned to the job, that is, direct access to the disks from the CPUs is made. The seek time to locate the proper position on any disk is assumed to be uniformly distributed between 0. and .075 seconds. Only one seek operation per disk can be performed at a time. Following the seek operation, a data transfer through the data channel is made. The transfer time is equal to .001*(2.5+U) where U is uniformly distributed between 0 and 25. After the transfer, the I/O request is considered satisfied.

Simulate the computing system to determine the residence time of jobs processed by the system, and the utilization statistics for the four disks, the input/output channel, and the two processors (CPUs). Also, the average use of memory is to be obtained. Statistics on the number of jobs waiting for a resource and the waiting time of jobs are also desired. The simulation is to be run for 12,000 seconds.

9-9. A machine tool processes two different types of parts. The time between arrivals of Type 1 parts is triangularly distributed with a mode of 30 minutes, a minimum of 20 minutes, and a maximum of 50 minutes. The interarrival time of Type 2 parts is a sample from a triangular distribution with a mode of 50 minutes, a minimum of 35 minutes, and a maximum of 60 minutes. Processing time for Type 1 parts is exponentially distributed with a mean of 20 minutes. For Type 2 parts processing time is a sample from a uniform distribution with a minimum of 15 minutes and a maximum of 20 minutes. Processing time includes an inspection of the completed part. Fifteen percent of the parts fail inspection and return to the end of the queue of parts awaiting processing. Assume that parts which fail inspection have a rework time equal to 90% of the previous processing time.

Include in the model a cart that transports parts from arrival to the processing area. Once the parts have passed inspection the same cart transports the finished product to the packaging area. No cart is required if a part requires reprocessing. The cart transports four parts at a time to the processing area. All transport times are 5 minutes. A packaged product includes one of each type of part. The packaging time is exponentially distributed for each of the two products with a mean of 20 minutes. There is only one cart and it is freed immediately after transporting the products. In addition, if more than three parts are waiting for the machine at a scheduled maintenance time, remove all but the first 3 parts for subcontracting. Make the probability of failing inspection 10 percent for Type 1 parts and 13% for Type 2 parts. Model and analyze this situation for 2400 minutes collecting utilization statistics and time spent in the system by a part.

Embellishment: Using the following data, replace the constant 5-minute travel time with the actual time that it takes for the cart to travel between stations. Assume that the cart remains at the station where it was last stopped until it is needed elsewhere. The cart travels at the rate of 100 feet per minute. The distances between the arrival and the machining areas is 45 feet and between the machining and packaging areas is 55 feet.

9.18 REFERENCES

1. Pritsker, A.A.B., *Introduction to Simulation and SLAM II*, Fourth Edition, Systems Publishing and John Wiley, 1995.

CHAPTER 10

Network Modeling With Continuous Variables

10.1 INTRODUCTION

Models are often classified as either discrete change, continuous change or combined discrete-continuous change. In discrete change models, the state of the model changes discretely at isolated points in time called event times. In a network model, the event times are imbedded in the network description and are equivalent to times at which an entity arrives to a node.

Continuous change models are characterized by variables defined in terms of equations that describe their behavior over time. Continuous models are built in Visual SLAM by describing the equations for the state variables in a user-written function called STATE and by having Visual SLAM call function STATE whenever updated values of the state variables are needed.

In this chapter we introduce the concept of state variables in order to illustrate how network models can be developed in conjunction with variables whose values change continuously with time. The defining equations for state variables are written in function STATE. Discrete changes can be made to state variables at

420

ASSIGN nodes in the network. A state variable can be monitored to detect when its value crosses a threshold. Such crossings are called state events and, when this occurs, an entity can be placed in the network to initiate any changes that are to take place. In this chapter, the concepts associated with state variables and state events are introduced.

10.2 STATE VARIABLES

A state variable has a value which changes, primarily, in accordance with a defining equation. The value of a state variable does not stay constant between event times but changes in accordance with the equation that describes its behavior over time. Examples of state variables are: the level of oil in a storage tank; the position of a projectile; the height of a cab on an overhead crane; and the probability that there are no items in the system at a particular time.

In the text that follows, Visual SLAM variables will be presented using brackets, the syntax used in C user inserts and in a network. The presentation of the coding of equations is in both Visual Basic and C.

The Visual SLAM variable SS[I] is used to represent state variable I. The derivative of state variable I is defined by the Visual SLAM variable DD[I], that is,

DD[I] = dSS[I]/dt

Visual SLAM solves for the values of state variables over time by taking steps in simulated time. The state variable value at each immediately preceding step is maintained as the Visual SLAM variable SSL[I] (in the C interface) or VS.SSL(I) (in Visual Basic). With these Visual SLAM variables, it is possible to write a difference equation for state variable I in function STATE in the following fashion:

VS.SS(I) = VS.SSL(I) + DTNOW *RATE(I)   'Visual Basic
SS[I] = SSL[I] + DTNOW*RATE[I];   /*C Version */

where DTNOW or TimeStep is the step size and RATE[I] is a user variable that specifies the rate of change of state variable I during DTNOW. This equation states that the value of state variable I at time TNOW is equal to the last value of state variable I plus the amount of change that would occur over time DTNOW. The value of RATE[I] could be specified as a function of other system variables. The Visual SLAM executive calls function STATE every time a step is to be made so that the updating of time is implicit in the equation given above for SS[I].

An alternative method for defining SS[I] is to define its derivative in function STATE. In this case the derivative is integrated by Visual SLAM to obtain the value of SS[I] at each step. Hence, an equivalent formulation for the above difference equation would be the following statement in function STATE:

$$VS.DD(I) = RATE(I) \qquad \text{'Visual Basic version}$$
$$DD[I] = RATE[I] \qquad \text{/* C version */}$$

The user may define SS[I] by either an algebraic expression, a difference equation or a DD[I] equation. Note that only one method for each variable is allowed. The Visual SLAM variables used to define the state variables and their derivatives in function STATE are defined below.

Visual Basic Variable Name	C Variable Name	Variable Description
VS.TNOW	TNOW	Time at which values of the state variables are being computed.
VS.TTLAST	TTLAST	Time at the beginning of the current step (the time at which the values for the state variables were last accepted).
VS.DTNOW	DTNOW	TNOW-TTLAST.
VS.SS(I)	SS[I]	Value of state variable I at time TNOW.
VS.SSL(I)	SSL[I]	Value of state variable I at time TTLAST.
VS.DD(I)	DD[I]	Value of the derivative of state variable I at time TNOW.
VS.DDL(I)	DDL[I]	Value of the derivative of state variable I at time TTLAST.

As mentioned above, to define a state variable by a differential equation, the user would write a defining equation in terms of DD[·]. For example, if the differential equation for state variable j is given by

$$dy_j / dt = Ay_j + B$$

the corresponding Visual SLAM statement is

$$DD[J] = A*SS[J] + B$$

where SS[J] represents y_j.

In this situation, the Visual SLAM processor calls function STATE many times within a step in order to obtain estimates of the derivatives (DD[J]) within the step. These estimates are used to compute SS[J] at TNOW from the equation

$$SS[J] = SSL[J] + \int_{TTLAS}^{TNOW} DD[J]dt$$

where TTLAS is the time at the beginning of the step and corresponds to the time at which SSL[J] was computed. The integration involved in the above equation is performed by a Runge-Kutta-Fehlberg (RKF) numerical integration algorithm in which a user-prescribed single-step accuracy specification is maintained (1,5,6). If the accuracy is not maintained, the step size is reduced and the integration recalculated as described in Chapter 13. This process is repeated if necessary until a user-specified minimum step size, DTMIN, is encountered.

10.3 CODING FUNCTION STATE

Function STATE is written to compute the current value of each state variable or its derivative. Visual SLAM permits state variables to be defined by state equations or derivative equations in function STATE. Function STATE is frequently called, especially if there are active derivative equations, and therefore should contain only essential code. It is most efficient if the state variables are numbered sequentially.

The state storage array consists of four one-dimensional arrays. The vectors SS[·] and DD[·] contain values associated with time TNOW. The vectors SSL[·] and DDL[·] contain values associated with time TTLAS, the most current value of simulated time for which model status has been completely updated. When the model status has been updated to TNOW, TTLAS is reset to TNOW.

The problem-specific definition of the state storage array is determined by the user. There are several policies regarding the writing of state equations that must be followed. The user inputs the variable NNEQD which is defined as the largest subscript used in a derivative equation. The second parameter on the CONTINUOUS statement is the number of equations defining SS variables directly, NNEQS. The largest subscript used in defining state equations is NNEQT, the sum of NNEQD and NNEQS. Therefore, equations defining the rate of change of state variables, that is, equations for DD[I], must satisfy the expression $0 \leq I \leq$ NNEQD. Equations defining SS[I] must satisfy the expression NNEQD $+ 1 \leq I \leq$ NNEQT. Thus, if there is an equation defining DD[M] and another defining SS[N], then M $\leq$ NNEQD; M < N; and NNEQD $+ 1 \leq$ N $\leq$ NNEQT. NNEQD, NNEQS, or both can be -1, meaning there are no DD defining equations or SS defining equations, respectively.

The above numbering policy can be summarized by the following four cases:

Case 1. NNEQD =-1; NNEQS = -1. No continuous variables are included in the simulation, that is, a discrete or network simulation is to be performed.

Case 2. NNEQD $\geq$ 0; NNEQS = 0. SS[0] through SS[NNEQD] state variables are defined by differential equations written for DD[I]. Visual SLAM uses an integration algorithm to compute SS[I]. Multiple calls to function STATE are made to evaluate DD[I] for use in the numerical integration algorithm.

Case 3. NNEQD = -1; NNEQS $\geq$ 0. SS[0] through SS[NNEQS] are defined by algebraic or difference equations written for SS[I]. The user must compute SS[I] in function STATE. In this case, the variable DD[I] is not used by Visual SLAM.

Case 4. NNEQD $\geq$ 0; NNEQS > 0. The first NNEQD+1 state variables, SS[0] through SS[NNEQD], are defined by differential equations, and the next NNEQS variables are defined by algebraic or difference equations. The evaluation procedure is a combination of cases (2) and (3) above.

In function STATE, the order in which the equations are written is left to the user, that is, a statement defining SS[5] can precede one defining DD[3]. Because Visual SLAM does not change the execution sequence of state equations, correct sequencing of state and derivative equations is the responsibility of the user. If the defining equations for DD[·] do not involve other DD[·] variables, any order is permitted and the integration procedure simultaneously solves for all DD[·] and corresponding SS[·] variables. Thus DD[1] = A * SS[1] + B * SS[2] and DD[2] = C * SS[1] + F * SS[2] can be written in either order, and the values obtained for DD[1], DD[2], SS[1] and SS[2] will be the same.

If the defining equations for DD[·] do involve other DD[·] variables, ordering becomes important. For example, if DD[3] = f(DD[5]), the equation for DD[5] must precede the equation for DD[3]. If there are simultaneous equations involving SS[·] variables, the user must develop an algorithm for solving the set of equations.

In function STATE, the equations for DD[·] and SS[·]can be written in a variety of forms. The equations

       DD[M] = RATE

and

       SS[M] = SSL[M] + DTNOW*RATE

are essentially equivalent (Visual SLAM sets DTNOW = TNOW-TTLAST). When an equation for DD[M] is written, values of SS[M] are obtained through the integration routine contained within Visual SLAM. Values of DDL[M] and SSL[M] are automatically maintained. The step size is automatically determined to meet specified accuracy requirements on the computation of SS[M] and tolerances on state-event occurrences. When the equation is written for SS[M], only SSL[M] is maintained by Visual SLAM. Accuracy requirements are not specified on SS[M], and the step size DTNOW for updating SS[M] is maintained at the maximum value specified by the user unless there is an intervening event. DTNOW is automatically reduced if there are intervening time-events, state-events, or a need to record a value of SS[M] for eventual communication (output).

The form of the equations for DD[·] and SS[·] is limited only by Visual Basic and C statement types. Thus, the user has a great deal of flexibility in defining the state variables for the model. Descriptions can be made conditional on time or on any model variable. State or time events could be used to trigger the change by resetting the rate values or by setting an indicator at the time of the event.

10.4 CONTINUOUS INPUT STATEMENT

When state variables are included in a Visual SLAM model, it is necessary to communicate to the Visual SLAM processor the following information: the number and type of state variables; limits on the step size to be taken when updating values of state variables; and whether messages associated with the accuracy of state variable evaluation are desired. The information about these quantities is given on the CONTINUOUS statement, and a description of the fields for this statement is now provided.

The largest subscript for a differential equation is specified by NNEQD. For state variables defined by difference or algebraic equations, the largest subscript is NNEQD+NNEQS. The user may specify the largest step size to be taken, DTMAX, and the smallest step size desired, DTMIN. These values control the step size set by Visual SLAM in meeting tolerance and accuracy requirements. No step will be taken smaller than DTMIN in order to achieve accuracy requirements or to detect a state event. The recording frequency specifies that values of the state variables are desired every DTSAV time units. Information on the error limits for numerical integration is specified by a relative error allowed (a fraction of the state variable value) and an absolute error allowed.

The Visual SLAM input statement and AweSim dialog box to specify values for models with state variables are as follows:

CONTINUOUS,NNEQD,NNEQS,DTMIN,DTMAX,DTSAV,ERRCHK,AAERR,RRERR;

The definitions of the variables on the CONTINUOUS statement are presented below along with their default values.

Variable	Definition	Default
NNEQD	Largest subscript for DD[·] when defined by a a derivative equation. (For efficiency, the derivative equations should be numbered sequentially.)	−1
NNEQS	Number of state variables that can be defined by state equations if NNEQD≥0. Otherwise, the largest subscript for SS[·].	−1
DTMIN	Minimum allowable step size; not used if NNEQD < 0 and NNEQS < 0.	infinite
DTMAX	Maximum allowable step size; not used if NNEQD < 0 and NNEQS < 0.	infinite
ERRCHK	Indicates type of error check in Runge-Kutta integration or in state-event crossing detection when a step size smaller than DTMIN is required. If FATAL is specified, then a fatal error occurs. If WARNING is specified, then a warning message is printed before proceeding. If NOWARNING is specified, then execution proceeds with no warning message given.	WARNING
AAERR	Absolute local truncation error allowed in Runge-Kutta integration. Used with RRERR to control accuracy; not used when NNEQD<0.	0.00001
RRERR	Relative local truncation error allowed in Runge-Kutta integration; used with AAERR to control accuracy.	0.00001

The numerical integration accuracy is controlled by the specification of AAERR and RRERR. The RKF algorithm estimates the single-step error for each variable defined by a differential equation. The Ith error estimate is compared to TERR where

$$TERR[I] = AAERR + ABS(SS[I])*RRERR$$

If the error estimate is less than or equal to TERR[I] for each I, the values of SS[I] are accepted. If not, the step size is reduced and the integration algorithm is reapplied. The default values of AAERR and RRERR are stringent and a significant reduction in running times can be achieved by liberalizing these values subject, of course, to the accuracy requirements of the simulation model.

10.5   STATE EVENTS

A state event is defined as a point in time at which an expression crosses a threshold. When a state event occurs, changes to the model and the variables in the model can be made. In this chapter, when a state event occurs, we will only consider the introduction of an entity into a network to initiate the desired status changes due to the occurrence of the state event. Note that state events can be caused by either state variables or network variables crossing a threshold.

A state event is defined in terms of a crossing expression, a direction of crossing and an expression that describes the threshold. In addition, a tolerance for the crossing is prescribed. Illustrations of state events are shown in Figure 10-1. In Figure 10-1(a), a positive crossing of state variable SS[3] of the threshold value 100 is shown. The crossing occurs when the value of SS[3] is below 100 at the end of one step (at time TTLAST) and equal to or above the value 100 at the end of the step (at time TNOW). In the figure, a tolerance TOL of 2 is shown. If the value of SS[3] is greater than 102 at the end of the step, then a crossing out of tolerance is indicated. In such a case, Visual SLAM would try to reduce the step size, DTNOW, and recalculate the value of the state variable for this shortened step. When this is done, a new value for TNOW is determined since the value given to DTNOW by Visual SLAM is smaller. Step size reductions will only be made as long as DTNOW is greater than DTMIN.

In Figure 10-1(b), an illustration of a negative crossing defining a state event is given. In this figure, the state event is defined as SS[2] crossing SS[1] in the negative direction with a tolerance of 0.01. The crossing is defined when the value of SS[2] is above SS[1] at the beginning of the step and equal to or below SS[1] at the end of the step. The concept of being within or out of tolerance for negative crossings is similar to that described for positive crossings.   State events can be defined for any Visual SLAM global expression.

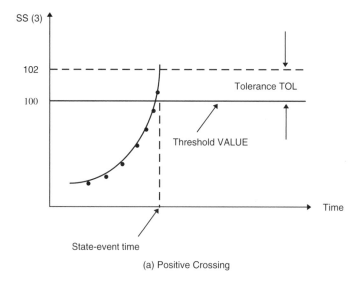

(a) Positive Crossing

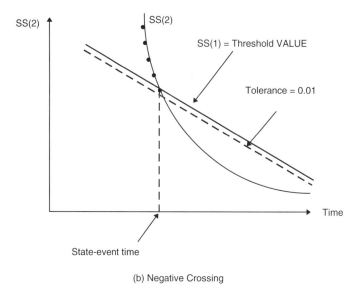

(b) Negative Crossing

Figure 10-1 Illustrations of positive and negative crossings defining state events.

10.6   DETECT NODE

A DETECT node, previously described for network variables in Chapter 7, can also be used for continuous variables. When the conditions for the state event are realized, the DETECT node is released and an entity with all attribute values equal to 0 is routed from the DETECT node in accordance with the M number of the DETECT node. The symbol for the DETECT node is given below.

The DETECT node provides the primary interface between the continuous and network portions of a model. When a DETECT node is included in the network model, it is released whenever the crossing variable, defined by the expression VALUE, crosses a threshold, defined by the expression THRESH in the direction specified by XDIR. The value of TOL specifies an interval beyond the threshold value for which a detection of a crossing is considered within tolerance. If a crossing occurs beyond the allowable tolerance, the Visual SLAM processor reduces the step size until the crossing is within tolerance or until the step size is reduced to the user prescribed minimum step size, DTMIN.

The DETECT node is also released whenever an entity arrives to it. A maximum of M emanating activities are initiated at each release. The statement format and AweSim dialog box for the DETECT node are as follows:

DETECT, VALUE, XDIR, THRESH, TOL, M;

where

VALUE	specifies the crossing variable and can be any Visual SLAM global expression
XDIR	is the crossing direction and can be specified as NEGATIVE, POSITIVE, or EITHER
THRESH	is a Visual SLAM global expression representing the threshold
TOL	is a numeric value which specifies the tolerance within which the crossing is to be detected.

DETECT Definition	⊠

Node Label: [   ]

Value: [   ] F(x)

Threshold: [   ] F(x)

Tolerance: INF

┌Crossing Direction───────────────────
  ○ Positive   ○ Negative   ⊙ Either

Max Branches to Take: 1

[OK]   [Cancel]

Label of this node. Used for branching and reports

One common use of the DETECT node is to specify or key the duration of an activity to the release of the DETECT node. In this way, the time an entity spends in an activity can be keyed to the time when a continuous state variable achieves a specified condition. This is illustrated by the following queueing model where the ACTIVITY completes service for the entity whenever the value of SS[1] crosses in the negative direction the value of SS[2] with a prescribed tolerance of 0.01. In this situation, the ACTIVITY could be the unloading of a tanker where SS[1] is the amount in the tanker and SS[2] is the amount to be left in the tanker after unloading.

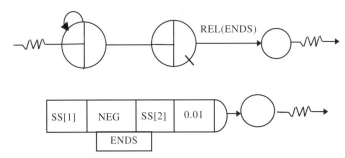

The above network segment operates in the following fashion. When SS[1] crosses SS[2] in a negative direction, node ENDS is released and an entity is created. Recall that SS[1] and SS[2] are varying in accordance with equations written in function STATE. The entity is immediately terminated since a TERM symbol follows the DETECT node. The release of the DETECT node ENDS causes the release(REL) of any entities in the activity following the QUEUE node whose duration is specified by REL(ENDS). Thus any entities being processed by this service activity are completed when the state event as represented by the DETECT node ENDS occurs. As discussed in Chapter 5, the duration specification REL(ENDS) only applies if an entity is currently engaged in the ACTIVITY. If DETECT node ENDS detects a crossing and no entity is being processed by the ACTIVITY, or by any other activity keyed to ENDS, then the crossing has no effect.

As another illustration of the DETECT node, consider the following network segments.

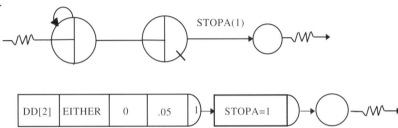

In these network segments, the service duration is specified as STOPA(1) to indicate that the entity in service is to leave the activity when an assignment of 1 is made to STOPA.

A DETECT node is used to monitor the value of DD[2], the derivative of state variable 2. When the derivative crosses 0 in either direction with a tolerance of .05, the DETECT node is released. Recall that a derivative crossing 0 indicates a maximum, minimum or point of inflection for the state variable. Thus, when one of these conditions occurs, an entity is put into the network following the DETECT node and, in the above situation, is routed to the ASSIGN node where STOPA is set equal to 1. When this assignment is made, service on the entities in the service activity would be completed. At this time, entities waiting in the QUEUE node would start service. These activities would not be completed until the next assignment of the value 1 to STOPA.

Through the use of STOPA(I), selective entities can be moved out of an activity by prescribing that an entity's duration be keyed to the value of I. For example the activity specification STOPA(ATRIB[1]) would cause only entities with ATRIB[1]= 1 to complete the activity when STOPA is assigned a value of 1 at the ASSIGN node.

10.7   EXAMPLE 10-1.   TANKER-REFINERY OPERATIONS

A fleet of 15 tankers carries crude oil from Valdez, Alaska to an unloading dock near Seattle, Washington (4). It is assumed that all tankers can be loaded simultaneously in Valdez, if necessary. In Seattle, there is only one unloading dock, which supplies a storage tank that feeds a refinery through a pipeline. The storage tank receives crude from a tanker at the dock at a constant rate of 300 thousand-barrels(tb)/day. The storage tank supplies crude to the refinery continuously at a constant rate of 150 tb/day. The unloading dock is open from the hours of 6 a.m. to 12 midnight. Safety considerations require the stopping of unloading of the crude when the dock is shut down. The completion of the tanker unloading occurs when the amount of crude remaining in the tanker is less than 7.5 tb.

The storage tank has a capacity of 2000 tb. When it is full, unloading is halted until the amount in the tank decreases to 80 percent of capacity. When the storage tank is nearly empty (less than 5 tb), supply to the refinery is halted until 50 tb is reached to avoid the possibility of frequent refinery start-ups and shut-downs. The characteristics associated with the tankers are listed below.

1.   Nominal carrying capacity is 150 tb.
2.   Travel time loaded is normally distributed with a mean of 5.0 days and standard deviation of 1.5 days.
3.   Travel time unloaded is normally distributed with a mean of 4.0 days and a standard deviation of 1 day.
4.   Time to load is uniformly distributed in the interval 2.9 to 3.1 days.

The initial conditions for the simulation are that the storage tank is half full and the tankers are to arrive at their loading points at 1/2 day intervals, starting with the first at time 0.

The objective of this example is to simulate the above systems for 365 days to obtain estimates of the following quantities:

1.   Unloading dock utilization.
2.   Loading dock utilization.
3.   Time refinery has a crude input available.
4.   Amount of crude in the storage tank.
5.   Tanker round trip time.
6.   Tanker waiting time.
7.   Number of tankers waiting for unloading.

Concepts Illustrated. This example illustrates the use of the DETECT node for modeling state-events in combined network-continuous simulation models. The use of a single state variable to represent the amount of crude oil to be unloaded simplifies the system state description. Since all tankers are scheduled to arrive at Valdez, abnormal initial conditions exist. MONTR statements are used to CLEAR statistics on days 65 and 165, and to obtain a summary report over the period from day 65 to day 165.

Visual SLAM Model. The tanker problem is simulated using a combined network-continuous model. The continuous variables are used to represent the level of crude oil in the tanker being unloaded and in the storage tank. The network is used to model the movement of tankers through the system and the interactions between the continuous and discrete elements of the system.

Two state variables are used in this simulation: SS[1], the amount of crude in a tanker at the unloading dock; and SS[2], the amount of crude in the storage tank. The state variable SS[1] represents the amount of crude available to be unloaded. SS[1] will be zero when no tanker is in the unloading dock; otherwise it will be equal to the amount of crude in a tanker that is in the unloading dock.

When a tanker leaves the unloading dock, SS[1] either becomes zero or is set equal to the amount of crude in the next tanker waiting to be unloaded. By defining SS[1] in this manner, a separate state variable for the amount of crude in each tanker need not be defined.

There are three XX variables which are used in the simulation to control the flow of crude between the unloading tanker and the refinery. Each of these variables represents a valve which is open when equal to 1.0 and closed when equal to 0. XX[1] is used to represent the dock input valve and is open between the dock operating hours of 6 a.m. to 12 midnight, and is closed otherwise. XX[2] is used to model the storage tank input valve and is closed whenever the storage tank crude level, SS[2], reaches the tank capacity of 2000 tb. It is reopened when the level of crude decreases to 1600 tb. XX[3] is used to represent the storage tank output valve and is closed whenever the storage tank crude level has decreased to less than 5 tb, thereby halting the flow to the refinery. XX[3] is reset to open when the crude level in the storage tank has increased to 50 tb, thereby restoring the flow of crude to the refinery. A schematic diagram depicting the arrangement of the three valves is provided in Figure 10-2. Note that XX[1] can be opened and closed by scheduling a time-event whereas XX[2] and XX[3] require the concept of a state-event.

SS(1)

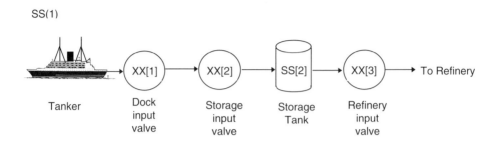

Figure 10-2 Crude oil flow from tanker to refinery.

The equations describing the state variables SS[1] and SS[2] are in the function STATE shown in Figure 10-3. The variable RateIn represents the flow rate of crude into the storage tank. It is set to zero if XX[1], XX[2], or SS[1] is zero, and is set equal to 300 otherwise. The variable RateOut, representing the flow rate of crude from the storage tank to the refinery, equals 150 if XX[3] = 1. and equals 0 if XX[3] = 0. Equations for state variables SS[1] and SS[2] are written as difference equations in terms of RateIn and RateOut. In this case, we are integrating the state equations explicitly in function STATE. An alternative would be to code function STATE in terms of the derivatives of the state variables as follows:

$$VS.DD(1) = - RateIn \qquad\qquad \text{'Visual Basic version}$$
$$VS.DD(2) = \ RateIn - RateOut$$

$$DD[1] = -RateIn; \qquad\qquad \text{/* C version */}$$
$$DD[2] = RateIn - RateOut;$$

In this case, the equations would be integrated by Visual SLAM using the Runge-Kutta-Fehlberg integration algorithm to determine SS[1] and SS[2].

The state equations for this example appear relatively simple but are deceptive since RateIn and RateOut have different values during the simulation because of the status of the system. These equations could be made more complex if RateIn or RateOut were functions of the type of crude or the level of crude in the storage tank and tanker. Since these aspects of the system do not add to the organizational aspects of the model, they are not included.

```
Public Sub STATE()
  Dim RateIn As Double
  Dim RateOut As Double

  ' if dock or storage input closed, or no waiting tanker
  If VS.XX(1) * VS.XX(2) * VS.SS(1) = 0# Then
     RateIn = 0#
  Else
     RateIn = 300#
  End If

  ' rate is zero if refinery input off - else 150
  RateOut = 150# * VS.XX(3)
  VS.SS(1)=VS.SSL(1)-VS.DTNOW*RateIn
  VS.SS(2)=VS.SSL(2)+VS.DTNOW*(RateIn-RateOut)

End Sub
```

Figure 10-3VB Function STATE written in Visual Basic for tanker example.

```
#include "vslam.h"
void SWFUNC STATE(void)
{

   double RateIn;
   double RateOut;

  /* if dock or storage input closed, or no waiting tanker */
   if (XX[1]*XX[2]*SS[1] == 0.0)      {
      RateIn = 0.0;
   }
   else                              {
      RateIn = 300.0;
   }

  /* rate is zero if refinery input off - else 150 */
   RateOut = 150.0 * XX[3];
   SS[1] = SSL[1] - DTNOW * RateIn;
   SS[2] = SSL[2] + DTNOW * (RateIn - RateOut);
   return;
}
```

Figure 10-3C Function STATE written in C for tanker example.

The network model for this example can be viewed as three subprocesses consisting of the tanker flow through the system, the start-up and shut-down of dock operations, and the state-events. Each of these subprocesses is modeled as a separate disjoint network.

The network for the tanker flow subprocess is depicted in Figure 10-4. The initial 15 tankers are created by the CREATE node at 0.50 day intervals, beginning with the first at time 0. The tankers proceed to the ASSIGN node labeled VLDZ where their arrival time to Valdez is marked as ATRIB[1]. The tankers then undertake the loading activity which is represented by ACTIVITY 1. The trip from Valdez to Seattle is modeled by ACTIVITY 2. Upon completion of ACTIVITY 2, the tankers then wait in file 1 at the AWAIT node for the resource DOCK. A single unit of resource DOCK is available as specified by the resource block. When the DOCK becomes available, the state variable SS[1] is set to 150 at the ASSIGN node indicating that there is 150 tb of crude available for unloading. The tanker then undergoes ACTIVITY 3 which represents the unloading activity. This ACTIVITY is completed at the next release of the node labeled ENDU. The node labeled ENDU is a DETECT node which is released when SS[1] crosses, in the negative direction, the threshold value of 7.5 which indicates that the state-event "end-of-unloading" has occurred.

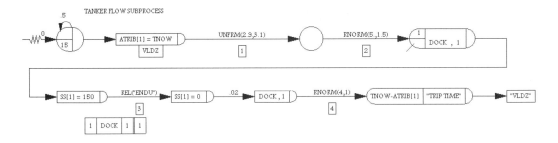

Figure 10-4 Tanker flow subprocess for tanker example.

At the completion of unloading, the tanker entity is routed to the ASSIGN node where SS[1] is set to 0, and then releases the DOCK at the FREE node after a delay of 0.02 days. This represents the time required to remove the tanker from the dock. The return trip to Valdez is modeled by ACTIVITY number 4. At the COLCT node, statistics are collected on the round trip time for the tanker which is then routed to the ASSIGN node labeled VLDZ to repeat the cycle through the network.

The network for the shift start-up and shut-down subprocess is depicted in Figure 10-5. The CREATE node inserts an entity into the network beginning at time 0.25 days (6 a.m.), and then daily thereafter. At the ASSIGN node, the dock input valve is opened by setting XX[1] equal to 1. The dock status remains open during the 0.75 days required for the entity to transverse the ACTIVITY before being closed at the ASSIGN node where XX[1] is reset to 0. The dock status remains closed until the next entity is inserted into the network at 6 a.m. the next day.

Figure 10-5 Shift start-up/shut-down subprocess for tanker example.

There are five possible conditions that could result in a state-event and these are listed below.

Condition	State-Event
The level of crude in the unloading tanker, SS[1], has decreased to 7.5.	Tanker unloading is completed
The level of crude in the storage tank, SS[2], has decreased to 5 tb.	Stop supply to refinery by setting XX[3] = 0
The level of crude in the storage tank has increased to 50 tb.	Start supplying refinery by setting XX[3] = 1
The level of crude in the storage tank has reached its capacity of 2000 tb.	Close input to the storage tank by setting XX[2] = 0
The level of crude in the storage tank has decreased to 1600 tb.	Open input to the storage tank by setting XX[2] = 1

These five state events are modeled by the five network segments depicted in Figure 10-6. The first network segment is used to detect the end of unloading state-event and causes the completion of ACTIVITY 3 whose duration is keyed to the release of the node labeled ENDU. The other four subnetworks are used to detect and process state-events which cause the opening and closing of the storage tank and refinery input valves. The tolerance for each state-event is set at 5. The value prescribed for a tolerance is set according to the accuracy with which a state-event should be detected. The value of the tolerance should also consider the value given to DTMIN and the maximum rate of change of the state variable. In this example, DTMIN = 0.0025 days and the maximum rate is 300 tb/day, hence tolerances of 0.75 tb or greater should enable detection of state-events within tolerance.

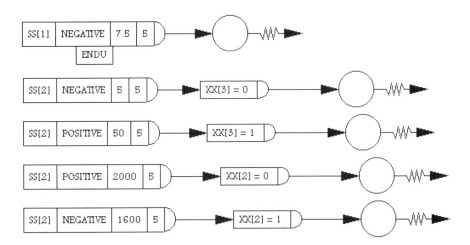

Figure 10-6 State event subprocesses for tanker example.

The input statements for this example are depicted in Figure 10-7. In addition to the network statements, the necessary control statements are included to obtain: 1) a plot of the crude level in an unloading tanker and the level in the storage tank; and 2) time-persistent statistics on the refinery input availability and the average crude level in the storage tank. The LIMITS statement specifies an index up to 3 for XX variables and an index up to 2 for real attributes. There are no LL, SZ, LTRIB or STRIB variables used. A negative 1 denotes the default for these limits. The INITIALIZE statement specifies that the model is to be simulated for 365 days. MONTR statements with the CLEAR option are used to clear statistics at time 65 and 165.

Summary of results. The Visual SLAM summary report for this example is given in Figure 10-8. As can be seen from the output statistics, the refinery is operated 100 percent of the time from day 165 to day 365. This high percentage of refinery utilization occurs at the expense of the tankers which wait on the average 1.5 days for the unloading dock. This is further illustrated by the file statistics which indicate that the average number waiting for the unloading dock is 1.6, and that as many as 5 tankers were waiting at one time. The resource statistics indicate that there was a tanker in the unloading dock 94 percent of the time. The average utilization of activity 3 shows that a tanker was unloading 92 percent of the time, with the remaining 2 percent of dock utilization due to dock exit time. Also available from the activity statistics is the average number of tankers being loaded as this quantity is the average utilization of activity 1. From the output, it is seen that approximately 3.15 tankers are being loaded and the maximum number of tankers loaded concurrently is 6.

```
GEN,"PRITSKER","TANKER FLEET",1/1/1996,1;
LIMITS,3,-1,-1,2,-1,-1;
TIMST,1,XX[3],"REFN INPUT AVAIL";
CONT,0,2,.0025,.25,.25;
RECORD,,out.raw,TNOW,"DAYS",{EXCEL},,,,
   {{SS[1],"TANKER  LEVEL", },{SS[2],"STORAGE LEVEL", }};
TIMST,2,SS[2],"STORAGE LEVEL";
INTLC,{ { SS[2], 1000 }, { XX[2], 1 }, { XX[3], 1 }, { XX[1], 0 } };
NETWORK;
;TANKER FLOW SUBPROCESS
;----------------------
      RESOURCE, ,DOCK,1,{ 1 };
      CREATE,.5,0, ,15;                      CREATE TANKERS
VLDZ: ASSIGN,{ { ATRIB[1], TNOW } };         MARK ARRIVAL TIME
      ACT,1,UNFRM(2.9,3.1), , , ,            "LOADING";
      GOON;                                  END OF LOADING
      ACT,2,RNORM(5.,1.5), , , ,             "TO SEATTLE";
      AWAIT,1,{ { DOCK, 1 } };               WAIT FOR DOCK
      ACTIVITY, , , ,                        "UNLOAD";
UNLOAD: ASSIGN,{{SS[1],150}};                RESET TANKER CRUDE LEVEL
      ACT,3,REL("ENDU"), , , ,               "UNLOADING";
      ASSIGN,{ { SS[1], 0 } };               TANKER CRUDE LEVER = 0
      ACT,,.02;
      FREE,{ { DOCK } };                     FREE THE DOCK
      ACT,4,RNORM(4,1), , , ,                "RETURN TRIP";
      COLCT, ,TNOW-ATRIB[1],"TRIP TIME";     COLLECT STATISTICS
      ACT, , , ,"VLDZ";                      BRANCH TO VLDZ
;SHIFT START UP/SHUT DOWN SUBPROCESS
;-----------------------------------
      CREATE,1.,,.25;
      ASSIGN,{ { XX[1], 1 } };               BEGIN SHIFT AT 6 A.M.
      ACT, ,.75;                                CONTINUE FOR 3/4 DAYS
      ASSIGN,{ { XX[1], 0 } };               CLOSE SHIFT AT MIDNIGHT
      TERM;
;
;STATE EVENT SUBPROCESSES
;-----------------------
ENDU:   DETECT,SS[1],NEGATIVE,7.5,5;          END OF UNLOADING ACTIVITY
      TERM;
      DETECT,SS[2],NEGATIVE,5,5;             STORAGE IS EMPTY
      ASSIGN,{ { XX[3], 0 } };               CLOSE REFINERY INPUT
      TERM;
      DETECT,SS[2],POSITIVE,50,5;            STORAGE BACK UP TO 50
      ASSIGN,{ { XX[3], 1 } };               OPEN REFINERY INPUT
      TERM;
      DETECT,SS[2],POSITIVE,2000,5;          CAPACITY REACHED
      ASSIGN,{ { XX[2], 0 } };               CLOSE STORAGE INPUT
      TERM;
      DETECT,SS[2],NEGATIVE,1600,5;          STORAGE BELOW 80%
      ASSIGN,{ { XX[2], 1 } };               OPEN STORAGE INPUT
      TERM;
      END;
;
INITIALIZE,0,365;
MONTR,CLEAR,65;
MONTR,CLEAR,165;
FIN;
```

Figure 10-7 Statement model for tanker example.

```
             ** AweSim SUMMARY REPORT **
        Simulation Project : TANKER FLEET
        Modeler : PRITSKER
        Date : 1/1/1996
        Scenario : TANKER

        Run number 1 of 1
        Current simulation time    : 365.000000
        Statistics cleared at time : 165.000000
```

```
          ** OBSERVED STATISTICS REPORT for scenario TANKER **
```

Label	Mean Value	Standard Deviation	Number of Observations	Minimum Value	Maximum Value
TRIP TIME	14.318	2.010	210	9.753	20.292

```
          ** TIME-PERSISTENT STATISTICS REPORT for scenario TANKER **
```

Label	Mean Value	Standard Deviation	Minimum Value	Maximum Value	Time Interval	Current Value
REFN INPUT AVAIL	1.000	0.000	1.000	1.000	200.000	1.000
STORAGE LEVEL	1810.021	109.544	1589.171	2004.743	200.000	1697.302

```
          ** FILE STATISTICS REPORT for scenario TANKER **
```

File Number	Label or Input Location	Avgerage Length	Standard Deviation	Maximum Length	Current Length	Avgerage Wait Time
1	RES. DOCK	1.648	1.274	5	2	1.562
0	Event Calendar	15.182	1.438	19	14	1.597

```
          ** ACTIVITY STATISTICS REPORT for scenario TANKER **
```

Activity Number	Label or Input Location	Avgerage Utililization	Standard Deviation	Entity Count	Maximum Utilization	Current Utilization
1	LOADING	3.146	1.362	208	6	3
2	TO SEATTLE	5.076	1.528	208	9	4
3	UNLOADING	0.920	0.272	209	1	1
4	RETURN TRIP	4.190	1.402	210	7	5

```
          ** RESOURCE STATISTICS REPORT for scenario TANKER **
```

Resource Number	Resource Label	Avgerage Utilization	Standard Deviation	Current Utilization	Maximum Utilization	Current Capacity
1	DOCK	0.941	0.236	1	1	1

Resource Number	Average Available	Current Available	Minimum Available	Maximum Available
1	0.059	0	0	1

```
          ** STATE VARIABLE REPORT **
```

Variable Index	SS[] Current Value	DD[] Current Value
0	0.000	0.000
1	83.191	
2	1697.302	

Figure 10-8 Visual SLAM summary report for tanker fleet model.

AweSim plots of the state variables during the initial and middle portions of the simulation are depicted in Figure 10-9. At the start of the simulation, all the tankers were scheduled to arrive at the loading dock at 0.50 day intervals. Thus, there were no tankers to be unloaded.

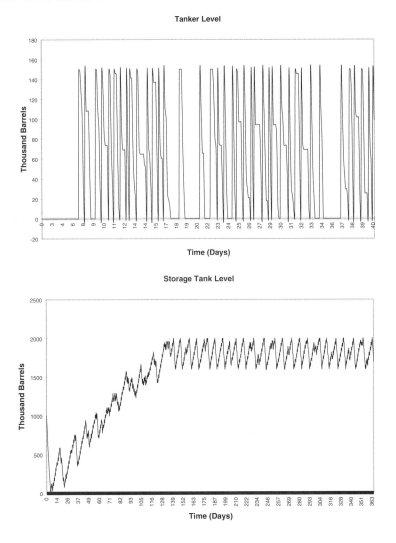

Figure 10-9 Plot of tanker level and storage tank level in tanker fleet model.

Since there are no tankers in the unloading dock initially, the amount in the storage tank is depleted by the amount being sent to the refinery. From the plot, this depletion continues until the first tanker arrives and begins unloading its crude. Since the input rate for the storage tank is greater than its output rate, the amount of crude in the storage tank increases as the tanker is being unloaded. Other tankers arrive and provide sufficient crude to replenish the storage tank after the initial depletion period.

As can be seen, the plots illustrate the combined discrete-continuous nature of the simulation. The storage level plot after time 120 illustrates the steady-state behavior of the system. The amount of crude in the storage tank oscillates between 1600 and 2000, and tankers are in the unloading dock waiting for storage space to become available to unload their crude.

10.8   EXAMPLE 10-2. A CHEMICAL REACTION PROCESS

A hydrogenation reaction is conducted in four reactors operating in parallel. Each reactor may be started, stopped, discharged, or cleaned independently of the others. A compressor with a constant molal flow rate provides a supply of hydrogen gas to the reactors through a surge pressure tank and individual valves for each reactor. The valve connecting each reactor to the surge tank is adjusted by controls that make the effective pressure in each reactor the minimum of surge tank pressure and critical pressure (100 psia). Figure 10-10 is a schematic representation of the compressor, surge tank, valves and reactors (2,3,4).

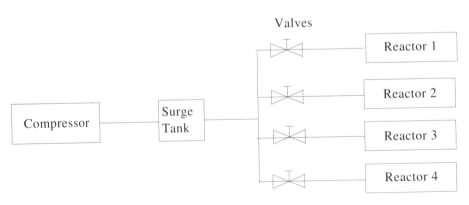

Figure 10-10 Schematic diagram for reactor example.

Initially the surge tank pressure is equal to 500 psia. Each reactor is charged with a fresh batch of reactant and the four reactors are scheduled to be turned on at half hour intervals beginning with reactor 1 at time 0. As a reaction proceeds, the concentration of the reactant decreases. As long as surge tank pressure remains above the critical pressure of 100 psia, the decrease in concentration is exponential. The concentration of each reactant is monitored until it decreases to 10% of its initial value at which time the reactor is considered to have completed a batch. At this time the reactor is turned off, discharged, cleaned, and recharged. The time to discharge a reactor is exponentially distributed with a mean time of one hour. The time to clean and recharge a reactor is normally distributed with a mean of one hour and a standard deviation of one-half hour.

The operating policy for the system prescribes that the last reactor started will be immediately turned off whenever surge tank pressure falls below the critical value of 100 psia. All other reactors that are on at that time will continue, but no reactor will be started if surge tank pressure is below a nominal pressure of 150 psia.

The objective for this example is to model and analyze a chemical reaction process that involves a continuous batch process subject to controls imposed by surge tank pressure. In addition to a plot of the operation of the process, statistics on the maintenance time, the number of reactors in use, and the surge tank pressure are to be obtained.

Concepts Illustrated. A network model is used to portray the status of a reactor when it is not processing a batch. While processing a batch, the concentration level in the reactor is described by a set of first order differential equations. Visual SLAM's numerical integration algorithm is used to obtain the values of the concentration levels. The status of a reactor is maintained on the network in the Visual SLAM variable ARRAY. In the equations describing the rate of change of concentration, the property VS.Array (in Visual Basic) or the function GETARY (in C) is employed to access the status of a reactor. DETECT nodes are used to monitor the continuous variables which can initiate state changes.

Visual SLAM Model. The Visual SLAM model of the reactor system consists of three parts: 1) equations describing the change of concentration level in each of the reactors; 2) reactor entities moving through activities that represent different states for the reactor; and 3) DETECT nodes for monitoring and detecting when reactor concentration and surge tank pressure cross thresholds.

The definitions of the parameters and variables of the model are given in Table 10-1. The basic equation for the rate of change in concentration of reactor I are

$$\frac{dSS[I]}{dt} = -RK[I]*PEFF*SS[I], \quad I= 1,4$$

where RK[I] is the reaction constant for reactor I and PEFF is the effective surge tank pressure. The Visual SLAM coding of this differential equation is directly obtained by substituting DD[I] for dSS[I]/dt. SS[5] is the state variable used to represent surge tank pressure. Using the definitions provided by Table 10-1, the model 's state equations describing the chemical reactor system are:

$$
\begin{aligned}
\text{PEFF} \quad &= \text{Minimum of (PCRIT,SS[5])} \\
\text{DD[I]} \quad &= \begin{cases} - RK[I]*SS[I] *PEFF & \text{if reactor I is on} \\ 0 & \text{if reactor I is off} \end{cases} \\
\text{F[I]} \quad &= -DD[I]*V[I] \\
\text{SUMF} \quad &= F[1] + F[2] + F[3] + F[4] \\
\text{DD[5]} \quad &= (RR*TEMP/VS*((FC*SUMFO)-SUMF) \\
&= RTV*(CMOLALFLOW-SUMF)
\end{aligned}
$$

The coding of these equations is performed in function STATE which is shown in Figure 10-11. As can be seen, there is a direct translation of the equations defined for the reactors to the code shown in function STATE. In the statement for DD[I], the variable dStatus is employed. When the reactor is idle, dStatus is 0 and when the reactor is working, dStatus is 1. In this way, the rate of change of concentration level is made 0 when the reactor is idle. In the network model, the Visual SLAM global array, ARRAY(1,I), is used to maintain the status of reactor I. In function STATE, the value for the status of reactor I is obtained by using the VS.Array (1,I) property in Visual Basic or Visual SLAM function GETARY(1,I) in C.

Table 10-1 Parameters and variables for chemical reaction model.

Model Parameters	Initial Value	Definition
RK[1] = XX [21]	0.03466	Reaction constant for product 1
RK[2] = XX [22]	0.00866	Reaction constant for product 2
RK[3] = XX [23]	0.01155	Reaction constant for product 3
RK[4] = XX [24]	0.00770	Reaction constant for product 4
V[1]= XX [25]	10.0	Volume of reactor 1
V[2]= XX [26]	15.0	Volume of reactor 2
V[3]= XX [27]	20.0	Volume of reactor 3
V[4]= XX [28]	25.0	Volume of reactor 4
VS	50.0	Volume of surge tank
RR	10.73	Gas constant
TEMP	550.0	System operating temperature
FC	0.19	Flow constant of compressor; FC * SUMFO is compressor molal flow rate
PNOM	150.0	Nominal pressure
PCRITICAL	100.0	Critical pressure
PEFF	–	Minimum of critical pressure and surge tank pressure
SUMFO	Calculated	Maximum possible molal flow of hydrogen to all reactors
RTV	RR * TEMP/VS	Composite reaction constant
CMOLALFLOW	FC * SUMFO	Compressor molal flow rate
Model Variables		
SS[1]	XX[1] = 0.1	Concentration of reactor 1
SS[2]	XX[2] = 0.4	Concentration of reactor 2
SS[3]	XX[3] = 0.2	Concentration of reactor 3
SS[4]	XX[4] = 0.5	Concentration of reactor 4
SS[5]	500.0	Surge tank pressure
DD[1],I=1,4	0.0	Derivative of SS[I] with respect to time
dFlow	0.0	Molal flow rate of hydrogen to reactor I
dSumFlow	0.0	Total molal flow of hydrogen to all reactors
LL[0]	0	Number of reactors on
ARRAY(1,I), I=1,4	0.0	A flag indicating whether reactor I is on (1.0) or off (0.0)

```
Const NUMREACTORS As Integer = 4
Const BASEXX As Integer = 21
Property Get PCRITICAL()
PCRITICAL = VS.XX(8)
End Property
Property Get CMOLALFLOW()
CMOLALFLOW = VS.XX(9)
End Property
Property Get RTV()
RTV = VS.XX(10)
End Property
Public Sub STATE()
    Dim dSumFlow As Double
    Dim PEFF As Double
    Dim dStatus As Double
    Dim dFlow As Double
    Dim i As Integer
      dSumFlow = 0#
' reactor constants start at XX(BASEXX)
' then velocities
    If VS.SS(NUMREACTORS + 1) < PCRITICAL Then
        PEFF = VS.SS(NUMREACTORS + 1)
    Else
        PEFF = PCRITICAL
    End If
' define the differential equations for concentrate in reactors
    For i = 1 To NUMREACTORS
        dStatus = VS.Array(1, i)
        VS.DD(i)=-VS.XX(BASEXX + i - 1) * VS.SS(i) * dStatus * PEFF
        dFlow = -VS.DD(i) * VS.XX(BASEXX + NUMREACTORS + i - 1)
        dSumFlow = dSumFlow + dFlow
    Next I
' set the surge tank pressure rate
 VS.DD(NUMREACTORS + 1) = RTV * (CMOLALFLOW - dSumFlow)
End Sub
```

Figure 10-11VB Function STATE in Visual Basic for chemical reactor process.

The network model depicting reactor status changes is shown in Figure 10-12. The gate PRESSURE is used to prohibit reactors from being started until the surge pressure is above the nominal value of 150 psia. Reactor entities waiting for the gate PRESSURE to open are placed in file 1. Several equivalences are defined between Visual SLAM variables and names employed on the network. Integer attribute 1, LTRIB[1], of the reactor entity is the reactor number and is given the name REACTOR. DISCHARGE is a sample from an exponential distribution with a mean of 1. C_AND_R represents the time to clean and recharge the reactor and is a sample from a normal distribution with mean 1 and standard deviation 0.5. PNOM, the nominal pressure, is equivalenced to XX[7] and PCRIT, the critical pressure, is equivalenced to XX[8].

```
#include "vslam.h"
#define NUMREACTORS 4
#define PCRITICAL  XX[8]    /* critical pressure */
#define CMOLALFLOW XX[9]    /* compressor molal flow rate */
#define RTV        XX[10]   /* composite reaction constant */

void SWFUNC STATE(void)
{
    static double * pdRK = NULL; /* reactor constants start at
                                    XX[21] */
    static double * pdV = NULL;  /* then velocities */
    double dSumFlow = 0.0;
    double PEFF;
    double dStatus;
    double dFlow;
    int i;

    if (!pdRK)                                        {
        pdRK = &(XX[21]);   /* reactor constants start at XX[21] */
        pdV = &(XX[21+NUMREACTORS]);  /* then velocities */
    }
    if (SS[5] < PCRITICAL)                            {
        PEFF = SS[5];
    }
    else                                              {
        PEFF = PCRITICAL;
    }

    /* define the differential equations for
       concentrate in reactors */
    for (i=1; i <= NUMREACTORS; I++)                  {
        dStatus = GETARY(1,i);
        DD[i] = (-(pdRK[i-1])) * SS[i] * dStatus * PEFF;
        dFlow = (-DD[i]) * (pdV[i-1]);
        dSumFlow += dFlow;
    }

    /* set the surge tank pressure rate */
    DD[NUMREACTORS+1] = RTV * (CMOLALFLOW - dSumFlow);
    return;
}
```

Figure 10-11C Function STATE written in C for chemical reactor process.

At a CREATE node, four reactor entities are generated at half-day intervals which are routed to an ASSIGN node where a reactor number is assigned from the count of the number of entities passing over activity 10. This assigns reactor numbers of 1, 2, 3 and 4 to the four entities created. The reactor entity is then sent to GOON node START which routes the entity to the AWAIT node LOWP if the surge pressure is less than the nominal pressure. If this is not the case, the status of the reactor is changed to busy and the number of reactors working, LL[0], is increased by one. The reactor number is recorded in LL[1] to identify the last reactor started.

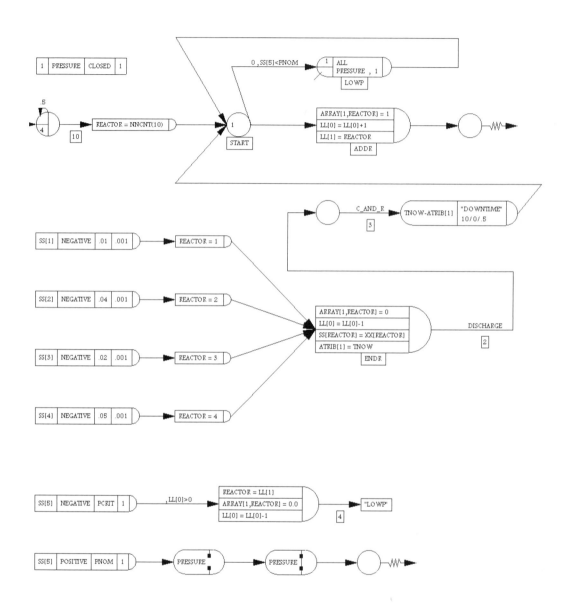

Figure 10-12 Network model for chemical reaction process.

When reactor I is busy, its concentration level is modeled by a continuous variable SS[I] which is defined in accordance with the equations in function STATE. Thus, the reactor entity is no longer required in the network so it is terminated following the ASSIGN node at which the appropriate status changes are made.

An entity will be recreated when the concentration level of a reactor decreases below its prescribed batch-ending threshold. For each reactor, the value of its concentration level crossing this threshold value is modeled at a DETECT node as shown in Figure 10-12. When the crossing is detected, a reactor entity is created and routed to an ASSIGN node where the reactor number is assigned. At ASSIGN node ENDR, the status of the reactor is changed to idle and the number of reactors busy is decreased by 1. The initial concentration of the reactor is reset by the statement SS[REACTOR] = XX[REACTOR].

To record the time the reactor starts its down period, ATRIB[1] is set equal to TNOW. Activities 2 and 3 model the discharge and clean and repair activities. Statistics on the discharge and clean and repair time are then collected at the COLCT node. The reactor entity is then routed to the GOON node START and the process is reapplied.

A DETECT node is used to monitor the surge pressure. When the surge pressure crosses the critical pressure, PCRIT, in the negative direction, an entity is routed to an ASSIGN node where the last reactor started, LL[1], is made idle. The entity created at the DETECT node is then used to represent the reactor made idle by routing it to the AWAIT node LOWP. The last DETECT node shown in Figure 10-12 is used to determine when the surge pressure crosses the nominal pressure in a positive direction. This state event opens the gate PRESSURE which allows all reactor entities waiting in file 1 to be routed to the GOON node START. The gate PRESSURE is then closed so that new arrivals to the AWAIT node LOWP are forced to wait in file 1.

This completes the description of the network model for the chemical reactor process. In Figure 10-13, the control statements for the model are provided. The CONTINUOUS statement shows that there are five differential equations and no state equations. The minimum step size is 0.001 days and the maximum step size is 0.1 days. The ARRAY statement establishes the status of each reactor as idle at the beginning of the simulation. The EQUIVALENCE statement allows for the use of names in the network model. The INTLC statement initializes the variables associated with the model. The concentration of the four reactors and the system pressure are plotted through the use of a RECORD statement. The nominal and critical pressure levels will also be plotted. The INIT statement indicates that a 300 day simulation run is desired. The network statements given in Figure 10-14 describe the flow of entities as presented in Figure 10-12.

```
;
;   Control Statements
;
GEN,"PRITSKER","CHEM REACTOR",1/1/1996;
LIMITS,28,-1,-1,1,1,-1;
TIMST,1,LL[0],"NO. BUSY REACT";
TIMST,2,SS[5],"SURGE PRESSURE";
CONTINUOUS,5,0,.001,.1,.1;
ARRAY,1,4,{ 0, 0, 0, 0 };
EQUIVALENCE,{{REACTOR,LTRIB[1]},{DISCHARGE,EXPON(1)}};
EQUIVALENCE,{{PNOM, XX[7]}, {PCRIT, XX[8]}, {C_AND_R, RNORM(1,.5)}};
;
;   XX(I) = INITIAL CONCENTRATION FOR REACTOR I, I=1,4
;   LL[0] = NUMBER OF BUSY REACTORS
;   LL[1] = LAST REACTOR STARTED, XX(7) = NOMINAL PRESSURE
;   XX(8) = CRITICAL PRESSURE, XX(9) = FCOMP, XX(10)=RTV
;   XX(21:24) = REACTION CONSTANTS 1-4
;   XX(25:28) = VOLUME OF REACTORS 1-4
;
INTLC,{ {SS[1], 0.1}, {SS[2], 0.4}, {SS[3], 0.2}, {SS[4], 0.5},
   { SS[5], 500 } };
INTLC,{ {XX[1], 0.1}, {XX[2], 0.4}, {XX[3], 0.2}, {XX[4], 0.5} };
INTLC,{ { XX[7], 150 }, { XX[8], 100 }, { XX[9], 4.352 }, { XX[10],
   118.03 } };
INTLC,{ {XX[21], 0.03466}, {XX[22], 0.00866}, {XX[23], 0.01155},
   { XX[24], 0.00770 } };
INTLC,{ {XX[25], 10}, {XX[26], 15}, {XX[27], 20}, {XX[28], 25} };
;
RECORD,,out.raw,TNOW,"TIME",{ EXCEL },,0,20,,{{   SS[1], "CONC 1" },
   { SS[2], "CONC 2" },{   SS[3], "CONC 3" },{   SS[4], "CONC 4" },
   { SS[5], "PRESSURE" },{   PNOM, "PNOM" },{   PCRIT, "PCRIT" }};
INIT,0,300;
;
  NETWORK;
FIN;
```

Figure 10-13 Control statements for chemical reaction process.

Summary of Results. The Visual SLAM Summary Report for this example is given in Figure 10-15. The statistics on downtime show that 282 maintenance operations were completed in the 300 hour simulation. For the 282 observations, the average downtime is 1.955 hours, which is not statistically different from the expected value of 2 hours. The statistics for time-persistent variables indicate that the average number of busy reactors is 1.8 and the average surge pressure is 357.1 psia.

```
GATE, ,PRESSURE,CLOSED,{1};
    CREATE,.5, , ,4;                          CREATE INITIAL BATCHES
      ACT,10;
    ASSIGN,{ { REACTOR, NNCNT(10) } };   ASSIGN REACTOR NUMBER
START: GOON,1;
      ACT, , ,SS[5]<PNOM,"LOWP";          IF PRESSURE<PNOM, GO TO LOWP
      ACTIVITY, , , ,"ADDR";              ELSE TO ADDR
LOWP: WAIT,1,{{PRESSURE,1}};              WAIT HERE IF PRESSURE TOO LOW
      ACTIVITY, , , ,"START";               TO START A BATCH
ADDR: ASSIGN,{{ARRAY[1,REACTOR],1},{LL[0],
          LL[0]+1},{LL[1],REACTOR}};   TURN ON REACTOR
    TERM;;
    DETECT,SS[1],NEGATIVE,.01,.001; STOP REACTOR 1: BATCH COMPLETE
    ASSIGN,{ { REACTOR, 1 } };
      ACT, , , ,"ENDR";
ENDR: ASSIGN,{{ARRAY[1,REACTOR],0},{LL[0],LL[0]-1},
      {SS[REACTOR],XX[REACTOR]},{ATRIB[1],TNOW}};
      ACT,2,DISCHARGE, , ,"DISCHARGE";
    GOON;
      ACT,3,C_AND_R, , , ,"CLEAN&RECHRG";
    COLCT, ,TNOW-ATRIB[1],"DOWNTIME",10,0,.5;
      ACTIVITY, , , ,"START";
  ;
    DETECT,SS[2],NEGATIVE,.04,.001;      STOP REACTOR 2: BATCH COMPLETE
    ASSIGN,{ { REACTOR, 2 } };
      ACT, , , ,"ENDR";
    DETECT,SS[3],NEGATIVE,.02,.001;      STOP REACTOR 3: BATCH COMPLETE
    ASSIGN,{ { REACTOR, 3 } };
      ACT, , , ,"ENDR";
    DETECT,SS[4],NEGATIVE,.05,.001;      STOP REACTOR 4: BATCH COMPLETE
    ASSIGN,{ { REACTOR, 4 } };
      ACTIVITY, , , ,"ENDR";
    DETECT,SS[5],NEGATIVE,PCRIT,1;         STOP LAST REACTOR STARTED IF
      ACT, , ,LL[0]>0;                      SURGE TANK PRESSURE FALLS
  ;                                       BELOW CRITICAL PRESSURE
    ASSIGN,{{REACTOR,INT(LL[1])},
       {ARRAY[1,REACTOR],0.0},{LL[0],LL[0]-1}};
      ACT,4, , ,"LOWP", ,"INTERRUPT";
    DETECT,SS[5],POSITIVE,PNOM,1;    ALLOW REACTORS TO PROCEED WHEN
    OPEN,PRESSURE;                        SURGE TANK PRESSURE RETURNS TO
    CLOSE,PRESSURE;                  NOMINAL PRESSURE
    TERM;
    END;
```

Figure 10-14 Network statement model for chemical reaction process.

From the file statistics, it is seen that on the average 0.298 reactors are waiting for surge pressure to build up and that the average waiting time for a reactor is approximately 0.384 hours. At the end of the simulation, there were no reactors waiting but during the simulation as many as 3 reactors are waiting for the gate PRESSURE to open.

```
** AweSim SUMMARY REPORT **
Simulation Project : CHEM REACTOR
  Modeler : PRITSKER
  Date : 1/1/1995
  Scenario : EX102
  Run number 1 of 1
  Current simulation time    : 300.000000
  Statistics cleared at time : 0.000000

            ** OBSERVED STATISTICS REPORT for scenario EX102 **

         Label        Mean      Standard   Number of   Minimum    Maximum
                      Value     Deviation  Observations  Value      Value

DOWNTIME              1.955      0.933        282        0.120      5.639

          ** TIME-PERSISTENT STATISTICS REPORT for scenario EX102 **

         Label      Mean    Standard   Minimum   Maximum    Time     Current
                    Value   Deviation   Value     Value    Interval   Value

NO. BUSY REACT     1.825     0.823     0.000     4.000    300.000    0.000
SURGE PRESSURE   357.119   331.306    49.478  1694.927    300.000  914.522

            ** FILE STATISTICS REPORT for scenario EX102 **

   File    Label or     Average   Standard   Maximum   Current   Average
  Number   Input Location Length  Deviation   Length    Length   Wait Time

    1      GAT. PRESSURE   0.298    0.555        3         0       0.384

            ** ACTIVITY STATISTICS REPORT for scenario EX102 **

Activity   Label or      Average   Standard   Entity   Maximum    Current
Number   Input Location Utilization Deviation Count  Utilization Utilization

  10     INITIAL BATCHES   0.000     0.000      4        1          0
  2      DISCHARGE         0.949     0.878     284       4          2
  3      CLEAN&RECHRG      0.918     0.838     282       3          2
  4      INTERRUPT         0.000     0.000     167       1          0

            ** GATE STATISTICS REPORT for scenario EX102 **

   Gate        Gate       Current    Percent
  Number      Label       Status     of Time
                                      Open
    1        PRESSURE      CLOSED     0.000

** STATE VARIABLE REPORT **

Variable       SS[]                DD[]
 Index     Current Value       Current Value

     0          0.000               0.000
     1          0.100               0.000
     2          0.400               0.000
     3          0.200               0.000
     4          0.500               0.000
     5        914.522             513.667
```

Figure 10-15 Visual SLAM Summary Report for chemical reaction model.

The activity statistics indicate there is about 1 reactor in the discharge and clean and repair activities. Specifically, the average number of reactors in the discharge operation is 0.949 and the average in cleaning and repair is 0.918. Since there is no resource restriction for discharge and clean and repair operations, the reactors could proceed in these activities in parallel. In fact, 4 reactors were discharged simultaneously during the simulation run and 3 reactors were cleaned and repaired simultaneously. If a restriction is placed on the number of concurrent cleaning and repair activities, then a decrease in the number of batches processed, 286, could be expected. The number of batches processed is the sum of the number of discharge operations plus the number of reactors currently being discharged and cleaned. Activity 4 in the network represents the detection of a surge pressure decreasing below the critical value which causes an interruption in the processing of a reactor. In this simulation, 167 entities traversed activity 4. This represents a large number of interruptions of the chemical reaction process and indicates that further design may be needed to eliminate some of the starting and stopping of reactors.

By dividing the average number of reactors in each state by the number of reactors in the system, we can obtain the percentage of time that reactors are in each possible state. This is shown below.

Possible State	Percent of Reactors in the State
Operating (from time-persistent statistics)	46
Waiting (from file statistics)	7
Downtime (from activity statistics)	47

With this type of information, a detailed assessment of the operation of the four reactors coupled through the surge tank can be made.

As expected, statistics on the gate PRESSURE show the percent of time opened as zero because the gate is closed immediately after it is opened. Figure 10-15 also provides the state and derivative variable values at the end of the simulation. In the model, the concentration level for a reactor is set to its initial concentration level while the reactor is being discharged and cleaned. This is done for plot display purposes. Thus, at the end of the simulation, all reactors have concentration levels at the initial amount. Surge pressure is 914.5 psia and increasing at a rate of 513.7 psia/hr. The numerical integration algorithm is sensitive to compiler accuracy, so results may vary slightly depending on the computer system on which a model including derivative equations is run.

Figure 10-16 shows plots of the concentration levels for each reactor and the normalized surge pressure using a default record interval. From the plots, it is seen that only reactor 1 is on initially and that pressure rose rapidly until reactor 2 is turned on at time 0.5. Reactor 1 is turned off because of a batch completion at about 0.7 hours. For display purposes, the concentration levels are plotted at their initial values while the reactors are off.

Beginning with the start of reactor 3 at time 1.0, surge tank pressure fell rapidly. There is an obvious change in rate in the pressure curve at time 1.5 when reactor 4 is started. Pressure first went critical at about 2.0 hours causing reactor 4 to be stopped since it was the last one started. At time 2.3, pressure increases above nominal and reactor 4 is restarted which quickly drives the pressure down again to the critical level at time 2.4. From Figure 10-16, it is seen how the controls and operating policies affect the batch time and batch processing. In addition, it shows that the length of the downtime can have a significant impact on the utilization of the reactors.

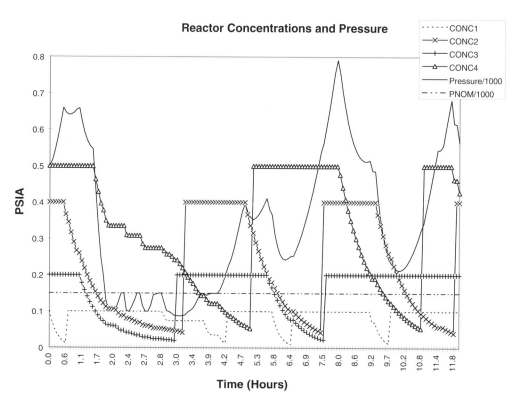

Figure 10-16 Plot of reactor concentrations over time.

To graphically see the variation of downtime, Figure 10-17 shows the AweSim histogram for downtime. This histogram shows a range of downtimes from a half hour to a downtime greater than five hours. The histogram illustrates that the downtime has a Poisson/normal shape as was expected since downtime is the sum of two random variables, one of which is normally distributed and the other exponentially distributed. Since the mean value of both distributions is one, the expected downtime is 2.0 hours with a variance equal to the sum of the variances of the individual components.

This example further illustrates the concepts in a combined network-continuous simulation. The summary reports and plots demonstrate the different types of information that can be obtained from a simulation of a combined model.

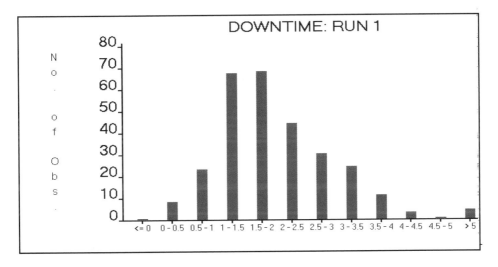

Figure 10-17 Histogram of downtime of reactors.

10.9 CHAPTER SUMMARY

In this chapter the concept of a state variable is introduced and the procedures for writing differential and difference equations in function STATE are described. The interface between a network model and state events is through the DETECT node. When a DETECT node establishes that a state event has occurred, the DETECT node is released and an entity is put into the network. A tanker refinery model is presented in which the flow of the tanker through operations is modeled in network form and the amount of crude oil in a tanker and storage tank is characterized by state variables. A second example involving the modeling of chemical reactors is presented. Pressure is modeled as a continuous variable and discharge, maintenance and recharge operations are modeled using network concepts. The framework provided by Visual SLAM to develop these combined network-continuous models involves only a few new constructs.

10.10 EXERCISES

10-1.   For the tanker refinery problem, assume that the rate of input to the storage tank decreases exponentially from the nominal value by the factor $1-e^{-x/5}$ where $x=SS[1]/150$. Determine the effects on the system due to this change in flow rate.

10-2.   For Example 10-1, develop equations that make the flow rate from tanker to storage tank a function of the level of crude in the tanker, the level of crude in the storage tank, and the viscosity of the crude in the tanker. Develop the code for function STATE to simulate the developed flow equations.

10-3.   For Example 10-1, it has been proposed that offshore unloading docks be built for unloading tankers at Seattle. Three such docks have been proposed, each of which can process at a rate two-thirds that of the current dock. Compare system operation between the three offshore unloading docks operating on only 1 shift versus the current unloading dock operating on a 3-shift basis.

10-4.   For the problem stated in Example 10-1, an elaboration of the refinery is to be made. Consider that the refinery consists of four phases, the first of which is processing. Crude is taken from the initial storage tank and processed in a processing unit at a rate of 150 tb/day. After processing, the material is stored in an intermediate storage tank (phase 2), after which it goes through a filtering unit (phase 3). The rate of filtering is dependent on the conditions of the filter. A filter has an expected life of 30 days. Initially, when the filter is new, the filter rate is 200 tb/day. The rate of flow through the filter decreases linearly until it is 100 tb/day after 30 days. The time to replace a filter is exponentially distributed with a mean of 0.5 day. The fourth phase of the refinery is a finished product storage tank. The finished product is removed from the tank according to the demand for the product, which is cyclic over an approximately 90-day period with a mean of 150 tb/day. All other characteristics of the system are identical to those presented in Example 10-1 except that the unloading dock works on a 24-hour schedule. Simulate the above system for 200 days, using different filter replacement policies to obtain the output requested in Example 10-1 and the following quantities: processor utilization, filter utilization, amount in intermediate storage tank, amount in final storage tank, and percentage of time that demand is lost. Initial conditions for the simulation are that the raw material storage tank is 50% full, the intermediate tank is 60% full, and the final storage tank is 40% full. The capacity of each storage tank is 2000 tb.

10-5.   For the tanker problem, discuss the changes necessary to model the following embellishments:

(a) Introduce a new super tanker into the fleet arriving empty at Valdez, Alaska on day 70. The new tanker has a capacity of 450 tb. The travel times for the super tanker are distributed according to the triangular distribution with a mode equal to the mean of the regular tankers. All other characteristics for the super tanker remain the same. Assume minimum and maximum travel times of 0.9 and 1.2 of the modal value, respectively.

(b) Retire the first three tankers that complete a round trip following the introduction of the new super tanker.

(c) Cause the super tanker to have priority over other tankers waiting for unloading at Seattle.

(d) The super tanker's unloading rate is a function of the level of crude in the super tanker, that is, dx/dt=-x where x is the amount of crude in the super tanker in thousands of barrels (tb).

10-6.   For the chemical reaction process described in Example 10-2, assume that the conditions under which reactors may be started when the surge tank pressure exceeds 150 psi are changed to allow only one reactor to start for each increase of 50 psi above the critical pressure. In addition, suppose that it is required to have a maintenance man available to clean the reactor. Rewrite the program under the condition that only one maintenance man is available and reactors requiring cleaning and recharging must wait if the maintenance man is busy. Determine the effect on throughput of the new control and requirement to have a maintenance man perform the cleaning and recharging.

10-7.   For Example 10-2, solve the differential equations in terms of the initial conditions and rewrite the simulation program to use the derived solution.

10-8.   A machine tool processes two different types of parts. The time between arrivals of Type 1 parts is triangularly distributed with a mode of 30 minutes, a minimum of 20 minutes, and a maximum of 50 minutes. The interarrival time of Type 2 parts is a sample from a triangular distribution with a mode of 50 minutes, a minimum of 35 minutes, and a maximum of 60 minutes. Processing time for Type 1 parts is exponentially distributed with a mean of 20 minutes. For Type 2 parts processing time is a sample from a uniform distribution with a minimum of 15 minutes and a maximum of 20 minutes. Processing time includes an inspection of the completed part. Fifteen percent of the parts fail inspection and return to the end of the queue of parts awaiting processing. Assume that parts which fail inspection have a rework time equal to 90% of the previous processing time. The machine tool tends to breakdown after 8 to 8 1/2 hours of use. That is, the rate of wear on the tool is dependent on the status of the machining operation (zero if idle, one if operating). When a breakdown occurs, processing stops and the part currently being processed returns to the end of the queue to be reworked. Repair time is normally distributed with a mean of 30 minutes and a standard deviation of 8 minutes. If the number of parts awaiting processing reaches four units, the processing time is decreased by 10%. (The machine operator works faster in an attempt to catch up.) In this event, the failure rate increases by 10%. When the number in the queue decreases to one unit, processing time and failure rate return to normal levels. Develop a Visual SLAM model to represent this situation, collecting statistics on the time spent in the system by a part. Simulate the system for 2400 minutes.

10.11 REFERENCES

1. Fehlberg, E., "Low-Order Classical Runge-Kutta Formulas with Step-Size Control and Their Application to Some Heat Transfer Problems," NASA Report TR R-315, Huntsville, Alabama, April 15, 1969.
2. Hurst, N. R., GASP IV: A Combined Continuous/Discrete FORTRAN based Simulation Language, Unpublished Ph.D. Thesis, Purdue University, Indiana, 1973.
3. Hurst, N. R. and A. A. B. Pritsker, "Simulation of a Chemical Reaction Process Using GASP IV," *SIMULATION*, Vol. 21, 1973, pp. 71-75.
4. Pritsker, A. A. B., *The GASP IV Simulation Language*, John Wiley, 1974.
5. Shampine, L. F., and R. C. Allen, Jr., *Numerical Computing: An Introduction*, W. B. Saunders, 1973.
6. Shampine, L. F. et al., "Solving Non-Stiff Ordinary Differential Equations--The State of the Art," *SIAM Review*, Vol. 18, 1976, pp. 376-411.

CHAPTER 11VB

Discrete Event Simulation
Using Visual Basic

11.1   INTRODUCTION

The network orientation presented in the previous chapters is a valuable approach to modeling a large class of systems. For systems requiring flexibility beyond that afforded by the network orientation, the discrete event orientation provides a general approach to simulation modeling. In this chapter, we describe and illustrate the basic concepts and procedures employed in constructing discrete event simulation models using Visual Basic functions within Visual SLAM.

11.2   DISCRETE EVENT ORIENTATION

The concepts of discrete event modeling were introduced in Chapter 2. The world view embodied in a discrete event orientation consists of modeling a system by describing the changes that occur in the system at discrete points in time. An isolated point in time where the state of the system may change is called an "event time" and the associated logic for processing the changes in state is called an "event." A discrete event model of a system is constructed by defining the event types that can occur and then modeling the logic associated with each event type. A dynamic portrayal of the system is produced by making the changes in states according to the logic of each event in a time-ordered sequence.

The state of a system in a discrete event model is similar to that of a network model and is represented by variables and by entities which have attributes and which belong to files. The state of the model is initialized by specifying initial values for the variables employed in the simulation, by creating the initial entities and by the initial scheduling of events. During execution of the simulation, the model moves from state to state as entities engage in activities. In discrete event simulation, system status changes only occur at the beginning of an activity when something is started or at the end of the activity when something is completed. Events are used to model the start and completion of activities.

The concept of an event which takes place instantaneously at a point in time and either starts or ends an activity is a crucial one. This relationship is depicted in Figure 11-1. Time does not advance within an event and the system behavior is simulated by state changes that occur as events happen.

When an event occurs, the state of the model can change in four ways: by altering the value of one or more variables; by altering the number of entities present; by altering the values assigned to one or more attributes of an entity; or by altering the relationships that exist among entities through file manipulations. Methods are available within Visual SLAM for accomplishing each of these changes. Note that an event can occur in which a decision is made not to change the state of the model. Schruben has developed a graphic methodology for portraying events and the conditions which define the relations between events (4).

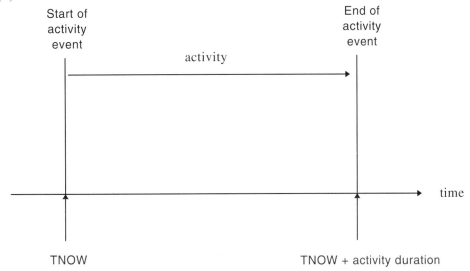

Figure 11-1   Relationship between activities and events.

Events are scheduled to occur at a prescribed time during the simulation. Events have attributes and are maintained in chronological order in a file. For example, when scheduling an end-of-service event, the attributes of the customer undertaking service are part of the event and are then made available at the time of the end-of-service event processing. Thus, if an entity undertakes a series of activities with the end of each activity represented by an event, the attributes of that entity will be associated with each event that is processed.

11.2.1   Event Model of a Queueing Situation

To illustrate the concepts involved in discrete event modeling, consider a bank with one teller where it is desired to obtain statistics on the time each customer spends in the system. Customers arrive at the system, wait for the teller, undergo service, and depart the system. For simplicity, if a customer is waiting, it will be assumed that there is no time delay between the time the service ends for one customer and begins for the next waiting customer. The states of the system will be measured by the number of customers in the system and the status of the teller. Two event types can be used to model the changes in system state: a customer arrival event and an end-of-service event. As a modeler, one must decide on the events that model the system. Here we assume all significant changes in system status can occur only at the arrival time of a customer or at the time that a service ends. In this model, it is assumed that the state of the system does not change between occurrences of these event times.

There is one activity in the model of this system consisting of the service activity. The service activity for a customer begins at either the time of arrival of the customer or at the time that the teller completes service for another customer. Therefore, the starting time for the service activity can be either in the customer arrival event or in the end-of-service event. The ending time for the service activity triggers the end-of-service event.

In constructing the event logic for this example, we employ the variable BUSY to describe the status of the teller where a value of 1 denotes busy and a value of 0 denotes idle. Customers are represented as entities with one attribute denoting the arrival time of the customer. This attribute is used in the model for collecting statistics on the time in the system for each customer in a fashion similar to the mark time employed in network modeling. The model employs a file ranked first-in, first-out (FIFO) for storing entities representing customers waiting for service when the teller is busy. The state of the model at any instant in time is defined by the value of the variable BUSY, location of the customer, the entities and attribute values of the entities.

The initialization logic for this example is depicted in Figure 11-2. The variable BUSY is set equal to 0 to indicate that the teller is initially idle. The arrival event corresponding to the first customer is scheduled to occur at time 0. Thus, the initial status of the system is empty and idle with the first customer scheduled to arrive at time 0.

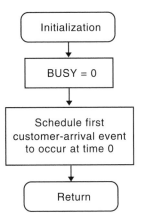

Figure 11-2   Initialization logic for bank teller problem.

The logic for the customer arrival event is depicted in Figure 11-3. The first action which is performed is the scheduling of the next arrival to occur at the current time plus the time between arrivals. Thus, each arrival will cause another arrival to occur at some later time during the simulation. In this way only one arrival event is scheduled to occur at any one time; however, a complete sequence of arrivals is generated.† The first attribute of the arrival entity associated with the event is then set equal to TNOW to mark the arrival time of the customer to the system. A test is then made on the status of the teller to determine if the service activity can begin or if the entity representing the customer must be placed in a file to wait for the teller. If service can begin, the variable BUSY is set equal to one, the end-of-service event for the current customer is scheduled and the event processing is completed. Otherwise, the entity and its attributes are placed in the file representing waiting customers and the event processing is completed.

---

† The next arrival event could also be read from an input device which contains an "historical" sequence of events. In this case, we refer to the simulation model as being "trace or data driven." Of course, the historical sequence could have been generated by a separate simulation model.

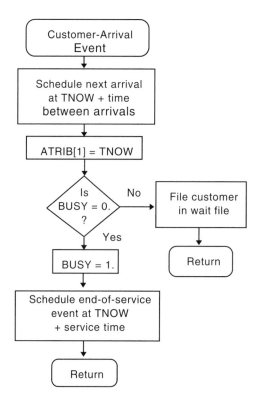

Figure 11-3 Customer arrival event logic for bank teller problem.

At each end-of-service event, statistics are collected on the time in the system for the customer completing service. The first waiting customer, if any, is removed from the wait file and placed into service. The logic for the end-of-service event is depicted in Figure 11-4. The variable TSYS, corresponding to the time in the system for this customer, is computed as TNOW - ATRIB[1]. Since ATRIB[1] was previously assigned the arrival time of the customer, TSYS is the elapsed time between the arrival and departure of the customer on which service was completed. A test is then made to determine if there are customers waiting for service. If not, the status of the teller is made idle by setting BUSY equal to 0 and the event processing is completed. Otherwise, the first customer entity is removed from the wait file. Processing of the customer is modeled by scheduling an end-of-service event to occur at the current time plus the service time.

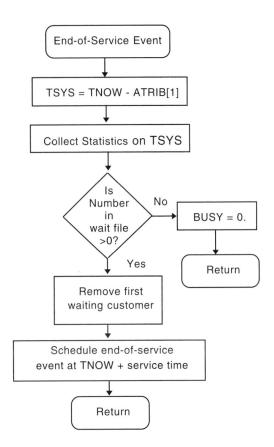

Figure 11-4   End-of-service event logic for the bank teller problem.

This simple example illustrates the basic concepts of discrete event simulation modeling. Variables and entities with their attributes and file memberships make up the static structure of a simulation model. They describe the state of the system but not how the system operates. The events specify the logic which controls the changes that occur at specific instants of time. The dynamic behavior is then obtained by sequentially processing events and recording status values at event times. Since status is constant between events, the complete dynamic system behavior is obtained in this manner. This example illustrates several important types of functions which must be performed in simulating discrete models. The primary functional requirement in discrete event simulation involves scheduling events, placing events in chronological order and advancing time. Other functional requirements which are illustrated by this example include mechanisms for file manipulations, statistics collecting and reporting and random sample generation. In Section 11-3, we describe the use of Visual SLAM for performing these and other functions in discrete event simulation modeling. First, we discuss how discrete-event modeling can be used to study inventory systems.

11.2.2 Event Modeling of Inventory Systems

To illustrate the generality of the event modeling approach, we now consider the analysis of inventory systems and indicate the event modeling procedures. All inventory systems involve the storage of particular items for future sale or use. Demands are imposed on an inventory by customers seeking supplies of items. A company must establish an inventory policy that specifies when an order for additional items should be placed (or manufactured), and how many of the items should be ordered at each order time. When the items stored in inventory are discrete units, simulation of the inventory system using the next event philosophy is quite natural. The primary system variables are the number of units in storage, called the *inventory-on-hand*, and the number of units that are theoretically on the books of the company, called the *inventory position*. The inventory position is equal to the inventory-on-hand, plus the number of units on order (the number due-in), minus the number of units that have been backordered by customers (the number due-out). The inventory-on-hand represents the number of units available to be sold to customers. The inventory position represents the number of units that are or will be available to the company for potential sale. Inventory decisions regarding when to place an order and how much to order are normally based on the inventory position. Other attributes associated with inventory situations are: the number of units sold, the number of orders placed, the number of lost sales and/or the number of backorders, and the number of times the inventory position is reviewed to make a decision whether to place an order.

The events associated with an inventory situation at which these attributes could change their value are: a demand by a customer for the items in inventory, a review of the status of the inventory position to determine if an order should be placed, the receipt of goods from the distributor to be placed in inventory and the satisfying of the customers' demands for the item. Each of these events could be modeled as a distinct event. However, several of the above can occur at the same point in time. When this happens, it is efficient to combine the events into a single event. For example, the satisfying of a customer demand would normally take place either when the customer demand is placed or when a shipment of units is received from the distributor. When this is done, the modeler assumes that the time delay in delivering a unit to a customer has an insignificant effect on the expected cost or profit associated with the inventory situation.

Customer demand events are normally modeled by specifying the time between customer demands. In this way, each demand event can be used to specify the time of the next demand. Then only the first demand event, which starts the demand process, and the time between demands would need to be specified.

Two types of review procedures to determine if an order should be placed are common in industry. A *periodic review procedure* specifies that a review should be performed at equally spaced points in time, for example, every month. The other review procedure involves the examination of the inventory position every time it decreases. This type of review is called *transaction reporting* and involves keeping a running log of the inventory position. When a transaction reporting review procedure is being studied, no separate review event is required since the inventory position can only be decreased when a customer demand occurs. Thus, the review procedure can be incorporated into the customer demand event.

The event involving the receipt of units from the distributor does not change the inventory position since the inventory position was increased when the units were ordered. However, the inventory-on-hand and the number of backorders could change when the receipt event occurs. The time at which the receipt event occurs is based on the time at which it was decided to place an order (at a review time) plus the time for processing the order and shipping the units. The time from the placing of the order to the receipt of the units is called the *lead time.*

The above general discussion of events that can occur in an inventory situation provides a general framework for simulating any inventory system. To obtain a simulation using Visual SLAM, it would only be necessary to write subroutines for each of the events required by the specific inventory situation. The points in time at which the individual events occur would be handled automatically by Visual SLAM using the time between events as specified by the user in the appropriate event routines. The user would schedule the next demand event (in a subroutine representing all demand events) and the receipt of units, if it was decided that an order was to be placed.

Of major importance in this modeling of systems is the absence of the need to specify the details about the interdemand time distribution, the lead time distribution, the number of units requested by a customer at a demand point, and so forth, when discussing the overall procedure for simulating an inventory system. This information is only important when simulating a specific system.

The Visual SLAM organizational structure for discrete event simulation allows the modeling of systems prior to data collection and, in fact, helps to specify the data required to analyze a system.

11.3   THE DISCRETE EVENT FRAMEWORK OF VISUAL SLAM

To simulate a discrete event model of a system using Visual SLAM, the analyst codes each discrete event as a Visual Basic subroutine. To assist the analyst in this task, Visual SLAM provides a set of support functions for performing all commonly encountered functions such as event scheduling, statistics collection and random sample generation. The advancing of simulated time (TNOW) and the order in which the event routines are processed are controlled by the Visual SLAM executive program. Thus, Visual SLAM relieves the simulation modeler of the task of sequencing events in their proper chronological order.

Each event is assigned a positive integer numeric code called the event code, in the same fashion as the event code defined at an EVENT node. The event code is mapped onto a call to the appropriate event function by subroutine EVENT(Code, Current) where the integer argument Code is the event code and Current is the current entity object. This function is written by the user as was discussed in Chapter 9VB and consists of a Select statement indexed on Code causing a transfer to the appropriate event function. An example of the EVENT routine is depicted in Figure 11-5 for a simulation model with two events consisting of an arrival event coded in function ARVL and assigned event code 1, and an end-of-service event coded in function ENDSV and assigned event code 2 .

```
Public Sub EVENT(Code As Long,Current As VSENTITY)
   Select Case Code
      Case 1
        Call ARVL(Current)   'Logic for Event Code 1 in ARVL
      Case 2
        Call ENDSV(Current) 'Logic for Event Code 2 in ENDSV
   End Select
 End Sub
```

Figure 11-5   Sample subroutine EVENT.

Two additional user-written routines which are commonly employed in discrete event simulation models are functions INTLC and OTPUT discussed in Chapter 9VB. Function INTLC is called by Visual SLAM before each simulation run and is used to set initial conditions and to schedule initial events. Function OTPUT is called at the end of each simulation and is used for end-of-simulation processing such as printing specific results for the simulation project.

The Visual SLAM next-event logic for simulating discrete event models is depicted in Figure 11-6. The Visual SLAM processor begins by reading the Visual SLAM input statements, if any, and initializing Visual SLAM variables. A call is then made to function INTLC which specifies additional initial conditions for the simulation. Visual SLAM has a version of function INTLC so that the user need not include function INTLC if no additional initialization is required. The processor then begins execution of the simulation by removing the first event from the event calendar. Events are ordered on the calendar based on low values of event times. The variable I is set equal to the event code and TNOW is advanced to the event time for the next event. Visual SLAM then calls the user-written subroutine EVENT which in turn calls the appropriate event subroutine. Following execution of the user-written event routine, a test is made to determine if the simulation run is complete. A discrete event simulation is ended if any of the following conditions are satisfied:

1.   TNOW is greater than or equal to TTFIN, the ending time of the simulation;
2.   no events remain on the event calendar for processing; or
3.   the Visual SLAM variable MSTOP has been set in a user-written routine to -1.

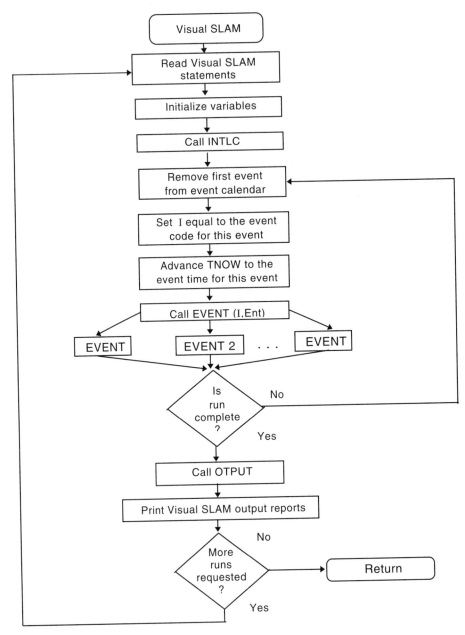

Figure 11-6   Visual SLAM next event logic for simulating discrete event models.

If the run is not complete, the new first event is removed from the event calendar and processing continues. Otherwise, a call is made to Function OTPUT. (As with INTLC, a version of OTPUT is included in Visual SLAM.) After the return from OTPUT, the Visual SLAM Summary Report is printed. A test is then made on the number of runs remaining. If more runs remain, control returns to initialization and the next simulation run is executed. Otherwise, a return is made from the Visual SLAM processor back to the main program.

The above description provides an overview of the Visual SLAM framework for simulating discrete event models. To write a discrete event simulation program, the user writes a subroutine EVENT(Code,Current) to decipher the event Code and to call the appropriate event function, and event routines to specify the changes that occur at event times. Functions INTLC and OTPUT are written if special initial conditions or end-of-simulation processing is required. Based on this overview of the Visual SLAM discrete event framework, we next describe the functional capabilities provided by Visual SLAM for assisting the analyst in developing the user-written functions. Table 11-1 summarizes the fundamental support functions described in Sections 11.4, 11.5 and 11.6.

11.4   SCHEDULING EVENTS

The Visual SLAM processor completely relieves the user of the responsibility for chronologically ordering the events on an event calendar. The user simply schedules events to occur, and Visual SLAM causes each event to be processed at the appropriate time in the simulation. Events are scheduled by calling the function **SCHDL(Event As Integer, Ent as VSENTITY,Time As Double) As VSENTRY**. A VSENTRY object holds an entity's file "placeholder" information while the entity is a file. The properties of a VSENTRY object include:

VSENTRY Property	*Definition*
Entity As VSENTITY	VSENTITY object for this entry
Next As VSENTRY	The entry following this one
Prev As VSENTRY	The entry preceding this one

Table 11-1. Fundamental Visual Basic Functions and Subroutines of Visual SLAM

User Written

Public Sub EVENT(Code As Long, Current As VSENTITY)

    To process event type Code for the entity whose object is Current.

Public Function INTLC(Run As Long) As Long

    To perform initialization for run number Run. Return True if the Run should be executed, False otherwise.

Public Function OTPUT(Run As Long) As Long

    To perform special end-of-run processing for run number Run. Return True if the next run should be made, False otherwise.

Provided by Visual SLAM

VSLAM Methods

COLCT(Value As Double, Collect As Integer) As Integer

    Records the value Value as an observation of the variable Collect.

DefineColct(Collect As Integer, ID As String, NCel As Integer, HLow As Double, _

        Hwid As Double) As Integer

    Defines a new observed statistic with identification number Collect, label ID, and a histogram with NCel cells, lower limit of HLow and cell width of HWid.

    ReturnsTrue if sucessful, False otherwise.

DefineEntity(EntType As Integer) As VSENTITY

    Creates a new entity and initializes its type.

FILEM (File As Integer, Current As VSENTITY) As VSENTRY

    Files the entity Current in file File. Returns the entity's placeholder in the file.

NNQ(File As Integer) As Long

    Returns the number of entries currently in file File.

RMOVE (File As Integer, Rank As Integer) As VSENTITY

    Removes the entity with rank Rank from file File and returns the entity object.

SCHDL(Event As Integer, Current As VSENTITY, Time As Double) As VSENTRY

    Schedules an event of type Event to occur at time TNOW+Time for the entity Current. Returns the placeholder of the event in the event calendar.

VSENTITY Methods

Clone(Type As Integer) As VSENTITY

    Clones the VSENTITY entity and gives it a new entity Type.

Terminate()

    Terminate the VSENTITY entity. The VSENTITY object should be set to Nothing after this function call.

The return value of function SCHDL is the event's "placeholder" object for the event calendar. The parameter Event denotes the event code of the event being scheduled, and Time denotes the number of time units from the current time, TNOW, that the event is to occur. The argument Ent, as with function EVENT, is a pointer to a VSENTITY object holding the attributes of the entity associated with the event. The properties of a VSENTITY object were discussed in Chapter 9VB.

An entity for which an event is to be scheduled is created with the function **DefineEntity(EntType As Integer) As VSENTITY**. The return value is the newly created ENTITY structure. The EntType parameter defines an entity type which is a special attribute that can be used to distinguish different types of entities.

To illustrate the use of functions SCHDL and Define Entity, consider the scheduling of a customer arrival event with event code 1 to occur at the current time plus a sample from an exponential distribution with mean of 5 and using random stream number 1. In addition, the entity representing the customer has its first real attribute value equal to 2.

The coding to accomplish this is as follows:

```
Set Enew =VS.DefineEntity(0)
Enew.ATRIB(1)=2#
Time = VS.EXPON(5.,1)
VS.SCHDL 1,Enew,Time
```

These statements will cause Visual SLAM to invoke the subroutine EVENT(I,Current) at time TNOW + EXPON(5.,1) with I equal to 1 and Current equal to Enew.

Another way to create an entity is to copy its structure from an existing entity with the function **Ent.Clone(Type As Integer) As VSENTITY.** The return value is the newly created VSENTITY object which is a new entity object copied from the entity object called Ent. The special entity type attribute, Type, may be set to be different for this clone.

As an example of the use of the Clone method, suppose that a copy is to be made of the entity object Enew created above, except that the copy should have an entity type of 1. An arrival event is to be scheduled for this entity, to occur at the current time plus a sample from a normal distribution with a mean of 7.5 and a standard deviation of 0.7 using random number stream 1. The following code fragment would accomplish the entity creation and event scheduling.

Set Ecopy = Enew.Clone(1)
Time = VS.RNORM(7.5,0.7,2)
 VS.SCHDL 1, Ecopy, Time

When an entity leaves the model, the VSENTITY object located at Ent is terminated with the statement **Ent.Terminate.**

11.5   FILE MANIPULATIONS

Entities which are grouped together because of a relationship are maintained in files. In network models, files are used to maintain entities waiting at QUEUE, AWAIT and PREEMPT nodes. Files are used extensively in discrete event simulation models and they can be shared with network models, that is, file 1 can be associated with a QUEUE node and also be accessed in a discrete event function. A file provides the mechanism for storing the attributes of an entity in a prescribed ranking with respect to other entities in the file.

In Visual SLAM, files are distinguished by integer numbers assigned to the files by the modeler. Visual SLAM automatically collects statistics on each file and provides the function NNQ(IFILE) which returns the number of entities in file IFILE. For example, NNQ(2) denotes the number of entities in file 2.

Associated with a file is a ranking criterion which specifies the procedure for ordering entities within the file. Thus, each entity in a file has a rank which specifies its position in the file relative to the other members in the file. A rank of one denotes that the entity is the first entry in the file. Possible ranking criterion for files are: first-in, first-out (FIFO); last-in, first-out (LIFO); high-value-first (HVF) based on the value of an expression; and low-value-first (LVF) based on the value of an expression. The ranking criterion for a file used by a network node is assumed to be FIFO unless otherwise specified using the PRIORITY statement described in Chapter 8. Files in a discrete event model may be defined and their ranking criterion specified using the PRIORITY statement. Alternatively, the modeler may create a new file and specifiy its attributes via a function call.

Visual SLAM provides the user with a set of functions for performing all file manipulations which are commonly encountered in discrete event simulations. We now describe the use of these functions for file manipulations where entities are referenced by their rank in the file.

11.5.1 Filing Entities

Function **FILEM(IFILE As Integer,Ent As VSENTITY) As VSENTRY** files an entity into file IFILE. Its return value is the placeholder of the newly filed entity. As an example of the use of function FILEM, the following statements cause an entity to be inserted into file 1 with its first attribute set equal to the current simulation time.

        Ent.ATRIB(1) = VS.TNOW
        VS.FILEM 1,Ent

11.5.2 Removing Entities from Files

Function **RMOVE (IFILE As Integer, Rank As Integer) As VSENTITY** removes an entity with rank Rank from file IFILE and returns the VSENTITY object of the entity just removed. As an example of the use of function RMOVE, the following statement removes the last entity in file 1 and returns the VSENTITY object Job.

        Job = VS.RMOVE(1, NNQ(1))

If the user attempts to remove an entity from file IFILE with rank greater than NNQ(IFILE), a Visual SLAM execution error results. Search functions to locate entities by its placeholder are described in Section 11.14.1.

11.5.3 User-Defined Files

The modeler may create a non-network file simply by using a PRIORITY control statement to define the file's ranking rule. Alternatively, a new file may be created by a call to the function **DefineFile(File As Integer, Label As String, Stats As BOOL,Type As Integer, Max As Integer, OrdCode As Integer, OrdArg As Long, TieCode As Integer, TieArg As Long) As VSFILE.**

Creating a file in this way allows one to give a file a name as well as a number, using the Label argument. The Stats argument, if set to FALSE, will suppress file statistics which would normally be collected. If the argument Max is not zero, then an error message will be given if the number in the file exceeds Max. The ranking rule is defined with the argument Type which is one of the following macro names:

> SUFILE_FIFO for a first-in-first-out ranking
> SUFILE_LIFO for a last-in-first-out ranking
> SUFILE_LIST for a sorted linked list
> SUFILE_HEAP for a sorted heap
> SUFILE_TREE for a sorted binary tree

If Type is not FIFO or LIFO but a sorted list, the modeler may use OrdCode, OrdArg, TieCode and TieArg to write a user-defined sorting algorithm. The return value for DefineFile is a VSFILE object.

Suppose we wish to define file number 4 for arriving customers with a FIFO ranking. Statistics are desired, and the file has no maximum capacity. The following function call would create the file:

DefineFile 4,"ArrivingCustomers", TRUE, SUFILE_FIFO, 0, 0, 0, 0, 0

11.5.4 Functions and Properties for Accessing File and Entry Pointers: MMFE, MMLE, Next and Prev

Entries in a file can be thought of as items on a list, customers in a queue or days on a calendar. The entries stored in a file are considered by Visual SLAM in a logical order, and their order is maintained by their VSENTRY "placeholder" objects. The properties of a VSENTRY object include:

VSENTRY Property	*Description*
Entity As VSENTITY	VSENTITY object for this entry
Next As VSENTRY	The entry following this one
Prev As VSENTRY	The entry preceding this one

A value of Nothing for the Prev or Next property indicates that no predecessor or no successor exists, respectively.

The object of the first entry in file IFILE is obtained by using the function **MMFE(IFILE As Integer) As VSENTRY.** The function **MMLE(IFILE As Integer) As VSENTRY** returns the object of the last entry in file IFILE. Thus the statement Set Ntry=VS.MMLE(3) defines Ntry as the object which is the placeholder of the last entry in file 3.

By knowing the placeholder of the first entry and by accessing the successor of the first entry, we can obtain the placeholder of the second entry. The Next property of a VSENTRY object is used to obtain the placeholder of an entry's successor in a file. In this way it is possible to proceed in a forward direction from a particular entry in a file until the last entry is encountered. The last entry in a file has no successor and, hence, the Next property of the last entry's VSENTRY object is set to Nothing. To search through a file from the last entry, MMLE(IFILE), to the first, the Prev property is used.

As an example of the use of these functions and properties, consider the problem of locating an entry in file 4 whose second integer attribute is equal to seven. We desire to locate the entry that is closest to the beginning of the file. The code for accomplishing this search is shown below.

```
' Search File 4 from the beginning for an entry
    Dim Enext As VSENTRY
    Dim Ent As VSENTITY
     Set Enext=VS.MMFE(4)
    Do While Enext <> Nothing
        Set Ent = Enext.Entity
        If Ent.LTRIB(2)=7 Then Exit Do
        Set Enext = Enext.Next
      Loop
```

In this code, the variable Enext is used to indicate the next entry to be tested for the desired condition. We start with the first entry in file 4 because the search is to start from the beginning of the file. If Enext is Nothing, then there are no entries in the file as function MMFE returns Nothing when the file is empty.

The Entity property is used to obtain the VSENTITY object for the entity whose VSENTRY object is Enext. Given this object, Ent, the second integer attribute of the entity can be accessed. LTRIB(2) for this entity is tested against the value 7 to determine if the prescribed condition is met. If it is, an exit is made from the Do loop. If the condition is not met, the successor entry is obtained through the use of the Next property. Upon exit from the Do loop, if

Enext is not Nothing, then Enext is the VSENTRY object and Ent the VSENTITY object for the desired entity.

If it is desired to search file 4 from the end of the file, then only minor changes are required in the code. The first entry to be tested is established as the last entry in the file, that is, Enext=VS.MMLE(4). In addition, it is necessary to obtain the next entry to be tested by using the Prev property, that is, Set Enext = Enext.Prev.

Several functions which are provided for use in searching a file for a specific entity are discussed in Section 11.13.1.

11.6   STATISTICS COLLECTION

In discrete event simulations, there are two distinct types of statistics: (1) statistics based on observations; and (2) statistics based on time-persistent variables. In this section, we describe the procedures employed in Visual SLAM discrete event simulations for collecting and estimating values associated with these two types of statistics.

11.6.1   Statistics Based on Observations

Statistics based on observations are statistics computed from a finite number of samples. Each sample value is considered as an observation. For example, in the bank teller problem, statistics on the time in the system for each customer are based on observations where each customer processed through the system is considered as one observation. These statistics depend only upon the value of each observation and not upon the time at which each observation is collected.

Each variable for which observation statistics are collected must be defined by the user with a call to the function **DefineColct(Collect As Integer, ID As String, NCe1 as Integer, HLow As Double, HWid As Double) As Integer** where:

Collect is an integer code associated with the variable used to distinguish
   variable types;

ID is an alphanumeric identifier which is printed on the Visual SLAM Summary
  Report to identify the output associated with the variable; and
NCel/HLow/HWid are histogram parameters specifying the number of interior
  cells, the upper limit for the first cell and the width of each cell. If these
  parameters are specified as zero then no histogram is prepared.

As an example, the following function call specifies that observation statistics are
to be collected on variable type 1, the results are to be displayed as TIME IN
SYSTEM, and a histogram is to be generated with 10 interior cells with the upper
limit for the first cell equal to 0 and with interior cell widths of 1.

> VS.DefineColct 1, "TIME IN SYSTEM", 10, 0#, 1#

Observations for each variable type defined by function DefineColct are collected
within the event functions by a call to function **COLCT(XVAL As Double, ICLCT
As Integer) As Integer** where the variable XVAL contains the value of the
observation and ICLCT is the integer code associated with the variable type. For
example, the following statement would cause one observation to be collected on the
variable TSYS which is coded as COLCT variable 1.

> VS.COLCT TSYS,1

Through inputs on the INITIALIZE statement, function COLCT can be used to
obtain statistics over simulation runs. The procedure for accomplishing this
involves not clearing the variables for which statistics over runs are desired. By
calling function COLCT with a value obtained at the end of each run, statistics
over runs are obtained. This call to function COLCT could be made from function
OTPUT. For example, if six collect variables are included in the model and we
specify that up to the 4th variable type should be cleared, then variables with codes
4, 5, and 6 would not be cleared at the end of a run. These three variables can then
be used to store values collected over multiple runs. Specifically, consider the
following definitions:

> VS.DefineColct 1, "V1", 0, 0#, 0#
> VS.DefineColct 2, "V2", 0, 0#, 0#
> VS.DefineColct 3, "V3", 0, 0#, 0#
> VS.DefineColct 4, "A1", 0, 0#, 0#
> VS.DefineColct 5, "A2", 0, 0#, 0#
> VS.DefineColct 6, "A3", 0, 0#, 0#

and the following input statement:

    INT, 0, 480, YES, 4;

This INIT statement specifies that collect variables 1, 2, and 3 should be cleared at the end of each run but collect variables 4, 5, and 6 should not. The following code in function OTPUT will provide observations on the average value of variables collected as V1, V2, and V3.

```
Public Function OTPUT (Run As Long) As Long
Dim I As Integer
For I=1 To  3
    VS.COLCT  VS.CCAVG(I),I + 3
Next I
OTPUT= TRUE
End Function
```

On each summary report printed, statistics based on observations are obtained for the variables A1, A2 and A3 which is the average of the average values for V1, V2 and V3 respectively. Thus, if a summary report is printed for three runs, the average of the three average values obtained for V1 is printed in the row whose descriptor is A1. If ten runs are made, the average of ten average values is obtained.

The above procedure can be used with all Visual SLAM status variables or with user defined variables. In Section 11.9, the functions for obtaining the average of any Visual SLAM status variable are described. In the above example, the function CCAVG was used. Similar functions exist for all other Visual SLAM statistics. As described in Chapter 8, a field on the COLCT node statement allows each COLCT node to have an index code so that the functions described in Section 11.9 can also be used to reference statistics collected at COLCT nodes.

11.6.2   Statistics on Time-Persistent Variables

Statistics on time-persistent variables refer to statistics maintained on variables which have a value defined over a period of time. For example, the variable BUSY in the bank teller example is used to denote the status of the teller over time. The fraction of time that BUSY equals 1 is the teller utilization. Therefore the utilization of the teller would be a time-persistent statistic.

Statistics on time-persistent variables are obtained in Visual SLAM discrete event simulations by the use of the TIMST statements. The TIMST input statement causes time-persistent statistics to be automatically accumulated by the Visual SLAM processor. This relieves the user of the burden of calling a function within the event routines to obtain time-persistent statistics. For example, to invoke time-persistent statistics on the variable XX[1], with the output identified as TELLER BUSY TIME, the user simply includes the following statement as part of the Visual SLAM input.

TIMST, 1, XX[1], TELLER BUSY TIME;

To improve the mnemonics within the coding of the event functions, the Visual Basic Property definition can be employed. For example, time-persistent statistics could be obtained on the Visual Basic variable BUSY by using the TIMST statement described above in conjunction with the following Property definition.

```
Property Get BUSY() As Long
BUSY = VS.XX(1)
End Property
```

To obtain a histogram on a time-persistent variable, values for the number of cells, upper limit of the first cell and a cell width are given in the last fields of the TIMST statement, that is, NCel,HLow,HWid. Each cell of the histogram gives the fraction of time that the time-persistent variable was in the range defined by the cell. For the teller utilization, we can obtain the fraction of time idle or busy in histogram form with the statement.

TIMST, 1, XX[1], TELLER BUSY TIME, 2,0,1;

11.7   VARIABLES

Variables which are employed in a Visual SLAM discrete event simulation model can be of two types: Visual SLAM variables; and user-defined variables. Visual SLAM variables are those defined by the Visual SLAM language. Table 11-2 summarizes the important Visual SLAM variables which are used in discrete event simulation models.

Table 11-2   Definitions of some important discrete event variables.

Variable	Definition
VS.MSTOP	Set by the user to -1 to stop a simulation run before TTFIN.
VS.NNRUN	The number of the current simulation run.
VS.TNOW	The value of current simulated time.
VS.TTBEG	The beginning time of the simulation.
VS.TTFIN	The ending time of the simulation.
VS.LL	The array of user-defined long global variables.
VS.XX	The array of user-defined double global variables.
VS.SZ	The array of user-defined string global variables.

11.8   INPUT STATEMENTS

In discrete event simulation models, input statements are required for specifying a project title, run length, file rankings, monitor events and the like. The input statements employed in discrete event models are identical to those described for network models in Chapter 8. Thus, a discrete event model will typically include a GEN statement, LIMITS statement and FIN statement plus any additional input statements required by the simulation model.

11.9   OUTPUT REPORTS

The results for each simulation run are summarized by the Visual SLAM summary report which is automatically printed by the Visual SLAM processor at the end of each simulation run. The Visual SLAM summary report for discrete event models is identical to that produced for network models with the network statistics omitted, and includes statistics on variables based on observations, statistics on time-persistent variables, file statistics, histograms, and plots. Definitions for the statistical quantities provided by the summary report are provided in Chapter 8.

The Visual SLAM processor also prints a trace report if the TRACE option has been specified using the MONTR statement. The Visual SLAM trace report for discrete-event models includes the event time, the event code, and any variables requested by the MONTR statement. Functions for retrieving values from the summary report writing functions are presented in Section 11.14.3.

11.9.1   Functions for Obtaining Values Associated with Statistical Estimates

Functions have been included in Visual SLAM to allow the user to access information related to statistical estimates during the execution of a simulation model. The first two letters of each function name represent one of the seven types of variables for which statistics are desired. The last three letters of the function name prescribes the statistic of interest. The seven types of variables are: variables based on observation (CC); time-persistent variables (TT); file variables (FF); resource variables (RR); group variables (GR); activity variables (AA); and gate variables (GG). The statistical quantities associated with these variables and their three letter codes are: average value (AVG); standard deviation (STD); maximum observed value (MAX); minimum observed value (MIN); number of observations (NUM); time period over which the time-persistent variable was observed (PRD); time of last change to a time-persistent variable (TLC), and percent of time opened (OPN).

The thirty-five functions included within Visual SLAM to obtain values associated with the variables and statistical quantities are presented in Table 11-2. These functions can be called from any Visual SLAM subprogram and the values can be used for decision making within Visual SLAM models.

The arguments to the Visual SLAM statistical calculation functions are always an integer. File numbers are prescribed for both discrete event and network models and there should be no ambiguity regarding the arguments for the file related functions. For resources, Visual SLAM or the modeler assigns a resource number to each resource block in a network model. This resource number is used as the argument to functions RRAVG, RRAVA, RRSTD, RRMAX, RRPRD, and RRTLC. Group and gate numbering is accomplished in the same manner as resources. For collect variables, numeric values are assigned by the user in discrete event models and by Visual SLAM or by the user in network models (for each COLCT node). If not specified by the user, Visual SLAM assigns a sequential numeric code for each COLCT statement starting with the first number above the highest user-assigned number. Thus, if there are three variables

Table 11-2 Visual SLAM statistical calculation functions.

Function	Description
Statistics for Variable Based on Observations (COLCT)	
CCAVG(ICLCT)	Average value of variable ICLCT.
CCSTD(ICLCT)	Standard deviation of variable ICLCT.
CCMAX(ICLCT)	Maximum value of variable ICLCT.
CCMIN(ICLCT)	Minimum value of varialbe ICLCT.
CCNUM(ICLCT)	Number of observations of variable ICLCT.
Statistics for Time-Persistent Variables (TIMST)	
TTAVG(ISTAT)	Time integrated average of variable ISTAT.
TTSTD(ISTAT)	Standard deviation of variable ISTAT.
TTMAX(ISTAT)	Maximum value of variable ISTAT.
TTMIN(ISTAT)	Minimum value of variable ISTAT.
TTPRD(ISTAT)	Time period for statistics on variable ISTAT.
TTTLC(ISTAT)	Time at which variable ISTAT last changed.
Queue Statistics	
FFAVG(IFILE)	Average number of entities in file IFILE.
FFAWT(IFILE)	Average waiting time in file IFILE.
FFSTD(IFILE)	Standard deviation for file IFILE.
FFMAX(IFILE)	Maximum number of entities in file IFILE.
FFPRD(IFILE)	Time period for statistics on file IFILE.
FFTLC(IFILE)	Time at which number in file IFILE last changed.
Resource Statistics	
RRAVG(IRSC)	Average utilization of resource IRSC.
RRAVA(IRSC)	Average availability of resource IRSC.
RRSTD(IRSC)	Standard deviation of utilization of resource IRSC.
RRMAX(IRSC)	Maximum utilization of resource IRSC.
RRPRD(IRSC)	Time period for statistics on resource IRSC.
RRTLC(IRSC)	Time at which status of resource IRSC last changed.
Activity Statistics	
AAAVG(IACT)	Average utilization of activity IACT
AAMAX(IACT)	Maximum utilization of activity IACT, or maximum busy time if activity IACT is a single-server activity.
AASTD(IACT)	Standard deviation of the utilization of activity IACT.
AATLC(IACT	Time at which the status of activity IACT last changed.
Gate Statistics	
GGOPN(IG)	Percent of time that gate IG was open.
GGTLC(IG)	Time at which the status of gate IG last changed.
Group Statistics	
GRPAVG (IGRP)	Average utilization of group IGRP.
GRPAVA (IGRP)	Average availability of group IGRP.
GRPSTD (IGRP)	Standard deviation of utilization of group IGRP.
GRPMAX (IGRP)	Maximum utilization of group IGRP.
GRPPRD (IGRP)	Time period for statistics on group IGRP.
GRPTLC (IGRP)	Time at which status of group IGRP last changed.

assigned codes 1, 2, and 3 by calls to DefineColct and two COLCT nodes, the average associated with the first COLCT node in the network description would be accessed by the statement

$$AVE = VS.CCAVG(4)$$

For time persistent-statistics, numeric values are assigned by the user or, if defaulted, by Visual SLAM in the order in which the TIMST input statements appear in the input list.

11.10   BUILDING DISCRETE EVENT MODELS

In the preceding sections, we described the discrete event framework of Visual SLAM and a set of subprograms which allows the user to perform the commonly encountered functions in discrete event simulation models. To construct a discrete event simulation model of the bank teller problem, the user must do the following:

1. Write subroutine EVENT to map the user-assigned event codes onto a call to the appropriate event routine.
2. Write function INTLC to initialize the model.
3. Write event routines to model the logic for the events of the model.
4. Prepare the input statements required by the problem.

11.11   ILLUSTRATION 11-1.   SERVING BANK CUSTOMERS

In this section, we illustrate how these Visual SLAM functional capabilities are used in constructing discrete event simulation models by describing the coding of the Visual SLAM discrete event model of the bank teller example. In the coding which follows, we assume that customers arrive at the bank with the time between arrivals given by an exponential distribution with a mean of 20 minutes and that the teller service time is uniformly distributed between 10 and 25 minutes. The operation of the bank teller system is to be simulated for a period of 480 minutes.

The event model of the bank teller problem contains two events: the customer arrival event and the end-of-service event. We will code the logic for the customer arrival event in function ARVL and assign it event code 1. The code for the logic for the end-of-service event will be written in function ENDSV and it will be referenced as event code 2. Thus, function EVENT, shown in Figure 11-7, is as depicted previously in Figure 11-5.

```
Public Sub EVENT(Code As Long, Customer As VSENTITY )
  Select Case Code
      Case 1
          Call ARVL (Customer)    ' Arrival event
      Case 2
          Call ENDSV (Customer) ' Departure event
  End Select
End Sub
```

Figure 11-7   Subroutine EVENT for bank teller problem.

The initialization logic for the bank teller problem is coded in function INTLC as depicted in Figure 11-8. LL(1) is set to zero to denote that the teller is initially idle. Next, the customer entity is created by function DefineEntity and the customer arrival event which has an event code of 1 is scheduled onto the event calendar to occur after 0.0 time units.

A set of observed statistics and a file for waiting customers are created. Collect variable 1 is given the label TIME IN SYSTEM and is to generate a histogram of 10 interior cells with the upper limit of the first cell at 0.0 and each interior cell width set to 4.0. File 1 is given the label "ArrivingCustomers", is to have statistics generated and is ranked first-in-first-out.

```
Public Function INTLC(Run As Long) As Long
   Dim Enew As VSENTITY

   ' Initialize the server to idle

     VS.LL(1) = 0

   ' schedule first arrival at time 0

   Set Enew = VS.DefineEntity(0)
   VS.SCHDL 1, Enew, 0#

   If Run = 1 Then
     ' create collect statistics and customer file
     VS.DefineColct 1, "TIME IN SYSTEM", 10, 0#, 4#
     VS.DefineFile 1,"ArrivingCustomers",_
        TRUE, SUFILE_FIFO, 0, 0, 0, 0, 0
   End If
   INTLC = True
End Function
```

Figure 11-8   Function INTLC for bank teller problem.

The logic for the customer arrival event is coded in subroutine ARVL and is presented in Figure 11-9. Figure 11-3 shows the logic in flowchart form. The Visual SLAM variable LL(1) is used to maintain the teller status, 1 if the teller is busy and 0 otherwise. The first function performed in the event is the rescheduling of the next arrival event to occur at the current time plus a sample from an exponential distribution with a mean of 20 and using stream 1. The first attribute of the currently arriving customer is then set equal to TNOW. A test is then made on the variable LL(1) to determine the current status of the teller. If LL(1) is positive, then the customer is placed in file 1 to wait for the busy teller. If LL(1) is 0, then the teller is idle. In this case, LL[1] is set to 1 to indicate that the teller is going to be busy and an end-of-service event is scheduled to occur at time TNOW plus a sample from a uniform distribution between 10 and 25 using stream 1. In either case, the customer entity is identified by an arrival time which is stored as attribute 1. Depending on LL(1), the customer entity is placed in file 1 or on the event calendar (file 0).

```
Public Sub ARVL(Customer As VSENTITY)
Dim ENext As VSENTITY

  Set ENext = Customer.Clone(1) ' schedule next arrival
  VS.SCHDL 1, ENext, VS.EXPON(20#, 1)

  'set attributes of arriving customer
  Customer.ATRIB(1)=VS.TNOW
  If VS.LL(1) > 0 Then       ' see if service can start
     VS.FILEM 1, Customer  ' busy server
  Else
     VS.LL(1) = 1              'schedule end of service
     VS.SCHDL 2, Customer, VS.UNFRM(10#, 25#, 1)
  End If
End Sub
```

Figure 11-9   Function ARVL for bank teller problem.

The logic for the end-of-service event is coded in subroutine ENDSV and is presented in Figure 11-10. Figure 11-4 shows the logic in flowchart form. The variable TSYS is set equal to the current time, TNOW, minus the first attribute of the current customer being processed. When an event is removed from the event calendar, the current entity object is passed to function EVENT. Since the value of the first attribute for this customer was set to the customer's time of arrival in the arrival event, the value of TSYS represents the elapsed time between the arrival and end-of-service events for this customer. A call is then made to function COLCT to collect statistics on the value of TSYS as collect variable 1. A test is made on the Visual SLAM function NNQ(1) representing the number of customers waiting for service in file 1. If the number of customers waiting is greater than zero, the first customer waiting is removed from file 1 and placed onto the event calendar. The end-of-service event, event code 2, is scheduled to occur at time TNOW plus the service time. If no customer is waiting, the status of the teller is changed to idle by setting the variable LL[1] to 0.

```
Public Sub ENDSV(Cdone As VSENTITY)
  Dim Cust As VSENTITY
  Dim TSYS As Double
  TSYS = VS.TNOW -Cdone.ATRIB(1) 'save time in system
  VS.Colct TSYS, 1
  Cdone.Terminate  ' terminate customer who is done
  If VS.NNQ(1) > 0 Then 'see if anyone is waiting
   Set Cust = VS.RMOVE(1, 1)      ' get customer waiting
   VS.SCHDL 2, Cust, VS.UNFRM(10#, 25#, 1) ' schedule
     end of service
  Else
   VS.LL(1) = 0  ' set server going idle
  End If
End Sub
```

Figure 11-10 Subroutine ENDSV for bank teller problem.

The input statements for this example are shown in Figure 11-11. The GEN statement specifies the analyst's name, project title, date, and number of runs. The LIMITS statement specifies that the model employs one LL variable and one attribute of type double per entity. The TIMST statement causes time-persistent statistics to be automatically maintained on the Visual SLAM variable LL[1] and the results to be displayed using the label Server Busy Time. The INIT statement specifies that the beginning time of the simulation is time 0 and that the ending time is time 480. The FIN statement denotes the end to all Visual SLAM input statements. This completes the description of the discrete event model of the bank teller system.

```
GEN,"PRITSKER","BANK TELLER",1/1/1996,1,
;
;Model uses 1 real entity attribute and 1 global LL variable
;
LIMITS,,1,,1;
;
;Collect statistics on LL[1], server utilization
;
TIMST,1,LL[1],"Server Busy Time";
INITIALIZE,0.0,480,YES;
FIN
```

Figure 11-11 Data statements for bank teller problem.

The coding of the bank teller problem illustrates the general use of Visual SLAM functional capabilities to code discrete event simulation models. Larger and more complicated models are developed in the same way and differ only in the number and complexity of the event functions. In the next sections, we present a discrete event example which is slightly more complicated and further illustrates discrete event modeling using Visual SLAM.

11.12   EXAMPLE 11-1. A DISCOUNT STORE OPERATION

A discount store has developed a new procedure for serving customers. Customers enter the store and determine the item they wish to purchase by examining display items. After selecting an item, the customer proceeds to a centralized area where a clerk takes the order and travels to an adjacent warehouse to pick up the item. Clerks will service as many as six customers at a time. The time for the clerk to travel to the warehouse is uniformly distributed between 0.5 and 1.5 minutes. The time to find an item depends on the number of items the clerk must locate in the warehouse. This time is normally distributed with a mean equal to three times the number of items to be picked up. The standard deviation is equal to 0.2 of the mean. Thus, if one item is to be obtained from the warehouse, the time to locate the item is normally distributed with a mean of 3 and a standard deviation of 0.6 minutes. The time to return from the warehouse is uniformly distributed within the range of 0.5 and 1.5 minutes. When the clerk returns from the warehouse, the sale is completed for each customer. The time to complete the sale is uniformly distributed between 1 and 3 minutes. The completion of sales for the customers is performed sequentially in the same order that requests for items were made of the clerk. The time between customer requests for items is assumed to be exponentially distributed with the mean of 2 minutes. Three clerks are available to serve the customers. A schematic diagram of the store operation is shown in Figure 11-12.

The objective of this simulation is to determine the utilization of the clerks, the time required to serve a customer from the time at which an item is requested until the completion of a sale, and the number of requests handled by a clerk for each trip to the warehouse. The simulation is to be run for 1000 minutes.

Visual SLAM model. The discrete event model for this example consists of a customer arrival event and an end-of-service event. At first glance, it may also appear that events are required to explicitly model each clerk's arrival to and departure from the warehouse. However, no specific interactions occur during the time that the clerk is filling a request, and therefore the explicit modeling of these intermediate points by event routines is not necessary. If competition for resources are involved in filling the requests, then a more detailed model of the procedure for locating items would be required. Such a situation would exist if resources are required in the warehouse, for example, a forklift truck.

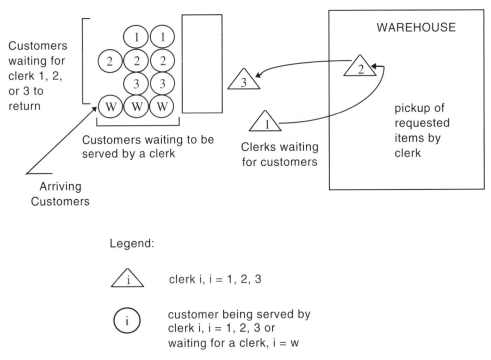

Figure 11-12 Schematic diagram of discount store operation.

There are five files employed in this example. The first four files are employed for storing the attributes of entities representing customers. Customers which arrive at the system when all clerks are busy are stored in file 4. Customers which have placed their orders and are waiting for clerk 1, 2, or 3 to return reside in files 1, 2, and 3, respectively. File 5 is employed for storing the attributes of entities representing free clerks waiting for customers to arrive. The VSENTITY

VSENTITY object Cust is utilized for filing and removing customers from the first four files and VSENTITY object Clerk is employed for filing and removing clerks from file 5. There is one attribute associated with the customer entities which is used to record the arrival time of the customer to the system. There is also one attribute associated with the clerk entities and it is used to denote the clerk as 1, 2, or 3.

The customer arrival event is assigned event code 1 and is coded in function ARVL. The end-of-service event is assigned event code 2 and is coded in function ENDSV. For easier reading, the names ARRIVAL and ENDSERVICE have been defined for the constants 1 and 2. Subroutine EVENT for this example is shown in Figure 11-13. It maps the event code onto the appropriate subroutine call.

```
Public Sub EVENT(Code As Long, Cust As VSENTITY)
    Select Case Code
      Case ARRIVAL ' customer entity
          Call ARVL(Cust)
      Case ENDSERVICE ' clerk entity
          Call ENDSV(Cust)
      Case Else
          VS.Error 1, "Unknown event code"
    End Select
End Sub
```

Figure 11-13 Sample function EVENT.

First, consider the logic associated with the customer arrival event. A flowchart for this event is depicted in Figure 11-14, and the coding is shown in Figure   11-15. Before processing the current arrival, the next arrival is scheduled to occur after an exponential time delay with a mean of 2 minutes by a call to function SCHDL. The arrival time of the current customer is then recorded as the first attribute of the entity. The disposition of the current customer request is determined based on the status of the clerks. A test is made on the number of free clerks waiting in file 5. If file 5 is empty, the customer must wait until a clerk becomes free. File 4 is used to store customers waiting for clerks. If the customer must wait, no further functions can be performed at the arrival event time and a return is made.

If a clerk is available, the order processing can be initiated. The first free clerk is removed from file 5. Function RMOVE returns the clerk entity object as Clerk. The user variable iClerk is then set to the first integer attribute of the clerk which corresponds to the clerk number. The current customer, whose object instance is Cust, is then inserted into file iClerk to wait for the return and end-of-service processing by clerk iClerk. Statistics are collected on the number of customers being served on each clerk trip which in this case is one. The statistics code for this collect variable is set as 2. The total time spent in traveling to the warehouse, in filling customer requests, returning from the warehouse, and completing the order is then computed as the variable dTemp. The end-of-service event is then scheduled to occur dTemp minutes later with the attributes of the clerk associated with the event.

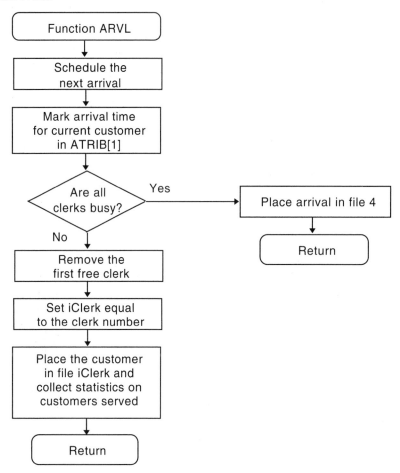

Figure 11-14 Flowchart of customer arrival event for discount example.

```
Public Sub ARVL(Cust As VSENTITY)
  Dim Clerk As VSENTITY
  Dim eNew As VSENTITY
  Dim dTemp As Double
  Dim iClerk As Integer

  ' schedule next arrival
  Set eNew = Cust.Clone(0)
  VS.SCHDL ARRIVAL, eNew, VS.EXPON(2#, 1)

  ' mark arrival time
  Cust.ATRIB(1) = VS.TNOW

  If VS.NNQ(5) = 0 Then
     ' all clerks busy.  wait for service
     VS.FILEM 4, Cust
  Else
     ' get first free clerk
     Set Clerk = VS.RMOVE(5, 1)
     iClerk = Clerk.LTRIB(1)

     ' place customer in this clerk's file
     VS.FILEM iClerk, Cust

     ' collect observation of 1 customer for this trip
     VS.Colct 1#, 2

     ' schedule end of service for clerk
     dTemp = VS.UNFRM(0.5, 1.5, 1)
     dTemp = dTemp + VS.RNORM(3#, 0.6, 1)
     dTemp = dTemp + VS.UNFRM(0.5, 1.5, 1)
     dTemp = dTemp + VS.UNFRM(1#, 3#, 1)
     VS.SCHDL ENDSERVICE, Clerk, dTemp
  End If
End Sub
```

Figure 11-15 Visual SLAM code for customer arrivals to discount store.

Next, consider the logic for the end-of-service event. A flowchart for this event is given in Figure 11-16 and the Visual SLAM coding is shown in Figure 11-17. The clerk entity object, Clerk, is used to set the user variable iClerk to the number of the clerk processing the end-of-service for the customer. The customer completing service is then removed from file iClerk and its object returned as Cust. The time in the system for the customer is computed and statistics are collected on this value as collect variable 1. A test is then made on the Visual SLAM function NNQ(iClerk) to determine if more customers remain.

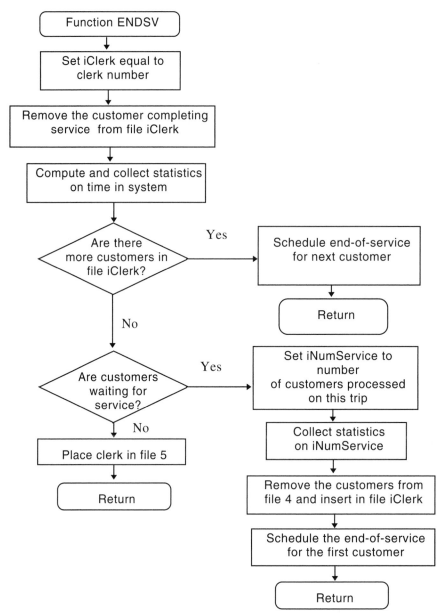

Figure 11-16 Flowchart of end-of-service event for discount store example.

```
Public Sub ENDSV(Clerk As VSENTITY)
    Dim Cust As VSENTITY
    Dim dVal As Double
    Dim dTemp As Double
    Dim iClerk As Integer
    Dim iNumService As Integer
    Dim i As Integer

    iClerk = Clerk.LTRIB(1)
    ' remove top customer from this clerk's list
    Set Cust = VS.RMOVE(iClerk, 1)
        ' collect time in system
        dTemp = VS.TNOW - Cust.ATRIB(1)
        VS.Colct dTemp, 1
        ' destroy customer
        Cust.Terminate
    ' see if anyone is waiting for this clerk
    If VS.NNQ(iClerk) > 0 Then
        ' more customers assigned to this clerk
        VS.SCHDL ENDSERVICE, Clerk, VS.UNFRM(1#, 3#, 1)
    ElseIf VS.NNQ(4) > 0 Then
        ' new customers waiting
        iNumService = VS.NNQ(4)
        If iNumService > MAXSERVICE Then
            iNumService = MAXSERVICE
        End If

        ' collect statistics on number of customers on this trip
        VS.Colct CDbl(iNumService), 2
        ' schedule end of service for first customer
        dVal = CDbl(iNumService * 3)
        dTemp = VS.UNFRM(0.5, 1.5, 1)
        dTemp = dTemp + VS.RNORM(dVal, dVal * 0.2, 1)
        dTemp = dTemp + VS.UNFRM(0.5, 1.5, 1)
        dTemp = dTemp + VS.UNFRM(1#, 3#, 1)
        VS.SCHDL ENDSERVICE, Clerk, dTemp

        ' move customers to this clerk's list
        For i = 1 To iNumService
            Set Cust = VS.RMOVE(4, 1)
            VS.FILEM iClerk, Cust
        Next i
    Else
        ' no customer waiting
        ' place clerk in idle clerk list
        VS.FILEM 5, Clerk
    End If
End Sub
```

Figure 11-17   Visual SLAM code for end-of-service event at discount store.

If NNQ(iClerk) is greater than zero, the end-of-service event for the next customer is scheduled. Otherwise, a test is made on NNQ(4) to determine if there are customers waiting to place their orders with a clerk. If customers are waiting, then the user variable iNumService is set to the number of customers to be processed and statistics are collected on this quantity as collect variable 2. These customers are then removed from file 4 and inserted into file iClerk to await end-of-service processing. The total time spent in traveling to the warehouse, in filling customer requests, returning from the warehouse, and completing the order for the first customer is then computed as dTemp. Note that the time to fill requests is obtained as a sample from a normal distribution with a mean dVal equal to the number of customers, iNumService, times 3. The standard deviation, STD, is two-tenths of the mean, that is, STD = 0.2*dVal. The end-of-service event for the first customer to be processed is then scheduled to occur dTemp minutes later. In the case where there are no customers waiting to place their orders, the clerk entity is placed in file 5 which is the file used for storing idle clerks.

Function INTLC is used to put the three clerks into file 5 as it is assumed that all clerks are idle at the beginning of the simulation run. The first customer arrival event is scheduled to occur at time 0.0 by calling SCHDL with an event code of 1. The constant definitions and listing of function INTLC are given in Figure 11-18. The input statements for this example are shown in Figure 11-19.

Summary of Results. The Visual SLAM Summary Report for this example is given in Figure 11-20. The report reveals that during the 1000 minutes of simulated operation, 517 customers were processed through the system with customers spending an average of 24.49 minutes in the system. The average number of customers per trip by each clerk was 3.040 with a total of 175 trips completed by the clerks. These results indicate that management should investigate the hiring of additional clerks or change the policy regarding the minimum or maximum number of customers a clerk should serve at one time.

Although the average utilization of the clerks is not directly provided by the report, this statistic can be estimated using the average length of file 5. Since idle clerks reside in file 5, the average number of busy clerks is the number of clerks minus the average number in file 5, that is, 2.927.

```
' events
Const ARRIVAL As Integer = 1
Const ENDSERVICE As Integer = 2

' limits
Const MAXCLERK As Integer = 3
Const MAXSERVICE As Integer = 6

Public Function INTLC(Run As Long) As Long
   Dim eNew As VSENTITY
   Dim szTemp As String
   Dim i As Integer
   INTLC = True

   If Run = 1 Then ' on first run,  define files
      ' create discrete files
      VS.DefineFile 4, "Customer Arrival", True, _
                       SUFILE_FIFO, 0, 0, 0, 0, 0
      VS.DefineFile 5, "Free Clerks", True, _
                       SUFILE_FIFO, 0, 0, 0, 0, 0
      For i = 1 To MAXCLERK
         szTemp = "Wait for Clerk " & CStr(i)
         VS.DefineFile i, szTemp, True, _
                       SUFILE_FIFO, 0, 0, 0, 0, 0
       Next i
       ' create collect statistics
       VS.DefineColct 1, "TIME IN SYSTEM", 0, 0#, 0#
       VS.DefineColct 2, "CUST PER TRIP", 10, 0#, 1#
   End If
       ' schedule arrival at time 0 of first customer
       Set eNew = VS.DefineEntity(0)
       VS.SCHDL ARRIVAL, eNew, 0#
       ' put initial idle clerks into free clerks file
       For i = 1 To MAXCLERK
          Set eNew = VS.DefineEntity(1)
          eNew.LTRIB(1) = i ' clerk number
          VS.FILEM 5, eNew
       Next i
  End Function
```

Figure 11-18 Function INTLC for discount store example.

```
GEN,"PRITSKER","DISCOUNT STORE",1/1/1996,1;
LIMITS,-1,-1,-1,1,1,-1;
INIT,0,1000;
FIN;
```

Figure 11-19 Input statements for discount store example.

```
** AweSim SUMMARY REPORT **

Simulation Project : DISCOUNT STORE
Modeler : PRITSKER
Date : 1/1/1996
Scenario : EX111

Run number 1 of 1
Current simulation time    : 1000.000000
Statistics cleared at time : 0.000000
```

```
        ** OBSERVED STATISTICS REPORT for scenario EX111 **

Label           Mean     Standard   Number of     Minimum   Maximum
                Value    Deviation  Observations  Value     Value

TIME IN SYSTEM  24.491   10.486        517        5.227     51.900
CUST PER TRIP    3.040    1.955        175        1.000      6.000
```

```
          ** FILE STATISTICS REPORT for scenario EX111 **

File   Label or        Average Standard  Maximum  Current Average
Number Input Location  Length  Deviation Length   Length  Wait Time

   1   Wait for Clerk 1 3.712   1.927      6        6      20.066
   2   Wait for Clerk 2 3.236   1.890      6        3      19.149
   3   Wait for Clerk 3 3.361   1.972      6        6      18.879
   4   Customer Arrival 2.648   2.783     17        1       5.371
   5   Free Clerks      0.073   0.295      3        0       1.816
```

Figure 11-20 Visual SLAM summary report for discount store example.

11.13   ADVANCED DISCRETE EVENT CONCEPTS

In this section, we present information on functions for searching files for entities, functions for report writing and functions for accessing statistical quantities.

11.13.1 Searching a File

In some cases the location of a specific entity of interest may not be known. Visual SLAM provides seven functions for searching a file and comparing each entry's placeholder object, entity number, event type, or specific attribute to a desired value. Each function is of type VSFILE, where an instance of a VSFILE object maintains the following information about a file:

VSFILE Property	*Description*
First As VSENTRY	Placeholder of the first entry in the file
Last As VSENTRY	Placeholder of the last entry in the file
Length As Long	Number of entities in the file
Capacity As Long	Capacity of the file (maximum length)
AvgLength As Double	Average length of the file
StdLength As Double	Standard deviation of the file length
MaxLength As Long	Maximum length of the file
MinLength As Long	Minimum length of the file
StatPeriod As Double	Time period over which file statistics were kept
StatTLC As Double	Time of the last change in file length
AvgWait As Double	Average waiting time in the file

Since Visual Basic coding requires a file object reference, the Visual SLAM object of a file can be obtained by the function **File(File As Integer) As VSFILE.** For example, a VSFILE object called "FileObj" would be set to the VSFILE object for File 1 by the following Visual Basic statements:

> Dim FileObj As VSFILE
> Set FileObj = VS.File(1)

The following examples of file searches return the VSENTRY object of a located entity in a VSENTRY object called "Loc". In each case, the first argument of the search function is the VSENTRY object of the entry at which the search should begin. If this argument is "Nothing", then the search will begin at the beginning of the file. If no matching entry is found, the function returns Nothing in each case. The VSFILE object used in each example is "FileObj" except in the case of the FindEvent function. This example uses the VSFILE object of the Visual SLAM event calendar which is returned by the VSLAM function Calendar(). The functions which compare attribute values use an integer code to define how an attribute should compare to the specified value. For ease of use, equivalent names beginning with SUFILTER have been provided.

FindEqEntity(Start As VSENTRY, Look As VSENTITY) As VSENTRY

Find the placeholder of the Look entity within the file with the search starting at the Start location.

Example: 'See If Ent is in file, set placeholder to Loc
　　　　　　Set Loc = FileObj.FindEqEntity(Nothing,Ent)

FindNEEntity(Start As VSENTRY, Look As VSENTITY) As VSENTRY

Find the placeholder of the next entity within the file which is not the Look entity with the search starting at the Start location.

Example: 'See if anything but Ent is in file
　　　　　　Set Loc = FileObj.FindNEEntity(Nothing,Ent)

FindEntity(Start As VSENTRY, Enum As Integer) As VSENTRY

Find the placeholder of the entry whose entity number attribute is Enum with the search starting at the Start location.

Example: 'find entity with Enum = 12
　　　　　　Set Loc = Fileobj.FindEntity(Nothing, 12)

FindEvent(Start As VSENTRY, Event As Integer) As VSENTRY

Find the placeholder of the next entity within the file which has event number Event with the search starting at the Start location.

Example: 'find event 5 on event calendar
　　　　　　Set Loc = VS.Calendar.FindEvent(Nothing,5)

FindAtrib(Start As VSENTRY, Index as Integer, Value as Double, Code As Integer) As VSENTRY

Find the placeholder of the next entity after Start which has Atrib(Index) *code* Value where *code* is SUFILTER_GT (>), SUFILTER_GE (>=), SUFILTER_LE (<=), SUFILTER_LT (<), SUFILTER_EQ (=) or SUFILTER_NE   (NOT =).
Example: 'look for entity with ATRIB(2)=3.4
         Set Loc = FileObj.FindAtrib(Nothing,2,3.4,SUFILTER_EQ)

FindLtrib(Start As VSENTRY, Index as Integer, Value as Long, Code As Integer) As VSENTRY

Find the placeholder of the next entity after Start which has Ltrib(Index) *code* Value where *code* is SUFILTER_GT (>), SUFILTER_GE (>=), SUFILTER_LE (<=), SUFILTER_LT (<), SUFILTER_EQ (=) or SUFILTER_NE   (NOT =).
Example: 'look for entity with LTRIB(2)=1000
         Set Loc = FileObj.FindLtrib(Nothing,2,1000,SUFILTER_EQ)

FindStrib(Start As VSENTRY, Index as Integer, Value as String, Code As Integer) As VSENTRY

Find the placeholder of the next entity after Start which has Strib(Index) *code* Value where *code* is SUFILTER_GT (>), SUFILTER_GE (>=), SUFILTER_LE (<=), SUFILTER_LT (<), SUFILTER_EQ (=) or SUFILTER_NE   (NOT =).
Example: 'find entity with STRIB(2)="PART1"
         Set Loc = FileObj.FindStrib(Nothing,2,"PART1",SUFILTER_EQ)

Given the VSENTRY object of a file entry, the Entity property of that object provides the entry's VSENTITY object (Section 11.5.4). For example, the third attribute of an entity whose VSENTRY object is Loc could be changed with the following Visual Basic statement:

Loc.Entity.ATRIB(3) = Loc.Entity.ATRIB(3)+100#

Recall that function RMOVE will remove a file entry based upon its rank in the file. In the case of an entity located via a file search function, the entity's VSENTRY object is known but not its rank. For this reason the VSENTRY function **Remove()** is provided. To remove an entity whose VSENTRY is Loc, for example, the following statement would be used:

  Loc.Remove   ' removes an entity based on its VSENTRY object.

11.13.2   Report Writing Functions

  A set of functions is contained within Visual SLAM to enable the user to obtain summary reports or sections of a summary report. These functions can be used to obtain summary information of a specific type. The output from a function corresponds to a specific section of the Visual SLAM summary report (see Chapter 8). The list of functions along with the definitions of their arguments is presented in Table 11-4.

  The terminology used in naming the functions is to append a specific letter onto the letters PRNT. Thus, PRNTF is used as the name of the function to print files and PRNTH is used as the name of the function to print histograms. The arguments to these functions have been standardized so that an argument value greater than zero requests a specific item to be printed. If the argument is given as a zero value then all items associated with the function are printed. In the case of PRNTF(IFILE), statistics on all files can be obtained by specifying a negative value for the argument IFILE.

  Listed below are examples of the use of the report writing routines.

Statement	*Description*
VS.SUMRY( )	Prints a complete summary report at time of calling (TNOW).
VS.PRNTF(3)	Prints statistics on file 3.
VS.PRNTT(0)	Prints statistics on all time-persistent variables.
VS.PRNTA(0)	Prints statistics on all network activities that were given activity numbers.

Table 11-4   Visual SLAM report writing functions.

Function	Description
PRNTA(Act As Integer)	Prints statistics for activity Act. If Act is zero, then statistics for all activities are printed.
PRNTB(Stat As Integer)	If Stat>0, prints the histogram associated with the time-persistent variable type Stat. If Stat=0, prints all time-persistent histograms.
PRNTC(Collect As Integer)	If Collect>0, prints statistics for COLCT variable Collect. If Collect=0, prints statistics statistics for all variables based on observation.
PRNTF(File As Integer)	If File>0, prints statistics for file File. If File=0, prints statistics for all files. If File<0, prints the contents of all files.
PRNTG(Gate As Integer)	If Gate>0, prints statistics on gate number Gate. If Gate=0, prints statistics on all gates.
PRNTH(Collect As Integer)	If Collect>0, prints the histogram for COLCT variable Collect. If Collect=0, prints all histograms.
PRNTO(Group as Integer)	If Group>0, prints statistics for group number Group. If Group=0, prints statistics for all groups.
PRNTR(Resource As Integer)	If Resource>0, prints statistics for resource number Resource. If Resource=0, prints statistics for all resources.
PRNTS()	Prints the contents of the state storage arrays SS[I] and DD[I].
PRNTT(Stat As Integer)	If Stat>0, prints statistics for time-persistent variable Stat. If Stat=0, prints statistics for all time-persistent variables.
SUMRY()	Prints the Visual SLAM Summary Report.

11.14 CHAPTER SUMMARY

This chapter presents the Visual SLAM discrete event simulation modeling procedures. The procedures for scheduling events, file manipulations, and statistical collection routines are described. A list of important discrete event variables is presented in Table 11-2. An illustration and an example of discrete event modeling using Visual SLAM are presented. The example involves a discount store where clerks perform multiple operations before completing service on customers.

The organization of a Visual SLAM program for discrete event modeling is illustrated in Figure 11-21. Table 11-5 summarizes the user-written and user-callable functions used with Visual SLAM.

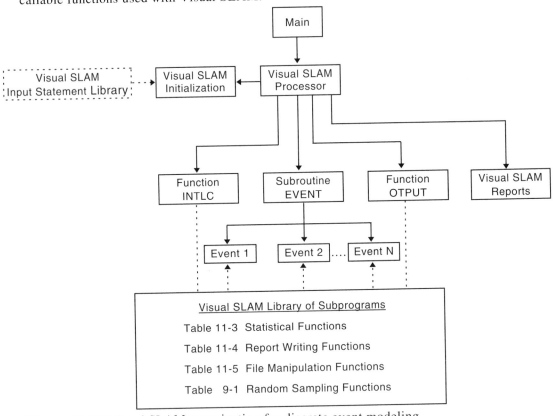

Figure 11-21 Visual SLAM organization for discrete event modeling.

Table 11-5. Summary of Visual Basic Routines Included in Visual SLAM

Function	Description
User Written	
Public Function ALLOC (Code As Long, First As VSENTRY) As VSENTRY	To process allocation rule Code at the AWAIT node for which First is the placeholder of the first entry. Returns the placeholder of the entry which should be released from the node, Nothing if allocations were not made.
Public Function ASSEMBLE (Code As Long, Node As VSNODE) As VSENTITY	To create the entity being assembled at the SELECT node whose object is VSNODE with the user-defined assembly rule Code. Returns the VSENTITY object of the newly assembled entity.
Public Sub BATCHSAVE (Code As Long, Form As VSENTITY, Add As VSENTITY)	To update the attributes of a batch entity whose object is Form when the entity whose object is Add arrives to a BATCH node with an attribute save criterion of User(Code).
Public Sub EVENT (Code As Long, User As VSENTITY)	To process event type Code for the entity whose object is User.
Public Function INTLC (Run As Long) As Long	To perform initialization for run number Run. Return True if the Run should be executed, False otherwise.
Public Function NQS (Code As Long, User as VSENTITY, Node As VSNODE) As Long	To process the SELECT node whose object is VSNODE and whose queue selection rule is NQS(Code). The entity whose object is User is the one which triggered the selection. Return the file number of the selected QUEUE.
Public Function NSS (Code As Long, User As VSENTITY, Node As VSNODE) As Long	To process the SELECT node whose object is VSNODE and whose server selection rule is NSS(Code). The entity whose object is User is the one which triggered the selection. Return the activity number of the selected service activity.
Public Function OTPUT (Run As Long) As Long	To perform special end-of-run processing for run number Run. Return True if the next run should be made, False otherwise.
Public Function USERF (Code As Long, User As VSENTITY) As Double	To return a value specified in a network as USERF(Code) and required by the entity whose object is User.
Provided by Visual SLAM	
VSLAM Methods	
COLCT(Value As Double, Collect As Integer) As Integer	Records the value Value as an observation of the variable Collect.
DefineColct (Collect As Integer, ID As String, NCel As Integer, HLow As Double, HWid As Double) As Integer	Defines a new observed statistic with identification number Collect, label ID, and a histogram with NCel cells, lower limit of HLow and cell width of HWid. Returns True if sucessful, False otherwise.

Table 11-5. (Continued)

Function	Description
DefineEntity(EntType As Integer) As VSENTITY	Creates a new entity and initializes its type.
DefineFile(File As Integer, Name As String, bStats As BOOL, Type As Integer, Max As Long, OrdCode As Integer,_OrdArg As Long, TieCode As Integer, TieArg As Long) As VSFILE	Creates a new file with file number File. Statistics are collected if bStats is True. The ranking rule, Type, is SUFILE_FIFO if first-in-first-out, SUFILE_LIFO if last-in-first-out, SUFILE_LIST if sorted linked list, SUFILE_HEAP if heap, SUFILE_TREE if sorted binary tree. An error message is generated if the number in the file exceeds Max. Max should be defined to be zero if there is no maximum. If Type specifies a sorted list, the user will write the ordering function ORDER with input parameters OrdCode, and OrdArg.
File(File As Integer) As VSFILE	Returns the VSFILE object for file File.
FILEM (File As Integer, User As VSENTITY) As VSENTRY	Files the entity User in file File. Returns the entity's placeholder in the file.
MMFE(File As Integer) As VSENTRY	Returns the placeholder to the first entry (rank 1) in file File.
MMLE(File As Integer) As VSENTRY	Returns the placeholder to the last entry (rank NNQ(File)) in file File.
NNQ(File As Integer) As Long	Returns the number of entries currently in file File.
RMOVE (File As Integer, Rank As Integer) As VSENTITY SCHDL(Event As Integer, User As VSENTITY, Time As Double) As VSENTRY	Removes the entity with rank Rank from file File and returns the entity object Schedules an event of type Event to occur at time TNOW+Time for the entity User. Returns the placeholder of the event in the event calendar.
VSFILE Methods	
FindEqEntity(Start As VSENTRY, Look As VSENTITY) As VSENTRY	Find the placeholder of the Look entity within the file, starting at the Start location.
FindNEEntity(Start As VSENTRY, Look As VSENTITY) As VSENTRY	Find the placeholder of the next entity within the file which is not the Look entity, starting at the Start location.
FindEntity(Start As VSENTRY, Enum As Integer) As VSENTRY	Find the placeholder of the entry whose entity number attribute is Enum, starting at the Start location.
FindEvent(Start As VSENTRY, Event As Integer) As VSENTRY	Find the placeholder of the next entity within the file which has event number Event, starting at the Start location.
FindAtrib(Start As VSENTRY, Index as Integer, Value as Double, Code As Integer) As VSENTRY	Find the placeholder of the next entity after Start which has ATRIB(Index) *code* Value where *code* is SUFILTER_GT (>), SUFILTER_GE (>=), SUFILTER_LE (<=), SUFILTER_LT (<), SUFILTER_EQ (=), or = SUFILTER_NE (NOT =).

Table 11-5. (Concluded)

Function	Description
FindLtrib(Start As VSENTRY, Index as Integer, Value as Long, Code As Integer) As VSENTRY	Find the placeholder of the next entity after Start which has LTRIB(Index) *code* Value where *code* is SUFILTER_GT (>), SUFILTER_GE (>=), SUFILTER_LE (<=), SUFILTER_LT (<), SUFILTER_EQ (=), or = SUFILTER_NE (NOT =).
FindStrib(Start As VSENTRY, Index as Integer, Value as String, Code As Integer) As VSENTRY	Find the placeholder of the next entity after Start which has STRIB(Index) *code* Value where *code* is SUFILTER_GT (>), SUFILTER_GE (>=), SUFILTER_LE (<=), SUFILTER_LT (<), SUFILTER_EQ (=), or = SUFILTER_NE (NOT =).
VSENTRY Method	
Remove() As Integer	Remove the entity at the VSENTRY placeholder from the file. The VSENTRY object may not be used after this call.
VSENTITY Methods	
Clone(Type As Integer) As VSENTITY	Clone the VSENTITY entity and give it a new entity Type.
Terminate()	Terminate the VSENTITY entity. The VSENTITY object should be set to Nothing after this function call.

11.15   EXERCISES

11-1.   Simulate a single server system where service is exponentially distributed with a mean service time of one hour and there are two types of arrivals. Arrival type 1 is an item of high priority and waits only for the processing of other high priority items. The time intervals between arrivals of high priority items is exponentially distributed with a mean time between arrivals of four hours. The time between arrivals of low priority items is also exponentially distributed, but has a mean time between arrivals of two hours. Obtain statistics regarding server utilization and information concerning the time in the system and in the queue for high and low priority items. Assume that service on low priority items is not interrupted to process high priority items.

Embellishment: Repeat the simulation with the assumption that high priority items interrupt the servicing of low priority items. Interrupted items are inserted at the beginning of the queue of low priority items. Show that the time remaining for those items interrupted is exponentially distributed with a mean time equal to the mean service time.

11-2.   Jobs arrive at a job shop so that the interarrival time is exponentially distributed with a mean time between arrivals of 1.25 hours. The time to process a job is uniformly distributed in the interval 0.75 to 1.25 hours. The time to process the jobs is estimated prior to the time the job is performed. Simulate the processing of jobs in the order of shortest processing time first. Obtain statistics describing the average time jobs are in the shop, the variation of the time the jobs are in the shop and the utilization of the server. Assume that the actual processing times for the jobs are equal to the estimates of the processing times. Repeat the simulation with jobs with the longest processing time performed first. Then carry out the simulation with the jobs processed in order of their arrival time. Compare the results.

Embellishment: Repeat the simulation for a situation in which the actual processing time is equal to the estimated processing time plus a sample drawn from a normal distribution with a mean of zero and a standard deviation of 0.2.

11-3.   Build a discrete event model for the two work stations in series described in Example 5-1.

Embellishment:

(a) Before subcontracting a unit, check the end-of-service times for the work stations. If the next end-of-service is within 0.1 hours of the current time, the unit is not subcontracted but returns to the work station in 0.2 hour.

(b) Redevelop the work station model under the assumption that the manufacturer only maintains 100 units. The time to failure for each unit is exponentially distributed with a mean of 40 hours. The time to repair a unit if subcontracted is triangularly distributed with a mode of 4, a minimum of 3, and a maximum of 6.

11-4.   Develop a discrete event simulation of the PERT network given in Example 7-1. Hint: The simulation of PERT networks involves a single event representing the end of an activity. Perform a simulation of the PERT network for 400 runs.

Embellishment: Estimate the probability that an activity is on the critical path in a run. This probability is referred to as a criticality index.

11-5.   Develop a discrete event model of the inventory situation presented in Example 5-1.

Embellishments:

(a) Make the lead time for the receipt of orders lognormally distributed with a mean of 3 and standard deviation of 1.

(b) Include in the model information that each customer may demand more than one radio. The additional number of radios demanded per customer is Poisson distributed with a mean of 2. Thus, the expected number demanded per customer is 3. Presume if there are insufficient radios to meet the total number of radios demanded by a customer, the entire order is backordered with probability 0.2.

(c) Convert the periodic review system to a transaction reporting system where the inventory position is reviewed after every sale or backorder.

(d) Make the mean time between customer demands a function of the number of lost sales and backorders. If the average number of lost sales and backorders per week is less than 1, the mean time between demands is 0.18 week. If the average number of lost sales and backorders is greater than 2, the mean time between demands is 0.22. Otherwise, the mean time between demands is 0.20.

(e) Add the following income and cost structure to the inventory situation. Radios sell for $65 and cost the store $40. An inventory carrying charge of $0.004 per dollar/week is used. The cost of placing an order for radios from the supplier is estimated to be $50. Each review of inventory costs $30. A lost sale results in a loss of goodwill and is estimated to cost $20. The cost for maintaining a backorder is $10. Run a simulation of this inventory situation for 312 weeks.

(f) Evaluate the effect of alternative inventory policies on average profit using the cost and income data provided in embellishment (e).

11-6. Build a discrete event model for the conveyor situation described in Exercise 9-5.

11-7. Build a discrete event model of the drive-in bank with jockeying described in Example 9-1. Embellishment: Enlarge the model by including the departure process of cars into the street next to the bank. Cars departing from the bank tellers can enter the street when a large enough gap exists between cars traveling on the street. The time between such gaps is uniformly distributed between 0.3 and 0.5 minutes. The space following the tellers is only sufficient to allow 3 cars to wait for a gap in the street traffic.

11-8. Embellishment to Example 11-1. Alter the discount store operation so that clerks wait for 1 minute before traveling to the warehouse to serve a single customer. Determine the effect of this new policy on customer waiting time and clerk utilization. Evaluate alternative time intervals for waiting for additional customers before traveling to the warehouse.

11-9. Embellishment to Example 11-1. In the simulation of the discount store operation, it has been determined that there is a probability that the clerk will return from the warehouse with an incorrect item. When this occurs the clerk immediately returns to the warehouse to obtain the correct item. The probability of retrieving an incorrect item is 0.15. In addition, there is a probability of 0.1 that the item requested was not in inventory. When this occurs, there is a probability of 0.25 that the customer will request a new item. Evaluate the effect of this new information on clerk utilization and customer waiting time.

11-10. For Exercise 11-4, determine the number of simulation runs that would be required to obtain a 95% probability that: (a) the estimate of the project duration is within 0.1 of a standard deviation of the theoretical project duration: (b) the estimate of the variance of the project duration is within 10% of the theoretical variance of the project duration; and (c) the difference between the observed and theoretical criticality indices is less than or equal to 0.005.

11-11.   Write the statements required to determine the location of the entry that satisfies the following conditions:

(a)   The entry in file 2 that has attribute 3 equal to 10.

(b)   The entry with the largest value of attribute 4 greater than 0 in file 1.

(c)   The entry whose third attribute is closest to 10 but does not exceed 10 in file 3.

(d)   In file 3, the entry whose third attribute is closest to 10 but is not less than 10.

(e)   The entry in file 4 whose second attribute is the largest. Entries with the value of attribute 2 less than 3 cannot be used.

11.16   REFERENCES

1.   Henriksen, J. O., "GPSS--Finding the Appropriate World-View," *Proceedings, 1981 Winter Simulation Conference*, 1981, pp. 505-516.

2.   Pritsker, A. A. B.., *Introduction to Simulation and SLAM II*, Fourth Edition, Systems Publishing and John Wiley, 1995.

3.   *Visual SLAM Quick Reference Manual*, Pritsker Corporation, 1996.

4.   Schruben, L., "Simulation Modeling with Event Graphs", *Communications of the ACM*, Vol. 26, 1983, pp. 957-963.

5.   Cornell, G. and T. Strain, *Visual Basic 4 Nuts and Bolts: For Experienced Programmers*, Osborne McGraw-Hill, 1995.

CHAPTER 11C

Discrete Event Simulation
Using C Functions

11.1   INTRODUCTION

The network orientation presented in the previous chapters is a valuable approach to modeling a large class of systems.   For systems requiring flexibility beyond that afforded by the network orientation, the discrete event orientation provides a general approach to simulation modeling. In this chapter, we describe and illustrate the basic concepts and procedures employed in constructing discrete event simulation models using the C language within Visual SLAM.

11.2   DISCRETE EVENT ORIENTATION

The concepts of discrete event modeling were introduced in Chapter 2. The world view embodied in a discrete event orientation consists of modeling a system by describing the changes that occur in the system at discrete points in time. An isolated point in time where the state of the system may change is called an "event time" and the associated logic for processing the changes in state is called an "event." A discrete event model of a system is constructed by defining the event types that can occur and then modeling the logic associated with each event type. A dynamic portrayal of the system is produced by making the changes in states according to the logic of each event in a time-ordered sequence.

The state of a system in a discrete event model is similar to that of a network model and is represented by variables and by entities which have attributes and which belong to files. The state of the model is initialized by specifying initial values for the variables employed in the simulation, by creating the initial entities and by the initial scheduling of events. During execution of the simulation, the model moves from state to state as entities engage in activities. In discrete event simulation, system status changes only occur at the beginning of an activity when something is started or at the end of the activity when something is completed. Events are used to model the start and completion of activities.

The concept of an event which takes place instantaneously at a point in time and either starts or ends an activity is a crucial one. This relationship is depicted in Figure 11-1. Time does not advance within an event and the system behavior is simulated by state changes that occur as events happen.

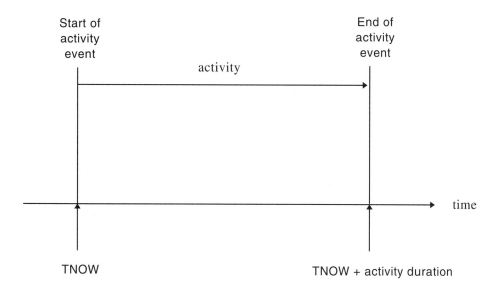

Figure 11-1   Relationship between activities and events.

When an event occurs, the state of the model can change in four ways: by altering the value of one or more variables; by altering the number of entities present; by altering the values assigned to one or more attributes of an entity; or by altering the relationships that exist among entities through file manipulations. Methods are available within Visual SLAM for accomplishing each of these changes. Note that an event can occur in which a decision is made not to change the state of the model. Schruben has developed a graphic methodology for portraying events and the conditions which define the relations between events (4).

Events are scheduled to occur at a prescribed time during the simulation. Events have attributes and are maintained in chronological order in a file. For example, when scheduling an end-of-service event, the attributes of the customer undertaking service are part of the event and are then made available at the time of the end-of-service event processing. Thus, if an entity undertakes a series of activities with the end of each activity represented by an event, the attributes of that entity will be associated with each event that is processed.

11.2.1 Event Model of a Queueing Situation

To illustrate the concepts involved in discrete event modeling, consider a bank with one teller where it is desired to obtain statistics on the time each customer spends in the system. Customers arrive at the system, wait for the teller, undergo service, and depart the system. For simplicity, if a customer is waiting, it will be assumed that there is no time delay between the time the service ends for one customer and begins for the next waiting customer. The states of the system will be measured by the number of customers in the system and the status of the teller. Two event types can be used to model the changes in system state: a customer arrival event and an end-of-service event. As a modeler, one must decide on the events that model the system. Here we assume all significant changes in system status can occur only at the arrival time of a customer or at the time that a service ends. In this model, it is assumed that the state of the system does not change between occurrences of these event times.

There is one activity in the model of this system consisting of the service activity. The service activity for a customer begins at either the time of arrival of the customer or at the time that the teller completes service for another customer. Therefore, the starting time for the service activity can be either in the customer arrival event or in the end-of-service event. The ending time for the service activity triggers the end-of-service event.

In constructing the event logic for this example, we employ the variable BUSY to describe the status of the teller where a value of 1 denotes busy and a value of 0 denotes idle. Customers are represented as entities with one attribute denoting the arrival time of the customer. This attribute is used in the model for collecting statistics on the time in the system for each customer in a fashion similar to the mark time employed in network modeling. The model employs a file ranked first-in, first-out (FIFO) for storing entities representing customers waiting for service when the teller is busy. The state of the model at any instant in time is defined by the value of the variable BUSY, location of the customer, the entities and attribute values of the entities.

The initialization logic for this example is depicted in Figure 11-2. The variable BUSY is set equal to 0 to indicate that the teller is initially idle. The arrival event corresponding to the first customer is scheduled to occur at time 0. Thus, the initial status of the system is empty and idle with the first customer scheduled to arrive at time 0.

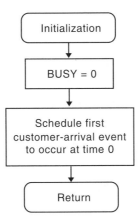

Figure 11-2   Initialization logic for bank teller problem.

The logic for the customer arrival event is depicted in Figure 11-3. The first action which is performed is the scheduling of the next arrival to occur at the current time plus the time between arrivals. Thus, each arrival will cause another arrival to occur at some later time during the simulation. In this way only one arrival event is scheduled to occur at any one time; however, a complete sequence of arrivals is generated.† The first attribute of the arrival entity associated with the event is then set equal to TNOW to mark the arrival time of the customer to the system. A test is then made on the status of the teller to determine if the service activity can begin or if the entity representing the customer must be placed in a file to wait for the teller. If service can begin, the variable BUSY is set equal to one, the end-of-service event for the current customer is scheduled and the event processing is completed. Otherwise, the entity and its attributes are placed in the file representing waiting customers and the event processing is completed.

---

† The next arrival event could also be read from an input device which contains an "historical" sequence of events. In this case, we refer to the simulation model as being "trace or data driven." Of course, the historical sequence could have been generated by a separate simulation model.

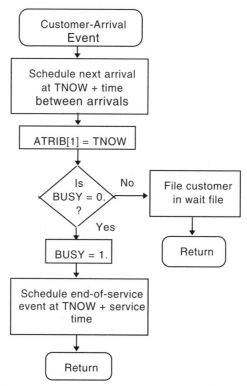

Figure 11-3 Customer arrival event logic for bank teller problem.

At each end-of-service event, statistics are collected on the time in the system for the customer completing service. The first waiting customer, if any, is removed from the wait file and placed into service. The logic for the end-of-service event is depicted in Figure 11-4. The variable TSYS, corresponding to the time in the system for this customer, is computed as TNOW - ATRIB[1]. Since ATRIB[1] was previously assigned the arrival time of the customer, TSYS is the elapsed time between the arrival and departure of the customer on which service was completed. A test is then made to determine if there are customers waiting for service. If not, the status of the teller is made idle by setting BUSY equal to 0 and the event processing is completed. Otherwise, the first customer entity is removed from the wait file. Processing of the customer is modeled by scheduling an end-of-service event to occur at the current time plus the service time.

This simple example illustrates the basic concepts of discrete event simulation modeling. Variables and entities with their attributes and file memberships make up the static structure of a simulation model. They describe the state of the system

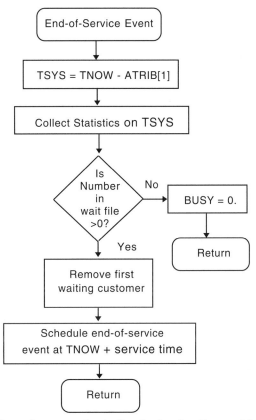

Figure 11-4   End-of-service event logic for the bank teller problem.

but not how the system operates. The events specify the logic which controls the changes that occur at specific instants of time. The dynamic behavior is then obtained by sequentially processing events and recording status values at event times. Since status is constant between events, the complete dynamic system behavior is obtained in this manner. This example illustrates several important types of functions which must be performed in simulating discrete models. The primary functional requirement in discrete event simulation involves scheduling events, placing events in chronological order and advancing time. Other functional requirements which are illustrated by this example include mechanisms for file manipulations, statistics collecting and reporting and random sample generation. In Section 11-3, we describe the use of Visual SLAM for performing these and other functions in discrete event simulation modeling. First, we discuss how discrete-event modeling can be used to study inventory systems.

11.2.2 Event Modeling of Inventory Systems.

To illustrate the generality of the event modeling approach, we now consider the analysis of inventory systems and indicate the event modeling procedures. All inventory systems involve the storage of particular items for future sale or use. Demands are imposed on an inventory by customers seeking supplies of items. A company must establish an inventory policy that specifies when an order for additional items should be placed (or manufactured), and how many of the items should be ordered at each order time. When the items stored in inventory are discrete units, simulation of the inventory system using the next event philosophy is quite natural. The primary system variables are the number of units in storage, called the *inventory-on-hand*, and the number of units that are theoretically on the books of the company, called the *inventory position*. The inventory position is equal to the inventory-on-hand, plus the number of units on order (the number due-in), minus the number of units that have been backordered by customers (the number due-out). The inventory-on-hand represents the number of units available to be sold to customers. The inventory position represents the number of units that are or will be available to the company for potential sale. Inventory decisions regarding when to place an order and how much to order are normally based on the inventory position. Other attributes associated with inventory situations are: the number of units sold, the number of orders placed, the number of lost sales and/or the number of backorders, and the number of times the inventory position is reviewed to make a decision whether to place an order.

The events associated with an inventory situation at which these attributes could change their value are: a demand by a customer for the items in inventory, a review of the status of the inventory position to determine if an order should be placed, the receipt of goods from the distributor to be placed in inventory and the satisfying of the customers' demands for the item. Each of these events could be modeled as a distinct event. However, several of the above can occur at the same point in time. When this happens, it is efficient to combine the events into a single event. For example, the satisfying of a customer demand would normally take place either when the customer demand is placed or when a shipment of units is received from the distributor. When this is done, the modeler assumes that the time delay in delivering a unit to a customer has an insignificant effect on the expected cost or profit associated with the inventory situation.

Customer demand events are normally modeled by specifying the time between customer demands. In this way, each demand event can be used to specify the time of the next demand. Then only the first demand event, which starts the demand process, and the time between demands would need to be specified.

Two types of review procedures to determine if an order should be placed are common in industry. A *periodic review procedure* specifies that a review should be performed at equally spaced points in time, for example, every month. The other review procedure involves the examination of the inventory position every time it decreases. This type of review is called *transaction reporting* and involves keeping a running log of the inventory position. When a transaction reporting review procedure is being studied, no separate review event is required since the inventory position can only be decreased when a customer demand occurs. Thus, the review procedure can be incorporated into the customer demand event.

The event involving the receipt of units from the distributor does not change the inventory position since the inventory position was increased when the units were ordered. However, the inventory-on-hand and the number of backorders could change when the receipt event occurs. The time at which the receipt event occurs is based on the time at which it was decided to place an order (at a review time) plus the time for processing the order and shipping the units. The time from the placing of the order to the receipt of the units is called the *lead time*.

The above general discussion of events that can occur in an inventory situation provides a general framework for simulating any inventory system. To obtain a simulation using Visual SLAM, it would only be necessary to write subroutines for each of the events required by the specific inventory situation. The points in time at which the individual events occur would be automatically handled by Visual SLAM using the time between events as specified by the user in the appropriate event routines. The user would schedule the next demand event (in a subroutine representing all demand events) and the receipt of units, if it was decided that an order was to be placed.

Of major importance in this modeling of systems is the absence of the need to specify the details about the interdemand time distribution, the lead time distribution, the number of units requested by a customer at a demand point, and so forth, when discussing the overall procedure for simulating an inventory system. This information is only important when simulating a specific system. The Visual SLAM organizational structure for discrete event simulation allows the modeling of systems prior to data collection and, in fact, helps to specify the data required to analyze a system.

11.3   THE DISCRETE EVENT FRAMEWORK OF VISUAL SLAM

To simulate a discrete event model of a system using Visual SLAM, the analyst codes each discrete event as a C function. To assist the analyst in this task, Visual SLAM provides a set of C functions for performing all commonly encountered functions such as event scheduling, statistics collection and random sample generation. The advancing of simulated time (TNOW) and the order in which the event routines are processed are controlled by the Visual SLAM executive program. Thus, Visual SLAM relieves the simulation modeler of the task of sequencing events in their proper chronological order.

Each event is assigned a positive integer numeric code called the event code, in the same fashion as the event code defined at an EVENT node. The event code is mapped onto a call to the appropriate event function by function EVENT(Code, peEnt) where the integer argument Code is the event code and peEnt is the pointer to the current entity structure. This function is written by the user as was discussed in Chapter 9C and consists of a switch statement indexed on Code causing a transfer to the appropriate event function. An example of the EVENT function is depicted in Figure 11-5 for a simulation model with two events consisting of an arrival event coded in function ARVL and assigned event code 1, and an end-of-service event coded in function ENDSV and assigned event code 2.

```
void EVENT(int Code, ENTITY *peCur)
{
 switch (Code)         {
  case 1: ARVL(peCur); /*Logic for Event Code 1 in ARVL */
     break;
  case 2: ENDSV(peCur);/*Logic for Event Code 2 in ENDSV*/
 }
}
```

Figure 11-5   Sample function EVENT.

Two additional user-written functions which are commonly employed in discrete event simulation models are functions INTLC and OTPUT discussed in Chapter 9C. Function INTLC is called by Visual SLAM before each simulation run and is used to set initial conditions and to schedule initial events. Function OTPUT is called at the end of each simulation and is used for end-of-simulation processing such as printing specific results for the simulation project.

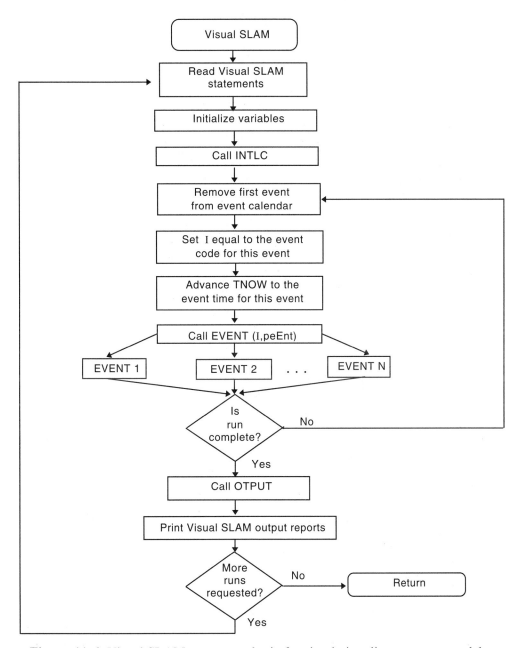

Figure 11-6 Visual SLAM next event logic for simulating discrete event models.

The Visual SLAM next-event logic for simulating discrete event models is depicted in Figure 11-6. The Visual SLAM processor begins by reading the Visual SLAM input statements, if any, and initializing Visual SLAM variables. A call is then made to function INTLC which specifies additional initial conditions for the simulation. Visual SLAM has a version of function INTLC so that the user need not include function INTLC if no additional initialization is required. The processor then begins execution of the simulation by removing the first event from the event calendar. Events are ordered on the calendar based on low values of event times. The variable I is set equal to the event code and TNOW is advanced to the event time for the next event. Visual SLAM then calls the user-written function EVENT which in turn calls the appropriate event routine.

Following execution of the user-written event routine, a test is made to determine if the simulation run is complete. A discrete event simulation is ended if any of the following conditions are satisfied:

1. TNOW is greater than or equal to TTFIN, the ending time of the simulation;
2. no events remain on the event calendar for processing; or
3. the Visual SLAM variable MSTOP has been set in a user-written routine to -1.

If the run is not complete, the new first event is removed from the event calendar and processing continues. Otherwise, a call is made to function OTPUT. (As with INTLC, a version of OTPUT is included in Visual SLAM.) After the return from OTPUT, the Visual SLAM Summary Report is printed. A test is then made on the number of runs remaining. If more runs remain, control returns to initialization and the next simulation run is executed. Otherwise, a return is made from the Visual SLAM processor back to the main program.

The above description provides an overview of the Visual SLAM framework for simulating discrete event models. To write a discrete event simulation program, the user writes a function EVENT(Code,peEnt) to decipher the event Code and to call the appropriate event function, and event routines to specify the changes that occur at event times. Functions INTLC and OTPUT are written if special initial conditions or end-of-simulation processing is required. Based on this overview of the Visual SLAM discrete event framework, we next describe the functional capabilities provided by Visual SLAM for assisting the analyst in developing the user-written functions. Table 11-1 summarizes the fundamental support functions described in Sections 11.4, 11.5 and 11.6.

Table 11-1. Fundamental C Functions of Visual SLAM

User Written

void SWFUNC EVENT(int iCode, ENTITY * peCurrent);

> To process event type iCode for the entity whose pointer is peCurrent.

BOOL SWFUNC INTLC(UINT uiRun);

> To perform initialization for run number uiRun. Return TRUE if the Run should be executed, FALSE otherwise.

BOOL SWFUNC OTPUT(UINT uiRun);

> To perform special end-of-run processing for run number uiRun. Return TRUE if the next run should be made, FALSE otherwise.

Provided by Visual SLAM

BOOL COLCT(double dVal, UINT uiCollect)

> Records the value dVal as an observation of the variable uiCollect.

BOOL su_colnew(UINT uiCollect, char*szID, UINT uiNCel,
    double dHLow, double dHWid)

> Defines a new observed statistic with identification number uiCollect, label szID, and a histogram with uiNCel cells, lower limit of dHLow and cell width of dHWid. ReturnsTRUE if sucessful, FALSE otherwise.

ENTRY*FILEM (UINT uiFile, ENTITY*peCurrent)

> Files the entity located at peCurrent in file uiFile. Returns the entity's placeholder in the file.

ULONG NNQ(UINT uiFile)

> Returns the number of entries currently in file uiFile.

ENTITY*RMOVE (UINT uiFile, ULONG ulRank)

> Removes the entity with rank ulRank from file uiFile and returns the entity pointer.

ENTRY*SCHDL(int iEvent, ENTITY*peCurrent, double dTime)

> Schedules an event of type iEvent to occur at time TNOW+dTime for the entity located at peCurrent. Returns the placeholder of the event in the event calendar (file 0).

ENTITY*su_entnew(int iEntType, double*adAttrib,long*alAttrib,
    char**aszAttrib)

> Creates a new entity and initializes its type and attributes. The attribute pointers are stored in the entity and should not be freed.

void su_entterminate(ENTITY*peUser)

> Terminates the entity pointed to by peUser and its attributes.

ENTITY*su_entclone(ENTITY*peUser,int iEntType)

> Creates a copy of the entity pointed to by peUser. iEntType, the entity type, is a special attribute, which may be different for this clone.

11.4   SCHEDULING EVENTS

The Visual SLAM processor completely relieves the user of the responsibility for chronologically ordering the events on an event calendar. The user simply schedules events to occur, and Visual SLAM causes each event to be processed at the appropriate time in the simulation. Events are scheduled by calling function SCHDL, whose prototype is:

ENTRY *SCHDL(int iEvent, ENTITY *peEnt, double dTime);

The ENTRY structure pointer is the location of an entity's file "placeholder" information while the entity is in a file.

The "placeholder" structure includes such information as the entity's rank, predecessor and successor in the file. The return value of function SCHDL is the pointer to the event's "placeholder" in the event calendar. The parameter iEvent denotes the event code of the event being scheduled, and dTime denotes the number of time units from the current time, TNOW, that the event is to occur. The argument peEnt, as with function EVENT, is a pointer to an ENTITY structure holding the attributes of the entity associated with the event. The elements of an ENTITY structure were discussed in Chapter 9C.

An entity for which an event is to be scheduled is created with the function su_entnew, whose prototype is:

ENTITY*su_entnew(int iEntType,double*ATRIB, long *LTRIB, char**STRIB);

The return value is the pointer to the newly created ENTITY structure. The iEntType parameter defines an entity type which is a special attribute that can be used to distinguish different types of entities. The remaining three parameters are pointers to arrays holding the three different types of attributes, double (identified in a network as ATRIB), long (referred to as LTRIB), and string (referred to as STRIB).

To illustrate the use of functions SCHDL and su_entnew, consider the scheduling of a customer arrival event with event code 1 to occur at the current time plus a sample from an exponential distribution with mean of 5 and using random stream number 1. In addition, the entity representing the customer has its first real attribute value equal to 2.

The coding to accomplish this is as follows:

```
peNew = su_entnew(0,NULL,NULL,NULL);
peNew->ATRIB[1]=2.;
dTime = EXPON(5.,1);
SCHDL(1,peNew,dTime);
```

These statements will cause Visual SLAM to invoke the function EVENT(I,peEnt) at time TNOW + EXPON(5.,1) with I equal to 1 and peEnt equal to peNew.

Another way to create an entity is to copy its structure from an existing entity with the function:

ENTITY *su_entclone (ENTITY *peEnt, int iEntType);

The return value is the pointer to a newly created ENTITY structure whose attributes are a copy of those of the entity pointed to by peEnt. The special entity type attribute, iEntType, may be set to be different for this clone.

When an entity leaves the model, the ENTITY structure located at peEnt is terminated with the statement **su_entterminate(ENTITY *peEnt);**. Function su_entterminate is of type void.

11.5   FILE MANIPULATIONS

Entities which are grouped together because of a relationship are maintained in files. In network models, files are used to maintain entities waiting at QUEUE, AWAIT, and PREEMPT nodes. Files are used extensively in discrete event simulation models and they can be shared with network models, that is, file 1 can be associated with a QUEUE node and also be accessed in a discrete event function. A file provides the mechanism for storing the attributes of an entity in a prescribed ranking with respect to other entities in the file.

In Visual SLAM, files are distinguished by integer numbers assigned to the files by the modeler. Visual SLAM automatically collects statistics on each file and provides the function NNQ(IFILE) which returns the number of entities in file IFILE. For example, NNQ(2) denotes the number of entities in file 2.

Associated with a file is a ranking criterion which specifies the procedure for ordering entities within the file. Thus, each entity in a file has a rank which specifies its position in the file relative to the other members in the file. A rank of one denotes that the entity is the first entry in the file. Possible ranking criterion for files are: first-in, first-out (FIFO); last-in, first-out (LIFO); high-value-first (HVF) based on the value of an expression; and low-value-first (LVF) based on the value of an expression. The ranking criterion for a file used by a network node is assumed to be FIFO unless otherwise specified using the PRIORITY statement described in Chapter 8. Files in a discrete event model may be defined and their ranking criterion specified using the PRIORITY statement. Alternatively, the modeler may create a new file and specifiy its attributes via a function call.

Visual SLAM provides the user with a set of functions for performing all file manipulations which are commonly encountered in discrete event simulations. We now describe the use of these functions for file manipulations where entities are referenced by their rank in the file. As described in Chapter 9C, the UINT variable type is an unsigned integer and the ULONG variable type is an unsigned long.

11.5.1 Filing Entities

The function FILEM with prototype **ENTRY *FILEM (UINT IFILE, ENTITY *peEnt);** files an entry into file IFILE. Its return value is the placeholder of the newly filed entry. As an example of the use of function FILEM, the following statements cause an entity to be inserted into file 1 with its first attribute set equal to the current simulation time.

```
PeEnt – >ATRIB[1] = TNOW;
FILEM(1,peEnt);
```

11.5.2 Removing Entities from Files

The function **ENTITY *RMOVE (UINT IFILE, ULONG NRANK);** removes an entity with rank NRANK from file IFILE and returns the pointer to the ENTITY structure for the entity just removed. As an example of the use of function RMOVE, the following statement removes the last entity in file 1 and returns the ENTITY structure pointer peJob.

peJob = RMOVE(1, NNQ(1));

If the user attempts to remove an entity from file IFILE with rank greater than NNQ(IFILE), a Visual SLAM execution error results. Search functions to locate an entity by its pointer are described in Section 11.13.1.

11.5.3 User-Defined Files

The modeler may create a non-network file simply by using a PRIORITY control statement to define the file's ranking rule. Alternatively, a new file may be created by a call to the function su_filnew, whose protype is

SIM_FILE*su_filnew(UINT File,char**Label,BOOL Stats,int iType,
UINT Max,UINT OrdCode,void*OrdArg,UINT TieCode, void*TieArg);

Creating a file in this way allows one to give a file a name as well as a number, using the Label argument. The Stats argument, if set to FALSE, will suppress file statistics which would normally be collected. If the argument Max is not zero, then an error message will be given if the number in the file exceeds Max. The ranking rule is defined with the which would normally be collected. If the argument Max is not zero, then an error message will be given if the number in the file exceeds Max. The ranking rule is defined with the argument iType, which is one of the following macro names:

> SUFILE_FIFO for a first-in-first-out ranking
> SUFILE_LIFO for a last-in-first-out ranking
> SUFILE_LIST for a sorted linked list
> SUFILE_HEAP for a sorted heap
> SUFILE_TREE for a sorted binary tree

If iType is not FIFO or LIFO but a sorted list, the modeler may use OrdCode, OrdArg, TieCode and TieArg to write a user-defined sorting algorithm. The return value for su_filnew is of type SIM_FILE, which is a pointer to the structure containing the file's attributes.

Suppose we wish to define file number 4 for arriving customers with a FIFO ranking. Statistics are desired, and the file has no maximum capacity. The following function call would create the file:

su_filnew(4,"Arriving Customers",TRUE,SUFILE_FIFO,0,0,NULL,0,NULL);

11.5.4 Functions for Accessing File and Entry Pointers: MMFE, MMLE, NPRED and NSUCR

Entries in a file can be thought of as items on a list, customers in a queue or days on a calendar. The entries stored in a file are considered by Visual SLAM in a logical order, and their order is maintained by their ENTRY* "placeholder" structures. Each entry potentially has a predecessor and successor entry in the file. ENTRY* pointers are used to keep track of each entry's predecessor and successor entry. A NULL value for a pointer indicates that no predecessor or no successor exists, respectively.

The pointer to the first entry in file IFILE is obtained by using the function MMFE with prototype **ENTRY*MMFE(UINT IFILE);**. The function MMLE with prototype **ENTRY*MMLE(UINT IFILE);** returns the pointer to the last entry in file IFILE. Thus the statement Ntry=MMLE(3); defines Ntry as the pointer to the placeholder structure of the last entry in file 3.

By knowing the pointer to the first entry and by accessing the successor of the first entry, we can obtain the pointer to the second entry. The function NSUCR with prototype **ENTRY*NSUCR(UINT IFILE,ENTRY*Ntry);** is used to obtain the pointer to the placeholder of the successor of Ntry in file IFILE. With this function it is possible to proceed in a forward direction from a particular entry in a file until the last entry is encountered. The last entry in a file has no successor and, hence, the function NSUCR would return a NULL value when the successor of the last entry is requested. To search through a file from the last entry, MMLE(IFILE), to the first, the function NPRED with prototype **ENTRY*NPRED (UINT IFILE,ENTRY*Ntry);** is used.

As an example of the use of these functions, consider the problem of locating an entry in file 4 whose second integer attribute is equal to seven. We desire to locate the entry that is closest to the beginning of the file. The code for accomplishing this search is shown below.

```
/* Search File 4 from the beginning for an entry
   ENTRY* Next;
   ENTITY* Ent;
   for (Next=MMFE(4); Next !=NULL; )
   {  Ent = su_sfnentity(Next);
      if (Ent->LTRIB[2]==7) break;
      Next = NSUCR(Next);
   }
```

In this code, the variable Next is used to indicate the next entry to be tested for the desired condition. We start with the first entry in file 4 because the search is to start from the beginning of the file. If Next is NULL, then there are no entries in the file as function MMFE returns NULL when the file is empty.

The function su_sfnentity is used to return the ENTITY* structure pointer for the entity whose ENTRY* structure pointer is Next. Given this pointer, Ent, the second integer attribute of the entity can be accessed. LTRIB[2] for this entity is tested against the value 7 to determine if the prescribed condition is met. If it is, a break is made from the for loop. If the condition is not met, the successor entry is obtained through the use of function NSUCR. Upon exit from the for loop, if Next is not NULL then Next is the ENTRY* pointer and Ent the ENTITY* pointer for the desired entity.

If it is desired to search file 4 from the end of the file, then only minor changes are required in the code. The first entry to be tested is established as the last entry in the file, that is, Next=MMLE(4). In addition, it is necessary to obtain the next entry to be tested by using function NPRED, that is, Next=NPRED(Next);.

11.6   STATISTICS COLLECTION

In discrete event simulations, there are two distinct types of statistics: (1) statistics based on observations; and (2) statistics based on time-persistent variables. In this section, we describe the procedures employed in Visual SLAM discrete event simulations for collecting and estimating values associated with these two types of statistics.

11.6.1   Statistics Based on Observations

Statistics based on observations are statistics computed from a finite number of samples. Each sample value is considered as an observation. For example, in the bank teller problem, statistics on the time in the system for each customer are based on observations where each customer processed through the system is considered as one observation. These statistics depend only upon the value of each observation and not upon the time at which each observation is collected.

Each variable for which observation statistics are collected must be defined by the user with a call to function su_colnew whose prototype is:

BOOL su_colnew (UINT uiCollect, char *szID, UINT uiNCe1, double dHLow, double dHWid);

where

uiCollect is an integer code associated with the variable used to distinguish variable types;

szID is an alphanumeric identifier which is printed on the Visual SLAM Summary Report to identify the output associated with the variable; and

uiNCel/dHLow/dHWid are histogram parameters specifying the number of interior cells, the upper limit for the first cell and the width of each cell. If these parameters are specified as zero, then no histogram is prepared.

Function su_colnew is of type BooL and returns TRUE if successful, FALSE otherwise. As an example, the following function call specifies that observation statistics are to be collected on variable type 1, the results are to be displayed as TIME IN SYSTEM, and a histogram is to be generated with 10 interior cells with the upper limit for the first cell equal to 0 and with interior cell widths of 1.

su_colnew (1, "TIME IN SYSTEM", 10, 0., 1.);

Observations for each variable type defined by function su_colnew are collected within the event functions by a call to function **COLCT(double XVAL,UINT ICLCT)** where the variable XVAL contains the value of the observation and ICLCT is the integer code associated with the variable type. For example, the following statement would cause one observation to be collected on the variable TSYS which is coded as COLCT variable 1.

COLCT(TSYS,1);

Function COLCT is of type BOOL and returns TRUE if successful, FALSE otherwise.

Through inputs on the INITIALIZE statement, function COLCT can be used to obtain statistics over simulation runs. The procedure for accomplishing this involves not clearing the variables for which statistics over runs are desired. By calling function COLCT with a value obtained at the end of each run, statistics over runs are obtained. This call to function COLCT could be made from function OTPUT. For example, if six collect variables are included in the model and we specify that up to the 4th variable type should be cleared, then variables with codes 4, 5, and 6 would not be cleared at the end of a run. These three variables can then be used to store values collected over multiple runs. Specifically, consider the following definitions:

```
su_colnew (1, "V1",0,0.,0.);
su_colnew (2, "V2" ,0,0.,0.);
su_colnew (3, "V3" ,0,0.,0.);
su_colnew (4, "A1" ,0,0.,0.);
su_colnew (5, "A2" ,0,0.,0.);
su_colnew (6, "A3" ,0,0.,0.);
```

and the following input statement:

```
INT, 0, 480, YES, 4;
```

This INIT statement specifies that collect variables 1, 2 and 3 should be cleared at the end of each run but collect variables 4, 5 and 6 should not. The following code in function OTPUT will provide observations on the average value of variables collected as V1, V2 and V3.

```
BOOL SWFUNC OTPUT (UNIT uiRun)
{
        int i;
        for (i=1;  i< = 3;  i++)
                COLCT (CCAVG (i) , i + 3);
        return TRUE;
}
```

On each summary report printed, statistics based on observations are obtained for the variables A1, A2 and A3 which is the average of the average values for V1, V2 and V3 respectively. Thus, if a summary report is printed for three runs, the average of the three average values obtained for V1 is printed in the row whose descriptor is A1. If ten runs are made, the average of ten average values is obtained.

The above procedure can be used with all Visual SLAM status variables or with user defined variables. In Section 11.9, the functions for obtaining the average of any Visual SLAM status variable are described. In the above example, the function CCAVG was used. Similar functions exist for all other Visual SLAM statistics. As described in Chapter 8, a field on the COLCT node statement allows each COLCT node to have an index code so that the functions described in Section 11.9 can also be used to reference statistics collected at COLCT nodes.

11.6.2   Statistics on Time-Persistent Variables

Statistics on time-persistent variables refer to statistics maintained on variables which have a value defined over a period of time. For example, the variable BUSY in the bank teller example is used to denote the status of the teller over time. The fraction of time that BUSY equals 1 is the teller utilization. Therefore the utilization of the teller would be a time-persistent statistic.

Statistics on time-persistent variables are obtained in Visual SLAM discrete event simulations by the use of the TIMST statements. The TIMST input statement causes time-persistent statistics to be automatically accumulated by the Visual SLAM processor. This relieves the user of the burden of calling a function within the event routines to obtain time-persistent statistics. For example, to invoke time-persistent statistics on the variable XX[1], with the output identified as TELLER BUSY TIME, the user simply includes the following statement as part of the Visual SLAM input.

TIMST, 1, XX[1], TELLER BUSY TIME;

To improve the mnemonics within the coding of the event functions, the C #define statement can be employed. For example, time-persistent statistics could be obtained on the C variable BUSY by using the TIMST statement described above in conjunction with the following #define statement.

#define BUSY XX[1]

To obtain a histogram on a time-persistent variable, values for the number of cells, upper limit of the first cell, and a cell width are given in the last fields of the TIMST statement, that is, NCel,HLow,HWid. Each cell of the histogram gives the fraction of time that the time-persistent variable was in the range defined by the cell. For the teller utilization, we can obtain the fraction of time idle or busy in histogram form with the statement.

TIMST, 1, XX[1], TELLER BUSY TIME, 2,0,1;

11.7   VARIABLES

Variables which are employed in a Visual SLAM discrete event simulation model can be of two types: Visual SLAM variables; and user-defined variables. Visual SLAM variables are those defined by the Visual SLAM language. Table 11-2 summarizes the important Visual SLAM variables which are used in discrete event simulation models.

Table 11-2 Definitions of some important discrete event variables.

Variable	Definition
MSTOP	Set by the user to -1 to stop a simulation run before TTFIN.
NNRUN	The number of the current simulation run.
TNOW	The value of current simulated time.
TTBEG	The beginning time of the simulation.
TTFIN	The ending time of the simulation.
LL	The array of user-defined long global variables.
XX	The array of user-defined double global variables.
SZ	The array of user-defined string global variables.

11.8   INPUT STATEMENTS

In discrete event simulation models, input statements are required for specifying a project title, run length, file rankings, monitor events and the like. The input statements employed in discrete event models are identical to those described for network models in Chapter 8. Thus, a discrete event model will typically include a GEN statement, LIMITS statement and FIN statement plus any additional input statements required by the simulation model.

11.9   OUTPUT REPORTS

The results for each simulation run are summarized by the Visual SLAM summary report which is automatically printed by the Visual SLAM processor at the end of each simulation run. The Visual SLAM summary report for discrete event models is identical to that produced for network models with the network statistics omitted, and includes statistics on variables based on observations, statistics on time-persistent variables, file statistics, histograms, and plots. Definitions for the statistical quantities provided by the summary report are provided in Chapter 8.

The Visual SLAM processor also prints a trace report if the TRACE option has been specified using the MONTR statement. The Visual SLAM trace report for discrete-event models includes the event time, the event code, and any variables requested by the MONTR statement. C functions for retrieving values from the summary report writing functions are presented in Section 11.14.3.

11.9.1   Functions for Obtaining Values Associated with Statistical Estimates

Functions have been included in Visual SLAM to allow the user to access information related to statistical estimates during the execution of a simulation model. The first two letters of each function name represent one of the seven types of variables for which statistics are desired. The last three letters of the function name prescribes the statistic of interest. The seven types of variables are: variables based on observation (CC); time-persistent variables (TT); file variables (FF); resource variables (RR); group variables (GR); activity variables (AA); and gate variables (GG). The statistical quantities associated with these variables and their three letter codes are: average value (AVG); standard deviation (STD); maximum observed value (MAX); minimum observed value (MIN); number of observations (NUM); time period over which the time-persistent variable was observed (PRD); time of last change to a time-persistent variable (TLC), and percent of time opened (OPN).

The thirty-five functions included within Visual SLAM to obtain values associated with the variables and statistical quantities are presented in Table 11-2 These functions can be called from any Visual SLAM subprogram and the values can be used for decision making within Visual SLAM models.

Table 11-3 Visual SLAM statistical calculation functions.

Function	Description
Statistics for Variable Based on Observations (COLCT)	
CCAVG(ICLCT)	Average value of variable ICLCT
CCSTD(ICLCT)	Standard deviation of variable ICLCT
CCMAX(ICLCT)	Maximum value of variable ICLCT
CCMIN(ICLCT)	Minimum value of varialbe ICLCT
CCNUM(ICLCT)	Number of observations of variable ICLCT
Statistics for Time-Persistent Variables (TIMST)	
TTAVG(ISTAT)	Time integrated average of variable ISTAT
TTSTD(ISTAT)	Standard deviation of variable ISTAT
TTMAX(ISTAT)	Maximum value of variable ISTAT
TTMIN(ISTAT)	Minimum value of variable ISTAT
TTPRD(ISTAT)	Time period for statistics on variable ISTAT
TTTLC(ISTAT)	Time at which variable ISTAT last changed
Queue Statistics	
FFAVG(IFILE)	Average number of entities in file IFILE
FFAWT(IFILE)	Average waiting time in file IFILE
FFSTD(IFILE)	Standard deviation for file IFILE
FFMAX(IFILE)	Maximum number of entities in file IFILE
FFPRD(IFILE)	Time period for statistics on file IFILE
FFTLC(IFILE)	Time at which number in file IFILE last changed
Resource Statistics	
RRAVG(IRSC)	Average utilization of resource IRSC
RRAVA(IRSC)	Average availability of resource IRSC
RRSTD(IRSC)	Standard deviation of utilization of resource IRSC
RRMAX(IRSC)	Maximum utilization of resource IRSC
RRPRD(IRSC)	Time period for statistics on resource IRSC
RRTLC(IRSC)	Time at which status of resource IRSC last changed
Activity Statistics	
AAAVG(IACT)	Average utilization of activity IACT
AAMAX(IACT)	Maximum utilization of activity IACT, or maximum busy time if activity IACT is a single-server activity
AASTD(IACT)	Standard deviation of the utilization of activity IACT
AATLC(IACT	Time at which the status of activity IACT last changed
Gate Statistics	
GGOPN(IG)	Percent of time that gate IG was open
GGTLC(IB)	Time at which the status of gate IG last changed
Group Statistics	
GRPAVG (IGRP)	Average utilization of group IGRP
GRPAVA (IGRP)	Average availability of group IGRP
GRPSTD (IGRP)	Standard deviation of utilization of group IGRP
GRPMAX (IGRP)	Maximum utilization of group IGRP
GRPPRD (IGRP)	Time period for statistics on group IGRP
GRPTLC (IGRP)	Time at which status of group IGRP last changed

The arguments to the Visual SLAM statistical calculation functions are always a numeric value of type UINT (unsigned integer). File numbers are prescribed for both discrete event and network models and there should be no ambiguity regarding the arguments for the file related functions. For resources, Visual SLAM or the modeler assigns a resource number to each resource block in a network model. This resource number is used as the argument to functions RRAVG, RRAVA, RRSTD, RRMAX, RRPRD, and RRTLC. Group and gate numbering is accomplished in the same manner as resoures. For collect variables, numeric values are assigned by the user in discrete event models and by Visual SLAM or by the user in network models (for each COLCT node). If not specified by the user, Visual SLAM assigns a sequential numeric code for each COLCT statement starting with the first number above the highest user-assigned number. Thus, if there are three variables assigned codes 1, 2, and 3 by calls to su_colnew and two COLCT nodes, the average associated with the first COLCT node in the network description would be accessed by the statement

$$AVE = CCAVG(4);$$

For time-persistent statistics, numeric values are assigned by the user or, if defaulted, by Visual SLAM in the order in which the TIMST input statements appear in the input.

11.10 BUILDING DISCRETE EVENT MODELS

In the preceding sections, we described the discrete event framework of Visual SLAM and a set of subprograms which allows the user to perform the commonly encountered functions in discrete event simulation models. To construct a discrete event simulation model of the bank teller problem, the user must do the following:

1. Write function EVENT to map the user-assigned event codes onto a call to the appropriate event function.

2. Write function INTLC to initialize the model.

3. Write event functions to model the logic for the events of the model.

4. Prepare the input statements required by the problem.

11.11   ILLUSTRATION 11-1.   SERVING BANK CUSTOMERS

In this section, we illustrate how these Visual SLAM functional capabilities are used in constructing discrete event simulation models by describing the coding of the Visual SLAM discrete event model of the bank teller example. In the coding which follows, we assume that customers arrive at the bank with the time between arrivals given by an exponential distribution with a mean of 20 minutes and that the teller service time is uniformly distributed between 10 and 25 minutes. The operation of the bank teller system is to be simulated for a period of 480 minutes.

The event model of the bank teller problem contains two events: the customer arrival event and the end-of-service event. We will code the logic for the customer arrival event in function ARVL and assign it event code 1. The code for the logic for the end-of-service event will be written in function ENDSV and it will be referenced as event code 2. Thus, function EVENT, shown in Figure 11-7, is as depicted previously in Figure 11-5.

```
#include "vslam.h"
void ARVL(ENTITY *peCust);
void ENDSV(ENTITY *peCust);
void SWFUNC EVENT(int iCode, ENTITY * peCust)
{
   switch (iCode)
   {
      case 1: ARVL(peCust);    /* Arrival event*/
              break;
      case 2: ENDSV(peCust); /* Departure event */
   }
}
```

Figure 11-7   Function EVENT for bank teller problem.

The initialization logic for the bank teller problem is coded in function INTLC as depicted in Figure 11-8. The variable LL[1] is set to zero to denote that the teller is initially idle.   Next, the customer entity is created by function su_entnew and the customer arrival event which has an event code of 1 is scheduled onto the event calendar to occur after 0.0 time units.

A set of observed statistics and a file for waiting customers are created.   Collect variable 1 is given the label TIME IN SYSTEM and is to generate a histogram of 10 interior cells with the upper limit of the first cell at 0.0 and each interior cell width set to 4.0. File 1 is given the label "Arriving Customers", is to have statistics generated and is ranked first-in-first-out.

```
BOOL SWFUNC INTLC(UINT uiRun)
{
  ENTITY * peNew;
  /* Initialize the server to idle */
    LL[1] = FALSE;
  /* schedule first arrival at time 0 */
  peNew = su_entnew(0,NULL,NULL,NULL);
  if (peNew)
    SCHDL(1,peNew,0.);
  if (uiRun == 1)
    /* create collect statistics and customer file*/
    {
     su_colnew(1, "TIME IN SYSTEM",10,0.0,4.0);
     su_filnew(1, "Arriving Customers", TRUE,
              SUFILE_FIFO,0,0,NULL,0,NULL);

    }
  return(TRUE);
}
```

Figure 11-8   Function INTLC for bank teller problem.

The logic for the customer arrival event is coded in function ARVL and is presented in Figure 11-9. Figure 11-3 shows the logic in flowchart form. The Visual SLAM variable LL[1] is used to maintain the teller status, TRUE (a macro defined to be 1) if the teller is busy and FALSE (zero) otherwise. The first function performed in the event is the rescheduling of the next arrival event to occur at the current time plus a sample from an exponential distribution with a mean of 20 and using stream 1. The first attribute of the currently arriving customer is then set equal to TNOW. A test is then made on the variable LL[1] to determine the current status of the teller. If LL(1) is TRUE, then the customer is placed in file 1 to wait for the busy teller. If LL[1] is FALSE, then the teller is idle. In this case, LL[1] is set to TRUE to indicate that the teller is going to be busy and an end-of-service event is scheduled to occur at time TNOW plus a sample from a uniform distribution between 10 and 25 using stream 1. In either case, the customer entity is identified by an arrival time which is stored as attribute 1. Depending on LL[1], the customer entity is placed in file 1 or on the event calendar (file 0).

```
void ARVL(ENTITY *peCust)
{
  ENTITY *peNext;
    peNext=su_entclone(peCust,1); /*schedule next arrival*/
    SCHDL(1,peNext,EXPON(20.,1));
    peCust->ATRIB[1]=TNOW;  /* set attributes of arriving
          customer */
    if (LL[1])          {     /* see if service can start*/
      FILEM(1,peCust);             /* busy server */
    }
    else              {
      LL[1] = TRUE;                  /*schedule end of service */
      SCHDL(2,peCust,UNFRM(10.,25.,1));
    }
}
```

Figure 11-9   Function ARVL for bank teller problem.

The logic for the end-of-service event is coded in function ENDSV and is presented in Figure 11-10. Figure 11-4 shows the logic in flowchart form. The variable TSYS is set equal to the current time, TNOW, minus the first attribute of the current customer being processed. When an event is removed from the event calendar, the pointer to the entity structure is passed to function EVENT. Since the value of the first attribute for this customer was set to the customer's time of arrival in the arrival event, the value of TSYS represents the elapsed time between the arrival and end-of-service events for this customer. A call is then made to function COLCT to collect statistics on the value of TSYS as collect variable 1. A test is made on the Visual SLAM function NNQ(1) representing the number of customers waiting for service in file 1. If the number of customers waiting is greater than zero, the first customer waiting is removed from file 1 and placed onto the event calendar. The end-of-service events, event 2, is scheduled to occur at time TNOW plus the service time. If no customer is waiting, the status of the teller is changed to idle by setting the variable LL[1] to FALSE.

```
void ENDSV(ENTITY *peCdone)
{
ENTITY *peCust;
 double TSYS;
 TSYS = TNOW - peCdone->ATRIB[1]; /*save time in system */
 COLCT(TSYS,1);
 su_entterminate(peCdone); /* terminate exiting customer*/

 if (NNQ(1)>0)  { /*see if anyone is waiting for teller */
   peCust = RMOVE(1,1);   /* get customer waiting */
   SCHDL(2,peCust,UNFRM(10.,25.,1)); /*schedule end of
                                      service */
 }
 else        [
   LL[1] = FALSE; /* set server going idle */
 }
}
```

Figure 11-10 Function ENDSV for bank teller problem.

The input statements for this example are shown in Figure 11-11. The GEN statement specifies the analyst's name, project title, date, and number of runs. The LIMITS statement specifies that the model employs one LL variable and one attribute of type double per entity. The TIMST statement causes time-persistent statistics to be automatically maintained on the Visual SLAM variable LL[1] and the results to be displayed using the label Server Busy Time. The INIT statement specifies that the beginning time of the simulation is time 0 and that the ending

time is time 480.   The FIN statement denotes the end to all Visual SLAM input
statements.   This completes the description of the discrete event model of the
bank teller system.

```
GEN,"PRITSKER","BANK TELLER",1/1/1996,1,
;
;Model uses 1 global LL variable and 1 real entity
attribute
;
LIMITS,,1,,1;
;
;Collect statistics on LL[1], server utilization
;
TIMST,1,LL[1],"Server Busy Time";
INITIALIZE,0.0,480,YES;
FIN
```

Figure 11-11 Data statements for bank teller problem.

The coding of the bank teller problem illustrates the general use of Visual SLAM
functional capabilities to code discrete event simulation models. Larger and more
complicated models are developed in the same way and differ only in the number
and complexity of the event functions. In the next sections, we present a discrete
event example which is slightly more complicated and further illustrates discrete
event modeling using Visual SLAM.

11.12   EXAMPLE 11-1.   A DISCOUNT STORE OPERATION

A discount store has developed a new procedure for serving customers.
Customers enter the store and determine the item they wish to purchase by
examining display items. After selecting an item, the customer proceeds to a
centralized area where a clerk takes the order and travels to an adjacent warehouse
to pick up the item. Clerks will service as many as six customers at a time. The
time for the clerk to travel to the warehouse is uniformly distributed between 0.5
and 1.5 minutes. The time to find an item depends on the number of items the clerk
must locate in the warehouse. This time is normally distributed with a mean equal
to three times the number of items to be picked up. The standard deviation is equal
to 0.2 of the mean. Thus, if one item is to be obtained from the warehouse, the time
to locate the item is normally distributed with a mean of 3 and a standard deviation
of 0.6 minutes. The time to return from the warehouse is uniformly distributed

within the range of 0.5 and 1.5 minutes. When the clerk returns from the warehouse, the sale is completed for each customer. The time to complete the sale is uniformly distributed between 1 and 3 minutes. The completion of sales for the customers is performed sequentially in the same order that requests for items were made of the clerk. The time between customer requests for items is assumed to be exponentially distributed with the mean of 2 minutes. Three clerks are available to serve the customers. A schematic diagram of the store operation is shown in Figure 11-12.

The objective of this simulation is to determine the utilization of the clerks, the time required to serve a customer from the time at which an item is requested until the completion of a sale, and the number of requests handled by a clerk for each trip to the warehouse. The simulation is to be run for 1000 minutes.

Visual SLAM model. The discrete event model for this example consists of a customer arrival event and an end-of-service event. At first glance, it may also appear that events are required to explicitly model each clerk's arrival to and departure from the warehouse. However, no specific interactions occur during the time that the clerk is filling a request, and therefore the explicit modeling of these intermediate points by event routines is not necessary. If competition for resources are involved in filling the requests, then a more detailed model of the procedure for locating items would be required. Such a situation would exist if resources are required in the warehouse, for example, a forklift truck.

There are five files employed in this example. The first four files are employed for storing the attributes of entities representing customers. Customers which arrive at the system when all clerks are busy are stored in file 4. Customers which have placed their orders and are waiting for clerk 1, 2, or 3 to return reside in files 1, 2, and 3, respectively. File 5 is employed for storing the attributes of entities representing free clerks waiting for customers to arrive. The ENTITY* pointer peCust is utilized for filing and removing customers from the first four files and ENTITY* pointer peClerk is employed for filing and removing clerks from file 5. There is one attribute associated with the customer entities which is used to record the arrival time of the customer to the system. There is also one attribute associated with the clerk entities and it is used to denote the clerk as 1, 2, or 3.

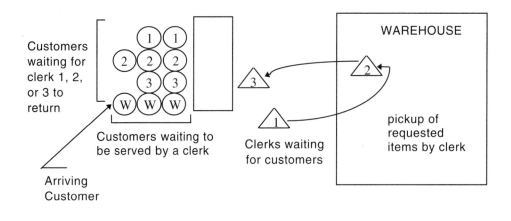

Customers waiting for clerk 1, 2, or 3 to return

Arriving Customer

Customers waiting to be served by a clerk

Clerks waiting for customers

WAREHOUSE

pickup of requested items by clerk

Legend:

clerk i, i = 1, 2, 3

customer being served by clerk i, i = 1, 2, 3 or waiting for a clerk, i = w

Figure 11-12 Schematic diagram of discount store operation.

The customer arrival event is assigned event code 1 and is coded in function ARVL. The end-of-service event is assigned event code 2 and is coded in function ENDSV. For easier reading, the macros ARRIVAL and ENDSERVICE have been defined for the constants 1 and 2. Function EVENT for this example is shown in Figure 11-13. It maps the event code onto the appropriate function call.

```
void SWFUNC EVENT(int iCode, ENTITY * peEnt)
{
    switch (iCode)
    {
        case ARRIVAL: /* customer entity */
            ARVL(peEnt);
        break;
        case ENDSERVICE: /* clerk entity */
            ENDSV(peEnt);
        break;
        default:
            su_error(1,"Unknown event code");
        break;
    }
}
```

Figure 11-13 Sample function EVENT.

First, consider the logic associated with the customer arrival event. A flowchart for this event is depicted in Figure 11-14, and the coding is shown in Figure 11-15. Before processing the current arrival, the next arrival is scheduled to occur after an exponential time delay with a mean of 2 minutes by a call to function SCHDL. The arrival time of the current customer is then recorded as the first attribute of the entity. The disposition of the current customer request is determined based on the status of the clerks. A test is made on the number of free clerks waiting in file 5. If file 5 is empty, the customer must wait until a clerk becomes free. File 4 is used to store customers waiting for clerks. If the customer must wait, no further functions can be performed at the arrival event time and a return is made.

If a clerk is available, the order processing can be initiated. The first free clerk is removed from file 5. Function RMOVE returns the pointer to the clerk entity as peClerk. The user variable iClerk is then set to the first integer attribute of the clerk which corresponds to the clerk number. The current customer, which is pointed to by peCust, is then inserted into file iClerk to wait for the return and end-of-service processing by clerk iClerk. Statistics are collected on the number of customers being served on each clerk trip which in this case is one. The statistics code for this collect variable is set as 2. The total time spent in traveling to the warehouse, in filling customer requests, returning from the warehouse, and completing the order is then computed as the variable dTemp. The end-of-service event is then scheduled to occur dTemp minutes later with the attributes of the clerk associated with the event.

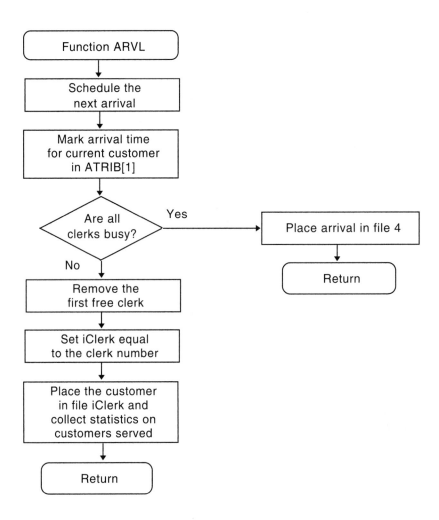

Figure 11-14 Flowchart of customer arrival event for discount example.

```
void ARVL(ENTITY *peCust)
{
    ENTITY * peClerk;
    ENTITY * peNext;
    double dTemp;
    int iClerk;

    /* schedule next arrival */
    peNext = su_entclone(peCust,0);
    SCHDL(ARRIVAL,peNext,EXPON(2.0,1));

    /* mark arrival time */
    peCust->ATRIB[1] = TNOW;
    if (NNQ(5)==0)                      {
        /* all clerks busy.  wait for service */
        FILEM(4, peCust);
    }
    else                                {
        /* get first free clerk */
        peClerk = RMOVE(5,1);
        iClerk = peClerk->LTRIB[1];

        /* place customer in this clerk's file */
        FILEM(iClerk, peCust);
       /* collect observation of 1 customer served this trip*/
        COLCT(1.0,2);

        /* schedule end of service for clerk */
        dTemp = UNFRM(0.5,1.5,1);
        dTemp += RNORM(3.0,0.6,1);
        dTemp += UNFRM(0.5,1.5,1);
        dTemp += UNFRM(1.0,3.0,1);
        SCHDL(ENDSERVICE,peClerk,dTemp);
    }
}
```

Figure 11-15 Visual SLAM code for customer arrivals to discount store.

Next, consider the logic for the end-of-service event. A flowchart for this event is given in Figure 11-16 and the Visual SLAM coding is shown in Figure 11-17. The pointer to the clerk entity structure, peClerk, is used to set the user variable iClerk to the number of the clerk processing the end-of-service for the customer. The customer completing service is then removed from file iClerk and its pointer set to peCust. The time in the system for the customer is computed and statistics are collected on this value as collect variable number 1. A test is then made on the

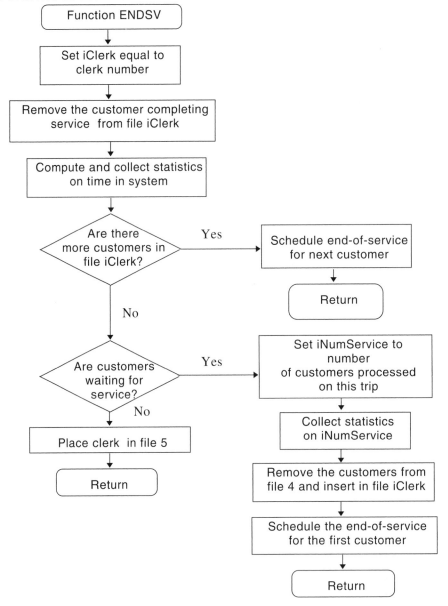

Figure 11-16 Flowchart of end-of-service event for discount store example.

```
void ENDSV(ENTITY *peClerk)
{
    ENTITY * peCust;
    double dVal;
    double dTemp;
    int iClerk;
    int iNumService;
    iClerk = peClerk->LTRIB[1];
    /* remove top customer from this clerk's list */
    peCust = RMOVE(iClerk, 1);
        /* collect time in system */
        dTemp = TNOW - peCust->ATRIB[1];
        COLCT(dTemp,1);
        /* terminate customer */
        su_entterminate(peCust);
    /* see if anyone is waiting for this clerk */
    if (NNQ(iClerk) > 0)
    {
        /* more customers assigned to this clerk */
        SCHDL(ENDSERVICE,peClerk,UNFRM(1.0,3.0,1));
    }
    else if (NNQ(4) > 0)
    {
        /* new customers waiting */
        iNumService = NNQ(4);
        if (iNumService > MAXSERVICE)
        {
            iNumService = MAXSERVICE;
        }
        /* collect stats on number of customers this trip */
        COLCT((double)iNumService,2);
        /* schedule end of service for first customer */
        dVal = (double) (iNumService * 3);
        dTemp = UNFRM(0.5,1.5,1);
        dTemp += RNORM(dVal,dVal*0.2,1);
        dTemp += UNFRM(0.5,1.5,1);
        dTemp += UNFRM(1.0,3.0,1);
        SCHDL(ENDSERVICE,peClerk,dTemp);
        /* move customers to this clerk's list */
        for (/* empty */; iNumService; iNumService--)
        {
            /* get next customer and place in this clerk's file */
            peCust = RMOVE(4,1);
            FILEM(iClerk, peCust);
        }
    }
    else
    {
        /* no customer waiting */
        /* place clerk in idle clerk list */
        FILEM(5,peClerk);
    }
}
```

Figure 11-17 Visual SLAM code for end-of-service event at discount store.

Visual SLAM function NNQ(iClerk) to determine if more customers remain. If NNQ(iClerk) is greater than zero, the end-of-service event for the next customer is scheduled.   Otherwise, a test is made on NNQ(4) to determine if there are customers waiting to place their orders with a clerk. If customers are waiting, then the user variable iNumService is set to the number of customers to be processed and statistics are collected on this quantity as collect variable number 2. These customers are then removed from file 4 and inserted into file iClerk to await end-of-service processing. The total time spent in traveling to the warehouse, in filling customer requests, returning from the warehouse, and completing the order for the first customer is then computed as dTemp. Note that the time to fill requests is obtained as a sample from a normal distribution with a mean dVal equal to the number of customers, iNumService, times 3. The standard deviation, STD, is two-tenths of the mean, that is, STD = 0.2*dVal. The end-of-service event for the first customer to be processed is then scheduled to occur dTemp minutes later. In the case where there are no customers waiting to place their orders, the clerk entity is placed in file 5 which is the file used for storing idle clerks.

Function INTLC is used to put the three clerks into file 5 as it is assumed that all clerks are idle at the beginning of the simulation run. The first customer arrival event is scheduled to occur at time 0.0 by calling SCHDL with an event code of 1. The listing of function INTLC is given in Figure 11-18. The input statements for this example are shown in Figure 11-19.

Summary of Results. The Visual SLAM Summary Report for this example is given in Figure 11-20. The report reveals that during the 1000 minutes of simulated operation, 517 customers were processed through the system with customers spending an average of 24.49 minutes in the system. The average number of customers per trip by each clerk was 3.040 with a total of 175 trips completed by the clerks. These results indicate that management should investigate the hiring of additional clerks or change the policy regarding the minimum or maximum number of customers a clerk should serve at one time.

Although the average utilization of the clerks is not directly provided by the report, this statistic can be estimated using the average length of file 5. Since idle clerks reside in file 5, the average number of busy clerks is the number of clerks minus the average number in file 5, that is, 2.927.

```
#include "vslam.h"
/* events */

#define ARRIVAL     1
#define ENDSERVICE 2
/* limits */

#define MAXCLERK    3
#define MAXSERVICE 6
/* prototypes */

void ARVL(ENTITY *peUser);
void ENDSV(ENTITY *peUser);

/****************************************************************
 *
 * FUNCTION: INTLC
 *
 ****************************************************************/

BOOL SWFUNC INTLC(UINT uiRun)
{
    ENTITY * peNew;
    char szTemp[30];
    int i;
    if (uiRun == 1) /* on first run,  define files */
    {
        /* create discrete files */
        su_filnew(4,"Customer Arrival", TRUE, SUFILE_FIFO, 0,
                            0, NULL, 0, NULL);
        su_filnew(5,"Free Clerks", TRUE, SUFILE_FIFO, 0,
                            0, NULL, 0, NULL);
        for (i=1; i <= MAXCLERK; i++)
        {
            sprintf(szTemp,"Wait for Clerk %d",i);
            su_filnew(i,szTemp, TRUE, SUFILE_FIFO, 0,
                            0, NULL, 0, NULL);
        }
        /* create collect statistics */
        su_colnew(1, "TIME IN SYSTEM",0,0.0,0.0);
        su_colnew(2, "CUST PER TRIP",10,0.0,1.0);
    }
        /* schedule arrival at time 0 of first customer */
        peNew = su_entnew(0,NULL,NULL,NULL);
        SCHDL(ARRIVAL,peNew,0.0);
        /* put initial idle clerks into free clerks file */
        for (i=1; i <= MAXCLERK; i++)
        {
            peNew = su_entnew(1,NULL,NULL,NULL);
            peNew->LTRIB[1] =  i; /* clerk number */
            FILEM(5, peNew);
        }
    return(TRUE);
}
```

Figure 11-18 Function INTLC for discount store example.

```
GEN,"PRITSKER","DISCOUNT STORE",1/1/1996,1;
LIMITS,-1,-1,-1,1,1,-1;
INIT,0,1000;
FIN;
```

Figure 11-19 Input statements for discount store example.

```
            ** AweSim SUMMARY REPORT **

Simulation Project : DISCOUNT STORE
Modeler : PRITSKER
Date : 1/1/1996
Scenario : EX111

Run number 1 of 1
Current simulation time   : 1000.000000
Statistics cleared at time : 0.000000

      ** OBSERVED STATISTICS REPORT for scenario EX111 **
```

Label	Mean Value	Standard Deviation	Number of Observations	Minimum Value	Maximum Value
TIME IN SYSTEM	24.491	10.486	517	5.227	51.900
CUST PER TRIP	3.040	1.955	175	1.000	6.000

```
      ** FILE STATISTICS REPORT for scenario EX111 **
```

File Number	Label or Input Location	Average Length	Standard Deviation	Maximum Length	Current Length	Average Wait Time
1	Wait for Clerk 1	3.712	1.927	6	6	20.066
2	Wait for Clerk 2	3.236	1.890	6	3	19.149
3	Wait for Clerk 3	3.361	1.972	6	6	18.879
4	Customer Arrival	2.648	2.783	17	1	5.371
5	Free Clerks	0.073	0.295	3	0	1.816

Figure 11-20 Visual SLAM summary report for discount store example.

11.13   ADVANCED DISCRETE EVENT CONCEPTS

In this section, we present information on functions for searching files for entities, functions for report writing and functions for accessing statistical quantities.

11.13.1 Searching a File

In some cases the location of a specific entity of interest may not be known. Function su_filfind, whose prototype is ENTRY*su_filfind (SIM_FILE*psfList, ENTRY* psfnStart, SF_FILTER compare,PVOID fpl); can be used to determine the placeholder of an entry for which a specific attribute, its pointer, or its event type bears a relationship designated by the user to a specified value. Definitions of the arguments to su_filfind for determining the placeholder of an entry are:

psfList   The pointer to the file to be searched.

psfnStart   The placeholder of the entry where the search begins. May be NULL, meaning that the search begins with the first entry in the file.

compare   A function which performs the comparison based on the argument fpl.

fpl   An argument for the *compare* function.

The psfList argument is a pointer to a structure of type SIM_FILE, which contains information about a file. Given a file number, the file pointer is returned by function *su_fnfile* whose prototype is:

SIM_FILE *su_fnfile(UINT uiFile);

The most common use of *su_filfind* is to search for an entity for whom an attribute bears a specified relationship (==,<=,>=,<,>,!=) to a given value. In this case, the third argument to *su_filfind* is the Visual SLAM comparison function *su_filterattrib*. The fourth argument to *su_filfind* is a pointer to a structure of type SU_FINDARG which holds the information needed to do the comparison. The elements of this structure are:

int iCompare   The type of comparison, one of SUFILTER_EQ, SUFILTER_LE, SUFILTER_GE, SUFILTER_LT, SUFILTER_GT or SUFILTER_NE. These are macro names for the appropriate integer values used by su_filterattrib.

int iAttribType   The type of attribute to compare, one of SUFILTER_DOUBLE, SUFILTER_LONG, or SUFILTER_STRING (more macro names for appropriate integer values).

ULONG ulAttribIndex   The offset in the specified attribute array. UCompare A union of comparison values. The element of the union to set is one of dVal, lVal, or szVal, depending on whether the attribute type is double, long, or string.

For example, the following code will search file 3, beginning with the first entry, and return the placeholder of the entry whose ATRIB[4] equals 10. It will return NULL if no such entry exists.

```
  SU_FINDARG stFind;                    /* Structure type declaration */
    stFind.iCompare = SUFILTER_EQ;     /* Structure element definitions */
    stFind.iAttribType = SUFILTER_DOUBLE;
    stFind.ulAttribIndex = 4;
    stFind.uCompare.dVal = 10.;
    psfIO = su_fnfile(3);                /* First argument for su_filfind */
    psfnCur = su_filfind(psfIO,NULL,
    su_filterattrib, &stFind);           /* The search */
```

Three additional comparison functions provided in Visual SLAM are given below.

Function	fpl Argument
su_filterEQentity	ENTITY pointer to the entity being matched
su_filterNEentity	ENTITY pointer to the entity being compared
su_filterevent	event number to be matched

The **compare** argument could also be a user-written filter function. Filter functions have the form:

$$BOOL\ filter(SIM\_FILE * psfList, ENTRY * peCur, PVOID\ fpl);$$

and return TRUE if the entry at peCur meets the criteria.

11.13.2 Report Writing Functions

A set of functions is contained within Visual SLAM to enable the user to obtain summary reports or sections of a summary report. These functions can be used to obtain summary information of a specific type. The output from a function corresponds to a specific section of the Visual SLAM summary report (see Chapter 8). The list of functions along with the definitions of their arguments is presented in Table 11-4.

The terminology used in naming the functions is to append a specific letter onto the letters PRNT. Thus, PRNTF is used as the name of the function to print files and PRNTH is used as the name of the function to print histograms. The arguments to these functions have been standardized so that an argument value greater than zero requests a specific item to be printed. If the argument is given as a zero value then all items associated with the function are printed. In the case of PRNTF(IFILE), statistics on all files can be obtained by specifying a negative value for the argument IFILE.

Listed below are examples of the use of the report writing routines.

Statement	Description
SUMRY( );	Prints a complete summary report at time of calling (TNOW)
PRNTF(3);	Prints statistics on file 3.
PRNTT(0);	Prints statistics on all time-persistent variables.
PRNTA(0);	Prints statistics on all network activities that were given activity numbers.

Table 11-4 Visual SLAM report writing functions.

Function	Description
BOOL PRNTA(UINT uiAct)	Prints statistics for activity uiAct. If uiAct is zero, then statistics for all activities are printed.
BOOL su_outactstat(FILE*pfFile, UINT uiAct)	Prints PRNTA statistics to file pfFile.
BOOL PRNTB(UINT uiStat)	If uiStat>0, prints the histogram associated with the time-persistent variable type iStat. If uiStat=0, prints all time-persistent histograms.
BOOL su_outtphist(FILE*pfFile, UINT uiStat)	Prints PRNTB statistics to file pfFile.
BOOL PRNTC(UINT uiCollect)	If uiCollect>0, prints statistics for COLCT variable number uiCollect. If uiCollect=0, prints statistics for all variables based on observation.
BOOL su_outcollect(FILE*pfFile, UINT uiCollect)	Prints PRNTC statistics to file pfFile.
BOOL PRNTF(UINT uiFile)	If uiFile>0, prints statistics for file uiFile. If uiFile=0, prints statistics for all files. If uiFile<0, prints the contents of all files.
BOOL su_outfilestat(FILE*pfFile, SIM_FILE*pList)	Prints PRNTF statistics to file pfFile. If pList is NULL, SIM_FILE*pList) prints statistics for all files.
BOOL su_outfilecontent	Prints contents of the file pointed to by pList to (SIM_FILE*plist,FILE*pfFile) the file pointed to by pfFile. If pList is NULL, prints the contents of all files.
BOOL PRNTG(UINT uiGate)	If uiGate>0, prints statistics on gate number uiGate. If uiGate=0, prints statistics on all gates.
BOOL su_outgatestat(FILE*pfFile UINT uiGate)	Prints PRNTG statistics to file pfFile.
BOOL PRNTH(UINT uiCollect)	If uiCollect>0, prints the histogram for COLCT variable uiCollect. If uiCollect=0, prints all histograms.
BOOL su_outcolhist(FILE*pfFile UINT uiCollect)	Prints PRNTH statistics to file pfFile.
BOOL PRNTO(UINT uiGroup)	If uiGroup>0, prints statistics for group number uiGroup. If uiGroup=0, prints statistics for all groups.
BOOL su_outgroupstat(FILE*pfFile, UINT uiGroup)	Prints PRNTO statistics to file pfFile.
BOOL PRNTR(UINT uiRes)	If uiRes>0, prints statistics for resource number uiRes. If uiRes=0, prints statistics for all resources.
BOOL su_outresstat(FILE*pfFile UINT uiRes)	Prints PRNTR statistics to file pfFile.
BOOL PRNTS(void)	Prints the contents of the state storage arrays SS[I] and DD[I].
BOOL su_outstate(FILE*pfFile)	Prints PRNTS output to file pfFile.
BOOL PRNTT(UINT uiStat)	If uiStat>0, prints statistics for time-persistent variable uiStat. If uiStat=0, prints statistics for all time-persistent variables.
BOOL su_outtpstat(FILE*pfFile, UINT,uiStat)	Prints PRNTT statistics to file pfFile.
BOOL SUMRY(void)	Prints the Visual SLAM Summary Report.

11.14   CHAPTER SUMMARY

This chapter presents the Visual SLAM discrete event simulation modeling procedures. The procedures for scheduling events, file manipulations, and statistical collection routines are described. A list of important discrete event variables is presented in Table 11-2. An illustration and an example of discrete event modeling using Visual SLAM are presented. The example involves a discount store where clerks perform multiple operations before completing service on customers. Table 11-5 summarizes the user-written and user-callable functions used with Visual SLAM.

The organization of a Visual SLAM program for discrete event modeling is illustrated in Figure 11-21.

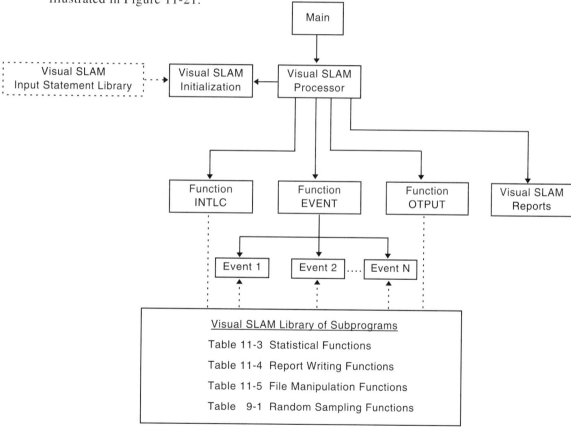

Figure 11-21 Visual SLAM organization for discrete event modeling.

Table 11-5. Summary of C Functions Included in Visual SLAM

Function	Description
User-Written	
ENTRY * SWFUNC ALLOC (int iCode,ENTRY* psfnFirst);	To process allocation rule iCode at the AWAIT node for which psfnFirst is the placeholder of the entry of the first entry. Returns the placeholder of the entry which should be released from the node, NULL if allocations were not made.
ENTITY * SWFUNC ASSEMBLE (int iCode, SN_NODE * pNode);	To create the entity being assembled at the SELECT node whose pointer is pNode with the user-defined assembly rule iCode. Returns the ENTITY pointer of the newly assembled entity.
void SWFUNC BATCHSAVE (int iCode, ENTITY*peForm, ENTITY*peAdd);	To update the attributes of a batch entity whose ENTITY pointer is peForm when the entity whose ENTITY pointer is peAdd arrives to a BATCH node with an attribute save criterion of User(iCode).
void SWFUNC EVENT (int iCode, ENTITY * peUser);	To process event type iCode for the entity whose pointer is peUser.
BOOL SWFUNC INTLC(UINT uiRun);	To perform initialization for run number uiRun. Return TRUE if the Run should be executed, FALSE otherwise.
UINT SWFUNC NQS (int iCode, ENTITY * peUser, SN_NODE * pNode);	To process the SELECT node whose pointer is pNode and whose queue selection rule is NQS(iCode). The entity whose pointer is peUser is the one which triggered the selection. Return the file number of the selected QUEUE.
UINT SWFUNC NSS (int iCode, ENTITY * peUser, SN_NODE * pNode);	To process the SELECT node whose pointer is pNode and whose server selection rule is NSS(iCode). The entity whose pointer is peUser is the one which triggered the selection. Return the activity number of the selected service activity.
BOOL SWFUNC OTPUT(UINT uiRun);	To perform special end-of-run processing for run number uiRun. Return TRUE if the next run should be made, FALSE otherwise.
double SWFUNC USERF (int iCode, ENTITY * peUser);	To return a value specified in a network as USERF(iCode) and required by the entity whose pointer is peUser.
Provided by Visual SLAM	
BOOL COLCT (double dVal, UINT uiCollect)	Records the value dVal as an observation of the variable uiCollect.
BOOL su_colnew (UINT uiCollect, char*szID, uiNCel, double dHLow, double dHWid)	Defines a new observed statistic with identification number uiCollect, label szID, and a histogram with uiNCel cells, lower limit of UINT dHLow and cell width of dHWid. ReturnsTRUE if sucessful, FALSE otherwise.
ENTRY*FILEM (UINT uiFile, ENTITY*peUser)	Files the entity located at peUser in file uiFile. Returns the entity's placeholder in the file.
ENTRY * MMFE(UINT uiFile)	Returns the pointer to the first entry (rank 1) in file uiFile.
ENTRY * MMLE(UINT uiFile)	Returns the pointer to the last entry (rank NNQ(uiFile)) in file uiFile.
ULONG NNQ(UINT uiFile)	Returns the number of entries currently in file uiFile.
ENTRY*NPRED (UINT uiFile, ENTRY*psfnCur)	Returns the placeholder of the entity in file uiFile which precedes the entity with the placeholder psfnCur.
ENTRY*NSUCR (UINT uiFile, ENTRY*psfnCur)	Returns the placeholder of the entity in file uiFile which succeeds the entity with the placeholder psfnCur.

Table 11-5. (continued)

Function	Description
ENTITY*RMOVE (UINT uiFile, ULONG ulRank)	Removes the entity with rank ulRank from file uiFile and returns the entity pointer.
ENTRY*SCHDL (int iEvent, ENTITY*peUser, double dTime)	Schedules an event of type iEvent to occur at time TNOW+dTime for the entity located at peUser. Returns the placeholder of the event in the event calendar (file 0).
ENTITY*su_entnew (int iEntType, double*adAttrib, long*alAttrib, char**aszAttrib)	Creates a new entity and initializes its type and attributes. The attribute pointers are stored in the entity and should not be freed.
void su_entterminate(ENTITY*peUser)	Terminates the entity pointed to by peUser and its attributes.
ENTITY*su_entclone(ENTITY*peUser,int iEntType)	Creates a copy of the entity pointed to by peUser. iEntType, the entity type, is a special attribute, which may be different for this clone.
SIM_FILE*su_filnew (UINT File, char*szLabel, BOOL bStats, int iType, UINT uiMax,UINT uiOrdCode, void*pvOrdArg,UINT uiTieCode, void* pvTieArg)	Creates a new file with file number File. Statistics are collected if bStats is TRUE. The ranking rule, iType, is SUFILE_FIFO if first-in-first-out, SUFILE_LIFO if last-in-first-out, SUFILE_LIST if sorted linked list, SUFILE_HEAP if heap, SUFILE_TREE if sorted binary tree. An error message is generated if the number in the file exceeds uiMax. uiMax should be defined to be zero if there is no maximum. If iType specifies a sorted list, the user will write the ordering function sw_order with input parameters uiOrdCode, and pvOrdArg. To assist in writing sw_order, six comparison functions are provided.
ENTRY*su_filfind (SIM_FILE*psfList, ENTRY*psfnStart, SF_FILTER compare,PVOID fpl)	Returns the placeholder of the next entity in the file pointed to by psfList which follows the entity with the placeholder psfnStart and matches the condition defined by SF_FILTER and fpl.
BOOL su_filremove (SIM_FILE*psfList,ENTRY*psfnCur)	Removes an entity given a file pointer and an entity placeholder, returning TRUE if no error was encountered.
SIM_FILE*su_fnfile(UINT uiFile)	Returns the pointer to file uiFile.
ENTITY*su_sfnentity(ENTRY*psfnCur)	Returns the pointer to the entity with the file placeholder psfnCur.

11.15   EXERCISES

11-1.   Simulate a single server system where service is exponentially distributed with a mean service time of one hour and there are two types of arrivals. Arrival type 1 is an item of high priority and waits only for the processing of other high priority items. The time intervals between arrivals of high priority items is exponentially distributed with a mean time between arrivals of four hours. The time between arrivals of low priority items is also exponentially distributed, but has a mean time between arrivals of two hours. Obtain statistics regarding server utilization and information concerning the time in the system and in the queue for high and low priority items. Assume that service on low priority items is not interrupted to process high priority items.

Embellishment: Repeat the simulation with the assumption that high priority items interrupt the servicing of low priority items. Interrupted items are inserted at the beginning of the queue of low priority items. Show that the time remaining for those items interrupted is exponentially distributed with a mean time equal to the mean service time.

11-2. Jobs arrive at a job shop so that the interarrival time is exponentially distributed with a mean time between arrivals of 1.25 hours. The time to process a job is uniformly distributed in the interval 0.75 to 1.25 hours. The time to process the jobs is estimated prior to the time the job is performed. Simulate the processing of jobs in the order of shortest processing time first. Obtain statistics describing the average time jobs are in the shop, the variation of the time the jobs are in the shop and the utilization of the server. Assume that the *actual* processing times for the jobs are equal to the *estimates* of the processing times. Repeat the simulation with jobs with the longest processing time performed first. Then carry out the simulation with the jobs processed in order of their arrival time. Compare the results.

Embellishment: Repeat the simulation for a situation in which the actual processing time is equal to the estimated processing time plus a sample drawn from a normal distribution with a mean of zero and a standard deviation of 0.2.

11-3. Build a discrete event model for the two work stations in series described in Example 5-1.

Embellishment:

(a) Before subcontracting a unit, check the end-of-service times for the work stations. If the next end-of-service is within 0.1 hours of the current time, the unit is not subcontracted but returns to the work station in 0.2 hour.

(b) Redevelop the work station model under the assumption that the manufacturer only maintains 100 units. The time to failure for each unit is exponentially distributed with a mean of 40 hours. The time to repair a unit if subcontracted is triangularly distributed with a mode of 4, a minimum of 3, and a maximum of 6.

11-4. Develop a discrete event simulation of the PERT network given in Example 7-1. Hint: The simulation of PERT networks involves a single event representing the end of an activity. Perform a simulation of the PERT network for 400 runs.

Embellishment: Estimate the probability that an activity is on the critical path in a run. This probability is referred to as a criticality index.

11-5. Develop a discrete event model of the inventory situation presented in Example 6-1.

Embellishments:

    (a) Make the lead time for the receipt of orders lognormally distributed with a mean of 3 and standard deviation of 1.

    (b) Include in the model information that each customer may   demand   more than one radio. The additional number of radios demanded per customer is Poisson distributed with a mean of 2. Thus, the expected number demanded per customer is 3. Presume if there are insufficient radios to meet the total number of radios demanded by a customer, the entire order is backordered with probability 0.2.

    (c) Convert the periodic review system to a transaction reporting system where the inventory position is reviewed after every sale or backorder.

    (d) Make the mean time between customer demands a function of the number of lost sales and backorders. If the average number of lost sales and backorders per week is less than 1, the mean time between demands is 0.18 week. If the average number of lost sales and backorders is greater than 2, the mean time between demands is 0.22. Otherwise, the mean time between demands is 0.20.

    (e) Add the following income and cost structure to the inventory situation. Radios sell for $65 and cost the store $40. An inventory carrying charge of $0.004 per dollar/week is used. The cost of placing an order for radios from the supplier is estimated to be $50. Each review of inventory costs $30. A lost sale results in a loss of goodwill and is estimated to cost $20. The cost for maintaining a backorder is $10. Run a simulation of this inventory situation for 312 weeks.

    (f) Evaluate the effect of alternative inventory policies on average profit using the cost and income data provided in embellishment (e).

11-6. Build a discrete event model for the conveyor situation described in Exercise 9-5.

11-7. Build a discrete event model of the drive-in bank with jockeying described in Example 9-1. Embellishment: Enlarge the model by including the departure process of cars into the street next to the bank. Cars departing from the bank tellers can enter the street when a large enough gap exists between cars traveling on the street. The time between such gaps is uniformly distributed between 0.3 and 0.5 minutes. The space following the tellers is only sufficient to allow 3 cars to wait for a gap in the street traffic.

11-8. Embellishment to Example 11-1. Alter the discount store operation so that clerks wait for 1 minute before traveling to the warehouse to serve a single customer. Determine the effect of this new policy on customer waiting time and clerk utilization. Evaluate alternative time intervals for waiting for additional customers before traveling to the warehouse.

11-9. Embellishment to Example 11-1. In the simulation of the discount store operation, it has been determined that there is a probability that the clerk will return from the warehouse with an incorrect item. When this occurs the clerk immediately returns to the warehouse to obtain the correct item. The probability of retrieving an incorrect item is 0.15. In addition, there is a probability of 0.1 that the item requested was not in inventory. When this occurs, there is a probability of 0.25 that the customer will request a new item. Evaluate the effect of this new information on clerk utilization and customer waiting time.

11-10. For Exercise ll-4, determine the number of simulation runs that would be required to obtain a 95% probability that: (a) the estimate of the project duration is within 0.1 of a standard deviation of the theoretical project duration: (b) the estimate of the variance of the project duration is within 10% of the theoretical variance of the project duration; and (c) the difference between the observed and theoretical criticality indices is less than or equal to 0.005.

11-11. Write the statements required to determine the location of the entry that satisfies the following conditions:

(a) The entry in file 2 that has attribute 3 equal to 10.

(b) The entry with the largest value of attribute 4 greater than 0 in file 1.

(c) The entry whose third attribute is closest to 10 but does not exceed 10 in file 3.

(d) In file 3, the entry whose third attribute is closest to 10 but is not less than 10.

(e) The entry in file 4 whose second attribute is the largest. Entries with the value of attribute 2 less than 3 cannot be used.

11.16 REFERENCES

1. Henriksen, J. O., "GPSS--Finding the Appropriate World-View," Proceedings, 1981 Winter Simulation Conference, 1981, pp. 505-516.

2. Pritsker, A.A.B., *Introduction to Simulation and SLAM II*, Fourth Edition, Systems Publishing and John Wiley, 1995.

3. *Visual SLAM Quick Reference Manual*, Pritsker Corporation, 1996.

4. Schruben, L., "Simulation Modeling with Event Graphs", Communications of the ACM, Vol. 26, 1983, pp. 957-963.

CHAPTER 12

Continuous Modeling

12.1   INTRODUCTION

Continuous modeling involves the characterization of the behavior of a system by a set of equations. The time-dependent portrayal of the variables described by the equations is one of the desired outputs from such models. The models can consist of sets of algebraic, difference, or differential equations and can contain stochastic components. The status of a system defined in this manner is changing continuously with time. Events may occur, however, and instantaneously affect the status of the system.

561

The continuous systems modeler has two basic tasks: 1) the development of the equation set and events that describe the time-dependent, stochastic behavior of the system; and 2) the evaluation of the equation set and events to obtain specific values of system behavior for different operating policies. A simulation language for continuous models assists in the first task by defining the format for the equation set. However, it is in task 2 that the simulation language has its greatest impact. The language provides the mechanisms for obtaining the values of the variables described by the equations. It does this by solving the equation set at a single point in time and by recording the values for future reporting. Time is then advanced in a step-wise fashion and the equations are again solved for the values of the variables at this new time, assuming knowledge of the variables at previous times. When events occur, the effect of the event is incorporated into the model and in the evaluation of the variable values. In this manner, the entire time history of the model variables are obtained. The procedures employed by Visual SLAM in supporting continuous system modeling are described in this chapter.

12.2   Visual SLAM ORGANIZATION FOR CONTINUOUS MODELING

Models of continuous systems involve the definition of state variables by equations and the definition of state events based on the values of state variables as presented in Chapter 10. The development of a Visual SLAM continuous simulation program requires the user to write function STATE for defining state equations, SEVNT input statements to prescribe the conditions that define state events, and function EVENT for modeling the consequences of the occurrence of state event I. Initial conditions are established by writing function INTLC or through INTLC input statements as described in Chapter 8. Specialized outputs of the system variables can be obtained by writing function OTPUT or through the RECORD input statement. A block diagram of the Visual SLAM organization for continuous models is shown in Figure 12-1.

The function of the main program is to call the Visual SLAM processor which controls the running of the simulation. The Visual SLAM processor first calls upon the standardized initialization routine to initialize Visual SLAM variables and to read Visual SLAM input statements that define the characteristics of the model. Other variables can be initialized in function INTLC which is called after the Visual SLAM input statements are read. The user can perform additional initialization functions in function INTLC.

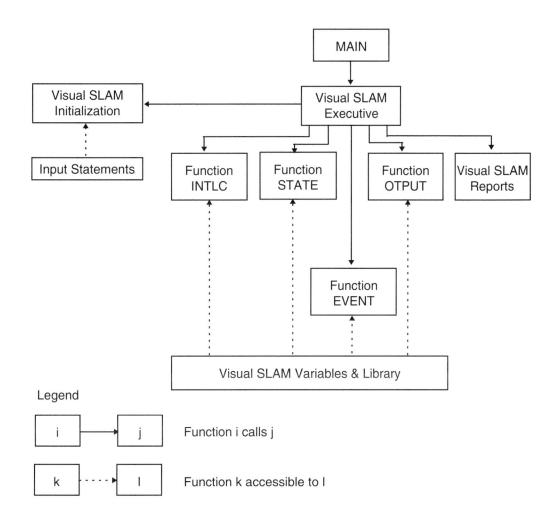

Figure 12-1   Visual SLAM organization for continuous modeling.

After initialization, the executive routine calls function STATE in order to obtain new values for the state variables. The state variables, SS[∙], and their derivatives, DD[∙], were defined in Section 10.2. The purpose of function STATE is to define the dynamic equations for the state variables. If only difference equations are used in function STATE, the executive routine will call

STATE at periodic intervals called steps unless an intervening event or information request is encountered. In function STATE, the state variable values at the end of the step are computed from the user-written equations. If differential equations are included in function STATE, then the executive routine calls function STATE many times within a step. In either case, values for the state variables at the end of a step are computed. The executive routine then tests if conditions defining state events are included in the model. These conditions are specified in terms of state variables crossing prescribed thresholds. The user specifies such conditions on SEVNT input statements. One input statement is required for each state condition definition. If a state event is detected, the executive routine calls function EVENT with the state event code that was specified on the SEVNT input statement. It is the user's responsibility to code the changes to be made to the system when a particular state event occurs. In Visual SLAM, the following types of changes are allowed:

1. Changes in the defining equations for the state variables;

2. Discrete changes in the values of the state variables;

3. Changes in the state variables and/or thresholds involved in state condition specifications;

4. Changes to Visual SLAM or non-Visual SLAM variables.

To record the performance of the system over time, the executive routine collects system status information throughout a simulation run. The information to be collected is specified by the user on TIMST and RECORD input statements. The frequency with which the information is recorded is user specified during the standardized initialization. The options are to record: at periodic intervals, when the value changes and at each call to function GPLOT.

The ending of the simulation can be specified either by a state-event condition or by a total simulation time. When the executive routine determines that the simulation is ended, function OTPUT is called. In OTPUT, the user can write a specialized output report and perform any end-of-simulation processing that is required. Following the call to function OTPUT, standardized summary reports are printed. These standardized summary reports include any statistical computations of values recorded during the simulation and the current value of the continuous variables.

As can be seen from the above description and from Figure 12-1, the Visual SLAM organization has decomposed a problem by specifying the functions within which the user must define the state variables and the potential changes to the state variables when state events occur. Superimposed on these functional elements are information processing statements and routines for detecting state variable crossings (SEVNT), recording state variable values (RECORD), initializing variables (INTLC), and reporting specialized output (OTPUT).

12.3   EXECUTIVE FUNCTION FOR CONTINUOUS SIMULATION MODELS

The executive function in Visual SLAM establishes the current simulation time, TNOW, and calls an appropriate user-written routine in accordance with the defined Visual SLAM organizational structure. If state variables are to be updated, the executive function defines the step size, DTNOW, and calls function STATE where the user has written equations that update state variables to time TNOW.

The executive function then determines if a state event has occurred, and, if it has, calls function EVENT(JEVNT,Ent) to communicate to the user that an event with code JEVNT has occurred. The executive routine also determines if the newly computed values are to be recorded as specified by a RECORD input statement. The next step size is then computed and the above procedure repeated.

12.4   ILLUSTRATION 12-1. CEDAR BOG LAKE

To illustrate the ease with which models of continuous systems can be analyzed using Visual SLAM, we present a model of Cedar Bog Lake that was developed by Williams (16).

The model includes three species, a solar energy supply (x_s), and the organic matter that forms a sediment on the lake bottom (x_0). These lake variables are modeled in terms of their energy content (calories/centimeter^2) and the energy transfers between the various lake variables and losses to the environment (x_e). The three species are plants (x_p), herbivores (x_h), and carnivores (x_c). The differential equations relating these species to the sediment and the solar energy source are shown below.

$$\frac{dx_p}{dt} = x_s - 4.03x_p$$

$$\frac{dx_h}{dt} = 0.48x_p - 17.87x_h$$

$$\frac{dx_c}{dt} = 4.85x_h - 4.65x_c$$

$$\frac{dx_o}{dt} = 2.55x_p + 6.12x_h + 1.95x_c$$

$$\frac{dx_e}{dt} = 1.00x_p + 6.90x_h + 2.70x_c$$

The values of the variables at time zero are: $x_p(0) = 0.83$, $x_h(0) = 0.003$, $x_c(0) = 0.0001$, $x_o(0) = 0.0$ and $x_e(0) = 0.0$.

The annual cycle in solar radiation is simulated using the following equation:

$$x_s = 95.9(1 + 0.635 \sin 2\pi t)$$

where t is time in years. These equations represent such processes as the predation of one species by another, plant photosynthesis, and the decaying of dead species. Energy transfers between lake entities and their environment are due to respiration and migration.

We will use Visual SLAM to illustrate the procedure for obtaining the values of the variables x_p, x_h, x_c, x_o, x_e, x_s over time. First, we make an equivalence between the model variables and the Visual SLAM state vector SS[$\cdot$] as shown below.

$$SS[1] = x_p \rightarrow DD[1] = \frac{dx_p}{dt}$$

$$SS[2] = x_h \rightarrow DD[2] = \frac{dx_h}{dt}$$

$$SS[3] = x_c \rightarrow DD[3] = \frac{dx_c}{dt}$$

$$SS[4] = x_o \rightarrow DD[4] = \frac{dx_o}{dt}$$

$$SS[5] = x_e \rightarrow DD[5] = \frac{dx_e}{dt}$$

and

$$SS[6] = x_s.$$

The entire Visual SLAM program consists of writing function STATE, and the input statements. Function STATE is given in Figure 12-2.

```
Const PI As Double = 3.14159
Public Sub STATE()
  VS.SS(6) = 95.9*(1# + 0.635*Sin(2#*PI*VS.TNOW))
  VS.DD(1) = VS.SS(6) - 4.03 * VS.SS(1)
  VS.DD(2) = 0.48 * VS.SS(1) - 17.87 * VS.SS(2)
  VS.DD(3) = 4.85 * VS.SS(2) - 4.65 * VS.SS(3)
  VS.DD(4) = 2.55*VS.SS(1)+6.12*VS.SS(2+1.95*VS.SS(3)
  VS.DD(5) = VS.SS(1) + 6.9 * VS.SS(2) + 2.7 * VS.SS(3)
End Sub
```

Figure 12-2VB Visual Basic form of STATE.

```
#include "vslam.h"
#include <math.h>
#define PI 3.14159

void SWFUNC STATE(void)
{
  SS[6]=95.9*(1.+0.635*sin(2.*PI*TNOW));
  DD[1]=SS[6]-4.03*SS[1];
  DD[2]=0.48*SS[1]-17.87*SS[2];
  DD[3]=4.85*SS[2]-4.65*SS[3];
  DD[4]=2.55*SS[1]+6.12*SS[2]+1.95*SS[3];
  DD[5]=SS[1]+6.9*SS[2]+2.7*SS[3];
}
```

Figure 12-2C   C version of STATE.

In function STATE, the set of differential equations is coded. The translation of the equations from the model to the Visual SLAM code is direct and normally does not require an excessive amount of work. The input statements for the model, shown in Figure 12-3, involve mainly the definitions of the variables to record on the RECORD input statement, and the CONTINUOUS statement as defined in Chapter 10. For this example, the CONTINUOUS statement specifies five differential equations (NNEQD), one state variable equation (NNEQS), a minimum step size (DTMIN) of 0.00025, and a maximum step size (DTMAX) of 0.025. The INTLC statement initializes the SS[·] values as prescribed by the problem statement, and the INITIALIZE statement specifies that the simulation should start at time zero and end at time 2. The plots requested through the RECORD statement are shown in Figure 12-4. This illustration demonstrates the ease of coding continuous models in Visual SLAM.

```
GEN,"PRITSKER","CEDAR BOG LAKE",1/1/1996,1,YES,YES;
;
;DEFINE 5 DIFFERENTIAL EQUATIONS AND 1 RATE EQUATION
;
CONTINUOUS,5,1,.00025,.025,.025;
;
;INITIALIZE THE CONTINUOUS VARIABLES
;
INTLC,{{SS[1],.83},{SS[2],.003},{SS[3],.0001},{SS[6],95.9}};
;
;PLOT SCALED CONTINUOUS VARIABLES
;
RECORD,,,TNOW,"TIME",{EXCEL},,,,,{{SS[1]/32,"PLANTS", },
              {SS[2],"HERBIVORES", },{SS[3],"CARNIVORES", },
              {SS[6]/160,"SOLAR ENERGY", }};
INITIALIZE,0,2.0;
FIN;
```

Figure 12-3   Input statements for the model.

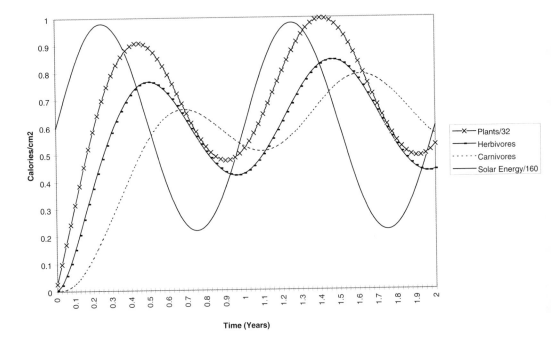

Figure 12-4   Plots requested through the RECORD statement.

12.5   COLLECTING TIME-PERSISTENT STATISTICS ON STATE VARIABLES

State variables and their derivatives are recomputed at the end of each step; hence, their values can be considered to be changing continuously over time. An average value for the variable can be computed by integrating the state variable and dividing by the time period of the integration. This could be accomplished by the Visual SLAM user through the definition of a new state variable. For example, if it is desired to obtain the average value of state variable 3, we could define state variable 10 to be the integral of state variable 3. The following statement coded in both Visual Basic and C language format would achieve the desired integration. (In the remainder of this chapter, C language format is used in textual references to Visual SLAM variables, that is, braces in place of parentheses and no object oriented prefixes.)

> VS.DD(10) = VS.SS(3)   'Visual Basic Statement
> DD[10] = SS[3];   /*C Statement * /

In function OTPUT, the average of SS[3] could be computed as SS[10]/TNOW.

To avoid the definition of new state variables to compute averages and to obtain second moments about the mean for state variables, Visual SLAM allows the use of the input statement TIMST to be used with state variables and their derivatives. The format for the TIMST input statement is

> TIMST,STAT#, EXPR,"ID",#CELLS,LOWER,WIDTH;

When EXPR is defined as an SS[·] or DD[·] variable, Visual SLAM assumes a linear function between the state variable values at the ends of steps and computes an average and standard deviation based on this linear approximation. The statistical estimates are included in the portion of the Visual SLAM Summary Report that presents information on time-persistent variables.

12.6   THE SEVNT INPUT STATEMENT

To assist the user in specifying state events, the Visual SLAM input statement SEVNT is provided. The SEVNT statement is a control statement that is analogous to the DETECT node in network models. SEVNT causes the detection of the crossings of one state variable against a threshold. A tolerance is specified for detecting the crossing. The crossing can be in the positive, the negative, or in both directions. The tolerance and direction of crossing are specified as fields in the SEVNT input statement. The format for the SEVNT input statement and the AweSim dialog box are given below.

SEVNT,JEVNT,EXPR,XDIR,THRESH,TOL;

where

JEVNT is a user supplied state event code;

EXPR is any expression involving Visual SLAM variables.

XDIR specifies crossing as: POSITIVE, NEGATIVE or EITHER;

THRESH is the crossing threshold and can be any global expression; and

TOL is a numeric value which specifies the tolerance within which the crossing is to be detected.

Below are three examples of the SEVNT statement:

1. Define state event 1 to occur when SS[3] crosses 100 in the positive direction with a tolerance of 2.0 (See Figure 10-1(a))

    SEVNT, 1 ,SS[3],POSITIVE, 100. ,2.0;

2. Define state event 2 to occur when SS[2] crosses SS[1] in the negative direction with a tolerance 0.01. (See Figure 10-1(b))

    SEVNT,2,SS[2],NEGATIVE,SS[1],0.01;

3. Define state event 4 to occur when DD[l] crosses 0.0 in either direction with a tolerance of 0.0.

    SEVNT,4,DD[1],EITHER,0.0,0.0;

    In this case, state event 4 detects minimums, maximums, or points of inflection of state variable 1. A tolerance of 0.0 insures that the minimum step size DTMIN will be used to detect the crossing if necessary.

When a crossing within tolerance is determined, the executive function calls function EVENT(JEVNT,Entity) to indicate that state event JEVNT has occurred. The second argument, Entity, is undefined in the case of state events, since there is no entity associated with a variable crossing a threshold. If a crossing occurs that is not within tolerance, the step size is automatically reduced and the above process is repeated until a crossing within tolerance is obtained or the minimum step size is used. The user would then code in function EVENT the logic involved and the system status changes required when such an event is detected.

In event routines, discrete changes to state variables can be made by changing the value of SS[J]. For example, the statement SS[3] = SS[3]+5.0 changes the value of state variable 3 by 5 units. In addition, parameters of equations and system status indicators used in STATE equations can be changed at event times. Thus, the values of coefficients and, in effect, the entire STATE equation structure could be changed at an event occurrence.

12.7   SIMULTANEOUS STATE EVENTS

Sometimes the processing logic associated with a state event depends upon knowledge concerning the possible occurrence of one or more additional state events at the same instant in time. Because of this, Visual SLAM provides the modeler with function SSEVT[N] which returns a code defining the status of state event N at the current time. The state event number, N, is the value of JEVNT prescribed by the user on SEVNT statements. The status code for state event N specifies whether the crossing variable crossed the threshold value during the last time advance, and if so, in what direction. In addition, the code denotes whether the minimum step size, DTMIN, permitted the crossing to be isolated within the prescribed tolerance. The codes returned from function SSEVT[N] are listed below.

Code	Definition
+2	crossing in the positive direction exceeding tolerance
+1	crossing in the positive direction within tolerance
0	no crossing
-1	crossing in the negative direction within tolerance
-2	crossing in the negative direction exceeding tolerance

As an example, consider that state event 4 has occurred and function EVENT has been called. If it is necessary to determine if state event 6 has also occurred then the value obtained from function SSEVT(6) will provide this information. The value of SSEVT(6) is one of the five codes listed above.

12.8   MODELING USING STATE VARIABLES

Function STATE can be used to model the state variables, employing any combination of DD[·] and SS[·] variables. The use of SS[·] to model difference equations is a straight translation of the difference equations, that is,

$$y_n = A * y_{n-1} + B$$

is equivalent to the Visual SLAM statement

SS[1]=A*SSL[l]+B;

where SS[1] is used to represent the value of y at time n, that is, y_n, and SSL[1] represents the value of y at time n-1, that is, y_{n-1}. Generalization to allow A and B to be functions of time is also direct. Higher order difference equations can be modeled. The translation of

$$y_n = A * y_{n-1} + B * y_{n-2} + C$$

is made by defining SS[1] to be y_n, then SSL[1] corresponds to y_{n-1}. Letting SS[2] = SSL[1] then SSL[2] corresponds to y_{n-2}. The value of y_n can be obtained as SS[l] using the following two state equations:

SS[1] = A * SSL[1] + B * SSL[2]+ C;
SS[2] = SSL[1];

State variables can also be used to model differential equations by means of an Euler integration method (1). In this case, the user must provide the integration method to solve the equations for the SS[·] variables. Consider the differential equation

$$\frac{dy}{dt} + A * y = B \div$$

or

$$y' = B - A * y .$$

Suppose that we know y at the point n - 1, and we call this value y_{n-1}^{o}. Then

$$y'_{n-1} = B - A * y_{n-1}^{o}.$$

If we assume that y'_{n-1} is a good approximation of y' between n-1 and n, then

$$y_n = y_{n-1}^{o} + h * y'_{n-1}$$

where h is the interval of time between points n-1 and n.   Substituting yields

$$y_n = y_{n-1}^{o} + h * (B - A * y_{n-1}^{o})$$

and

$$y_n = y_{n-1}^{o} * (1 - h * A) + h * B.$$

In terms of Visual SLAM variables, this becomes

SS[1] = SSL[1]*(1.- DTNOW*A) + DTNOW*B

since DTNOW is the time interval between calculations of state variables. The Visual SLAM user can employ more advanced Euler type integrators by coding them in function STATE. If the equations involving the SS[·] variables cannot be written sequentially due to an interdependence of the variables, the user must provide the means for solving them. For example, the Gauss-Seidel procedure (2,11) could be used. Visual SLAM does not provide such a method since convergence is highly dependent on the set of equations.

12.9   MODELING USING DERIVATIVES OF STATE VARIABLES

Visual SLAM uses a Runge-Kutta-Fehlberg (RKF) algorithm to integrate the equations of function STATE written in terms of the DD[·] variables. The RKF algorithm is used to obtain a solution to a set of simultaneous first-order ordinary differential equations of the form

$$y'_j(t) = f(_1 y_1, y_2, \ldots, Y_m, t), \quad j = 1, 2, \ldots, m$$

where

$$y'_j(t) = \frac{dy_j(t)}{dt}.$$

In Visual SLAM, these equations would be expressed in the following form:

DD[J]=f$_j$(SS[1],SS[2], . . ., SS[M], TNOW), J=1, 2, . . ., M.

For example, if

$$y'_1(t) = a_1 y_1 + b_1 y_2$$

and

$$y'_2(t) = a_2 y_1 + b_2 y_2,$$

the corresponding Visual SLAM coding would be

DD[1]=A1*SS[1]+B1*SS[2];

and

DD[2]=A2*SS[1]+B2*SS[2];

Higher order differential equations can be modeled by putting the equations in canonical form. Thus, if an nth order differential equation of the form

$$x^{(n)}(t) = f(x, x', x^{(2)}, \ldots, x^{(n-1)}, t)$$

is to be modeled using Visual SLAM, N variables SS[J], J = 1, 2, . . . ,N, must be defined as follows:

SS[1] = x

SS[2] = x' = DD[1]

SS[3] = x$^{(2)}$ = DD[2]

.

.

.

$$SS[N] = x^{(n-1)} = DD[N-1]$$

By substitution, DD[N] =f(SS[1], SS[2],...,SS[N],t). With these equations, SS[1] is the solution to the nth order differential equation. As an example, consider the second order equation

$$x^{(2)}(t) = Ax'(t) + Bx(t) + C.$$

Let   SS[1]= x(t)

and   DD[1] = x'(t) = SS(2)

then   DD[2] = $x^{(2)}$(t)

In Visual SLAM, this would be coded in function STATE as

DD[1] =SS[2];

DD[2] = A*SS[2] + B * SS[1] + C; /*C Statements*/

VS.DD(1) = VS.SS(2)

VS.DD(2) = A* VS.SS(2)+B*VS.SS(1)+C 'Visual Basic Statements

12.10   NUMERICAL INTEGRATION IN VISUAL SLAM

The integration method provided by Visual SLAM is a fourth (fifth) order, variable step size Runge-Kutta routine for integrating systems of first-order ordinary differential equations with initial values. The particular constants and error estimation used are from Fehlberg(4) as further described by Shampine and Allen(11).

The Runge-Kutta-Fehlberg (RKF) method provides the specific capability of numerically integrating a system of first-order ordinary differential equations of the form

$$\frac{dy(t)}{dt} = f(y(t);t)$$

with initial conditions $y(t_o)$. In this section $y(t)$ is a vector, and the above equation represents a system of first-order simultaneous differential equations. Given the equation for $dy(t)/dt$, simulation can be used to obtain the time history of $y(t)$. This is accomplished by considering $y(t)$ as a function of the derivatives of $y(t)$ using a Taylor series expansion. A Taylor series expansion allows the writing of a function in terms of the derivatives of the function where the accuracy with which the series represents the function is related to the order of the terms in the series. The error of the series approximation can be estimated by evaluating the first term omitted from the series approximation. In this way by evaluating the derivatives, $dy(t)/dt$, the values of $y(t)$ can be estimated. This procedure for estimating $y(t)$ is embodied in the RKF algorithm.

The RKF algorithm is a one step procedure involving six function evaluations over a step of size h. Let $t_1=t_o+h$. The procedure as implemented in Visual SLAM for computing $y(t_1)$ involves the evaluation of the following equations:

$$a_1 = hf(y(t_o);t_o)$$

$$a_2 = hf(y(t_o)+\frac{1}{4}a_1;t_o+1/4h)$$

$$a_3 = hf(y(t_o)+\frac{3}{32}a_1+\frac{9}{32}a_2;t_o+\frac{3}{8}h)$$

$$a_4 = hf(y(t_o)+\frac{1932}{2197}a_1-\frac{7200}{2197}a_2+\frac{7296}{2197}a_3;t_o+\frac{12}{13}h)$$

$$a_5 = hf(y(t_o)+\frac{439}{216}a_1-8a_2+\frac{3680}{513}a_3-\frac{845}{4104}a_4;t_o+h)$$

$$a_6 = hf(y(t_o)-\frac{8}{27}a_1+2a_2-\frac{3544}{2565}a_3+\frac{1859}{4104}a_4-\frac{11}{40}a_5;t_o+\frac{1}{2}h)$$

$$EERR = \frac{1}{360}a_1-\frac{128}{4275}a_3-\frac{2197}{75240}a_4+\frac{1}{50}a_5+\frac{2}{55}a_6$$

$$y(t_o+h) = y(t_o)+\frac{25}{216}a_1+\frac{1408}{2565}a_3+\frac{2197}{4104}a_4-\frac{1}{5}a_5$$

$$TERR = AAERR + RRERR*|y(t_o+h)|$$

where AAERR and RRERR are the user-specified absolute and relative error values provided on the Visual SLAM CONTINUOUS statement.

In the above equations, the a_i values can be considered as changes to y(t) at the end of the step based on derivative evaluations at intermediate points within the step. The equation for $y(t_o+h)$ is a weighted average of these changes added to $y(t_o)$. Thus, a_1 is the change that would occur if the derivative at the beginning of the step was used to project the value at the end of the step; a_2 is the change based on the derivative at the quarter step; a_3 is the change based on the derivative at three-eights of the step; a_4 is the change based on the derivative at twelve-thirteenths of the step; and a_5 is the change based on the derivative at the end of the step. Note that a_6 is not used in the computation of the value at the end of the step but only used in the calculation of the estimated error, EERR. The allowed error, TERR, is based on the estimated value of the state variable at the end of the step. The computation indicated above involves multiple evaluations of the function f which corresponds to the computation of DD[·] as specified in function STATE. These evaluations are made by Visual SLAM through calls to function STATE. Prior to each call, the step size, DTNOW, is set as a fraction of h and the values of the state variables, SS[·], are computed.

The RKF algorithm employed in Visual SLAM estimates the local error by simultaneous computation of fourth and fifth order approximations. This method permits the step size to be changed with little additional computation. A derivation and description of Runge-Kutta methods are contained in most books on numerical analysis (1,12). In the above procedure a_j is a vector and EERR is computed for each state variable defined by a differential equation. Only if the EERR $\leq$ TERR for all such state variables will the $y(t_1)$ be accepted.

In the RKF procedure, a variable step size is employed. Let Q be equal to the largest value of |EERR|/TERR for any state variable defined by a differential equation. If Q > 1.0, the values are not accepted and h is reduced. If Q $\leq$ 1.0, the values are accepted and, depending on the value of Q, the next step size may be increased. If the step is accepted or rejected, the new step size is related to the value of $h/Q^{1/5}$. The new step size is maintained within the user-specified minimum and maximum allowable step sizes, that is,

$$DTMIN \leq h_{new} \leq DTMAX$$

Runge-Kutta integration has three advantages that make it an appropriate method for Visual SLAM. First, it is widely used and well-documented. For example, most CSSLs provide Runge-Kutta integration. Second, it is easy to change the step size with a Runge-Kutta routine. This is very important in a combined simulation where events are not normally spaced uniformly in time. The third advantage is closely related to the second. Runge-Kutta integration is self-starting, thus there is no loss of efficiency when restarting from an event. This is of critical importance in a combined simulation.

12.11 TIME ADVANCE PROCEDURES

In Visual SLAM, the amount by which simulated time is advanced depends on the type of simulation (network, continuous, discrete) being performed and the values of specific variables at the current point in simulated time.

In a network or discrete simulation, time is advanced from one event to the next event. In this case, the time interval between events is TNEXT-TNOW where TNEXT is the time of the next event. Time is advanced from TNOW to TNEXT by resetting TNOW equal to TNEXT and assuming that the system status has remained constant between events. Since status at TNOW is always accepted, there is no need to maintain system status values at TTLAST, and TNOW can be used as both the last update point and then as the new event time, that is, TTLAST is neither required nor used.

For a continuous simulation, the variable DTFUL is the value for a full step size. If all the equations for state variables are written in terms of SS[·], the variable representing the time advance increment, DTNOW, will normally be set equal to DTFUL. The time at the beginning of the step is TTLAST, and the time at the end of the proposed step is TNOW, that is, TNOW = TTLAST + DTNOW. DTFUL remains constant at the maximum step size prescribed by the user, DTMAX, unless an event occurs within the step.

The size of a step is also reset (decreased) if Visual SLAM determines that the step would cause a state event to be passed. Thus, if the value of a state variable at time TTLAST + DTNOW results in the crossing of a threshold beyond allowable tolerances, the step size is reduced. If the tolerance is still not met, the step size continues to be reduced until the value of DTFUL is set equal to a user-prescribed minimum step size, DTMIN. Note that DTFUL can be less than DTMIN if TNEXT-TTLAST < DTMIN. Further note that a fixed step size can be specified for a simulation involving only SS[·] variables in which there are no time events by specifying DTMIN = DTMAX.

The most complex time advance procedure occurs when variables defined by DD[·] equations are included in a Visual SLAM simulation program. In this case, all the considerations described above pertain; in addition, the full step size, DTFUL, is divided into fractions so that the time advance increment, DTNOW, proceeds as required by the RKF algorithm. The SS[·] variables are evaluated at these intermediate points within the step and used by Visual SLAM in the integration of the equations for DD[·]. These intermediate values for SS[·] and DD[·] allow error estimates to be made and simultaneous differential equations to be evaluated.

The variable DTACC is defined as the next step size to be used, based on allowable error specifications. Initially, DTACC is set equal to DTMAX. Whenever the accuracy of the integration algorithm does not meet the user's prescribed accuracy, as defined by an absolute error value AAERR and a relative error value RRERR, the value of DTACC is recomputed. At the start of each step, DTFUL is set equal to DTACC. The decreasing of DTACC when accuracy is not met is permitted only until DTACC becomes less than DTMIN, at which time DTACC is set equal to DTMIN. If the specified accuracy cannot be achieved using DTMIN, the following conditions specified in the CONTINUOUS statement define the appropriate action:

N   Proceed without printing a warning message;
W   Proceed after printing a warning message;
F   Terminate the simulation after printing a fatal error message.

When all state variables are within the accuracy specifications to a significant extent, DTACC is increased by a factor that is dependent on the ratio of the estimated error to the allowed error. In this way, the step size is increased when good estimates for the state variables are obtained by the integration algorithm. In no case will Visual SLAM allow DTACC to become greater than DTMAX.

It is obvious that the time advance procedures included within Visual SLAM involve many variables with many interactions between these variables, Visual SLAM automatically advances time for the user on the basis of the input values prescribed for DTMIN and DTMAX and the accuracy requirements (AAERR and RRERR) when DD[·] equations are specified. The calculation of DTFUL, DTNOW, and DTACC, as well as the next discrete event time, TNEXT, are internally computed in Visual SLAM.

12.11.1   Use of DTNOW

A note of caution is in order regarding the use of DTNOW in function STATE. DTNOW is the value of the time increment through which Visual SLAM updates the state variables over a full step of size DTFUL. In many cases, DTNOW = DTFUL. In other cases, this is not so. In fact, if two events occur at the same time, DTNOW will assume a value of zero for the second event processed. Thus, DTNOW should not be used in the denominator of any equation in function STATE. However, DTNOW should be used in any equation in function STATE in which the state variable is updated by a rate multiplied by the increment in time for which the update is being performed.

12.11.2   Summary of Time Advance Procedure

A summary of the time advance procedures used in Visual SLAM is given below. If derivative equations are included (NNEQD > 0), then

DTFUL = min[DTACC; TNEXT-TTLAST; time to next state event],
DTNOW = f(DTFUL),
TNOW = TTLAST + DTNOW,
max DTACC = DTMAX,
min DTACC = DTMIN, and
min (full step size to next state event) = DTMIN.

If derivative equations are not included (NNEQD = 0), but state equations   are (NNEQS > 0), then
DTFUL = min[DTMAX; TNEXT-TTLAST; time to next state event],
DTNOW = DTFUL,
TNOW = TTLAST + DTNOW,
min (full step size to next state event) = DTMIN, and
DTACC is not used.

If NNEQD=0 and NNEQS=0, then DTFUL, DTNOW, DTACC, and TTLAST are not used and TNOW is the time of the current event being processed. In this case only time events are possible.

12.12   Example 12-1. PILOT EJECTION

The pilot ejection system of an aircraft that is flying level and at a constant velocity is to be simulated. This example is frequently cited in the literature and is referred to as the pilot ejection model. The specific version described here is extracted from Reference 3. The pilot ejection system, when activated, causes the pilot and his seat to travel along rails at a specified exit velocity V_E at an angle θ_E backward from vertical. After traveling a vertical distance Y_1, the seat becomes disengaged from its mounting rails and at this point the pilot is considered out of the cockpit. When this occurs, a second phase of operation begins during which the pilot's trajectory is influenced by the force of gravity and atmospheric drag. A critical aspect of this phase is whether the pilot will clear the tail of the aircraft.

The tail is 60 feet behind and 12 feet above the cockpit. Graphical and mathematical descriptions of the two phases are shown in Figure 12-6 along with a legend for the variables of the model.

The objective of this simulation is to determine the trajectory of a pilot ejected from an aircraft to assess whether he would hit the tail of the aircraft. This information is desired for a fixed ejection velocity and angle for the two aircraft velocities: 900 feet/second and 500 feet/second.

Concepts Illustrated. The purpose of this example is to introduce the use of Visual SLAM for the preparation of a continuous simulation model. The coding of function STATE is illustrated. The procedures for programming different run termination conditions within a run and for making multiple runs are demonstrated. On each run, two plots are prepared and printed. On one of the plots, altitude versus distance is graphed to illustrate the plotting of a state variable against an independent variable other than time.

Visual SLAM Model. The pilot ejection model is simulated using continuous variables. The equations describing the state variables and their derivatives are programmed in function STATE. The conditions for state events are defined on SEVNT input statements. Since this is a continuous model, no time events are involved. The initial conditions for the simulation will be set in function INTLC.

A RECORD statement is used to specify the outputs desired to portray the trajectory of the pilot as he leaves the aircraft. A RECORD statement will also be used to obtain the data to plot the pilot's relative position from the aircraft over time, and his speed and direction over time.

The major programming effort for this example is expended in writing function STATE where the equations describing the pilot ejection model are coded. Table 12-1 presents a listing of the Visual SLAM variables that are equivalent to the variables presented in Figure 12-5 and discussed in the problem statement.

The coding of the equations presented in Figure 12-5 using Visual SLAM variables is shown below.

DD[1] = SS[3]*COS(SS[4])-XX[1]
DD[2] = SS[3]*SIN(SS[4])
DD[3] = 0.0   SS[2] < Y1
DD[4] = 0.0   SS[2] < Y1
DD[3] = -DeltaX/Mass - Gravity * Sin(SS[4]),   SS[2] ≥ Y1
DD[4] = - Gravity * COS (SS[4])/SS[3],SS[2] ≥ Y1
where
        DeltaX = 0.5*RHO*CD*XS*SS[3]*SS[3]

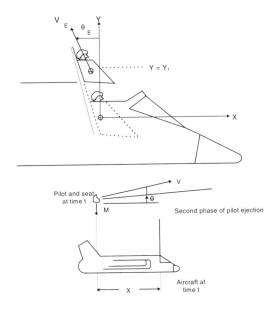

Variable	Definition	Equations
X	Horizontal distance from point of ejection	$\dfrac{dX}{dt} = V\cos\theta - V_A$
Y	Vertical distance from point of ejection	$\dfrac{dX}{dt} = V\sin\theta$
Y_1	Vertical distance above point of ejection where first phase ends	$\dfrac{dV}{dt} = 0,\ 0 \le Y < Y_1$
V_A	Velocity of aircraft	$\dfrac{d\theta}{dt} = 0,\ 0 \le Y < Y_1$
V	Pilot and seat velocity	
θ	Angle for pilot and seat movement	
V_E	Ejection velocity	
θ_E	Angle of ejection	$D = \dfrac{1}{2} pc_d S V^2$
M	Mass of pilot and seat	$\dfrac{dV}{dt} = -\dfrac{D}{M} - g\sin\theta,\ Y \ge Y_1$
$\rho,\ c_d,\ S$	Parameters of the model	$\dfrac{d\theta}{dt} = -\dfrac{g\cos\theta}{V},\quad Y \ge Y_1$

Figure 12-5 Graphical and mathematical description of a pilot ejection model.

Table 12-1 Variables for pilot ejection model.

Problem Statement	Visual SLAM	Initial Value
X	SS[1]	0.0
dX/dt	DD[1]	Computed
Y	SS[2]	0.0
dY/dt	DD[2]	Computed
V	SS[3]	Computed
dV/dt	DD[3]	0.0
θ	SS[4]	Computed
$d\theta/dt$	DD[4]	0.0
c_d	Drag	1.0
g	Gravity	32.2 ft/sec^2
ρ	AirDensity	2.3769x 10^{-3} slug/ft^3
θ_E (rad)	ATemp	15./57.3
θ_E (deg)	AEject	15.0
V_A	XX[1]	Input
V_E	VEject	40.0 ft/sec
M	Mass	7 slugs
S	Area	10.0 ft^2
Y_I	Y1	4.0 ft

When SS[2] $\geq$ Y1, the pilot is released from the cockpit and the second set of equations for DD[3] and DD[4] is used. Since the relative position of the pilot during the simulated period of interest will always exceed Y1 after he is released, the test of whether SS[2] is greater than Y1 can serve for specifying when the equations for DD[3] and DD[4] are to be used. In the coding to follow, the global variable LL[1] is used to indicate this condition.

The coding for function STATE is shown in Figure 12-6. It should be noted that DD[l], DD[2], DD[3], and DD[4] are functions of both SS[3] and SS[4]. The RKF integration algorithm of Visual SLAM simultaneously solves for the desired SS[·] values, and the multiple dependence is taken into account. The order of coding the DD[·] equations will not affect the results obtained in this example.

```vb
Public Sub STATE()
    Dim DeltaX As Double
    Const Mass = 7#          ' mass of pilot and seat
    Const Gravity = 32.2 ' gravitational constant
    Const Drag = 1#          ' coefficient of drag
    Const Area = 10#         ' projected area of the pilot and seat
    Const AirDensity = 0.0023769 ' air density

    ' define the differential equations for rates of change of:
    '    DD[1] - horizontal distance of pilot from point of ejection
    '    DD[2] - vertical distance of pilot from point of ejection
    '    DD[3] - pilot and seat velocity
    '    DD[4] - angle of pilot and seat movement
    '    XX[1] - plane velocity

    VS.DD(1) = VS.SS(3) * Cos(VS.SS(4)) - VS.XX(1)
    VS.DD(2) = VS.SS(3) * Sin(VS.SS(4))

    If VS.LL(1) > 1 Then
        DeltaX = 0.5 * AirDensity * Drag * Area * VS.SS(3) * VS.SS(3)
        VS.DD(3) = (-DeltaX) / Mass - Gravity * Sin(VS.SS(4))
        VS.DD(4) = (-Gravity) * Cos(VS.SS(4)) / VS.SS(3)
    End If
End Sub
```

Figure 12-6VB Subroutine STATE in Visual Basic for pilot ejection model

```c
void SWFUNC STATE(void)
{
    double DeltaX;
    const double Mass = 7.0;         /* mass of pilot and seat */
    const double Gravity = 32.2;     /* gravitational constant */
    const double Drag = 1.0;         /* coefficient of drag */
    const double Area = 10.0;/*projected area of the pilot and seat */
    const double AirDensity = .0023769; /* air density */

    /* define the differential equations for rates of change of:  */
    /*    DD[1] - horizontal distance of pilot from point of ejection*/
    /*    DD[2] - vertical distance of pilot from point of ejection*/
    /*    DD[3] - pilot and seat velocity                         */
    /*    DD[4] - angle of pilot and seat movement                */
    /*    XX[1] - plane velocity                                  */

    DD[1] = SS[3] * cos(SS[4]) - XX[1];
    DD[2] = SS[3] * sin(SS[4]);

    if (LL[1] > 1)
    {
        DeltaX = 0.5 * AirDensity * Drag * Area * SS[3] * SS[3];
        DD[3] = (-DeltaX)/Mass - Gravity * sin(SS[4]);
        DD[4] = (-Gravity) * cos(SS[4]) / SS[3];
    }

    return;
}
```

Figure 12-6C Function STATE in C for pilot ejection model.

In function STATE, DD[3] and DD[4] are not set to zero since this is done in the initialization routines. When SS[2] ≥ Y1, a state event is coded to change the value of LL[1] to 2. Initially LL[1] = 1. When LL[1] = 2, the values of DD[3] and DD[4] will be recomputed for each call to function STATE. Three conditions define state events. A state event occurs when the pilot achieves a relative height of Y1 with respect to the aircraft. When this occurs, the equations governing the pilot's movement are altered as described above. The other two state events are for stopping the simulation. When the pilot is 60 feet behind the cockpit, he will be beyond the tail. When the pilot is 30 feet above the airplane, he is well above the 12 foot high tail. In either case, the simulation is halted. In terms of the Visual SLAM variables, these conditions are SS[1] ≤ -60 and SS[2] ≥ 30. The other condition for stopping involves time exceeding four seconds. This is accomplished through the INITIALIZE input statement by setting TTFIN = 4.

The establishment of the conditions for state events is made using statement type SEVNT. The input statements for the three conditions are shown below:

        SEVNT,1,SS[1],NEGATIVE,-60.,0.0;
        SEVNT,1,SS[2],POSITIVE,30,0.0;
        SEVNT,2,SS[2],POSITIVE,4,0.0;

The first SEVNT statement specifies that state event 1 occurs when SS[1] crosses the value -60 in the negative direction with zero tolerance. This corresponds to the pilot passing the tail in the X-direction. A tolerance of zero is used to force Visual SLAM to use the minimum step size when SS[1] exceeds the value of -60. In this way, a precise determination of when the state event occurs can be obtained. State event 1 represents one of the conditions by which the simulation run will be terminated. The second statement specifies that state event 1 will also occur when SS[2] crosses the value 30 in the positive direction with a tolerance of zero. This statement corresponds to the run termination condition that the pilot exceeds a vertical distance of 30 feet above the cockpit.

The third state event input statement corresponds to the pilot achieving a vertical distance, SS[2], of four feet. The crossing is prescribed to be in a positive direction and again a zero tolerance is specified to force Visual SLAM to detect the point at which the pilot leaves the aircraft with as much precision as possible. In this manner, the switching from one equation set to another will be accomplished with the precision specified by the input value for DTMIN. This third SEVNT statement prescribes state event 2 to be the event code associated with the pilot leaving the cockpit.

The effects associated with the occurrence of state events are modeled in function EVENT(Code,Current). Since only state events are processed by the EVENT routine, the argument Current will be null and is not used. When Code=1, we request a stopping of the simulation by setting MSTOP negative.

When Code=2, we desire to change the equations for DD[3] and DD[4]. This latter change is prescribed in function STATE to occur when the value of LL[1] is set to 2. The coding for function EVENT is shown in Figure 12-7. Since the code required to model the state events associated with this problem is extremely short, both state events are programmed directly in function EVENT using a switch or Select statement to decode state event codes. When a termination condition is reached, the Visual SLAM variable MSTOP is set to -1 to indicate to the Visual SLAM executive that the run should be terminated. When state event 2 occurs, LL[1] is set to 2 to cause the desired change to be made in the equations written in function STATE. This completes the description of function EVENT for the pilot ejection model.

```
'*  Visual BASIC VERSION OF SUBROUTINE EVENT
Public Sub EVENT(Code As Integer, Current As VSENTITY)
   Select Case Code
      Case 1 ' event 1.  things went far enough
         VS.MSTOP = -1
      Case 2 ' event 2.  ready for second phase of flight
         VS.LL(1) = 2
      Case Else
         VS.Error 3, "Unknown event code"
   End Select
End Sub
```

Figure 12-7VB Subroutine EVENT in Visual Basic for pilot ejection model.

```
/*  C VERSION OF FUNCTION STATE

void SWFUNC EVENT(int Code, ENTITY * User)
{
   switch (Code)
   {
      case 1: /* event 1.  things went far enough */
         MSTOP = -1;
      break;
      case 2: /* event 2.  ready for second phase of flight */
         LL[1] = 2;
      break;
      default:
         su_error(3,"Unknown event code");
      break;
   }
}
```

Figure 12-7C Function EVENT in C for pilot ejection model.

Function INTLC is used to initialize the simulation before each run. The plane velocity, XX[1], has already been defined for the run through an INTLC control statement. The initial position of the pilot relative to the aircraft cockpit is at the origin, that is, SS[1] = 0.0 and SS[2] = 0.0. These values are automatically established in the Visual SLAM initialization process. The pilot's initial velocity vector, caused by pushing the ejection button, is given by the following equations:

$$V_{initial} = \sqrt{(V_A - V_E \sin\theta_E)^2 + (V_E \cos\theta_E)^2}$$

and

$$\theta_{initial} = \tan^{-1}(\frac{V_E \cos\theta_E}{V_A - V_E \sin\theta_E}).$$

These initial values are set equal to SS[3] and SS[4] at the beginning of each simulation run since ejection is initiated at time zero. The initial values of the derivatives of the state variables are obtained when the Visual SLAM executive calls function STATE at time zero. The last statement in function INTLC sets the value of LL[1] to 1 to indicate that the pilot has not left the cockpit at the beginning of each run.

A listing of the input for this example is shown in Figure 12-9. The first input record describes the general information (GEN statement type) and indicates that two runs are to be made. The INITIALIZE statement specifies that the beginning time for a run (TTBEG) is to be zero and that the ending time (TTFIN) is to be four. Default values for other variables on the INITIALIZE statement are to be used. Information regarding the number of equations, step size, , and accuracy of the RKF algorithm are provided on the CONTINUOUS input statement. Specifically, the following values are prescribed: NNEQD = 4; NNEQS = 0; DTMIN = 0.0001; DTMAX = 0.01; W = Warning; AAERR = 0; and RRERR = 0.000005.

With these values for the variables, there are four differential equations and no difference or state equations. The minimum step size is 0.0001 seconds and the maximum step size is 0.01 seconds. When a state event cannot be detected within specified tolerances or when the RKF numerical integration algorithm cannot meet accuracy specifications, warning messages are to be printed. The simulation is to be continued even when these conditions are detected. The accuracy requirement for the numerical integration algorithm has a zero value for the absolute error (AAERR) and a five millionth value for the relative error (RRERR).

```
Public Function INTLC(Run As Long) As Long
    Const VEject = 40#     ' ejection velocity
    Const AEject = 15#     ' angle of ejection
    Dim ATemp As Double
    Dim VX As Double
    Dim VY As Double

    ' calculate values
    ATemp = AEject / 57.3                ' convert to radians
    VX = VS.XX(1) - VEject * Sin(ATemp)
    VY = VEject * Cos(ATemp)
    VS.SS(3) = Sqr(VX* VX+ VY*VY) ' initial velocity pilot and seat
    VS.SS(4) = Atn(VY / VX)            ' initial angle of pilot and seat

    VS.LL(1) = 1

    INTLC = True
End Function
```

Figure 12-8VB Visual Basic Function INTLC for pilot ejection model.

```
#include <math.h>
#include "vslam.h"

BOOL SWFUNC INTLC(UINT uiRun)
{
    const double VEject = 40.;     /* ejection velocity */
    const double AEject = 15.;     /* angle of ejection */
    double ATemp;
    double VX;
    double VY;


    /* calculate values */
    ATemp = AEject / 57.3;                /* convert to radians */
    VX    = XX[1] - VEject * sin(ATemp);
    VY    = VEject * cos(ATemp);
    SS[3] = sqrt(VX*VX+VY*VY);/*initial velocity pilot and seat */
    SS[4] = atan(VY/VX);         /*initial angle of pilot and seat */
    LL[1] = 1;

    return(TRUE);
}
```

Figure 12-8C Function INTLC written in C for pilot ejection model.

The next two input statements refer to the recording of values for eventual tabling and plotting. The first RECORD statement specifies that the state variable

SS[1] is to be the independent variable and it is to be labeled as X POS. An AweSim plot of the dependent variable versus the independent variable is desired. Default values are prescribed for the next three fields of the RECORD. With default values, the plot will be started at TTSTART = TTBEG = 0 and completed at TTEND = TTFIN = 4. Variable values will be recorded at intervals of .01 seconds. Only one dependent variable is to be recorded for each value of the independent variable. The dependent variable is SS[2] which is to have a label of Y POS.

```
 1 GEN,"PRITSKER","PILOT EJECTION",1/1/1996,2;
 2 INITIALIZE,0,4;
 3 LIMITS,9,1;
 4 CONTINUOUS,4,,.0001,.01,,WARNING,0.,.000005;
 5 RECORD,,,SS[1],"X POS",{AWESIM},,,,,.01,
       {{SS[2],"Y POS.", }};
 6 RECORD,,,TNOW,"TIME",{AWESIM,TABLE},,,,,.02,
       {{SS[1],"X POS.", },{SS[2],"Y POS.",},
       {SS[3],"SPEED",},{SS[4],"THETA", }};
 7 SEVNT,1,SS[1],NEGATIVE,-60.0,0.0;
 8 SEVNT,1,SS[2],POSITIVE,30.0,0.0;
 9 SEVNT,2,SS[2],POSITIVE,4.0,0.0;
10 INTLC,{{XX[1],900}};
11 SIMULATE;
12 INTLC,{{XX[1],500}};
13 FIN;
```

Figure 12-9 Data input and statements for pilot ejection model.

A second RECORD statement prescribes that an AweSim plot and table are desired with the independent variable being current time, TNOW. The label for TNOW is to be TIME. The dependent variables for the plot are prescribed to be SS[1] through SS[4].

The next three input statements describe the state event conditions; these were described in detail previously. The INTLC statement assigns the value of XX[1], aircraft velocity. The SIMULATE statement indicates that the execution of the first run is to be initiated. Following the reading of the SIMULATE statement, the first run is executed. After the first run is completed, Visual SLAM will read the next input statement, which specifies the aircraft velocity for the second run. The next input statement is FIN which specifies that this is the last Visual SLAM statement of the program.

Before examining Visual SLAM outputs for this example, we describe the sequence in which the subprograms are invoked. The executive reads in the input statements, initializes Visual SLAM variables, and calls functions INTLC and

STATE. The executive then controls the simulation by advancing time in steps. During each step advance, the RKF algorithm integrates the DD[·] equations coded in STATE to evaluate SS[·] values at select time points within the step and at the end of the step.

When accuracy is acceptable, Visual SLAM tests if any state events occurred because of the updating of the state variables. The state events are those that were defined on SEVNT input statements. If a state event was passed, the step size is reduced and the above process is repeated with a new but smaller step size. If a state event ends the step, function EVENT is called. If the state event is one that ends the simulation, MSTOP is set to -1 in EVENT and Visual SLAM ends the run by calling OTPUT and SUMRY. Visual SLAM also checks TNOW against TTFIN and if TNOW ≥ TTFIN, the simulation run is ended.

Summary of Results. Intermediate results for the first simulation, in which the aircraft velocity was 900 feet/second, are shown in Figure 12-10. Because a zero tolerance was specified on the SEVNT input statements for detecting crossings, warning messages that tolerances could not be met are not unexpected. The messages could have been suppressed by specifying an N in the field for warning messages on the CONTINUOUS input statement. Each message will refer to the line in the control file which defined the state event. There is no message regarding the state event defined by Line 9 of the control file, which means that Visual SLAM was able to calculate exactly the time at which the pilot left the cockpit. The message reporting the occurrence of the state event defined by Line 7 of the control file indicates that the simulation ended at time 0.433942.

```
Intermediate results for run 1

Warning (0.433942): Specified tolerance exceeded for state event.

        File : CEX131.CON, Line : 7
```

Figure 12-10 Intermediate results showing diagnostic messages for pilot ejection model.

Figure 12-11 is the plot of the pilot's position relative to the aircraft cockpit which is obtained in accordance with the first RECORD input statement. Note that the independent variable on the first plot is not time but distance (X Position) and that it is monotonically non-increasing. With Visual SLAM, the independent variable must be monotonically non-increasing if DTPLT < 0 and monotonically non-decreasing if DTPLT > 0. From the first plot, it is seen that the pilot clears the cockpit (Y = 4.0) at about X = -1.0. At X = -30.0, Y is approximately 10.6, and at X = -60.0, Y is approximately 12.8. With the tail being 12 feet high, there are design problems with the ejection system when the aircraft velocity is 900 feet/second. If desired, the precise values for X and Y could have been obtained by requesting a table in addition to the plot in the RECORD statement. Since precise values are printed out for plot-table 2, this was not done.

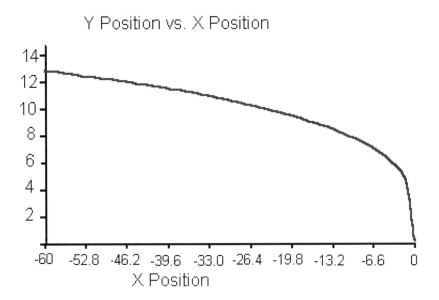

Figure 12-11 AweSim plot of pilot's position relative to aircraft for an aircraft velocity of 900 feet/second.

The table from the second RECORD statement through time 0.25 is presented in Figure 12-12. In this table, the state variables are given as a function of time. The state event representing the pilot leaving the cockpit is at time 0.1035, after which the X position increases rapidly. The summary report for this run reports that at the ending time of the simulation, 0.4339, the value SS[2], Y position, is 12.82. This shows that the ejected pilot is less than 1 foot above the tail when the simulation ends indicating a need for a design change.

TIME	X POS.	Y POS.	SPEED	THETA	Run #
0.000000	0.000000	0.000000	890.486592	0.043403	1
0.010000	-0.103520	0.386372	890.486592	0.043403	1
0.020000	-0.207040	0.772745	890.486592	0.043403	1
0.030000	-0.310561	1.159117	890.486592	0.043403	1
0.040000	-0.414081	1.545489	890.486592	0.043403	1
0.050000	-0.517601	1.931862	890.486592	0.043403	1
0.060000	-0.621121	2.318234	890.486592	0.043403	1
0.070000	-0.724641	2.704606	890.486592	0.043403	1
0.080000	-0.828161	3.090979	890.486592	0.043403	1
0.090000	-0.931682	3.477351	890.486592	0.043403	1
0.100000	-1.035202	3.863723	890.486592	0.043403	1
0.110000	-1.166717	4.248212	881.847765	0.043169	1
0.120000	-1.421756	4.624365	868.826049	0.042804	1
0.130000	-1.804851	4.991834	856.183026	0.042433	1
0.140000	-2.312304	5.350823	843.902416	0.042057	1
0.150000	-2.940573	5.701527	831.968859	0.041675	1
0.160000	-3.686268	6.044135	820.367853	0.041288	1
0.170000	-4.546138	6.378826	809.085689	0.040896	1
0.180000	-5.517066	6.705772	798.109406	0.040498	1
0.190000	-6.596061	7.025139	787.426735	0.040095	1
0.200000	-7.780250	7.337086	777.026052	0.039686	1
0.210000	-9.066875	7.641766	766.896343	0.039272	1
0.220000	-10.453283	7.939325	757.027158	0.038852	1
0.230000	-11.936924	8.229904	747.408579	0.038427	1
0.240000	-13.515344	8.513639	738.031183	0.037996	1
0.250000	-15.186181	8.790661	728.886018	0.037560	1

Figure 12-12 State variables versus time for pilot ejection model with an average velocityof 900 feet/second.

12.13   EXAMPLE 12-2.   WORLD DYNAMICS

The world model analyzed in this example was defined by Forrester (7). An extensive analysis of an extended version of this model has been reported by Meadows (8). World Dynamics is an aggregate model of world interactions to illustrate the behavior of a set of defined variables depending on whether population growth is eventually suppressed by a shortage of natural resources, pollution, over-crowding, or an insufficient food supply. The model portrays the world interactions by five interrelated state variables: population SS[1]; natural resources SS[2]; capital investment SS[3]; capital-investment-in-agriculture fraction SS[5]; and pollution SS[4]. Table 12-2 defines the variables that are used in this example. The equations for the model are presented in the discussion of function STATE.

Concepts Illustrated. The primary objective of this example is to illustrate the coding of the World Dynamics model in Visual SLAM. Systems Dynamics (6) models are easily built using Visual SLAM and extensions to include discrete events are straightforward (9,14). Difference equations are used to define the state variables.

Visual SLAM Model. The major Visual SLAM coding required for Systems Dynamics problems is for function STATE. State variables are written in terms of rate components and "auxiliary" values that may be required for the computation of the rate components. Using the definitions of Table 12-2, the statements for the rate components as defined by Forrester are:

$$BR = SS[1]*BRN*BRFM*BRMM*BRCM*BRPM$$
$$DR = SS[1]*DRN*DRMM*DRPM*DRFM*DRCM$$
$$NRUR = SS[1]*NRMM$$
$$CIG = SS[1]*CIM*CIGN$$
$$CID = SS[3]*CIDN$$
$$POLG = SS[1]*POLN*POLCM$$
$$POLA = SS[4]/POLAT$$

where all variables on the right-hand side are previous values of state variables or values already obtained in function STATE. These equations are coded in function STATE using the C variable reference SS[i] as shown or the Visual Basic reference, VS.SS(i).

The above equations illustrate that Forrester hypothesized multiplicative relationships in the computation of rate components. For example, birth rate, which is a component rate to be used in the computation of population, is equal to the product of the current population, birth rate normal, birth-rate-from-food multiplier, birth-rate-from-material multiplier, birth-rate-from-crowding multiplier, and birth-rate-from-pollution multiplier. Each of the multipliers are in turn computed from other variables. For example, BRFM, birth-rate-from-food multiplier, is obtained from a table function with the independent variable being the food ratio, FR. FR in turn is equal to a product of terms divided by food normal. Each of these relations is included in function STATE.

Table 12-2 Definition of variables for world dynamics model.

Variable†	Definition
BR	Birth rate
BRCM	Birth-rate-from-crowding multiplier
BRFM	Birth-rate-from-food multiplier
BRMM	Birth-rate-from-material multiplier
BRPM	Birth-rate-from-pollution multiplier
CFIFR	Capital fraction indicated by food ratio
SS[3]	Capital investment, CI
SS[5]	Capital-investment-in-agriculture fraction, CIAF
CID	Capital-investment discard
CIG	Capital-investment generation
CIM	Capital-investment multiplier
CIQR	Capital-investment-from-quality ratio
CIR	Capital-investment ratio
CIRA	Capital-investment ratio in agriculture
CR	Crowding ratio
DR	Death rate
DRCM	Death-rate-from-crowding multiplier
DRFM	Death-rate-from-food multiplier
DRMM	Death-rate-from-material multiplier
DRPM	Death-rate-from-pollution multiplier
ECIR	Effective-capital-investment ratio
F	Food
FC	Food coefficient
FCM	Food-from-crowding multiplier
FPCI	Food potential from capital investment
FPM	Food-from-pollution multiplier
FR	Food ratio
MSL	Material standard of living
SS[2]	Natural Resources, NR
NREM	Natural-resources-extraction multiplier
NRFR	Natural-resources-fraction remaining
NRI	Natural-resources, initial
NRMM	Natural-resources-usage-from-material-multiplier
NRUR	Natural-resources-usage-rate
SS[1]	Population, P

Table 12-2   Definition of variables for world dynamics model. (continued)

Variable†	Definition
PD	Population density
SS[4]	Pollution, POL
POLA	Pollution absorption
POLCM	Pollution-from-capital multiplier
POLG	Pollution generation
POLR	Pollution ratio
POLS	Pollution standard
QL	Quality of life
QLC	Quality of life from crowding
QLF	Quality of life from food
QLM	Quality of life from material
QLP	Quality of life from pollution
QLS	Quality of life standard

†The letters, I, N, and T when added to the variable name respectively denote initial, normal, and table, for example, BRN is birth rate normal.

With the above rate components, new values for the state variables can be computed using the following statements:

$$SS[1] = SS[1] + DTNOW*(BR-DR)$$
$$SS[2] = SS[2] + DTNOW*(-NRUR)$$
$$SS[3] = SS[3] + DTNOW*(CIG-CID)$$
$$SS[4] = SS[4]+DTNOW*(POLG-POLA)$$
$$SS[5] = SS[5] + DTNOW*(CFIFR*CIQR-SS[5])/CIAFT$$

The equation for population SS[1] indicates that the population projected to time TNOW is equal to the population at TTLAST, plus the time interval times the rate of change of population. The time interval is DTNOW = TNOW - TTLAST and the rate of change of population is equal to the birth rate, BR, minus the death rate, DR. The above equations are coded directly in function STATE, shown in Figure 12-14, and together with the statements for evaluating the "auxiliaries" comprise the World Dynamics model.

Function INTLC, shown in Figure 12-13, initializes the variables that specify the starting conditions for the run.

```c
void SWFUNC STATE(void)
{
    NRFR  = SS[2] / NRI;
    CR    = SS[1] / (LA * PDN);
    CIR   = SS[3] / SS[1];
    NREM  = GTABL(5,NREMT,NRFR,0.,1.,.25);
    ECIR  = CIR * (1. - SS[5]) * NREM / (1. - CIAFN);
    MSL   = ECIR / ECIRN;
    BRMM  = GTABL(6,BRMMT,MSL,0.,5.,1.);
    DRMM  = GTABL(11,DRMMT,MSL,0.,5.,.5);
    DRCM  = GTABL(6,DRCMT,CR,0.,5.,1.);
    BRCM  = GTABL(6,BRCMT,CR,0.,5.,1.);
    CIRA  = CIR * SS[5] / CIAFN;
    FPCI  = GTABL(7,FPCIT,CIRA,0.,6.,1.);
    FCM   = GTABL(6,FCMT,CR,0.,5.,1.);
    POLR  = SS[4] / POLS;
    FPM   = GTABL(7,FPMT,POLR,0.,60.,10.);
    FR    = FPCI * FCM * FPM * FC / FN;
    CIM   = GTABL(6,CIMT,MSL,0.,5.,1.);
    POLCM = GTABL(6,POLCMT,CIR,0.,5.,1.);
    POLAT = GTABL(7,POLATT,POLR,0.,60.,10.);
    CFIFR = GTABL(5,CFIFRT,FR,0.,2.,.5);
    QLM   = GTABL(6,QLMT,MSL,0.,5.,1.);
    QLC   = GTABL(11,QLCT,CR,0.,5.,.5);
    QLF   = GTABL(5,QLFT,FR,0.,4.,1.);
    QLP   = GTABL(7,QLPT,POLR,0.,60.,10.);
    NRMM  = GTABL(11,NRMMT,MSL,0.,10.,1.);
    CIQR  = GTABL(5,CIQRT,QLM / QLF,0.,2.,.5);
    DRPM  = GTABL(7,DRPMT,POLR,0.,60.,10.);
    DRFM  = GTABL(9,DRFMT,FR,0.,2.,.25);
    BRFM  = GTABL(5,BRFMT,FR,0.,4.,1.);
    BRPM  = GTABL(7,BRPMT,POLR,0.,60.,10.);
    BR    = SS[1] * BRN * BRFM * BRMM * BRCM * BRPM;
    DR    = SS[1] * DRN * DRMM * DRPM * DRFM * DRCM;
    NRUR  = SS[1] * XNRUN * NRMM;
    CIG   = SS[1] * CIM * CIGN;
    CID   = SS[3] * CIDN;
    POLG  = SS[1] * POLN * POLCM;
    POLA  = SS[4] / POLAT;
    QL    = QLS * QLM * QLC * QLF * QLP;

    SS[1] = SS[1] + DTNOW * (BR - DR);
    SS[2] = SS[2] - DTNOW * NRUR;
    SS[3] = SS[3] + DTNOW * (CIG - CID);
    SS[4] = SS[4] + DTNOW * (POLG - POLA);
    SS[5] = SS[5] + DTNOW * (CFIFR * CIQR - SS[5]) / CIAFT;

    return;
}
```

Figure 12-13C Function STATE in C for world model.

```
Public Sub STATE()
     NRFR = VS.SS(2) / NRI
     CR = VS.SS(1) / (LA * PDN)
     CIR = VS.SS(3) / VS.SS(1)
     NREM = GTABL(5, NREMT(), NRFR, 0#, 1#, 0.25)
     ECIR = CIR * (1# - VS.SS(5)) * NREM / (1# - CIAFN)
     MSL = ECIR / ECIRN
     BRMM = GTABL(6, BRMMT(), MSL, 0#, 5#, 1#)
     DRMM = GTABL(11, DRMMT(), MSL, 0#, 5#, 0.5)
     DRCM = GTABL(6, DRCMT(), CR, 0#, 5#, 1#)
     BRCM = GTABL(6, BRCMT(), CR, 0#, 5#, 1#)
     CIRA = CIR * VS.SS(5) / CIAFN
     FPCI = GTABL(7, FPCIT(), CIRA, 0#, 6#, 1#)
     FCM = GTABL(6, FCMT(), CR, 0#, 5#, 1#)
     POLR = VS.SS(4) / POLS
     FPM = GTABL(7, FPMT(), POLR, 0#, 60#, 10#)
     FR = FPCI * FCM * FPM * FC / FN
     CIM = GTABL(6, CIMT(), MSL, 0#, 5#, 1#)
     POLCM = GTABL(6, POLCMT(), CIR, 0#, 5#, 1#)
     POLAT = GTABL(7, POLATT(), POLR, 0#, 60#, 10#)
     CFIFR = GTABL(5, CFIFRT(), FR, 0#, 2#, 0.5)
     QLM = GTABL(6, QLMT(), MSL, 0#, 5#, 1#)
     QLC = GTABL(11, QLCT(), CR, 0#, 5#, 0.5)
     QLF = GTABL(5, QLFT(), FR, 0#, 4#, 1#)
     QLP = GTABL(7, QLPT(), POLR, 0#, 60#, 10#)
     NRMM = GTABL(11, NRMMT(), MSL, 0#, 10#, 1#)
     CIQR = GTABL(5, CIQRT(), QLM / QLF, 0#, 2#, 0.5)
     DRPM = GTABL(7, DRPMT(), POLR, 0#, 60#, 10#)
     DRFM = GTABL(9, DRFMT(), FR, 0#, 2#, 0.25)
     BRFM = GTABL(5, BRFMT(), FR, 0#, 4#, 1#)
     BRPM = GTABL(7, BRPMT(), POLR, 0#, 60#, 10#)
     BR = VS.SS(1) * BRN * BRFM * BRMM * BRCM * BRPM
     DR = VS.SS(1) * DRN * DRMM * DRPM * DRFM * DRCM
     NRUR = VS.SS(1) * XNRUN * NRMM
     CIG = VS.SS(1) * CIM * CIGN
     CID = VS.SS(3) * CIDN
     POLG = VS.SS(1) * POLN * POLCM
     POLA = VS.SS(4) / POLAT
     QL = QLS * QLM * QLC * QLF * QLP

     VS.SS(1) = VS.SS(1) + VS.DTNOW * (BR - DR)
     VS.SS(2) = VS.SS(2) - VS.DTNOW * NRUR
     VS.SS(3) = VS.SS(3) + VS.DTNOW * (CIG - CID)
     VS.SS(4) = VS.SS(4) + VS.DTNOW * (POLG - POLA)
     VS.SS(5) = VS.SS(5)+VS.DTNOW*(CFIFR * CIQR - VS.SS(5))/ CIAFT
End Sub
```

Figure 12-13VB Subroutine STATE in Visual Basic for world model.

```c
BOOL SWFUNC INTLC(UINT uiRun) {
    BOOL bContinue = TRUE;
    int i;

    if (uiRun == 1) {
        /* set experiment parameters */
        for(i=0;i<6;i++) BRCMT[i]=GETARY(1,i+1);
        for(i=0;i<5;i++) BRFMT[i]=GETARY(2,i+1);
        for(i=0;i<6;i++) BRMMT[i]=GETARY(3,i+1);
        for(i=0;i<7;i++) BRPMT[i]=GETARY(4,i+1);
        for(i=0;i<5;i++) CFIFRT[i]=GETARY(5,i+1);
        for(i=0;i<6;i++) CIMT[i]=GETARY(6,i+1);
        for(i=0;i<5;i++) CIQRT[i]=GETARY(7,i+1);
        for(i=0;i<6;i++) DRCMT[i]=GETARY(8,i+1);
        for(i=0;i<9;i++) DRFMT[i]=GETARY(9,i+1);
        for(i=0;i<11;i++)DRMMT[i]=GETARY(10,i+1);
        for(i=0;i<7;i++) DRPMT[i]=GETARY(11,i+1);
        for(i=0;i<6;i++) FCMT[i]=GETARY(12,i+1);
        for(i=0;i<7;i++) FPCIT[i]=GETARY(13,i+1);
        for(i=0;i<7;i++) FPMT[i]=GETARY(14,i+1);
        for(i=0;i<5;i++) NREMT[i]=GETARY(15,i+1);
        for(i=0;i<11;i++) NRMMT[i]=GETARY(16,i+1);
        for(i=0;i<7;i++) POLATT[i]=GETARY(17,i+1);
        for(i=0;i<6;i++) POLCMT[i]=GETARY(18,i+1);
        for(i=0;i<11;i++) QLCT[i]=GETARY(19,i+1);
        for(i=0;i<5;i++) QLFT[i]=GETARY(20,i+1);
        for(i=0;i<6;i++) QLMT[i]=GETARY(21,i+1);
        for(i=0;i<7;i++) QLPT[i]=GETARY(22,i+1);
    }

    /* set BRN */
    BRN = XX[10];

    /* initialize values */
    dPI   = 1.65e9;
    ECIRN = 1.;
    NRI   = 900.e9;
    XNRUN = 1.;
    DRN   = .028;
    LA    = 135.e6;
    PDN   = 26.5;
    FC    = 1.;
    FN    = 1.;
    CIAFN = .3;
    CII   = .4e9;
    CIGN  = .05;
    CIDN  = .025;
    POLS  = 3.6e9;
    POLI  = .2e9;
    POLN  = 1.;
    CIAFI = .2;
    CIAFT = 15.;
    QLS   = 1.;
    SS[1]   = dPI;
    SS[2]   = NRI;
    SS[3]   = CII;
    SS[4]   = POLI;
    SS[5]   = CIAFI;

    return(bContinue);
}
```

Figure 12-14C Function INTLC in C for world model.

```
Public Function INTLC(Run As Long)         For i = 1 To 11
As Long                                        NRMMT(i) = VS.Array(16, i)
    Dim bContinue As Long                  Next i
    Dim i As Integer                       For i = 1 To 7
                                               POLATT(i) = VS.Array(17, i)
    bContinue = True                       Next i
                                           For i = 1 To 6
    If Run = 1 Then                            POLCMT(i) = VS.Array(18, i)
        'set experiment parameters         Next i
                                           For i = 1 To 11
        For i = 1 To 6                         QLCT(i) = VS.Array(19, i)
            BRCMT(i) = VS.Array(1, i)      Next i
        Next i                             For i = 1 To 5
        For i = 1 To 5                         QLFT(i) = VS.Array(20, i)
            BRFMT(i) = VS.Array(2, i)      Next i
        Next i                             For i = 1 To 6
        For i = 1 To 6                         QLMT(i) = VS.Array(21, i)
            BRMMT(i) = VS.Array(3, i)      Next i
        Next i                             For i = 1 To 7
        For i = 1 To 7                         QLPT(i) = VS.Array(22, i)
            BRPMT(i) = VS.Array(4, i)      Next i
        Next i                         End If
        For i = 1 To 5
            CFIFRT(i) = VS.Array(5, i)     'set BRN
        Next i                             BRN = VS.XX(10)
        For i = 1 To 6
            CIMT(i) = VS.Array(6, i)       'initialize values
        Next i                             dPI = 1650000000#
        For i = 1 To 5                     ECIRN = 1#
            CIQRT(i) = VS.Array(7, i)      NRI = 900000000000#
        Next i                             XNRUN = 1#
        For i = 1 To 6                     DRN = 0.028
            DRCMT(i) = VS.Array(8, i)      LA = 135000000#
        Next i                             PDN = 26.5
        For i = 1 To 9                     FC = 1#
            DRFMT(i) = VS.Array(9, i)      FN = 1#
        Next i                             CIAFN = 0.3
        For i = 1 To 11                    CII = 400000000#
            DRMMT(i) = VS.Array(10, i)     CIGN = 0.05
        Next i                             CIDN = 0.025
        For i = 1 To 7                     POLS = 3600000000#
            DRPMT(i) = VS.Array(11, i)     POLI = 200000000#
        Next i                             POLN = 1#
        For i = 1 To 6                     CIAFI = 0.2
            FCMT(i) = VS.Array(12, i)      CIAFT = 15#
        Next i                             QLS = 1#
        For i = 1 To 7                     VS.SS(1) = dPI
            FPCIT(i) = VS.Array(13, i)     VS.SS(2) = NRI
        Next i                             VS.SS(3) = CII
        For i = 1 To 7                     VS.SS(4) = POLI
            FPMT(i) = VS.Array(14, i)      VS.SS(5) = CIAFI
        Next i
        For i = 1 To 5                     INTLC = bContinue
            NREMT(i) = VS.Array(15, i) End Function
        Next i
```

Figure 12-14VB Function INTLC in Visual Basic for world model.

A listing of input statements for this example is shown in Figure 12-15.

```
GEN,"PRITSKER","WORLD MODEL",1/1/1996,1;
LIMITS,10,-1,-1,2,-1,-1;
CONTINUOUS,-1,5,.2,.2,,WARNING,.00001,.00001;
INITIALIZE,1900.,2100.;
RECORD,TNOW,"TIME",{AWESIM,EXCEL},8,{{SS[1]/1.E9,"POP",},
{SS[3]/1.E9,"CI",},SS[2]/1.E11,"NR",},{SS[4]/1.E9,"POL",}};
ARRAY,1,6,{1.05,1,.9,.7,.6,.55};
ARRAY,2,5,{0,1,1.6,1.9,2};
ARRAY,3,6,{1.2,1,.85,.75,.7,.7};
ARRAY,4,7,{1.02,.9,.7,.4,.25,.15,.1};
ARRAY,5,5,{1,.6,.3,.15,.1};
ARRAY,6,6,{.1,1,1.8,2.4,2.8,3};
ARRAY,7,5,{.7,.8,1,1.5,2};
ARRAY,8,6,{.9,1,1.2,1.5,1.9,3};
ARRAY,9,9,{30,3,2,1.4,1,.7,.6,.5,.5};
ARRAY,10,11,{3,1.8,1,.8,.7,.6,.53,.5,.5,.5,.5};
ARRAY,11,7,{.92,1.3,2,3.2,4.8,6.8,9.2};
ARRAY,12,6,{2.4,1,.6,.4,.3,.2};
ARRAY,13,7,{0.5,1.0,1.4,1.7,1.9,2.05,2.2};
ARRAY,14,7,{1.02,.9,.65,.35,.2,.1,.05};
ARRAY,15,5,{0,.15,.5,.85,1};
ARRAY,16,11,{0,1,1.8,2.4,2.9,3.3,3.6,3.8,3.9,3.95,4};
ARRAY,17,7,{.6,2.5,5,8,11.5,15.5,20};
ARRAY,18,6,{.05,1,3,5.4,7.4,8};
ARRAY,19,11,{2,1.3,1,.75,.55,.45,.38,.3,.25,.22,.2};
ARRAY,20,5,{0,1,1.8,2.4,2.7};
ARRAY,21,6,{.2,1,1.7,2.3,2.7,2.9};
ARRAY,22,7,{1.04,.85,.6,.3,.15,.05,.02};
INTLC,{{xx[10],0.04}};
FIN;
```

Figure 12-15   Listing of input statements of world model.

Summary of Results. The plotted output for the world model is shown in Figure 12-16. In running this simulation, no external excitation of the system is introduced. For stable systems, the dynamic behavior exhibited is due to the transients of the model. When the model is simulated for a longer period of time, all levels reach their steady state values.

World Dynamics

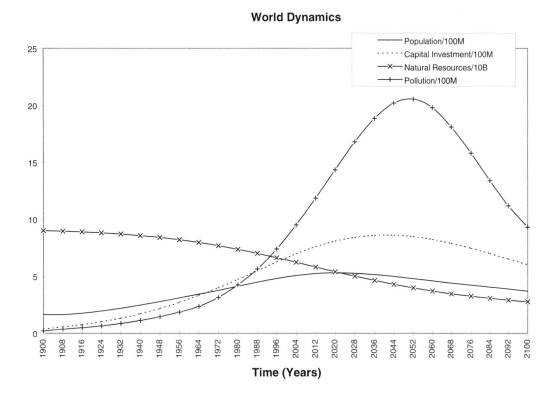

Figure 12-16 Plot of dynamic behavior of world model for a birth rate normal
value of 0.04.

12.14   CHAPTER SUMMARY

This chapter presents the continuous simulation procedures of Visual SLAM. The
definition of state variables is given and the methods for writing differential and
difference equations are prescribed. A detailed description of Visual SLAM's time
advance procedure is presented. The use of Visual SLAM to model a pilot ejecting
from an aircraft is presented as Example 12-l. As an example of the use of Visual
SLAM for building Systems Dynamics models, the coding for Forrester's World
Dynamics model is presented as Example 12-2.

12.15   EXERCISES

12-1.   Experiment with the model of Cedar Bog Lake.
Embellishments:
(a) Superimpose a normally distributed random variation with a mean of 0, and a standard deviation of 9 on the solar energy supplied to the lake ecosystem that occurs every 0.025 years; (b)Determine the effects of a step increase of 20% in the solar energy input to the lake ecosystem; (c) Suppose that 20% of the energy losses to the lake sediment are considered as fertilizer and are reflected in the rate of change in plant energy. Determine the effect of this change in lake ecosystem structure on the behavior of the model; (d) Superimpose the following control policies on the natural environment: stock the lake with carnivores by 0.3 cal/cm2 every tenth of a year; replenish the lake with 0.2 cal/cm2 of herbivores when the population of carnivores increases above 0.6 cal/cm2; and spray the lake to reduce the plant population by 70% every 0.5 year. Simulate Cedar Bog Lake under the above control strategies.

12-2.   Use Visual SLAM to compute a value of y for the following equation:

$$y = \int_{3}^{6} 0.0012193 \ x(x-3)^7 dx$$

Integrate to obtain y and compare with the value obtained from Visual SLAM.

12-3.   Modify the pilot ejection model of Example 12-1 to allow for a two-pilot aircraft. The second pilot ejects from the aircraft 1 sec after the first pilot. The second pilot is located 7 feet behind the first pilot. Simulate the system for an aircraft speed of 500 feet/second to determine if the pilots maintain a separation of 5 feet and if the pilots clear the aircraft. Assume all parameters used in Example 12-1 hold for the two pilot situation.

12-4.   A mass is suspended by a spring and a dashpot. The mass is subjected to a vertical force, f(t), and the vertical movement of the mass is described by

$$my'' + k_2 y' + k_1 y = f(t)$$

where   y is the spring displacement,
y' is the derivative of y with respect to time,
y" is the second derivative of y with respect to time,
m is the mass,
k_1 is the spring constant, and
k_2 is the dashpot constant

Run a 60 second simulation to obtain a plot of the vertical movement of the mass when m = 1, k_1 = 1.0, and k_2 = 0.3, f(t) = 1.0 for all t.
Embellishments:

(a) Rerun the simulation when f(t) = sin 2πt.

(b) Rerun the simulation when f(t) is sampled every 5 seconds from a uniform distribution whose range is 0.5 to 1.5.

12-5. A bank has a drive-in teller whose service time is exponentially distributed with a mean time of 0.5 minutes. Customer interarrival time is also exponentially distributed with a mean of 0.4 minutes. Only 1 car can wait for the drive-in teller, that is, customers that arrive when 1 car is waiting balk from the system and do not return. Letting $p_n(t)$ = the probability that n customers are in the system (queue plus service) at time t, the following equations can be derived

$$\frac{dp_0(t)}{dt} = -2.5*p_0(t) + 2.0*p_1(t)$$

$$\frac{dp_1(t)}{dt} = -2.5*p_0(t) - 4.5*p_1(t) + 2.0*p_2(t)$$

and

$$\frac{dp_2(t)}{dt} = -2.5*p_1(t) - 2.0*p_2(t)$$

Assume that at t=0 there are no customers in the system and, hence, the teller is idle. Develop a Visual SLAM model to obtain the expected number in the system, E[N(t)], for t=0,2,4,6,..., 100 where

$$E[N(t)] = \sum_{i=0}^{2} i*p_i(t)$$

Prepare a table and plot for $p_j(t)$ and E[N(t)] using a record interval of 0.05.

12-6. Develop a simulation model to portray a single server finite queueing system with exponential interarrival and service times. For a maximum of 20 in the system, plot the transient values for selected probabilities, and the expected value and variance of the number in the system. Also plot the average value of the expected number in the system observed at 5 minute intervals. Let the arrival rate be 4 units/minute and the service rate be 5 units/minute (10).

12-7. Use Visual SLAM to analyze Forrester's model of industrial dynamics (5).

12-8. For the world model presented as Example 13-2, incorporate the following events (9):

Event	Effect	Event Code
Food shortage occurs every 20 years and lasts 4 years	Decreases food ratio to 70% of its "normal" value over a 4-year period and population by 10% immediately	1
Discovery of new resources (or equivalent technological development), occurs in 1975	Increases natural resources immediately by 50%	2
Worldwide epidemic, occurs in 1980	Decreases population by 15% and capital investment by 20%	3
Legislative controls go into effect against pollution, occurs 5 years after pollution threshold is reached	Set indicator so that controls are in effect which will decrease POLCM by 75%	4
End of food shortage, occurs 4 years after event 1	Reset indicator to restore food ratio to normal value	5
Initiate zero population growth drive, occurs when population threshold is reached	Decrease birth rate by 15% when population exceeds $2.5*10^9$ (TOL = $1.5*10^8$)	6
Initiate legislation to correct pollution, occurs when pollution threshold is reached	Schedule event 4 to occur in 5 years when pollution exceeds $5*10^8$ (TOL = $5*10^7$)	7
Begin conservation measures to protect supply of natural resources, occurs when natural resources threshold is reached	Set conversation indicator that that will cause NRMM to be decreased by 10% when natural resources decrease below $7*10^{12}$ (TOL = $1.05*10^{12}$)	8

12-9.   The equation for the current i in a series electrical system is shown below.

$$L\frac{d^2i}{dt^2} + R\frac{di}{dt} + \frac{i}{c} = \omega E \sin \omega t.$$

Develop the equations for simulating the current *i* in Visual SLAM form. When the current exceeds the value A, a fuse is blown. Develop the statements that would detect the time at which the fuse would be blown. Assume that the tolerance on the current is 0.1*A.

12-10.   The equations modeling the height of a dropped ball y_1 are

$$\frac{dy_1}{dt} = y_2$$

$$\frac{dy_2}{dt} = -g$$

where g=32.2. The initial height of the ball is 4 feet and its initial speed is 0. When the ball hits the ground, it reverses direction and has only 0.80 of its speed. Model this bouncing ball to observe the first eight times it hits the ground. Compare with the calculated bounce times (15) of (0.4984, 1.2960, 1.9340, 2.4444, 2.8527, 3.1794, 3.4407, 3.6498). Develop a plot which shows the position of the ball over time.

12-11.   Model a swinging pendulum to determine its position, $y_1(t)$, and the times it reaches the maximum angular displacement. The equation for the pendulum is:

$$\frac{d^2y_1}{dt^2} = 2k^2y_1^3 - (1 + k^2)y_1$$

where k = 0.5, $y_1(0) = 0$ and $dy_1(0)/dt = 1$.

12.16   REFERENCES

1.   Carnahan, B., H. A. Luther, and J. O. Wilkes, *Applied Numerical Methods*, John Wiley, 1969.

2.   Conte, S. D. and C. de Boor, *Elementary Numerical Analysis*, McGraw-Hill, 1972.

3.   *CONTROL DATA MIMIC--A Digital Simulation Language Reference Manual*, Publication No. 44610400, Revision D, Control Data Corporation, Minneapolis, Minn., 1970.

4.   Fehlberg, E., "Low-Order Classical Runge-Kutta Formulas with Step-Size Control and Their Application to Some Heat Transfer Problems," *NASA Report TR R-315*, Huntsville, Alabama, April 15, 1969.

5.   Forrester, J. W., *Industrial Dynamics*, John Wiley, 1961.

6.   Forrester, J. W., *Principles of Systems*, Wright-Allen Press, 1971.

7.   Forrester, J. W., *World Dynamics*, Wright-Allen Press, 1972.

8.   Meadows, D. H., D. L. Meadows, J. Randers, and W. W. Behrens, III, *The Limits to Growth*, Potomac Associates, 1972.

9.   Pritsker, A. A. B., "Three Simulation Approaches to Queueing Studies Using GASP IV," *Computers & Industrial Engineering*, Vol. 1, 1976, pp. 57-65.

10.   Ralston, A., *A First Course in Numerical Analysis*, McGraw-Hill, 1965.

11.   Shampine, L. F. and R. C. Allen, Jr., *Numerical Computing: An Introduction*, W. B. Saunders, 1973.

12.   Shampine, L. F. et al., "Solving Non-Stiff Ordinary Differential Equations-The State of the Art," *SIAM Review*, Vol. 18, 1976, pp. 376-411.

13.   Talavage, J. J. and M. Triplett, "GASP IV Urban Model of Cadmium Flow," *Simulation*, Vol. 23, 1974, pp. 101-108.

14.   Thompson, S., "Rootfinding and Interpolation with Runge-Kutta-Sarafyan Methods," *Transactions of SCS*, Vol. 2, 1985, pp. 207-218.

15.   Williams, R. B., "Computer Simulation of Energy Flow in Cedar Bog Lake, Minnesota Based on the Classical Studies of Lindeman," in *Systems Analysis and Simulation in Ecology*, B. C. Patten, Ed., Academic Press, 1971.

CHAPTER 13

Combined Modeling

13.1   INTRODUCTION

Systems are often classified as either discrete change, continuous change, or combined discrete-continuous change, according to the mechanism by which the state space description of the system changes with time. In discrete change systems, the state of the system changes discretely at event times. As previously described, discrete change systems can be modeled with Visual SLAM using a network, discrete event or combined network-discrete event orientation. In contrast, continuous change systems are characterized by variables defined through state and derivative equations and the variables are assumed to change continuously with time. Continuous systems are modeled with Visual SLAM by describing the dynamics of the system as a set of differential or difference equations. In combined discrete-continuous change systems, the state of the system may change discretely, continuously, or continuously with discrete jumps superimposed. Changes to status variables and to the model configuration are made at event times. For combined modeling, an event is defined as a point in time beyond which the status of the system cannot be projected with certainty (6).

607

Thus, status variables can change without an event occurring as long as the change is made in a prescribed manner. Also, an event could occur and no change be made. Events that occur at a specified point in time are defined as time events. They are commonly thought of in terms of next event simulation. Events that occur when the system reaches a particular state are called state events. Unlike time events, they are not scheduled in the future but occur when state variables meet prescribed conditions. In Visual SLAM state events can initiate time events, and time events can initiate state events.

In this chapter, examples of combined modeling are presented. The features of Visual SLAM that facilitate the use of alternative modeling viewpoints are described. No new modeling elements are presented. The Visual SLAM interfaces for combined modeling have been introduced in previous chapters and they are reviewed in the next section. The processing logic to integrate discrete and continuous models is described.

13.2   VISUAL SLAM INTERFACES

This section summarizes information on the interfaces between network, discrete event, and continuous models. The variables SS, DD, XX, LL, SZ, II, ATRIB, LTRIB, STRIB, ARRAY and TNOW provide for the transfer of values of status variables throughout a Visual SLAM model. The functions NNACT, NNCNT, NNQ, NNRSC, NRUSE and NNGAT provide the method for accessing the status of network elements in discrete event and continuous submodels. The function USERF provides a means for writing Visual Basic or C code to establish a value to be used in a network model. USERF can replace any Visual SLAM status variable in a network model. The functions FREE, ALTER, OPEN and CLOSX are used to change the status of network elements from user-written Visual Basic or C subprograms. The subprograms ALLOC, SEIZE, NQS and NSS provide a method for incorporating advanced decision logic when modeling resource allocations and server and queue selection procedures.

The DETECT node and SEVNT statement provide mechanisms to monitor state variables and to detect state events. They provide the interface between changes in status variables in any modeling viewpoint and the invoking of function EVENT. The EVENT node is the direct interface for this capability between a network model and discrete event subprograms. Inserting entities into a network from a discrete event is accomplished through the use of function ENTER and function ARRIVE. Function ARRIVE places an entity at any node in a network. Function ENTER places an entity in a network at an ENTER node and provides a graphical portrayal of an entity being inserted into a network. Within a discrete event, entities can be manipulated through the use of the file processing routines. This includes entries on the event calendar. Entities in activities can be made to complete an activity from a discrete event by invoking function STOPA.

The above describes the constructs available in Visual SLAM to interface models developed from alternative viewpoints. Clearly, Visual SLAM has been designed to foster and facilitate the combined modeling of systems.

13.3   USING ALTERNATIVE MODELING VIEWPOINTS

Experience has shown that the education of an individual is the prime determinant of the modeling viewpoint used on a particular problem. It is one of the clearest examples of the impact of the educational process on problem-solving capabilities. Electrical engineers, mechanical engineers, chemical engineers and physicists tend to be continuous modelers. Computer scientists tend to be process or network oriented as do management and business people. Operations researchers and industrial engineers are basically discrete simulation modelers. An underlying hypothesis that establishes the need for Visual SLAM is that there is not one best viewpoint when modeling a system.

When using Visual SLAM, the primary question is not which modeling viewpoint to take, but how to start to solve the problem. As demonstrated throughout this book, models developed in Visual SLAM are easily embellished. The interfaces between modeling viewpoints provide the flexibility to include constructs from each viewpoint into an existing model. Models, like systems, evolve and change to meet new specifications and conditions. As a model grows, the need for new modeling viewpoints and concepts becomes greater. The flexibility provided by Visual SLAM to perform combined modeling is a long term advantage of strategic importance.

13.4   VISUAL SLAM PROCESSING LOGIC FOR COMBINED MODELS

The processing logic employed by Visual SLAM for simulating combined models is depicted in Figure 13-1. The processor begins by interpreting the Visual SLAM

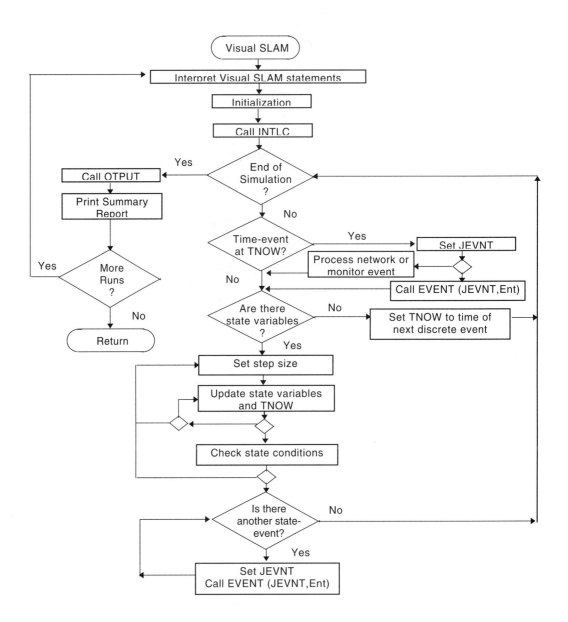

Figure 13-1   Visual SLAM processing logic for combined models.

input statements. This is followed by an initialization phase including a call to the user-written function INTLC for establishing user-defined initial conditions for the simulation. During the initialization phase, the processor schedules an entity arrival event for each CREATE node to occur at the time of the first release of the CREATE node. These events are filed on the event calendar in the order in which the CREATE nodes appear in the statement model.

In addition, entities initially in QUEUE nodes are created and end-of-activity events are scheduled for the service activities following the QUEUE nodes. All attribute values of these created entities are zero. Events placed on the event calendar through calls to function SCHDL made in function INTLC are then put on the event calendar.

After processing function INTLC or after any increase in TNOW, a test is made for one of the following end-of-simulation conditions:

1. TNOW is greater than or equal to the ending time specified for the simulation.

2. The value of MSTOP has been set to a negative value.

3. A TERMINATE node has reached its specified terminate count in the network portion of the model.

4. There are no events on the event calendar and there are no continuous variables in the model.

If the simulation run is ended, statistics are calculated, a call is made to function OTPUT, and the Visual SLAM Summary Report is written. A test is then made to determine if additional runs are to be executed. If there are, the next run is initiated. If all simulation runs have been completed, Visual SLAM prepares the Multiple Run Summary Report and ends execution.

If none of the end-of-simulation conditions is satisfied, the Visual SLAM processor determines if there is a time event at the current time. If there is, JEVNT is set to the event code of the current event. Events may be user-defined, through EVENT nodes or calls to function SCHDL, or they may be Visual SLAM network or monitor events. A small diamond is shown in Figure 13-1 to represent logical tests on internal Visual SLAM variables. For user events, function EVENT is called directly. In function EVENT, the modeler performs the transfer necessary to process the event associated with JEVNT. For network and monitor events, the Visual SLAM processor performs the necessary operations. All network events are associated with entity arrivals to a node. The functions necessary to process an entity arriving to a node are precoded and the updates to network status variables are made automatically in accordance with the parameters specified for the node. As part of this nodal processing, events are placed on the calendar in accordance with the node type. For example, an entity arrival to a FREE node may reallocate the freed resources to other entities, place the other entities in activities, and schedule an end-of-activity event for the entity arriving to the FREE node.

Following the processing of a time event, continuous variables are updated and state-event conditions checked since threshold crossings can be caused by discrete changes made in the event routines. If no continuous variables are included in the model, TNOW is updated to the time of the next discrete event and the end-of-simulation conditions are checked. If continuous variables are included in the model, a step size is established and the values of the SS variables are updated by calls to function STATE. If differential equations are involved, then multiple calls to function STATE are made within the step. If accuracy is not met, the step size is reduced. After the updating of the continuous variables, a check is made on state event conditions. If there is not a state event to be processed, a test for the end-of-simulation is made. If a variable exceeds a threshold beyond tolerance then the step size is reduced and the updating process is repeated. If there is a state event to be processed, the event code JEVNT is set, and a call is made to function EVENT. Following the return from function EVENT, a test for another state event is processed as multiple state events can occur at the same time.

The processing logic presented in Figure 13-1 gives an overview of how combined simulation is performed. It is important to note that the values of continuous variables are always updated before a time event is processed. In this way, decisions in a time event are based on the current values of continuous variables. Following the processing of a time event, the state variables are updated in accordance with any changes made to parameters or other state variables in the model. For display convenience, the flowchart does not include the details with regard to the setting of the step size, accuracy checking, out-of-tolerance state-event detection, and the recording of values at save times.

13.5   EXAMPLE 13-1.   SOAKING PIT FURNACE

Steel ingots arrive at a soaking pit furnace (1,4,7) in a steel plant with an interarrival time that is exponentially distributed with mean of 2.25 hours. The soaking pit furnace heats an ingot so that it can be economically rolled in the next stage of the process. The temperature change of an ingot in the soaking pit furnace is described by the following differential equation.

$$\frac{dh_i}{dt} = (H - h_i) * C_i$$

where h_i is the temperature of the ith ingot in the soaking pit; C_i is the heating time coefficient of an ingot and is equal to X+.1 where X is normally distributed with mean of .05 and standard deviation of 0.01; and H is the furnace temperature which is heated toward 2600°F with a heating rate constant of 0.2, that is,

$$\frac{dH}{dt} = (2600.-H) * 0.2$$

The ingots interact with one another in that adding a "cold" ingot to the furnace reduces the temperature of the furnace and thus changes the heating time for all ingots in the furnace. The temperature reduction is equal to the difference between furnace and ingot temperatures, divided by the number of ingots in the furnace. There are 10 soaking pits in the furnace. When a new ingot arrives and the furnace is full, it is stored in an ingot storage bank. It is assumed that the initial temperature of an arriving ingot is uniformly distributed in the interval from 400 to 500°F. All ingots put in the ingot storage bank are assumed to have a temperature of 400°F upon insertion into the soaking pit. The operating policy of the company is to continue heating the ingots in the furnace until one or more ingots reach 2200°F. At such a time all ingots with a temperature greater than 2000°F are removed. The initial conditions are that there are six ingots in the furnace with initial temperatures of 550, 600, 650, 700, 750 and 800°F. Initially, the temperature of the furnace is 1650°F, and the next ingot is due to arrive at time 0.

The objective is to simulate the above system for 500 hours to obtain estimates of the following quantities:

1. Heating time of the ingots;

2. Final temperature distribution of the ingots;

3. Waiting time of the ingots in the ingot storage bank; and

4. Utilization of the soaking pit furnace.

Concepts Illustrated. This example illustrates the stopping of an ACTIVITY in a network model due to the occurrence of a state event through the use of a STOPA activity duration specification and a call to function STOPA. A RESOURCE is used to model the soaking pits.

Visual SLAM Model. The furnace problem is described using a combined network, discrete event and continuous model. A network is employed to model the ingot arrival process, the ingot storage bank, the soaking pit activity, and the exit from the system. A time event initiated through an arrival to an EVENT node is used to insert ingots into the furnace. A state event ends the soaking activity and causes ingots to be removed from the furnace. Continuous state variables model the temperature of the ingots in the furnace and the temperature of the furnace. The status of the pits in the furnace is maintained in the Visual SLAM vector LL. If pit I is occupied by an ingot, LL[I] is set to 1; otherwise LL[I] is equal to 0 which indicates that the pit is empty. The continuous portion of the model employs twelve state variables. The first ten state variables are used to model the temperature of the ingot in each of the ten soaking pits. If soaking pit I is occupied, SS[I] equals the temperature of the ingot in pit I, otherwise SS[I] is set equal to 0. The temperature of the furnace is modeled as state variable SS[11] which is given the equivalent name TEMP_FURNACE. State variable SS[12], given the name TEMP_MAX, is set equal to the maximum temperature of all ingots in the furnace. The equations for the temperatures of each ingot and the furnace are coded in function STATE in terms of their derivatives as shown in Figure 13-2. The value of SS[12], representing the maximum ingot temperature, is initially set to 0. In a For loop, each ingot temperature is compared to the value of SS[12], and SS[12] is reset to the temperature of the ingot as appropriate. Also each value of DD[I] is calculated as the rate of change of the temperature for the ingot in the Ith pit. Note that if the Ith pit is empty, then LL[I] equals 0, and therefore DD[I] is set to 0. The variable InPit[I] holds the ENTITY reference to the ingot in pit I. Attribute 3 of the ingot entity is the normally distributed heating coefficient for the ingot in pit I which is set in the discrete event portion of the model. It is assumed that the ingot has material properties that affect its heating rate. Following the exit from the For loop, DD[11] is set equal to the rate of change of the temperature in the furnace. This variable is given the equivalent name DELTA_FURNACE.

The network model for this example is depicted in Figure 13-3. The ingot arrivals are created at the CREATE node with the arrival time marked as ATRIB[1]. The time between arrivals of the ingot entities is exponentially distributed with a mean of 2.25 hours. The ingots continue to the ASSIGN node where ATRIB[2] is set equal to a sample from a uniform distribution between 400 and 500 which represents the initial temperature of the ingot. The ingots then wait, if necessary, in file 1 for one unit of resource PIT. Once the ingot has seized a PIT, it proceeds to the EVENT node labeled LOAD where an event with code 1 is invoked. This event determines the pit number of the available pit, sets the status of the pit to occupied, sets the initial temperature for the ingot, and sets ATRIB[3] of the entity equal to the heating coefficient for the ingot and LTRIB[1] equal to the pit number. If the ingot has waited in the storage bank, statistics are collected on the waiting time and ATRIB[1] is re-marked as TNOW.

In addition, the temperature of the furnace is reduced appropriately as the result of adding an ingot to the furnace. The logic for this event is coded in the LOADP case of function EVENT and is described following the discussion of the network model.

```
Public Sub STATE()
   Dim iPit As Integer

' monitor the temperature in each pit and store the highest
 ' pit temperature in TEMP_MAX

   TEMP_MAX = 0#

   For iPit = 1 To NUMPITS
      If VS.LL(iPit) = 1 Then
If VS.SS(iPit) > TEMP_MAX Then
            TEMP_MAX = VS.SS(iPit)
         End If
         VS.DD(iPit)=(TEMP_FURNACE-VS.SS(iPit))*InPit(iPit).ATRIB(3)
      Else
         VS.DD(iPit) = 0# ' unoccupied pit
      End If
   Next iPit
   DELTA_FURNACE = (2600# - TEMP_FURNACE) * 0.2
End Sub
```

Figure 13-2VB   Subroutine STATE for furnace example in Visual Basic.

```
   void SWFUNC STATE(void)
   {
      int iPit;

      /* monitor the temperature in each pit and store the highest
            temperature in TEMP_MAX                          */
      TEMP_MAX = 0.0;

      for (iPit=1; iPit <= NUMPITS; iPit++)           {
         if (LL[iPit]>0)                              {
            /* pit is occupied */
            if (SS[iPit] > TEMP_MAX)
                  TEMP_MAX = SS[iPit];
            DD[iPit]=(TEMP_FURNACE-SS[iPit])*InPit[iPit-1]->ATRIB[3];
         } else
            DD[iPit] = 0.0; /* unoccupied pit */
      }
      DELTA_FURNACE = (2600.0 - TEMP_FURNACE) * 0.2;

      return;
   }
```

Figure 13-2C Function STATE for furnace example in C.

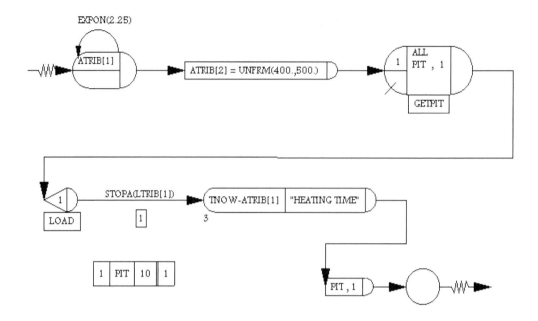

Figure 13-3 Network model for furnace example.

Following processing at the EVENT node, the ingot undertakes ACTIVITY 1 representing the soaking activity. The duration of this ACTIVITY is indefinite and is terminated from within a discrete event when stopping conditions are satisfied. This is modeled in the event EXITP case of function EVENT with a call to function STOPA(NTC) where NTC is equal to the PIT number. The invocation of function STOPA(I) causes the ingot in pit I to complete ACTIVITY 1. When any ingot's temperature is greater than or equal to 2200°, ACTIVITY 1 is completed for each ingot I with SS[I] greater than or equal to 2000° in event EXITP. This event is initiated as a state event when SS[12] exceeds 2200°F within a tolerance of 50° as prescribed on the SEVNT statement depicted below.

SEVNT,2,SS(12),POSITIVE,2200. ,50;

Following the completion of the soaking activity, the ingots proceed to a COLCT node where interval statistics are collected on the heating time for the ingot using the time reference contained in ATRIB[1]. An ingot entity is routed to the FREE node where a PIT is released. The entity is then terminated from the system.

The events for this example are coded in function EVENT(I). Two cases are provided for: case 1 for the LOAD event and case 2 for the EXITP event. Recall that the LOAD event is initiated from within the network model by ingots arriving to the EVENT node with code 1, and the EXITP event is initiated as a state event from within the continuous model by the maximum ingot temperature reaching 2200°F.

The coding for the EVENT routine is given in Figure 13-4. In the coding for Case 1 the pit number, iPit, in which the ingot is to be inserted, is set equal to the first iPit such that LL[iPit] equals 0. The variables associated with pit iPit are then initialized and ATRIB[3] is set equal to the heating coefficient. If the ingot waited in the storage bank, statistics are collected on the wait time using COLCT variable number 2, the temperature of the ingot is set to 400°F, and ATRIB[1] is re-marked at TNOW. The ingot is placed in the pit which causes the temperature of the furnace to be reduced by the difference in temperature between the ingot and the furnace divided by the number of ingots in the furnace (including the new one).

The coding for Case 2, the EXITP event, is invoked when one of the ingots has a temperature greater than or equal to 2200°F. The temperature of each pit, iPit, is tested against the desired temperature of 2000°F. If the ingot in pit iPit has reached 2000°, the variable LL[iPit] is set to zero to denote the pit has been emptied, statistics are collected on the temperature of the ingot exiting the pit as COLCT variable number 1, and the temperature of the pit is set equal to 0. A call is then made to function STOPA(iPit) which causes the entity representing the ingot in pit iPit to complete ACTIVITY 1 in the network model.

The initial conditions for the simulation are established in function INTLC depicted in Figure 13-5. The temperature of the furnace is initialized to 1650°F and six ingots with initial temperatures of 550, 600, 650, . . ., 800°F are inserted into file 1 of the AWAIT node through multiple calls of the statement ARRIVE("GETPIT",eNew). To initialize non-network COLCT statistics prior to the first run, function DefineColct (in Visual Basic) or su_colnew (in C) is called twice. Note that the definition of COLCT variable 1 specifies that a histogram be generated with 20 interior cells, with the upper limit of the first cell equal to 2000°F, and cell width of 10°F.

```
Public Sub EVENT(Code As Long, Ent As VSENTITY)
  Dim iPit As Integer
  Dim dReduce As Double
  Select Case Code
     Case LOADP ' load into pit
         ' determine available pit
         For iPit = 1 To NUMPITS
            If VS.LL(iPit) = 0 Then
               Exit For
            End If
         Next iPit
         If iPit > NUMPITS Then
            ' this should never happen
            VS.Error 1, "LOAD event called when no pits available"
            Exit Sub
         End If
         ' turn pit on, set initial temp.and heating coeff.,save pit #
         Set InPit(iPit) = Ent
         VS.LL(iPit) = 1
         With InPit(iPit)
           VS.SS(iPit) = .ATRIB(2) ' temp
           .ATRIB(3)=VS.RNORM(0.05, 0.01, 1) + 0.1 ' heating coeff
           .LTRIB(1) = iPit
           ' see if ingot has been waiting
           If .ATRIB(1) < VS.TNOW Then
              ' collect how long it has been waiting
              VS.Colct VS.TNOW - .ATRIB(1), 2
              VS.SS(iPit)=400# ' assume has cooled to min temperature
              .ATRIB(1) = VS.TNOW ' start count of how long in pit
           End If
         End With
         ' reduce furnace temperature
         dReduce = (TEMP_FURNACE - VS.SS(iPit)) / CDbl(VS.NNACT(1) + 1)
         TEMP_FURNACE = TEMP_FURNACE - dReduce
     Case EXITP ' pit is done heating ingot.  This is a state event
         For iPit = 1 To NUMPITS
            If VS.LL(iPit) >0 And VS.SS(iPit) >= 2000# Then
               ' this ingot is done
               VS.Colct VS.SS(iPit), 1
               ' clear pit
               Set InPit(iPit) = Nothing
               VS.LL(iPit) = 0
               VS.SS(iPit) = 0#
               VS.STOPA (iPit) ' stop heating
            End If
         Next iPit
     Case Else
         VS.Error 2, "Unknown event code"
  End Select
End Sub
```

Figure 13-4VB Subroutine EVENT for furnace example in Visual Basic.

```
void SWFUNC EVENT(int Code, ENTITY * Current)  {
   int iPit;
   double dReduce;

   switch (Code)                                              {
      case LOAD: /* load into pit */
         /* determine available pit */
         for (iPit=1; iPit <= NUMPITS; iPit++)             {
            if (LL[iPit]==0)
               break;
         }
         if (iPit > NUMPITS)                               {
            /* this should never happen */
            su_error(1,"LOAD event called when no pits available");
            break;
         }

         /* turn pit on, set initial temp. and heating coeff.,save pit # */
         LL[iPit] = 1;
         InPit[iPit-1] = Current;
         SS[iPit] = Current->ATRIB[2]; /* temp */
         Current->ATRIB[3]=RNORM(0.05,0.01,1)+0.1;/*heating coeff*/
         Current->LTRIB[1] = iPit;

         /* see if ingot has been waiting */
         if (Current->ATRIB[1] < TNOW)                       {
            /* collect how long it has been waiting */
            COLCT(TNOW - Current->ATRIB[1], 2);
            SS[iPit]=400.0;/* assume has cooled to min tempature */
          Current->ATRIB[1]=TNOW;/*start count of how long in pit */
         }

         /* reduce furnace tempature */
         dReduce = (TEMP_FURNACE-SS[iPit]) / (double)(NNACT(1)+1);
         TEMP_FURNACE -= dReduce;
      break;

      case EXITP:/* pit is done heating ingot.this is a state event */
         for (iPit=1; iPit <= NUMPITS; iPit++)             {
            if (LL[iPit] > 0 && SS[iPit] >= 2000.0)        {
               /* this ingot is done */
               COLCT(SS[iPit],1);

               /* clear pit */
               LL[iPit] = 0;
               InPit[iPit-1] = NULL;
               SS[iPit] = 0.0;
               STOPA(iPit); /* stop heating */
            }
         }
      break;
      default:
         su_error(2,"Unknown event code");
      break;
   }
}
```

Figure 13-4C   Function EVENT for furnace example in C.

```
Public Function INTLC(Run As Long) As Long
    Dim eNew As VSENTITY
    Dim i As Integer
    Dim szTemp As String
    Dim dTemp As Double
' empty pits
    For i = 1 To NUMPITS
        Set InPit(i) = Nothing
        VS.LL(i) = 0
    Next i
' initial furnace tempature
    TEMP_FURNACE = 1650#
' start 6 ingots in furnace
        dTemp = 550#
        For i = 1 To 6
            dTemp = dTemp + 50#
            Set eNew = VS.DefineEntity(0)
            If IsObject(eNew) Then
                eNew.ATRIB(1) = VS.TNOW
                eNew.ATRIB(2) = dTemp
                VS.ARRIVE "GETPIT", eNew ' entity arrives to await node
            End If
        Next i
If Run = 1 Then
        ' create collect statistics
        VS.DefineColct 1, "HEATING TEMP", 20, 2000#, 20#
        VS.DefineColct 2, "WAITING TIME", 0, 0#, 0#
    End If
INTLC = True
End Function
```

Figure 13-5VB   Function INTLC for furnace example in Visual Basic.

```
#include "vslam.h"

/* events */
#define LOAD  1
#define EXITP 2

/* limits */
#define NUMPITS 10

#define TEMP_FURNACE  SS[NUMPITS+1]
#define DELTA_FURNACE DD[NUMPITS+1]
#define TEMP_MAX      SS[NUMPITS+2]

ENTITY * InPit[NUMPITS]; /* the ingot in each pit */

BOOL SWFUNC INTLC(UINT uiRun)
{
```

Figure 13-5C   Function INTLC for furnace example in C.

```
    BOOL bContinue = TRUE;
    ENTITY * peNew;
    int i;
    double dTemp;

    /* empty pits */
    for (i=0; i < NUMPITS; i++)              {
        InPit[i] = NULL;
        LL[i+1] = 0;
    }

    /* initial furnace tempature */
    TEMP_FURNACE = 1650.0;

    /* start 6 ingots in furnace */
    for (i=0, dTemp = 550.0;
        i < 6;
        i++, dTemp += 50.0)                     {
      peNew = su_entnew(0,NULL,NULL,NULL);
      if (peNew)                            {
        peNew->ATRIB[1] = TNOW;
        peNew->ATRIB[2] = dTemp;
        ARRIVE("GETPIT",peNew); /* entity arrives to await node */
      }
    }

    if (uiRun == 1)                          {
      /* create collect statistics */
      su_colnew(1, "HEATING TEMP",20,2000.0,20.0);
      su_colnew(2, "WAITING TIME",0,0.0,0.0);
    }

    return(bContinue);
}
```

Figure 13-5C Function INTLC for furnace example in C (continued).

The input statements for this example are shown in Figure 13-6. Time-persistent statistics are specified for state variable SS[11].

Summary of Results. The Visual SLAM Summary Report for this example is included as Figure 13-7. The report reveals that during the 500 hours of simulated time, 238 ingots are processed and the average heating time is 19.96 hours. The heating time for ingots varied between 10.29 and 29.49 hours. The variation in the heating time is due to the coupling of the equations of the system through the furnace temperature and to the random component of the equation that is associated with the ingot, that is, the normal sample used to define the heating coefficient. The average waiting time for ingots in the cold ingot bank is 15.66 hours.
```
 GEN,"PRITSKER","INGOT PROBLEM",1/1/1996,1;
```

```
LIMITS,-1,10,-1,4,1,-1;
CONTINUOUS,11,5,.1,10;
TIMST,1,SS[11],"FURNACE TEMP.";
SEVNT,2,SS[12],POSITIVE,2200,50.;
NETWORK;

INIT,0,500;
FIN;

;   Furnace Example Network Statement Listing

    RESOURCE,1,PIT,10,{1};
    CREATE,EXPON(2.25), ,ATRIB[1];
        ACTIVITY;
    ASSIGN,{ { ATRIB[2], UNFRM(400.,500.) } };
        ACTIVITY;
GETPIT: AWAIT,1,{{PIT,1}},ALL, ,NONE;
        ACTIVITY, , , ,"LOAD";
LOAD: EVENT,1;
        ACTIVITY,1,STOPA(LTRIB[1]), , , ,"SOAKING ACTI";
    COLCT,3,TNOW-ATRIB[1],"HEATING TIME";
        ACTIVITY;
    FREE,{{PIT, }};
        ACTIVITY;
    TERM;
    END;
```

Figure 13-6 Input statements for furnace example.

Note that the waiting time statistics are collected only for the 210 ingots that waited. The determination of whether to include the zero waiting time of the ingots that went directly into the furnace is a modeling question that must be decided by the analyst. If waiting times with and without zero values are desired, then two calls to function COLCT can be incorporated into the program.

From both the activity and resource statistics sections of the summary report, it is seen that the average number of pits in use was 9.74. At the end of the simulation, all ten pits were being utilized. These results show that the system is overloaded and that new procedures or additional resources are required. From the file statistics output, the average number of ingots in the storage bank is 6.63 and the maximum number is 19. Thus, a storage area for at least 19 ingots is required. The state and derivative variables portray the final conditions of the simulation. At 500 hours, the furnace temperature was 2308°F and increasing at 58°F/hour. The corresponding value for each ingot in a pit is shown in the summary report. A histogram of the temperatures of the ingots removed from the pit is shown in Figure 13-8. The histogram reveals that 90 percent of the ingot temperatures were greater than 2100°F. This clustering is due to the stopping decision that requires at least one ingot to have a temperature of 2200° before any ingot can be removed from the furnace. Thirty eight percent of the ingots reached the 2200°F limit.

```
                ** AweSim SUMMARY REPORT **

  Simulation Project : INGOT PROBLEM
  Modeler : PRITSKER
  Date : 1/1/1996
  Scenario : EX131

  Run number 1 of 1
  Current simulation time    : 500.000000
  Statistics cleared at time : 0.000000

             ** OBSERVED STATISTICS REPORT for scenario EX131 **

  Label            Mean        Standard    Number of     Minimum      Maximum
                   Value       Deviation   Observations  Value        Value

  HEATING TEMP     2176.563    53.928         238         2000.801     2249.725
  WAITING TIME     15.657       9.828         210            0.100       36.755
  HEATING TIME     19.962       2.923         238           10.291       29.490

             ** TIME-PERSISTENT STATISTICS REPORT for scenario EX131 **

  Label            Mean        Standard    Minimum     Maximum     Time       Current
                   Value       Deviation   Value       Value       Interval   Value

  FURNACE TEMP.    2111.519    280.965     649.054     2498.183    500.000    2308.748

             ** FILE STATISTICS REPORT for scenario EX131 **

  File    Label or        Average    Standard    Maximum   Current   Average
  Number  Input Location  Length     Deviation   Length    Length    Wait Time

  1       RES. PIT        6.630      5.176         19        3        13.530

             ** ACTIVITY STATISTICS REPORT for scenario EX131 **

  Activity Label or       Average     Standard   Entity   Maximum      Current
  Number  Input Location  Utilization Deviation  Count    Utilization  Utilization

  1       SOAKING ACTI    9.736       0.879       238       10          10

             ** RESOURCE STATISTICS REPORT for scenario EX131 **

  Resource Resource  Average     Standard   Current      Maximum      Current
  Number  Label      Utilization Deviation  Utilization  Utilization  Capacity

  1       PIT        9.736       0.879      10           10           10

  Resource Average   Current    Minimum   Maximum
  Number  Available  Available  Available Available

  1       0.264      0          0         6

             ** STATE VARIABLE REPORT **

  Variable    SS[]            DD[]
  Index       Current Value   Current Value

  0           0.000           0.000
  1           1442.032        130.595
  2           1390.585        127.704
  3           1416.533        129.224
  4           2012.445         40.808
  5           1384.840        127.351
  6           2023.247         40.634
  7           2008.950         40.868
  8           2029.372         40.544
  9           1414.456        129.107
  10          1452.730        131.134
  11          2308.748         58.250
  12          2029.372
```

Figure 13-7 Visual SLAM summary report for furnace example.

```
** OBSERVED STATISTICS HISTOGRAM REPORT **

  Observed Histogram Number 1
  Label: HEATING TEMP
  Number of Observations: 238

Observed    Relative     Cumulative    Upper Cell
Frequency   Frequency    Frequency     Limit

       0    0.000        0.000         2000.000
      10    0.042        0.042         2020.000
       6    0.025        0.067         2040.000
       1    0.004        0.071         2060.000
       3    0.013        0.084         2080.000
       2    0.008        0.092         2100.000
       2    0.008        0.101         2120.000
       6    0.025        0.126         2140.000
      21    0.088        0.214         2160.000
      42    0.176        0.391         2180.000
      55    0.231        0.622         2200.000
      61    0.256        0.878         2220.000
      21    0.088        0.966         2240.000
       8    0.034        1.000         2260.000
       0    0.000        1.000         2280.000
       0    0.000        1.000         2300.000
       0    0.000        1.000         2320.000
       0    0.000        1.000         2340.000
       0    0.000        1.000         2360.000
       0    0.000        1.000         2380.000
       0    0.000        1.000         2400.000
       0    0.000        1.000         INFINITY
```

Figure 13-8   Histogram of ingot temperatures.

13.6   EXAMPLE 13-2. A CONTINUOUS FLOW CONVEYOR

A sparkplug packing line modeled by Henriksen(5) consists of a conveyor belt which transports sparkplugs at the rate of 999 per minute over a conveyor belt that feeds five machines. Each machine can process 333 plugs per minute. The flow from the conveyor to the machines is automatic. The time to transport a plug between two adjacent machines is 9 seconds. If a plug is not packed by one of the five machines, it flows into a barrel for future packing. Each packing machine has stoppages due to jams. The jamming of a machine occurs after it has packed between 200 and 600 sparkplugs. The time to repair a jammed machine is uniformly distributed between 6 and 24 seconds. The initial conditions for the system are that all machines are idle. It takes 18 seconds to build up to a rate of

999 sparkplugs per minute or 16.65 plugs per second before the first machine. The processing of plugs by the first machine starts at this time. It is desired to evaluate the system design by estimating the utilization of the machines and the number of sparkplugs that flow into the barrel.

Concepts Illustrated. State variables are used to model the amount of production since the last jam for each packing machine. A state variable maintains the number of sparkplugs that fall into the barrel at the end of the conveyor belt. DETECT nodes are used to monitor the number of sparkplugs packed by each machine and to detect when the machine jams. Events contain the logic for stopping a machine, starting a machine, and changing the flow of sparkplugs on the conveyor belt at points along the conveyor belt.

Visual SLAM Model. When building a combined model, it is normally easier to begin the modeling process with a definition and development of the continuous variables and equations (7). The Visual SLAM model defines SS[M] as the number of plugs packed since the last unjamming of machine M and SS[11] as the number of plugs falling into the barrel. A DETECT node is used to determine when the number of plugs packed by a machine exceeds a threshold value which is maintained in SS[5+M] for machine M. For this state event, an entity is inserted into the network and routed to an EVENT node to stop the packing of plugs by the machine. One DETECT node is employed for each machine. The discrete event portion of the model involves three events. A stop machine event called STOPM sets a status variable LL[5+M] to indicate that machine M is in a jammed state and not packing plugs. The flow of plugs to the machine is then diverted and scheduled to arrive at the next machine after a 9 second transport time on the conveyor. A start machine event, START, is scheduled to occur at the failure time plus the time to unjam the machine. The START event changes the status variables for the machine and, if there is a flow of parts to the machine, schedules a decrease in the flow of parts along the conveyor. A third event models the flow changes on the conveyor to a point in front of each machine. Detailed logic is included in this routine to specify if the flow change causes the machine to go to an idle status; to a packing status; or that a flow change should be made to a downstream point on the conveyor. The events of the model are listed below.

Event Code	Equivalence Name	Definition
1	STARTMACH	Start machine because it is unjammed.
2	STOPMACH	Stop machine because of jam.
3	FLOWCHANGE	Change of rate of flow of sparkplugs on the conveyor.

The variables of the model are listed below.

Variable	Definition
NUMMACH	Number of Machines = 5.
LL[M]	Status of Machine M: 0→NOTWORKING; 1→WORKING.
LL[M+NUMMACH]	Jam Status of Machine M: 1→JAMMED; 0→NOT JAMMED.
SS[M]	Number of sparkplugs packed since last jam of Machine M.
SSBARREL	An index, NUMMACH *2+1
SS [SSBARREL]	Number of sparkplugs in barrel.
XX[1]	Production flow rate into barrel.
SS[M+NUMMACH]	Number of sparkplugs that define the threshold for the jamming event for machine M.
MFlowRate[M]	Flow rate on conveyor before Machine M.
LTRIB[1]	Machine number.
ATRIB[1]	Change in flow rate.
FLOWRATE	Flow rate on conveyor, 5.55 plugs/sec.

Figure 13-9 gives the code for subroutine STATE. For each machine, the number of plugs packed is prescribed by the following difference equation

$$SS[M] = SSL[M] + DTNOW*LL[M]*FLOWRATE$$

where LL[M] is the status of machine M and FLOWRATE is the plug flow rate.

```
Public Sub STATE()
   Dim iMach As Integer

   For iMach = 1 To NUMMACH
      VS.SS(iMach)=VS.SSL(iMach)+VS.DTNOW*VS.LL(iMach)*FlowRate
   Next iMach
VS.SS(SSBARREL) = VS.SSL(SSBARREL) + VS.DTNOW * VS.XX(1)
End Sub
```

Figure 13-9VB Subroutine STATE for flow conveyor model in Visual Basic.

```
void SWFUNC STATE(void) {
   int iMach;
   for (iMach=1; iMach <= NUMMACH; iMach++) {
     SS[iMach] = SSL[iMach] + DTNOW*LL[iMach]*FLOWRATE;
   }
   SS[SSBARREL] = SSL[SSBARREL] + DTNOW * XX[1];
   return;
}
```

Figure 13-9C Function STATE for flow conveyor model in C.

The production into the barrel is also defined as a difference equation with the rate given by XX[1]. Figure 13-10 presents Function INTLC where the initial values and conditions for the simulation are established. Subroutine EVENT is shown in Figure 13-11.

```
Public Function INTLC(Run As Long) As Long
    Dim eNew As VSENTITY
    Dim iMach As Integer
    Dim i As Integer
    ' machines start idle
    For iMach = 1 To NUMMACH
        VS.SS(iMach) = 0#
        VS.SS(iMach + NUMMACH) = VS.UNFRM(VS.XX(2), VS.XX(3), 2)
        VS.LL(iMach) = 0
        VS.LL(iMach + NUMMACH) = 0
        MFlowRate(iMach) = 0#
    Next iMach
    ' schedule 3 flow increases
    For i = 1 To 3
        Set eNew = VS.DefineEntity(0)
        eNew.LTRIB(1) = 1 ' start at first machine
        eNew.ATRIB(1) = FlowRate
        VS.SCHDL FLOWCHANGE, eNew, 18#
    Next i
    INTLC = True
End Function
```

Figure 13-10VB   Function INTLC for flow conveyor model in Visual Basic.

```
BOOL SWFUNC INTLC(UINT uiRun)  {
    BOOL bContinue = TRUE;
    ENTITY * peNew;
    int iMach;
    int i;

    /* machines start idle */
    for (iMach=1; iMach <= NUMMACH; iMach++)         {
        SS[iMach]       = 0.0;
        SS[iMach+NUMMACH]      = UNFRM(XX[2],XX[3],2);
        LL[iMach]        = FALSE;
        LL[iMach+NUMMACH]          = FALSE;
        MFlowRate[iMach-1] = 0.0;
    }

    /* schedule 3 flow increases */
    for (i=0; i < 3; i++)          {
        peNew = su_entnew(0,NULL,NULL,NULL);
        if (peNew)        {
            peNew->LTRIB[1] = 1; /* start at first machine */
            peNew->ATRIB[1] = FLOWRATE;
            SCHDL(FLOWCHANGE,peNew,18.0);
        }
    }
return(bContinue);
}
```

Figure 13-10C   Function INTLC for flow conveyor model in C.

```
Public Sub EVENT(Code As Long, Current As VSENTITY)
Select Case Code
Case STARTMACH ' unjam a machine
   Call STRTMACH(Current)
Case STOPMACH ' stop a machine due to jamming (detect node)
   Call STPMACH(Current)
Case FLOWCHANGE
   Call FLWCHANGE(Current)
Case Else
   VS.Error 2, "Unknown event code"
End Select
End Sub
```

Figure 13-11VB EVENT routine in Visual Basic for flow conveyor model.

```
void SWFUNC EVENT(int iCode, ENTITY * Current)
{
   switch (iCode)
   {
      case STARTMACH: /* unjam a machine */
         STRTMACH(Current);
         break;
      case STOPMACH:
         STPMACH(Current);
         break;
      case FLOWCHANGE:
         FLWCHANGE(Current);
         break;
   }
}
```

Figure 13-11C EVENT routine in C for flow conveyor model.

Figure 13-12 presents the code for the first event case, STARTMACH. The variable iMach is the machine number which is obtained from LTRIB[1] of the entity Current passed to the EVENT routine. Machine status is then set to not jammed, that is, LL[iMach+NUMMACH]=0. A test is then made to determine if plugs are flowing to the machine and, if not, the packing status of the machine is not changed. If plugs are flowing to the machine, the status of the machine is set to packing by setting LL[iMach] = 1. This change causes fewer plugs to be routed on the conveyor and a flow change to the next machine is scheduled to occur in 9 seconds by calling SCHDL with an event code of 3.

```
Public Sub STRTMACH(Current As VSENTITY)
Dim iMach As Integer

iMach = Current.LTRIB(1)
VS.LL(iMach + NUMMACH) = 0
If MFlowRate(iMach) >= (FlowRate - 0.001) Then
    VS.LL(iMach) = 1
    ' reduce downstream flow rate
    Current.LTRIB(1) = Current.LTRIB(1) + 1
    Current.ATRIB(1) = 0# - FlowRate
    VS.SCHDL FLOWCHANGE, Current, 9#
Else
    Current.Terminate ' done with this entity
End If
End Sub
```

Figure 13-12VB Event routine written in Visual Basic for restarting a machine.

```
void STRTMACH(ENTITY * peCurrent)
{
    int iMach;
    iMach = peCurrent->LTRIB[1];
    JAMMED(iMach) = FALSE;
    if (ad_FlowRate[iMach-1] >= FLOWRATE-.001)  {
            MACHON(iMach) = TRUE;
     /* reduce downstream flow rate */
            peCurrent->LTRIB[1]++;
            peCurrent->ATRIB[1] = 0.0 - FLOWRATE;
            SCHDL(FLOWCHANGE,peCurrent,9.0);
        } else
            /* done with this entity          */
            su_entterminate(peCurrent);
}
```

Figure 13-12C Event routine written in C for restarting a machine.

The coding for the stop machine event, STOPMACH, is given in Figure 13-13. This logic is invoked when a DETECT node determines that the number of parts produced exceeds the jam number defining the threshold. Machine status is set to idle and to jammed. The number of plugs packed since the last jamming is reset to 0 by setting SS[iMach] to 0. A potential start for the machine is scheduled through a call to SCHDL with event code 1 to occur in a uniformly distributed time between 6 and 24. When a machine is stopped, a flow change to the next machine is scheduled by a call to SCHDL with an event code of 3 to indicate a flow change is required.

```
Public Sub STPMACH(Current As VSENTITY)
Dim iMach As Integer
Dim eNew As VSENTITY

iMach = Current.LTRIB(1)
VS.LL(iMach + NUMMACH) = 1
VS.LL(iMach) = 0
VS.SS(iMach) = 0#

' schedule repair
Set eNew = Current.Clone(0)
VS.SCHDL STARTMACH, eNew, VS.UNFRM(6#, 24#, 1)

If MFlowRate(iMach) >= (FlowRate - 0.001) Then
    ' reduce downstream flow rate
    Set eNew = Current.Clone(0)
    eNew.LTRIB(1) = eNew.LTRIB(1) + 1
    eNew.ATRIB(1) = FlowRate
    VS.SCHDL FLOWCHANGE, eNew, 9#
End If
End Sub
```

Figure 13-13VB Event routine written in Visual Basic for stopping a machine.

```
void STPMACH (ENTITY*Current)
{ /* stop a machine due to jamming (detect node) */
   ENTITY * peNew;
   int iMach;

   iMach = Current->LTRIB[1];
   JAMMED(iMach)   = TRUE;
   MACHON(iMach)   = FALSE;
   MACHPACK(iMach) = 0.0;
        /* schedule repair */
   peNew = su_entclone(Current,0);
   if (peNew)
       SCHDL(STARTMACH,peNew,UNFRM(6.,24.,1));
   if (ad_FlowRate[iMach-1] >= FLOWRATE-.001)    {
       /* reduce downstream flow rate */
       peNew = su_entclone(Current,0);
       peNew->LTRIB[1]++;
       peNew->ATRIB[1] = FLOWRATE;
       SCHDL(FLOWCHANGE,peNew,9.0);
     }
}
```

Figure 13-13C Event routine in C for stopping a machine due to jamming.

Figure 13-14 presents a flowchart of the flow change event, FLOWCHANGE. The local variables iMach and dChange are established as the machine number and the amount of change for which the flow change event is occurring. If iMach is greater than NUMMACH, no further machines are on the conveyor and XX[1], the rate into the barrel, is updated by the value of dChange. Otherwise, the flow change is made on the conveyor before machine iMach. If machine iMach is jammed, the flow change is passed on down the conveyor to the next machine. If the flow change is positive and machine iMach is working, or if the flow change is negative but there is still flow to machine iMach, the flow change is passed on to the next machine. If the flow change is positive and the machine is not working, then the flow change allows machine iMach to start working. If the flow change is negative and there is no flow to the machine, the flow change is also passed on to the next machine. This is necessary because the flow before a machine could be 0 but positive changes down the conveyor could have been scheduled from earlier flow changes. To further clarify this point, it is possible for all five machines to be working concurrently even though the flow rate on the conveyor can support a maximum of three machines working. This occurs, for example, when machines 1 and 2 are jammed and are then repaired in a short period of time so that machines 4 and 5 begin processing using the overflow during the times that machines 1 and 2 were jammed and are packing when machines 1 and 2 come back on line.

The coding for the FLWCHANGE routine is shown in Figure 13-15. This code follows the logic presented in the flowchart for a FLOWCHANGE event. The network input statements and control statements for this model are shown in Figure 13-16. Network statements are used to monitor and detect when the number of plugs packed at a machine exceeds a value specifying the jamming threshold. Disjoint networks for each machine are included. For machine 1, a DETECT node is used to detect SS[1] crossing SS[7] in the positive direction. SS[7] is a sample from a uniform distribution in the range XX[2] to XX[3]. An INTLC statement is used to set XX[2] to 200 and XX[3] to 600. When the detection of this state event occurs, an entity is sent to an ASSIGN node which identifies machine 1 as being jammed by setting LTRIB[1]=1. The next threshold value, SS[7], is then set and a transfer to the EVENT node with event code 2 is made. In event 2, machine 1 is stopped and SS[1] is reset to 0 since no plugs have been packed since the last jamming. Also, in event 2 the status of machine 1 is changed to idle by setting LL[1] to 0. This causes the rate of plugs packed by machine 1 to become 0 in the equation for SS[1] which is included in subroutine STATE.

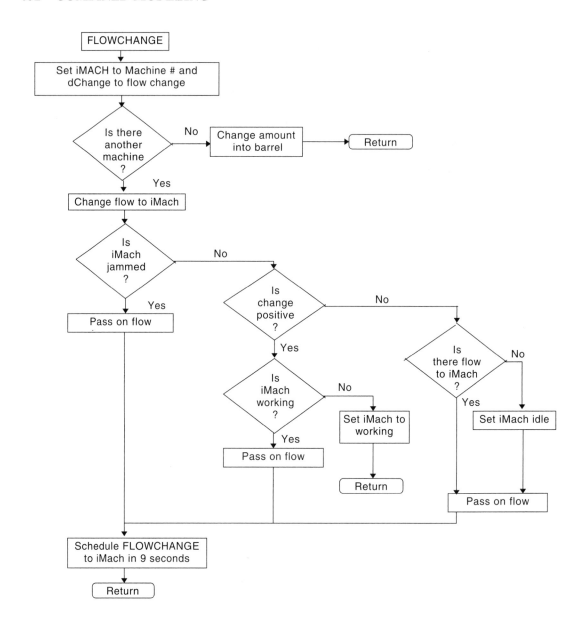

Figure 13-14 Flowchart of FLOWCHANGE logic.

```
Public Sub FLWCHANGE(Current As VSENTITY)
Dim iMach As Integer
Dim dChange As Double

iMach = Current.LTRIB(1)
dChange = Current.ATRIB(1)

' see if this is machine flow or barrel flow
If iMach <= NUMMACH Then
   ' machine flow change
   MFlowRate(iMach) = MFlowRate(iMach) + dChange
   If MFlowRate(iMach) < 0# Then
       MFlowRate(iMach) = 0#
   End If

   If Not VS.LL(iMach + NUMMACH) = 1 And Not _
       VS.LL(iMach) = 1 And dChange > 0# Then
   ' machine starting up again
       VS.LL(iMach) = 1
       Current.Terminate ' done with this entity
   Else
     If Not VS.LL(iMach + NUMMACH) = 1 And dChange <= 0# And _
         MFlowRate(iMach) < 0.001 Then
         ' flow is stopping
         VS.LL(iMach) = 0
     End If
     ' schedule downstream flow change
     Current.LTRIB(1) = Current.LTRIB(1) + 1
     VS.SCHDL FLOWCHANGE, Current, 9#
   End If
Else  ' barrel flow change
   VS.XX(1) = VS.XX(1) + dChange
   If VS.XX(1) < 0# Then
       VS.XX(1) = 0#
   End If
   Current.Terminate ' done with this entity
End If
End Sub
```

Figure 13-15VB Flow change logic written in Visual Basic.

```
void FLWCHANGE(ENTITY*peCurrent)
{   double dChange;
    int iMach;

    iMach = peCurrent->LTRIB[1];
    dChange = peCurrent->ATRIB[1];
  /* see if this is machine flow or barrel flow */
    if (iMach <= NUMMACH)                           {
        /* machine flow change */
        ad_FlowRate[iMach-1] += dChange;
        if (ad_FlowRate[iMach-1] < 0.0)
            ad_FlowRate[iMach-1] = 0.0;
        if (!JAMMED(iMach) && !MACHON(iMach) && dChange > 0.0)
{
        /* machine starting up again */
          MACHON(iMach) = TRUE;
          su_entterminate(peCurrent); /* done with this entity
*/
        } else
{
            if (!JAMMED(iMach) && dChange <= 0.0 &&
                    ad_FlowRate[iMach-1] < 0.001)
              /* flow is stopping */
              MACHON(iMach) = FALSE;
          /* schedule downstream flow change */
          peCurrent->LTRIB[1]++;
          SCHDL(FLOWCHANGE,peCurrent,9.0);
          }
      } else /* barrel flow change */
{
        RATEBARREL += dChange;
        if (RATEBARREL < 0.0)
              RATEBARREL = 0.0;
        su_entterminate(peCurrent); /* done with this entity
*/
      }
  }
```

Figure 13-15C Flow change logic written in C.

The control statements for this model show that there are 3 XX variables and 10 LL variables used and that there are 2 attributes per entity (one real and one integer). Statistics are collected on the utilization of the machines as specified on the TIMST statements. The average rate of plugs into the barrel is also obtained in this fashion. A plot of the number of plugs packed since the last jamming and the number of plugs going into the barrel is obtained through specifications on RECORD statement. The INIT statement sets the run length at 6000 seconds. The

CONTINUOUS statement indicates that there are no differential equations, 11 state variables, and that the minimum step size is to be one tenth of a second. This model of the conveyor system illustrates the use of network, discrete event and continuous modeling viewpoints.

```
;   Control Statement Listing for Flow Conveyor Model
    GEN,"PRITSKER","CONT_CONV_FAIL",1/1/1996,1;
    LIMITS,3,10,-1,1,1,-1;
    TIMST,1,XX[1],"RATE IN BARREL";
    TIMST,2,LL[1],"MTIME FOR 1";
    TIMST,3,LL[2],"MTIME FOR 2";
    TIMST,4,LL[3],"MTIME FOR 3";
    TIMST,5,LL[4],"MTIME FOR 4";
    TIMST,6,LL[5],"MTIME FOR 5";
    RECORD,,,TNOW,"TIME",{EXCEL},,2500,3000,10,
        {{SS[1],"S1",  },{SS[2],"S2",  },{SS[3],"S3",  },
        {SS[4],"S4",  },{SS[5],"S5",  },{SS[11],"BARREL",}};
    INTLC,{{XX[2],200},{XX[3],600}};
    NETWORK;
    INITIALIZE,0,6000,YES;
    CONTINUOUS,-1,11,.1;
    FIN;

;   Network Statement Listing for Flow Conveyor Model
    DETECT,SS[1],POSITIVE,SS[6],1;
    ACTIVITY;
    ASSIGN,{{LTRIB[1],1},{SS[6],UNFRM(XX[2],XX[3],2)}};
    ACT, , , ,"EVNT";
EVNT: EVENT,2;
    ACTIVITY;
    TERM;
    DETECT,SS[2],POSITIVE,SS[7],1;
    ACTIVITY;
    ASSIGN,{{LTRIB[1],2},{SS[7],UNFRM(XX[2],XX[3],2)}};
    ACT, , , ,"EVNT";
    DETECT,SS[3],POSITIVE,SS[8],1;
    ACTIVITY;
    ASSIGN,{{LTRIB[1],3},{SS[8],UNFRM(XX[2],XX[3],2)}};
    ACT, , , ,"EVNT";
    DETECT,SS[4],POSITIVE,SS[9],1;
    ACTIVITY;
    ASSIGN,{{LTRIB[1],4},{SS[9],UNFRM(XX[2],XX[3],2)}};
    ACT, , , ,"EVNT";
    DETECT,SS[5],POSITIVE,SS[10],1;
    ACTIVITY;
    ASSIGN,{{LTRIB[1],5},{SS[10],UNFRM(XX[2],XX[3],2)}};
    ACTIVITY, , , ,"EVNT";
    END;
```

Figure 13-16 Control and network statements for flow conveyor model.

Summary of Results. In Figure 13-17, the flow of sparkplugs through the packing machines and into the barrel is shown for the time period between 2500 and 2800 seconds. The solid line without tick marks represents the processing of sparkplugs on Machine 1. At time 2500, Machine 1 has produced approximately 310 spark plugs during its current cycle. At time 2510, Machine 1 becomes jammed and its next cycle begins at time 2520 after it is unjammed. The number of sparkplugs packed until Machine 1 will jam again is approximately 400 which occurs at time 2600. The peak of each curve represents the number of sparkplugs that are packed before a jam occurs. This value is a sample from uniform distribution between 200 and 600 spark plugs. During the 300 seconds for which the graph is displayed, there were no periods of time at which sparkplugs were not available to Machine 1. A similar pattern for the packing of sparkplugs through Machines 2 and 3 is observed with different levels at which the machines become jammed. For Machine 4, it is seen there are periods where the curve is flat indicating that there were no inputs being delivered to Machine 4 from the conveyor belt. This is even more dramatic for Machine 5 where from time 2560 to time 2660, Machine 5 is not packing due to lack of input. The flow into the barrel is shown by the line with small squares on it. It is seen that from time 2500 to approximately 2670, no sparkplugs   flowed   into   the   barrel.   Throughout   the   300

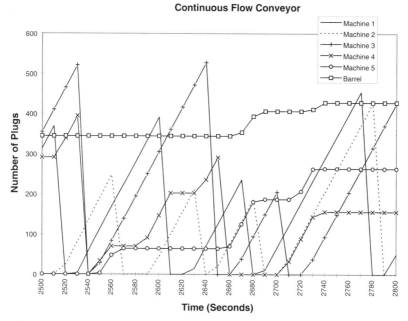

Figure 13-17   Plot of state variables for continuous flow conveyor model.

second interval, only 75 sparkplugs were not processed by the 5 machines. Figure 13-17 provides graphical information to understand the operation of the continuous flow conveyor.

The Visual SLAM summary report for this example is shown in Figure 13-18. The time-persistent statistics provide the machine busy time and the rate of sparkplugs into the barrel. The rate of plugs into the barrel is about one plug every 8.5 seconds. This value is obtained from the reciprocal of the estimate of the mean rate into the barrel. The plug rate into the barrel can also be obtained by dividing the ending value of SS[11] by the time period for the simulation, that is, 702 by 6000 seconds. This small rate into the barrel results from having sufficient machines available to pack plugs. The utilization time for machine 5 is a low 11.4 percent. The utilization for machine 4 is also low, less than 40 percent, which indicates that a design change should be considered.

If we remove machine 5, the average rate of plugs into the barrel will increase by the product of its packing rate and its utilization. Removal of machine 5 does not change the utilization of the other machines. The removal of machine 4 will change the utilization of machine 5. To some extent, the operation of the sparkplug line employs the conveyor as a buffer area for the machines. By removing machine 4, the buffer area on the conveyor for machine 5 can contain up to 18 seconds supply of plugs for processing by machine 5. This will increase the utilization of machine 5 but will also increase the rate of flow into the barrel.

The utilization of machines 1, 2 and 3 are all over 80 percent. Intuitively, the utilization of these machines should be statistically the same as the input rate to the machines after the initial warmup period is 5.55 plugs per second. The variation in utilization values is due to different settings of plug thresholds and the random generation of machine unjamming times. An expected value analysis of the machine utilization time shows that machine utilization should be approximately 83 percent. This value is arrived at by dividing the expecting jamming threshold, 400 plugs, by the plug packing rate of 5.55. This yields an expected time until jamming of approximately 72 seconds. The expected time to unjam a machine is 15 seconds which results in a working plus idle cycle for a machine of 87 seconds. Since the input flow on the conveyor is always available to machines 1, 2 and 3, the utilization of these machines should be approximately 72 divided by 87 or 82.8 percent. The values presented in Figure 13-18 are not significantly different from this value.

```
            ** AweSim SUMMARY REPORT **

    Simulation Project : CONT_CONV_FAIL
    Modeler : PRITSKER
    Date : 1/1/1996
    Scenario : EX142

    Run number 1 of 1
    Current simulation time   : 6000.000000
    Statistics cleared at time : 0.000000

        ** TIME-PERSISTENT STATISTICS REPORT for scenario EX142 **

Label            Mean     Standard   Minimum    Maximum    Time       Current
                 Value    Deviation  Value      Value      Interval   Value

RATE IN BARREL   0.117    0.799      0.000      11.100     6000.000   0.000
MTIME FOR 1      0.822    0.382      0.000      1.000      6000.000   0.000
MTIME FOR 2      0.806    0.395      0.000      1.000      6000.000   1.000
MTIME FOR 3      0.827    0.379      0.000      1.000      6000.000   1.000
MTIME FOR 4      0.394    0.489      0.000      1.000      6000.000   0.000
MTIME FOR 5      0.114    0.318      0.000      1.000      6000.000   0.000

        ** STATE VARIABLE REPORT **

Variable     SS[]            DD[]
Index        Current Value   Current Value

   0             0.0
   1             0.0
   2           265.9
   3           365.6
   4           180.8
   5           226.3
   6           543.8
   7           569.3
   8           405.6
   9           452.6
  10           459.6
  11           701.6
```

Figure 13-18 Summary report for continuous flow conveyor model.

13.7   CHAPTER SUMMARY

This chapter summarizes the modeling approaches of Visual SLAM and demonstrates how Visual SLAM supports alternative world views. Two examples of combined modeling are presented. The first example involves the heating of ingots in a soaking pit furnace, and the second example describes the modeling of a flow conveyor system using continuous variables.

13.8   EXERCISES

13-1.   A drag of ingots arrives at the soaking pit on the average every 1.75 hours. The distribution of times between arrivals is exponential. A drag consists of ten ingots. All ten ingots in the drag have the same temperature which is lognormally distributed between 300°F and 600°F with a mean of 400°F and standard deviation of 50°F. Upon arrival, the ingots may be charged directly into an available pit or they may be placed in a waiting-to-be-charged queue. The temperature of the arriving ingots decreases with the square root of the time they must wait, that is, temperature = old temperature-SQRT(waiting time) * 157°. When an ingot reaches a temperature of 150°F, it is assumed cold. Charging practice dictates that cold ingots may not be charged into any pit at a temperature of greater than 750° since this causes surface cracks and, hence, poor quality. Hot ingots (over 150°F) may be charged into any temperature pit. It is assumed that the pit temperature after charging is equal to a weighted average of the pit and ingot temperatures (new pit temperature = 0.7* old pit temperature + 0.3* temperature of ingots in drag), and from then on varies according to the equation dT/dt=2600-T. When the pit temperature reaches 2200°F, the ingots are ready to soak and the pit temperature remains at this temperature for 2 hours. After the soak time, the ingots are removed and the pit is available to be reloaded. If nothing can be loaded, the pit temperature changes according to the equation dT/dt=600-T. There are four independent pits and each pit has a capacity of five ingots. (Note: Ingots can be processed in units of 5 which saves on computer storage and processing.)

The initial conditions for the simulation are:

1.   Pit temperatures are 1150°F, 800°F, 1500°F, and 1000 °F

2.   The pits whose temperatures are 1150°F and 800°F are loaded with 5 ingots. The other pits are not charging.

3.   The first drag is scheduled to arrive at time zero. Simulate the soaking pit system for 400 hours to obtain estimates of the following quantities: heating time for ingots; waiting time for ingots; the number of ingots waiting (total and by temperature class); and the number of loaded pits.

   Embellishments: Clear statistics at time 100 and obtain summary reports at times 200, 300 and 400 hours. Give priority to processing the cold ingots at times 200 and 300, that is, if cold ingots are waiting assign pit(s) to process the cold ingots. Evaluate the policy of making one of the pits a processor of cold ingots. Simulate the system if the sum of the temperatures of the pits is restricted to 7000°F due to energy considerations.

13-2.   Model and simulate a gas station attendant providing service to arriving customers. The time between arrivals of customers is exponentially distributed with a mean value of 4 minutes. The service station employs one attendant whose service rate is dependent on the number of customers waiting for his service. The relationship between service rate S and number in queue N is given below

```
S= 1.2exp(0.173N)                        N <   5
S= 1.2(0.25exp(-0.305(N-5)) +0.5)        N >=  5
```

The nominal amount of service time required by each customer is an exponentially distributed random variable with a mean of 3.5 minutes. The attendant works off this nominal service time at rate S. Analyze this queueing situation for 1000 minutes to obtain statistics on the following quantities: the time a customer spends in the queue, the time a customer spends at the gas station, the fraction of time the attendant is busy, and the number of customers waiting in the queue of the server. A plot is to be made that illustrates the status of the server, the number in the queue, and the remaining service time for a customer.

13-3.   For the continuous flow conveyor example, assume that the time until the next jam on a machine is uniformly distributed between 200/5.55 and 600/5.55 seconds. Discuss how this information could be used in modeling the sparkplug situation.

13-4   Build a model of the sparkplug packing line in which the sparkplugs arrive in trays every 20 seconds and each tray contains 333 sparkplugs. Arrivals are to the first machine with the first arrival scheduled to occur at 18 seconds. When a machine becomes jammed, the sparkplugs remaining in the tray are placed back on the conveyor and routed to the next machine. Perform a simulation of this situation for 6000 seconds and compare the results with those obtained in Example 13-2.

13-5.   Redesign the sparkplug packaging line presented in Example 13-2 to eliminate one of the machines. The machines may be placed in any location along the conveyor belt. The input rate of sparkplugs to the first packing machine changes every 1000 seconds and is a sample from the following probability mass function: (0.25,888); (0.5,999), and (0.25,1110).

13-6.   For the drive-in bank example with jockeying, Example 9-1, the system description is enlarged to include a limited waiting area for cars departing the bank into the street. Space for five cars exists between the tellers and the street. A bank customer will pull out into the street traffic if a gap of 0.4 time units is perceived in the street traffic until the next car arrives. However, as the customer waits, shorter gaps become acceptable. For wait times of .25, .50, .75, and 1.0 time units, the gap time that is acceptable is 0.4, 0.3, 0.2, and 0.1 time units. If a gap is not acceptable, the customer waits for an acceptable gap. The time between arrivals of cars on the street is exponentially distributed with a mean of 0.3 time units. The departure point from the bank is located within six car lengths of a traffic light. Thus, if six cars are waiting for the light to turn green, the bank exit is blocked. The traffic light has a red/green cycle that stays green for 0.65 time units and then red for 0.5 time units. Assume cars will only go through the light when the light is green. The time to pass through the light is 0.125 time units when a car is waiting for the light to turn green. Time to pass through the light decreases by 80 percent for each successive car waiting in the line. Develop a model that embellishes the bank teller system with jockeying to include the features described above. Consider the time in the system for the bank customer to be from the time of arrival to the bank until the customer passes through the street traffic light. Determine the number of times a customer's anxiety level results in an acceptance of a gap that is less than 0.25 time units.

13-7.   A flexible manufacturing system performs machining operations on castings. The FMS consists of ten horizontal milling machines which can perform any of three operations. Castings arrive to the FMS every 22 minutes. For each casting it is necessary to perform operations 10, 20, and 30 and the processing time for these operations are 120, 40, and 56 minutes respectively. The ten milling machines can be dedicated to the performing of one or more operations. A flexible milling machine can do all three operations. One cart is available to move the castings to the milling machines and the central inspection station. The time for the cart to move from the inspection station to station 1 is 0.3 minutes. This is also the time for the cart to move from machine 10 to the inspection station. Movement from mill 5 to mill 6 is around a bend and this takes 0.6 minutes. Movement between all other stations takes 0.2 minutes. The cart always travels from the inspection station to station I and then back around to the inspection station. After each operation, the casting is inspected and the inspection time is 10 minutes. There are two inspectors available to inspect the castings. Castings arrive to the inspection station and are immediately assigned a destination upon arrival. Develop a model of this system to determine the throughput of castings for two 40 hour shifts.

13.9   REFERENCES

1.   Ashour, S. and S. G. Bindingnavle, "An Optimal Design of a Soaking Pit Rolling Mill System," *Simulation*, Vol. 18,1972, pp. 207-213.

2.   Cellier, F. E. and A. A. B. Pritsker, "Teaching Continuous Simulation Using GASP", *Simulation*, Vol. 34, 1980, pp. 137-139.

3.   Cellier, F. E., *Continuous Systems Modeling*, Springer-Verlag, 1991.

4.   Duket, S. D. and C. R. Standridge, "Applications of Simulation: Combined Models", *Modeling*, Issue No. 19, December 1983, pp. 20 29.

5.   Henriksen, J. O., "GPSS - Finding the Appropriate World-View*," Proceedings, 1981 Winter Simulation Conference*, 1981, pp. 505-516.

6.   Pritsker, A. A. B., *Introduction to Simulation and SLAM II*, Fourth Edition, Systems Publishing and John Wiley, 1995.

7.   Pritsker, A. A. B., Modeling for Simulation Analysis, *Handbook of Simulation*, J. Banks, Ed., John Wiley, 1997, to be published.

CHAPTER 14

AweSim Simulation Support System

14.1   INTRODUCTION

Throughout this book, a problem-solving approach based on modeling and simulation is presented. The fundamental assumption is that additional information is generated through the building and exercising of a model that explains or characterizes the operation of a system. Simulation languages such as Visual SLAM provide both a world view for building such models and a computer program for exercising and analyzing them. However, as described in Chapter 3, these modeling and analysis tasks are only two phases of a problem-solving project.

To support a total simulation project, additional tools and techniques are required. A simulation project involves data management, model management, scenario generation, verification, validation, output analysis, documentation and the presentation of results and recommendations. To support these project functions, database tools and graphics capabilities are required. In this chapter, we present the issues relating to the need for a simulation support system and an overview of AweSim. AweSim provides an integrated problem solving environment on personal and desktop computers using a Windows interface (2).

14.2 WHOM WOULD A SIMULATION SUPPORT SYSTEM SUPPORT?

A major problem in designing a simulation support system is identifying the characteristics of its users. There are many individuals involved in the design, development, and use of a simulation model. Five overlapping groups requiring support are: the language installers; the language maintainers; the model builders; the model users; and the decision makers. For the type of simulation support system discussed in this chapter, only the model builders, model users, and decision makers are addressed. With respect to how individuals in these groups might use a decision support system, the following categorization was developed (9): the hands-off user; the requester; the hands-on user; and the renaissance decision maker.

The *hands-off* user reads the reports that are generated but is not in direct contact with the support system either through requests or knowledge of its underpinnings. The hands-off user employs an intermediary for modeling and simulation. He or she frames the questions, interprets the results, and uses the answers to make decisions. The *requester* is not concerned with how the answers are obtained but realizes that they provide additional information that is helpful in making decisions. The *hands-on* user views the support system as an extension of himself or herself and employs direct on-line access to the system using predetermined interfaces and models. The *renaissance* decision maker functions as part of a team, is comfortable talking in terms of database systems and modeling and is adept at making decisions. The renaissance decision maker knows how to set requirements for information, can prescribe the types of reports he or she wants and can ask questions concerning the details of a model. With the increased use of personal computers, a greater number of simulationists are hands-on users and renaissance decision makers.

14.3   SUPPORTING THE MODELING TASK

The modeling approach recommended in this book is an iterative one. A model is defined, developed, refined, updated, modified, and extended. One of the secrets to being a good modeler is the ability to re-model (6). A simulation support system must provide the environment to allow for this approach. To support re-modeling, models should be easily recalled and cataloged. The model building process should be interactive and graphical. Current models should be available as the basis for future models. A documentation trail regarding model development should be maintained. All this suggests that models be stored along with inputs and outputs in a form that provides referencing, copying and query capabilities.

14.4   SUPPORTING THE DATA MANAGEMENT TASKS

The data management activities associated with a simulation project involve the storage, retrieval and organization of system data, maintaining experimental control specifications, and preparing simulation generated outputs (9,13). The system data can be used directly in the model or to estimate model parameters. It is frequently used for comparison and for validation purposes. Data from a simulation run is generated in accordance with the control statements which specify the experimental scenario under which the run is made. It is desirable to have the experimental specifications accessible for use with different models. The simulation outputs should reference both the experimental specifications and the model from which it is generated. Both raw data and summary data are typically stored for future reference and use. Procedures are required to access, edit, concatenate and display data. This frequently occurs when it is desirable to use operational data as inputs to a financial model. It is also useful to be able to access the simulation outputs for presentation in spreadsheets or as inputs to other models.

The form of the simulation data should not differ from the form of the actual system data. Thus, any analysis performed on system data should be appropriate for model data and vice versa. A major difference is that the simulated data can be reproduced and, if the model is a stochastic one, additional simulated historical records can be obtained by exercising the model repeatedly.

14.5 SUPPORTING ANALYSIS AND REPORTING TASKS

Analysis of data involves the browsing, sorting, selection and computation of values. These are standard functions associated with file management. For a simulation project, data is typically related to time. Analysis of data outputs at a particular time for one or more runs is commonplace. Alternatively, data from within a single run are sometimes grouped into subintervals or batches in order to study the behavior during the subinterval. Subintervals of special interest are an initial time period and an ending time period. In the former case the system is starting from an atypical state, and it may be of interest to determine how long it takes to transition to a specified or a steady state. The time period just before the ending of a simulation run may also require special processing. In some projects, it is necessary to estimate the dry-up or close-down time for system operations. Procedures for interrogating the data obtained from a simulation run are needed to explore such situations within runs and over multiple runs.

Support should also be provided to transform automatically the outputs of the simulation runs into inputs for statistical analysis procedures such as regression analysis, analysis of variance (ANOVA), autoregressive time series programs, and curve fitting programs. The support system should provide the capability to output the data to other programs and be capable of working with different output devices.

14.6 SUPPORTING THE VISUALIZATION TASK USING ANIMATION

The visualization of the status of variables, resources and entities contained within a model has become increasingly important. At the simplest level, a plot of the value of a variable as a function of time provides a visualization of the equations or logic that govern the dynamic behavior of the variable. Other types of display include the positions and the status of resources and entities. Positions are displayed by refreshing screens and showing new locations. Status changes are indicated through color changes, numeric value changes or by displaying icons that indicate a particular type of status. When the above forms of vizualization are integrated in a dynamic display of the operational changes that occur during a simulation, an animation of the model is created. The animation can be displayed on a static background representing the system under study. In some cases the background is imported to the screen from CAD diagrams.

Trace data describing system operation includes data that portrays the state changes that occur over time. A dynamic characterization of the state changes can be presented visually as a form of animation in which icons move, change color, and are added or deleted from the picture. In this sense, an animation is a dynamic presentation of the changes in state of the system over time. To obtain an animation, it is necessary to diagram a facility which represents the system and the icons which represent the elements of the system. Such a facility diagram is an abstraction of the real system, hence it is a model of the system. It is a model that is built for the purpose of displaying a visualization of a system and fits the model category referred to in Chapters 1 and 15 as explanatory.

A simulation support system should provide the tools to convert either system data or simulation output data into a form which portrays the state changes on a facility diagram. Although this can be done as part of the simulation language, it tends to complicate the modeling process and is not a recommended approach to the visualization task. Any support task that complicates the modeling process should be avoided. Another approach is to use the facility diagram as the modeling language. Although intriguing, this approach requires that a limited scope of application be developed for the language, for example, manufacturing systems. A third approach is to use the constructs of the simulation language as the basis for the facility diagram (3,6). This approach requires that the viewer of the animation have some familiarity with the simulation language, for example, the network portion of Visual SLAM. An approach which eliminates these disadvantages involves the use of animation actions. The actions translate the changes occurring in status variables to displays on a facility diagram. By changing the actions, different animations can be obtained which present different features or aspects of a simulation run.

The visualization process can be run in either a concurrent or post simulation mode. The concurrent mode provides an excellent way to understand, debug and verify the running of the model. It also aids in modifying and enhancing the model. The post simulation model allows for faster simulations and assists in developing new operating policies and presenting results in visual form to managers and customers.

14.7   AWESIM OVERVIEW

AweSim is a program that supports the range of tasks required to perform a simulation project. AweSim also provides integrating capabilities to store, retrieve, browse and communicate with externally written software applications. The architecture of AweSim is shown in Figure 14-1. The most fundamental feature of the AweSim architecture is its openness and interconnectivity to databases, spreadsheets and word processing programs such as Microsoft Office. Each of the AweSim components is discussed in this chapter. Since AweSim is built in Visual Basic and C/C++, programs written in these languages are easily incorporated into its architecture. The use of standard programs built in C/C++ or Visual Basic are easily added as components of AweSim. In particular, it is common to create a tailored user interface to AweSim components using Visual Basic. The details on the capabilities of AweSim are contained in the *AweSim User's Guide* (2). In this chapter the capabilities that support problem solving using simulation are described through illustrations and examples. The open-ended architecture of AweSim is demonstrated. The possible uses and ways of using AweSim are unlimited. All features are accessible from the AweSim Executive Window through the pull-down menus and dialog boxes shown in Figure 14-2.

An AweSim project consists of one or more scenarios, each of which represents a particular system alternative. In Figure 14-2, the name of the scenario is EX51. A scenario is comprised of components. Software programs called builders are provided by AweSim to create each component. The procedures included in AweSim follow the guidelines for standard Windows and Visual Basic interfaces. It is assumed that these types of personal computer capabilities are familiar to the reader and specific details can be learned by using AweSim. In this chapter, an overview is provided of AweSim capabilities for supporting problem solving when Visual SLAM is the modeling language.

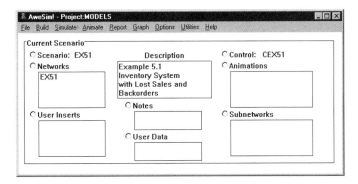

Figure 14-2 AweSim Executive Window

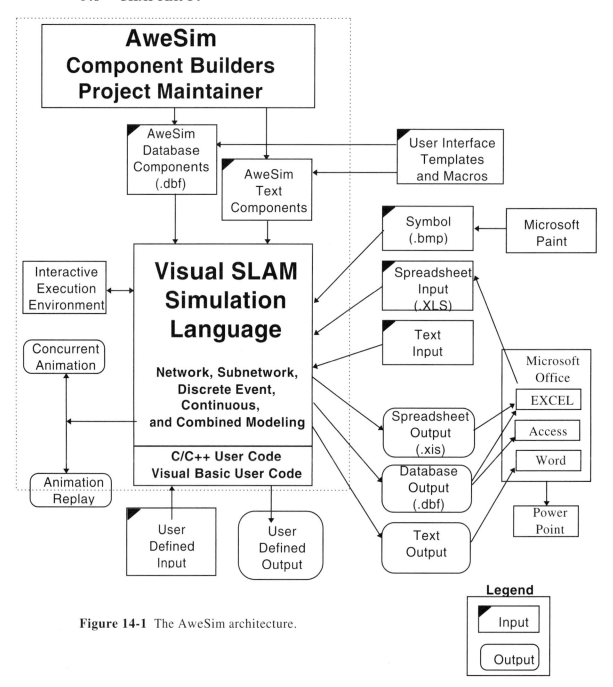

Figure 14-1 The AweSim architecture.

AweSim's Project Maintainer determines if a model translation or compilation is required. Each time the modeler requests a run, the Project Maintainer examines changes made to the current scenario to determine if any components have been modified and indicates whether translating tasks should be performed. The Project Maintainer then allows the user to specify whether these tasks should be done prior to performing the requested function. Multiple tasks may be performed in parallel while a simulation is executed in the background. The simulation modeler can switch between tasks by using a mouse to click in the appropriate window. The use of the MS Windows interface simplifies learning and provides the foundation for combining application programs using that interface.

14.7.1   AweSim Project Terminology

AweSim supports problem resolution within a project structure. The project consists of one or more scenarios with each scenario being an alternate way to improve the system being considered on the project. Each scenario consists of one or more networks, subnetworks, user data files, user inserts, animations, notes, a control and a description. The elements of a scenario are referred to as components. Components can be shared among scenarios of a project and may also be used in different projects. The maintenance and management of components is an important feature of AweSim.

The AweSim executive window as shown in Figure 14-2 contains an action bar with nine items: File, Build, Simulate, Animate, Report, Graph, Options, Utilities and Help. The File item has a pull-down list for accomplishing the following tasks: defining a new project; opening an existing project; saving the current components under the current project name; saving the current project under a new name, that is, Save As; exiting AweSim; and providing information about AweSim.

From the executive window, after a project is opened, the list of scenarios that have been developed for the project can be obtained by clicking on the radio button next to the word Scenario. For each scenario, there can be multiple networks, animations, user data and user inserts. To simulate a scenario, the components to be included in the running of this scenario are made current. Radio buttons on the executive window are used for this purpose. First, the list of possibilities for each component are displayed for the selected scenario. Basically, there are two categories for each component: current and available. An available component is one that has been built and which can be made current by selecting it and adding it to the list of current components. Once the component is current, it can be selected to be part of the scenario to be run. A current component can be removed from the current list by selecting the Remove button. Other options relating to the selection of a component are: develop a new component and open an existing component. To leave the selection process without making a selection, a Cancel button is made available. To make a selection, an OK button is used. The above description applies for the components: Network, Subnetwork, Animation and User Data. For the Control component, only one set of control statements can be employed when running a scenario. When clicking on the Control radio button, a list of controls available for the project is provided. Selection of the control to be used on the scenario is made by selecting the control and then clicking on the Set Current button. In addition to setting a control as current, a new control can be built or an existing control can be opened from the Control Selection screen. As is true throughout AweSim, a Cancel button is available to return to the previous screen or an OK button is used to confirm that a selection has been made.

For User Inserts, the procedure depends on whether C or Visual Basic is the language employed for writing the user inserts. If C is used, the procedure described above applies. In Visual Basic, selecting user inserts invokes the Visual Basic environment. The project icon of Visual Basic is then used to obtain a list of the user inserts written in Visual Basic. By selecting the user insert and clicking on the View Code button, the user insert code becomes current and displayed.

Returning to the Action bar, the selection of the Build item provides direct access to the AweSim builders for: networks; subnetworks; controls; user inserts; notes; animation; and user data. Basically, this is an alternative route to the selection process described above for the radio buttons on the AweSim executive window.

The Simulate element on the AweSim action bar provides a means to: run a simulation of the current scenario; translate components of the current scenario; compile the user code in user inserts specified for the current scenario; and to link user code. The Translate, Link and Compile items are made available in case it is only desired to perform these operations for specific components of the scenario. If it is desired to run a simulation then AweSim's Project Maintainer will automatically perform the tasks necessary to bring the scenario components up-to-date so that a simulation run can be made on the current components selected. When Run is selected, the required updates are listed with a check mark displayed for those elements that require updating. The Project Maintainer gives the user an option to perform the update or to bypass it.

The Animate item is used to run a postprocess animation from a capture file generated by a prior simulation run. The Project Maintainer performs a similar function for Animate as was described for Run listed under the Simulate item with the same alternatives provided.

The selection of Report from the action bar provides a means to display a selected network; subnetwork; control; user insert; note; animation; or user data for the current project. The last item on the drop-down menu list is to report outputs obtained from a run of Visual SLAM. The Outputs include the: Echo Check report; Intermediate Output reports; Summary report; Animation report; and Multi-Summary report.

The Graph item provides a means to obtain graphs from scenarios that have been run. The Options item selection displays the following list: AweSim; Graphs; Runs; Simulate; and Compile. The AweSim option relates to turning on the Project Maintainer and/or Sound associated with AweSim. The Graphs option allows project-wide selection of the type of graph to be displayed. For example, make all graphs three-dimensional, have an X- or Y-grid, display data points, have a graphic frame and so on. The Runs option provides a means to select the runs from which graphs and summary reports are to be displayed. The list of available runs is presented for the current scenario. A selection of a run number as current indicates that graphs are to be produced for that run number. Any runs selected as current for the Report option will be included in a concatenated summary report.

The Simulate option provides a means to select whether an animation is to be performed and the type of animation desired: concurrent or postprocess. The Simulate option also provides the opportunity to turn on the Interactive Execution Environment.

The Utilities action item provides the following capabilities: a complete list of all scenarios; networks; subnetworks; user inserts; animations; notes; controls; data; and symbols for the current project; a means to copy any AweSim component; a means to import or export a component of a project including components previously developed for SLAMSYSTEM; the ability to rename an existing AweSim component and a procedure for deleting an AweSim component.

The last item on the action bar is Help which provides an index on help items, help on the keyboard and procedures for using Help.

In addition to the features described above, AweSim, as a integrated Windows product, is supported by the many capabilities of Microsoft Windows and Microsoft Office and the application programs that run under a Windows environment.

14.8   BUILDING NETWORKS IN AWESIM

In AweSim, a network builder is used to construct Visual SLAM networks and subnetworks interactively. Figure 14-3 shows a symbol window superimposed on a network window. This screen is obtained by selecting ADD from the drop-down menu under the edit function of the network builder window. In the symbol window, the AWAIT node is shown in reverse video to indicate that it is the current option being selected. The AWAIT node symbol is displayed on the right. After the AWAIT node is selected, AweSim requests a location for the AWAIT node. A dialog box is then presented that contains the fields for the AWAIT node as shown in Figure 14-4. The dialog boxes for each network element were described in previous chapters. Initially, values are given for fields which have defaults. The dialog box is completed by selecting a field and typing the desired input for the field. The dialog box can be filled in at the time the AWAIT node is selected or it can be edited at a later time.   After the OK button is selected, AweSim places the AWAIT node in the network with its fields filled in with current values.

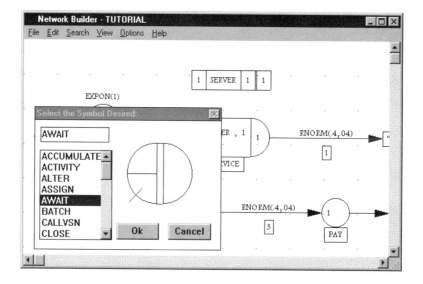

Figure 14-3 Network builder windows.

On-line error checking is performed upon completion of the dialog box so that input errors can be corrected immediately.

The "Clipboard" can be used for copying a set of symbols to other positions in the network or to other networks or applications. Symbols may be repositioned by selecting and dragging them with a mouse. The Network Builder also facilitates model building by providing context-sensitive help and search capabilities. Options are available for placing symbols at grid points, selecting symbol colors and flowcharting models by defaulting symbol parameters. A model may be built as separate networks to facilitate reuse and project management. Such disjoint networks are associated with a scenario and are concatenated at run time.

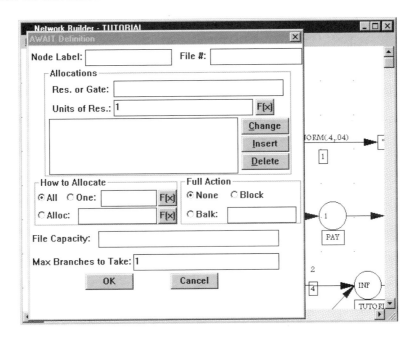

Figure 14-4 Window and dialog box for AWAIT node fields.

A network created with AweSim is stored in a database for integration with other Visual SLAM statements and models, that is, control statements and program inserts. A list of network model names is maintained to facilitate their retrieval using an AweSim utility. Networks and control statements can be copied and given different names to provide a starting point for new models. Discrete events are referenced as inserts and are given a name so that the code can be copied and used in different scenarios and projects.

14.9   BUILDING CONTROL STATEMENTS WITH AWESIM

Control statements are used to define experimental conditions such as the number of runs to make, run length and when to clear statistics after a warmup period. Other control functions include the ability to set Visual SLAM variables, prescribe random number seeds, queueing priorities and initial queue populations. A model's control statements are established in the AweSim Control Builder.

As an example of the control dialog box input to AweSim, the form to complete the GEN statement is presented in Figure 14-5. Behind the GENERAL statement window is a window displaying the current list of control statements. The statement which is currently being edited, the GEN statement, is shown in reverse video. HELP is available to obtain a definition of any field. In Figure 14-5, HELP, on the field where the cursor is located, is provided at the bottom of the dialog box. Descriptions of all fields on the GEN Control statement are available using HELP as shown in Figure 14-6. A separate dialog box is available for each of the Visual SLAM control statements as discussed in Chapter 8.

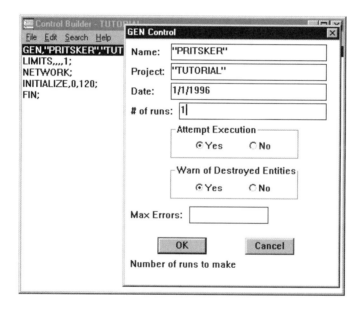

Figure 14-5 Control statement windows.

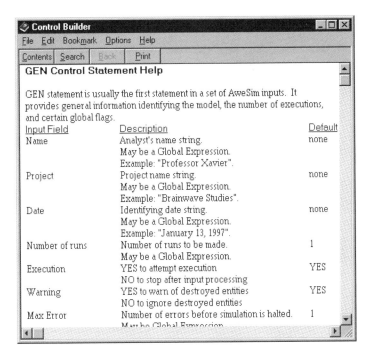

Figure 14-6 Help for GEN control statement.

14.10   INTERACTIVE EXECUTION ENVIRONMENT

The AweSim Interactive Execution Environment (IEE) provides an interface with an executing simulation to examine, modify, save or load the current system status. In this way, the IEE supports the debugging of a model under construction and verification of a completed model. For example, during a simulation it is possible to monitor variable values, statistics or the contents of a queue (file). The times at which status is monitored can be established by advancing time in a stepwise fashion or by setting specific times as breakpoints. This is accomplished using the IEE executive window shown in Figure 14-7. The executive window has an action bar and five pushbuttons shown at the bottom of the window. The pushbuttoms cause the simulation to: restart(|◀), pause (||), step ◀|), continue ◀) and advance ◀||). The display area is divided into 3 sections:

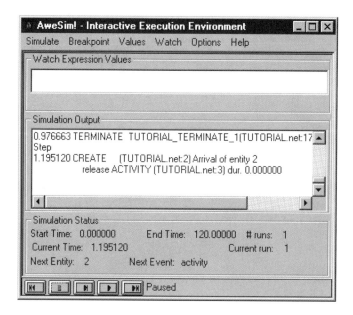

Figure 14-7 Interactive Execution Environment executive window.

1. A Watch window which displays the value of monitored expressions as established using the Watch action bar item;
2. A Simulation Output window which displays messages written by the simulator as a result of IEE commands, simulation trace options or progress indicator updates; and
3. A Simulation Status window displays TTBEG and TTFIN, the run number and the current time whenever the simulation pauses or, if the continuous update option is selected, whenever simulated time advances. The number of the next entity and the next event type are also displayed.

The IEE action bar provides a means to control a simulation while it is running. The functions that can be performed from the items on the action bar are described below.

Item	*Functions Under Item*
Simulate	Stops/continues a simulation run interactively. Also provides Save/Load capability. A saved model status may be loaded and be the starting status of a run. Functions may also be selected using pushbuttons at the bottom of the window which restart, pause, step, continue or advance the simulation.

Breakpoint   Sets/cancels model pause condition based on values of system variables which are set using dialog boxes.

Values   Monitors the value of system variables. May also call Visual SLAM functions and manipulate Visual SLAM files. File contents can be displayed including the attributes of entities.

Watch   Defines/cancels variables to be displayed when the simulation pauses or when continuous update is selected. May also remove the Watch window to allow more room for simulation output.

Options   Sets on/off flags for a diary file, the Visual SLAM trace and a continuous update.

Help   Provides information on the other action bar items. Describes the expressions which may be used for breakpoints, monitors and displays in the Watch window.

The best way to become familiar with IEE operations is use it on a project. Examples of IEE dialog boxes and descriptions of the pull down list for each action bar item are given in the AweSim User's Guide (3).

14.11   OUTPUT ANALYSIS AND PRESENTATION

AweSim provides the capability for comparing simulation outputs from multiple scenarios both graphically and textually. A report browser allows alternative textual outputs to be compared side by side. Graphically, output may be viewed in the form of bar charts, histograms, pie charts and plots. Bar charts can be used to display the value of a statistic across scenarios. It is possible to view multiple windows of graphical output at the same time as shown in Figure 14-8. Observations, summaries of observations, graphical and textual information from AweSim can be exported to other Windows applications packages such as EXCEL, WORD or statistical analysis programs for additional analysis and for inclusion in presentations and reports. This is illustrated in the examples included in this chapter.

Another capability of AweSim is that it can display output reports while input files are displayed. For example, a step-by-step operation of the simulation can be viewed along with the model to verify that the model is running as specified or expected. In this regard, AweSim automatically generates a report describing all model actions. It may be customized to only include events of interest. This textual and graphical output provides a means to compare model performance to actual system performance. Model validation is supported by AweSim in this manner.

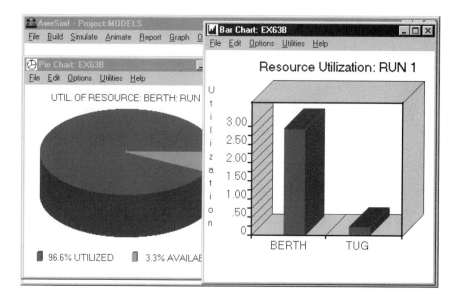

Figure 14-8 Multiple windows for Visual SLAM outputs.

14.12   BUILDING ANIMATIONS WITH AWESIM

As discussed in Section 14-6, animations provide a visual perspective of a model and of the operation of the system as reflected in the model. One of the uses of animation is in the support of model verification and validation. Through the watching of animations, logical inconsistencies in the model can be uncovered. For example, bottlenecks are easily seen, machines that are starved for incoming work are easily identified and deadlock situations in which two resources or entities require a resource held by the other can be detected. The greatest advantage of animation is in communicating the operations of a model between and among developers, users and decision makers. In addition to the advantages of communication and support for verification and validation tasks, animations provide motivation during model creation and lead to the making of strong recommendations. Pitfalls associated with animation relate to a distortion of detail, the length of time required to prepare an animation and the increase in simulated time required to obtain a full view or an appropriate view of a complete simulation run.

In AweSim, animations are created by importing a background screen and using forms to create animation commands that relate simulation events to animation actions. Computer programming is not required to obtain an animation although animations can be enhanced with user-written code. In AweSim, multiple animation screens can be developed and displayed simultaneously along with plots, bar charts, histograms and trend charts. The animations can be presented as the simulation is running, that is, as a concurrent animation, or trace data that drives an animation can be stored to present the animation in a post-process mode. In the post-process mode, simulations are run without incurring the processing time required to update a graphic screen every time a change is made in the simulation.

As mentioned above, animations are built using animation constructs called actions. Many of these actions correspond directly to elements in a Visual SLAM network model. For example, activities, resources, queues and global variables (either as counters, plots or bar graphs) have corresponding action elements in the animation builder. Specifically, an ACTIVITY action shows the movement of a symbol for a time specified by an ACTIVITY in a network. The modeler defines a symbol, the location of a graphical path where movement of the symbol is to be shown and the number of an activity in the Visual SLAM model. The rate of movement is then made a function of the activity time.

Animation actions related to Visual SLAM constructs are listed in Table 14-1. General animation actions are presented in Table 14-2. The actions listed in Table 14-1 are special cases of the actions listed in Table 14-2. For example, the Activity action is a special case of the MoveSymbol action where the time to perform the action is an activity's duration. Similarly, the Queue action is a special case of the ModifyBuffer action and the Graph, Tank and Utilization actions are special cases of the UpdateChart action.

Actions, locations and symbol constructs are all defined by using dialog boxes. These dialog boxes are similar to the ones used in the network builder. To illustrate the basic animation capabilities of AweSim, two examples using previously built network models are presented. Although these examples do not show the full animation capabilities of AweSim, they illustrate the process by which animations are obtained.

Table 14-1 Animation actions related to Visual SLAM constructs.

Action	Description
Activity	Move a symbol along a path for the duration of an activity.
Graph	Display a time-persistent variable as a plot.
Monitor	Monitor a Visual SLAM expression and display its value at a point.
Queue	Define a queue, display the number currently in the queue at a point and display symbols representing entities in the queue along a path.
Resource	Monitor a resource's status and place symbols representing each type of status (busy, idle, preempted, unavailable).
Tank	Display the value of a Visual SLAM expression as the height of a bar.
Text	Place a text string at a point when a specified event occurs.
Utilization	Display a resource's utilization as a the height of a bar.

Table 14-2 General animation actions.

Action	Description
FillArea	Fill an area of the screen with a solid color.
ModifyBuffer	Add or remove symbols from a buffer.
MoveItem	Adjust an item's position, velocity and /or acceleration.
MoveSymbol	Move a symbol along a path.
PlaceString	Place a number or character string at a point.
PlaceSymbol	Place a symbol at a point.
UpdateChart	Prepare and display a bar chart, histogram or plot.

   To develop an animation for the TV inspector problem, a variant of the network shown in Figure 4-7 is imported into the Animation Buider of AweSim. By zooming out on the network, the labels and parameters of the network are masked which is done only to facilitate the viewing of animation actions directly on the nodes and branches of the network. Activity actions are then placed on the network directly over the five branches representing activities. This is shown in Figure 14-9.

   These Activity actions are used to portray the movement of TVs over the branches of the network. Activity numbers were added to each branch in the Visual SLAM model to allow activity animation actions to reference an activity number. Through a setting in the animation builder, entities are shown to move for a short period of time over branches that have zero time durations. The symbol selected to represent a TV entity is a black box. Symbol information is input to AweSim through a dialog box following a request to add an Activity action to the animation facilities screen.

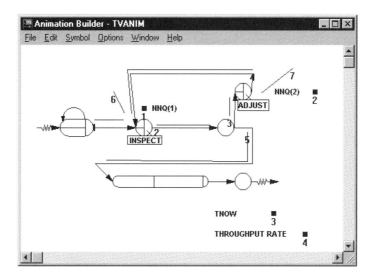

Figure 14-9 Animation actions superimposed on the Visual SLAM network from Example 4-2.

Queue actions are included on the network facility diagram near the queue nodes with labels INSPECT and ADJUST. The Queue actions are shown in lines leading to the QUEUE nodes. Each waiting TV entity will be displayed as a black box positioned along the line. The squares to the right of the text "TNOW" and "THROUGHPUT RATE" indicate the two locations where numeric values will be displayed. The specific values are prescribed by PlaceString actions. The TV inspection throughput rate is computed as the number of entities completing activity 5, NNCNT(5), divided by the current time TNOW. Similarly, the values for the number in file 1 and file 2 representing the number of TVs waiting for inspection and adjustment respectively will be displayed at the locations shown.

When the simulation is run, the action and specification information is removed from the screen and the symbols and variables at their current value are displayed dynamically to provide an animation of the model. Figure 14-10 presents a snapshot of the animation after 140.039 minutes of simulated time. From Figure 14-10 it is seen that there are no TV's waiting for inspection; three TVs are waiting for adjustment; two TVs are being inspected; one TV is being adjusted; and the average TV throughput rate is 0.193 per minute.

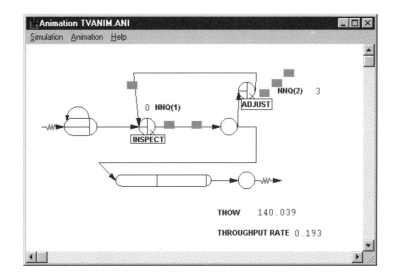

Figure 14-10 Animation snapshot of TV inspection and adjustment model.

As a second example of a network animation, the inventory situation modeled in Example 5-1 is presented. Activity, PlaceString and Queue actions are superimposed on the networks shown in Figure 14-11. In addition a Graph action is used to show a plot of the inventory position of radios over time. Figure 14-12 shows a snapshot of the animation after 150.341 weeks of simulated time. During this time, there were 34 lost sales and on the average 2.922 radios were sold per week. From the plot of inventory position, an order was recently placed. The order has not arrived as can be observed by the entity on the second activity (representing the lead time delay) on the lower network. There were three sales backordered when the order was placed, and an additional two backorders have occurred since the order was placed. These are shown waiting at the AWAIT node in the upper network. This accounts for the inventory position being 70 when the inventory policy is to order up to a stock control level of 72. These two examples illustrate the ease with which animations can be obtained on Visual SLAM networks using AweSim. When a general facility diagram is imported, the addition of animation actions follows the same procedures as described above.

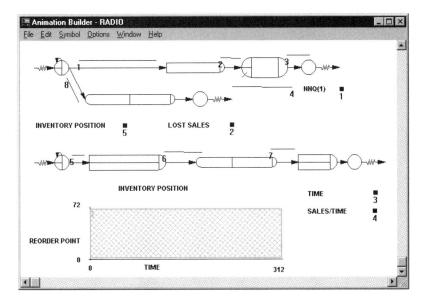

Figure 14-11 Animation actions superimposed on the Visual SLAM network from Example 5-1.

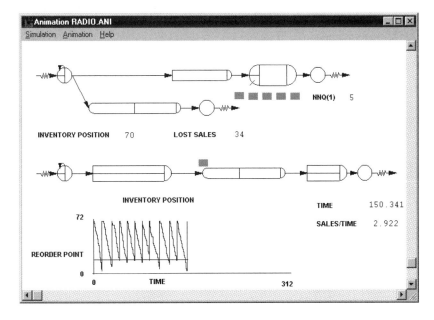

Figure 14-12 Animation snapshot of inventory situation network.

AweSim supports changing the symbol representing the entity that moves through the model. This is accomplished by either defining a symbol for each action; or defining a Symbol Group to provide a reference table to identify a symbol with an entity type. The EDIT pull down menu which is part of the Animation Builder allows animation facility diagrams to be edited in a direct manner. For further details relative to the buildng and editing of animation facility diagrams and their use, the AweSim User's Guide should be consulted (2).

Examples of animations are given in the color inserts in Chapter 15, pages 715-718 with the project descriptions provided on pages 708-711.

14.13   THE AWESIM DATABASE AND ITS USE

During the running of a simulation, data from Visual SLAM is stored in the AweSim database. Table 14-3 is a listing of the AweSim database tables and index file names. The table extension is .dbf and index files with the extension .cdx allow index searches that can be performed on the table. In this section, the procedures for accessing the database tables listed in Table 14-3 which do not have the .fpt extension are described.

To transfer a database table into an Excel spreadsheet, the procedure is to invoke EXCEL and to request that a file be opened. The type of file to be opened will have the .dbf extension. Thus to put statistics regarding all numbered activities of a Visual SLAM network model contained in scenario EX51, the file EX51\activity.dbf should be opened. This spreadsheet will have a row for each numbered activity containing the information as described in Table 14-4.

To append an AweSim table to ACCESS, the first step is to open an ACCESS database and then to select the option "Link Table". This will link an AweSim table to the ACCESS database. Next, set the "Files of Type:" field to the database file format Microsoft FoxPro. In the filename, enter the AweSim table name for a desired scenario and table, for example,

\PROJECTS\MODELS\EX51\SYSTIME.DBF

The table SYSTIME.DBF contains observed values from directory PROJECTS, project MODELS, scenario EX51 based on a DOCOLCT control statement which records the time at which a sample observation is made, its simulation run number and its value at that time. To complete the linking, close the window that was opened to define a new table, click "OK" on the message that appears to use the default record identifier and click "OK" on the message that indicates that the table has successfully been linked. Lastly, click on "CLOSE" to stop the linking process. The linked table now appears in the list of tables for the ACCESS database and the name is preceded with an arrow and a fox to indicate that it is a linked FoxPro table.

Table 14-3 Database table and index file names

Base	Tab	Index	Memo	Description
<project>	.dbf	.cdx	.fpt	Main project table (only one row)
SCENARIO	.dbf	.cdx		Main scenario table for project
SCENNET	.dbf	.cdx		Scenario-Network association table
SCENSUB	.dbf	.dcx		Scenario-Subnetwork association table
SCENUI	.dbf	.cdx		Scenario-User Insert association table
SCENNOTE	.dbf	.cdx		Scenario-Note association table
SCENDATA	.dbf	.cdx		Scenario-User Data association table
SCENANIM	.dbf	.cdx		Scenario-Animation association table
NETWORKS	.dbf	.cdx		Networks list table
ANIMS	.dbf	.cdx		Animation list table
network\<network>	.dbf	.cdx	.fpt	Network statement main table
subnet\<subnetwork>	.dbf	.cdx	.fpt	Subnetwork statement main table
control\<control>	.dbf	.cdx	.fpt	Control statement main table
listanim\<animation>	.dbf	.cdx	.fpt	Animation statement main table
<scenario>\run	.dbf	.cdx		Scenario's run information table
<scenario>\activity	.dbf	.cdx		Scenario's activity statistics table
<scenario>\batch	.dbf	.cdx		Scenario's batch statistics table
<scenario>\colstat	.dbf	.cdx		Scenario's colct statistics table
<scenario>\file	.dbf	.cdx		Scenario's file statistics table
<scenario>\gate	.dbf	.cdx		Scenario's gate statistics table
<scenario>\group	.dbf	.cdx		Scenario's group statistics table
<scenario>\resource	.dbf	.cdx		Scenario's resource statistics table
<scenario>\service	.dbf	.cdx		Scenario's service activity statistics table
<scenario>\tpstat	.dbf	.cdx		Scenario's time-persistent statistics table
<scenario>\colhist	.dbf	.cdx		Scenario's colct histogram table
<scenario>\tphist	.dbf	.cdx		Scenario's time-persistent histogram table
<scenario>\<name>	.dbf			Raw data from DOCOLCT and RECORD statements

To write data to the AweSim database, a WRITE node or WRITE statement can be used directly in the Visual SLAM model by using the extension .dbf.

Table 14-4   Activity Statistics Table (<scenario>/activity.dbf)

Key	Name	Type	Description
*	Scenario	C(8)	Scenario name
*	Run	INT	Run number
*	Instance	C(32)	Instance name
*	Activity	INT	Activity Statistic number
	ID	C(32)	Activity ID
	Complete	INT	Number of entities to complete activity
	Current	INT	Number of entities currently on activity
	Min	INT	Minimum number on activity
	Max	INT	Maximum number on activity
	Mean	FLOAT	Average number on activity
	StdDev	FLOAT	Standard deviation of number on activity

14.14   INTEGRATION OF AWESIM WITH OTHER SOFTWARE

AweSim works with other software programs in an integrated manner. For example, AweSim is built on a relational database which is accessible with standard tools such as Dbase, Access, FoxPro and Excel. Input data is easily moved from an Excel worksheet to the AweSim input tables. Output data is stored in AweSim output tables which are directly available for creating custom reports using standard tools. In addition to standard output data, raw data from the simulation is stored in standard database or Excel format for analysis, manipulation or presentation. Data used to create AweSim output graphics can also be exported "on the fly" to an output file for use in any tool accepting comma-delimited input.

Modelers often want to drive their simulation models from historic data. The AweSim project framework includes a user data element as part of the scenario definition. This data element may contain schedule, routing or facility configuration information. It can be read in a Visual SLAM model during a simulation run. This data can be created in a spreadsheet or the built-in data editor provided with AweSim.

An AweSim animation can use graphics created from other programs. As previously discussed, the graphical elements employed by the animation program can be created using Computer-Aided Design(CAD), drawing or paint programs. Bitmap files can be used directly while other formats can be used after converting them to a .bmp format with a graphical translation program.

The output charts and plots created by AweSim can be exported to other applications through the Windows clipboard or directly using Visual Basic or MS Office procedures. Examples of these capabilities are demonstrated in Example 14-1. In addition, the standard trace output of Visual SLAM or values generated from Subroutine UMONT have been used to generate vector-graphics animations.

The standard output reports are often exported to other packages for communication or analysis purposes. For example, an analyst can place sections of the standard AweSim report in a spreadsheet program and then add revenue and cost data to produce a financial report.

Two examples of custom reports generated from AweSim database tables are shown in Figure 14-13 and Figure 14-14. Using the Excel functions TINV, DAVERAGE and DSTDEV the formula for calculating a confidence interval may be built into a spreadsheet macro. Figure 14-13 shows the result of applying the spreadsheet to the RESOURCE.DBF file created by five runs of Example 5-4. A second example uses the SERIES function of Excel to create a pie chart of resource utilization as shown in Figure 14-14. Although AweSim will prepare a pie chart from the same data, Excel provides a wide range of formatting tools to enhance the presentation of output data.

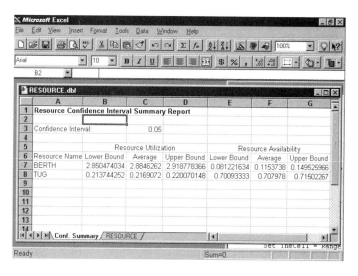

Figure 14-13 Excel confidence interval macro output.

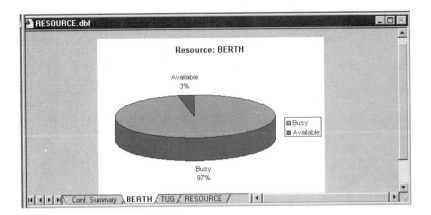

Figure 14-14 Excel pie chart macro output.

14.15   EXAMPLE 14-1. LIVER TRANSPLANTATION POLICY EVALUATION

Organs for transplantation are a scarce life-saving resource. The number of cadaveric donors has not kept pace with increasing demand. The United Network for Organ Sharing (UNOS) is a not-for-profit organization with all its Board of Directors, committees and officers being volunteers from the transplantation community. UNOS operates a nationwide system to procure and allocate human organs to potential recipients. It is an on-line system which maintains a list of waiting patients for an organ, matches a donor organ with potential transplant recipients and prepares a ranked list of feasible patients for the donor organ in compliance with a prescribed policy. Pritsker Corporation in conjunction with UNOS developed the UNOS Liver Allocation Model, ULAM, for assessing proposed policies for allocating livers (4). The material presented in this example is based on ULAM with major changes made to reduce the size and scope of the model.

The policy to be evaluated allocates a liver to a terminally ill liver patient using a single national list. Patients waiting on the list are classified into three status types:

1.   Status 1 patients are referred to as acute patients who have within the last six weeks encountered a life-threatening liver disease that is not curable without a liver transplant;

2. Status 2 patients have a chronic liver disease and have been hospitalized for at least five consecutive days;

3. Status 3 patients have a life-threatening liver disease and are continuously monitored by a physician but do not meet the criteria for being a Status 2 patient.

Patients on the waiting list are located at transplant centers throughout the United States. Historical records are available relative to the characteristics of the patients at the transplant center locations. The arrival of donors can be to any of 2,000 donor hospitals throughout the United States. Organ Procurement Organizations (OPOs) are responsible for recovering organs and maintaining contact with transplant centers. In this example only the allocation of livers is considered. Patients on the waiting list may have a health status change, be transplanted or die. The Status 1 patients do not make transitions to Status 2 or 3 because of the acute nature of their illness. Status 2 patients typically do not transition from a chronic state to an acute state but 20 percent do improve sufficiently to leave the hospital and become Status 3 patients. When Status 3 patients register into a hospital, they can become Status 2 patients after 5 days in the hospital. Patients who die are classified as Status 4.

The policy to be evaluated specifies that a liver be allocated to waiting patients who have the same blood type as the donor. The order in which the patients are to be ranked are by status with a liver being allocated to Status 1 patients before Status 2 patients before Status 3 patients. A secondary ranking of patients within a given status is to be done on the basis of the total amount of time that the patient has been on the waiting list. At the beginning of the simulation, there is an initial list of patients waiting.

The objective of this example is to simulate the above system to obtain estimates of the following quantities:

1. Number of pre-transplant patient deaths and their waiting time
2. Number of post-transplant patient deaths and their waiting time
3. Number of transplanted patients that survive for more than two years and their waiting time
4. Waiting time of patients by status until they are transplanted
5. Distance that organs travel from the donor hospital to the transplant hospital.

Concepts Illustrated. This example illustrates the use of the program integration capabilities of AweSim to: provide input data for a model; store model outputs for presentation using Excel; and build animations illustrating the allocation of organs to waiting patients. Outputs are stored in a database to facilitate the computation and display of performance measures. A MATCH node is used to determine the patient to which an arriving liver is to be allocated. A ranking of entities in a queue based on primary and secondary priority variables is demonstrated with the first priority being status and the secondary ranking based on waiting time.

Visual SLAM Model. The transplantation system is simulated using a network model with user inserts. The network model represents the flow of patients and livers through the system. When the liver is transplanted into a patient, the patient's future condition is determined based on a survival time projection. While waiting, patient changes in status are modeled by a probability of status change and a time to make the status change. When a status change occurs, the patient is reranked on the list of waiting patients. If a patient dies on the waiting list, the patient is removed from the waiting list and statistics are collected on the patient as a pre-transplant death. The Visual SLAM network model is shown in Figure 14-15.

In describing the Visual SLAM model, the network flow will be emphasized. The attribute structure for this example is shown below.

Attribute Structure

	Index	*Description*
ATRIB	0	Arrival time of a liver entity
	1	Arrival time of a patient entity
	2	x-coordinate of location of transplant center
	3	y-coordinate of location of transplant center
	4	x-coordinate of donor hospital
	5	y-coordinate of donor hospital
LTRIB	0	Status code of patient: 1, 2 or 3
	1	Next status code of patient: 2, 3, or 4
	2	Time of next status change
	3	Blood type: 1=A, 2=B, 3=O or 4=AB.

There are two types of entities in the model: patients and livers. For a patient entity, attribute 1 is the arrival time which is the registration time for a patient. It is used to collect statistics on waiting time and also to calculate the priority ranking expression for a patient on the waiting list. Attributes 2 and 3 are the x- and y-coordinates of the location of the transplant center to which the patient arrived. LTRIB[0] is the initial status code for the arriving patient. LTRIB[3] is the blood type of both the patient and liver entities and can be 1(A), 2(B), 3(O) or 4(AB). For the liver entity, ATRIB[4] and ATRIB[5] are the coordinates of the donor hospital. When a patient is transplanted, the attributes of the patient and liver entities are combined to provide the attributes of a transplanted patient.

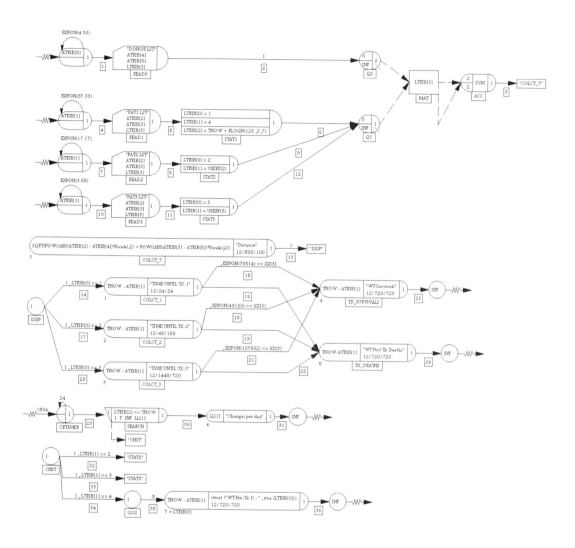

Figure 14-15 Visual SLAM network model for transplantation analysis, Example 14-1.

In Figure 14-15, the arrival time of the liver entity is established as ATRIB[0] and the time between arrivals of liver organs is specified at the CREATE node. READ node READ0 is used to read a file which contains attributes for liver entities. ATRIB[4] and ATRIB[5] and LTRIB[3] are established by reading the information from a file. The liver entity is then routed to QUEUE node Q2 where it is allocated to a waiting patient. The coordinates of the donor hospital are read in as ATRIB[4] and ATRIB[5] and these will be used to collect statistics on the donated liver travel distance and in an animation that shows the transfer of livers to patients throughout the United States.

The arrival of patients is separated into arrivals by status type. Prior to running the Visual SLAM program, files were constructed with the attributes necessary to describe the type of patient arriving for a given status. The attributes read from the file are the x- and y-coordinates of the transplant center to which the patient arrives and the patient's blood type. The random construction of files to represent a set of characteristics for entities is referred to as "bootstrapping."

The patient entity is sent to an ASSIGN node where the patient's current status is set. The value of the next status for the patient, LTRIB[1], and the time at which the status change will occur, LTRIB[2], are set in user function 1 which is described following the description of the network.

For each status code, patient entities are routed to QUEUE node Q1 where they are inserted into the file 1 waiting list in accordance with the priority ranking rule defined for file 1 on a Priority Control statement. The ranking rule is set equal to the patient's status code minus a value which is proportional to the patient's waiting time. The patient's waiting time is the current time minus the patient's arrival time, that is, TNOW - ATRIB[1]. Since we are using the waiting time to compute a priority ranking value, it is convenient to normalize the waiting time by dividing by TNOW. This maintains the same order of the entities but yields a ranking value as (TNOW - ATRIB[1])/TNOW or, equivalently, 1 - ATRIB[1]/TNOW. Since at any time during the simulation, the waiting time is computed at a given instant, TNOW is a constant for such calculations. Because of this, any constant value can be used for ranking in place of TNOW as long it is larger than the arrival time of the entity. A convenient value to use is the ending time for the simulation, that is, TTFIN. By subtracting this waiting time factor from the status code, a combined ranking expression is obtained which ranks patient entities by status code first and then, within status code, to those patient entities that have waited the longest. Thus, the ranking expression for the PRIORITY statement for file 1 is prescribed as LTRIB[0]−(1−ATRIB[1]/TTFIN).

A MATCH node MAT is used to match an arriving liver entity with a waiting patient with the same blood type who has the highest value of the ranking expression. The matched entities are routed from the MATCH node to an ACCUMULATE node where the attributes of the two entities are combined. The transplanted patient entity is then routed to COLCT node DISP where the distance between the donor hospital and the patient transplant center is collected and the patient entity is routed according to the status code at which the patient was transplanted, LTRIB[0]. Three COLCT nodes are used to obtain the waiting time until transplant by status type. Following each COLCT node is an activity which has a condition that represents the 2-year survivability of the transplanted patient. An exponential survivability function has been assumed for the time to death for each patient type. For Status 1 patients, the mean time to death after being transplanted is 78,514 hours or approximately 9 years. For Status 2 patients, the mean time to death is 49,120 hours or approximately 5.6 years. And for Status 3 patients, the mean time to death is 107,802 hours or approximately 12.3 years. The condition involves drawing a random sample from the survivability function and testing it against a threshold which for this scenario is 2 years. The global variable XX[3] is used as the threshold value and it is set on an INTLC statement. Statistics are then collected on the waiting time of transplant patients according to whether they survived or whether they died.

By using a condition on an activity rather than simulating the time until death, the simulation run length can be shortened. In essence, this procedure is a projection of an outcome with respect to transplanted patients and makes it unnecessary to run the simulation until the outcome occurs. This completes the description of the patient portion of the model.

A disjoint network is used to model the status change process. At 4 a.m. each day, the patients waiting in file 1 are reviewed to see if their status change was projected to occur prior to that time. This is accomplished by examining LTRIB[2] of the patient entity. To accomplish this reviewing of patients, a CREATE node creates one entity at 4 a.m. of the first simulated day and routes it to FINDAR node SEARCH. The FINDAR node initiates a search through file 1 and a testing of the value of LTRIB[2] to determine whether it is less than or equal to TNOW. If the value is less than or equal to TNOW, the patient entity that is making a status change is removed from file 1 and routed to GOON node CHST where it is further routed to ASSIGN nodes, STAT2 or STAT3, based on its changed status code, LTRIB[2]. At nodes STAT2 and STAT3, the current status of the patient is reset and the next transition state and time are established in function USERF. If the patient is making a transition to Status 4, the death state, then statistics are collected on the number and waiting time of a pre-transplant death categorized by status at death. The pre-transplant death waiting times are collected at a single COLCT node by making the COLCT node number an expression, 6+LTRIB[0], and concatenating a string with LTRIB[0] as the output identifier. This entity is then terminated from the simulation.

After searching through all patient entities waiting in file 1, the timer entity is routed to a COLCT node where the number of status changes per day, LL[1], is recorded. The value of LL[1] is obtained from the FINDAR node where it was specified as the FOUND parameter. The timer entity is then terminated.

The user code for this example is shown in Figures 14-16 and 14-17. Function USERF is used to model a Semi-Markov process in which patients in Status 2 have a probability of transitioning to Status 3 or to Status 4, death. Patients in Status 3 can transition to Status 2 or to Status 4. The arguments for function USERF are Code, the status code of the patient, and Patient, the patient entity object. Since a transition probability will be needed independent of which transition is made, Prob is set equal to a random number upon entering USERF. A Select Case statement based on Code then transfers to Case 2 or Case 3. At Case 2, 20% of Status 2 patients transition to Status 3. Thus, if Prob is less than or equal to 0.2 then USERF is set equal to 3. Since LTRIB[1] is set equal to USERF in the network, LTRIB[1] will be set to 3. When a transition is made from Status 2 to Status 3, the transition time is equal to the current time plus a sample from the lognormal distribution with mean of 1440 hours and a standard deviation of 365. If the patient does not transition to Status 3 then the next status of the patient is set to 4 and the time of the transition to set to TNOW plus a sample from an exponential distribution with mean of 4380 hours.

```
Public Function USERF(Code As Long, Patient As VSENTITY)
   Dim Prob
   On Error GoTo Bad
   Prob = VS.DRAND(10)
   Select Case Code
      Case 1
         Exit Function
      Case 2
         If Prob <= 0.2 Then
            USERF = 3
            Patient.LTRIB(2) = VS.TNOW + VS.RLOGN(1440#, 365#, 7)
            Exit Function
         Else
            USERF = 4
            Patient.LTRIB(2) = VS.TNOW + VS.EXPON(4380#, 7)
            Exit Function
         End If
         Exit Function
      Case 3
         If Prob <= 0.6 Then
            USERF = 2
            Patient.LTRIB(2) = VS.TNOW + VS.RLOGN(4380#, 730#, 7)
            Exit Function
         Else
            USERF = 4
            Patient.LTRIB(2) = VS.TNOW + VS.EXPON(8760#, 7)
            Exit Function
         End If
         Exit Function
   End Select
Bad:
   VS.Out True, True, "Unknown USERF code "
   VS.Out True, True, Str(Code)
   End Function
```

Figure 14-16 Function USERF for Example 14-1.

Similar code is provided for transitions from Status 3 where, if the probability is less than or equal to 0.6, a transition is made to Status 2 with a time equal to TNOW plus a sample from a lognormal distribution with a mean 4,380 hours and a standard deviation 730 hours. If the Status 3 patient makes a transition to

Status 4, then the time at which the transition is made is TNOW plus a sample from an exponential distribution with a mean of 8,760 hours or 1 year. This completes the description of function USERF.

Function INTLC, shown in Figure 14-17, is used in this example to provide an initial list of 200 patients in file 1. Fifteen hundred hours was selected as the start time of the simulation because the earliest arrival time of the 200 patients was within this 1500 hour time interval. In this way, it is possible to avoid negative arrival times as part of the input data.

```
Public Function INTLC(Run As Long) As Long
    Dim atribute1 As Double       'arrival time
    Dim atribute2 As Double       'x-coord of transplant center
    Dim atribute3 As Double       'y-coord of transplant center
    Dim ltribute3 As Integer      'blood type of patient
    Dim Status As Integer         'status 1, 2, or 3
    Dim I As Integer
    Dim Pat As VSENTITY

    On Error GoTo Bad
    INTLC = 1
    Open "init.lst" For Input As #1
    For I = 1 To 200
        Input #1, atribute1
        Input #1, atribute2
        Input #1, atribute3
        Input #1, ltribute3
        Input #1, Status
        Set Pat = VS.DefineEntity(Status)
        Pat.ATRIB(1) = atribute1
        Pat.ATRIB(2) = atribute2
        Pat.ATRIB(3) = atribute3
        Pat.LTRIB(3) = ltribute3
        Call VS.ARRIVE("STAT" + Format(Status, "#"), Pat)
    Next I
    Close #1
    Exit Function
Bad:
    VS.Out True, True, "Error in INTLC"
    INTLC = 0
End Function
```

Figure 14-17 Function INTLC for Example 14-1.

Basically, function INTLC contains a For loop with I going from 1 to 200. The attributes of patients arriving before the start of the simulation are taken from an initial list. A patient entity, Pat, is created using the Visual SLAM method DefineEntity and the read-in attributes are placed in Pat.ATRIB(·) and Pat.LTRIB(·). Pat is routed to node STAT1, STAT2 or STAT3 to assign additional attributes using the Visual SLAM method ARRIVE. For run 1, the initial patients were distributed as 5 Status 1, 35 Status 2 and 160 Status 3 patients.

The control statements for this example are shown in Figure 14-18. The INTLC statement sets XX[3] to 17520 hours or 2 years which is the threshold for the survivability calculations of the patient. The INITIALIZE statement sets the beginning time of the simulation to 1500 hours and the ending time to 19020 hours which provides a simulation interval of 2 years. The priority statement establishes the priority for file 1 to be low value first based on the expression derived earlier in this section.

```
REPORT,100,YES,YES,EVERY(1),{{ALL,2}};
GEN,"Pritsker","ULAMJR",09/01/96,10,YES,YES;
LIMITS,5,5,,5,4,5;
INTLC,{{xx[3],17520}};
INITIALIZE,1500,19020,YES;
PRIORITY,{{1,LVF(LTRIB[0] - (1-ATRIB[1]/TTFIN))}};
NET;
FIN;
```

Figure 14-18 Control statements for Example 14-1.

Summary of Results. The policy being simulated involves a single national list in which patients are allocated a liver based on their medical status first and patients of the same status selected based on longest waiting time. The allocation requires identical blood matching between the organ donor and the patient. First, we examine the flow of patients through the liver organ transplantation network. An Excel spreadsheet for the number of entities that traversed each activity is shown in Figure 14-19. Column one represents the first run. The entity count for Activities 4, 7 and 10 indicates the arrival of 187 Status 1 patients, 1,001 Status 2 patients and 4,787 Status 3 patients during the two year simulation period. The total number of arriving patients is 6,175 including the initial 200 waiting patients. The number of liver arrivals is obtained from activity 1 as 4,056. Thus, livers were available to transplant approximately 66% of the arriving and initial patients. Of the patients transplanted, 3,156 survived for greater than two years to give a transplantation survival fraction of 0.778. There were 900 patients who died after transplantation and 699 patients who died while waiting for a transplant. This constitutes 26% of the patients. The flow of entities over the ten runs is simulated with the standard error of the number of entities completing an activity always being less than 4.2% of the average.

| | RUN NUMBER | | | | | | | | | | | | |
ACTIVITY	1	2	3	4	5	6	7	8	9	10	AVG	STD	STDERR
1 LIVER1	4056	4042	3883	4028	3928	4044	4131	3940	4047	4049	4015	74.29	23.493
2 LIVER2	4056	4042	3882	4027	3928	4044	4131	3940	4047	4049	4015	74.47	23.550
3 DIST	4056	4042	3882	4027	3928	4044	4131	3940	4047	4049	4015	74.47	23.550
4 ST1	187	196	202	178	193	175	181	183	182	166	184	10.60	3.353
5 ST1	187	196	202	178	193	175	181	183	182	166	184	10.60	3.353
6 ST1	192	201	207	183	198	180	186	188	187	171	189	10.60	3.353
7 ST2	1001	976	1000	1062	1025	1046	1001	1009	1029	985	1013	26.90	8.508
8 ST2	1001	976	1000	1062	1025	1046	1001	1009	1029	985	1013	26.90	8.508
9 ST2+3	2053	2136	2383	2404	2481	2169	1921	2322	2357	2149	2238	178.46	56.435
10 ST3	4787	4837	4759	4765	4864	4774	4734	4774	4879	4896	4807	56.99	18.021
11 ST3	4787	4837	4759	4765	4864	4774	4734	4774	4879	4896	4807	56.99	18.021
12 ST2+3	4953	5008	4943	4934	5034	4940	4897	4949	5049	5075	4978	58.80	18.594
13 TX_PAT	4056	4041	3882	4027	3928	4044	4131	3940	4047	4049	4015	74.43	23.537
14 TX_ST1	189	197	205	180	196	178	180	186	186	169	187	10.61	3.354
15 SURVIVAL_1	146	150	166	151	163	139	147	150	154	140	151	8.72	2.758
16 DIED_1	43	47	39	29	33	39	33	36	32	29	36	5.96	1.886
17 TX_ST2	1946	2012	2204	2298	2351	2040	1851	2153	2232	1996	2108	163.45	51.687
18 SURVIVAL_2	1392	1398	1583	1617	1683	1427	1312	1526	1568	1392	1490	121.44	38.403
19 DIED_2	554	614	621	681	668	613	539	627	664	604	619	46.24	14.624
20 TX_ST3	1921	1832	1472	1549	1381	1826	2100	1601	1629	1884	1720	226.96	71.770
21 SURVIVAL_3	1618	1544	1265	1300	1206	1560	1739	1354	1385	1606	1458	178.30	56.384
22 DIED_3	303	288	207	249	175	266	361	247	244	278	262	51.36	16.242
23 TERM	3156	3092	3014	3068	3052	3126	3198	3030	3107	3138	3098	58.27	18.427
24 TERM	900	949	867	959	876	918	933	910	940	911	916	30.04	9.501
29 1st_Change	730	730	730	730	730	730	730	730	730	730	730	0.00	0.000
30 DAYCLOCK	730	730	730	730	730	730	730	730	730	730	730	0.00	0.000
31 TERM	730	730	730	730	730	730	730	730	730	730	730	0.00	0.000
32 CHG->2	1017	1125	1348	1307	1421	1088	885	1278	1293	1129	1189	167.22	52.880
33 CHG->3	6	11	24	9	10	6	3	15	10	19	11	6.40	2.022
34 PreTxD	699	770	834	752	878	770	707	790	799	772	777	53.58	16.943
35 PreTxD	699	770	834	752	878	770	707	790	799	772	777	53.58	16.943
36 TERM	699	770	834	752	878	770	707	790	799	772	777	53.58	16.943

Figure 14-19 Entity counts on activities for 10 runs.

A partial AweSim Summary Report for the first of 10 runs is shown in Figure 14-20. Statistics from file 1 show that the number of patients waiting for a liver transplant after two years is 1,420 which means that the waiting list grew by 1,220 patients in the two year period.

For the run, the impact of this policy can be summarized as follows: for Status 1 patients 189 of the 189 Status 1 patients receive a transplant. (There were 5 acute patients on the initial waiting list.) The average waiting time for these patients is 28.16 hours, slightly more than a day. This of course does not include transportation and surgical time for the liver to be sent to the transplant center where the patient resides. The analysis of Status 2 and Status 3 patients is more involved as patients transplanted in Status 2 arrive to the system as either a Status 2 or Status 3 patient. The average waiting time of the 1,946 status 2 patients transplanted is 2,241 hours. Presumably the waiting time is less for a patient that arrived as a Status 2 and then transplanted as Status 2 (approximately 1,017 patients). The waiting time of the 1,921 patients transplanted in Status 3 is 2,599 hours. In this case, there were only 6 Status 2 patients that transitioned to Status 3 so that the waiting time is from a more homogenous population.

```
              ** AweSim SUMMARY REPORT **

      Simulation Project : ULAMJR
      Modeler : Pritsker
      Date : 09/01/96
      Scenario : ULAMJR

      Run number 1 of 10
      Current simulation time   : 19020.000000
      Statistics cleared at time : 1500.000000

            ** OBSERVED STATISTICS REPORT for scenario ULAMJR **
         Label          Mean     Standard   Number of  Minimum    Maximum
                        Value    Deviation  Observations Value     Value

      TIME UNTIL TX-1    28.16     105.70       189       2.04     1403.97
      TIME UNTIL TX-2  2241.45    2148.11      1946       2.00     7226.69
      TIME UNTIL TX-3  2599.33    1210.55      1921     943.68     8203.58
      WT Survivals     2358.80    1751.68      3156       2.00     8203.58
      WT Post Tx Death 2129.01    1894.58       900       2.01     7713.83
      Changes per day     2.36       2.43       730       0.00       12.00
      Distance         1167.04     833.85      4056       0.00     3397.02
      WT Pre-Tx D - 1   144.72       1.85         3     143.11      146.75
      WT Pre-Tx D - 2  1924.39    1977.95        51       9.75     5515.57
      WT Pre-Tx D - 3  2204.04    2009.29       645      19.65    11471.12

            ** FILE STATISTICS REPORT for scenario ULAMJR **

      File   Label or    Average   Standard  Maximum  Current  Average
      Number Input Location Length Deviation Length   Length  Wait Time

      1      QUEUE  Q1     847.01    351.96     1433     1420    2061.62
      2      QUEUE  Q2       0.00      0.00        1        0       0.00
      0      Event Calendar   5.81      1.09      205        5       3.25
```

Figure 14-20 Partial AweSim Summary Report for Example 14-1.

Looking at some of the other observed statistics, it is seen that the waiting time for those patients that survived and the waiting time for those patients that died after being transplanted are approximately the same. This result could be observed directly from the model as the determination of whether a patient survived or died following transplantation is determined following the calculation of the waiting time for the patient. Thus, the model assumes that there is no statistical difference in the mean waiting time for these 2 statistics. The larger value of the maximum waiting time for those patients surviving is based on the larger number of surviving patients, that is, 3,156 survivals and 900 post-transplant deaths.

The number of status changes per day was 2.36 for the 730 days on which status changes could occur. For these status changes, 699 were pre-transplant deaths, 6 were transitions from Status 2 to Status 3, and 1,017 were transitions from Status 1 to Status 2. Note, however, that on one day there were 12 status changes made. The waiting time of patients who died while waiting on the list is 145 hours for Status 1 patients, 1,924 hours for Status 2 patients and 2,204 hours for Status 3 patients. This is to be expected as Status 3 patients have the lowest priority for receiving a liver.

Although the data in this example is hypothetical, it does present the dilemma involved in allocating a scarce life-saving resource. In actuality, there is a need to increase the number of donors making the general public aware that the number of donors is even more scarce than that presented in this example. Not only are there many performance measures that must be taken into account in selecting a liver allocation policy, but policies need to be developed that balance utility of an organ placement with the equity involved in treating all patients in the same manner. Simulation is a tool that has supported policy selection in this complex medical environment (4,5).

14.16   ILLUSTRATIONS OF AWESIM INTERFACES

The AweSim Executive Window is an interface for a modeler to the functions which support the creation and execution of a Visual SLAM model. Using Visual Basic, the modeler may create an alternative interface for the end user. Such an interface might include COMMAND buttons to modify input, initiate the simulation, browse outputs, print outputs or to transfer to MicroSoft EXCEL, Word or PowerPoint application programs. By providing the Visual Basic code for these COMMAND buttons, list boxes and dialog boxes, a customized user interface to Visual SLAM programs can be easily developed. As an example of such a custom interface, Figure 14-21 provides the user interface to the UNOS Liver Allocation Model (ULAM) to select a policy (scenario), to set the run length and a time to clear statistics, to edit or reset input data, and to simulate, animate or view output.

The ULAM user interface also provides a means to create new policies or edit existing policies. The screen for editing or creating a policy is shown in Figure 14-22 which provides many options to the user based on the characteristics included in the Visual SLAM model. Figure 14-23 presents the ULAM user interface for policy configuration management. For programs that will have a high usage by nonsimulationists, it is normally a good practice to include an interface for configuration management of output files and the database by allowing the deletion of previously run policies. An example of this type of user interface is shown in Figure 14-23.

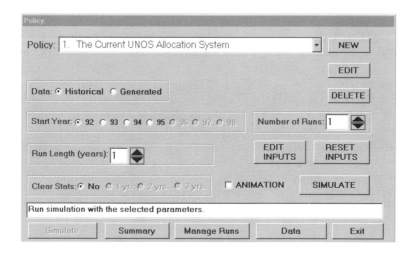

Figure 14-21 ULAM user interface.

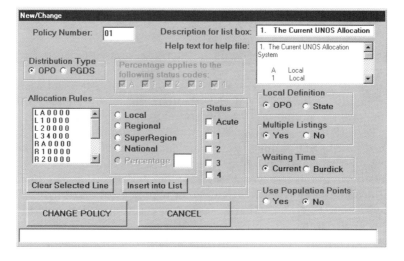

Figure 14-22 ULAM user interface for policy creation and editing.

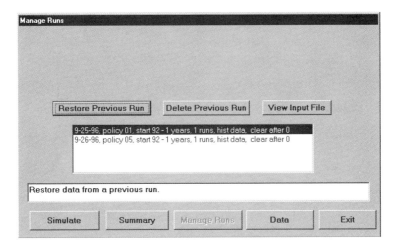

Figure 14-23 ULAM interface for output file management.

In Figure 14-24 transfers to components of ULAM and to the application programs PRIME (10) and ULAMFIT (1,11) are shown. This user interface allows the preparation, generation and use of external application programs.

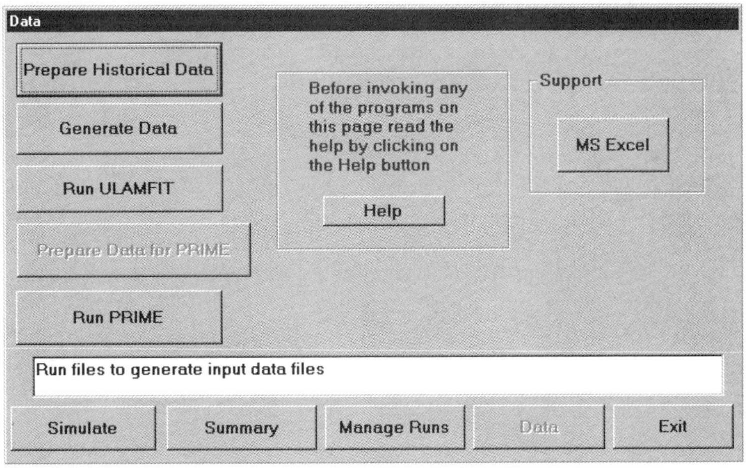

Figure 14-24 ULAM interface for data fitting programs..

In Figures 14-25 and 14-26, two animations from Example 14-1 are presented which are interfaces to the individuals in the transplantation industry.

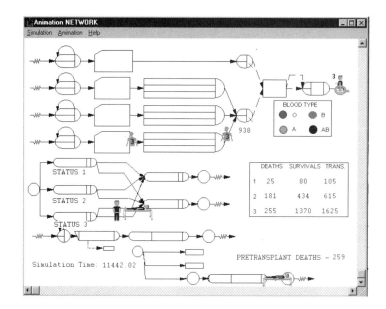

Figure 14-25 Network animation of ULAM model.

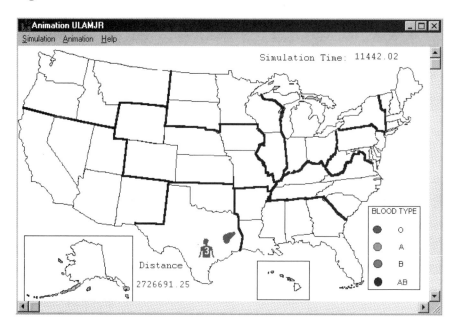

Figure 14-26 Geographic animation of ULAM model.

14.17 EXAMPLE 14-2 RETIREMENT PLANNING

The model described in this example is derived from Parker and evolved from his previous work in integrating Systems Dynamics and SLAM II simulations (2). The example is illustrative of a wide range of financial modeling initiatives which require the concepts of combined simulation. In this example, it is desired to determine the length of time that funds in a retirement account can support a couple in retirement. Basically, the monthly change in the retirement account is dependent on the income earned from outside investments plus the interest from the retirement account minus expenses. The couple starting retirement have a fixed outside monthly income of $2,000 which includes social security payments plus a random amount of income which averages $200 and is exponentially distributed. The monthly interest from the retirement account is based on the interest rate which is 6 percent a year or 0.5 percent per month. The interest rate varies from month to month in a normally distributed manner with a standard deviation of .05 percent.

Expenses per month are from two main sources: a home mortgage and living expenses. The home mortgage is $1,500 a month. The miscellaneous living expenses are estimated to be $3,500 on the average but vary between $3,000 and $4,000 per month, uniformly distributed. For the retiring couple, the basic question is how long will their $500,000 retirement account last under these conditions? The couple is also considering planning for a vacation every year and the purchase of a new car every 5 years. They estimate that a vacation would cost them $2,000 each year with a variation of at most $300, normally distributed. They also have been buying a car every 5 years with a price of $20,000 on the average and a variation of at most $3,000, normally distributed. Another worry of the couple is the impact of inflation on their retirement funds. They are interested in knowing how long the funds would last given all the conditions above if inflation increases by 3 percent per year.

Concepts Illustrated. Nonsimulation-based financial modeling tends to be done in a static, nonprobabilistic way. Simulation offers the opportunity to incorporate dynamic characteristics of cash flows and to include the random nature of future events. In this example, the basic question posed by the couple is modeled and then the model is embellished to include the events associated with vacations and car purchases. Inflation is then added to the model. The models are coded in the C language. The basic model and the 2 embellishments define 3 scenarios. AweSim's capabilities to compare outputs across different scenarios is illustrated. A user interface using Visual Basic is presented to demonstrate how variables in the Visual SLAM model can be changed through an interface to allow users to change input parameters to the model.

Visual SLAM Model. The modeling of cash flows is accomplished by defining a state variable to represent the retirement account and by developing a difference equation that computes the current value of the retirement account as the previous month's value plus the difference in the dollars added to the account and the dollars used for expenses. Equivalence statements are used to improve the readability of the model. The embellishments involve adding events to the basic difference equation evaluations.

Preprocessor directives provide for equivalences between model names and Visual SLAM variables using #define statements. The preprocessor directives are given in Figure 14-27 and show that RETIREMENT_ACCOUNT is defined as SS[1]. The coding of the basic retirement model is contained in function STATE as shown in Figure 14-28. The difference equation to compute the amount in the RETIREMENT_ACCOUNT is the last statement in the function and shows that it is equal to the previous value of the RETIREMENT_ACCOUNT plus the product of the time interval DTNOW and the rate at which funds are coming in plus the retirement interest minus the expenses. The four statements preceding the equation for RETIREMENT_ACCOUNT are used to compute the rates at which the retirement account is increased and decreased in accordance with the problem statement. The coding follows directly from the problem statement. This completes the description of the coding required for the basecase of the retirement simulation model.

```
#define RETIREMENT_ACCOUNT SS[1]
#define MONTHLY_INTEREST_RATE XX[1]
#define MORTGAGE_PAYMENT XX[2]
#define PAYMENTS_LEFT XX[3]
#define MISC_EXPENSES UNFRM(3000.,4000.,3)
```

Figure 14-27 Preprocessor directives for Example 14-2.

The coding to add discrete events to the continuous model requires: 1) changing the preprocessor directives as shown in Figure 14-29 to define new variables; 2) writing function INTLC to define vacation, new car and inflation events and to schedule them to occur for the first time, and 3) writing function EVENT as shown in Figure 14-30. In function EVENT, events are used to reduce the retirement account in accordance with taking a vacation, buying a new car, changing the value of the inflation factor yearly and ending mortgage payments when the mortgage is paid off. (Not employed in the three scenarios.) In function

EVENT, the inflation factor is multiplied by the inflation multiplier to get a new inflation factor which is then applied in function STATE to increase both the variable funds coming in and the miscellaneous expenses which are dependent on the current inflation period. The embellished version of function STATE is shown in Figure 14-31.

```
void SWFUNC STATE()
{
 double RETIREMENT_INTEREST;
 double FUNDS_COMING_IN;
 double EXPENSES;
/*
 *****INCOME************
 */

       MONTHLY_INTEREST_RATE=RNORM(.005,.0005,1);
       RETIREMENT_INTEREST=RETIREMENT_ACCOUNT*
                                    MONTHLY_INTEREST_RATE;
       FUNDS_COMING_IN=2000.+ EXPON(200.,1);
/*
 *****EXPENSES*************************************
 */
       EXPENSES=MISC_EXPENSES+MORTGAGE_PAYMENT;
 /*
 *****ACCOUNT LEVEL EQUATION****************************
 */
       RETIREMENT_ACCOUNT=RETIREMENT_ACCOUNT+DTNOW*
            ((FUNDS_COMING_IN+RETIREMENT_INTEREST)-EXPENSES);
}
```

Figure 14-28 Coding for function STATE for Example 14-2.

```
#define RETIREMENT_ACCOUNT SS[1]
#define MONTHLY_INTEREST_RATE XX[1]
#define MORTGAGE_PAYMENT XX[2]
#define PAYMENTS_LEFT XX[3]
#define MISC_EXPENSES UNFRM(3000.,4000.,3)
#define INFLATION_FACTOR XX[4]
#define INFLATION_MULTIPLIER 1.03
```

Figure 14-29 Changing preprocessor directives to add new variables.

The control statements for the retirement model are shown in Figure 14-32. EQUIVALENCE statements are used to prescribe names for the RECORD, TIMST and INTLC statements. The INITIALIZE statement specifies that the retirement model be run for 360 months.

```
void SWFUNC EVENT(int iCode, ENTITY * Current)
{
switch (iCode)
  {
   case 1:
   /* Event Type 1: Mortgage paid off
   */
     MORTGAGE_PAYMENT = 0.;
     break;
   case 2:
   /* Event Type 2:  Vacation
     Spend about $2000 and schedule one for next year
   */
      RETIREMENT_ACCOUNT= RETIREMENT_ACCOUNT - RNORM(2000.,100.,2);
      SCHDL (2, Current, 12.);
      break;
   case 3:
  /*  Event Type 3: New Car
     Spend about $20000, schedule another one after 5 years
   */
      RETIREMENT_ACCOUNT RETIREMENT_ACCOUNT - RNORM(20000.,1000.,2);
      SCHDL (3, Current, 60.);
      break;
   case 4:
  /*   Event Type 4: Annual adjustment for inflation
  */
      INFLATION_FACTOR=INFLATION_FACTOR*INFLATION_MULTIPLIER;
      SCHDL (4, Current, 12.);
      break;
   case 10:
   /* State Event: No more money
   */
      MSTOP = -1;
      break;
   default:
      su_error (1, "Unknown event code.");
   }
}
```

Figure 14-30 Function EVENT for Example 14-2.

To facilitate the changing of parameters of the retirement model, a Visual
Basic user interface as shown in Figure 14-33 is included as part of this AweSim
project. This interface allows values to be inserted into text boxes. A simulate
button is available to initiate the running of the simulation program. The building
of the Visual Basic interface is shown in Figure 14-34 and involves standard
Visual Basic techniques associated with text boxes and text commands. The
translation of the values from the text boxes to Visual SLAM is achieved by
placing the user prescribed values into a file and reading them in function INTLC
as shown in Figure 14-35.

```
void SWFUNC STATE()
{
 double RETIREMENT_INTEREST;
 double FUNDS_COMING_IN;
 double EXPENSES;
/*
 *****INCOME*************/

      MONTHLY_INTEREST_RATE=RNORM(.005,.0005,1);
      RETIREMENT_INTEREST=RETIREMENT_ACCOUNT*
                                    MONTHLY_INTEREST_RATE;
      FUNDS_COMING_IN=2000.+ EXPON(200.,1)*INFLATION_FACTOR;

/*
 *****EXPENSES************************************** */

      EXPENSES=MISC_EXPENSES*INFLATION_FACTOR+MORTGAGE_PAYMENT;
  /*
  *****ACCOUNT LEVEL EQUATION*****************************/
      RETIREMENT_ACCOUNT=RETIREMENT_ACCOUNT+DTNOW*
          ((FUNDS_COMING_IN+RETIREMENT_INTEREST)-EXPENSES);
}
```

Figure 14-31 Embellished version of function STATE.

```
GEN,"PARKER","RETIREMENT",7/4/1996,1,Y,Y;
LIMITS,500,-1,-1,1,-1,-1;
CONTINUOUS,,1,1,1,1;
EQUIVALENCE,{{RETIREMENT_ACCOUNT,SS[1]},
            {MONTHLY_INTEREST_RATE,XX[1]}};
EQUIVALENCE,{{MORTGAGE_PAYMENT,XX[2]},{PAYMENTS_LEFT,XX[3]}};
EQUIVALENCE,{{INFLATION_FACTOR,XX[4]}};
RECORD,,out.raw,TNOW,"TIME",{AWESIM,EXCEL},,0,360,1,
                {{RETIREMENT_ACCOUNT,"RETIREMENT $", }};
INTLC,{{RETIREMENT_ACCOUNT,500000.},
      {MONTHLY_INTEREST_RATE,.005}};
INTLC,{{MORTGAGE_PAYMENT,1500.},{PAYMENTS_LEFT,360}};
INTLC,{{INFLATION_FACTOR,1}};
SEVNT,10,SS[1],NEGATIVE,0,100;
INITIALIZE,,360,Y;
FIN;
```

Figure 14-32 The control statements for Example 14-2.

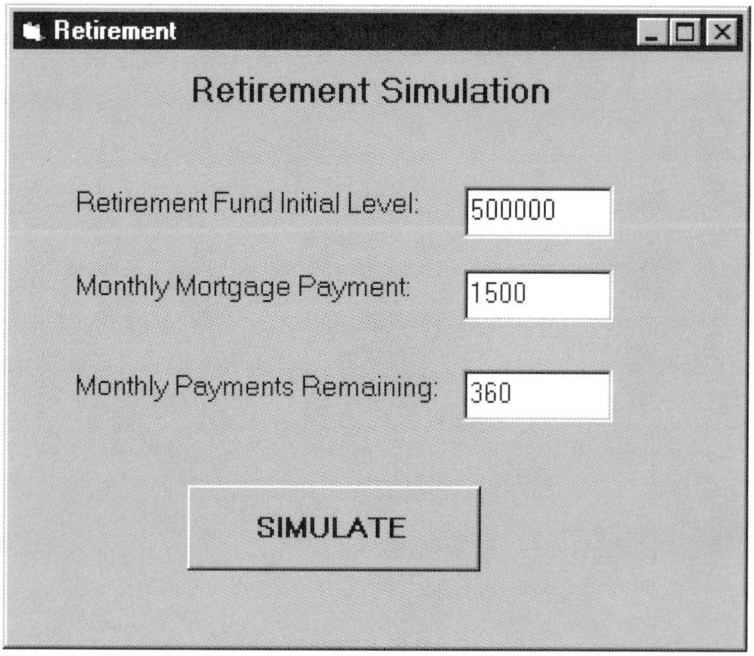

Figure 14-33 Visual Basic user interface for Example 14-2.

Summary of Results. The main question posed by retirees is how long a retirement account is able to provide funds. Figure 14-36 shows the decrease in the retirement account for the three scenarios: BASECASE, EVENTS and INFLATED. For BASECASE, the retirement account is sufficient to support the retirees over a 360 month period and still have approximately $200,000 remaining in the account. When vacations and new cars are added in scenario EVENTS, the retirement account is depleted after 305 months. With a 3% inflation factor, the retirement account in scenario INFLATED is depleted after 204 months. Each of the plots shown in Figure 14-36 is for a single run. Multiple runs should be made in order to provide an expected number of months at which the retirement account is depleted. Figure 14-36 was prepared by placing the values obtained from the RECORD statement that are stored in the AweSim database into Excel and using Excel's charting capability to prepare the graphic. Figure 14-37 is an AweSim bar chart showing the number of months for which the retirement account has a positive value for the 3 scenarios.

```
Attribute VB_Name = "frm_retire"
Attribute VB_Creatable = False
Attribute VB_Exposed = False
Option Explicit

Private Sub cmd_sim_Click()
    Dim retval As Long
    Dim simroot As String

    simroot = Environ("AWESIM")

    Open "retire.dat" For Output As #1            'Open File.
    Print #1, txt_init.Text                  'Write initial level.
    Print #1, txt_monthly.Text               'write monthly payment
    Print #1, txt_numrem.Text         'write number of payments remaining
    Close #1
    retval = Shell(simroot + "\bin\execute retire", 1)        'start
simulation on scenario retire
  End Sub


  Private Sub Command1_Click()
    End
  End Sub


  Private Sub Form_Load()
    Dim init As Single
    Dim monthly As Single
    Dim num As Integer

    ' read in initial values
    Open "retire.dat" For Input As #1
    Input #1, init
    Input #1, monthly
    Input #1, num
    Close #1

    txt_init.Text = init
    txt_monthly.Text = monthly
    txt_numrem.Text = num
  End Sub
```

Figure 14-34 Building of a Visual Basic user interface for Example 14-2.

```
BOOL SWFUNC INTLC(UINT uiRun)
{
/* Schedule first vacation after one year, first
   new car after five years*/

ENTITY* PaidOff,*Vacation,*NewCar,*Inflation;
FILE* fp

PaidOff = su_entnew(0,NULL,NULL,NULL);
Vacation = su_entnew(0,NULL,NULL,NULL);
NewCar = su_entnew(0,NULL,NULL,NULL);
Inflation = su_entnew(0,NULL,NULL,NULL);

SCHDL(1,PaidOff,PAYMENTS_LEFT);
SCHDL(2,Vacation,12.);
SCHDL(3,NewCar,60.);
SCHDL(4,Inflation,12.);
su_colnew(1, "PAYOUT PERIOD",0,0.0,0.0);

/*  Read input data file */
if ((fp = fopen("RETIRE.DAT","r"))==NULL)   {
   SU_OUT(TRUE,TRUE,"Error opening file RETIRE.DAT.");
   exit(1);
}
fscanf(fp,"%lf",&SS[1]);
fscanf(fp,"%lf",&XX[2]);
fscanf(fp,"%lf",&XX[3]);
fclose(fp);
return TRUE;
}
```

Figure 14-35 Function INTLC for Example 14-2.

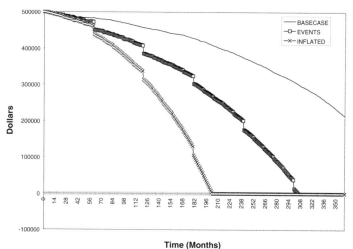

Figure 14-36 Decrease in retirement account for three scenarios

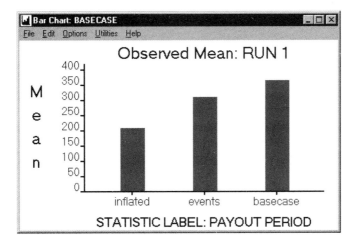

Figure 14-37   AweSim bar chart for Example 14-2.

14.18 CHAPTER SUMMARY

A simulation support system provides tools for performing simulation projects. The tools relate to the management of data and models and their use in making decisions. For management to accept the outputs of a simulation project, the models developed on a project must augment the managers understanding of the problem situation. A simulation support system provides a mechanism through which a decision maker can gain knowledge of the definition of an alternative and how its selection may affect performance in a changing environment. This chapter describes how AweSim provides support for the many tasks on a simulation project and demonstrates how it is used in the modeling and simulation process described in Chapter 3. Examples of the use of AweSim with Visual SLAM models for health care policy selection and financial planning are presented.

14.19 EXERCISES

14-1.   Develop an explanatory model that defines the functions of a simulation support system and how they relate to one another. For each function define its inputs, outputs, resources, and controls.

14-2.   Define each of the data elements discussed in this chapter and build an information model that characterizes the relations between the data elements.

14-3.   Discuss the hypothesis that it is easier to support the analysis and reporting tasks than the modeling tasks in a simulation project.

4-4.   Develop a set of concepts that could display the movement of entities on a Visual SLAM network.

14-5.   Prepare a detailed specification for a simulation support system.

14-6.   Decision support systems categorize decisions as structural, semistructural and unstructured. Decisions are also described in terms of an organizational level as being part of: strategic planning, management control and operational control. Discuss how simulation can support decisions in these categories and assess the need for having a simulation support system according to the category of the decision.

14-7.   Explore the Awesim database and the Visual SLAM Summary Report and prepare tables in the form of Table 14-4 which describe the following: <scenario>\file; <scenario>\resource; and <scenario>\colstat.

14-8.   Develop a Visual Basic template to retrieve data from the AweSim database.

14-9.   Embellish the model of organ transplantation, Example 14-1, for the following conditions: a) make the transition times from status to status dependent on the length of stay in a status. b) change the policy to allocate livers to the patient that has waited the longest. c) change the policy to allocate livers to the patient who is closest to the donor hospital with ties broken by longest waiting time first.

14-10.   Develop an AweSim interface for job shop scheduling problems for the Visual SLAM model presented in Example 7-2.

14-11.   Perform a sensitivity analysis for the Retirement Planning model, Example 14-2, for the following parameters: a) initial retirement account value; b) the inflation rate; c) the interest rate; d) the distribution of variable expenses.

14.20 REFERENCES

1.   Kuhl, M. E., J. R. Wilson and M. A. Johnson, "Estimation and Simulation of Nonhomogeneous Poisson Processes Having Multiple Periodicities," *Proceedings, Winter Simulation Conference,* 1995, pp. 374-383.

2   Parker, S. R., "Military Force Structure and Realignment through Dynamic Simulation," Unpublished Ph.D. Thesis, Purdue University, 1994.

3. Pritsker Corporation, *AweSim Total Simulation Project Support User's Guide*, July 1996.
4. Pritsker, A. A. B. et al, "Organ Transplantation Policy Evaluation", *Pro-ceedings, 1995 Winter Simulation Conference*, pp. 1314-1323.
5. Pritsker, A. A. B., O. P. Daily and K. D. Pritsker, "Using Simulation to Craft a National Organ Transplantation Policy," *Proceedings, 1996 Winter Simulation Conference*.
6. Pritsker, A. A. B., *Introduction to Simulation and SLAM II*, Fourth Edition, Systems Publishing and John Wiley, 1994.
7. Schruben, L., *SIGMA: A Graphical Simulation System*, boyd & fraser, 1991.
8. Standridge, C.R., "Performing Simulation Projects with The Extended Simulation System (TESS)", *Simulation*, December 1985, pp. 283-291.
9. Standridge, C. R. and A. A. B. Pritsker, *TESS: The Extended Simulation Support System*, Halsted Press (John Wiley), 1987.
10. Wagner, M. A. F. and J. R. Wilson, "Graphical Interactive Simulation Input Modeling with Bezier Distributions," *ACM Transactions on Modeling and Computer Simulation*, V. 5, 1995, pp. 163-184.
11. Wilson, J. R. and M. E. Kuhl, *User's Guide for ULAMFIT: Estimation Program for ULAM Arrival Processes*, Pritsker Corporation, 1995.
12. Witte, T., T. Claus and K. Helling, *Simulation von Produktionssystemen mit SLAM*, Addison-Wesley, 1994.
13. Yancey, D.P., C.N. Busch and J.P. Whitford, *IDSS Build 1, Final Technical Report*, Volume 1, Pritsker & Associates, Inc. and WPAFB Materials Laboratory, 1984.
14. Zeigler, B.P., *Theory of Modelling and Simulation*, John Wiley, 1976.
15. Zeigler, B.P., *Multifacetted Modelling and Discrete Event Simulation*, Academic Press, 1984.

CHAPTER 15

Applications of Simulation

15.1   INTRODUCTION

Simulation has been used to study such wide ranging topics as urban systems, economic systems, business systems, production systems, biological systems, social systems, transportation systems, health care delivery systems, and many more. Table 15-1 presents areas in which simulation methods are currently being used. Simulation is one of the most widely-used industrial engineering, management science and operations research techniques employed by industry and government.

Table 15-1 Modeling and simulation application areas.

Type of System	Design, Planning and Operational Issues
Manufacturing Systems	Plant design and layout
	Continuous improvement
	Capacity management
	Agile manufacturing evaluation
	Scheduling and control
	Materials handling
Transportation Systems	Railroad system performance
	Truck scheduling and routing
	Air traffic control
	Terminal and depot operations
Computer and Communication Systems	Performance evaluation
	Workflow generation and analysis
	Reliability assessment
Project Planning and Control	Product planning
	Marketing analysis
	Research and development performance
	Construction activity planning
	Scheduling project activities
Financial Planning	Capital investment decision-making
	Cash flow analysis
	Risk assessment
	Balance sheet projections
Environmental and Ecological Studies	Flood control
	Pollution control
	Energy flows and utilization
	Farm management
	Pest control
	Reactor maintainability
Health Care Systems	Supply management
	Operating room scheduling
	Manpower planning
	Organ transplantation policy evaluation

The continuing development of simulation languages has been an important factor in this growth. Another major factor is the flexibility of simulation modeling when compared, for example, to the structural restrictions imposed by a mathematical programming formulation of a problem. Even when an analytic model can be applied to a problem, simulation is frequently used to study the practical implications of the assumptions underlying the analytic model. In this chapter, general simulation application areas are described and capsule summaries of specific simulation projects performed at Pritsker Corporation or its clients are given. The summaries demonstrate that simulation is a value-added technique. They also provide a discussion of problem types for which simulation has been used in actual decision-making situations, and the types of questions that have been answered by using simulation. The procedures employed in building the specific simulation models described are contained in the referenced papers.

This text provides procedures for developing models. The design of models for industrial use involves representing a system using extensive insight and logical thinking. Such system models are larger in size, but conceptually not more complex, than those that are presented in this book. A significant point when developing a simulation model is the understanding that there are alternative approaches to building a model. Thus, as the examples illustrate, it is not necessary to conform to any fixed set of rules when modeling. Using new and novel approaches is encouraged. Remember, it is easy to add to a simulation model or to use a first pass model to set the specifications for a second pass model. Do not hesitate to design when modeling and to make modeling an essential part of design and analysis. In all cases, it is necessary to establish both a purpose for modeling and the measures that evaluate performance.

15.2 PERFORMANCE MEASURES

The performance of a system is measured by its effectiveness and efficiency in achieving system objectives. The objectives of different types of systems vary and performance measures across areas of simulation applications are not the same. The applications presented in this chapter provide information on the benefits obtained from modeling and simulation. To provide general information on the inputs to the computation of benefits, we present a discussion of performance measures for manufacturing systems. A taxonomy of performance measures for different classes of systems would be a research contribution to the fields of engineering and management.

15.2.1 Performance Measures for Manufacturing Systems

In many situations, objectives are established in terms of a level of cost effectiveness or system profitability. Inputs to such measures of performance are: price and cost values; and measures of the operations of a system. The calculation of a system performance measure involves the combining of these two types of inputs. We will focus on measures of operational performance since simulation is more commonly used to estimate such values. Once obtained, they can be combined with the dollar values and used to estimate monetary performance.

For manufacturing systems, measures of operational performance can be grouped in to four categories:

1. Measures of throughput
2. Measures of ability to meet deadlines
3. Measures of resource utilization
4. Measures of in-process inventory

Throughput is the output produced in a given period of time. Another name for this measure is the production rate. *System capacity* is often defined as the maximum throughput that can be obtained.

The ability to meet deadlines is measured by product lateness, tardiness, or flowtime. Lateness is the time between when a job is completed and when it was due to be completed. Tardiness is the lateness of a job only if it fails to meet its due date; otherwise, it is zero. Flowtime is the amount of time a job spends in the system. In some cases, the total time it takes to complete all jobs is of importance. This time is referred to as the makespan. These measures are indications of the effectiveness and efficiency of the system in satisfying customer orders.

System resources include personnel, materials, machines, and work space. The utilization of these resources, as measured by the fraction of time they are productive, is another measure of system effectiveness. Measures of resource utilization relate the degree to which a system is operating at capacity.

The final category of manufacturing performance measures is concerned with the buildup of raw materials and unfinished parts during production. This buildup, called in-process inventory or work in process (WIP), is usually due to parts waiting for available resources. Since inventory requires storage space, often a critical resource in itself, and also ties up capital, in-process inventory requirements are of great importance in manufacturing operations assessment.

The measures outlined above provide the basis for evaluating diverse objectives. By concentrating on measures of operational performance, we bypass the question of identifying the objectives of system planning, which by necessity are situation dependent. However in many situations objectives are satisfied when performance measures reach prescribed levels.

15.3   CAPITAL EXPENDITURE EVALUATION IN THE STEEL INDUSTRY

Bethlehem Steel Corporation was considering a design for new facilities for improving the steel-making process. Included in the design were new operations involving the melting of scrap and the desulfurization of hot metal. The analysis was to determine the need for additional hot metal carriers, called submarines, to support the proposed new operations. (4,11)

A discrete event simulation model was developed consistent with the objectives of evaluating a proposed capital expenditure and involved modeling the various operations associated with delivering hot metal from a set of blast furnaces (BF) to a set of basic oxygen furnaces (BOF). A schematic diagram of the operations model is shown in Figure 15-1. The submarines serve as materials handling equipment which transport the hot metal through a series of operations before returning to perform the set of tasks again. The demand for hot metal carriers depends on the casting times of the blast furnaces and the new scrap melter. Casting times are scheduled but actual performance times depend on the hot metal characteristics. Not having submarines available when a cast is ready is a dangerous and expensive situation and could cause a furnace to be shut down.

Scheduling rules were incorporated for routing the submarines through the desulfurization operation, if necessary, and to hot metal ladles which provided inputs to the basic oxygen furnaces. Submarines were also required to transfer hot metal from the scrap melter. A decision rule was also incorporated into the model for determining if an insufficient number of submarines would be available to accommodate the next cast from a blast furnace. When this situation occurs, a submarine dumps its hot metal and returns immediately to serve a blast furnace.

The simulation model showed, in contrast to earlier studies recommending the purchase of three submarines, that by altering the scheduling rules, the current number of submarines could support the new operations. Thus, the simulation analysis resulted in a recommendation which led to an avoidance of a capital expenditure of over one million dollars. In addition, procedures were suggested by which further improvements in the total steelmaking process could be made.

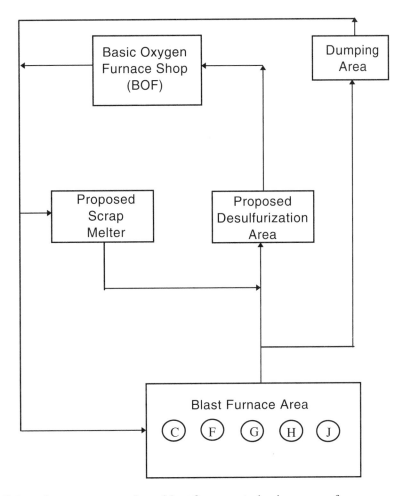

Figure 15-1 Submarine movements from blast furnaces to basic oxygen furnace.

15.7 DESIGN OF A CORN SYRUP REFINERY

A.E. Staley Manufacturing Company built an $85 million corn wetmilling plant in Lafayette, Indiana. The plant was engineered with a flexible end-product mix capability which would permit Staley to respond to changes in the demand for various types of corn sweeteners. Prior to building the plant, a proposed design was developed that is depicted in Figure 15-2. As can be seen from the figure, the process involves two evaporation steps, one carbon refining step, and one ion exchanger step. Also shown are the required material flows from step to step. Water is used extensively in the process. Since it is recycled and contains sweeteners, it is referred to as sweetwater. In addition, storage tanks are required for maintaining balanced operations through the process. A combined discrete event-continuous model of the system was built to determine the size of the storage tanks, evaporators, and ion exchanger (24, 25).

The model was exercised and the most cost effective size of the various units was determined. Since large, special purpose equipment is involved, a lead time of over eighteen months is typical, and simulation was the only feasible way to evaluate the proposed design. In addition to the sizing study, system parameters were investigated for both a manual and a computerized control system. One control system model included the setting of valves to regulate sweetwater-source flows from different tanks, each having a different concentration level. It was presumed that the concentration level in each sweetwater tank could be assessed hourly. With knowledge of the concentration levels, a linear programming blending model was developed and imbedded in the simulation to set valves in order to maximize the profitability associated with the end-product (the end-product is a function of the component saccharide distributions which can change as a function of the concentration in the sweetwater tanks and the process control parameters). Thus, after using the simulation to finalize the design of the plant, it was used to identify the most economical control strategy compatible with production quality and volume requirements. These results were incorporated into the refinery's operating process control procedures.

15.5 RISK ANALYSIS OF PIPELINE CONSTRUCTION

The construction of a pipeline basically involves: 1) preparing a site for laying pipe, 2) laying the pipe, and 3) welding sections of the pipe together. Supporting operations for pipeline construction involve the building, dismantling, and moving of campsites; the construction of roads and other transportation facilities; and relandscaping the site. When pipeline construction is performed in Alaska, the adverse weather conditions must be considered when planning the construction project. A network model was developed consisting of the pipeline construction activities, and transportation facility development activities (9, 20).

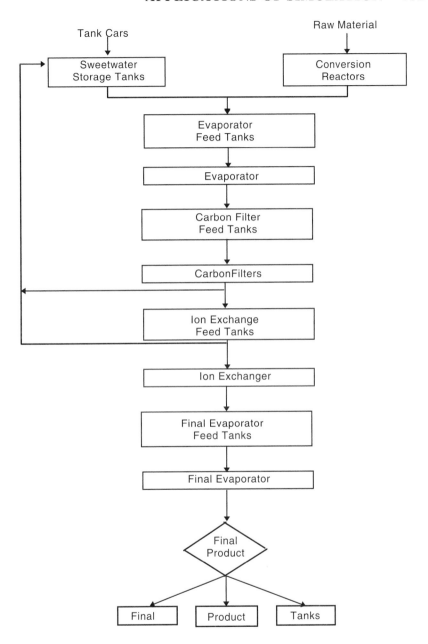

Figure 15-2 Proposed block diagram design of a corn syrup refinery.

The effects of weather conditions on construction activities were also included in the model. A risk analysis was performed to determine the probability of completing pipeline construction by specified due dates. A cost analysis was also performed to determine potential overrun conditions. The analysis indicated that both time and cost overruns could be expected. The effects of changing the activity schedule and construction rates were also evaluated.

15.6   EVALUATING SECURITY FORCES AT A SPORTING EVENT

In conjunction with the Los Angeles Sheriff's Department, a model was developed to determine the number and location of security forces necessary to respond to disturbances that might occur at the Rose Bowl (8). The model portrayed disturbances such as fights, fires and terrorism as discrete events requiring the services of security forces. Detailed graphics were developed to display the location and routing of the security forces and how they respond to the disturbances. Local law enforcement personnel assisted in developing the algorithms for establishing staff levels and the routing of the security forces. The algorithms were developed on an iterative basis with the modeler and personnel from the Sheriff's Department assessing different strategies. The benefits of the project included a 25 percent reduction in the required security forces at the Rose Bowl and an understanding of the policies and procedures employed in protecting and controlling a large crowd. Simulation analysis of this type have been performed for evaluating disaster response plans. An animation facility diagram of a football stadium with medical and police personnel positioned to respond to periodic and random events is shown in Figure 15-3.

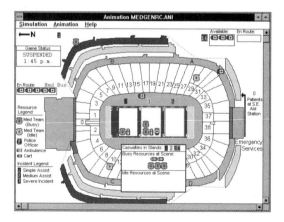

Figure 15-3 AweSim animation for displaying security response actions.

15.7   EVALUATION OF THE MANUFACTURE OF A ROCKET SYSTEM

Vought Corporation of Grand Prairie, Texas, developed a plan to manufacture the Multiple Launch Rocket System (MLRS) for the U.S. Army (19). The MLRS weapon was used extensively in Desert Storm engagements. The MLRS vehicle is comprised of a tracked vehicle (similar to a personnel carrier) carrying a launch pod container holding six rockets. Vought's manufacturing operations would be located in two buildings, the metal parts building and the load, assembly, and pack building. A schematic diagram of the facility is shown in Figure 15-4. Operations performed in the Metal Parts Building include the fabrication of the necessary detail parts, assembly of the launch pod container, and production of the motor case. Operations performed in the load, assembly and pack building include loading the warhead with grenades, joining the warhead and motor case, and loading each container with six rockets.

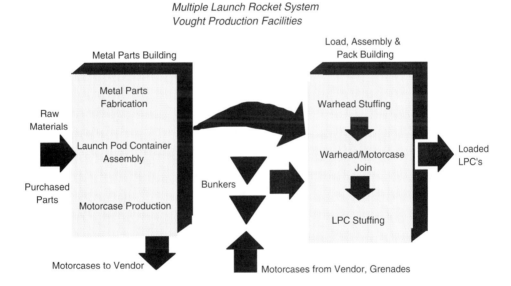

Figure 15-4 Schematic diagram of multiple launch rocket system manufacturing process.

The tasks performed on the project included:

- Verify the production rates of both buildings.
- Size storage space requirements for key buffer areas.
- Gather statistics on labor and machine utilization.
- Determine production "dry-up" time for key pieces of equipment.
- Develop a graphic output format to communicate the capabilities of the model to Army and management personnel.
- Provide the capability for follow-up analysis by Vought personnel.

The model of the load, assembly, and pack building identified a potential bottleneck and was used to verify the redesign of the buffer causing the problem.

The models of the two buildings validated production capabilities for a normal rate of production (two eight-hour shifts a day) and surge production rates (two ten-hour and three eight-hour shifts a day). Vought Corporation was awarded the contract by the Army to produce the rocket system. The computer modeling analysis was cited by the Army as a determinant in awarding the contract to Vought.

15.8 WORK FLOW ANALYSIS IN AN INSURANCE COMPANY

The work flow system of a regional service office involves the processing of property and casualty insurance claims through a centralized computer information system (14, 20). The various types of forms are routed through fourteen distinct operating units or departments within the regional service office which employs over 150 personnel. The system was modeled as a complex queueing situation to identify the bottlenecks of the work flow and to assist in investigating the effects of certain managerial decisions. A network model aided in estimating the consequences of specific actions contemplated or anticipated by management. The procedural changes investigated were:

1. Changes in the volume of each type of work handled by the regional service office;
2. Changes in the composition and requirements of the work input;
3. Changes in priority rules for the processing of work in the same operating unit;
4. Changes in the pathways of the work flow system;
5. Reallocation of personnel among the different departments; and
6. Changes in total processing times of customer requests due to training programs in specific areas.

This is an example of how simulation is used to perform business process reengineering (BPR).

15.9   PUBLIC HEALTH POLICY SELECTION

The United Network for Organ Sharing (UNOS) was formed in 1984 as a nationwide system to match human organs to potential transplant patients. UNOS operates the national system for data collection on patients and organs and establishes U.S. organ allocation policies. Organs for transplantation are a scarce resource. How to allocate such a scarce and valuable resource is very complex. Issues revolve around what is an equitable, efficient and effective means of organ distribution with the tradeoffs being between utility and equity. UNOS continuously searches for policies that balance all aspects of this complex situation.

Since an organ allocation policy is a procedure that lists all potential recipients to receive the organ, issues arise relating to the medical status, personal characteristics (blood type, for example), time a patient has been waiting and the location of the patient relative to the location of the organ donor. The issues have medical, patient and system consequences with respect to utility and equity. Pritsker Corporation and UNOS have created a model named ULAM for UNOS Liver Allocation Model which includes many component modules for simulating patient and donor arrivals, matching and ranking patients, and predicting the future status of patients (21). The modeling and simulation techniques used in building ULAM include: fitting arrival processes having trend and seasonal components using nonhomogeneous Poisson processes having exponential rate functions; fitting distributions to transition time data; application of variance reduction techniques using common streams and prior information; organizing data structures for efficient searching and ranking capabilities; using boot-strapping techniques for attribute sampling; and building submodels employing biostatistical procedures such as Kaplan-Meier and logistic regression. The characterization of performance measures within a complex political, economic and social environment was a major challenge (22). A sample of the types of outputs produced by ULAM are: percentage of patients surviving transplantation; number of pre-and post-transplant deaths; number of patient-years in each medi-cal status; distance organs travel for transplantation; and waiting time by patient and regional characteristics.

After assessing over 80 proposed policies, UNOS through its committees and Board of Directors were able to select a new policy for liver allocations.

15.10   EVALUATION OF AIR TERMINAL CARGO FACILITIES

Managers of the military airlift system need a way of measuring the productive capacity of aerial port cargo processing. Specifically, the managers need to determine the effects of fluctuating demands for airlift cargo on a terminal's ability to meet the demand in a timely manner. Resource utilization is also an important factor.

At a terminal, cargo arrives by truck or by aircraft. The arriving cargo is off loaded and sorted by shipment type, destination, and priority. The sorted cargo is moved to various in-process storage areas where it is held until some form of consolidation is possible. Once consolidated, it is weighed, inspected, and stored. Its status can then be classified as "movement-ready." When movement-ready cargo is selected for a mission, it is transferred to a staging area where it is combined with the other cargo assigned to the mission and defined as a load. The load is then processed by cargo loading equipment, K-loaders, and transferred to the aircraft. A schematic diagram of an air terminal is shown in Figure 15-5. A network model of this situation was constructed to answer the following procedural questions (1, 5, 6):

1. Is it worthwhile to introduce automation equipment in ports to improve processing capacity?
2. Where should new equipment be located?
3. How many aircraft can a port load simultaneously?
4. During contingencies, what additional resources will be required to support an increase in the level of air traffic?

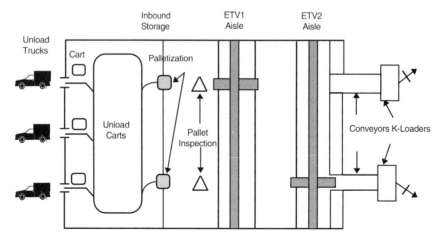

Figure 15-5 Schematic diagram of air terminal.

15.11 DESIGN OF REFINERY OFFSITE SYSTEMS

A simulation program was developed during the initial planning of a significant expansion and upgrading of the Raffinor Refinery at Mongstad in Norway (from 4.5 million tons per year to 6.5 million tons per year). The objective of the project was to design a system of lines, pumps, blenders, component tanks, product tanks and jetties which minimizes the total operating cost for the expected refinery production and shipping pattern. A schematic diagram and an aggregate block diagram of the offsite facility are shown in Figure 15-6. The refinery produces a flow of components which are stored in tanks. With a modern refinery, upgrading processes are employed to generate a large number of blending components that provide a number of different products. For example, the expansion at Raffinor involved over 60 component streams to produce as many as 40 different products. The products were loaded over seven berths to approximately 2000 ships annually.

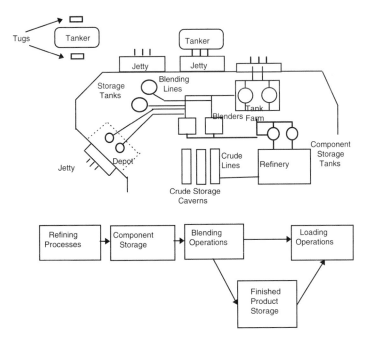

Figure 15-6 Descriptive diagram of a refinery offsite facility.

The project was a large effort and the simulation model was only a part of a total program. The various components of the program are listed below (12). Note that items 5 and 6 below use operational performance measures to calculate management performance measures.

1. Refinery and petro-chemical planning system including a generalized refinery linear programming package.
2. Refinery operating plan preprocessor to develop production schedules.
3. Marine operating plan preprocessor which is a combined distribution linear program with embedded heuristic logic.
4. Refinery offsites operations simulator includes a network model to portray the arrival of ships and the effects of weather. The flow of components in the system is modeled using continuous concepts. The setting and the termination of product blending, shiploading and offloading are modeled as discrete events.
5. Facilities investment cost estimator for the overall determination of the investment cost of the facility.
6. Refinery offsite profitability analysis to perform the profitability analysis including the costs of investment, demurrage, and capital.

The simulation program has been used for the analysis of a number of different offsite systems with the main objectives to size tankage to decide the number of jetties required, and to evaluate the consequences of bad weather on the performance of different fleets. The proper operation of the model was determined through comparison with existing data. Program results and operating statistics comparisons showed that the program accurately represented the operation of the offsite system (13).

15.12 INJECTION BODY FMS DESIGN EVALUATION

A manufacturer of castings desired to evaluate alternative milling machine center configurations to achieve a production goal of 157,000 finished castings per year. A flexible manufacturing system (FMS) was designed to perform machining operations on the castings and is shown in Figure 15-7. Castings are initially loaded onto pallets which can carry 16 parts each and sent to one of two lathes on a conveyor. Upon completion of the turning operation, the parts are transported, again by conveyor, to a wash/load area before being sent to the machining center on a wire-guided vehicle. (18, 26)

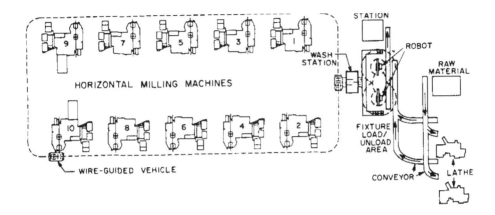

Figure 15-7 A flexible milling machine system.

The machining center consists of ten identical horizontal milling machines which can perform any one of three operations. The three operations are referred to as OP10, OP20, and OP30. For a particular part type, the milling machines are set up to be either dedicated to performing one operation or flexible so that any of the three operations can be performed.

Two types of fixtures, A and B, are used in this system. Fixture A is used for OP10 and Fixture B is used for OP20 and OP30.

Before a set of parts is routed for OP10 machining, each part in that set is attached to fixture A and sent through the wash station. When buffer space becomes available at one of the machines capable of performing OP10, this set of parts is transported to that machine's input buffer. After the parts have been machined, they are returned to the wash/load area. The parts are then attached to fixture B to await OP20. The same procedure is used for OP30 except that the parts are rotated 180 degrees on the same fixture. After all three machining operations have been completed, the parts are sent to final inspection before departing the system.

The objectives of the simulation study are to evaluate system balance and productivity, determine the need for additional equipment, determine which resources, if any, could be eliminated and to evaluate the number of dedicated versus flexible machines required. Tooling costs are much higher if a machine is used to perform all three operations.

With a configuration consisting of nine dedicated machines and one flexible machine, simulation results revealed that a wire-guided vehicle, four fixtures and several sets of tools could be eliminated while achieving the desired production goal of 157,000 finished castings per year.

An animation of a manufacturing system including the FMS described above is shown on page 715 The status of the machines is indicated by color changes.

15.13 PACKAGING AND MANUFACTURING ANIMATIONS

A general model (PACKAGING) has been developed of packaging lines consisting of high speed conveyor networks that bring products to machines with production rates in the thousands per minute (10). PACKAGING supports designers in controlling the flow and density of products by changing conveyor and machine speeds based on the status of system sensors. The animation on the bottom half of page 715 illustrates rates of product flow, the blocking and starving of machines, and the effectiveness of the control system.

Two additional animations of SLAM II models of FMS operations of Caterpillar and Mazak Corporation are shown on page 716. The top animation shows an FMS Yoke Cell where the effects of fixture assignments and operator availability impacted cell throughput. The animation on the bottom of the page shows an FMS coupled with a high rise storage for fixtures. The simulation model developed for Mazak is used to show how the response time for the part and fixture shuttle of Mazak machines can improve system performance.

15.14 SURGICAL SUITE PLANNING

The Surgical Suite Planning Model is a tool to evaluate surgical suite operations. Hospitals use it to improve the utilization of their facility and personnel and to become more responsive to patients and surgeons (16). The animations on pages 717 and 718 were used to help doctors and schedulers understand patient flow and resource schedules. A sequence of four snapshots shows the waiting room, gurneys with patients on them, personnel, and occupancy in 16 operating rooms and a post-operative recovery area.

The people represented by green icons are doctors, nurses are represented by white icons and anesthesiologists are represented by the red icons. At time 7:00 a.m. on Tuesday, the first snapshot shows two operations ongoing, two operating rooms being cleaned and two operating rooms attended to by nurses. At time 7:31 a.m. on Tuesday, a greater level of activity is seen with four operations in progress and two about to start. Six other operating rooms are being prepared and there has been an increase in the number of RNs on duty. In the snapshot at time 9:01 a.m., it is seen that there are ten operations in progress with one operation about to begin, one patient is waiting, and six patients are in post-operative recovery. In the fourth snapshot taken on Tuesday at 1:40 p.m., one operation is ongoing in operating room 2, one patient is waiting for an RN or a technician and one person is in post-operative recovery.

The SLAM II model for scheduling operating rooms included many complex logical features including block scheduling associated with specific physician specialties and constraints on the types of uses of operating rooms due to equipment and facility requirements. The primary performance measures included in the model are: room utilization; nurse, anesthesiologist and support utilization; time from room request until room scheduling; and the time from the scheduled start of service until actual start of service. The proper balancing of these measures will tend to maintain high utilization of costly resources and provide efficient service to patients and staff. High variability of patient volume, service times and case mix cause balancing difficulties. The model has been successfully used in different hospitals for the following purposes: to evaluate the impact of a changing case mix; to perform cost/service tradeoffs; to reduce the time from walk-in to room placement in emergency areas; to redesign and size a labor and delivery facility; and to analyze lease versus buy decisions for ventilators.

15.15   USES OF MODELS

Throughout this chapter, emphasis has been placed on the use of modeling and simulation to enhance performance or solve problems. The model-based problem solving process was presented in Chapter 2 as being driven by a system-specific purpose. The purpose for modeling can also be viewed at a functional level. The following list illustrates functional levels to which simulation modeling has been applied:

- as *explanatory devices* to understand a system or problem;
- as a *communication vehicle* to describe system operation;

- as an *analysis tool* to determine critical elements, components and issues and to estimate performance measures;

- as a *design assessor* to evaluate proposed solutions and to synthesize new alternative solutions;

- as a *scheduler* to develop on-line operational schedules for jobs, tasks and resources;

- as a *control mechanism* for the distribution and routing of materials and resources.

- as a *training tool* to assist operators in understanding system operations; and

- as a *part of the system* to provide on-line monitoring, status projections and decision support.

Since simulation modeling can be used at each of these levels and across a wide spectrum of systems, many types of outputs and analysis capabilities are associated with simulation models.

15.16   CHAPTER SUMMARY

In this chapter, the types of applications of simulation have been presented. Eleven situations in which simulation was useful in problem solving or performance enhancement are described. Different types of performance measures for each situation were presented. From the material presented, it can be seen that simulation is a practical tool of wide-spread use.

15.17   EXERCISES

15-1.   Select two of the applications presented in this chapter and describe the modeling approach that you would use in resolving the specified problem. Define the necessary entities, attributes, processes, activities and files that you would employ. List the variables on which you would collect statistical information.

15-2   Categorize the thirteen applications presented in this chapter by class of sponsor, simulation model type, and simulation modeling approach. Develop other categories for simulation models.

15-3.   Rank the thirteen applications given in this chapter according to difficulty of the modeling effort; difficulty of obtaining data for the model; difficulty in applying the results; and potential benefit from using the model.

15-4.   Develop specifications for a network simulation language which can be used to build simulation models to evaluate materials-handling equipment.

15-5.   Categorize the areas listed in Table 15-1 according to the courses you have taken during your academic studies.

15-6.   Develop a list of performance measures for the Department of Defense.

15.18   REFERENCES

1.   Auterio, V. J., "Q-GERT Simulation of Air Terminal Cargo Facilities," *Proceedings, Pittsburgh Modeling and Simulation Conference,* Vol. 5, 1974, pp. 1181-1186.

2.   Castillo, D. and J. K. Cockran, "A Microcomputer Approach for Simulating Truck Haulage Systems in Open Pit Mining," *Computers in Industry*, 1987, pp. 37-47.

3.   Clark, T.D. and C. Waring, "A Simulation Approach to Analyis of Emergency Services and Trauma Center Management", *Proceedings of the 1987 Winter Simulation Conference*, pp. 925-931.

4.   Cobb, A. E., and A. A. B. Pritsker, "Simulated Overview for an Itegrated Steelmaker, *Proceedings, AISE Hot End Scheduling and Simulation for Optimum Steel Production Conference*, 1996

5.   Duket, S. D.and C. R. Standridge, "Applications of Simulation: Combined Models," *Modeling, The Simulation Technical Committee Newsletter* (IEEE), No. 190, Dec. 1983.

6.   Duket, S. D. and D. B. Wortman, "Q-GERT Model of the Dover Air Force Base Port Cargo Facilities," MACRO Task Force, Military Airlift Command, Scott Air Force Base, Illinois, 1976.

7.   Dzakuma, J.M. and D.L. Harris, "Computer Modeling of Sheep Reproduction," *Journal of Animal Science*, 1989, No. 67, pp. 2197-2221.

8.   Erdbruegger, D. D., W. G. Parmelee, and D. W. Starks, "SLAM II Model of the Rose Bowl Staffing Plans," *Proceedings, Winter Simulation Conference*, 1982, pp. 127-135.

9.   Federal Power Commission Exhibit EP-237, "Risk Analysis of the Arctic Gas Pipeline Project Construction Schedule," Vol. 167, Federal Power Commission, 1976.

10.   Gittlitz, S., "A Case Study: Simulation of Packaging Line Control Logic," *Proceedings of the 1990 Winter Simulation Conference*, pp. 699-706.

11.   Hanna, J., P. Tanner, J. Barbus, "The Evolution (1981 - Present) of Process Simulation and Scheduling of Steelmaking at Burns Harbor," *Proceedings, AISE Hot End Scheduling and Simulation for Optimum Steel Production Conference*, 1996

12.   Kristiansen, T. K. and A. Landsnes, "Design of Refinery Offsite Systems by Simulation," *Proceedings, IMACS Conference*, Vol. 2, 1985, pp. 293-296.

13.   Kristiansen, T. K. and H.W. Poos, "Discrete Event Simulation of Refinery Offsite Systems," National Petroleum Refiners Association Computer Conference, 1990.

14.   Lawrence, K. D. and C. E. Sigal, " A Work Flow Simulation of a Regional Service Office of a Property and Casualty Insurance Company with Q-GERT," *Proceedings, Pittsburgh Modeling and Simulation Conference*, Vol. 5, 1974, pp. 1187-1192.

15.   Leemis, L., et.al., "Job Shop Configuration Optimization at Tinker Air Force Base," *Simulation*, June 1990, pp. 287-290.

16.   Lewellen, G. and J. Mishler, "Simulation Analysis of an Operating Room Scheduling System," Health Care Information and Management Systems Society Conference, October, 1989.

17.   McBeath, D.F. and W.S. Keezer, "Simulation in Support of Software Development," *Proceedings of the 1993 Winter Simulation Conference*,   pp. 1143-1151.

18.   Musselman, K. J., "Computer Simulation: A Design Tool for FMS," *Manufacturing Engineering,* Vol. 93, 1984, pp. 117-120.

19.   Pritsker, A. A. B., "Applications of SLAM," *IIE Transactions,* Vol. 14, 1982, pp. 70-77.

20.   Pritsker, A. A. B., "Applications of Simulation," in *Operational Research '84: Proceeding of IFORS*, J. B. Brans, Ed., Elsevier Science, 1984, pp. 908-920.

21.   Pritsker, A.A.B., et.al., "Organ Transplantation Policy Evaluation," *Proceedings of the 1995 Winter Simulation Conference*, pp. 1314-1323.

22.   Pritsker A. A. B., O. P. Daily and K. D. Pritsker, "Using Simulation to Craft a National Organ Transplantation Policy," *Proceedings of the 1996, Winter Simulation Conference.*

23.   Sarosky, T. and T. Wilcox "Simulation of a Railroad Intermodel Terminal," *Proceedings of the 1994 Winter Simulation Conference*, pp. 1233-1238.

24.   Schooley, R. V., "Simulation in the Design of a Corn Syrup Refinery," *Proceedings, Winter Simulation Conference*, 1975, pp. 197-204.

25.   Schuman, R. E., E. L. Janzen and W. H. Dempsey, "Applications of GASP IV Simulation," Presentation to ORSA/TIMS Combined Chicago Chapters, November 16, 1977.

26.   Wortman, D. B., and J. R. Wilson, "Optimizing a Manufacturing Plant by Computer Simulation," *Computer-Aided Engineering*, Vol. 3, 1984, pp. 48-54.

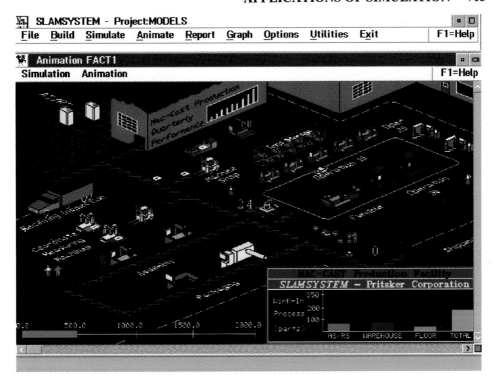

A manufacturing system animation.

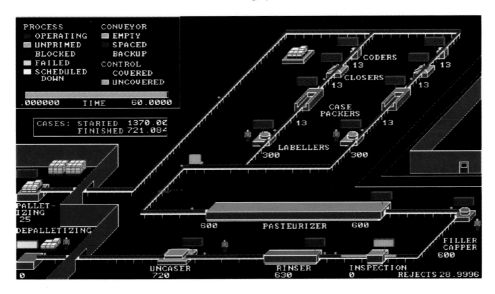

PACKAGING system animation illustration.

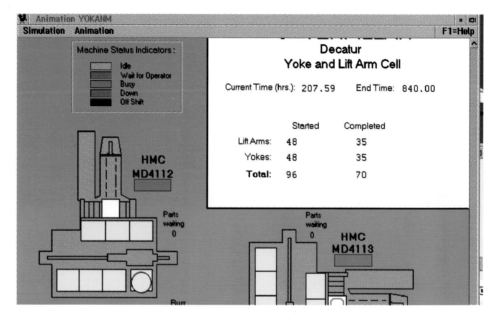

Animation of an FMS and high rise storage.

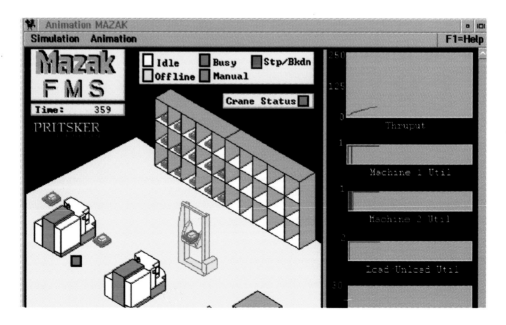

Animation of an FMS yoke cell.

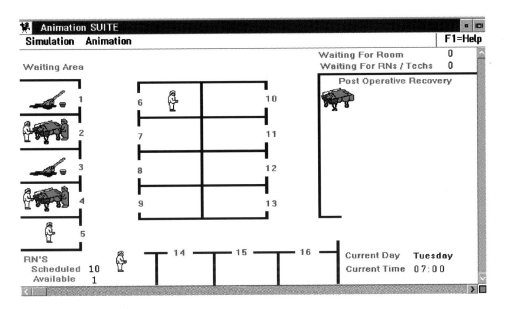

Snapshot of an operating room animation at 7:00 a.m.

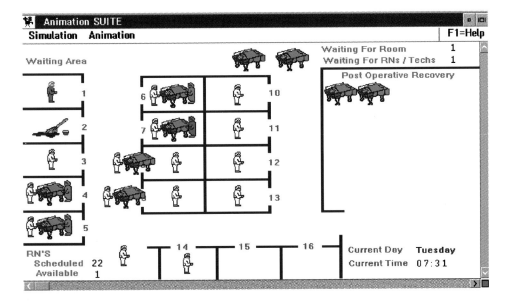

Snapshot of an operating room animation at 7:31 a.m.

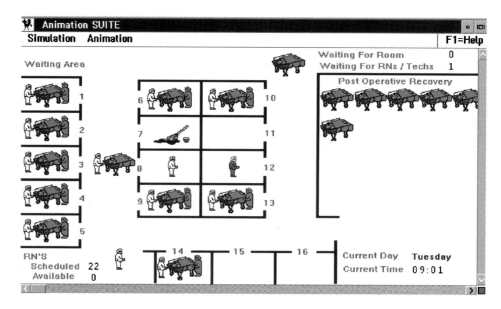

Snapshot of an operating room animation at 9:01 a.m.

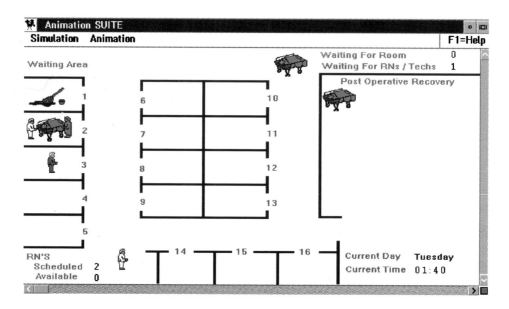

Snapshot of an operating room animation at 1:40 p.m.

Random Sampling from Distributions

16.1 INTRODUCTION

Throughout this text, we have dealt with models which contain variables that are characterized by distributions. In Chapter 1, we discussed data acquisition procedures. In Chapter 14, the storing of data in a database for analysis or for direct use in models is described. The increased use of data collection hardware on the manufacturing shop floor or in service establishments establishes new horizons for modelers and establishes a need for further research on data characterization.

A model that is developed for analysis by simulation can employ input data in different forms. The data need not be characterized by a distribution function. The data can be used directly which results in a trace-driven simulation. The data can be grouped, and samples can be obtained from the grouped data. Alternatively, the data can be fit by a theoretical distribution and random samples can be obtained by sampling from the distribution. This last topic is the central concern of this chapter.

First, a discussion is given of the most commonly used theoretical distributions including graphs of their density functions and a rationale for their use in models. The question of when to use a distribution to represent data is then posed. The remainder of the chapter discusses procedures for generating random numbers and random samples.

16.2 DISTRIBUTIONS

Distributions have underlying characteristics which make them appropriate to represent a random process or activity. We refer to a distribution that comes up repeatedly as a standard distribution. We describe these standard distributions in this section. For a more formal discussion and graphical description of distributions, the books "Statistical Methods in Engineering" by Hahn and Shapiro (14) and "Statistical Distributions" by Hastings and Peacock (15) are recommended.

Throughout the discussion, the following variable definitions will be used:

X = the random variable
$f(x)$ = the density function of X
$p(x)$ = probability mass function of X.
a = minimum;

b = maximum;

m = mode;

μ = mean = E [X]

σ^2 = Variance = E[(X-μ)^2]

σ = standard deviation

α = a parameter of the density function

β = a parameter of the density function

For the density functions with parameters not prescribed by the mean and standard deviation, we provide equations to relate the mean and standard deviation to the parameters.

16.2.1 Uniform Distribution

The uniform density function specifies that every value between a minimum and a maximum value is equally likely. The use of the uniform distribution often implies a complete lack of knowledge concerning the random variable other than that it is between a minimum value and a maximum value. Thus, the probability of a value being in a specified interval is proportional to the length of the interval. Another name for the uniform distribution is the rectangular distribution. Figure 16-1 gives the density function for the uniform distribution and its graph.

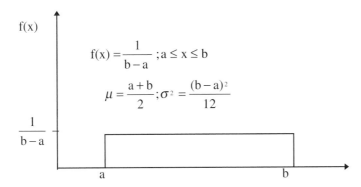

$$f(x) = \frac{1}{b-a} \; ; a \le x \le b$$

$$\mu = \frac{a+b}{2} ; \sigma^2 = \frac{(b-a)^2}{12}$$

Figure 16-1 Uniform density function and illustration.

16.2.2   Triangular Distribution

The triangular distribution contains more information about a random variable than the uniform distribution. For this distribution, three values are specified: a minimum, a mode, and a maximum. The density function consists of two linear parts: one part increases from the minimum value to the modal value; and the other part decreases from the modal value to the maximum value. The average associated with a triangular density is the sum of the minimum, mode and maximum values divided by 3. The triangular distribution is used when a most likely value can be ascertained along with minimum and maximum values, and a piecewise linear density function seems appropriate. Figure 16-2 gives the density function for the triangular distribution and its graph.

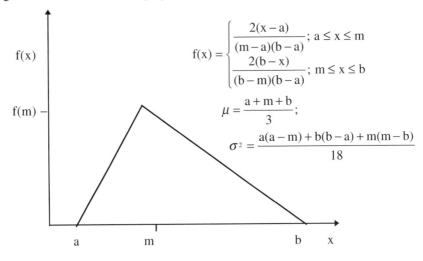

$$f(x) = \begin{cases} \dfrac{2(x-a)}{(m-a)(b-a)}; & a \le x \le m \\ \dfrac{2(b-x)}{(b-m)(b-a)}; & m \le x \le b \end{cases}$$

$$\mu = \frac{a+m+b}{3};$$

$$\sigma^2 = \frac{a(a-m)+b(b-a)+m(m-b)}{18}$$

Figure 16-2 Triangular density function and illustration.

16.2.3   Exponential Distribution

If the probability that one and only one outcome will occur during a small time interval Δt is proportional to Δt and if the occurrence of the outcome is independent of the occurrence of other outcomes then the time between occurrences of outcomes is exponentially distributed. Another way of saying the above is that an activity characterized by an exponential distribution has the same probability of being completed in any subsequent period of time Δt. Thus, if the activity has been ongoing for Δt time units, the probability that it will end in the next Δt time units is the same as if it had just been started. This is a lack of conditioning of the remaining time on the amount of time expended is referred to as the Markov or forgetfulness property. The exponential distribution has one of the largest variances of the standard distribution types as its variance is the square of its mean. The exponential distribution is easy to manipulate mathematically and is assumed for many studies because of this property. Figure 16-3 gives the density function for the exponential distribution and its graph.

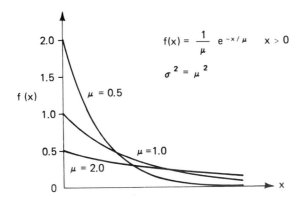

Figure 16-3 Exponential density function and illustrations.

16.2.4 Poisson Distribution

The Poisson distribution is a discrete distribution and usually is used to model the number of outcomes occurring in a specified time period. If the duration of time between outcomes is exponentially distributed and they occur one at a time, the number that occur in a fixed time interval can be shown to be Poisson distributed. Thus, if the interarrival distribution is exponential, the number of arrivals will be Poisson distributed. The Poisson distribution is frequently used as an approximation to the binomial distribution where the binomial distribution is used to represent a series of independent Bernoulli trials, that is, an outcome of a trial is go-nogo, success-failure or yes-no. When the mean value of the Poisson distribution is large, its distribution function approaches that of the normal distribution. Figure 16-4 gives the Poisson probability mass function and illustrates its form.

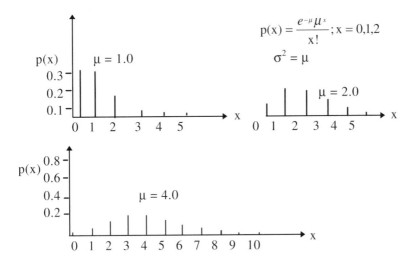

Figure 16-4   Poisson probability mass function and illustrations.

16.2.5   Normal Distribution

The normal or Gaussian distribution is the most prominent distribution in probability and statistics. Justification for the use of the normal distribution comes from the Central Limit Theorem which specifies that under very broad conditions the distribution of the average or sum of I independent observations from any distribution approaches a normal distribution as I becomes large. Thus, when dealing with phenomena that are related to sums of random variables, approximation by a normal distribution should be considered.

Because of the Central Limit Theorem, it is easy to see why the normal distribution has received a great amount of attention and use in applications of probability and statistics. There is another reason for the heavy use of the normal distribution. The normal distribution also has the advantage of being mathematically tractable and consequently many techniques of statistical inference such as regression analysis and analysis of variance have been derived under the assumption of an underlying normal density function.

As discussed in Section 16.2.4, the normal distribution is a good approximation to the Poisson distribution for a large mean value. Figure 16-5 gives the density function for the normal distribution and illustrates the distribution for selected values of the mean and standard deviation.

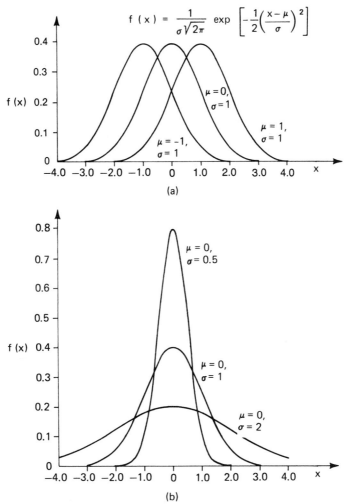

Figure 16-5 Normal density function and illustrations.

16.2.6   Lognormal Distribution

The lognormal distribution is the distribution of a random variable whose natural logarithm follows the normal distribution (3). The lognormal distribution is appropriate for a multiplicative type process in the same manner that the normal distribution is applicable for additive type processes. By use of the Central Limit Theorem, it can be shown that the distribution of the product of independent positive random variables approaches a lognormal distribution.

If a set of data is transformed by taking the logarithm of each data point, and if the transformed data points are normally distributed, then the original data is said to be lognormally distributed. The lognormal distribution has been used as an appropriate model in a wide variety of situations from biology to economics. It is an appropriate model for processes where the value of an observed variable is a random proportion of the previous observed value. Examples of such processes include the distribution of personal incomes, inheritances and bank deposits, and the distribution of particle sizes.

Figure 16-6 gives the density function for the lognormal distribution and illustrates the distribution for selected values of the mean and variance.

16.2.7   Erlang Distribution

The Erlang distribution is derived as the sum of independent and identically distributed exponential random variables. It is a special case of the gamma distribution and as such the density function, illustrations and remarks concerning the gamma distribution described in the next section apply to the Erlang distribution. The Erlang distribution is used extensively in queueing theory when an activity or service time is considered to occur in phases with each phase being exponentially distributed.

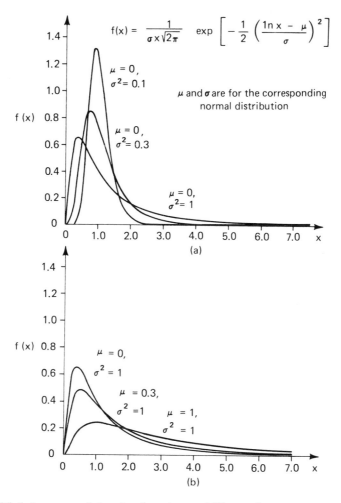

$$f(x) = \frac{1}{\sigma x \sqrt{2\pi}} \exp\left[-\frac{1}{2}\left(\frac{\ln x - \mu}{\sigma}\right)^2\right]$$

$\mu = 0,$
$\sigma^2 = 0.1$

μ and σ are for the corresponding
normal distribution

$\mu = 0,$
$\sigma^2 = 0.3$

$\mu = 0,$
$\sigma^2 = 1$

(a)

$\mu = 0,$
$\sigma^2 = 1$

$\mu = 0.3,$
$\sigma^2 = 1$

$\mu = 1,$
$\sigma^2 = 1$

(b)

Figure 16-6 Lognormal density function and illustrations

16.2.8 Gamma Distribution

The gamma distribution is a generalization of the Erlang distribution where conceptually the number of sums of exponential variables need not be integer valued. Gamma distributed times can take on values between zero and infinity. By different parameter settings, the gamma distribution can be made to take on a variety of shapes and, hence, can represent many different physical processes. The chi-square distribution is also a special case of the gamma distribution where a chi-square random variable is the sum of squared normal random variables. Thus, special cases of the gamma are the chi-square distribution, the Erlang distribution and, hence, the exponential distribution.

Figure 16-7 gives the density function for the gamma distribution and illustrates the density function for selected values of its parameters.

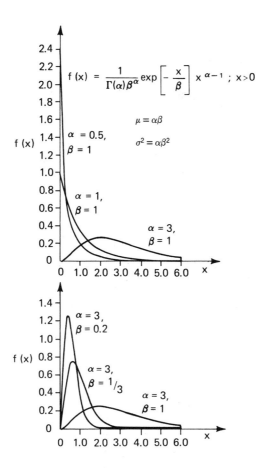

Figure 16-7 Gamma density function and illustrations.

16.2.9 Beta Distribution

The beta distribution is defined over a finite range and can take on a wide variety of shapes for different values of its parameters. It can be bell shaped, symmetric or asymmetric, or it can be U-shaped within the finite range. For U-shaped beta functions, the value of the density function goes to infinity as the ends of its range are approached. A simple variant of the beta distribution is referred to as the Pareto distribution which has been used to characterize income distributions. Figure 16-8 gives the density function for the beta distribution and illustrates the density function for selected values of its parameters.

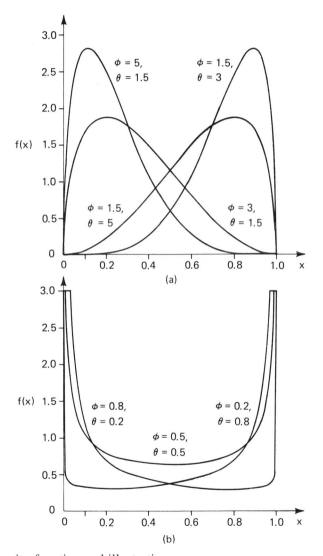

Figure 16-8 Beta density function and illustrations

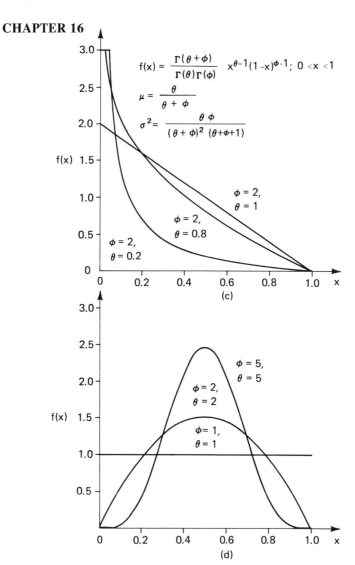

Figure 16-8 Beta density function and illustrations (continued)

Since the beta distribution is defined over a finite interval, it has been used to describe situations which have a finite range. Examples of this are density functions related to percentages and probability estimates. Frequently, the beta distribution is used as the priori distribution of the parameter of a binomial process by Bayesian statisticians. Another use of the beta distribution is as the descriptive density function associated with an activity duration in PERT.

16.3   USING DISTRIBUTIONS TO REPRESENT DATA

When the underlying nature of a variable is not understood, then it is necessary to pose the question as to whether a distribution should be used to represent the data. If this question is answered in the affirmative then a procedure for determining the distribution form is required. If it is decided not to use a theoretical distribution then a sampling procedure from the empirical data or a quasi-empirical distribution is required.

The fundamental question associated with using a distribution to represent the data is whether a model of the data, that is, the distribution, provides more information than the direct use of the data. The resolution of this question requires an investigation of the validity of the model used to fit the data and statistical tests of the fit of the model. The advantage of building a model is that it extends the range of the data and allows for values beyond those observed. It also tends to smooth the frequency of occurrence of variable values. Further, it may provide insight into ways of using the variable or improving the system characteristic which the variable represents. The pitfalls of using a theoretical distribution as a model of a variable are well-described by Fox (13) and are included in the discussion below.

If an empirical distribution is used to characterize the data, then sampling from the empirical distribution will in the long run approximate the data. The sampling from a theoretical distribution that models the data allows alternate samples to be obtained which extends the information content of the data. The validity question relates to whether or not the theoretical distribution fits the underlying distribution from which the data come. It also relates to the purpose for modeling and whether the system under study is to be exercised by data values other than those that have been observed.

Statistical tests of the fit of a theoretical distribution to the data leave much to be desired. Goodness-of-fit tests such as the Chi-square and Kolmogorov-Smirnov have a low probability of rejecting a fit. In addition, distribution fitting procedures typically involve looking at the data and then sequentially attempting to fit theoretical distributions to the data. In this regard, the warning given by Feller (10) with regard to the law of logistic growth should be mentioned: ". . . the only trouble with the theory is that not only the logistic distribution but also the normal, the Cauchy and other distributions can be fitted to the same material with the same or better goodness-of-fit . . . Most contradictory theoretical models can be supported by the same observational material."

Bratley, Fox and Schrage (8) point out "statistics associated with tandem goodness-of-fit tests have unknown distributions". They further state that "estimating the tails of distributions accurately from a limited amount of data is impossible". Based on these pitfalls, they recommend fitting a quasi-empirical distribution which is piecewise linear with exponential tails. A program developed by Wagner and Wilson (31) provides a means to fit a polynomial function described by Bezier curves to the data (32).

If the above pitfalls are not bothersome, then a theoretical distribution can be fit with the aid of a computer package (20). Typically, a graphical overlay of the theoretical distribution is displayed on a histogram of the data. A visual inspection is then made to assess the fit.

16.4   PROCEDURES FOR GENERATING RANDOM SAMPLES

The state-of-the-art for generating random samples on digital computers is advanced. Fishman provides an extensive categorization of Monte Carlo techniques and relates the research and issues between Monte Carlo techniques and computer simulation (11). The material in this section follows the excellent survey by Schmeiser.

There are four fundamental approaches for random sample generation:

1.   Inverse transformation;
2.   Composition;
3.   Acceptance/Rejection; and
4.   Special Properties.

Each of the approaches use as inputs independent samples from a uniform distribution distributed over the interval (0,1). These uniform samples are called random numbers and they provide the basic source of randomness in simulation experiments. Definitions and procedures for generation random numbers are presented in Section 16.5.

16.4.1   The Inverse Transformation Method

The simplest and most fundamental technique which forms the basis for generating samples is the *inverse transformation method* (11,28). This method uses the fundamental information that for the distribution function F(X), the random variable $R = F(X)$ is uniformly distributed on the unit interval [0,1]. Thus, to generate a random sample of X, we generate a random number r and solve the equation $r=F(x)$ for the corresponding value of $x=F^{-1}(r)$. The proof for the validity of the method is straightforward (8,28) and is based on the following reasoning. Let R=F(X) have distribution function G. Then, for $0 \leq r \leq 1$, we have

$$G(r) = \mathbf{P}[F(X) \leq r] = \mathbf{P}[X \leq F^{-1}(r)] = F(F^{-1}(r)) = r.$$

Thus, R is uniformly distributed on [0,1].

To illustrate the method for a continuous distribution, consider the generating of a sample from the exponential distribution. The distribution function for the exponential is $F(x) = 1 - e^{-\lambda x}$ where $1/\lambda$ is the mean of the exponential distribution. Setting F(x) equal to r and then solving for x yields

$$x = -(1/\lambda) \, ln(1-r)$$

Hence, if r is uniformly distributed in the range 0 to 1, then x given by the above equation is exponentially distributed with a mean value of $1/\lambda$.

The inverse method is also applicable to discrete distributions. For example, consider the following probability mass function: p(0)= 0.25; p(1)= 0.50 ; and p(2)= 0.25. The cumulative distribution function, F(X), is depicted in Figure 16-9. To obtain a sample from the above distribution, a random number is generated in the range 0 to 1, and the graph is entered at this ordinate value. The resulting random sample is then obtained by tracing across the graph to the cumulative curve, and then down to the x-axis. For example, the random number 0.81 yields a random sample of 2 as shown. The intuitive justification for this procedure is that 25 percent of the random numbers are in the interval (0,0.25), 50 percent in (0.25,0.75) and 25 percent in (0.75,1.00) which is the desired distribution function. An arbitrary but consistent decision should be made at the break points.

The difficulty with the inverse transformation method lies in finding the inverse transformation. In some cases, the method leads to a simple explicit transformation as was illustrated for the exponential distribution. However, there are continuous distributions that do not have closed-form inverse functions.

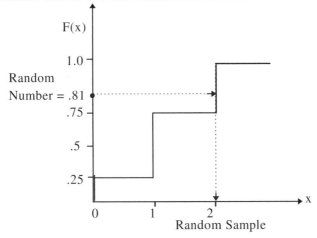

Figure 16-9 Illustration of the inverse transform method for obtaining a sample from a given distribution.

16.4.2   Acceptance/Rejection Method

The acceptance/rejection approach to generating random samples involves generating samples from a distribution and then rejecting (discarding) some of the samples in such a way that the remaining samples have the desired distribution. The procedure starts with the generation of two random numbers. The first random number is used to calculate a proposed random sample, x. This sample value is then inserted into the equation for the density function f(x). The second random number is used to obtain a random value t(x) from a function that majorizes or covers the density function. If t(x) is larger than f(x) then x is rejected as a sample from f(x). If the value of t(x) is smaller, x is accepted. In this way, samples are accepted based on the height of the density function which is the property desired from the random sampling procedure. The acceptance/rejection method for generating random samples is similar to the use of.the Monte Carlo method to evaluate integrals (11).

Acceptance/rejection methods have been developed for both discrete and continuous distributions. The efficiency of the method depends on the amount of rejection required. Research has concentrated on majorizing functions which reduce the value of the test function t(x) used for the acceptance/rejection decision. The acceptance/rejection method has been used for obtaining random samples from most of the standard distributions including normal, gamma and beta (1,2,28).

16.4.3   The Composition Method

The composition method assumes that the density function can be written as a weighted sum of component distribution functions with the sum of the weights totaling one. The inverse transformation method can be used to select one of the subdistributions. A sample is then drawn from that subdistribution and it becomes the sample for the distribution. By repeated sampling, each of the subdistributions are selected in accordance with the weights and, hence, the samples are generated in accordance with the total distribution.

As described above, the composition method may employ the inverse transformation method to select a subdistribution and any sampling procedure to obtain a random sample from the subdistribution. The acceptance/rejection method is frequently used where majorizing functions are defined for portions of the distribution function. This illustrates that combinations of the methods for generating random samples are sometimes used.

16.4.4   Methods Employing Special Properties

In some cases, a distribution will have a special property or be related to another distribution from which it is easier to obtain a random sample. Examples of this are:

- A lognormal sample computed from e^y where y is a sample from the normal distribution;
- An Erlang sample as the sum of exponential samples;
- A beta sample as the ratio of gamma samples;
- A binomial sample as a sum of Bernoulli trials;
- A negative binomial sample as a sum of geometric samples;
- A normal sample as a sum of uniform samples;
- A Cauchy sample as the ratio of two independent standard normal samples;
- A chi-square sample, if the degrees of freedom are even, can be obtained from an Erlang sample. If the degrees of freedom are odd, add the square of a standardized normal to a chi-square sample which has one less degree of freedom;
- An F-distribution sample as the ratio of two chi-square samples; and
- A t-distribution sample as the ratio of a standardized normal sample to a chi-square sample.

In other situations, relationships are derived in order that random samples may be obtained. One such case relates normal random variables to uniform random variables (7).

Another special situation involves sampling from a distribution with specified limits. If a sample is desired from a truncated distribution between the specified limits a and b then generate a sample and, if it is within the prescribed limits, accept the sample. If it is outside the limits, reject the sample and repeat the procedure. Alternatively, the random numbers can be restricted to values between $F_x(a)$ and $F_x(b)$ and the inverse transformation procedure used. A mixed truncated distribution assumes that samples between a and b are desired, and a sample that exceeds either limit is set equal to the limiting value. To obtain samples from a mixed truncated distribution, accept a sample if it is within the limits specified. If the value is larger than b, set the sample to b. If the value is less than a, set the sample to a. Note that the moments of a truncated or mixed distribution may be different than those of the underlying distribution.

Parameterized distributions have been developed to represent systems of distributions, for example, Pearson (23) and Johnson (17). Schmeiser and Deutsch developed a system of distributions for which the inverse transformation can be used to obtain samples (27). Wagner and Wilson (32) use Bezier functions to represent different functional forms or different data sets and use the inverse transformation or numerical integration to obtain sample values. Wilson et al (18,33) have developed procedures for fitting time series using nonhomogeneous Poisson processes (NHPP) including trends and cycles and provides methods to sample from the resulting stochastic processes.

16.4.5   Implementing Random Sampling Procedures

The algorithms for obtaining samples from a distribution are many. Extensive research is being performed in this area. New algorithms are continually being proposed and tested which provide improved computer efficiency. The methods and equations used in Visual SLAM to obtain random samples are presented in Table 16-1. In the table, R denotes a random number.

The inverse transformation method is used to obtain a sample from the uniform distribution. The uniform distribution is typically specified in terms of a range with a low value, ULO, and a high value, UHI. Samples within this range are equally likely. The arguments for function UNFRM are ULO and UHI. For the uniform distribution, these values can be specified in terms of the mean and standard deviation as follows:

$$ULO = \mu - \sqrt{3}\sigma$$

$$UHI = \mu + \sqrt{3}\sigma$$

The inverse transformation method is also used to obtain a sample from the triangular distribution. For the triangular distribution, two equations are involved depending on whether the density function is increasing or decreasing. To obtain samples from the normal distribution, a transformation of variables developed by Box and Muller (7) is used in conjunction with a sample rejection(1). The procedure generates pairs of normal samples.

A sample from an exponential distribution is obtained using the inverse transformation. In taking the inverse, the value (1-R) is required. Since (1-R) is equivalent to a random number, the value R is used directly in the formula for the exponential sample.

A sample from a Poisson distribution is generated based on the relationship between the exponential distribution and the Poisson distribution. The mean number of events occurring in time t for a Poisson distribution with a mean rate of arrivals U is Ut. By setting t equal to one, we can generate exponential samples with mean time l/U until the sum of the values of the exponential samples exceeds 1. Then one less than the number of samples generated is an observation from the Poisson distribution. The procedure presented in Table 16-1 to obtain a sample from the Poisson distribution has been derived from the following inequality

$$t_1 + t_2 + ... + t_N < 1 < t_1 + t_2 + ... + t_{N+1}$$

where t_i is a sample from an exponential distribution with mean time l/U.

An Erlang random variable is the sum of independent and identically distributed exponential random variables. The arguments of function ERLNG are specified in terms of the exponential parameters. EMN is the mean of the underlying exponential random variable and XK is the number of exponential random variables included in the sum. If the mean and standard deviation of the Erlang distribution are known, then EMN = σ^2/μ and XK= μ/EMN. Samples from the Erlang distribution are obtained by summing K exponential samples with each sample having a mean time of U. The mean of the Erlang distribution would then be KU. The equation to obtain a sample from the Erlang distribution employs the inverse transformation for obtaining samples from the exponential distribution and then summing up the values. The equation shown in Table 16-1 makes use of the information that the sum of logarithms is equal to the logarithm of the product.

A sample from a lognormal distribution is obtained by using the relationship that the natural logarithm of a lognormal random variable is normally distributed. The equations that relate the mean and variance of the normal distribution to the mean and variance of the lognormal distribution are shown in Table 16-1.

The gamma distribution is a generalization of the Erlang distribution in which the second parameter need not be an integer. The arguments for function GAMA in terms of the mean and standard deviation of the gamma distribution are:

$$\text{BETA} = \frac{\sigma^2}{\mu} \text{ and ALPHA} = \frac{\mu}{\text{BETA}}.$$

Samples from a gamma distribution are obtained using a combined approach. The second parameter of the gamma distribution is a shape parameter. When the shape parameter is small, an acceptance/rejection technique proposed by Jöhnk (5) is employed. For intermediate values of the shape parameter, a method proposed by Fishman (12) and modified by Tadikamalla (29,30) is used. For shape parameter values greater than 5, a weighted selection of Erlang samples is employed (5). If the shape parameter is an integer, then Function Erlang should be used for efficiency purposes.

A sample from a beta distribution is obtained as the ratio of two gamma samples. The beta distribution is defined over a finite region and can take on many shapes. The Visual SLAM function BETA generates samples in the range 0 to 1. Thus, it is necessary for the user to make the transformation of a general beta distribution to a beta distribution in the range 0 to 1 through the following equations:

$$\mu = \frac{\mu_\beta - \text{BMIN}}{\text{BMAX} - \text{BMIN}}$$

$$\sigma^2 = \frac{\sigma_\beta^2}{(\text{BMAX-BMIN})^2}$$

where μ_β and σ_β^2 are the untransformed mean and variance of the beta distribution and BMIN and BMAX are the end points for the beta distribution.

With this transformation the arguments for Function BETA are:

$$\text{THETA} = \frac{\mu 2}{\sigma 2}(1 - \mu) - \mu$$

$$\text{and PHI} = \text{THETA} \left(\frac{1 - \mu}{\mu} \right)$$

In order to obtain a sample in the range BMIN to BMAX,BETAT, the following equation should be used:

BETAT = BETA(THETA,PHI) * (BMAX - BMIN) + BMIN.

Samples from a Weibull distribution are obtained using the inverse transformation method. Note that there are alternative definitions for the Weibull distribution function. The form of the Weibull distribution function used in Visual SLAM is shown in Table 16-1. It is the alternative definition of the Weibull function used in SLAM II. When converting SLAM II models to Visual SLAM, the

SLAM II scale parameter α should be replaced with $\alpha^{1/\beta}$ for the Visual SLAM algorithm.

Visual SLAM obtains samples from a probability mass function by comparing a random number against the cumulative distribution function. When the random number falls in the appropriate range, the corresponding sample value is returned from function DPROB.

Table 16-1 Visual SLAM random sampling procedures.

Uniform Distribution
        Function Name: UNFRM(A, B, I)
        Method: Inverse transformation
        Equation: UNFRM = A + (B − A) *R

Triangular Distribution
        Function Name: TRIAG(A, D, B, I)
        Method: Inverse transformation (27)
        Equations:

$$\text{For } 0 \le R \le \frac{D-A}{B-A} \text{ ; TRIAG = A+SQRT } ((D - A) * (B - A) * R)$$

$$\text{For } \frac{D-A}{B-A} < R \le 1; \text{ TRIAG = B - SQRT}((B -D) * (B-A) * (1.-R))$$

Normal Distribution
    Function Name: RNORM (U,S,I)
    Method: Transformation of variables and sample rejection (2,8)
    Procedure: Normal samples are generated in pairs.

        Let A = 2.*R_1 - 1. and B = 2.*R_2 - 1.
        Let W = A*A + B*B
        If W > 1.0, repeat procedure
        If W $\le$ 1.0 then
                $RNORM_1$ = (A*SQRT(−2.*LOG(W)/W))*S+U
                $RNORM_2$ = (B*SQRT(−2.*LOG(W)/W))*S+U

Exponential Distribution
    Function Name: EXPON(U,I)
    Method: Inverse transformation
    Equation: EXPON = −U*LOG(R)

Table 16-1 Visual SLAM random sampling procedures(continued).

Poisson Distribution

   Function Name: NPSSN(U,I)

   Method: The number of exponential samples in a unit interval (27)

   Procedure: Set the sample value, NPSSN, equal to the first value of N such that

$$\prod_{n=1}^{N} R_n \geq e^{-U} > \prod_{n=1}^{N+1} R_n$$

   where R_n is the nth pseudorandom number.

Erlang Distribution

   Function Name: ERLNG(U,K,I)

   Method: Sum K exponential samples each having a mean equal to U

   Equation: ERLNG = - U*LOG ($\prod_{i=1}^{K} R_i$)

Lognormal Distribution

   Function Name: RLOGN(U,S,I)

   Method: Use a sample, N, from a normal distribution in the equation $L = e^N$.
         It can be shown that if N is normally distributed L is lognormally
         distributed (4).

   Equation: RLOGN = EXP(RNORM(μ_N, σ_N,I))

      where σ_N^2 = LOG (S^2/U^2+1.)

      and μ_N = LOG U – .5 σ_N^2

Gamma Distribution

   Function Name: GAMA(β,α,I)

   Method: The method for obtaining a sample from a gamma distribution is a
         function of the parameter α. More efficient methods are employed as α is
         increased. When α is an integer, Function ERLNG should be employed.

            For $0 < \alpha < 1$, the method of Jöhnk is employed (6)

            For $1 \leq \alpha < 5$, the method of Fishman (13) as modified by
                        Tadikamalla is employed (33, 34)

            For $\alpha \geq 5$, a weighted selection of Erlang samples is employed.

   Procedure: For $0 < \alpha < 1$:

      Let X = R_1**(1./ α) and Y = R_2**(1./(1.- α))

      If X + Y $\leq$ 1, compute W = X/(X+Y). Otherwise recompute X and Y.

      Let GAMA = W*(-LOG(R_3))*β

      For $1 \leq \alpha < 5$;

Table 16-1 Visual SLAM random sampling procedures(continued).

> Let a = [α] and b = α - [α]
>
> Compute X = (α/a)*(-LOG($\prod_{i=1}^{a} R_i$))
>
> If R_{a+1} > (X/α)^b exp(-b*(X/α-1.)), recompute X.
>
> Otherwise GAMA = X*β
>
> For α ≥ 5:
>
> If R_1 ≥ α - [α], GAMA = ERLNG (β, [α],I)
>
> If R_1 < α - [α], GAMA = ERLNG (β, [α] + 1,I)

Beta Distribution

Function Name: BETA (α,β,I)

Method: Transformation of variables where the beta sample is the ratio of two gamma samples (12)

Equation: BETA = G1/(G1 + G2)

where G1 - GAMA (1, α,I) and G2 = GAMA (1, β,I)

and if μ_g and σ_g are given

then α = $\mu(\mu-\mu^2)/ \sigma^2-\mu$

and β = α(1−μ)/μ

where μ = (μ_g-min)/(max-min)

and $\sigma^2 = \sigma_g^2$ /(max-min)^2.

Weibull Distribution

Function Name: WEIBL (α, β, I)

Method: Inverse transformation (15)

Equation: WEIBL = α*(−LOG(R))**(1./ β)

where α is a scale parameter and β is a shape parameter,

as defined by the distribution function F(W) = 1−exp[−(w/β)^α]

Probability Mass Function

Function Name: DPROB(CPROB, VALUE, NVAL, I)

Method: Inverse transformation

Procedure: Set DPROB equal to VALUE(N) when

CPROB(N-1)< R ≤ CPROB(N) where CPROB(0) = 0.0 and N = 1 to NVAL

16.5   GENERATING PSEUDORANDOM NUMBERS

As discussed in the last section, generating random samples from a distribution on a digital computer normally requires one or more uniform random samples between 0 and 1, and then to transform the uniform sample (or samples) into a new sample from the desired distribution. Independent samples that are uniformly distributed in the interval 0 to 1 are called random numbers.

There are at least three methods for obtaining random numbers for digital simulation. The first method is to read a table of random numbers (29) into the computer and then treat the random numbers as data for the simulation problem. The major shortcomings of this method are related to the relative slowness of computers in reading data from an external device and the need to store large tables. A second method is to employ a physical device such as a vacuum tube which generates random noise. A major objection to this method is that the simulation results are not reproducible, thereby complicating model verification and controlled experimentation with model parameters. The third and preferred method is to employ a recursive equation which generates the (i+1)st random number from previous random numbers. Since the sequence of numbers is produced deterministically by an equation, they are not truly random, and therefore are referred to as "pseudorandom" numbers. From our perspective and approach to simulation, Lehmer's definition (21) of pseudorandom numbers is appealing, " . . . a vague notion embodying the idea of a sequence in which every term is unpredictable to the uninitiated and whose digits pass a certain number of tests . . . depending somewhat on the uses to which the sequence is to be put.."

The properties desirable in a pseudorandom number generator are:

1. The numbers should be uniformly distributed in the interval (0,1);
2. The numbers should be independent and, hence, no correlation should exist in a sequence of random numbers;
3. Many numbers should be generated before the same number is obtained. This is referred to as the period or cycle length of the generator;
4. A random number sequence should be reproducible. This implies that different starting values or seeds should be permitted to allow different sequences or streams to be generated;
5. The generator should be fast; and
6. A low storage requirement is preferred.

The technique which best satisfies these properties is referred to as the congruential method.

A linear congruential method employs the following recursive equation:

$$z_{i+1} = (az_i+b)(\text{mod } c) \qquad\qquad i=0,1,2,\dots$$
$$r_{i+1} = z_{i+1}/c$$

where z_0 is the seed value and r_i is the ith pseudorandom number. This equation denotes that the unnormalized random number, z_{i+1}, is equal to the remainder of (az_i+b) divided by c where z_i is the previous unnormalized random number, z_0 is an initial value or seed, and a, b, and c are constants. In Exercise 16-2, an equation for computing the (i+1)st unnormalized random number is given. The assignment of values to the constants a, b, and c has been the subject of intensive research. Fishman (11) presents an excellent review of how to set the constants and the procedures for testing random number generators. In Table 16-2, we summarize the suggested rules for setting a, b, and c for congruential random number generators. In Chapter 6 of Bratley, Fox and Schrage, the implementation and testing of random number generators is described. Schrage's portable random number generator (8) is also presented which is included in the basic Visual SLAM package. The function that generates random numbers in Visual SLAM is DRAND(ISTRM). The function XRN(ISTRM) returns the value of the last random number generated.

In simulation modeling, it is frequently desirable to employ several random number streams within the same model. For example, separate random number streams could be employed in a queueing system to model the arrival and service process. In this manner, the same sequence of arrival times can be generated without regard to the order in which service is performed. Thus, different service procedures could be evaluated for the same sequence of arrivals. Random number generators provide for parallel streams by allowing the modeler to provide a different seed value for each stream to be employed.

16.6 TESTS FOR RANDOMNESS

The statistical validity of the results of a simulation model are dependent upon the degree of randomness of the random number generator employed. Because of this, many statistical procedures have been developed for testing random number generators. However, as noted by Hull and Dobell (16) ". . . no finite class of tests can guarantee the general suitability of a finite sequence of numbers. Given a set of tests, there will always exist a sequence of numbers which passes these tests but which is completely unacceptable for some particular application." This reservation

Table 16-2   Linear congruential random number generators.[a]

Mixed Congruential Generators

A full period of 2^B before recycling will be obtained on a computer that has B bits/word for the generator

$$z_{i+1} = (az_i + b) \,(\text{mod } c)$$

when $c = 2^B$; b is relatively prime to c; that is, the greatest common factor of b and c is 1; and $a \equiv 1(\text{mod } 4)$ or $a = 1 + 4k$ where k is an integer.

Multiplicative Congruential Generators

A maximal period of 2^{B-2} before recycling will be obtained on a computer that has B bits/word for the generator

$$z_{i+1} = az_i(\text{mod } c)$$

when $c = 2^B$; $a = \pm 3 + 8k$ or $a = 1 + 4k$ for k integer; and z_0 is odd.

Fishman refers to these generators as maximal period multiplicative generators.

For multiplicative congruential generators a period of c-1 can be obtained by setting c equal to the largest prime in 2^B and making the coefficient a, a primitive root of c. In some instances 2^B-1 is the largest prime in 2^B. For a to be a primitive root of c, the following equation must be satisfied

$$a^{c-1} = 1 + ck$$

where k is an integer and for any integer q<c-1, $(a^q-1)/c$ is nonintegral. These generators are referred to as prime modulus multiplicative congruential generators.

---

[a] The material contained in this table is based on Fishman (11).

does not present a serious problem as a simulation analyst only desires the properties of randomness that were previously described.

Both analytical and empirical tests have been used to investigate the randomness properties of random number generators. These include the Frequency Test, Serial Test, Gap Test, Sum-of-Digits Test, Runs Test, as well as many others. Empirical results from the use of the tests are contained in Lewis (21) and Fishman (11). Fishman and Law and Kelton (19) describe the spectral (9) and latticed (6,22) procedures for measuring the performance of congruential random number generators with regard to their departure from the desired randomness properties.

16.7 CHAPTER SUMMARY

This chapter has described standard distributions which are important in modeling random processes. The topics of fitting distributions to data and obtaining samples from distributions is introduced. Extensive research on these topics has been and continues to be performed. Procedures are available to obtain samples from empirical, quasi-empirical, and theoretical distributions and from time series data with trends and periodicities.

16.8 EXERCISES

16-1. Use the multiplicative congruential method to generate a sequence of ten random numbers with c = 256, a = 13, b = 0 and z_0 = 51.

16-2. Given that $z_{i+1} = (az_i + b)(\mod c)$, show that z_{i+1} is only a function of z_0, a, b and c, that is, $z_{i+1} = (a^{i+1} z_0 + b(a^{i+1} - 1)/(a-1))(\mod c)$. Compute z_9 for the values given in Exercise 16-1 using this formula.

16-3. Use the inverse transform method to transform the uniform random numbers from Exercise 16-1 into samples from the continuous distribution whose probability density function is:

$$f(x) = \begin{cases} \dfrac{3x^2}{8}, \text{if } 0 \le x \le 2 \\ 0, \text{otherwise} \end{cases}$$

16-4. Use the inverse transformation method to transform the random samples from Exercise 16-1 into samples from the discrete distribution defined by the following probability mass function:
P(0) = 1/5; P(1) = 1/5; P(2) = 2/5; and P(3) = 1/5.

16-5. Write a Visual SLAM function for obtaining a sample from a truncated exponential distribution.

16-6. Show that the maximum of two random numbers is triangularly distributed.

16-7. Develop a procedure for modeling batch arrivals where the time between arrivals is exponential and the number of entities per arrival is Poisson.

16-8.   Test to see if the time between arrivals is exponential if 100 arrivals are generated in 1000 minutes by randomly selecting an interarrival time from the current time to the 1000 minute ending time. The current time is the sum of the interarrival times generated.

16-9.   Research the question of generating samples from a bivariate normal distribution. Embellishment: Expand your research to the consideration of procedures for obtaining samples from other multivariate distributions.

16-10.   Develop a function for use in Visual SLAM that generates samples from an ARMA process.

16-11.   Test Schmeiser's (26) approximate method for generating standardized random normal deviates which uses

RNORMS=(R**0.135 -(1.-R)**0.135)/0.1975.

16.9   REFERENCES

1.   Ahrens, J. H. and U Dieter, "Computer Methods for Sampling from the Exponential and Normal Distributions," *Comm. ACM*, Vol. 15, 1972, pp. 873-882.

2.   Ahrens, J. H. and U. Dieter, "Computer Methods for Sampling from Gamma, Beta, Poisson and Binormial Distributions," *Computing*, Vol. 12, 1974, pp. 223-246.

3.   Aitchison, J. and J. A. C. Brown, *The Lognormal Distribution*, Cambridge Press, 1957.

4.   Banks, J., J. S. Carson II, B. L. Nelson, *Discrete-Event System Simulation*, Second Edition, Prentice-Hall, 1995.

5.   Berman, M. B., *Generating Random Variates from Gamma Distributions with Non-Integer Shape Parameters*, The RAND Corporation, R-641-PR, November 1970.

6.   Beyer, W. A., R.B. Roof and D. Williamson, "The Lattice Structure of Multiplicative Congruential Pseudo-Random Vectors," *Math. Comp.*, Vol. 25, 1971, pp. 345-363.

7.   Box, G. E. P. and M. A. Muller, "A Note on the Generation of Random Normal Deviates," *Annals of Math. Stat.*, Vol. 29, 1958, pp. 610-611.

8.   Bratley, P., B. L. Fox, and L. E. Schrage, *A Guide to Simulation*, Second Edition, Springer-Verlag, 1987.

9. Conveyou, R. R. and R. D. MacPherson, "Fourier Analysis of Uniform Random Number Generators," *J.ACM,* Vol. 14, 1967, pp. 100-119.

10. Feller, W., *An Introduction to Probability Theory and Its Applications*, John Wiley, 1950.

11. Fishman, G. S., *Monte Carlo: Concepts, Algorithms, and Applications,* Springer, 1996.

12. Fishman, G. S., "Sampling from the Gamma Distribution on a Computer," *Comm. ACM*, Vol. 19, 1976, pp. 407-409.

13. Fox, B. L., "Fitting 'Standard' Distributions to Data is Necessarily Good: Dogma or Myth?," *Proceedings, Winter Simulation Conference*, 1981, pp. 305-307.

14. Hahn, G. J. and S. S. Shapiro, *Statistical Methods in Engineering*, John Wiley, 1967.

15. Hastings, N. A. J. and J. B. Peacock, *Statistical Distributions*, Butterworth, 1975.

16. Hull, T. E. and A. R. Dobell, "Random Number Generators," *SIAM Review*, Vol. 4, 1962, pp. 230-254.

17. Johnson, N. L., "Systems of Frequency Curves Generated by Methods of Translation," *Biometrika*, Vol. 36, 1949, pp. 149-176.

18. Kuhl, M. E., J. R. Wilson and M. A. Johnson, "Estimation and Simulation of Nonhomogeneous Poisson Processes Having Multiple Periodicities," ," *Proceedings, Winter Simulation Conference,* 1995, pp. 374-383.

19. Law, A. M. and W. D. Kelton, *Simulation Modeling and Analysis*, McGraw-Hill, 1982.

20. Law, A. M. and S. D. Vincent, *ExpertFit User's Guide*, Averill M. Law & Associates, Tucson, AZ, 1995.

21. Lewis, T. G., *Distribution Sampling for Computer Simulation*, D.C. Heath and Co., 1975.

22. Marsaglia, G., "The Structure of Linear Congruential Sequences," in *Applications of Number Theory to Numerical Analysis*, S.K. Zaremba, ed., Academic Press, 1972.

23. Pearson, K., "Contributions to the Mathematical Theory of Evolution, II. Skew Variations in Homogeneous Material," *Philosophical Transactions of the Royal Society of London, Series A*, Vol. 186, 1895, pp. 343-414.

24. Ramberg, J. S., P.R. Tadikamalla, E. J. Dudewicz and E. F. Mykytka, "A Probability Distribution and Its Uses in Fitting Data," *Technometrics*, Vol. 21, 1979, pp 201-214.

25. RAND Corporation, *A Million Random Digits with 1,000,000 Normal Deviates*, Free Press, 1955.

26. Schmeiser, B. W., "Approximations to the Inverse Cumulative Normal Function for Use on Hand Calculators," *App. Stat.*, Vol. 28, 1979, pp. 175-176.

27. Schmeiser, B. W. and S. T. Deutsch, "A Versatile Four Parameter Family of Probability Distributions Suitable for Simulation," *AIIE Transactions*, Vol.9, 1977, pp. 176-182.

28. Schmeiser, B. W., "Random Deviate Generation: A Survey," *Proceedings, Winter Simulation Conference,* 1980, pp. 79-90.

29. Tadikamalla, P. R., "Computer Generation of Gamma Random Variables," *Comm. ACM*, Vol. 21, 1978, pp. 419-421.

30. Tadikamalla, P. R., "Computer Generation of Gamma Random Variables, II," *Comm. ACM*, Vol. 21, 1978, pp. 925-927.

31. Wagner, M. A. F., and J. R. Wilson, "Using Bivariate Bezier Distributions to Model Simulation Input Processes," IIE Transactions, 1996.

32. Wagner, M. A. F. and J. R. Wilson, "Recent Developments in Input Modeling with Bezier Distributions," *Proceedings, Winter Simulation Conference*, 1996.

33. Wilson, J. R. and M. E. Kuhl, *User's Guide for ULAMFIT: Estimation Program for ULAM Arrival Processes*, Pritsker Corporation, 1995.

CHAPTER 17

Statistical Aspects of Simulation

17.1   STATISTICAL QUESTIONS FACING SIMULATORS

A simulation model portrays the dynamic behavior of a system over time. A model is built to provide results that resemble the outputs from the real system. Thus, the statistical analysis of the outputs from a simulation is similar to the statistical analysis of the data obtained from an actual system. The main difference is that the simulation analyst has more control over the running of the simulation model. Thus he can design experiments to obtain the specific output data necessary to answer the pertinent questions relating to the system under study.

There are two types of questions that relate to the outputs of simulation models:

1. What is the inherent variability associated with the simulation model?
2. What can be inferred about the performance of the real system from the use of the simulation model?

The first question relates to an understanding of the model and verifying that it performs as designed. The sensitivity of the model outputs to changes in input and model parameters is of interest. The precision of the outputs with respect to the inherent probability distributions employed is a basic part of this type of question.

The second question relates to the validity of the model and to its usefulness. The answer to the second type of question usually involves describing the system performance variables and making statistical computations related to the performance variables. Thus, tables and plots are constructed and viewed as if they were possible outputs from the real system. The computations and statistical analyses made are similar to those performed on data obtained from the real system. If decision-making is based on the probability of occurrence of an outcome or on an average value, such quantities are estimated from the simulation. If the variability of a random variable is important, it is estimated in the same manner as is done in the real system. This mode of simulation analysis is the most common one found in current applications. The fact that a single simulation run represents one sample or time series of a stochastic process is no more bothersome than the fact that an historical record represents only a single time series.

Answering the first type of question involves a detailed statistical analysis to obtain information on the precision and sensitivity of the model. Basically we explore the type of output that would be obtained if the simulation was performed again or run for a longer period of time. In doing this, we recognize that the simulation model is a stochastic one and that the random elements of the model will produce outputs that are probabilistic. This type of analysis can be unfamiliar to the industrial manager since the analysis involves advanced statistical terminology. In addition, more precise responses can be obtained by changing experimental conditions, for example, by performing more runs.

Because the second type of question is system and, hence, model specific, there are no general forms of analysis that can be recommended beyond the standard statistical procedures. The first type of question has been explored extensively, and we provide a description of the techniques that we have found to be useful in this chapter. We would have preferred to present these techniques in a handbook fashion, with detailed examples illustrating each procedure. However, the field has not progressed to such a point, and we can only describe the specific types of problems and current approaches to their resolution. Two excellent surveys of statistical analysis of simulation results are given by Welch (81) and Wilson (87). The books by Bratley, Fox, and Schrage (9) and Law and Kelton (56) provide illustrations of the use of statistical techniques to analyze simulation outputs.

17.1.1 Definition of Terms

During a simulation, observations of variables of interest are to be recorded. Each potential observation is a time-based sample so that the observations can be considered to be random variables. To provide a standard set of terms, we make the following definitions regarding such random variables:

Let

I = the number of intervals, iterations, or individual observations. The word batch or interval will be used in a generic sense in the remainder of this chapter to mean any of the above.

T_i = ending time of the ith interval, $i=1,2,\ldots,I$ with T_0 defined as the start time of the first interval.

N_i = the number of observations in the ith interval, $i = 1,2,\ldots,I$.

$X_i(t)$ = value of X at time t in interval i; $t \in [T_{i-1},T_i]$.

$X_i(n)$ = value of X for nth observation in interval i; $n = 1,2,\ldots,N_i$.

Examples of $X_i(t)$ are the amount of inventory on-hand at time t and the number of customers in a system at time t. These variables were previously referred to as time-persistent variables. Examples of $X_i(n)$ are the time in the queue for the nth customer and the inventory on-hand when the nth receipt of an order arrives. These variables were previously referred to in conjunction with observations. Note that I, T_i, and N_i are usually treated as constants but in some instances may be random variables.

A *stochastic process*† is a set of ordered random variables. Thus $\{X_i(t), t \in [0, \infty)\}$ and $\{X_i(n), n=1, 2, \ldots, \infty\}$ are stochastic processes. A *realization* of a stochastic process is the set of sample paths assumed by the stochastic process. A *time series* is a finite realization of a stochastic process. In simulation terms, each run produces a time series for each stochastic process of interest.

The literature pertaining to stochastic processes and time series is extensive (12,68). Here, we only present a brief, informal background to introduce the topic.

A stochastic process is said to be *stationary* if the underlying joint distribution of the random variables in the process remains the same as time progresses, that is, if the random mechanisms producing the process are time invariant. This is referred to as the strictly stationary property (or *strong stationarity*). A special type of stationarity is referred to as *covariance stationarity* which requires all the means, μ_t, and covariances, R_{st}, of the random variables of the process to be finite and covariances separated by h time units to be equal, that is,

$$\mu_t = E[X_i(t)]$$
$$R_{st} = E[(X_i(s)-\mu_s)(X_i(t)-\mu_t)]$$

and

$$R_{st} = R_{rq} \quad \text{if } |t-s| = |q-r| = h$$

A covariance stationary process is also referred to as stationary in the wide sense or as mean square stationarity or as second-order stationarity.

Tests for the stationarity of a sequence are not well developed. The simplest and most frequently used evaluation is to consider the physics or underlying procedures associated with the phenomenon producing the data. If the basic physical factors which generate the phenomenon are time invariant then typically we accept the stationarity of the resulting data. If we believe trends or seasonality factors are involved, then differencing techniques are employed to remove such time-variant behavior.

An *ergodic* process is one from which the properties of the random variables in the process can be estimated from a single time series. A covariance stationary process is ergodic in the mean and autocovariance if the following two conditions hold (39)

$$\lim_{T \to \infty} \frac{1}{T} \sum_{s=-T+1}^{T-1} R_s = 0$$

and

---

† In this text, we do not differentiate between a stochastic process and a stochastic sequence.

$$\lim_{T \to \infty} \frac{1}{T} \sum_{s=-T+1}^{T-1} R_s^2 = 0$$

The following important result regarding sequences of sample means is given by Parzen (68). A sequence of sample means, $\{\overline{X}_s, s = 1, 2, \ldots \infty\}$, may be shown to be ergodic if $Var[\overline{X}_s] \to 0$ as $s \to \infty$.

The significance of this result for simulation analysts is that the sample mean is approximately equal to the process mean if the variance of the sample mean approaches zero as the length of the sample increases.

17.2 IMPORTANCE OF THE VARIANCE OF THE SAMPLE MEAN, VAR[$\overline{X}_I$]

The sample mean is the average of the I random variables X_i as given below.

$$\overline{X}_I = \frac{\sum_{i=1}^{I} X_i}{I}$$

The notation, $\overline{X}_I$, is employed to indicate that the mean is a random variable that is based on the sum of I random variables. Typically, in simulation studies, we are interested in comparing $\overline{X}_I$ values for different alternatives using a test of hypothesis or in setting confidence limits on the value of $\overline{X}_I$ for a single alternative. To accomplish either of these tasks, it is necessary to calculate the variance of the sample mean denoted by $Var[\overline{X}_I]$. Extensive research has been performed on methods for estimating $Var[\overline{X}_I]$ from the time series output associated with a simulation. Procedures have also been suggested for obtaining smaller estimates of $Var[\overline{X}_I]$ which allow more precise statements about $\overline{X}_I$ to be made. These topics are discussed in Sections 17.3 and 17.4 respectively. In this section, we present the background information and formulas that are pertinent to the understanding of the significance of the variance of the sample mean.

17.2.1 Notation

In our exploration of $\overline{X}_I$, we propose the notation that X_i be a random variable associated with interval or batch i. We will use the term batch throughout this chapter where a batch is an undefined quantity that can be a single observation, a set of observations in a subinterval during a run, or an entire run (replication). How a batch is defined is dependent on the procedures employed in the simulation to compute the sample mean which in turn is based on the test of hypothesis to be performed or the confidence interval to be set. Possible definitions for X_i are given below.

A derived observation: $X_i = \begin{cases} 1, \text{success on batch i} \\ 0, \text{failure on batch i} \end{cases}$

A time-averaged value for batch i:

$$X_i = \frac{1}{T_i - T_{i-1}} \int_{t=T_{i-1}}^{T_i} X_i(t)\,dt$$

An observation-averaged value for batch i:

$$X_i = \frac{1}{N_i} \sum_{n=A_i}^{A_{i+1}} X_i(n)$$

$$\text{where} \quad A_i = \sum_{j=1}^{i-1} N_j \text{ and } A_1 = 0$$

Note that the latter two definitions involve the computation of an average within a batch. To simplify the presentation of the formulas to be derived, we will not take advantage of this information during the presentation of formulas. In Section 19.3 where specific calculation methods are proposed, this subject will be discussed.

17.2.2   Formulas for Var $[\overline{X}_I]$

Starting with the definition of the variance, we can derive the following expressions (all summations are from 1 to I)

$$\text{Var}[\overline{X}_I] = E[(\overline{X}_I - E[\overline{X}_I])^2]$$

$$= E\left[\left(\frac{\sum_i X_i}{I} - E\left[\frac{\sum_i X_i}{I}\right]\right)^2\right]$$

$$= \frac{1}{I^2} E\left[\left(\sum_i X_i - E\left[\sum_i X_i\right]\right)\left(\sum_j X_j - E\left[\sum_j X_j\right]\right)\right]$$

$$= \frac{1}{I^2} E\left[\sum_i (X_i - E[X_i]) \cdot \sum_j (X_j - E[X_j])\right]$$

$$= \frac{1}{I^2} E\left[\sum_i \sum_j (X_i - E[X_i])(X_j - E[X_j]) \right]$$

$$= \frac{1}{I^2} \sum_i \sum_j E[(X_i - E[X_i])(X_j - E[X_j])]$$

$$= \frac{1}{I^2} \sum_i \sum_j \text{Cov}[X_i, X_j] \tag{17-1}$$

$$= \frac{1}{I^2} \left(\sum_i \text{Var}[X_i] + \sum_i^I \sum_{\substack{j \\ j \neq i}}^I \text{Cov}[X_i, X_j] \right)$$

If X_i and X_j are independent for all i and j and $\text{Var}[X_i] = \sigma^2$ for all i then

$$\text{Var}[\overline{X}_I] = \frac{1}{I^2} \sum_i^I \sigma^2 = \frac{1}{I} \sigma^2 \tag{17-2}$$

From this equation, we note that when independence applies, $I*\text{Var}[\overline{X}_I] = \sigma^2$, a constant, and that $\text{Var}[\overline{X}_I]$ decreases in proportion to $1/I$. We will return to this observation shortly.

Under the assumption of independence and mild regularity conditions on X_i, the central limit theorem specifies that for large I the distribution of $\sqrt{I}(\overline{X}_I - \mu)/\sigma$ converges to a normal distribution with mean 0 and variance 1, that is, $N(0,1)$. If the X_i are also normally distributed then $\overline{X}_I$ is in fact normally distributed and $(\overline{X}_I - \mu)/\sqrt{S_X^2/I}$ has a t-distribution with $I-1$ degrees of freedom where S_X^2 is an estimator of σ^2. From this information, an exact confidence interval for $\overline{X}_I$ can be constructed. Note that by making X_i a batch average as discussed above, an assumption of normality for X_i is reasonable. Fishman (26) provides the following equation for the variance of S_X^2:

$$\text{Var}[S_X^2] = \sigma^4 \left(\frac{2}{I-1} + \frac{\gamma_2}{I} \right) \tag{17-3}$$

where γ_2 is the excess kurtosis (fourth central moment divided by the square of the second central moment minus three.) Eq. 17-3 indicates the amount of variability that may be expected in the estimate of the underlying process variance.

When $\text{Cov}[X_i, X_j]$ cannot be assumed to be zero, but we can assume a covariance stationary process, then $\text{Cov}[X_i, X_j] = R_{j-i} = R_h$. Using this notation in Eq. 17-1 and by combining terms, we can obtain

$$\text{Var}[\overline{X}_I] = \frac{1}{I} \sum_{h=1-I}^{I-1} \left(1 - \frac{|h|}{I}\right) R_h \qquad (17\text{-}4)$$

Substituting $\sigma^2 = R_o$ and $R_{-h} = R_h$ into Eq. 19-4 yields

$$\text{Var}[\overline{X}_I] = \frac{1}{I} \left\{ \sigma^2 + 2 \sum_{h=1}^{I-1} \left(1 - \frac{h}{I}\right) R_h \right\} \qquad (17\text{-}5)$$

Procedures for estimating $\text{Var}[\overline{X}_I]$ using this equation are discussed in Section 17.3.5.

If the autocovariance decays exponentially (a common and reasonable assumption is that $R_h = R_o \alpha^{|h|}$ for $0 < \alpha < 1$) then it can be shown that

$$\lim_{I \to \infty} I\,\text{Var}[\overline{X}_I] = \sum_{h=-\infty}^{\infty} R_h = m \qquad (17\text{-}6)$$

From Eq. 17-6, it is seen that as the number of batches increases the $\text{Var}[\overline{X}_I]$ decreases in proportion to $1/I$. Comparing Eq. 17-6 with Eq. 17-2, we observe that the underlying process variability, σ^2, is related to the sum of all covariances. Throughout this text, we refer to this quantity by the symbol m. Since the value of m is not based on the number of batches I, an estimate of m for a process permits the estimation of $\text{Var}[\overline{X}_I]$ for any I.

17.2.3   Interpreting Var $[\overline{X}_I]$

As mentioned above, $\text{Var}[\overline{X}_I] \to m/I$ for large I and under appropriate assumptions. Based on this, we can picture the distribution of $\overline{X}_I$ over time as shown in Figure 17-1. There are several observations to be made from Figure 17-1. First, $\overline{X}_I$ is a random variable and, hence, the values estimated are sample values. When making a simulation replication, one should expect a different value of $\overline{X}_I$ to result with the precision based on $f(\overline{X}_I)$ and, hence, $\text{Var}[\overline{X}_I]$. The length of a run or the number of batches can change $f(\overline{X}_I)$, that is, $f(\overline{X}_I)$ depends on I and the distribution of X_i. For the same run length, different estimators may be based on a different number of batches. Furthermore, the three distributions shown in Figure 17-1 all are shown with the same $E[\overline{X}_I]$. This need not be the case as biased estimators can be and are used. Thus, when comparing estimators for $\text{Var}[\overline{X}_I]$ under different experimental conditions, we need a basis to compare the estimates. The criterion used for comparison in most research efforts are m and the mean square error of the sample mean (34) denoted by $\text{MSE}[\overline{X}_I] = E[(\overline{X}_I - \mu_x)^2]$.

Unfortunately, equations for the computation of m for non-Markov processes have not been derived. For the number in the system in an M/M/1 queueing situation, Fishman (26) computes $m = 6840$ for the case in which the arrival rate, λ,

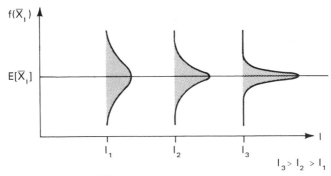

Figure 17-1 Distribution of $\overline{X}_I$.

equals 4.5 and the service rate, μ, equals 5. Also if $\lambda = 2.0$ and $\mu = 2.25$ then m = 361. For the M/M/∞ situation (68), m = $2\lambda/\mu^2$. A procedure has been developed for obtaining values of m for finite state Markov processes† (32,40).

The MSE[$\overline{X}_I$] is a criterion that combines the Var[$\overline{X}_I$] and the bias associated with $\overline{X}_I$. This is seen in the following development:

$$\begin{aligned}
\text{MSE}[\overline{X}_I] &= E[(\overline{X}_I - \mu_X)^2] \\
&= E[(\overline{X}_I - E[X_I] + E[\overline{X}_I] - \mu_X])^2] \\
&= E[(\overline{X}_I - E[\overline{X}_I])^2] + E[(E[\overline{X}_I] - \mu_X])^2] \\
&= \text{Var}[\overline{X}_I] + (\text{Bias}[\overline{X}_I])^2
\end{aligned}$$

(17-7)

When there is bias‡ associated with $\overline{X}_I$, then the probability that the theoretical mean is covered by (contained in) a confidence interval differs from a prescribed value due to the offset caused by the bias. The "coverage" is defined as the probability that the theoretical mean is covered by an interval centered at $E[\overline{X}_I]$ or $\overline{X}_I$. When estimators are employed which are unbiased, then MSE($\overline{X}_I$) reduces to Var[$\overline{X}_I$] and the coverage is the same as the value associated with the confidence interval. We are now ready to examine proposed procedures for estimating Var[$\overline{X}_I$].

† For finite state Markov processes, it is also shown that m is a function of both λ and μ and that $m(a\lambda, a\mu) = (1/a)[m(\lambda, \mu)]$. Glynn proves (32) that this result holds for countable state Markov processes like the M/M/1 queueing situation. Hence, to compute m for the M/M/1 queue with $\lambda/\mu = 0.9$ but with $\lambda = 4$, $\mu = 40/9$ then a = 8/9 and m = 9/8(6840) = 7695.

‡ A bias could exist if the underlying process was not covariance stationary or if $\overline{X}_I$ was computed using a ratio estimator (see Section 17.3.3).

17.3   PROCEDURES FOR ESTIMATING VAR[$\overline{X}_I$]

As discussed in the previous section, the variance of the sample mean plays a fundamental role in the reliability of simulation output. The estimation of Var[$\overline{X}_I$] from a single simulation run is complicated due to the dependence of the samples that are used in the computation of $\overline{X}_I$. A considerable amount of research has been performed regarding the estimation of Var[$\overline{X}_I$]. This research has resulted in five basic approaches which are listed below:

1. *Replication*—employ separate runs with each run being considered as a batch. From run i, we obtain a value of X_i and the Var[$\overline{X}_I$] is estimated using Eq. 17-2;
2. *Subintervals*—divide a run into equal batches (subintervals) and compute X_i as an average for batch i. Assume each X_i is independent and use Eq. 17-2 for estimating Var[$\overline{X}_I$];
3. *Regenerative cycles*—divide a simulation run into independent cycles by defining states where the model starts anew. Estimate the Var[$\overline{X}_I$] based on observed values in the independent cycles;
4. *Parametric modeling*—fit an equation(s) to the output values or a function of the output values obtained from a run. Derive an estimate of Var[$\overline{X}_I$] from the equations that model the simulation output;
5. *Covariance/spectral estimation*—estimate the autovariance from the sample output and use these in a spectral analysis or directly in Eq. 17-5 to estimate Var[$\overline{X}_i$].

Each of these five procedures will now be presented.

17.3.1   Replications

In this procedure, a value x_i of the random variable X_I is computed on run i. As discussed in Section 17-2.1, the variable X_i could be: the mean number of units in the system on run i; the mean time in the system per customer; or a binomial variable that represents the number of successes in a run. The mean of the X_i values over I runs is used as an estimate of the parameter of interest, that is,

$$\overline{X}_I = \frac{\sum\limits_{i=1}^{I} X_i}{I} \qquad (17\text{-}8)$$

An estimate of $\text{Var}[X_i]$, S_X^2, is then obtained using standard procedures as

$$S_X^2 = \frac{1}{I-1} \sum_{i=1}^{I} (X_i - \overline{X}_I)^2 = \frac{1}{I-1} \sum_{i=1}^{I} X_i^2 - \frac{1}{I(I-1)} \left(\sum_{i=1}^{I} X_i \right)^2 \qquad (17\text{-}9)$$

Equation 17-9 provides an estimate of the variability associated with a random sample obtained from each run. Since each run is an independent replication, an estimate of the variance of the sample mean can be obtained as shown in Eq. (17-10).

$$S_{\overline{X}}^2 = S_X^2 / I \qquad (17\text{-}10)$$

Based on $S_{\overline{X}}^2$ and $\overline{X}_I$ and using the central limit theorem, probability statements about the parameter of interest can be made after observations are taken. Tests of hypotheses can also be made based on these theoretic considerations.

The replication procedure has the desirable property that samples are independent. Another advantage is that it can be used for both terminating and steady-state analysis where a terminating analysis is one that is performed for a specific finite time period.† The disadvantages associated with replications are: 1) each replication contains a startup segment which may not be representative of stationary behavior; and 2) only one sample, X_i, is obtained from each replication which could mean that extensive information about the variable of interest is not being gleaned from the data. This is particularly the case when X_i is computed as a mean value for the run.

17.3.2 Subintervals

The approach to estimating the variance of $\overline{\overline{X}}_I$ using subintervals is to divide a single simulation run into batches. If each batch has b samples of $X_i(n)$ then a batch sample mean, X_i, is computed from

$$X_i = \frac{\sum_{n=1}^{b} X_i(n)}{b} \qquad (17\text{-}11)$$

---

† Law (54) states "we have concluded from talking with simulation practitioners that a significant proportion of real-world simulations are of the terminating type. This is fortunate because it means classical statistical analysis is applicable . . .".

If the subintervals are independent then Eq. 17-8, 17-9 a n d 17-10 are used to estimate $E[X_i]$, $Var[\overline{X}_i]$, $Var[\overline{X}_i]$, respectively.† The assumption of independence is typically made in simulation analyses even though there exists an autocovariance between the values at the end of one subinterval and those at the beginning of the next subinterval. This variance can cause a positive covariance between batch means. By making the batch size b larger, the covariance between the sample batch means should decrease. Procedures for determining the batch size such that the covariance between adjacent batch means is insignificant have been developed by Mechanic and McKay (59), Law and Carson (55), and Fishman (27,28). Schriber and Andrews (74) have proposed a modification to Fishman's algorithm.

Fishman's proposed procedure involves recomputing the batch values by doubling the batch size b until the null hypothesis that the $X_{i,b}$ for i=1,2, . . . , I_b are iid is accepted, where the subscript b is appended to X_i to indicate the dependence of it on the batch size. He recommends the use of the test statistic

$$C_b = 1 - \sum_{i=1}^{I_b-1} (X_{i,b} - X_{i+1,b})^2 \quad 2 \cdot \sum_{i=1}^{I_b} (X_{i,b} - \overline{X}_{I_b})^2$$

where I_b = number of batches when the batch size is b.

For large b, C_b is approximately the estimated autocorrelation coefficient between consecutive batches.

If the $X_{i,b}$ are independent and normally distributed then C_b has a mean of zero, a variance of $(I_b-2)/(I_b^2-1)$, and a distribution that is close to normal for b as small as 8. Thus, if these conditions hold, a standard test using normal tables can be applied. If $\{X_{i,b}\}$ has a monotone autocovariance function then a one-sided test is appropriate: otherwise a two-sided test is in order.

Several procedural details are necessary when using the above approach to setting the batch size. The observed values $x_i(n)$ must be recorded in order to compute $x_{i,b}$ for different values of b. Any non-representative values of $x_i(n)$ at the beginning of a run should be truncated before applying the test (see Section 17.5.2). An initial batch size needs to be set. Fishman recommends setting $I_b=1$ initially. Schmeiser has concluded that an I_b value between 10 and 30 is reasonable for most simulation situations (72). He also states that the initial value of I_b for Fishman's algorithm could be much larger with almost no deterioration in the confidence intervals.

---

† It can be shown that if the subintervals are independent, m associated with X_1, denoted $m(X_1)$, is $\frac{1}{b}*m(X_1(n))$ where $m(X_1(n))$ is the m value associated with individual observations.

The advantages of using subintervals to estimate the variance of the sample mean are that a single run can be used to obtain an estimate and only one transient period is included in the output (or required to be deleted). The disadvantage of the procedure is in establishing the batch size, b, which makes the subintervals independent. Note that for a fixed number of observations, increasing the batch size decreases the number of batches and, hence, could yield larger estimates of $Var[\overline{X}_I]$. Schmeiser's results (72) alleviate this difficulty by suggesting a number of batches, 10 to 30, that is reasonable. Another disadvantage involves the boundaries of a batch. Care must be taken in computing batch averages when an observation spans more than a single batch, for example, an arrival in batch i that leaves the system during batch $i+1$.

17.3.3 Regenerative Method

The regenerative method (16,29,44) is similar to the subinterval method in that it divides a simulation run into intervals which are referred to as cycles. A cycle starts when a specific state of the system is reached in which future behavior is independent of the past behavior. When a return is made to such a state, the cycle ends and one independent observation of each quantity of interest is obtained. By defining cycles in this manner, independent samples from the model are obtained and the covariance problem encountered when using subintervals is avoided. A different statistical problem arises, however, in that the length of a cycle is not predetermined but is a random variable.

The most commonly used regeneration point in queueing studies is a return to a status where servers are idle and no customers are waiting. If the next customer arrival is processed in a consistent fashion then each time a customer arrives to an empty system is a regeneration point and the start of a regeneration cycle. In inventory models, a possible regeneration point is when the inventory position is equal to a stock control level.

By construction, each cycle of a simulation run will be independent and we can base the estimates of the sample mean on cycle values. Following the development by Crane and Lemoine (17), let

$Y_i =$ the value of interest in the ith cycle, for example, the sum of customer waiting times in the ith cycle†; and

---

† The value of interest could also be a time-integrated variable, that is, the time-integrated number in the system during the ith cycle.

L_i = the length of the ith cycle, for example, the number of customers or the cycle time.

If X_{ik} is the kth sample on the ith cycle and we perform the simulation run until there are I cycles, then the following two equations hold

$$Y_i = \sum_{k=1}^{L_i} X_{ik} \tag{17-12}$$

and

$$\sum_{i=1}^{I} L_i = N \tag{17-13}$$

where N = total number of samples (a random variable).

The average of all the samples for a simulation run, $\overline{X}_I$, would normally be computed as shown in Eq. 17-14.

$$\overline{X}_I = \frac{\sum_{i=1}^{I} \sum_{k=1}^{L_i} X_{ik}}{N} \tag{17-14}$$

By substituting in the variables from Eqs. 17-12 and 17-13 into Eq. 17-14, we illustrate that $\overline{X}_I$ can be considered as the ratio of cycle averages.

$$\overline{X}_I = \frac{\sum_{i=1}^{I} \sum_{k=1}^{L_i} X_{ik}}{N} = \frac{\sum_{i=1}^{I} Y_i}{\sum_{i=1}^{I} L_i} = \frac{\sum_{i=1}^{I} Y_i/I}{\sum_{i=1}^{I} L_i/I} = \overline{Y}_I/\overline{L}_I \tag{17-15}$$

Since the number of samples per cycle is a random variable, we cannot specify both the number of cycles and the total number of samples. In such a case, we are using a ratio estimator which can be shown to be biased (26).

An estimate of the variance of $\overline{X}_I$ can be computed using Eq. 17-16

$$S_{\overline{X}}^2 = \frac{S^2}{(\overline{L}_I\sqrt{I})^2} \tag{17-16}$$

where

$$S^2 = S_Y^2 - 2\overline{X}_I S_{YL} + \overline{X}_I^2 S_L^2$$

and

$$S_Y^2 = \frac{1}{I-1} \sum_{i=1}^{I} (Y_i - \overline{Y}_I)^2 \ ,$$

$$S_L^2 = \frac{1}{I-1} \sum_{i=1}^{I} (L_i - \overline{L}_I)^2 ,$$

$$S_{YL} = \frac{1}{I-1} \sum_{i=1}^{I} (Y_i - \overline{Y}_I)(L_i - \overline{L}_I) \ .$$

As noted above $\overline{X}_I$ is a biased estimator. To alleviate the problem of bias with ratio estimators, a Jackknife estimator (36,46) can be used which eliminates the bias term of order $1/I$. The equation for the Jackknife estimator of the sample mean is given in Eq. 17-17

$$\overline{J} = \frac{1}{I} \sum_{i=1}^{I} J_i \qquad (17\text{-}17)$$

where J_i is referred to as a psuedo-value computed from

$$J_i = I \overline{X}_I - (I-1) \sum_{\substack{j=1 \\ j \neq i}}^{I} Y_j \Big/ \sum_{\substack{j=1 \\ j \neq i}}^{I} L_j$$

The J_i are considered to be independent and identically distributed so that confidence intervals for $\overline{X}_I$ can be constructed using estimates of $\overline{J}$ and $S_{J_i}/\sqrt{I}$.

The advantages of the regenerative method are that independent and identically distributed random variables for each cycle are obtained. Thus, standard statistical procedures can be used for tests of hypothesis and confidence interval calculations. However, to use the procedure, a regenerative point must be established for which the expected time between returns is finite and for which sufficient cycles are observed to achieve a reasonable confidence interval. As illustrated by the arc sine law presented in Chapter 2, Section 2 (69) this may not be an easy determination. An additional advantage is that the problems of determining a start-up procedure are avoided as statistical collection can begin when a regeneration point is reached which, if possible, could be the initial conditions specified. Disadvantages of the procedure are the added computations and the bias associated with the estimator for the sample mean.

17.3.4 Parametric Modeling

Parametric modeling involves the building of a model to describe the outputs from a simulation model. Values of the estimates of quantities of interest are then obtained through computations made on the parametric model. The procedure for employing parametric modeling involves the collection of sample values from a simulation and then fitting an equation(s) to the observed data values. This approach is similar to the one used when attempting to describe real world systems by fitting equations to data obtained from the system.

To provide further rationale for using this approach, consider a single server queueing situation in which customers are processed on a first-come, first-serve basis. If the variable of interest is the waiting time of a customer, we could write an equation that describes the waiting time of the $(j+1)$st customer in terms of the waiting time of the jth customer, the interarrival time random variable and the service time random variable. Such an equation can be developed based on the pictorial sketch shown below.

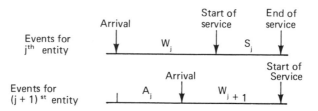

In this sketch, it is assumed that the $(j+1)$st entity arrives before the end of service for the jth entity. By equating the variables from the two lines given in the sketch, we obtain the following equation

$$W_{j+1} = \begin{cases} W_j + S_j - A_j & \text{if } A_j < W_j + S_j \\ 0 & \text{otherwise} \end{cases}$$

where

W_j is the waiting time of the jth entity,
S_j is the service time of the jth entity, and
A_j is the interarrival time between the jth and $(j+1)$st entity.

If we had simulated a queueing system and saved the observed values of W_j, S_j, and A_j and were sufficiently astute to derive a model for W_{j+1} such as the one given above, then we could use it to obtain information concerning the waiting time of customers.†

---

† This model is a convenient one for introducing sampling procedures and for performing research on the waiting time associated with a single server queueing situation. Since it is difficult to embellish, it is not a good model for teaching modeling procedures.

The above model development was presented to provide a rationale for attempting to fit a model to sample data. Past research on parametric modeling of simulation output has primarily been through the use of autoregressive (AR) models. Fishman has done extensive analyses of such models (29). Since the values obtained from the execution of a simulation model can be considered as time series data, we recommend the use of the Box-Jenkins methodology for model identification and estimation (8). An excellent discussion of this methodology is provided by Mabert (58). The Box-Jenkins methodology attempts to derive a parametric model of the sample data using an equation of the following form:

$$Y_t = \sum_{k=1}^{p} \phi_k Y_{t-k} - \sum_{l=1}^{q} \theta_l U_{t-l} + U_t \; ; t = 1, 2, \ldots, n \qquad (17\text{-}18)$$

where

$$Y_t = X(t) - E[X(t)]$$

and

U_t is white noise, that is, $E[U_t] = 0$ and

$$E[U_t U_{t-l}] = \begin{cases} \sigma_U^2 & l=0 \\ 0 & \text{otherwise} \end{cases}$$

The model of Eq. 17-18 is referred to as a combined autoregressive and moving average (ARMA) model. If all the terms which have a coefficient θ_l in Eq. 17-18 are deleted, then an autoregressive model of order p is obtained (AR(p)). An autoregressive model expresses Y_t as a linear combination of previous values of the time series plus a white noise component.

If all the terms with a coefficient of ϕ_k are deleted from Eq. 17-18, then a moving average model is obtained. The moving average model expresses Y_t as a linear combination of the past q error terms. This is referred to as a moving average model of order q and is designated as an MA(q) model.

The Box-Jenkins methodology provides procedures for identifying the order of an autoregressive model, p, and the order of a moving average model, q. In addition, procedures have been computerized for obtaining the best estimates of ϕ_k and θ_l. The program for making such computations can be obtained from The Ohio State University Data Center or The University of Wisconsin. The outputs from this program provide values for θ_l and ϕ_k and an estimate of the variance of the white noise, σ_U^2. With these estimates, an estimate of the variance of the sample mean can be computed as shown in Eq. 17-19

$$s_{\bar{X}}^2 = \frac{\widehat{m}}{n} \qquad (17\text{-}19)$$

where

$$\hat{m} = \hat{\sigma}_U^2 \frac{\left(1 - \sum_{l=1}^{q} \hat{\theta}_l\right)^2}{\left(1 - \sum_{k=1}^{p} \hat{\phi}_k\right)^2}$$

In our experience, parametric modeling of the time series obtained from a simulation model has not produced reliable estimates of the variance of the sample mean. This could be related to a non-stationary behavior of the time series and a non-normality of the individual observations. Significantly improved results have been obtained by building parametric models using a time series consisting of batch means. By using batch means, assumptions regarding stationarity and normality are alleviated. Andrews and Schriber (3) have developed a procedure for automatically fitting an ARMA model to estimate m.

Schruben, taking a different approach, computes a standardized time series for the output data by forming cumulative sums of the difference between the average and the observations (75). Statistical output measures are then developed from the standardized time series. This approach has the advantage of transforming the data into a familiar form.

The advantage of using parametric modeling is that an equation describing a variable of interest is obtained. Further analyses using the derived model can provide new insights into the system being simulated. The main disadvantage of parametric modeling is the lack of knowledge of the reliability of the model. Building a parametric model of a simulation model takes the analysis one step further away from the real system and requires much care on the part of the analyst.

17.3.5   Estimating Covariances and the Use of Spectral Analysis

In Section 17.2.2, we showed that

$$\text{Var}[\overline{X}_I] = \frac{1}{I}\left[R_o + 2\sum_{h=1}^{I-1}\left(1 - \frac{h}{I}\right)R_h\right]$$

Thus, if estimates of the autocovariances, R_h, can be obtained, we could compute

$$s_{\overline{X}}^2 = \frac{1}{I}\left[\hat{R}_o + 2\sum_{h=1}^{I-1}\left(1 - \frac{h}{I}\right)\hat{R}_h\right]$$

In the literature, the following three alternative equations have been proposed for computing $\hat{R}_h$:

$$A_h = \frac{1}{I-h} \sum_{i=1}^{I-h} (X_i - \overline{X}_I)(X_{i+h} - \overline{X}_I)$$

$$B_h = \frac{1}{I} \sum_{i=1}^{I-h} X_i X_{i+h} - \frac{1}{I-h} \left(\sum_{i=1}^{I-h} X_i \right) \left(\sum_{i=1}^{I-h} X_{i+h} \right)$$

$$C_h = \frac{1}{I} \sum_{i=1}^{I-h} (X_i - \overline{X}_I)(X_{i+h} - \overline{X}_I)$$

When a time series is short and the end points differ significantly from $\overline{X}_I$, B_h has been recommended as the estimator. In simulation studies, the time series is normally long and B_h is not employed.

The estimator A_h has intuitive appeal as it averages $(I-h)$ values. However, A_h has a larger mean square error than C_h. C_h has the disadvantage that it is a biased estimator. The current consensus is that for a time series with large I, C_h should be used to estimate R_h.

The past research on estimating the autocovariances dealt primarily with the sample variables, $X_i(t)$ or $X_i(n)$. These variables are highly correlated and estimates of the autocovariances are highly correlated. Thus, if a large value is obtained for the estimator of R_o, we would expect a high value relatively for the estimator of R_h. In simulation experiments, this phenomenon has been observed by Duket (20). The use of batch values, X_i, as recommended previously will alleviate this correlation in the estimates of the autocovariances.

An alternative procedure is to employ spectral analysis. The *spectrum* is defined as

$$g(\lambda) = \frac{1}{2\pi} \sum_{h=-\infty}^{\infty} R_h e^{-i\lambda h} \qquad -\pi \leq \lambda \leq \pi \qquad (17\text{-}20)$$

and the *spectral density function* as

$$f(\lambda) = g(\lambda)/R_o$$

The inverse transform of $g(\lambda)$ is given by

$$R_h = \int_{-\pi}^{\pi} g(\lambda) e^{i\lambda h} d\lambda$$

and can be used to obtain values of R_h.
For h=0, this yields

$$R_o = \int_{-\pi}^{\pi} g(\lambda) d\lambda$$

Thus, the underlying variance of the process can be thought of as consisting of nonoverlapping contributions at frequency λ. A large value of $g(\lambda)$ indicates variability in the process at frequency λ or periodically at $2\pi/\lambda$.

As discussed in Section 17.2, it can be shown for many systems that

$$\lim_{I \to \infty} I \, \text{Var}[\overline{X}_I] = m = \sum_{h=-\infty}^{\infty} R_h$$

Letting $\lambda=0$ in Eq. 17-20 yields

$$g(0) = \frac{1}{2\pi} \sum_{h=-\infty}^{\infty} R_h$$

and, hence,

$$m = 2\pi \, g(0)$$

Thus, if $g(0)$ can be estimated, an estimate of m can be obtained.

Extensive research has been performed on obtaining estimates of the spectrum for time series. The main difficulties involve the determination of the number of covariances to include in the computation, and the weighting function (lag window) to apply to the estimated autocovariance obtained from finite observations. Weighting functions have been developed by Bartlett, Tukey, and Parzen; others are referred to as the Rectangular and Variance weighting functions (21).

The advantage of the spectral approach is the extensive research that has been performed on spectral methods. The main disadvantage is that point estimates obtained from the spectrum, that is, at $\lambda=0$, are known to be unreliable. Employing data grouped into a single batch observation, as previously suggested, should diminish this reservation (41,61,81).

17.4   VARIANCE REDUCTION TECHNIQUES

The variance of the sample mean is a derived measure of the reliability that can be expected if the simulation experiment is repeatedly performed. It has been shown that longer runs should produce smaller estimates of $\text{Var}[\overline{X}_I]$. Thus, in some sense, the value of $\text{Var}[\overline{X}_I]$ is dependent on experimental procedures and calculations. Variance reduction techniques (VRT) are methods that attempt to reduce the estimated values of $\text{Var}[\overline{X}_1]$ through the setting of special experimental conditions or through the use of prior information. An excellent survey of variance reduction techniques has been published by Wilson (88). Nelson and Schmeiser (66) have attempted to characterize the underlying structure of the variance reduction process.

17.4.1 Antithetic Sampling

Eq. 19-1 for $\text{Var}[\overline{X}_1]$ contains terms involving the $\text{Cov}[X_iX_j]$. If $\text{Cov}[X_iX_j]$ can be made negative then the $\text{Var}[\overline{X}_1]$ will be reduced. Since X_i and X_j are functions of pseudorandom numbers, it has been suggested that if $X_i = f(r_1, r_2, \ldots, r_q)$ then letting $X_j = f(1-r_1, 1-r_2, \ldots, 1-r_q)$ will induce a negative covariance between X_i and X_j. Obtaining a negative covariance depends on the function f, which reflects a transformation of random numbers into sample values by the simulation model. Clearly, a general result regarding the use of the antithetic values can not be provided. However, in experiments, a variance reduction has been observed when such antithetic sampling is employed. The generation of the antithetic stream of random numbers: $1-r_1, 1-r_2, \ldots, 1-r_q$, is easily accomplished when using a multiplicative congruence random number generator of the form

$$z_k = az_{k-1} \bmod(c) \quad k=1,2,\ldots$$

and

$$r_k = z_k/c$$

It can be shown (46) that if

$$z'_0 = c - z_0$$

is used as a starting value for a sequence of random numbers then†

$$z'_k = c - z_k$$

and, hence,

$$r'_k = \frac{z'_k}{c} = 1 - r_k.$$

---

† Care is required when doing this with packaged random number generators that may add 1 to a seed value or that store the initial seed value as a real number.

In **AWESIM**, an antithetic sequence is obtained by specifying a negative initial seed value on the SEEDS control statement, that is, $-z_0$.

The application of antithetic samples within a batch or even within a run is not recommended. The manipulation of batches to produce antithetic samples could cause a distortion of the basic process and seems not to be warranted. Other proposed procedures appear more palatable. For example, perform pairs of independent runs in which antithetic streams are used on the second run of the pair. For a sequence of arrivals, let the kth interarrival time be based on r_k in the first run of a pair and based on $1-r_k$ on the second run of a pair. When doing this, the variance calculation for 2I runs is simplified by combining values across pairs of runs. If X_i' is the antithetic value for X_i, then

$$\text{Var}[\overline{X}_I] = \text{Var}\left(\frac{\sum_{i=1}^{I}(X_i+X_i')}{2I}\right) = \text{Var}\left(\frac{\sum_{i=1}^{I}U_i}{I}\right)$$

where

$$U_i = \frac{X_i+X_i'}{2}$$

When combined in this fashion, covariance terms between runs need not be computed.

Another suggestion that is in the spirit of antithetic sampling (28) is to switch the streams employed for interarrival times and service times in alternate runs. To see that this induces antithetic behavior, note that long interarrival times reduce potential congestion whereas long service times increase potential congestion. Results of the application of antithetic sampling are summarized by Kleijnen (46). Typically, the results are for small-scale simulation models. Kleijnen defines a measure of variance reduction as a percentage change, that is, if $\text{Var}_R[\overline{X}_I]$ is obtained using a VRT then

$$\text{Percent Variance Reduction} = \frac{\text{Var}[\overline{X}_I] - \text{Var}_R[\overline{X}_I]}{\text{Var}[\overline{X}_I]} * 100$$

Hammersley and Handscomb (39), Tocher (80), and Fishman (26) define variance reduction as a ratio, that is

$$\text{Variance Reduction} = \frac{\text{Var}[\overline{X}_I]}{\text{Var}_R[\overline{X}_I]}$$

Before ending this discussion of antithetic sampling, two important points should be mentioned. First, although the correlation between antithetic random numbers is $-1.$, the correlation between samples based on such numbers may not be -1. If the samples are from a symmetric distribution, the correlation will be -1. If the samples are from an exponential distribution, Fishman (26) shows the correlation between antithetic samples is -0.645. A similar increase in the negative correlation is obtained for other distributions.

The second point involves the simulation model. If the model involves a square or higher order even relation then the introduction of a negative correlation can result in a positive contribution to the variance of the sample mean.

17.4.2 Common Streams

A typical practice when performing a simulation is to employ historical data as the driving force. As an example, the time of arrivals of jobs to a computer could be maintained and used to define the arrival times and job characteristics for a simulation of the computer center. Simulations involving the use of historical data are sometimes referred to as *trace-driven*. Recognizing that the historical arrival pattern is a single time series, it is apparent that its repeated use reduces the variation of the output from a simulation model. By starting different simulation runs with the same random number seed, that is, employing a common stream, a similar variance reduction can be obtained. Care is required when employing trace-driven or common streams in that the complete variability associated with the system being modeled is not incorporated in the model. The analyst should ensure that the single time series employed by such a practice is representative of the stochastic process being modeled.

A more appealing use of common streams is when comparing alternatives. In this situation, the variance of a difference between sample means is of interest, that is

$$\mathrm{Var}[\overline{X}_I^{(1)} - \overline{X}_I^{(2)}] = \mathrm{Var}[\overline{X}_I^{(1)}] + \mathrm{Var}[\overline{X}_I^{(2)}] - 2\mathrm{Cov}[\overline{X}_I^{(1)}, \overline{X}_I^{(2)}]$$

where $\overline{X}_I^{(k)}$ is the sample mean for the alternative k. By using common streams, the $\mathrm{Cov}[\overline{X}_I^{(1)}, \overline{X}_I^{(2)}]$ should be positive and a reduction in the variance of the difference should be obtained. The use of a common stream here only presumes that the time series generated affects both alternatives in a similar manner. Extreme care must be taken if common streams are employed in conjunction with antithetic sampling techniques as a variance increase has been observed under several situations (46).

17.4.3   Prior Information

The Rao-Blackwell theorem presented in Hogg (43) can be interpreted as specifying that a variance reduction can be obtained by estimating the sample mean based on a conditioned random variable. One procedure for implementing this approach is to employ analytic results in the estimation process. We present two illustrations of this procedure.

It is well known that for a wide class of queueing situations, Little's formula (57,79) holds

$$L = \lambda W$$

where

L is the expected number in a system

W is the expected time in the system

λ is the effective arrival rate to the system, that is, the number of arrivals that are eventually served per unit time.

In a run, the average number of entities in a queue, $\overline{N}$, will be equal to the product of the observed arrival rate, λ_0, in the run and the average waiting time of all entities passing through the queue, $\overline{T}$. Notationally, we can write $\overline{N} = \lambda_0 \overline{T}$. This equation can be developed by observing that the time integrated number in the queue is equal to the sum of the waiting times (assuming at the end of the run all entities leave the queue). Based on this information, we could compute

$$\text{Var}[\overline{N}] = \lambda^2 \, \text{Var}[\overline{T}]$$

assuming λ is a known value. This equation provides the basis for an indirect estimator of the variance of the average number in the system by multiplying the estimate of $\text{Var}[T]$ obtained from a simulation by the value of λ^2. The rationale for the variance reduction is the use of the theoretical arrival rate λ in the estimation of $\text{Var}[N]$. In the actual simulation, a sampling process is used and a sample arrival rate would be drawn for the entire simulation. If λ is treated as an independent random variable, the relevant equation would be

$$\text{Var}[\overline{N}] = \text{Var}[\lambda]\text{Var}[\overline{T}] + E^2[\lambda]\text{Var}[\overline{T}] + \text{Var}[\lambda]E^2[\overline{T}]$$

and, hence, we expect a variance reduction by assuming that λ is a constant, that is, $\text{Var}[\lambda] = 0$.

The above establishes that a variance reduction should occur but another question still remains. Should we estimate $\text{Var}[\overline{N}]$ directly and use it to obtain an indirect estimate of $Var[\overline{T}]$ or vice versa? Law (53) considered five equations that relate the first moments of number in system, number in queue, time in system, time in queue, and work content in system. Using estimates obtained from regenerative procedures, he showed analytically, assuming steady-state values are of interest, that for the $M/G/1$ queueing situation, it is more efficient (less variance of the sample means) to use indirect estimators based on the variance of the time in the system.

A second example of the use of prior information is based on the work of Carter and Ignall (10). This study involved the analysis of an inventory situation in which backorders were allowed. For such studies, the expected number of backorders must be estimated. However, backorders may be infrequent and long simulations may be required to obtain low variance estimates of the average number of backorders. The Carter and Ignall approach was to derive an expression for the expected number of backorders given the inventory position at the beginning of a period prior to demands being met. For period t, they showed that

$$E[B_t|A_t] = E[D_t] - A_t + \sum_{d=0}^{A_t} (A_t-d)P[D_t=d]$$

where

  B_t is the number of backorders in period t
  A_t is the inventory position at beginning of period t
  D_t is the demand in period t.

An estimate of the average backorders in the simulation was obtained by observing the values of A_t and solving the above equation for $E[B_t|A_t]$ for t=1,2, . . . ,T. Average values for the T periods could then be obtained.

The above procedure resulted in variance reduction ratios of 3.89 and 8.79 for two different parameter settings. The procedure is a direct application of the Roa-Blackwell theorem in which the prior information concerning the distribution of the demand, D_t, is used in estimating the average number of backorders.

The use of prior information as a variance reduction technique is appealing because it allows the combining of analytical and experimental procedures. Since direct estimation is always possible, a check on the variance reduction is easily made. Since the reliability of results is being considered, the question of why there should be multiple estimates of the variance of the sample mean should not be bothersome. Remember the question raised in the first section of this chapter was related to the variability expected if the simulation experiment is repeated? This implicitly assumes that the same procedures for statistics collection and analysis are used when computing the variance.

The difficulty associated with the use of prior information involves the derivation of equations upon which to base the computations of the sample values.

17.4.4   Control Variates as a VRT

The concept associated with control variates is the identification of a variable, say Y, that has a positive covariance with the variable of interest, say X. If such a control variable exists and if we can derive the theoretical expectations associated with the control variable, then a variance reduction for the variable of interest can be obtained. To see how this is accomplished, consider the following equation that combines the sample means $\overline{X}_I$ and $\overline{Y}_I$ to form a new random variable, $\overline{Z}_I$:

$$\overline{Z}_I = \overline{X}_I + (E[Y] - \overline{Y}_I)$$

clearly, $E[\overline{Z}_I] = E[\overline{X}_I]$ if an unbiased estimator for $E[Y]$ is used. Looking now at variances, we have

$$\text{Var}[\overline{Z}_I] = \text{Var}[\overline{X}_I] + \text{Var}[\overline{Y}_I] - 2\,\text{Cov}[\overline{X}_I,\overline{Y}_I]$$

From this equation, we see that $\text{Var}[\overline{Z}_I] < \text{Var}[\overline{X}_I]$ if $\text{Var}[\overline{Y}_I] < 2\,\text{Cov}[\overline{X}_I,\overline{Y}_I]$.

Extensive research has been performed on the theoretical aspects of control variates (46,63). Generalizations to multiple control variates with weighting coefficients have been explored, that is,

$$\overline{Z}_I = \overline{X}_I + \sum_{k=1}^{K} w_k(E[Y_k] - \overline{Y}_{Ik})$$

However, little practical application of control variates has been reported. Typical control variates suggested are input variables (assuming the output variables are positively correlated with the input variables) and models derived by applying limiting assumptions to the simulation model.

The control variate procedure is easy to comprehend and should be considered further. However, application experience is necessary in order to properly evaluate its significance (85,86).

17.4.5   Other Variance Reduction Techniques

In a section on variance reduction techniques, we feel called upon to mention stratified sampling and importance sampling procedures. These VRT have been used in Monte Carlo studies (39,80) and in standard sampling experiments (14). An excellent review of the procedures and attempts to apply them is contained in

Kleijnen (46). Based on a review of the literature, it is our opinion that these techniques require further refinement before they can be applied in advanced simulation applications. Therefore, only a brief review of the techniques is presented.

Stratified Sampling Procedure.   Stratified sampling procedures involve the definition of a variable y from which the stratification classes G_k can be defined. The random samples for X_i are then stratified by examining y_i corresponding to the ith observation and classifying X_i to be in the kth strata if $y_i \in G_k$. It is assumed that $p_k = P(y \in G_k)$ is known and the sample mean based on stratification is computed as

$$\overline{X}_{ST} = \sum_k p_k \overline{X}_k$$

where $\overline{X}_k$ is the sample mean for the kth strata. It can be shown that $\overline{X}_{ST}$ is an unbiased estimator of μ_x. It can also be shown that (14,46)

$$Var[\overline{X}_{ST}] = \sum_k p_k^2 Var[\overline{X}_k] \leq Var[\overline{X}]$$

so that a variance reduction may be obtained through stratification. Greater variance reductions are obtained when the absolute differences between the strata means, μ_k, and population mean, μ_x, are large.

Importance Sampling Procedure.   Importance sampling involves a redefinition of the variable of interest by defining a new density function that gives more weight to the values of X that contribute the most to the expected value. For example, assume we are going to estimate the expected value of g(X) where X is a random variable whose density function is f(x). From the "law of the unconscious statistician" (71), we have

$$E[g(X)] = \int_x g(x)f(x)dx$$

Rewriting the above by defining the density h(x), we have

$$E[g(X)] = \int_x \frac{g(x)f(x)}{h(x)} h(x)dx$$

In importance sampling, this result is used to estimate the sample mean by selecting values of x in accordance with h(x) and then computing a sample value equal to [g(x)f(x)]/[h(x)] for the value of x selected. The estimate of the sample average is obtained by summing these values and dividing by the number of values generated.

17.5   START-UP POLICIES

The initial conditions for a simulation model may cause the values obtained from the model to be different from those obtained after a startup period. If the system being modeled has a natural termination time, then such a transient response is anticipated and the values obtained during the startup period, although different, would be representative of the outputs obtained from the real system. However, when steady-state performance is to be estimated, the initial responses can adversely influence the estimators of steady-state performance. This latter problem is the one discussed in this section.

Startup policies are used for setting the initial conditions for the simulation model and specifying a procedure for establishing a truncation point, d, at which sample values should begin to be included in the estimators being computed. Basically, the initial-condition setting attempts to provide a starting point that requires only a limited amount of data truncation to be performed, that is, one that allows a small value of d to be employed. The truncation point specification involves two considerations. The deletion of initial values tends to reduce the bias of the output estimators. Deletion of values may, however, increase the estimate of the $\mathrm{Var}[\bar{X}_I]$ as it would be based on fewer observations. This latter assertion assumes that the deleted values are samples that have a variability similar to the variability associated with steady-state samples. This may not be the case.

From the above discussion, it appears that a trade-off is required in evaluating startup policies between bias reduction and variance reduction. Thus, it seems natural to employ the mean square error and the coverage as evaluation measures for startup policies. A procedure has been developed to make such an evaluation and the reader is referred to Wilson and Pritsker (83,84) for a summary of past research and for further details regarding this trade-off analysis.

In this section, we present various proposed initial condition rules and truncation procedures. Before doing so, several observations are in order. The use of startup policies should be considered in conjunction with the estimation procedure. If estimators are to be obtained using regenerative methods then the startup policy decision is an easy one, that is, start the run in the regenerative state so that the first cycle starts immediately and no truncation is required. If the estimation procedure is based on a single time series then the startup policy is only applied once and it is not too inefficient to truncate. However, if replication is used, the startup policy is used repetitively and great care is needed in establishing it.

Another observation involves past research on startup policies. Theoretical results (7,25) are only available for small, well-behaved models. For such models. the variability associated with sample values during startup is not too different from the steady-state variability. Thus, the theoretical research tends to indicate that no truncation should be performed. Practical applications, however, indicate this is not the case and that truncation is a reasonable policy to follow. This is especially true when dealing with job shops or conveyor systems in which many sequential operations must be performed before the system is "loaded". These points bring the discussion back to initial condition setting.

17.5.1   Initial Condition Setting

The ideal initial condition setting would be to sample from the steady-state distributions that underlie the simulation model and set the initial conditions based on the sample values obtained. Repeated use of this procedure would ensure sound statistical estimates of steady-state performance. This is clearly a "catch 22" situation as knowledge of the steady-state distribution would preclude the need for the simulation model. To avoid such a situation, three basic rules have been proposed for setting the initial state of the system:

1. Start the system "empty and idle";
2. Start the system at the steady-state mode; and
3. Start the system at the steady-state mean.

Rule 1 has the advantage of being easy to implement. It has the disadvantage in application studies of not being a good representative state. For small scale models, such as the $M|M|1$ queueing situation, it is a good representative state as "empty and idle" is the modal state.

Rule 2 specifies that the most likely state, that is, the state with the highest probability of occurring, should be the starting condition. Through experimental analysis, it was selected as the best initial condition for the models evaluated (83). The main disadvantage is the inability to determine the modal state for a large model.

Rule 3 recommends that the starting state be the expected or average state. The advantage of this rule is that the average state can be approximated through the making of a pilot study or by analyzing a related but analytically tractable model. Intuitively, starting in the expected state should provide initial samples that have a representative variability. However, there have been no published results which indicate that starting a simulation in the "average" state produces better statistical estimators.

17.5.2   Truncation Procedures

The simplest truncation procedure is to specify a time at which the collection of sample data is to be initiated. Actually, in simulation models, such a rule is implemented by discarding all sample values collected up to the truncation point. This is the case in SLAM II, and truncation is implemented by either including a MONTR statement in the input with the CLEAR option specified or by directly calling subroutine CLEAR at the time truncation is desired.

The question that arises for setting the truncation point is how to specify the time at which truncation should be made. One approach, which is perhaps the most common in applications, is to make a pilot run and select a time based on the pilot run. Although not normally done on a formal basis, the analyst considers such quantities as the number of consecutive times sample values have increased or decreased, differences between successive batch averages and successive cumulative averages, and crossings of averages by the sample values. An approach proposed by Welch (81) is to perform a set of pilot runs and select a time based on the sequence of averages computed over the runs at equally spaced points in time. Graphing the sequence of averages helps to select the truncation time. Welch (81) graphically shows the effect of using 5, 25, and 100 runs in determining a truncation point for an example problem. He also advocates smoothing the data using a moving average procedure. Many authors have attempted to formalize these concepts and to provide a truncation rule that can be used in the simulation model for detecting when the conditions for truncation are met by the time series values for a given run.

Papers that survey and evaluate some of these rules are available (31,83,84). A limited summary of these rules is presented in Table 17-1. Most evaluations have been made on small models and indicate that truncation should not be employed. For the reasons cited earlier, these results may not apply for large-scale models.

Table 17-1 Truncation rules.†

Proposer	Rule
Conway(15)	Set d so that x(d+1) is neither the maximum nor the minimum of the values $\{x(n) : n=d+1, \cdots, N\}$
Fishman(25)	Set d=n when $\{\text{sgn}(x(t) - \overline{x}_n) : t=0,1,2, \cdots n\}$ contains k runs where k is a parameter to be specified. This rule corresponds to setting d=n when the time series $\{x(t) : t=0,1,2, \cdots n\}$ has crossed $\overline{x}_n$ at least (k − 1) times.
Schriber(73)	Set d=n when the batch means for the k most recent batches of size b all fall within an interval of length ϵ.
Fishman(25)	Set d so that the number of observations deleted is "equivalent" to one independent observation where the number of dependent observations to independent observations is given by m/R_o. Thus set $d=m/R_o - 1$.
Gordon(35)	Make k replications to compute Var $[\overline{x}_n]$, n=1,2, $\cdots$. Set d= n for which Var $[\overline{x}_n]$ begins to fall off as 1/n.
Gafarian(31)	Set d equal to the smallest n for which x(n) is neither the maximum nor minimum of all preceding observations $\{x(t) : t=0,1,2, \cdots, n\}$.

† The notation used in this table suppresses the batch number subscript and employs lower case letters as the rules depend directly on the sample values observed.

In the application of the proposed truncation rules, four issues should be kept in mind:

1. The expected value of a sample average lags the expected values of the process variable if the system is initially empty and leads it if the system is loaded to capacity (21);
2. Crossings of averages are not as likely as anticipated;
3. Truncation rules are extremely sensitive to parameter settings. Also, parameter setting procedures are not available for many proposed rules (82); and
4. For a long initial startup period, the application of a truncation rule can be time-consuming and, hence, expensive.

These issues account for the lack of use of truncation procedures in applications and the direct use of a truncation time for clearing statistics. A promising technique that alleviates these difficulties is to use cumulative sums as proposed by Schruben (76). Truncation rules have been explored by Schruben based on this work and quality control procedures.

17.6   STOPPING RULES

Determining the length of a simulation run as specified in terms of the number of batches is a complex problem. If we are willing to assume that $\overline{X}_I$ is unbiased and that $Var[\overline{X}_I] = \sigma_{\overline{X}}^2/I$ then the number of batches I required to obtain a $(1-\alpha)$ confidence that the mean μ_X is contained in a prescribed interval can be computed using standard statistical formula. Symbolically, suppose we desire

$$P[\overline{X}_I - g \leq \mu_X \leq \overline{X}_I + g] \geq 1 - \alpha$$

where g is a prescribed half-length for the confidence interval. Letting $Z = \sqrt{I}(\overline{X}_I - \mu_X)/\sigma_X$, we have

$$P\left[|Z| \leq \frac{g\sqrt{I}}{\sigma_X}\right] \geq 1 - \alpha$$

with equality holding for the smallest value of I, say I*. Assuming I* is large enough so that the central limit theorem applies, we have

$$I^* = \left(\frac{\sigma_X}{g} Z_{\alpha/2}\right)^2$$

where

$$Z_{\alpha/2} \text{ is such that } \frac{1}{\sqrt{2\pi}} \int_{Z_{\alpha/2}}^{x} e^{-y^2/2} \, dy = \alpha/2$$

This equation for I* requires knowledge of σ_X. A common trick is to specify g in relative terms of σ_X, that is, let $g = v\sigma_X$ for $v > 0$. In this case, I* can be computed without knowledge of σ_X. Values of I* for combinations of v and α are given in Table 17-2.

From Table 17-2, we see that it requires almost 400 batches to obtain a 95 percent confidence interval that μ_X is within $(\overline{X}_I - 0.1\,\sigma_X, \overline{X}_I + 0.1\,\sigma_X)$. Similar analyses can be performed for determining the sample size to have a prescribed confidence interval on the variance or on a probability value.

Throughout this chapter, we have proposed the use of a batch mean as the sample value X_I. Because of this, the assumptions required in the above procedure are

Table 17.2 Values of I* for combinations of v and α.

I* v	α 0.02	0.05	0.10
0.01	54093	38416	27060
0.10	541	384	271
0.20	135	96	68
0.50	22	15	11

tenable. If the independence assumption is not appropriate, then we can use $\text{Var}[\overline{X}_I] = m/I$ and replace σ_X in the above equations by m.

Typically, s_X is used in place of σ_X (or $\hat{m}$ for m) in which case $\sqrt{I}(\overline{X}_I - \mu)/s_X$ has a t-distribution. In simulation studies, I is usually large enough to assume that the normal approximation to the t-distribution holds. To set I* before the simulation is started, a value of s_X is required. In some cases, pilot studies are performed to obtain a value for s_X from which I* is estimated. A more general approach is to use a sequential stopping rule.

A sequential stopping rule specifies a condition that when satisifed will yield the desired objective. Starr (78) has shown that if the X_i are iid normal random variables that

$$P\{\overline{X}_{I*} - g \le \mu \le \overline{X}_{I*} + g\} \ge \begin{cases} 0.928 \text{ for } 1-\alpha = 0.95 \\ 0.985 \text{ for } 1-\alpha = 0.99 \end{cases} \tag{17-21}$$

when I* is set according to

$$I* = \min\{I : I \ge 3 \text{ and odd}; s_X^2 \le Ig^2/t_{a/2,I-1}^2\} \tag{17-22}$$

where $t_{a/2,I-1}$ corresponds to the $1-\alpha/2$ fractile of the student t-distribution with I−1 degrees of freedom, for example, $t_{.025,10} = 2.228$.

The degradation in the confidence interval occurs because the test is being sequentially applied. Fishman (28) proposes the use of Eq. 17-22 without the requirement for I to be odd, since the requirement for I to be odd is due to the intractability of the analysis when I is even. The use of Eq. 17-22 in a simulation experiment requires a table of t-values, a prescription for g, a batch size specification and then the periodic testing of computed values of s_x until its value is below that required in Eq. 17-22. When this occurs, the confidence interval as specified by Eq. 17-21 holds.

When a relative specification is desired, that is, $-v\mu \le \overline{X}_I - \mu \le v\mu$ where $v > 0$, Nadas (64) has shown that the stopping rule

$$I^* = \min \{I : s_{\overline{X}}^2 \le [(Iv\overline{x}_I/t_{a/2,I-1})^2 - 1]/(I - 1)\} \qquad (17\text{-}23)$$

will result in a limiting confidence interval of

$$\lim_{v \to 0} P[\overline{X}_{I\bullet}/(1+v) \le \mu_X \le \overline{X}_{I\bullet}/(1-v)] = 1-\alpha$$

Note that for large I and $g = v\overline{x}_I$, the stopping rule given by Eq. 17-23 approximates the rule given by Eq. 17-22.

Since there is a degradation in the coverage associated with the use of the stopping rules specified by Eq. 17-22 and Eq. 17-23, we recommend for important decisions that I* be established not as the minimum number of batches for which the condition on $s_{\overline{X}}^2$ holds, but as the value of I for which the condition holds a second time. Typically, this should only require one additional batch to be obtained but it may require more. Using this rule should help to compensate for both the degradation expected from Eq. 17-21 and the inherent optimism (smaller variance) estimates) associated with the calculation of $s_{\overline{X}}^2$ based on the assumption of iid batch observations.

In addition to determining the sample size to meet desired confidence interval specifications, there are practical issues associated with the stopping of a simulation run. Such questions involve the consideration of what to do about entities in the model at the end of a run. The answers to such questions are problem specific. If such entities are representative of the other entities on which statistics were collected, then the further processing of them should not matter. However, if they are atypical or if some information has been collected on them, then their processing should be considered. For example, in a job shop where a shortest processing time rule was employed, the jobs remaining at the end of a run could be those jobs whose processing times are extremely long. Not processing such jobs would lead to a bias in the statistics on time in system. Care must be taken to avoid such a situation.

A more general procedure for establishing a stopping condition involves the concept of marginal return. It has been proposed that a run should be stopped when the marginal improvement in potential profits based on the run decreases below the marginal costs associated with continuing the run (30,44). Although this is a good general concept, assessing potential profits and calculating marginal costs can be difficult.

17.7   STATISTICAL INFERENCE

In simulation studies, inferences or predictions concerning the behavior of the system under study are to be made based on experimental results obtained from the simulation. Because a simulation model contains random elements, the outputs from the simulation are observed samples of random variables. As a consequence, any assertions which are made concerning the operation of the system based on simulatin results should consider the inherent variability of the simultion outputs. This variability is summarized or taken into account by the use of confidence intervals, tolerance limits or through hypothesis testing.

17.7.1   Confidence Intervals

In Section 17.2.2, we discussed methods for estimating the mean and variance parameters of a population based on a sample record. The estimates were calculated as a single number from the sample record and are referred to as *point estimates*. In general, an estimate will differ from the true but unknown parameter as the result of chance variations. The use of a point estimate has the disadvantage that it does not provide the decision maker with a measure of the accuracy of the estimate. A probability statement which specifies the likelihood that the parameter being estimated falls within prescribed bounds provides such a measure and is referred to as confidence interval or an interval estimate.

The parameter of primary interest in simulation analysis is the population mean. In the classical development of the confidence interval for the mean, it is assumed that the samples are independent and identically distributed (iid). Hence, by the Central Limit Theorem, the sample mean, $\overline{X}_I$, is approximately normally distributed for sufficiently large I. As stated previously, the assumption of independence is not a necessary condition for the application of the Central Limit Theorem.

If we assume that $\overline{X}_I$ is normally distributed, then the statistic

$$Z = \frac{\overline{X}_1 - \mu}{\sigma_{\overline{x}}}$$

is a random variable which is normally distributed with a mean of zero and standard deviation of one. Furthermore,

$$P[-Z_{\alpha/2} < Z < Z_{\alpha/2}] = 1 - \alpha$$

where $Z_{\alpha/2}$ is the value for Z such that the area to its right on the standard normal curve equals $\alpha/2$. Hence, we can assert with probability $1-\alpha$ that

$$\overline{X}_1 - Z_{\alpha/2} \cdot \sigma_{\overline{x}} < \mu < \overline{X}_1 + Z_{\alpha/2} \cdot \sigma_{\overline{x}} \qquad (17\text{-}24)$$

that is, a proportion, $1-\alpha$, of confidence intervals based on I samples of x should contain (cover) the mean μ. This proportion is called the coverage probability.

The above formula assumes knowledge of the standard deviation of the mean, $\sigma_{\overline{x}}$, which is usually unknown. If we use the sample standard deviation of the mean, $S_{\overline{x}}$, to estimate $\sigma_{\overline{x}}$, we can develop a similar relationship by noting that the statistic

$$t = \frac{\overline{X}_1 - \mu}{S_{\overline{x}}}$$

is a random variable having a student t-distribution with I-1 degrees of freedom. Hence, a $1-\alpha$ confidence interval for μ using the estimate $S_{\overline{x}}$ is given by

$$\overline{X}_1 - t_{\alpha/2, I-1} S_{\overline{x}} < \mu < \overline{X}_1 + t_{\alpha/2, I-1} S_{\overline{x}} \qquad (17\text{-}25)$$

where $t_{a/2, I-1}$ is a critical value of the t-statistic with (I-1) degrees of freedom.

If the samples X_i are iid, the confidence intervals given by 17-24 and 17-25 are modified by the substitutions

$$\sigma_{\overline{x}} = \frac{\sigma_x}{\sqrt{I}} \qquad (17\text{-}26)$$

and

$$S_{\overline{x}} = \frac{S_x}{\sqrt{I}} \qquad (17\text{-}27)$$

respectively.

Methods for determining $S_{\overline{x}}$ for use in Expression 17-25 in the case of autocorrelated samples are described in Section 17.3. The most direct approach is to organize the experiment to obtain independent observations which can be accomplished through replicating the simulation or organizing the data into batches.

17.7.2 Tolerance Intervals

A tolerance interval provides a range for an observation or for an average of a set of observations. Remember that the observation and its average are random variables. Because we are setting an interval on a random variable, it is necessary to specify the fraction of samples of the random variable that is desired to be within the tolerance interval and then to further specify the confidence with which we desire the fraction of samples to be contained within the interval. Hence, we specify that, with $(1-\delta)$ probability, we desire a range such that $(1-\varepsilon)$ fraction of observations of $\overline{X}_I$, each based on a sample size of I, will fall in the tolerance interval. Wilson (87) developed the following formula for such a range:

$$\overline{X}_I \pm Z_{\varepsilon/2} Q \frac{S_x}{\sqrt{I}}$$

where $Z_{\varepsilon/2}$ is a critical value of the normal distribution corresponding to a $(1-\varepsilon)$ confidence, and Q is given by

$$Q = \frac{(2I+1)}{2I} \sqrt{\frac{(I-1)}{\chi^2_{\delta,I-1}}}$$

where $\chi^2_{\delta,I-1}$ is a critical value from the chi-square distribution with $(1-\delta)$ confidence and $(I-1)$ degrees of freedom.

In an experiment consisting of I runs, Wilson also derived the following tolerance interval formula that the probability is at least $(1-\delta)(1-\varepsilon)$ that a single additional observation X_{I+1} will fall in the interval

$$\overline{X}_I \pm Z_{\varepsilon/2} Q S_x$$

17.8 DESIGN OF EXPERIMENTS

A simulation run is an experiment in which an assessment of the performance of a system is estimated for a prescribed set of conditions. In the jargon of design of experiments, the conditions are referred to as factors and treatments where a treatment is a specific level of a factor. The literature in the field of design of experiments is extensive (13,49,65). The purpose of this section is to present the issues relating to the design of expenments, but not to present the details as to how one should design a simulation experiment. The statistical techniques associated with the design of experiments are well documented. Applications of the procedures of analysis of variance (ANOVA); the Shapiro-Wilk test for testing normality assumptions; or the Newman-Keuls test for investigating all pairs of means are not considered to be significantly different in simulation studies from their use in other areas (2) .

The major problem involved in simulation experiments is associated with the definition of the inference space associated with the simulation model. Making a priori assessment of how widely the results obtained from the simulation model are to be applied, and developing a thorough understanding of the inferences that can be made, are the most neglected aspects of the design of experiments associated with simulation studies. A possible reason for this is the inclusion of factors in the experiment that relate to the multitude of alternatives open to the analyst and the extensive number of experimental controls that must be set when performing the experiment. In previous sections of this chapter we have discussed some of these experimental controls such as: starting conditions; sampling procedures; run length; batch size; and estimation procedures. Documented examples which include all these factors are not available; however, the survey by Kleijnen is extensive and highly recommended (49). Also there is an excellent article which presents the details of an experimental design and analysis of simulations to evaluate scheduling rules (11).

In general, the objectives of simulation experiments are to:
1. obtain knowledge of the effects of controllable factors on experimental outputs;
2. estimate system parameters of interest;
3. make a selection from among a set of alternatives; and
4. determine the treatment levels for all factors which produce an optimum response.

When multiple factors are involved the approach to the first two items listed above is to select one of the many possible experimental designs and to hypothesize a model for the analysis of variance for the experimental design selected. The experimental design specifies the combination of treatment levels along with the number of replications for each combination for which the simulation model must be exercised. Using the data obtained from the experiment, the parameters of the hypothesized model are determined along with the estimation of the error terms. Interaction plots are then drawn to ascertain the joint effects of the various factors. The significance of each factor is then judged based on the derived model, and from this, estimates of system parameters of interest can be calculated. This procedure is reminiscent of the parametric modeling approach described earlier in this chapter for a single performance measure of interest. Kleijnen has used regression techniques to develop metamodels of simulation outputs. The metamodels are then used to investigate alternatives characterizing different parameter settings (48,50,51). Kleijnen has applied this approach with success (49).

In the problem of making a choice among alternatives, the statistical procedures or ranking and selection are used. Kleijnen(47) and Dudewicz(19) present state-of-the-art reviews that summarize past research in this area and how it can be used in simulation analysis. Many procedures have been developed for specifying the sample size required in order to select the alternative whose population mean is greater than the next best population mean by a prescribed value with a given probability. The test procedures involve the computation of the sample mean based on the sample size specified and the selection of the largest sample mean observed. Bechhofer developed this approach which is referred to as the indifference zone approach (4,5)

An alternative approach involves grouping the alternatives into statistically equivalent subsets. The procedures involved in making subset selections are given by Gupta who also compares subset selection with the indifference zone approach (37,38).

A final topic relating to the design of experiments is the selection of a best alternative. This problem differs from those previously described in that we are trying to determine the values for the controllable variables which either maximize or minimize an objective function. For example, in the analysis of a periodic review inventory system, we might wish to employ simulation to determine the values for the stock control level, reorder point, and time between reviews which minirnize the average monthly cost of the inventory system.

Although the principles of optimization using simulation experiments are essentially the same as for optimization of mathematical expressions, there are some differences which must be considered. Since the response from a simulation typically involves random variables, the objective function or constraint equations written as a function of the simulation response will also be random variables. As a consequence, it is necessary to formulate response constraints as probability statements and to make statistical interpretations of the objective function value.

There have been two basic approaches to optimization using simulation models. The first approach involves a direct evaluation of the independent variables using the simulation model. Farrell (22) divides these techniques into three categories: mathematically naive techniques such as heuristic search, complete enumeration, and random search; methods appropriate to unimodal objective functions such as coordinate search, and pattern search; and methods for multimodal objective functions.

The second approach to optimization using simulation is response surface methodology (60,70). In this method we fit a surface to experimental observations using a factorial design in the vicinity of an initial search point. We then apply an optimization algorithm such as the gradient method to determine the optimum values of the controllable variables relative to the fitted equation. The optimum values for the fitted surface are then used to define the next search point. Biles has applied this procedure sequentially in a search for optimal decision values (6). A modular FORTRAN program for simulation optimization using first and second order response surfaces has been developed by Smith (77).

17.9 CHAPTER SUMMARY

Two distinct aspects of simulation output analysis involve the accuracy and reliability of the sample values obtained. The main emphasis of this chapeer is on reliability. The importance of $Var[\overline{X}_1]$ in simulation studies is established. It is recommended that the reliability of simulation outputs be based on observations of batch or cycle averages rather than on individual sample values. Five methods for estimating the variance of sample means, $Var[\overline{X}_1]$, based on I batches are presented. Variance reduction techniques, startup policies, stopping rules, and the design of simulation expenments are described. Overall, this chapter provides both detailed practical results and suggestions for the important statistical problems facing a simulation analyst.

17.10 EXERCISES

17-1. Define the following terms: Reliable; Batch; Stochastic Process; Ergodic; Stationary; Steady State; Time Series; Sample Mean; Average; Expectation; Mean Square Error; Kurtosis; Spectrum; Regeneration Point; Parametric Modeling: Spectral Density Function; ARMA Model; White Noise; VRT; Stratified Sampling; Catch-22; and Bias.

17-2. A drive-in bank has two windows, each manned by a teller and each has a separate drive-in lane. The drive-in lanes are adjacent. From previous observations, it has been determined that the time interval between customer arrivals during rush hours is exponentially distributed with a mean time between arrivals of 0.25 time units. Congestion occurs only during rush hours, and only this period is to be analyzed. The service time is exponentially distributed for each teller with a mean service time of 0.4 time unit. It has also been shown that customers have no preference for a teller if the waiting lines are equal. At all other times, a customer chooses the shortest line. After a customer has entered the system, he may not leave until he is serviced. However, he may change lanes if he is the last customer in his lane and a difference of two customers exists between the two lanes. Because of parking space limitations, only nine cars can wait in each lane. These cars, plus the car of the customer being serviced by each teller, allow a maximum of twenty cars in the system. If the system is full when a customer arrives, he balks and is lost to the system.

The initial conditions are as follows:

1. Both drive-in tellers are busy. The initial service time for each teller is exponentially distributed with mean of 0.4 time unit.

2. The first customer is scheduled to arrive at 0.1 time unit.

3. Two customers are waiting in each queue.

Theoretical Steady-State Results

Steady-state probabilities: (0.1123, 0.1796, 0.1437, 0.1150, 0.0920, 0.0736. 0.0589, 0.0471, 0.0377, 0.0301, 0.0241, 0.0193, 0.0154, 0.0123, 0.0099, 0.0079. 0.0063, 0.0050, 0.0040, 0.0032, 0.0026)

Number in system: Mean = 4.232; Variance = 15.83; and m = 177.4.

Determine the simulation run length required to obtain estimates that are within 10 percent of the theoretical values.

17-3. Simulate the system described in Exercise 17-2 to obtain estimates of the variance of the sample mean and the value of m for each of the following random variables:

1. The number of customers in the system, and

2. The time a customer spends in the system.

Develop estimates for Var($\overline{X}_I$) and m using both replication and subinterval sampling procedures. Select a total amount of simulation time on which to base your estimates and give a rationale for your selection. The same amount of simulation time should be used for each procedure.

Embellishments: (a) Perform a spectral analysis of the experimental data.

(b) Use regenerative techniques to obtain the requested estimates.

(c) Use parametric modeling techniques to build a model of the simulated data. (d) Obtain 95% confidence limits for m using the information that $(k-1)\,\hat{m}/m$ is Chi-square distributed with $(k-1)$ degrees of freedom.

17-4. Compare the use of the observed data values and batched observations in the embellishments to Exercise 17-3.

17-5 Evaluate the effect of making the initial conditions for the system described in Exercise 17-2 to be the modal state.

17-6. Evaluate the effect of starting in the expected state. Evaluate three truncation rules for the system described in Exercise 17-2. Embellishment: Develop a truncation rule and evaluate it.

17-7.   Perform four experiments each consisting of ten runs of length 200 time units on the bank teller simulation model, Exercise 17-2. In experiment 1, use random number stream 1 for arrival times and stream 2 for service times. In experiment 2, use stream 1 again for arrivals but the antithetic values from stream 2. In experiment 3, employ antithetic values from both streams 1 and 2. In experiment 4, use stream 1 for arrival times and stream 3 for service times.

Define $X_k^{(i)}$ to be the average computed on run k of experiment i where X could be either the average number in the system, $\overline{N}$, or the average time in the system, $\overline{W}$.

(a) Calculate $\text{Var}[\overline{Z}]$ where $\overline{Z}_k = [X_k^{(i)} + X_k^{(j)}]/2$ using pairs of runs from experiments 1 and 2 and experiments 1 and 3.

(b) Calculate $\text{Var}[X_k^{(i)} + X_k^{(j)}]$ for j = 2 and 4 and i =1.

(c) For each experiment, use the prior information that $\overline{N} = \lambda_E \overline{W}$ to obtain a variance reduction where λ_E is the effective arrival rate after balking occurs.

17-8.   Apply the sequential stopping rule suggested in Section 17.6 to the bank teller model, Exercise 17-2, to obtain a 95 percent confidence interval that has a half length, g, of 0.25. Embellishment: Apply the sequential stopping rule procedure to obtain a 95 percent confidence that the half length is 10 percent of the true mean value.

17-9.   Perform Exercises 17-2 through 17-8 for Example 5-2, the inspection and adjustment of television sets model.

17-10.   For the single channel queueing situation, evaluate the variance reduction obtained from switching the streams used for generating arrival and service times.

17-11.   For the bank teller simulation model, stratify customers based on their service time and then compute the variance of the average time in the system. Compare these results with those obtained without stratification.

17-12.   Develop and apply an optimization procedure for setting the reorder point, stock control level and time between reviews for the inventory model and cost values given in embellishment (e) of Exercise 11-5.

17-13.   Discuss the issues involved in performing an analysis of variance on experiments that involve the use of common streams and antithetic samples.

17.11   REFERENCES

1.   Anderson, T. W., *The Statistical Analysis of Time Series*, John Wiley, 1970.
2.   Anderson, V. L. and R. A. McLean, *Design of Experiments: A Realistic Approach*, Marcel Dekker, 1974.

3. Andrews, R. W. and T. J. Schriber, "ARMA Based Confidence Intervals for Simulation Output Analysis," *American Journal of Mathematical and Management Science*, Vol. 4, 1984, pp. 345-374.

4. Bechhofer, R. E., "A Single-Sample Multiple Decision Procedure for Ranking Means of Normal Populations with Known Variances," *Ann. Math. Staf.*, Vol. 25, 1954, pp. 16-39.

5. Bechhofer, R. E., "Selection in Factorial Experiments," *Proceedings, Winter Simulation Conference*, 1977, pp. 65-70.

6. Biles, W. E., "Integration-Regression Search Procedure for Simulation Experimentation," *Proceedings, Winter Simulation Conference*, 1974, pp. 491-497.

7. Blomqvist, N., "On the Transient Behavior of the Gl/G/ 1 Waiting-Times," *Skandinavisk Aktuarietidskrift*, Vol. 53, 1970, pp. 118-129.

8. Box, G. E. P. and G. M. Jenkins, Time Series Analysis: Forecasting and Control, Holden-Day, 1970.

9. Bratley, P., B. L. Fox, and L. E. Schrage, *A Guide to Simulation*, Second Edition, Springer-Verlag, 1987.

10. Carter, G. and E. J. Ignall, "A Variance Reduction Technique for Simulation," *Management Science*, Vol. 21, 1975, pp. 607-616.

11. Chang, Y., R. S. Sullivan, J. R. Wilson, and U. Bagchi, "Experimental Investigation of Real Time Scheduling in Flexible Manufacturing Systems," *Annals of OR*, Vol. 3, 1985, pp. 355-377.

12. Cinlar, E., *Introduction to Stochastic Processes*, Prentice-Hall, 1975.

13. Cochran, W. G. and G. M. Cox, *Experimental Designs,* John Wiley, 1957.

14. Cochran, W. G., *Sampling Techniques*, Third Edition, John Wiley, 1977.

15. Conway, R., "Some Tactical Problems in Digital Simulation," *Management Science*, Vol. 10, 1963, pp. 47-61.

16. Crane, M. A. and D. L. Iglehart, "Simulating Stable Stochastic Systems I: General Multiserver Queues," *J. ACM*, Vol. 21, 1974, pp. 103-113.

17. Crane, M. A. and A. Lemoine, An Introduction to the Regenerative Method for Simulation Analysis, *Technical Report No. 86-23*, California Analysis Corporation, Palo Alto, CA., October 1976.

18. Diananda, P. H., "Some Probability Limit Theorems with Statistical Applications," *Proceedings, Cambridge Phil. Soc.*, Vol. 49, 1953, pp. 239-246.

19. Dudewicz, E. J., "New Procedures for Selection Among (Simulated) Alternatives," *Proceedings, Winter Simulation Conference*, 1977, pp. 58-62.

20. Duket, S., Simulation Output Analysis, unpublished MS Thesis, Purdue University, December 1974.

21. Duket, S. and A. A. B. Pritsker, "Examination of Simulation Output Using Spectral Methods," *Mathematics and Computers in Simulation*, Vol. XX, 1978, pp. 53-60.

22. Farrell, W., "Literature Review and Bibliography of Simulation Optimization," *Proceedings, Winter Simlllation Conference*, 1977, pp. 116-124.

23. Feller, W., *An Introduction to Probability Theory and Its Applications*, Vol. 1, Second Edition, John Wiley, 1957.

24. Feller, W., *An Introduction to Probability Theory and Its Applications*, Vol. 2, John Wiley, 1972.

25.   Fishman, G. S., "A Study of Bias Considerations in Simulation Experiments," *Operations Research,* Vol. 20, 1972, pp. 785-790.

26.   Fishman, G. S., *Monte Carlo concepts, Algorithms and Applications,* Springer-Verlag, 1996.

27.   Fishman, G. S., "Grouping Observations in Digital Simulation," *Management Science*, Vol. 24, 1978, pp. 510-521.

28.   Fishman, &. S., *Principles of Discrete Event Simulation*, John Wiley, 1978.

29.   Fishman, G. S., "Statistical Analysis for Queueing Simulation," *Management Science*, Vol. 20, 1973, pp. 363-369.

30.   Fishman, G. S., "The Allocation of Computer Time in Company Simulation Experiments," *Operations Research*, Vol. 16, 1968, pp. 280-295.

31.   Gafarian, A. V., Ancker, C. J., and Morisaku, T. The Problem of the Initial Transient with Respect to Mean Value in Digital Computer Simulation and the Evaluation of Some Proposed Solutions, *Technical Report No. 77-1*, University of Southern California, 1977.

32.   Glynn, P. W., "Some Asymptotic Formulas for Markov Chains with Applications to Simulation," *Journal of Statistical Computation and Simulation*, Vol. 19, 1984, pp. 97-112.

33.   Glynn, P. W., "On the Role of Generalized Semi-Markov Processes in Simulation Output Analysis," *Proceedings, Winter Simulation Conference*, 1983, pp. 39-42.

34.   Goldenberger, A. S., *Econometric Theory*, John Wiley, 1964.

35.   Gordon, G., *System Simulation*, Prentice-Hall, 1969.

36.   Gray, H. L. and W. R. Schucany, *The Generalized Jackknife Statistic*, Marcel Dekker, 1972.

37.   Gupta, S. S. and S. Panchapakesan, "On Multiple Decision (Subset Selection) Procedures, *Journal of Math and Physical Sciences*, Vol. 6, 1972, pp. 1-71.

38.   Gupta, S. S. and J. C. Hsu, "Subset Selection Procedures with Special Reference to the Analysis of 2-Way Layout: Application to Motor Vehicle Fatality Data," *Proceedings, Winter Simulation Conference*, 1977, pp. 80-85.

39.   Hammersley, J. M. and D. C. Handscomb, *Monte Carlo Methods*, Methuen, 1964.

40.   Hazen, G. and A. A. B. Pritsker, "Formulas for the Variance of the Sample Mean in Finite State Markov Processes," *Journa/ of Statistical Computation and Simulation*, Vol. 12, 1981, pp. 25-40.

41.   Heidelberger, P. and P. D. Welch, "A Spectral Method for Confidence Interval Generation and Run Length Control in Simulations," *Comm. ACM*, Vol. 24, 1981, pp. 233-245.

42.   Hoel, P. G., *Elementary Statistics*, Second Edition, John Wiley, 1966.

43.   Hogg, R. V. and A. T. Craig, *Introduction to Mathematical Statistics*, Macmillan, 1970.

44.   Kabak, I. W., "Stopping Rules for Queueing Simulations," *Operations Research*, Vol. 16, 1968, pp. 431-437.

45.   Karlin, S. and H. Tayler, *A First Course in Stochastic Processes*, Academic Press, 1975.

46.   Kleijnen, J. P. C., *Statistical Techniques in Simulation: Part I,* Marcel Dekker, 1974.

47.   Kleijnen, J. P. C., *Statistical Techniques in Simulation, Part Il,* Marcel Dekker, 1975.

48.   Kleijnen, J. P. C., A. J. van den Burg, and R. Th. van der Ham, "Generalization of Simulation Results," *European Journal of Operational Research*, Vol. 3, 1979, pp. 50-64.

49.   Kleijnen, J. P. C., *Statistical Tools for Simulation Practitoners*, Marcel Dekker, 1986.

50.   Kleijnen, J. P. C., "Regression Metamodel Summarization of Model Behaviour," *Encyclopedia of Systems and Control*, Pergamon, Press, 1982.

51.   Kleijnen, J. P. C., and W. Van Groenendael, *Simulation: A Statistical Perspective*, John Wiley, 1992.

52.   Law, A. M., Confidence Intervals for Steady-State Simulations, I: A Survey of Fixed Sample Size Procedures, *Technical Report 78-5*, University of Wisconsin, 1978.

53.   Law, A. M., "Efficient Estimators for Simulated Queueing Systems," *Management Science*, Vol. 22, 1975, pp. 30-41.

54.   Law, A. M., Statistical Analysis of the Output Data from Terminating Simulations, *Technical Report 78-4*, University of Wisconsin, 1978.

55.   Law, A. M. and J. S. Carson, III, "A Sequential Procedure for Determining the Length of a Steady State Simulation," *Operations Research*, Vol. 27, 1979, pp. 1011-1025.

56.   Law, A. M. and W. D. Kelton, *Simulation Modeling and Ana/ysis*, Second Edition, McGraw-Hill, 1991.

57.   Little, J. D. C., "A Proof of the Queueing Formula L=lW," *Operations Research*, Vol. 9, 1961, pp. 383-387.

58.   Mabert, V. A., An Introduction to Short Term Forecasting Using The Box-Jenkins Methodology, *AIIE Monograph Series*, AIIE-PP C-75-1, Atlanta, Georgia, 1975.

59.   Mechanic, H. and W. McKay, "Confidence Intervals for Averages of Dependent Data in Simulations II," *Technical Report 17-202*, IBM Advanced Systems Development Division, August 1966.

60.   Meyer, R. H., *Response Surface Methodology*, Allyn & Bacon, 1971. 75. 76. 77. *Conference*, 1977, pp. 176-184.

61.   Moeller, T. L. and P. D. Welch, "A Special Based Technique for Generating Confidence Intervals from Simulation Outputs," *Proceedings, 1977 Winter Simulation Conference*, 1977, pp. 176-184.

62.   Moran, P. A. P., "Some Theorems on Time Series, I," *Biometrika*, Vol. 34, 1947, pp. 281-291 .

63.   Moy, W, A., "Practical Variance Reducing Procedures for Monte Carlo Simulations," in *Computer Simulation Experiments with Models of Economic Systems* by T. H. Naylor, John Wiley, 1971.

64.   Nadas, A., "An Extension of a Theorem of Chow and Robbins on Sequential Confidence Intervals for the Mean," *Ann. Math. Stat.*, Vol. 40, 1969, pp. 667-671.

65.   Nelson, B. L., Statistical Analysis of Simulation Results, in *Handbook of Industrial Engineering*, Second Edition, G. Salvendy, Ed., John Wiley, 1992, pp. 2567-2593.

66.   Nelson, B. L. and B. W. Schmeiser, "Variance Reduction: Basic Transformations," *Proceedings, Winter Simulation Conference*, 1983, pp. 255-258.

67.   Page, E. S., "On Monte Carlo Methods in Congestion Problems; II; Simulation of Queueing Systems," *Operations Research*, Vol. 13, 1965, pp. 300-305.

68.   Parzen, E., *Stochastic Processes*, Holden-Day, 1962.

69.   Pritsker, A. A. B., *Introduction to Simulation and SLAM II*, Fourth Edition, Systems Publishing and John Wiley, 1995.

70.   Ravindrin, R., D. T. Phillips, and J. J. Solberg, *Operations Research: Principles and Practice*, Second Edition, John Wiley, 1987.

71.   Ross, S., *A First Course in Probability*, Macmillan, 1976.

72.   Schmeiser, B., "Batch Size Effects in the Analysis of Simulation Output," *Operations Research*, Vol. 307 1982, pp. 556-568.

73.   Schriber, T. J., *Simulation Using GPSS*, John Wiley, 1974.

74.   Schriber, T. J., *An Introduction to Simulation Using GPSS/H*, John Wiley, 1991.

75.   Schruben, L. W., "Confidence Interval Estimation Using Standardized Time Series," *Tech Report 518*, School of QR.I.E., Cornell University, 1982.

76.   Schruben, L. W., "Detecting Initialization Bias in Simulation Output," *Operations Research*, Vol. 30, 1982, pp. 569-590.

77.   Smith, D. E., Automated Response Surface Methodology in Digital Computer Simulation (U), *Volume 1: Program Description and User's Guide (U)*, Office of Naval Research, Arlington, VA: September 1975.

78.   Starr, N., "The Performance of a Seauential Procedure for the Fixed-Width Interval Estimation of the Mean," *Ann. Math. Stat.*, Vol. 37, 1966, pp. 36-50.

79.   Stidham, S., Jr., "L=λW: A Discounted Analog and a New Proof," *Operations Research*, Vol. 20, 1972, pp. 1115-1126.

80.   Tocher, K. D., *The Art of Simulation*, Van Nostrand, 1963.

81.   Welch, P. D., "The Statistical Analysis of Simulation Results," in *Computer Performance Modeling Handbook*, S. S. Lavenberg, Ed., Academic Press, 1983.

82.   Wilson, J. R., A Procedure for Evaluating Startup Policies in Simulation Experiments, unpublished M. S. Thesis, Purdue University, December 1977.

83.   Wilson, J. R. and A. A. B. Pritsker, "A Survey of Research on the Simulation Startup Problem," *Simulation*, Vol. 31, 1978, pp. 55-58. 84.

84.   Wilson, J. R. and A. A. B. Pritsker, "A Procedure for Evaluating Startup Policies in Simulation Experiments," *Simulation*, Vol. 31., 1978, pp. 79-89.

85.   Wilson, J. R. and A. A. B. Pritsker, "Experimental Evaluation of Variance Reduction Techniques for Queueing Simulation Using Generalized Concomitant Variables," *Management Science*, Vol. 30, 1984, pp. 1459-1472.

86.   Wilson, J. R. and A. A. B. Pritsker, "Variance Reduction in Queueing Simulation Using Generalized Concomitant Variables," *Journal of Statistical Computation and Simulation*, 1984, pp. 129-153.

87.   Wilson, J. R., "Statistical Aspects of Simulation," *Proceedings, IFORS, 1984*, pp. 825-841 .

88.   Wilson, J. R., "Variance Reduction Techniques for Digital Simulation," *American Journal of Mathematical and Management Sciences*, Vol. 4, 1984, pp. 277-312.

Author Index

Subject Index